THE COLLECTED LETTERS OF
THOMAS HARDY

VOLUME SIX

1920–1925

Already published

THE COLLECTED
LETTERS OF
THOMAS HARDY

EDITED BY

RICHARD LITTLE PURDY

AND

MICHAEL MILLGATE

VOLUME SIX

1920—1925

CLARENDON PRESS · OXFORD
1987

Oxford University Press, Walton Street, Oxford OX2 6DP

Oxford New York Toronto
Delhi Bombay Calcutta Madras Karachi
Petaling Jaya Singapore Hong Kong Tokyo
Nairobi Dar es Salaam Cape Town
Melbourne Auckland

and associated companies in
Beirut Berlin Ibadan Nicosia

Oxford is a trade mark of Oxford University Press

Published in the United States
by Oxford University Press, New York

British Library Cataloguing in Publication Data

Hardy, Thomas, 1840–1928
The collected letters of Thomas Hardy.
Vol. 6: 1920–1925
1. Hardy, Thomas, 1840–1928—Biography
2. Novelists, English—19th century—Biography
I. Title   II. Purdy, Richard Little
III. Millgate, Michael
823'.8   PR4753
ISBN 0–19–812623–9

Library of Congress Cataloging-in-Publication Data
(Revised for volume 6)
Hardy, Thomas, 1840–1928.
The collected letters of Thomas Hardy.
Includes indexes.
Contents: v. 1. 1840–1892.—v. 2. 1893–1901.
—[etc.]—v. 6. 1920–1925.
1. Hardy, Thomas, 1840–1928—Correspondence.
2. Novelists, English—19th century—Correspondence.
I. Purdy, Richard Little, 1904–   . II. Millgate, Michael.
PR4753.A42 1978 823'.8 77-30355
ISBN 0–19–812470–8 (v. 1)

Set by Hope Services, Abingdon, Oxon
Printed in Great Britain
at the Alden Press, Oxford

CONTENTS

CHRONOLOGY

1840	2 June	Born, eldest child of Thomas and Jemima (Hand) Hardy, at Higher Bockhampton, Dorset.
1856	11 July	Articled to John Hicks, Dorchester architect.
1862	17 Apr	Goes to London; soon employed in architectural office of Arthur Blomfield.
1867	20 July	Returns to Dorset because of ill health; again employed by Hicks.
1868	9 June	Completes final draft of 'The Poor Man and the Lady' (later destroyed).
1869	May	Employed by Weymouth architect, G. R. Crickmay.
1870	7 Mar	Goes to St. Juliot, Cornwall, to inspect church; meets Emma Lavinia Gifford for the first time.
1871	25 Mar	*Desperate Remedies* pub. (3 vols.) by Tinsley Brothers.
1872	March	In London lodgings, working for the architect T. Roger Smith.
	June	*Under the Greenwood Tree* pub. (2 vols.) by Tinsley Brothers.
	15 Aug	First instalment of *A Pair of Blue Eyes* in September number of *Tinsleys' Magazine*.
1873	late May	*A Pair of Blue Eyes* pub. (3 vols.) by Tinsley Brothers.
	21 Sept	Suicide of Horace Moule at Cambridge.
	December	First instalment of *Far from the Madding Crowd* in the *Cornhill Magazine*.
1874	17 Sept	Marries Emma Lavinia Gifford at St. Peter's Church, Paddington; honeymoon in France.
	6 Oct	Takes rooms at St. David's Villa, Hook Road, Surbiton.
	23 Nov	*Far from the Madding Crowd* pub. (2 vols.) by Smith, Elder.
1875	22 Mar	Moves to 18 Newton Road, Westbourne Grove, London.
	15 Aug	Moves to West End Cottage, Swanage, Dorset.
1876	early March	Moves to 7 Peter (or St. Peter) Street, Yeovil, Somerset.
	3 Apr	*The Hand of Ethelberta* pub. (2 vols.) by Smith, Elder.
	3 July	Moves to Riverside (or Rivercliff) Villa, Sturminster Newton, Dorset.
1878	22 Mar	Moves to 1 Arundel Terrace, Trinity Road, Upper Tooting.
	4 Nov	*The Return of the Native* pub. (3 vols.) by Smith, Elder.
1880	23 Oct	Beginning of serious illness.
	26 Oct	*The Trumpet-Major* pub. (3 vols.) by Smith, Elder.
1881	25 June	Moves to Lanherne, The Avenue, Wimborne, Dorset.
	early December	*A Laodicean* pub. (3 vols.) by Sampson Low.
1882	late October	*Two on a Tower* pub. (3 vols.) by Sampson Low.
1883	June	Moves to Shire-Hall Lane, Dorchester.

1885	29 June	Moves to Max Gate (designed by himself), just outside Dorchester.
1886	10 May	*The Mayor of Casterbridge* pub. (2 vols.) by Smith, Elder.
1887	15 Mar	*The Woodlanders* pub. (3 vols.) by Macmillan.
	March–April	Visits Italy.
1888	4 May	*Wessex Tales* pub. (2 vols.) by Macmillan.
1891	30 May	*A Group of Noble Dames* pub. by Osgood, McIlvaine.
	late November	*Tess of the d'Urbervilles* pub. (3 vols.) by Osgood, McIlvaine.
1892	20 July	Death of Thomas Hardy, sen.
1893	19 May	In Dublin; first meeting with Florence Henniker.
1894	22 Feb	*Life's Little Ironies* pub. by Osgood, McIlvaine.
1895	4 Apr	First vol. of Wessex Novels edn. pub. by Osgood, McIlvaine.
	1 Nov	*Jude the Obscure* pub. by Osgood, McIlvaine.
1897	16 Mar	*The Well-Beloved* pub. by Osgood, McIlvaine.
1898	December	*Wessex Poems* pub. by Harper & Brothers.
1901	mid-November	*Poems of the Past and the Present* pub. by Harper & Brothers.
1904	13 Jan	*The Dynasts*, Part First, pub. by Macmillan.
	3 April	Death of Jemima Hardy.
1906	9 Feb	*The Dynasts*, Part Second, pub. by Macmillan.
1908	11 Feb	*The Dynasts*, Part Third, pub. by Macmillan.
1909	3 Dec	*Time's Laughingstocks* pub. by Macmillan.
1910	June	Receives the Order of Merit.
1912	30 Apr	First two vols. of Wessex Edition pub. by Macmillan.
	27 Nov	Death of Emma Lavinia Hardy.
1913	24 Oct	*A Changed Man and Other Tales* pub. by Macmillan.
1914	10 Feb	Marries Florence Emily Dugdale at St. Andrew's Church, Enfield.
	17 Nov	*Satires of Circumstance* (including 'Poems of 1912–13') pub. by Macmillan.
1915	24 Nov	Death of Mary Hardy, the elder of his sisters.
1917	30 Nov	*Moments of Vision* pub. by Macmillan.
1922	23 May	*Late Lyrics and Earlier* pub. by Macmillan.
1923	15 Nov	*The Famous Tragedy of the Queen of Cornwall* pub. by Macmillan.
1925	20 Nov	*Human Shows, Far Phantasies, Songs, and Trifles* pub. by Macmillan.
1927	21 July	Address at Dorchester Grammar School stone-laying: last public appearance.
1928	11 Jan	Dies at Max Gate.
	2 Oct	*Winter Words* pub. by Macmillan.
	2 Nov	*The Early Life of Thomas Hardy* pub. under the name of Florence Emily Hardy.
1930	29 Apr	*The Later Years of Thomas Hardy* pub. under the name of Florence Emily Hardy.

ACKNOWLEDGEMENTS FOR
VOLUME SIX

In the course of collecting and editing the letters in this sixth volume the editors have incurred many obligations. Our thanks are due first of all to the authorities of the following institutions for the assistance they have given and for permission to publish manuscripts in their possession:

Albert A. and Henry W. Berg Collection, New York Public Library, and Mrs. Lola L. Szladits; University of Birmingham; Bodleian Library; Boston Public Library; University of Bristol; British Library; British Library of Political and Economic Science; University of California, Los Angeles; King's College, Cambridge; University of Chicago; Central Zionist Archives; Colby College Library, Waterville, Maine, and Dr. J. Fraser Cocks III; Columbia University Library and Mr. Kenneth A. Lohf; Cornell University;

Dorset County Museum, Dorchester, and Mr. R. N. R. Peers; Eton College, School Library, and Mr. Michael Meredith; Fitzwilliam Museum, Cambridge; Thomas Hardy Society, Dorchester; Harvard University, Houghton Library; University of Illinois, Urbana; Indiana University; Keats-Shelley Memorial Association; University of Kentucky, W. Hugh Peal Collection, and Ms. Claire McCann;

Allen Lane Foundation; University of Leeds, Brotherton Library, and Mr. Christopher Sheppard; Library of Congress; National Library of Scotland; National Trust (Stourhead); New York University, Fales Library, Bobst Library, and Dr. Theodore Grieder; Princeton University Library; Queen's College, Oxford;

Royal Library, Windsor, with the gracious permission of Her Majesty the Queen; Royal Literary Fund; Royal Society of Literature; Society for the Protection of Ancient Buildings; University of Southern California; University of Texas at Austin, Harry Ransom Humanities Research Center, and Ms Cathy Henderson; Victoria and Albert Museum; Wiltshire Record Office; Yale University, Beinecke Library, and Miss Marjorie G. Wynne.

We owe a special debt of gratitude to the following collectors and private owners who have made manuscripts in their possession available to us:

Mr. Frederick B. Adams, Mr. Celadon August, Dr. C. J. P. Beatty, Lord Bridges, Mrs. G. Bugler, Messrs. W. & R. Chambers, Mrs. Ada Murray Clarke, Canon C. P. Cowley, Mr. J. Stevens Cox, Mr. T. R. M. Creighton, Mrs. Norton Downs, Professor C. H. Gifford, Mr. R. Greenland, Mr. David Holmes, Professor Mary Jacobus, Mr. W. M. King, Mrs. Michael MacCarthy, Mrs. Sheila Mannion, Mr. Roger Morgan, the Revd. G. R. K. Moule, Miss F. F. Quiller-Couch, Mr. Gordon N. Ray, Mme Romain Rolland, Mr. J. S. Sample, Mrs. Stewart-Mackenzie, Mr. Robert H. Taylor, Mr. T. Trafton, Mrs. Richard Tyler, Mrs. Mildred Wheatcroft.

To the following we offer our grateful thanks for help of many kinds, especially in tracing manuscripts and resolving problems of annotation:

Mr. and Mrs. Frederick B. Adams, Professor Peter Allen, Mr. John Antell, Professor John Baird, Mrs. Celia Barclay, Dr. and Mrs. C. J. P. Beatty, Professor Karl Beckson, Mr. Alan Bell, Mr. Alan Clodd, Mrs. Nancy Coffin, Professor Michael Collie, Professor Thomas J. Collins, Professor Eleanor Cook, Mrs. Jane Cooper, Professor Pierre Coustillas, Mr. Peter W. Coxon, Mr. Nigel Cross, Mr. H. Lovat Dickson, Dr. Howard Garber, Mrs. Shelagh Garland, Miss Helen Garton, Dr. James Gibson, Mrs. Carole Gillin, Dr. Robert Gittings, Mr. Ronald Greenland, Professor Gordon S. Haight, Dr. Desmond Hawkins, Mr. David Holmes, Professor Samuel Hynes, Professor Heather Jackson, Professor J. R. de J. Jackson, Professor W. J. Keith, Professor Martin Kreiswirth, Mr. Richard Landon, Miss Patience-Anne W. Lenk, Professor Charles Lock, Mr. Desmond MacCarthy, Lord Macmillan, Mr. Michael Meredith, Professor Jane Millgate, Professor W. W. Morgan, the Revd. David Nash, Mr. Stephen R. Parks, Mr. John Pentney, Mr. Charles P. C. Pettit, Mr. Michael Rabiger, Mr. Gordon N. Ray, Mr. Henry Reed, Mrs. Isabelle Robinson, Professor J. M. Robson, Mr. P. C. Roscoe, Professor S. P. Rosenbaum, Professor Ann Saddlemyer, Professor Eric Salmon, Professor Robert C. Schweik, Mrs. Carola Shephard, Mr. and Mrs. J. P. Skilling, Mrs. Sofija Skoric, Mrs. Virginia Surtees, Mrs. Lillian Swindall, Mrs. Ann Thwaite, Professor Judith Wittenberg, Miss Marjorie G. Wynne, the Revd. J. M. C. Yates.

Professor Millgate has again been greatly aided in his work on this volume by the generous and sustained support of the Social Sciences and Humanities Research Council of Canada. That support has made available the expert typing and word-processing services of Mrs. Freda Gough and Ms. Gail Richardson and the efficient research assistance of Ms. Pamela Dalziel, Dr. Gary Harrington, and, especially, Ms. Lesley Mann, Mr. Lawrence Miller, and Mr. Keith Lawson, all three of whom have made a substantial contribution to the present volume.

Professor Millgate also particularly acknowledges the researches so willingly and ably undertaken on his behalf by Mr. and Mrs. William Jesty and the late Mr. Malcolm Tomkins and the independent proof-readings carried out by Ms. Pamela Dalziel (for this volume) and Mr. David Holmes (for the two previous volumes).

Our best thanks, finally, must go to the Trustees of the Thomas Hardy Estate for their grant of an 'exclusive licence' to collect, edit, and publish Hardy's letters, and to Mr. R. N. R. Peers, Curator of the Dorset County Museum and its Hardy Memorial Collection, for assistance of every sort, most generously given.

September 1986

R.L.P
M.M.

LIST OF ABBREVIATIONS

TH	Thomas Hardy
ELH	Emma Lavinia Hardy
FEH	Florence Emily Hardy

Adams	Frederick B. Adams, private collection
Berg	Berg Collection, New York Public Library
BL	British Library
Colby	Colby College, Waterville, Maine
DCM	Dorset County Museum
LC	Library of Congress
Leeds	University of Leeds, Brotherton Collection
NLS	National Library of Scotland
NYU	New York University, Fales Library
SPAB	Society for the Protection of Ancient Buildings
Taylor	Robert H. Taylor, private collection
Texas	University of Texas at Austin, Humanities Research Center
UCLA	University of California, Los Angeles

D.N.B.	*Dictionary of National Biography*
EL	Florence Emily Hardy, *The Early Life of Thomas Hardy* (London, 1928)
LY	Florence Emily Hardy, *The Later Years of Thomas Hardy* (London, 1930)
Millgate	Michael Millgate, *Thomas Hardy: A Biography* (New York, 1982; Oxford, 1982)
Purdy	Richard Little Purdy, *Thomas Hardy: A Bibliographical Study* (London, 1954, 1968, 1978); where no page is indicated, the reference is to the editor's private collection.
Wessex edn.	Wessex Edition, 24 vols. (London, 1912–31)

For the full names of other private and institutional owners of Hardy letters, see Acknowledgements, pp. viii–ix.

1920

To SYDNEY COCKERELL
MAX GATE, | DORCHESTER. | Jan 6: 1920. 5 p.m.

My dear Cockerell:

Have just received your telegram, & am sorry you are laid up, but I hope it is not very serious. Florence is on her way back from London, where she has been for 2 days, & she will be disappointed that you are not coming just yet. I hope the remainder of your household are fairly well. I have returned from a wet walk to Stinsford with my sister-in-law who is staying here. Mrs Hanbury at Kingston Maurward is ill, you will be sorry to hear. I have kept all right so far this winter, but won't brag. My wife will write more at length when she arrives. I am posting this hasty line at our gate, it being too wet to go further. Best wishes for the year from

Yours sincerely
Thomas Hardy.

Text MS. Victoria and Albert Museum.
Cockerell: Sydney Carlyle Cockerell, director of the Fitzwilliam Museum, Cambridge; see IV.178.   *Florence*: Florence Emily Hardy, TH's second wife (subsequently referred to as FEH); see letter of 1 Sept 20.   *sister-in-law*: FEH's younger sister Eva Dugdale, a nursing sister, currently working at the new Children's Hospital in Swanage, Dorset.   *Mrs Hanbury*: Effield Dorothy Hanbury, *née* Jeune (see V.188), wife of Cecil Hanbury, owner of Kingston Maurward House, near Dorchester.   *at our gate*: the post-box installed for TH's convenience in the garden wall of Max Gate, just outside the front gate, was bricked up after his death.

To EDMUND GOSSE
Max Gate: Thursday eveng | 8: 1: 1920

My dear Gosse:

This is very nice of you, to patronize the Gloucester. We have the honour of knowing the managing director, & if I had been aware I would have told him to put you in George the Third's room. The hotel was, as I need not say, the famous Gloucester Lodge; & as ghosts are just now in fashion perhaps you will see the spirits not only of George & Charlotte, but of Miss Burney, Pitt, Eldon, &c, &c, all of whom walked the passages there in their lifetime.

Florence is flying off to the Hunt Ball this evening with our neighbours the Cecil Hanburys, & as no doubt she will be tired to morrow I suggest that we lunch with you & Mrs Gosse Saturday, all being well. By the way we have a telephone in this house, so should this be inconvenient, or weather be very bad, you can ring us up—we are 43 Dorchester. (I ought to say that I personally am uncallable, not being able to hear what is said, but somebody would answer.)

Always yours
Thomas Hardy.

Text MS. Adams.
Gosse: Edmund Gosse, poet and man of letters, one of TH's oldest friends; see I.110.   *the Gloucester*: the Gloucester Hotel, Weymouth.   *managing director*:   Major Herbert John Groves, a former mayor of Weymouth and, like TH, a Justice of the Peace for Dorset.   *ghosts . . . fashion*: see, e.g., letter of 30 June 20.   *Miss Burney*: Frances Burney, later Madame d'Arblay (1752–1840), novelist, held the post of Second Keeper of the Queen's Robes, 1786–90; *D.N.B.*   *Pitt*: William Pitt (1759–1806), statesman, Prime Minister 1783–1801, 1804–6; *D.N.B.*   *Eldon*: John Scott, 1st Earl of Eldon (1751–1838), Lord Chancellor 1801–6, 1807–27; *D.N.B.*   *George*: King George III (1738–1820); *D.N.B.*   *Charlotte*: Queen Charlotte Sophia (1744–1818); *D.N.B.*   *in their lifetime*: i.e., during the early years of the nineteenth century when King George III and Queen Charlotte used the Lodge as a summer residence; see V.185 and *The Dynasts*, Part First, Act IV, Scene 1.   *the Cecil Hanburys*: see letter of 6 Jan 20.   *Mrs Gosse*: Ellen ('Nellie') Gosse, *née* Epps; see IV.239.   *a telephone*: installed late in 1919; see V.291.

To JOHN MIDDLETON MURRY

MAX GATE, | DORCHESTER. | Jan. 9: 1920

Dear Mr Murry:
    The book has come, & I thank you for the kind gift. I shall read it by degrees, so will make no remark on it now.
    I feel a sad sense of shortcoming at your good opinion of my writings & myself. I fear you do not know what a feeble person I really am, & how I have been weighted in the race—a race that was not worth running on my own account, though I am not sorry I have run it for the sake of one or two others.

Most sincerely
Th: Hardy.

P.S. I want some day to get "When I set out for Lyonnesse" set to music—to a pretty country tune that common people can sing. If anybody wants to do it please let me know. Th: H.

Text MS. Berg.
Murry: John Middleton Murry, critic and author; see V.298.   *The book*: Murry's vol. of essays, *The Evolution of an Intellectual* (London, 1920), inscribed to TH.   *your good opinion*: Murry's letter to TH of 5 Jan 20 (DCM) had spoken of him as the inspiration and champion of the younger generation of writers.

To MACMILLAN & CO.

MAX GATE, | DORCHESTER. | Jan 12. 1920

When the enclosed is printed off, please send Mr Hardy a few slips to distribute to friends who have bought the book.

for T.H.

Text MS. BL.
Macmillan & Co.: TH's publishers since 1902.   *the enclosed*: evidently a proof of the errata slip to the one-vol. edn. of TH's *Collected Poems* (1919), originally sent to Sir Frederick Macmillan 22 Nov 19 (see V.342).   *for T.H.*: the entire MS. is, however, in TH's hand.

To SIEGFRIED SASSOON

Max Gate | Jan. 15: 1920

My dear Sassoon:

I send a line to wish you may be well sped on your journey by whatever gods there be. Also to thank you for the poem, which I have hardly read yet, but shall of course.

I doubt if you will pick up many ideas over there. As a witty man once said, "it's just the same as here, except of course the language."

I am not doing much beyond keeping old things going. At this moment, by a coincidence, I am reading over proofs for a reprint of a novel suggested by an experience I had exactly 50 years ago—in its bare outline I mean—"A Pair of Blue Eyes". The people shadowed forth in the story being now all, alas, dead, I am able to give lights here & there on the locality, &c., which I had to obscure when the book was written.

Well: I repeat that we both wish you every success in your outing. Tell Turner I don't forget him.

Always yours
Thomas Hardy.

Text   MS. Eton College.
Sassoon: Siegfried Loraine Sassoon, poet and prose writer; see V.201.   *your journey*: Sassoon was about to embark on a two-months' lecture tour of the United States; see chaps. 18–22 of *Siegfried's Journey* (London, 1945).   *the poem*: presumably 'The Passing Show', *New Statesman* 10 Jan 1920.   *a witty man*: in Oscar Wilde's story 'The Canterville Ghost' the narrator remarks that 'we have really everything in common with America nowadays, except, of course, language'.   *Blue Eyes*": the novel, first pub. 1873, drew largely upon TH's courtship of his first wife, whom he met in Cornwall in 1870; TH was reading proofs of the book prior to its appearance in the Mellstock Edition (see letter of 29 Jan 20).   *Turner*: Walter James Redfern Turner, poet and journalist (see V.313), with whom Sassoon had just begun to share a house.

To EDMUND GOSSE

Max Gate: | Jan. 22: 1920

My dear Gosse:

We are glad to learn that you got away from the shades of George & Charlotte without misadventure.

This is very interesting that you tell me about your life in Weymouth. I had not the faintest idea that your father did so much zoological work there. The town should be proud, & would be if it knew, to have his name connected with it: perhaps the fact could be got into a guide book some day.

As nearly as I can judge, at the date you mention, 1853, I was at Mr. Last's Academy for Young Gentlemen, reading Eutropius & Caesar. Curiously enough I remember my father driving to Weymouth on business one day about that very year (there was no railway further than Dorchester then) & taking me with him as a treat; so that you may certainly have "brushed up against a boy called T.H." in the streets there—though not a "big" boy, for I was small & delicate, & had scarcely started off growing & reaching the robust condition into which I plunged between then & my 21st year.

I wish I had seen your father's first Aquarium. The first one I saw was a year or two after 1853, in a private house near here.

I am enclosing a list of Errata for you to put into that volume of Collected Poems. They were embodied in the Wessex Edn but On account of the war some parts of this book were printed at one time & some at another.

Always sincerely
Thomas Hardy.

Text MS. Adams.
George & Charlotte: see letter of 8 Jan 20.   *your life in Weymouth*: Gosse's letter to TH of 18 Jan 20 (DCM) is printed in Evan Charteris, *The Life and Letters of Sir Edmund Gosse* (London, 1931), 460–2; it describes childhood visits to Weymouth with his father, Philip Henry Gosse (see I.110).   *Last's*: Isaac Glandfield Last (1814–66), Dorchester schoolmaster; see *EL*, 28–31.   *Eutropius & Caesar*: TH's library included the *Breviarum Historiae Romanae* of Eutropius and an 1854 edn. of Caesar's *Commentaries on the Gallic War*.   *father . . . business*: TH's father (see I.3) was a mason and bricklayer, later a small builder.   *first Aquarium*: Philip Henry Gosse's invention of a marine aquarium was described in his *A Naturalist's Rambles on the Devonshire Coast* (1853) and elaborated upon in *The Aquarium* (1854).   *house near here*: unidentified, but probably Kingston Maurward; see Millgate, 46–7.   *list of Errata*: see letter of 12 Jan 20; the printed slip still accompanies this letter.   *some at another*: work on the one-vol. *Collected Poems* began in 1909; see IV.4.

To THE SECRETARY OF THE NAVY LEAGUE

Jan. 24. 1920

I am sorry to say that I do not belong to a Naval family, though I have many friends both in the English and American navies. All that I can state with certainty is that both Admiral Sir Thomas Hardy's family and my own have been Dorset for centuries, dwelling within a few miles of each other, and that they are reputed to come from the same ancestry, as is antecedently probable for several reasons. But they branched apart long before the Admiral's time.

He had no direct descendant in the male line, having left two daughters only.

Text Typed transcript (made for contemplated inclusion of letter in *Later Years*) DCM.
Secretary: the General Secretary of the Navy League, 1919–22, was Admiral Ronald Arthur Hopwood (1868–1949).   *English and American navies*: see, e.g., *LY*, 147, 231.   *Admiral . . . Hardy's*: Sir Thomas Masterman Hardy, Bt. (1769–1839), Nelson's flag-captain at Trafalgar; *D.N.B.*   *two daughters only*: with one of whom TH was in correspondence in 1877; see *EL*, 154.

To CHARLES MORGAN

MAX GATE, | DORCHESTER. | January 25. 1920.

Dear Mr Morgan:

I am sorry to have had to delay my reply for a few days. We still hope to come, weather permitting, but the doctor says that he cannot sanction my going by car, the roads being unusually bad just now, and full of holes in places. So that we will not accept the very kind offer of the Society to fetch us, but appear unceremoniously at the railway station. We have accepted accommodation at our friends the Raleighs who have obligingly offered it, and we have also to spend a little time with our other friends the Giffords.

At the risk of seeming fussy I am compelled to tell you that for physical and other reasons I shall probably be unable to stay through the whole performance, and therefore must ask you to let me be placed in some obscure box or (failing that) behind in the wings, from which I can come out at any time without notice. My wife can sit in front of the house of course with the rest of the audience. As I shall be there, if at all, as a mere private spectator and not as author, and without any hand in the production, this will be of no moment—indeed most appropriate for one who not only deserves no credit for the production, but had no idea that The Dynasts could be used for the stage in any degree.

I hope you will excuse these tedious details from a very old man, and am,

Yours sincerely,
Th: Hardy.

Text   MS. (typewritten, with envelope in FEH's hand) Roger Morgan.
Morgan: Charles Langbridge Morgan, novelist and playwright (see V.349), currently stage-manager of the Oxford University Dramatic Society's production of TH's *The Dynasts*. For his account of TH's visit to Oxford see *LY*, 203–9.   *my reply*: to Morgan's letter of 19 Jan 20 (DCM).   *the Raleighs*: Sir Walter Alexander Raleigh (see III.245) was Merton Professor of English Literature at Oxford.   *the Giffords*: the widow and daughters of the late Archdeacon Edwin Hamilton Gifford (see I. 31), ELH's uncle; see letters of 14 Feb and 14 June 20 to Margaret Gifford.

To CHARLES MORGAN

MAX GATE, | DORCHESTER. | 27: 1: 1920

Letter received. Many thanks. Quite satisfactory. Expect us unless anything unusual occurs in the interim.

Th: H.

Text   MS. (postcard) Roger Morgan.
Expect us: TH and FEH arrived in Oxford by train on 9 Feb 1920, as planned; in addition to attending the performance of *The Dynasts* TH received an Honorary D.Litt. from the University of Oxford. See *LY*, 201–3, and (for TH's reaction to *The Dynasts*) Marguerite Roberts, *Hardy's Poetic Drama and the Theatre* (New York, 1965), 68–9.

To THE REVD. G. H. MOULE

MAX GATE, | DORCHESTER. | 28 Jan. 1920.

Many thanks for letter & particulars about repairing the old church, with which kind of work I sympathize. "Reparation" is far better than "Restoration".

Sincerely yrs
Th: H.

Text   MS. (postcard) the Revd. G. R. K. Moule.
Moule: the Revd. George Herbert Moule (1876–1949), son of Horace Moule's younger brother Arthur Evans Moule (see I.244); he was subsequently vicar of Stinsford, 1936–42.   *letter*: of 20 Jan 20 (DCM).   *old church*: Moule was currently vicar of Damerham, near Salisbury; he said in his letter that the 'reparation' of the church was being conducted on 'very conservative lines'.

To SIR FREDERICK MACMILLAN

MAX GATE, | DORCHESTER. | 29th. January 1920.

Dear Sir Frederick:

Certainly charge Mr William Drake one guinea for including "Men who march away" in his volume. I have never heard of him. And please make it a condition that he print it either from the "Collected Poems", or the "Satires of Circumstance"-volume which you have lately added to the 6/- uniform edition—for I think that after the first edition of "Satires of Circumstance" a word or line was amended, and he possibly has the first edition.

I forget if I told you how much I like the Mellstock edition. I did not infer from the page you sent to show the type that it would come out so handsomely.

The printers are sending proofs of "A Pair of Blue Eyes" for this edition, and since the corrections are only a word here and there I thought I might as well send them straight back to save trouble: if otherwise let me know, as they have only got to the middle. I don't think it necessary for me to see any more of the prose.

In respect of the 7 volumes of verse (31 to 37) in the same edition, what do you think about my reading them over? The Clarks are quite excellent printers, but as no human printer, or even one sent from Heaven direct, can be trusted with verse, I don't mind reading them, since, unlike prose, there is so little on each page in poetry that I can soon run through them. On the other hand if the Mellstock edition is one merely for collectors which nobody will read it may not matter. I shall be glad for you to decide.

One other matter. I enclose a letter, which I don't know how to answer, to get your opinion on it as to whether it is worth taking notice of, and if so, whether you would do the best you can. "The Distracted Preacher"—the story he refers to—occurs in the volume called Wessex Tales. The writer of the letter does not appear to be a member of the firm he alludes to—possibly he is a sort of agent.

Yours sincerely,
Thomas Hardy.

Text   MS. (typewritten) BL.
Macmillan: Sir Frederick Orridge Macmillan, publisher (see I.132), TH's most trusted adviser during these later years.   *Drake*: William A. Drake (1899–1965), American author.   *in his volume*: Macmillan wrote 28 Jan 20 (Macmillan letterbooks, BL) to say that Drake had requested permission to include the poem in an anthology (unidentified) to be distributed in England.   *make it a condition*: Macmillan & Co.'s letter to Drake of 30 Jan 20 (Macmillan letterbooks, BL) followed TH's instructions.   *Mellstock edition*: the 37-vol. de luxe edn. of TH's works pub. by Macmillan 1919–20; see Purdy, 287–8.   *The Clarks*: the Edinburgh printing firm of R. & R. Clark; see letter of 9 Dec 25.   *enclose a letter*: of 7 Jan 20 (DCM) from the Swedish writer August Georg Brunius (1879–1926), seeking permission to adapt TH's story 'The Distracted Preacher' for filming in Sweden; see letter of 31 Jan 20.

To SIR FREDERICK MACMILLAN

MAX GATE, | DORCHESTER. | January 31st. '20.

Dear Sir Frederick:

I agree that you ask of the Swedish gentleman £50 for the film rights in "The Distracted Preacher". I am, in fact, quite vague on whether he means for Sweden only—the legends, or synopses, attached to the pictures being in Swedish—or not.

As to proofs of the verse-volumes, it is certainly safer that I should read them, and whenever the printers begin to send them, which will be with Vol. 31 (containing Part I of "The Dynasts") I shall be ready for them.

Very sincerely yours,
Thomas Hardy.

Text MS. (typewritten) BL.
Swedish gentleman: August Brunius (see letter of 29 Jan 20); Macmillan had suggested the fee in his letter to TH of 28 Jan 20 (Macmillan letterbooks, BL).   *the verse-volumes*: see letter of 29 Jan 20; Macmillan, in his 28 Jan letter, had recommended that the poetry proofs for the Mellstock edn. should 'pass under your eye' but agreed to instruct the printer to send no more proofs of the prose.

To LADY ILCHESTER

Max Gate, | Dorchester. | February 5: 1920

My dear Lady Ilchester:

The book arrived to-day, & I must thank you & Lord Ilchester very warmly for a gift which I shall be greatly interested in reading, as will my wife, who was, as you may know, a writer of reviews in the papers. As I am going away for a few days I shall not plunge deeply into the pages till I get home again about the middle of next week, but content myself with glimpses.

I must congratulate its author on it having apparently already "caught on", to judge from the review of it occupying the place of honour in The Times Literary Supplement to-day. Perhaps he will be urged on to become a regular historian like Macaulay.

I dare say Lady Mary feels excited over the prospect of being abroad for 5 months! May she have a successful tour & safe return.

With kind regards I am

Very sincerely yours
Thomas Hardy.

Text Typed transcript (by Henry Reed) Purdy.
Ilchester: Lady Helen Mary Theresa Fox-Strangways, Countess of Ilchester; see IV.191. *The book*: Henry Fox, First Lord Holland, His Family and Relations (2 vols., London, 1920), by Lady Ilchester's husband, Giles Stephen Holland Fox-Strangways, sixth Earl of Ilchester. *writer of reviews*: FEH had published several reviews of new novels in the *Sphere*, edited by Clement Shorter.   *Supplement to-day*: the anonymous review, headed 'Henry Fox and His Contemporaries', appeared on the front page.   *like Macaulay*: Thomas Babington Macaulay, first Baron Macaulay (1800–59), historian; D.N.B.   *Lady Mary*: Lady Mary Theresa Fox-Strangways, the Ilchesters' elder daughter; see V.186.   *successful tour*: Lady Ilchester's letter of 3 Feb 20 (DCM) gives no details of her daughter's prospective travels.

To EVELYN GIFFORD

MAX GATE, | DORCHESTER. | 14: 2: 1920

My dear Evelyn:

You will remember my promising to send you the scenes selected by the O.U.D.S. from The Dynasts. But I found on looking at the play-bill that they were given there, so that you can easily mark them in your copy of the book from the play-bill, & see what they skipped, which you may find interesting. Best thanks for the bookplate.

Sincerely yours
Thomas Hardy.

Text   MS. C. H. Gifford.
Gifford: Evelyn Hamilton Gifford (see V.189), ELH's cousin, whom TH had recently seen in Oxford; see letter of 25 Jan 20.   *O.U.D.S.*: Oxford University Dramatic Society; see letter of 25 Jan 20.

To BLANCHE CRACKANTHORPE

MAX GATE, | DORCHESTER. | Feb 15: 1920

Dear Mrs Crackanthorpe;

I must send a line to tell you that we have got back from Oxford, & while there made the acquaintance of your friend Mr Morgan, & saw the play which he did so much for. Owing to the hurry of our sojourn I had only a brief talk with him, but he is a very good fellow indeed.

I was sorry you could not come, as was he. My wife send kindest regards.

Always yours
Th: Hardy.

Text   MS. (with envelope) Roger Morgan.
Crackanthorpe: Blanche Alethea Crackanthorpe, literary hostess; see IV.89. She had written Morgan a letter of introduction to TH in December 1919; see V.349.   *the play*: see letter of 25 Jan 20.   *wife send*: TH means 'wife sends'.

To EDWARD CLODD

Max Gate | 22: 2: 1920

My dear Clodd:

Very many thanks for your kind congratulations. It all went off quite pleasantly, the time of my being in Oxford for another reason having been chosen to save me trouble.

The undergrads' perfomance of the play was really excellent, & it was a delight to see their enthusiasm in doing it.

I hope the inhaling of east coast air continuously, instead of intermittently as formerly, has set you back years in your calendar.

You probably are aware that your book "If a man die" is one of a batch forming the text of an article on Modern Spiritualism in the January Quarterly.

Sincerely yrs
Th: Hardy.

Text MS. (correspondence card) Purdy.
Clodd: Edward Clodd, rationalist author; see I.237. He had been a close friend of TH's for many years.   *congratulations*: on TH's honorary degree from Oxford; see letter of 27 Jan 20.
"If a man die": Clodd's *The Question: "If a Man Die, Shall He Live Again?" Job. XIV. 14. A Brief History and Examination of Modern Spiritualism* (London, 1917).   *an article*: Hugh Elliot, 'Modern Spiritualism', *Quarterly Review*, January 1920; Clodd's book is reviewed along with four others.

To JOHN MIDDLETON MURRY

Max Gate | 23: 2: 1920

Dear Mr Murry:

Many thanks. These things seem to come as a gift, for I cannot feel that such intangible ware as thought-beats can weigh against a solid commodity.

My mind is quite vacant of any new poem, nor can I find one already written, beyond some lines I have long promised. I will, of course, bear your wish in mind. I gather that The Athenaeum has quite caught on, & I am glad.

Yrs sincerely
Th: Hardy.

Text MS. Berg.
These things: specifically, payment for his poem 'According to the Mighty Working' in the *Athenaeum* of 4 Apr 1919; Murry, as editor, wrote on 22 Feb 20 (DCM) to apologize for not having sent the money sooner.   *bear your wish in mind*: see letter of 7 Apr 20.

To FLORENCE HENNIKER

MAX GATE, | DORCHESTER. | Feb 28: 1920

My dear friend:

Yes: you conjecture rightly: we had a very pleasant time at Oxford. The undergrads who form the O.U.D.S. took us in hand & treated us as their property, putting a taxi at our disposal from morning to night all the time. There were improvements on the London performance—notably in the scenery; & the fact of the characters (110 in all, I think, & all speaking ones) being young, & many of them handsome, lent a great freshness & vivacity to their exhibition. Professional actors might have envied the breathless silence with which some of the scenes were followed, & the large use of handkerchiefs at points of tragedy.

We did not go by motor after all. The doctor said he could not sanction it, the roads being just at that time full of holes & mud: yet a man went from here by road a few days after & said the journey was comfortable enough. We stayed at Sir W. Raleigh's, the late professor of English Literature, though we might have put up at the Giffords. However we went to see them.

So Milner requires a garage to walk about in on wet days. Our Wessex, too, is very exacting. He sleeps in a room which has an anthracite stove that burns night & day; but if it goes out by chance in the small hours he promptly comes scratching at the bedroom door to induce us to come down & light it for him, as if it were unreasonable to expect him to sleep without a fire.

I wonder if you will be a fixture at Sussex Place. It is certainly a better side of the park to live on than the South. The Gosses came about 6 weeks ago & stayed at the Gloucester Hotel Weymouth: they visited us here, & we them: I think the air strengthened Mrs Gosse, as Weyth air does many people.

We have had of late great trouble with servants: they come & picnic for a month or two, & then leave, to picnic in somebody else's house. We have been reading Ld Ilchester's book on Henry Fox which he was kind enough to send. Lady I. wanted to know what I thought of it, & I have told her. It is a very thorough & sincere piece of work, & interesting. Best love from both.

Your affectte friend
Th: H.

Text   MS. DCM.
Henniker: Florence Ellen Hungerford Henniker, novelist; see II.11. TH had been deeply attracted to her when they first met in 1893.   *at Oxford*: see letters of 25 and 27 Jan 20. *Raleigh's, the late professor*: since Raleigh (see letter of 25 Jan 20) remained Merton Professor until his death in 1922, TH was perhaps using 'late' in the sense of 'lately' or 'of late'; cf. 'her late visit' in letter to Mrs. Henniker of 22 Dec 20.   *Giffords*: see letters of 25 Jan and 14 Feb 20. *Milner*: one of Mrs. Henniker's dogs, presumably named for Viscount Milner (see letter of 14 Jan 21 to Cock).   *Wessex*: the Max Gate dog, a wire-haired terrier; see V.8.   *Sussex Place*: 3 Sussex Place, Lancaster Gate, Mrs. Henniker's current London address.   *the park*: Hyde Park.   *Gosses ... Weymouth*: see letter of 8 Jan 20.   *Ld Ilchester's book*: see letter of 5 Feb 20.

To CLEMENT SHORTER

MAX GATE, | DORCHESTER. | March 7: 1920

Dear Clement Shorter:

The books have duly arrived—every one: though when those lonely two first came I doubted if the rest of the family would follow, & fancied a possibly ruined set impending.

Many thanks for such a birthday present, which you are certainly not justified in making to a solitary person you may seldom see much of in the future, & when the birthday itself hangs fire as yet—at least here: though I have been eighty for two or three years in the newspapers, & in American for ten or twelve; & out west in some places I died several years ago, to judge from queries by the correspondents of the papers there.

Yours sincerely
Thomas Hardy.

Text   MS. Princeton.
Shorter: Clement King Shorter, journalist; see I.245.   *The books*: unidentified.   *in American*: an apparent slip for 'America', though TH could have meant 'in American newspapers'.

To JOHN SLATER

March 7. 1920

My dear Slater:

It is very curious that yesterday at lunch I said apropos of nothing: "I never hear or see anything of John Slater nowadays". And lo, here is a letter from you!

As to your question whether I should like to be nominated as an Hon. Fellow of the R.I.B.A. I really don't know what to say. Age has naturally made me, like Gallio, care for none of these things, at any rate very much, especially as I am hardly ever in London. But at the same time I am very conscious of the honour of such a proposition, and like to be reminded in such a way that I once knew what a T square was. So, shall I leave the decision to your judgment? But if you think there would be any doubt in the mind of any member of the Council, please don't propose it.

Your letter recalls those times we had in Bedford Street together. Are there any such amiable architects now as Roger Smith was? Not many. Also, what became of Conder?—the one who had such a keen sense of humour.

Text Typed transcript (for inclusion in *LY*) DCM.
Slater: John Slater (1847–1924), architect, vice-president of Royal Institute of British Architects 1900–4.　　*like Gallio*: an allusion to Acts 18: 17.　　*to your judgment*: see letter of 29 Apr 20.　　*Bedford Street . . . Smith*: Professor Thomas Roger Smith (see I.50), the architect for whom TH worked in the 1870s, had offices in Bedford Street; Slater was articled to Smith and later co-authored a book with him.　　*Conder*: Josiah Condor, architect, is evidently intended; he worked with Smith in the early 1870s, entered the service of the Imperial Japanese Government in 1876, and died in Tokyo in 1920.

To MAURICE MACMILLAN

MAX GATE, | DORCHESTER. | March 23rd. 1920.

Dear Mr Macmillan:

I am told that children's books are a good advertisement for poetry, and therefore suggest that you let the people who want the three poems have them for half-a-guinea each, or if they want one, a guinea. But please do as you think best.

I hope you have now quite recovered from your indisposition.

Yours sincerely,
Thomas Hardy.

Text MS. (typewritten) BL.
Macmillan: Maurice Crawford Macmillan, publisher; see III.261.　　*people . . . three poems*: the request had come from Ethel Louisa Fowler, compiler of *The Daffodil Poetry Book* (London, 1920); the poems were 'The Going of the Battery', 'Song of the Soldiers' Wives', and 'The Souls of the Slain'.

To THOMAS HUMPHRY WARD

MAX GATE, | DORCHESTER. | April 3: 1920

Dear Mr Humphry Ward:

I did not suspect when we last corresponded that I should be writing the next time to express sympathy with you in such a great loss.

My wife & I last saw Mrs Ward at the house in Grosvenor Place, one afternoon, & have always remembered how vigorous & zestful she seemed in all relating to literature. But Alas!

My letter is belated, for I thought that while you were ill a delay would be better. I gather that you are mending, & hope it to be rapidly.

Sincerely yours
Thomas Hardy.

Text MS. NYU.
Ward: Thomas Humphry Ward, journalist and author; see III.90.   *great loss*: Ward's wife, Mary Augusta Ward, the novelist (see I.263), died 24 Mar 1920.   *Grosvenor Place*: the Wards left 25 Grosvenor Place in August 1919, having lived there for almost 30 years.

To JOHN MIDDLETON MURRY

MAX GATE, | DORCHESTER. | April 7th. 1920.

Dear Mr Murry:

Since you wrote kindly asking me for another poem I have found some verses which at first I thought would only suit publication in a *daily* paper dated April 30th. But I find that by accident there will be an Athenaeum on April 30th. next, and therefore I shall have pleasure in sending you the verses for serial use in that number, if it is not already made up. If it should be I will wait till I can find something else for the opportunity of appearing in your pages, as the aforesaid poem would lose some of whatever point it may have if it were published at another date. I can let you have it at once if you say there is room on April 30.

Yours sincerely,
Thomas Hardy.

P.S. I am presupposing you will care for it! Th. H.

Text MS. (typewritten) Berg.
some verses: TH's poem 'The Maid of Keinton-Mandeville', described as 'A tribute to Sir Henry Bishop on the sixty-fifth anniversary of his death: April 30, 1855', appeared in the *Athenaeum*, 30 Apr 1920; the typed MS. of the poem still accompanies this letter.   *P.S. . . . for it!*: postscript added in TH's hand.

To F. B. FISHER

MAX GATE, | DORCHESTER. | 13th. April 1920.

Dear Dr. Fisher:

I have signed the young woman's book on the strength of your recommendation & return it herewith. I notice that the author repeats the unaccountable error that "Wessex" in my books means the county of Dorset, although, as is stated continually in them, it has its ancient meaning as to extent, and many of the stories and poems are located outside Dorset altogether; and I may mention that one story, "The Romantic Adventures of a Milkmaid" (in the volume entitled "A Changed Man") has its scene near Tiverton.

By the way, is any member of the Holder family left at Tiverton? The late Colonel Holder, a connection of mine by marriage, lived there some time. Perhaps you could tell me if he died there, or is buried in the churchyard.

I remember the illness you speak of, which your skill pulled me through. I hope you keep well yourself. It seems from your letter that you do.

Sincerely yours,
Th. Hardy.

P.S. Old age compels me to dictate letters nowadays, which please excuse.
P.P.S. Your letter containing stamps has just been received. It was thoughtful of you to send them, but you should not have troubled. I remember when you came to Dorchester. Th H.

Text MS. (typewritten) DCM.
Fisher: Frederick Bazley Fisher, TH's doctor for many years prior to his retirement in 1910; see II.272.   *young woman's book*: unidentified.   *near Tiverton*: the Devonshire town from which Fisher had written—and in which he had been born.   *late Colonel Holder*: Cecil Holder, a son of ELH's brother-in-law, the Revd. Caddell Holder (see I.13), by his first marriage; he was living in Tiverton in the 1880s. See letter of 3 May 20 and letter of 12 June 20 to Hicks.   *illness you speak of*: according to Fisher's brief memoir in C. M. Fisher, *Life in Thomas Hardy's Dorchester 1888–1908* (Beaminster, Dorset, 1965), this 'serious illness' occurred in the late 1880s but was not allowed to become public knowledge.   *letter containing stamps*: dated 13 Apr 20 (DCM).   *I . . . Dorchester.*: final sentence added in TH's hand.

To GEORGE MACMILLAN

MAX GATE, | DORCHESTER. | April 15. 1920.

Dear Mr Macmillan:

I am in your hands in the matter of raising the price of the Wessex Edition to 10/6 a volume on account of the cost of production, and as you assure me that the extra price will not bring more profit I agree to the author's royalty remaining at 1/6 as now.

It is a curious question how far the public will go in accepting the necessary increase in the price of nearly all books before they leave off buying. I fancy more and more people will go back to the plan of borrowing at circulating libraries, as in the days of the three-volume novel, when the libraries were almost the sole purchasers.

I have, by the way, a few corrections to five or six of the volumes, which it would be a pity not to embody when you reprint. There may be none in those you think of reprinting now; but at any rate a list of the errata shall be in your hands by Monday morning. They are trifling, and cause no over-running.

Always sincerely yours,
Thomas Hardy.

Text MS. (typewritten) BL.
Macmillan: George Augustin Macmillan, publisher; see II.108.   *in your hands*: TH in this paragraph accepts the situation as set out in Macmillan's letter of 14 Apr 20 (Macmillan

letterbooks, BL); the previous price had been 7/6 a vol. and Macmillan was anxious that the new price should not go above 10/6.   *a few corrections*: see letter of 18 Apr 20.

To GEORGE MACMILLAN

MAX GATE, | DORCHESTER. | April 18. 1920

My dear Macmillan:

I send as promised the corrections for your reprint of the Wessex edition. As you will see, they do not refer to many of the volumes.

Many thanks for your letter.

Always sincerely
Thomas Hardy

Text   MS. (typewritten) BL.
the corrections: a list of these—a 4-page carbon typescript with additions in TH's hand—is in DCM, annotated by TH, '[Sent up Apl 18. 1920]'; two further lists, written entirely in TH's hand, record changes sent directly to the printers on 15 and 26 May 1920 (DCM).

To CHARLES SPEYER

MAX GATE, | DORCHESTER. | 24th. April 1920.

Dear Mr Speyer:

I have pleasure in sanctioning your publication of "When I set out for Lyonesse" to your music. It is not necessary to ask the Messrs Macmillan.

I think I told you, though I am not sure, that the correct reading of the lines is the one in the little "Golden Treasury" selection from my poems, or my "Collected Poems" in one volume, or the volume of the "Wessex" Edition entitled "Satires of Circumstance".

I have not been near the places you mention since last summer. No doubt they are looking well now.

You will pardon one of my age sending a machine-written letter.

Yours very truly,
Th: Hardy.

Text   MS. (typewritten, with envelope in FEH's hand) NYU.
Speyer: Charles Anthony Speyer, composer; see V.289.   *to your music*: it appeared later that year as the first of Speyer's *Six Selected Lyrics*; see V.289.   *Treasury" selection*: TH's *Selected Poems* of 1916, pub. in Macmillan's Golden Treasury Series.   *places you mention*: in his letter of 22 Apr 20 (DCM) Speyer expressed the hope that the Dorset uplands Pilsdon Pen and Golden Cap were 'putting on their spring garb'.

To GEORGE MACMILLAN

MAX GATE, | DORCHESTER. | April 27th. 1920.

Dear Mr Macmillan:

I have received the enclosed letters from Mr Hugo Vallentin, who appears to be a literary agent,—of what repute I do not know. Do you think it would be well to enter into some arrangement with the Swedish publishers through him, or that it should be made with the publisher Mr Andelsforlaget himself? Or to do nothing in the matter? I really don't like to give you the trouble of acting for me in it, but as his office is near yours he could easily call on you, and it might soon be concluded.

Two of my novels, Far from the Madding Crowd (which I believe you arranged for) and, I think, A Group of Noble Dames, have already been translated into Swedish; but no others, so far as I remember.

Yours very sincerely,
Thomas Hardy.

Text MS. (typewritten) BL.
literary agent: Hugo Maurice Valentin (1888–1963) was known later as a Swedish historian and leading Zionist; his two letters to TH, of 14 and 26 Apr 20, relate to some proposed Swedish translations of TH's novels. See letter of 21 May 20.   *Mr Andelsforlaget*: as Macmillan pointed out in his reply (29 Apr 20, Macmillan letterbooks, BL), the name 'Svenska Andelsförlaget' mentioned by Valentin simply meant 'the Swedish Publishing Company'.
near yours: Valentin had written from a London address, 16A John Street, Adelphi.   *into Swedish*: both these vols. appear to have been first pub. in 1920.

To JOHN SIMPSON

Max Gate, Dorchester, 29th April 1920.

Dear Mr. Simpson,

It has given me much pleasure to renew mental contact, as I may call it, with the R.I.B.A. after so many years through your kindness in sending the *Journal* of that body, in which I have been greatly interested to read the opening remarks in your article on "A War Memorial of the Last Century." You may be amused to learn that I had quite forgotten the little episode you quote from "A Laodicean," and have no more idea than you why the two Fellows of the Institute did not suspect foul play in noting the singular resemblance of the two designs. Well, as you say, the matter is closed. As I have informed the Secretary, I feel truly honoured by nomination to the Hon. Fellowship.

Believe me, sincerely yours,
Thomas Hardy.

Text *Journal of the Royal Institute of British Architects*, 8 May 1920, 329.
Simpson: John William Simpson (1858–1933), architect, president of the R.I.B.A. 1919–21; D.N.B.   *Last Century.*": Simpson's article (*Journal of the R.I.B.A.*, 24 Apr 1920) was dedicated to TH and written on the occasion of his election as an Honorary Fellow of the R.I.B.A.   *the two designs*: Simpson had remarked on the failure of the 'Fellows of the Royal Institute of British Architects' to comment on the similarity of the designs submitted to them by the hero, George Somerset, and by his dishonest rival, James Havill, in TH's *A Laodicean* (Wessex edn., 188).

To F. B. FISHER

Max Gate | Dorchester | May 3: 1920

Dear Dr Fisher:

Many thanks for information about the Holders. I don't know the present generation of the family, but, as I may have told you, the Revd C. Holder, Rector of St Juliot, Cornwall, Colonel Holder's father, married my late wife's sister.

If you should be meeting Mrs Rawlings she might inform you if she was the only child of the Colonel.

I will bear in mind that you still do consulting work, & am,

Sincerely yrs
Th: Hardy.

Text MS. DCM.
about the Holders: see letter of 13 Apr 20; Fisher reported (22 Apr 20, DCM) that Cecil Holder was not buried in Tiverton but that a daughter of his, Mrs. Rawlings, still lived nearby.   *consulting work*: Fisher had offered his services to TH in his 22 April letter.

To HAROLD CHILD

MAX GATE, | DORCHESTER. | 4th. May 1920.

Dear Mr Child:

(I use the universal printing-engine now, which I am sure you will excuse in one of my years.)

I am rather appalled at the prospect of my 80th. birthday—and an article thereon.—However, I daresay that in your judicious hands it may not be alarming.

As to the letter I wrote to Mr Shorter about my mother at the time of her death, I should object to it, or any other letter to him, being published or alluded to. As you will well know, one is apt at such times to write more freely than at others. I do not remember what I said in the letter, but if it concerned any facts of her life I can give you at first hand all that I should like to be mentioned—or my wife can. She will send them to you if you wish.

In respect of myself personally I am most averse to anything like an "interview," and have been for many years. Such details as it would be reasonable to print, if people want them, (would that it were impossible to print any!) she could also send you, and you could mould them into shape and good size, by warming up and adding some of the ideas that went to the making of your little book on my writings.

All this seems as if I did not wish you to come and see us—but that is not so by any means. At present, as in the perversity of things has happened before, we are in the turmoil of having repairs done to the house (postponed so many years owing to the war), but that difficulty may perhaps be overcome if you would like to run down. However a conversation with me anent the birthday does not seem to be really necessary; and I would rather you came when that date is quite past, and no newspaper copy is in question at all.

I have never printed anything about my early years of authorship &c. more than appears in Who's-Who and such publications. But absurd paragraphs have been published in the gossip-papers purporting to be my history. For instance, quite lately, an educated man at Oxford wrote to inquire if he might take it to be true, as reported, that the story of "Jude the Obscure" was my personal history. Curiously enough, that particular novel has hardly a single fact of my own life in it, or any sort of resemblance to my experiences.

If then, you say that such detail as we furnish will satisfy you for using as a skeleton of your article they shall be forwarded, on the understanding that you do not say how you came by them.

    Believe me,

Yours sincerely,
Th: Hardy.

Text   MS. (typewritten) Adams.
Child: Harold Hannyngton Child, author and critic; see III.333.   *article thereon*: Child's 'Thomas Hardy', *Bookman* (London), June 1920.   *letter . . . to Mr Shorter*: possibly that dated 8 Apr 04 (III.118–19).   *little book*: Child's *Thomas Hardy* (London, 1916). *educated man at Oxford*: Archie Stanton Whitfield, who wrote from Exeter College, Oxford, on 30 Oct 19 (DCM); FEH's reply, written 'at [TH's] request', is quoted in *LY*, 195–6, and mentioned by Whitfield himself in his published lecture, *Thomas Hardy: The Artist, the Man, and the Disciple of Destiny* (London, 1921).

To R. B. MARSTON

May 15: 1920

Dear Mr Marston:

    The paragraph in the Times to which you allude in your letter of the 12th. relates to a correspondence I had with the Society of Authors some years ago on the question of their acting as literary executors. I have not thought or heard anything of the matter of late, & I do not know why it should be revived just now. Possibly somebody else has written about it to them. It has no reference to any personal need of mine, my former correspondence with the Society having been in the interest of other authors.

    It is however worth while to know the Public Trustee's views on the subject, & I am obliged to you for forwarding his letter, which is returned with the pamphlet.

Yours very truly

R. B. Marston Esq.

Text   MS. (pencil draft) DCM.
Marston: Robert Bright Marston (1853–1927), publisher and authority on angling.   *in the Times*: *The Times*, 7 May 1920, noted that the annual report of the Incorporated Society of Authors contained an inquiry from TH (the society's president) as to whether the society could act as a trustee and literary executor for a deceased member.   *his letter*: i.e., a letter from the Public Trustee Office to Marston on the question of whether the Public Trustee could be designated as an author's trustee and literary executor; TH copied out the letter (DCM) before returning it to Marston.   *the pamphlet*: issued by the Public Trustee Office.

To SIR ANTHONY HOPE HAWKINS

[Mid-May 1920]

Dear Anthony Hawkins.

    I have learned that we are to have the pleasure of a visit from you on June 2, and much hope that this is really the case. The last time I saw you was, I think, across a huge blue table at Wellington House, Buckingham Gate, on that memorable afternoon in September 1914, the yellow sun shining in upon our confused deliberations in a melancholy manner that I shall never forget.

Of course the necessity of a deputation is rather, well, make-believe, to a person who goes about bicycling (though in mitigation let me state that I don't bicycle *far* nowadays). I ought to be a dignified figure sitting in a large arm-chair (gilded for choice) with a foot-stool. However, I didn't begin it, and at any rate shall be delighted to see you, and a bad reason is better than none.

Text Fragment, Charles Mallet, *Anthony Hope and His Books* (London, 1935), 243.
Date From internal evidence.
Hawkins: Anthony Hope Hawkins ('Anthony Hope'), novelist; see II.246. He was knighted in 1918.   *on June 2*: Hawkins was a member—with Augustine Birrell (see II.83) and John Galsworthy—of a deputation from the Incorporated Society of Authors which visited Max Gate on TH's 80th birthday; see letter of 23 Aug 20, also *LY*, 212–13, and Mallet, 243.   *in September 1914*: when they, together with other writers, were asked by the government to assist in the public articulation of British war aims; see V.47 and *LY*, 163.

To JOHN MIDDLETON MURRY

MAX GATE, | DORCHESTER. | 18: 5: 1920

Dear Mr Murry:
Many thanks for the cheque. I should feel very uncomfortable at taking any payment for the use of such a short poem if I had not received some letters from people who tell me they like it, so I suppose they do.
I am so glad to hear that the Athenaeum makes headway. I consider it quite a "live" paper, & I marvel at your energy in keeping it going so briskly, & at the same time doing your own particular work outside the paper.

Sincerely yours
Thomas Hardy.

Text MS. Berg.
short poem: see letter of 7 Apr 20.

To JOHN GALSWORTHY

Max Gate. | May 19, 1920.

My dear Galsworthy,
I am delighted to hear that you are coming to see us on June 2, as one of a deputation, and though the reason was not altogether a necessity the result is as it should be. As it seems you are coming by Great Western from Paddington we will meet the train here and bring you out straight to our house to lunch, so please don't go eating any before you arrive.
I must congratulate you on your new play, which I have not seen, though good critics (I don't mean professional) tell me it is very fine. One friend of mine—Sir George Douglas—who is very independent in his ideas, writes: "I have seen *three times* one really fine and finely acted play; Galsworthy's *Skin Game*."
I am reading *Tatterdemalion* (for which many thanks; did I acknowledge

it?)—though as usual my wife is further on than I. However I will leave that till I see you.

Always sincerely
Thomas Hardy.

Text   H. V. Marrot, ed., *The Life and Letters of John Galsworthy* (London, 1935), 494.
Galsworthy: John Galsworthy, novelist and playwright; see III.202.   *deputation*: see letter of mid-May 20 to Hawkins.   *new play*: Galsworthy's *The Skin Game*, first performed at the St. Martin's Theatre 21 Apr 1920.   *Douglas*: see letter of 20 Nov 21; he wrote 2 May 20 (DCM).   *Tatterdemalion*: Galsworthy's short story volume *Tatterdemalion* (London, 1920).

To LEONARD REES

MAX GATE, | DORCHESTER. | 20th. May 1920.

Dear Sir:

I have been hunting for something I might send for May 30 in answer to the request you honour me with, but I cannot find a suitable contribution, having used up a few weeks ago all I had available, and I am unable to write a thing offhand.

A message to your readers, even if not uncalled for, is inadvisable, as it brings demands from other papers for messages, and their resentment if one is not sent.

I may have incurred yours by this answer. If so I must bear it. However if anything suitable turns up later on I will let you have it with pleasure.

Yours very truly,
Thomas Hardy.

Leonard Rees, Esq.

Text   MS. (typewritten) Purdy.
Rees: Leonard Rees (1856–1932), journalist, editor of the *Sunday Times* 1901–32.   *honour me with*: Rees wrote 17 May 20 (DCM) to seek from TH a contribution to the *Sunday Times* of 30 May 1920, just prior to TH's 80th birthday.   *let you have it*: TH sent nothing, however, and the *Sunday Times* marked the occasion with a short article by Edmund Gosse.

To SIR FREDERICK MACMILLAN

MAX GATE, | DORCHESTER. | 21st. May 1920.

Dear Sir Frederick:

I am sending back the agreement for the Swedish translations, signed. It seems fair enough, especially as the publishing company might have helped themselves to the books without saying anything. (I am not sure if I ought to have put on a 6d. stamp or not). Many thanks for seeing to the matter.

This reminds me of a kindred one. I remember you saying some time ago that you would consider any question or difficulty that I might meet with in respect of publication in America, and give me the benefit of your opinion thereon. I am just now rather puzzled on a point of that sort. I could send up particulars, but I don't like to do so till I hear that you are not too busy to look over them. Perhaps when you are not you will kindly let me know.

Yours sincerely,
Thomas Hardy.

Text MS. (typewritten) BL.
Swedish translations: see letter of 27 Apr 20.   *without saying anything*: Macmillan pointed out, 19 May 20 (Macmillan letterbooks, BL), that TH's books were not in fact protected by copyright in Sweden.   *6d. stamp*: as Stamp Duty on the contract.   *let me know*: Macmillan replied, 26 May 20 (Macmillan letterbooks, BL), that he would be glad to advise TH; see letter of 28 May 20.

To HAROLD CHILD

MAX GATE, | DORCHESTER. | Saturday morning | 22: 5: 1920

Dear Mr Child:
Here it is back at once. The facts are all right, & as for the opinions & estimate, I am glad that you are responsible for them & not I! There is no objection to what you propose to insert. I write in haste, to catch the morning post. Believe me

Always yours
Thomas Hardy.

Text MS. Adams.
back at once: evidently a draft of Child's article; see letter of 4 May 20.

To WILBUR CROSS

MAX GATE, | DORCHESTER. | May 26th. 1920.

Dear Mr Cross:
I am greatly obliged by the advance proof of Mr Fletcher's poem, which I think very beautiful and characteristic.
As for my contributing to the Yale Review, it is what I should much like to do, but my productions are limited nowadays and I fear to promise.
With thanks for the honour of your request,
I am,

Sincerely yours,
Thomas Hardy.

Text MS. (typewritten, with envelope in FEH's hand) Yale.
Cross: Wilbur Lucius Cross (1862–1948), scholar and teacher, editor of *Yale Review*, subsequently Governor of Connecticut.   *Mr Fletcher's poem*: John Gould Fletcher (1886–1950), American poet; his 'The Black Rock', dedicated 'To Thomas Hardy', appeared in *Yale Review*, July 1920.   *your request*: in Cross's letter of 10 May 20 (Purdy).

To SIR FREDERICK MACMILLAN

MAX GATE, | DORCHESTER. | May 28: 1920

My dear Macmillan:
It occurred to me a day or two ago that it would be better if Wessex Poems preceded Time's Laughingstocks in the Mellstock edition, being more

correct chronologically; & that the suggestion might be in time I wrote straight to the printers, in case they should be taking it in hand. If you agree with me will you let them know?

I am enclosing what I promised to send. I hope it won't bore you, but am terribly afraid it will! What I am personally most interested in is how to get our Collected edition of the poetry circulated in America. However, you will see from the memoranda what I mean.

Sincerely yours
Thomas Hardy.

Text   MS. BL.
the suggestion: it was adopted.   *promised to send*: see letter of 21 May 20; still accompanying this letter is a typed 5-page summary of TH's contractual relations with Harper & Brothers since the international copyright agreement of July 1891, together with a list of questions on which TH was seeking advice and a summary by Macmillan & Co. of their American sales of TH's poetry since 1917.

To PETER GILES

Max Gate, | Dorchester. | 3rd June, 1920.

My Dear Sir,

My sincere thanks for the kind message from yourself and the University on the occasion of my birthday.

I had hoped to be frequently in Cambridge after receiving the honour of the degree. But the war came and hindered travelling; and now I am almost past taking journeys.

Very truly yours,
Thomas Hardy.

Text   *Cambridge Review*, 9 June 1920, 395.
Giles: Peter Giles (1860–1935), philologist, master of Emmanuel College, Cambridge, 1911–35, vice-chancellor 1919–21.   *the degree*: TH received an Honorary Litt.D. from Cambridge in 1913; see IV.259–60 and *LY*, 156–7.

To FLORENCE HENNIKER

Max Gate | June 4: 1920

My dear friend:

We are delighted to hear that you are coming to Weymouth on July 1. I should have written to-day in answer to your kind telegram on my birthday, even if you had not added this pleasant letter. I was going to write last night, but some people came in just at the moment. You know how I valued having it, I am sure you do!

Yes: it was amusing to have the deputation. I had never been deputated (?) before, so I was not at all dignified. But, as you know, I never am.

Yes: they *did* come to lunch. I was rather tired—not by them, for no less tiresome people can be conceived—but by the messages, & by strangers unexpectedly entering. I may tell you, since you allude to the King's message, that he has sent another to-day, thanking me for my good wishes for *his* birthday, which I expressed in my reply.

I saw the paragraph about the publishers. I wonder if it was true. Will you kindly thank Anna for her message as well. How very good of her. I am so sorry to hear of her sprained arm. I use Eliman's Embrocation for such accidents, but a relative uses a much stronger application—Jacob's Oil, or some such name. However I need not tell you of these things.

Florence has gone to Weymouth this very afternoon for an hour, taking Wessex. He so implores to be taken that it is hard to leave him at home. We will do anything to help you get there, if you will let us know. F. is splendid in managing such things. She often finds rooms for friends. Some rooms are good there, & some bad. Weymouth air is very good in summer, & probably you will not mind a few trippers beginning to come. (August is their great month.)

Lady Ir will be so glad to have you near. She always asks when we see her if we have heard lately. She & Ld I. sent a combined wire on Wedny which I must thank them for.

Barrie has just sent a note to say he is coming to morrow night for the week end. Believe me

Ever your affectionate

Tho. H.

By a curious chance the printers are reprinting just now: & you may imagine how full my hands are. Th: H.

Text MS. DCM.
deputation: see letter of mid-May 20 to Hawkins.   *in my reply*: TH's telegram to Lord Stamfordham (the King's private secretary), 2 June 20, reads, 'Please convey to His Majesty respectful thanks for message & best wishes for his birthday tomorrow Thomas Hardy' (Royal Library, Windsor).   *paragraph about the publishers*: unidentified.   *Anna*: Anna Hirschmann, Mrs. Henniker's personal maid; see V.99.   *Lady Ir . . . Ld I.*: Lady Ilchester . . . Lord Ilchester; see letter of 5 Feb 20.   *Barrie*: Sir James Barrie; see letter to him of early Aug 21. *reprinting*: FEH, writing to Rebekah Owen (see II.147), 12 June 20 (Colby), speaks of TH as busy with proofs for the Mellstock edn. (see letter of 29 Jan 20).

To SIR FREDERICK MACMILLAN

MAX GATE, | DORCHESTER. | June 7th. 1920.

Dear Sir Frederick Macmillan:

I am greatly obliged to you for going into the question of America. I think I can write now more definitely to them, and I will let you know how I get on. Please keep the details I sent up, as I have a copy.

I had quite forgotten that you were circulating the poems over there in the way you describe—which of course is quite satisfactory. No doubt the readers will get hold of them in time, but they take rather a long while to comprehend editions it seems, and probably it accounts for their asking me where they can get them, etc.

I must also thank you for your good wishes, which are not the less valued for arriving next day. My wife sends her kind regards and I am

Sincerely yours,

Thomas Hardy.

Text MS. (typewritten) BL.
question of America: see letters of 21 and 28 May 20; Macmillan (2 June 20, Macmillan letterbooks, BL) had responded with information about Harper & Brothers' delay in bringing out its version of the Wessex edn.   *way you describe*: Macmillan, in the same letter, reminded TH that Macmillan's New York house was circulating the one-vol. *Collected Poems* in the United States.

To DOROTHY ALLHUSEN

MAX GATE, | DORCHESTER. | June 8: 1920

My dear Dorothy:

How very kind of you to send me good wishes, & to remember beforehand to send them when the time came. Not many do.

Yes: I have a heap of letters, & that, unfortunately, makes my reply to yours a very hurried affair. I am not sure, but I hope to see your mother for a day or two later on: I should like to very much; but I have reached an age at which plans are provisional only. You have not yet!

Your experiences abroad must be painfully interesting. You must tell us about them when you come. Florence sends her love, & I am

Your affectte old friend
Th: Hardy.

Text MS. (with envelope) Purdy.
Allhusen: Osma Mary Dorothy Allhusen, *née* Stanley; see I.257.   *good wishes*: in her letter of 31 May 20 (DCM).   *beforehand*: i.e., ahead of the actual day.   *your mother*: Lady St. Helier; see letter of 28 Jan 23.   *experiences abroad*: Mrs. Allhusen reported that she had just returned from France, having visited 'all the Battlefields from Festubert to Verdun'.   *when you come*: Mrs. Allhusen said that if TH were not coming to London she would hope to see him in Dorchester during the summer.

To EDITH BATESON

MAX GATE, | DORCHESTER. | June 8: 1920

Dear Madam:

I am deeply obliged to you for the charming little model suggested by my poem, "Often when Warring", that you have been kind enough to send. We have put it up in the drawing room, & it has already been seen by some judges, who think highly of it, as I do myself.

Believe me

Sincerely yours
Thomas Hardy.

Miss Edith Bateson.

Text MS. (with envelope) Fitzwilliam Museum.
Bateson: Edith Bateson (d. 1938), sculptor and painter, daughter of William Henry Bateson (*D.N.B.*), master of St. John's College, Cambridge, and sister of Mary Bateson (*D.N.B.*), the historian.   *when Warring*": an anti-war poem, first pub. 1917; in her letter of 3 June 20 (DCM) Miss Bateson referred to the 'model' (evidently a small sculpture) as 'The Enemy's Kiss'.

To A. C. BENSON

MAX GATE, | DORCHESTER. | June 8: 1920

Dear Dr Benson:

I send my very warm thanks for the kind wishes & congratulations that reached me last week from yourself & the College. I have decided that it was worth while to live to be eighty to discover what friends there were about me up & down the world, & my judgment against the desirability of being so long upon earth is therefore for a time at least suspended. An incidental pleasure is that I now discover you to be at head quarters as usual after your long illness: I felt that you would be, sooner or later, but I determined not to trouble you with a letter of inquiry to which you must of necessity return an indefinite answer. I am rejoiced that you are there again.

How I wish I could be often at dear old Magdalene. But the war, after taking away the spirit to go anywhere while it lasted, has left behind complications that get more troublesome with the years, & my powers of locomotion naturally do not increase. I shall always remember those few pleasant days we had with you just on the eve, or near it, of that mad convulsion, which did more mischief in five years than a University can mend in a hundred I fear.

You are now in the middle of the May Week bustle, which I hope will not touch you much personally. My wife sends her kindest regards & a message that you are to be careful against over-exertion. Believe me

Always sincerely yours
Thomas Hardy.

Text   MS. (with envelope) Texas.
Benson: Arthur Christopher Benson, man of letters; see I.280.   *the College*: Magdalene College, Cambridge, of which Benson was master (1915–25) and TH an honorary fellow. *long illness*: Benson spoke of his 'long and depressing' illness when writing to TH, 2 June 20 (DCM); it was, in fact, a mental breakdown from which he had as yet imperfectly recovered. *few pleasant days*: in November 1913, when TH was installed as an honorary fellow; see IV.314–16 and *LY*, 158.

To SIR HENRY AND LADY HOARE

MAX GATE, | DORCHESTER. | 9: 6: 1920.

Dear Sir H. & Lady Hoare:

My sincere thanks for your kind & handsome present on my birthday, & your good wishes. Alas that I should have to be brief, but you will understand. We hope we may see you this summer.

Most truly yours
Thomas Hardy.

Text   MS. (correspondence card, with envelope) Wiltshire Record Office.
Hoare: Sir Henry Hugh Arthur Hoare, Bt., and his wife Alda, of Stourhead, Wiltshire; see IV.75.   *present*: unidentified.

To JOHN LANE

MAX GATE, | DORCHESTER. | June 9th. 1920.

Dear Mr Lane:

I send my sincere thanks as soon as possible—which is not very soon, by the way—for Mrs Lane's and your good wishes. Also for the mysterious goblet inscribed to the mysterious namesake of mine. He must, or may, have been a jockey; though if riding so late as 1876 I surely should have heard of him.

Anyhow, no woman ever took the trouble to inscribe her love for me on a cup of crystal—of that you may be sure: and it is best on the whole to leave the history of the glass in vague obscurity.

I hope you both are well in that ideal London site of yours, and my wife desires you to give her kindest regards to Mrs Lane.

Believe me,

Sincerely yours,
Th: Hardy.

P.S. You will understand why I have to dictate. Th: H.

Text MS. (typewritten) Colby.
Lane: John Lane, publisher; see I.239.   *Mrs Lane's*: Annie, *née* Eichberg, Lane's American-born wife; see letter to her of 7 Feb 25.   *a jockey*: it appears from the revised excerpt from this letter in *LY*, 213, that this assumption was based on 'the diagrams' also etched on the glass. *no woman*: Lane, writing 31 May 20 (DCM), speculated that the goblet had been intended as a gift to TH 'from some fair but probably shy admirer'.   *London site*: Lane wrote from 8 Lancaster Gate Terrace.   *P.S. . . . dictate.*: added in TH's hand.

To JOHN MIDDLETON MURRY

MAX GATE, | DORCHESTER. | June 10: 1920.

Best thanks to Athenaeum Staff & yourself. You will understand this regretful & compulsory brevity.

Th: Hy

Text MS. (postcard) Texas.
Best thanks: evidently for a congratulatory message on TH's 80th birthday.

To J. C. SQUIRE

MAX GATE, | DORCHESTER. | June 10: 1920.

Many thanks. Alas that such brevity shd be compulsory! but you will understand.

Th: H.

Text MS. (postcard) Taylor.
Squire: John Collings Squire, poet and man of letters; see V.322.   *Many thanks*: for birthday greeting.

To JOHN ACLAND

MAX GATE, | DORCHESTER. | June 12: 1920

Dear Captain Acland:

I must thank you, both on your personal account, & as the representative of the County Museum, for your kind letter on my birthday. I should have replied sooner, but you will quite understand that my correspondence has been rather heavy this past week or two. When your own birthday comes round please accept the same good wishes from me.

Believe me,

Always sincerely yrs
Thomas Hardy.

Text MS. DCM.
Acland: Captain John Edward Acland, curator of the Dorset County Museum; see III.262.

To G. LOWES DICKINSON

MAX GATE, | DORCHESTER. | June 12; 1920

Dear Mr Lowes Dickinson:

I am sending a brief—too brief—reply to your kind letter of greeting, or re-greeting. I quite remember your visit to us that afternoon: if it was in 1918, & I suppose it must have been, how time flies.

It is a great pleasure to me to know that my poems appeal to you. But lest I should be made unduly vain by this knowledge it happens that I am just now immersed in the drudgery of correcting blunders (partly mine, partly printers') for a reprint—& my sight is not so good as it was. My wife's kindest regards.

Sincerely yours
Thomas Hardy.

Text MS. Celadon August.
Dickinson: Goldsworthy Lowes Dickinson (1862–1932), historian and philosophical writer; *D.N.B.*   *kind letter*: of 2 June 20 (DCM).   *your visit*: its precise date has not been established.   *appeal to you*: Dickinson wrote that TH's poetry made 'an appeal . . . so intimate' that he had felt him to be 'a spiritual ally' even before they met.   *reprint*: evidently the poetry vols. of the Mellstock edn. (see letter of 4 June 20); although this was a reset edn. the contents were not themselves new.

To CHARLES GIFFORD

MAX GATE, | DORCHESTER. | June 12: 1920

Dear Mr Gifford:

I fear I am rather late in thanking you for the good wishes you sent on my birthday. When yours comes along please accept the same from me.

This about your "Recollections" is interesting. I hope your excellent mother comes into them. I seem to know her through having heard such praise of her by Emma, & of the delightful times she used to have at your house. However perhaps your public life will be more to the point in a book for general readers.

My wife & I both send kind regards to Léonie. We were somewhat invaded last week, but I am thankful to say that is over. I hope your rheumatism does not trouble you much now. My trouble is that I cannot leave off anything in the hottest weather without getting twinges. But you are a boy to me.

Always sincerely yours
Thomas Hardy.

P.S. You will not, of course, come this way without letting us know: nor Léonie. T.H.

Text MS. C. H. Gifford.
Gifford: ELH's cousin Charles Edwin Gifford, former Paymaster-in-Chief, Royal Navy; see II.17 and IV.237.   *"Recollections"*: Gifford's 'Recollections of a Naval Secretary', pub. in six instalments in *Chambers's Journal*, 14 Aug–27 Nov 1920.   *your excellent mother*: Emlin Gifford, *née* Rowe, wife of Gifford's father (ELH's uncle) George Mitchell Gifford.   *Léonie*: Gifford's elder daughter Leonora Randolph Gifford (1881–1968).   *boy to me*: Gifford was born in 1843.

To JOHN GEORGE HICKS

MAX GATE, | DORCHESTER. | 12th. June 1920.

Dear Colonel Hicks:

I must thank you for your kind congratulations on my birthday. Your letter interested me much, for of course I remember you as a boy—inconveniently smart sometimes at riddles &c., I may say. But we used to call you George (that is, if you are the fair-haired one I think you are); but now you put John in front—your uncle's name.

Another point that puzzles me is, how it comes about that your aunt Louisa was the rector's wife at St Juliot. My brother-in-law Holder was rector there for 20 years till he died in 1882, his first wife being named Anne, and his second Helen—my sister-in-law. Probably your aunt's husband succeeded him? Anyhow it is a very odd coincidence that I first got to know St Juliot through your uncle John and that his (?) sister should have gone there long after his disassociation from the place, and after my relations too had left it.

It may be, however, that Mr John Hicks's original connection with the church restoration was in some way the cause of your aunt being there later—though I don't quite see how.

The scene of "A Pair of Blue Eyes" is, as you surmise, St. Juliot and its neighbourhood—so far as it is anywhere.

Yours sincerely,
[signed] Thomas Hardy.

Text MS. (typed draft or transcript, on Max Gate stationery) DCM.
Hicks: John George Hicks, currently assistant secretary of the Imperial Service College; he was the son of the Revd. James Hicks, vicar of Piddletrenthide, Dorset, 1845–88, and nephew of John Hicks, the architect to whom TH was apprenticed in Dorchester in 1856 (see V.198 and Millgate, 54–6).   *Your letter*: of 2 June 20 (DCM).   *fair-haired one*: Hicks had a brother, just over a year older, named William.   *your aunt Louisa*: not, apparently, the sister of Hicks's father but of Hicks's mother.   *Holder*: the Revd. Caddell Holder; see I.13.   *Anne*: Holder's first wife, who died, aged 60, in 1867.   *Helen*: Helen Holder, *née* Gifford, ELH's sister; see II.271.   *succeeded him*: Holder's successor as rector of St. Juliot was the Revd.

William Henry Leicester, whose wife does indeed appear to have been named Louisa.   *through your uncle John*: John Hicks made the original architectural inspection of St. Juliot Church, although the restoration was not taken in hand until after his death; see Millgate, 121.   *[signed]*: square brackets in original.

To WILLIAM ROTHENSTEIN

MAX GATE, | DORCHESTER. | June 12: 1920

Dear Mr Rothenstein:

I am sending a brief acknowledgement of the receipt of your good wishes—briefer than it ought to be, but you will understand. Of course I now remember you for a great many years, & know what a reader you have been.

I have lost the scent of pictorial art nowadays, rather puzzled at its drift. I don't suppose I shall ever catch on again.

Kind regards to Mrs Rothenstein (whose portrait I saw somewhere lately)

Sincerely yours
Th: Hardy.

Text   MS. (with envelope) Harvard.
Rothenstein: William Rothenstein, artist; see II.149.   *good wishes*: in Rothenstein's letter of 2 June 20 (DCM).   *Mrs Rothenstein*: Alice Mary Rothenstein, actress; see III.98.

To SIR ROBERT PEARCE EDGCUMBE

MAX GATE, | DORCHESTER. | June 14: 1920

Dear Edgcumbe:

I send a line—though I am late in doing it—to thank you for your kind message on my birthday; & also for the Western Mercury with your interesting article. It reminds me that a maternal ancestor of mine established a paper in Cornwall called The West Briton, somewhere between 100 & 150 years ago. What became of the paper I never heard.

Your survey of the advance in what we call civilization since 1860 might be supplemented by a prophetic article on our probable retrogression during the next 60 years to the point from which we started (not to say further)—to turnpike-road travelling, high postage, scarce newspapers (for lack of paper to print them on), oppression of one class by another, etc., etc.

Very truly yours
Thomas Hardy.

Text   MS. Texas.
Edgcumbe: Robert Pearce Edgcumbe, former Dorchester banker and politician; see I.180.
interesting article: it has not been traced in the *Western Weekly Mercury*, however, and was perhaps published pseudonymously.   *maternal ancestor*: Christopher Childs, mining engineer, brother of TH's great-grandmother; see V.216 and *EL*, 8.   *The West Briton*: published weekly in Truro, Cornwall, from 1810 to the present; see *The Personal Notebooks of Thomas Hardy*, ed. Richard H. Taylor (London, 1978), 274.

To MARGARET GIFFORD

MAX GATE, | DORCHESTER. | June 14: 1920

Dear Mrs Gifford:

I must send a line in reply to your & Daisy & Evelyn's kind telegram on my birthday—though I am rather late in doing it. But you will understand why, & you would be amused to hear how we got through the time.

We learnt from Mr Jeune when he called here that you were away from Oxford for a change. We hope Evelyn has quite recovered by this time, & that you are all well.

My wife sends her love to all, & I am

Ever yours sincerely
Thomas Hardy.

Text MS. C. H. Gifford.
Gifford: Margaret Symons Gifford, *née* Jeune (1839–1924), second wife of ELH's uncle, the late Archdeacon Edwin Hamilton Gifford (see I.31).   *Daisy*: Margaret Gifford, Mrs. Gifford's elder daughter; see letter to her of 31 Dec 20.   *Evelyn's*: her younger daughter; see letter of 14 Feb 20.   *Mr Jeune*: John Frederic Symons Jeune (see V.164), Mrs. Gifford's brother.   *quite recovered*: she died, however, in September 1920; see *LY*, 214.

To THE REVD. J. H. DICKINSON

MAX GATE, | DORCHESTER. | June 15: 1920

Dear Mr Dickinson:

It was a great pleasure to me to get your good wishes on my birthday, as also to my wife, who having been a friend of Emma's has naturally been always interested in St. Juliot & its associations.

It is satisfactory to learn that you have annexed Lesnewth, & curious, inasmuch as I myself annexed it as "East Endelstow" when I wrote "A Pair of Blue Eyes"—that is, so far as the story has any reality, this being confined to its topographical features. Though readers will look in vain for the mansion I put in, the fact being, if I remember rightly, that I imported the building bodily from some 20 miles off—Lanhydrock, I fancy. But as it is more than 45 years ago that the romance appeared, I am vague.

I used, of course, to know the church quite well, & have a vivid recollection of going there on more than one Sunday evening in summer with Miss Gifford when I was visiting at St. J., & the churchwarden lighting the candles for the evening hymn. But these things are passing to "the land where all things are forgotten".

It is very kind of you to wish to see us again. But I don't know. For though I am quite active, travelling is much slower now than it was, so that distances have been lengthened. We both send kind regards to your sister.

Very sincerely yours
Thomas Hardy.

Text MS. (with envelope) Berg.
Dickinson: John Harold Dickinson, rector of St. Juliot; see IV.262.   *Emma's*: i.e., ELH, TH's first wife (see I.131); TH met her, as Emma Lavinia Gifford, at St. Juliot in

1870.   *annexed Lesnewth*: Dickinson reported in his letter of 2 June 20 (DCM) that the neighbouring parish of Lesnewth had been added to his responsibilities.   *Lanhydrock*: the former seat of the Robartes family, just S. of Bodmin.   *for the evening hymn*: see TH's poem 'The Young Churchwarden' and Millgate, 128.   *things are passing*: TH first wrote 'things have passed'.   *are forgotten"*: from the version of Ps. 88: 12 in the Book of Common Prayer.   *your sister*: also living at St. Juliot.

To SIR HENRY NEWBOLT

MAX GATE, | DORCHESTER. | 21 June 1920

My dear Newbolt:

Hearty thanks for letter & telegram—from both of us. I am disappointed at not being able to be present, owing to this sudden rheumatism—not very violent, but incapacitating. I have no idea where I caught the cold that brought it on. However, old gents of 80 must expect such.

My interest in Salisbury Cathedral, which is of course architectural, has lasted ever since 1860, when it began with me, on visiting it as an architect's pupil; & I remember well my first sight of its unrivalled outline—through a driving mist that nearly hid the top of the spire. At that time the interior, as arranged by Wyatt, was still untouched by Scott, the organ being over the screen. The result was that a greater air of mystery & gloom hung over the interior than does now, & it looked much larger from the subdivision—as buildings always do.

Kindest regards to Lady Newbolt from both of us, & with renewed thanks for your offer of hospitality I am

Sincerely yours

Thomas Hardy.

Text MS. Texas.
Newbolt: Henry John Newbolt, poet and man of letters; see III.21 and V.189.   *to be present*: Newbolt (20 June 20, Texas) had invited TH and FEH to stay with him near Salisbury and attend, on 24 June, a service marking the 700th anniversary of the founding of Salisbury Cathedral.   *Wyatt*: James Wyatt (1746–1813), architect; *D.N.B.*   *Scott*: Sir George Gilbert Scott (1811–78), architect; *D.N.B.*   *Lady Newbolt*: Margaret Edina Newbolt, *née* Duckworth.

To J. H. MORGAN

MAX GATE, | DORCHESTER. | June 28: 1920.

Dear General Morgan:

I was delighted to receive a letter from you at the time of my birthday, apart from the subject of it, for which accept my warm thanks. I should have sent them sooner, but as it happened a whole series of proofs for a reprint coincided with the addition to my correspondence for the other reason.

Yes: Oxford has honoured me with a degree, & was so considerate as to choose the time for conferring it that at which I had arranged with the young barbarians of the O.U.D.S. to be there to see their performance of The Dynasts. It was an extremely pleasant visit, & everybody was very kind.

As you may have shifted into the vague from the address you gave, things being so very uncertain over there, I will make this but a brief letter. My wife sends kindest regards. Please let us know your whereabouts from time to time, & believe me

Sincerely yours
Thomas Hardy.

Text MS. Purdy.
Morgan: John Hartman Morgan, lawyer and author; see III.94. *letter from you*: dated 3 June 20 (DCM). *of The Dynasts*: see letters of 25 and 27 Jan 20. *over there*: Morgan was still in Berlin at this date, serving on the Inter-Allied Commission of Control for enforcement of the disarmament provisions of the Treaty of Versailles.

To EDWARD CLODD

Max Gate, | Dorchester. | June 30: 1920

My dear Clodd:

I am now sending supplementary thanks for your kind letter on my birthday—my hasty postcard having been all I was able to write at the date—as you no doubt understood: & I can also send at the same time my best wishes to you on your anniversary, & that there may be as many happy returns of it as nature with her highest efforts can allow.

We saw your article in the Daily News on the spiritualistic craze, & some so-called answers to your arguments by correspondents of the Daily Graphic. Apart from scientific & other reasons against such communications the one fact of a "medium" being necessary would, one might think, discredit them, since, in at least half these performances the medium has been proved to be an impostor.

Our ancestors used to burn these mediums—or witches as they were then called; but we reward them—a more humane, though more mischievous, treatment. When the Witch of Endor called up Samuel we are not told what he paid her, but the case is of course an exact parallel to present practice, for one clearly gathers that Saul did not *see* Samuel, who conversed with him *through* the witch—as now. She was afraid, when she knew him: but now they are not afraid!

I daresay you go to London oftener than I do—to dinners & other genial gatherings. May you be able to go long. With kindest regards to Mrs Clodd I am

Very sincerely yours
Thomas Hardy.

Text MS. (with envelope) Purdy.
kind letter: of 31 May 20 (DCM). *hasty postcard*: it has not been traced. *your anniversary*: Clodd was 80 on 1 July 1920. *in the Daily News*: Clodd's 'From Beyond the Veil. Are "Spirit Messages" Sub-Conscious?', *Daily News*, 28 June 1920, a review of the Revd. George Vale Owen's *The Life Beyond the Veil* (London, 1920). *Daily Graphic*: where Clodd had just pub. two articles, 'Spiritualism. An Exposure', 22 June 1920, and 'Spiritualism. Credulous Advocates', 23 June 1920; the letters to which TH refers appeared in the issues of 25 and 29 June. *called up Samuel*: 1 Sam. 28: 11–14. *Mrs Clodd*: Phyllis Clodd, *née* Rope, Clodd's second wife; see V.81.

To EMMA DUGDALE

Max Gate | Dorchester. | July 2: 1920

My dear Mrs Dugdale:

I must write a line to tell you how grieved I was to hear of your illness. I am glad that Florence went to see you, & am much relieved to learn to-day—as she is too—that you are considerably better. I sincerely hope that you will soon be quite yourself again.

I take this opportunity of thanking you & Mr Dugdale, & also Connie, for your kind letters to me on my birthday. I have been postponing this reply to them day by day ever since they came, but have been so overwhelmed with correspondence & messages that I have not been able to do so till this late time. However better late than never.

I hear that you are likely to come in this direction soon, & shall be delighted to see you.

Yours affectionately
Thomas Hardy.

Text MS. (with envelope) Purdy.
Dugdale: Emma Dugdale, *née* Taylor, FEH's mother; see IV.246.   *see you*: at her home in Enfield, Middlesex.   *Mr Dugdale*: Edward Dugdale, FEH's father; see V.33.   *Connie*: Constance Dugdale, one of FEH's sisters; see letter to her of 2 June 25.

To MADELEINE ROLLAND

MAX GATE, | DORCHESTER. | July 4: 1920

Dear Miss Rolland:

I valued nobody's good wishes for my birthday more than yours; yet I daresay I seem to you rather remiss in not answering your kind letter till now. But I have had a great deal to attend to, &, alas, I am not so young as I was & so prompt in correspondence.

Since you made those excellent translations of my novels I have confined my attention almost entirely to verse. What a pity it is that verse should be in so many, indeed, nearly all cases, untranslateable. However, I hope some day to send you two or three short lyrics that you may experiment upon turning them into French prose or verse—of course only for your own amusement.

I well remember your mother & liked her very much. Do you recall what a wet day we had on our first meeting, at Salisbury? I sympathize deeply with you in your loss of her.

Certainly whenever you come to England you must visit us here. My wife says she will be glad to make your acquaintance.

I am much honoured by your pupils' study of my novels, & ask you to believe me

Always sincerely yours
Thomas Hardy.

P.S. I have also written a note to your brother Mr Romain Rolland. Th: H.

Text MS. (with envelope) Mme Rolland.
Rolland: Madeleine Rolland, translator, sister of Romain Rolland; see II.145.   *kind letter*: of

6 June 20 (DCM).   *translations of my novels*: the only one to appear in book form was *Tess d'Urberville* (see II.278–9); see, however, II.177–8, 224, and III.225.   *your mother*: Marie Rolland, *née* Courot (1845–1919), whom TH met when he first met Mlle Rolland herself at Salisbury in September 1897 (see II.173–4).   *your pupils' study*: Mlle Rolland reported that her pupils, students at the Sorbonne, were studying TH's novels and feeling 'their tragic grandeur'.   *Romain Rolland*: the French novelist, music critic, and dramatist (1866–1944), who had also written (12 June 20, DCM) on the occasion of TH's 80th birthday; TH's 'note' has not been traced.

To FLORENCE HENNIKER

Max Gate | July 7: 1920

My dear friend:

Yes: Thursday afternoon at 2, or as soon after as you can manage, at the Dorchester Museum, an easy place for an appointment, as we can read the papers, &c, during a few minutes of waiting; & you can look at the relics if you should get there a minute or two before us.

As to the weather, to-day it seems doubtful. If bad to-morrow morning a discussion can be carried on over the telephone on what is to be done. I would suggest that, if persistently wet up to, say 4 o'clock, & then fine, you might still come to Dorchester, & we could go across to Stinsford, &c. going to Lyme the next day, or some other.

I enclose an amusing cutting from The Outlook which a Press-Cutting agency has sent to Florence. She gives you her love, & says she will be so glad to see you again.

Always yours sincerely
Th. H.

Text MS. DCM.
Yes: TH is responding to Mrs. Henniker's letter of 6 July 20 (DCM) from the Royal Hotel, Weymouth; see letter of 4 June 20.   *from The Outlook*: evidently A. Wyatt Tilby's 'The New Literary Criticism', *Outlook*, 3 July 1920, which humorously employs the methods of the Baconians to 'prove' that TH's works had in fact been written by Arthur James Balfour, the former prime minister (see II.185).

To GEORGE MACMILLAN

MAX GATE, | DORCHESTER. | 10th. July 1920.

Dear Mr Macmillan:

I am quite willing that the poem "The Darkling Thrush" should be included in the proposed volume of "Prayers for Church & Nation". I will leave it to you to say whether a charge of a guinea should be made, or the permission be granted free.

I enclose a letter I have received from Madrid. I do not know whether the writer is a bona fide publisher or a speculative translator. If you think him the former I suppose he may be allowed to produce the two books in Spanish at the same price for each as that paid by another Spanish publisher for the right to translate "A Pair of Blue Eyes". That was carried out by yourselves, which is why I send on the present request; but please do not attend to it if troublesome.

Yours very sincerely,

Thomas Hardy.

Text   MS. (typewritten) BL.

quite willing: TH is replying to Macmillan's enquiry of 9 July 20 (Macmillan letterbooks, BL).   *& Nation"*: the Revd. W. B. Trevelyan's *Prayers for Church and Nation* (London, 1921); the poem appears, without its title and under the general heading 'Courage and Hope', in an appendix devoted to 'Selections from Various Authors'.   *the writer*: identified in Macmillan's letter to TH of 12 July 20 (Macmillan letterbooks, BL) as J. Pius Cartillo, a Spanish publisher.   *two books*: unidentified; the next work of TH's to be translated into Spanish was *The Well-Beloved*, pub. in Madrid as *La bien amada* in 1921.   *another Spanish publisher*: see V.209.

To HELEN GIFFORD

MAX GATE, | DORCHESTER. | July 13: 1920

Dear Miss Gifford:

Certainly mention me as a reference if you care to. I trust that your proposed change will result in further successes.

We are hoping for a fine day as a great & unusual treat, to be able to motor to Lyme Regis.

I have mislaid your letter, & am sending this through your father, lest my memory should not serve me as to your exact address.

Believe me

Always yrs sincerely

Th: Hardy.

Text   MS. C. H. Gifford.

Gifford: Helen Gifford (1887–1964), teacher, younger daughter of Charles Gifford.   *your proposed change*: currently joint headmistress of the Allenswood School, Wimbledon (see V.344), she founded shortly after this date the Marie Souvestre School at Benfleet Hall, Sutton, Surrey.

To HOWARD BLISS

July 17. 1920

Dear Sir:

In reply to your inquiry I write for Mr Hardy, who is much pressed by correspondence, to inform you that his poem "The Night of Trafalgar" is part of his epic-drama "The Dynasts", of which the complete MS. is in the British Museum, & the song as there first written being bound up with the other pages could not of course be separated from them. If you look into the printed volume you will see where it comes. The replica that you possess which is precisely like the original was made by Mr Hardy—for one of the Red Cross sales during the war.

In respect of the poem "The Oxen", which originally appeared in "The Times", the reprint made at Hove was unauthorized though not objected to.

It is one of a considerable number produced for distribution among the soldiers, as Mr Hardy was informed. His best thanks for your good wishes

Yours truly
F.E

Text   MS. (pencil draft) DCM.

Bliss: J. Howard Bliss (1894–1977), musician and art collector, younger brother of Sir Arthur Bliss, the composer; he built up a distinguished collection of books and manuscripts by TH.   *your inquiry*: Bliss wrote 16 July 20 (DCM) to ask if the MS. of 'The Night of Trafalgar', sent to the Red Cross Sale in 1915 and recently acquired by him, was in fact the original MS.   *reprint made at Hove*: Bliss also enquired how many copies of this pamphlet (Hove, 28 December 1915) had been printed; see Purdy, 175.   *among the soldiers*: this claim was also made for other Hove reprints of TH's works; see Purdy, 158.

To FLORENCE HENNIKER

MAX GATE, | DORCHESTER. | Aug. 5: 1920

My dear friend:

I have found a copy of Two on a Tower in the edition you like, & I am sending it with this. But instead of assisting you to make up your set of these novels I ought really to be making you read my more serious & later books. However you must have your own way, I suppose.

We were glad to hear that you & Anna got back comfortably, in spite of the mishap with the engine. It was rather a pity that you had not many really fine days in Weymouth, but if you had waited till now you would have fared no better. I hope, & so does Florence, that you will find a place somewhere in this direction—not further from here than you could compass in a day, & back. We missed you very much the first few days after you left: that's the worst of seeing old friends.

A poet & his wife—two quite young people—are going to descend upon us on bicycles this month, & stay a night—so they tell us. But as she has lately had a baby it seems rather a wild project of theirs. Their scheme is to bicycle from Oxford into Devon.

Florence's mother is immensely improved by Weymouth air. I wish she could stay longer.

Believe me, ever affectionately yrs
Th: H.

We are reading Jane Austen: but *you* are to read T. on a T. On looking into it it seems rather clever. Th. H.

Text   MS. DCM.

edition you like: probably the Osgood, McIlvaine 'Wessex Novels' edn. of 1895.   *Anna*: see letter of 4 June 20.   *poet & his wife*: Robert Graves (1895–1986) and his wife Nancy Nicholson (1900–77); see Graves, *Goodbye to All That: An Autobiography* (London, 1929), 374–9.   *Florence's mother*: see letter of 2 July 20.   *reading Jane Austen*: specifically, *Northanger Abbey*, *Persuasion*, and *Emma*; see *Friends of a Lifetime: Letters to Sydney Carlyle Cockerell*, ed. Viola Meynell (London, 1940), 306. See also letter of 26 Oct 20.

To EDWARD CLODD

FROM THO. HARDY, | MAX GATE, | DORCHESTER. | 12: 8: '20.

Have written to Thring—I hope with good results.

We have read Inge's book—I think him something of a trimmer; but that's no novelty.

Am sorry you have lost your taste for London. But it will come back—In haste,

Yrs sincerely
T.H.

Text MS. (postcard) Leeds.

Thring . . . results: see letter of 23 Aug 20; although the subject of this earlier letter to Thring is not known, Clodd may have suggested that the illuminated address from the Society of Authors, currently on view at Hatchard's bookshop, ought to be delivered to TH without further delay.   *Inge's book*: the Very Revd. William Ralph Inge (1860–1954; *D.N.B.*), Dean of St. Paul's; the book was presumably his *Outspoken Essays* (London, 1919).

To ETHEL COWLEY

MAX GATE, | DORCHESTER. | Sunday. [15 August 1920]

Dear Mrs Cowley:

I send my idea for the setting up of the old font. I find it to be of almost exactly the same date as the one in Martinstown Church, and have therefore adopted the design of that font in its lower part. To attempt anything more elaborate would I think be a mistake, as what the original was can be only matter of conjecture. It is however probable that it resembled the Martinstown one.

I find that the present marble font dates from about 1730 or 1740, and it is therefore of some antiquity: it was the gift of Mrs Pitt. By taking away a row of chairs there would be room for both the fonts, which would add to the interest of the church's history.

Believe me,

Yours sincerely,
Th: Hardy.

Text MS. (typewritten, with envelope in FEH's hand) Canon Cowley.   *Date* From postmark.

Cowley: Ethel Florence Cowley (d. 1961), wife of the Revd. H. G. B. Cowley, vicar of Stinsford (see letter to him of 11 Nov 20).   *old font*: the original Norman font of Stinsford church had been discovered, broken into pieces, under rubbish in the churchyard (see V.3–4); for TH's drawing, see *The Architectural Notebook of Thomas Hardy*, ed. C. J. P. Beatty (Dorchester, 1966), fo. [115].   *Martinstown Church*: i.e., the church of Winterborne St. Martin, Dorset, visited by TH on 14 August 1920; see *Architectural Notebook*, fo. 116.   *Mrs Pitt*: Grace Amelia Morton Pitt (d. 1836), second wife of William Morton Pitt (1754–1836), owner of Kingston Maurward House, near Dorchester.   *both the fonts*: only the Norman font is now in the church, however, the marble font (in which TH was baptized) having been declared surplus in 1945.

To G. HERBERT THRING

MAX GATE, | DORCHESTER. | August 23: 1920

Dear Mr Thring:

The address from the Members of the Council, representing the Society of Authors all, has reached me safely, and though I knew its contents—its spiritual part—on my actual birthday when the deputation came here, I did not realize its bodily beauty till now.

As to the address itself, I can only confirm by this letter what I told the deputation by word of mouth—how much I have been moved by such a mark of good feeling—affection as I may truly call it—in the body of writers whose President I have had the distinction of being for many years—a do-nothing president, a roi fainéant, I very greatly fear, in spite of their assurances! However, the Society has been good enough to take me as worth this tribute, & I thank them heartily for it & what it expresses. It will be a cheering reminder of bright things whenever I see it or think of it, which will be often & often. Believe me

Theirs & yours ever sincerely
Thomas Hardy.

Text   MS. (draft) DCM.
Thring: George Herbert Thring, secretary to the Incorporated Society of Authors; see III.8. He wrote 20 Aug 20 (DCM).   *The address*: an illuminated address (DCM) presented by the Society to TH, its president, to mark his 80th birthday; its text was pub. in *The Times*, 2 June 1920, but the address itself was not available to the deputation which called at Max Gate on that date (see letters of mid-May 20 to Hawkins and 12 Aug 20).   *do-nothing president*: TH used double underlining to indicate that the initial letter of 'president' should be typed as a capital; the entire draft shows extensive revision.

To W. M. COLLES

August 25. 1920

Dear Mr Colles:

I have been so burdened with correspondence of late that this delay in replying to your letter was unavoidable.

As to the request you make, my messages to the American people were so friendly during the war, & before it, that I fear I can say nothing now which I have not said already, either directly or indirectly. A person detached from politics can hardly write practically on questions of international relationships.

I am glad to hear that you are still actively engaged on literary matters, & remain

Yours very truly

W. M. Colles Esq.

Text   MS. (pencil draft) DCM.
Colles: William Morris Colles, literary agent; see I.241.   *request you make*: Colles (12 Aug 20, DCM) said that he was to be London correspondent of 'a Press Service organised in the United States in the British interests' and hoped for a message from TH which would help to prevent the two countries from drifting apart 'owing to alien machinations'.   *my messages*: TH's reference is unclear.

To BENJAMIN HUEBSCH

MAX GATE, | DORCHESTER. | August 30th. 1920.

Dear Sir:

I fear that I have too long neglected to acknowledge a kind and most welcome cable of congratulation which reached me on my 80th. birthday, sent from "The Freeman" and fourteen eminent American writers. May I now, though late, tender to you and those ladies and gentlemen my thanks and a deep sense of appreciation of their good wishes, and the hope that poetry and literature may ever form an unbreakable link between the two great English-speaking nations.

I also have to thank you for the copies of the Freeman you have kindly sent—which I am reading with interest.

Yours very truly,
Thomas Hardy.

To the Editor of The Freeman.

Text MS. (typewritten) LC.
Huebsch: Benjamin W. Huebsch (1876–1964), American publisher, currently editor of the *Freeman*, a New York weekly. TH perhaps expected this letter to be published, but it seems not in fact to have appeared in the *Freeman*.   *cable of congratulations*: in DCM; the text was pub. in the *New York Times*, 2 June 1920.   *American writers*: among them Sherwood Anderson, Theodore Dreiser, Robert Frost, and Amy Lowell (see letter to her of 7 Mar 23).

To FLORENCE HARDY

Max Gate | Sept 1. [1920] | 4.30.

My dearest F:

Nothing has happened here—& I only write that you may not be anxious. I went to Talbothays yesterday.

I suppose Miss Scudamore will call presently. Colonel Tweedie died on Saturday & was buried yesterday. I have been doing the Post Office tablet all the morning.

Ever yours
Th: H.

There are one or two letters but as they seem of no importance I don't enclose them—one seems a receipt from Harrods. I sent on a letter yesterday to you at Club.

5.30

Miss Scudamore has just called for Wess.

Text MS. Purdy.   *Date* From internal evidence.
Hardy: Florence Emily Hardy (FEH), *née* Dugdale, whom TH married, as his second wife, in 1914; see III.179 and V.8.   *Talbothays*: the house near West Stafford, Dorset, where TH's brother and surviving sister lived; it was designed by TH himself.   *Miss Scudamore*: Joyce Maud Scudamore (d. 1977, aged 85), a close friend of FEH's and the niece of TH's friend Hermann Lea (see letter to him of 3 Oct 24).   *Colonel Tweedie*: John Lannoy Tweedie (1842–1920), soldier, of Dorchester.   *Post Office tablet*: a war memorial tablet for the Dorchester Post Office; see letter of 30 Oct 20.   *at Club*: the Lyceum Club, a London club for professional women of which FEH was a member.   *Wess*: i.e., the dog Wessex.

To EDMUND BLUNDEN

Max Gate | Dorchester | 2 Sept 1920.

Dear Mr Blunden:

I have just received "The Waggoner" for which I much thank you. As I should like to read the poems slowly I have not stopped to do this before writing, lest the delay should make you think me indifferent.

Sincerely yours
Thomas Hardy.

Text MS. (with envelope) Texas.
Blunden: Edmund Blunden (1896–1974), poet and critic, whom TH did not meet until the summer of 1922. *"The Waggoner"*: Blunden's *The Waggoner, and Other Poems* (London, 1920).

To EDGAR MITCHELL

MAX GATE, | DORCHESTER. | Sept 20: 1920

My dear Sir:

I have received the copies of The Hampshire Independent & your accompanying letter: for which I thank you. I shall read the articles with interest, & hope you will find some of the places mentioned in the Collected Poems under their real names worthy of a visit while you are in Wessex.

Yours very truly
Th: Hardy.

Edgar A. Mitchell Esq.

Text MS. Eton College.
Mitchell: Edgar A. Mitchell, journalist, of Southampton. *accompanying letter*: of 19 Sept 20 (DCM). *the articles*: in fact a two-part article, 'The Interpreter of Modern Wessex. A Few Notes on Mr. Hardy and His Novels', pub. in the *Hampshire Independent*, 11 and 18 Sept 1920, over the initials 'E.A.M.'.

To SIR FREDERICK MACMILLAN

MAX GATE, | DORCHESTER. | September 22nd. 1920.

Dear Sir Frederick:

The proposal of the Medici Society seems all right, and I am inclined to accept it if you are. As to how it will affect the Golden Treasury edition you are the better judge. That one quarter of the receipts as royalty from the Society should go to yourselves is quite reasonable, and I agree.

I think the edition has been reprinted since I sent you a few corrections to bring it into accord with the Wessex Edition, so that they will have the right text to print from. I think I do not possess a copy of your last impression of the selections, so shall be glad to have one at your convenience.

In respect of the Messrs Harper reprinting the Wessex Edition as the "Anniversary Edition" (a name of their own), I told them in July that I wished them to make it complete by the addition of the last volume—"Satires of Circumstance and Moments of Vision,"—by arrangement with your New

York house. I have not heard from them since, but suppose they have proceeded with the matter.

Believe me,

Yours sincerely,
Thomas Hardy.

Text MS. (typewritten) BL.
proposal . . . Society: for a limited edn. of TH's *Selected Poems*, to be pub. by the Medici Society's Riccardi Press (London, 1921).   *Treasury edition*: i.e., the original *Selected Poems*, first pub. 1916.   *I agree*: Macmillan made this suggestion in his letter of 21 Sept 20 (Macmillan letterbooks, BL).   . *"Anniversary Edition"*: it was not, however, textually identical with the Wessex edn.; see Purdy, 286.   *with your New York house*: the extra vol. was in fact printed from the plates of the original Macmillan edns.; see Purdy, 286.

To J. J. FOSTER

MAX GATE, DORCHESTER. | 23 Sept. 1920

Dear Mr Foster:

Proof returned herewith. I could not think of any additions. If you object to the word "hobby" you can insert "study".

I heard of your being at Weymouth, & hope the air was a good change.

Yours very truly
Th: Hardy.

Text MS. Princeton.
Foster: Joshua James Foster, antiquary; see I.160.   *Proof*: of Foster's *Wessex Worthies* (London, 1921), to which TH contributed an 'Introductory Note'; see Purdy, 320–1.   *insert "study"*: the text as pub. shows that Foster did prefer his undertaking to be described as a 'study' rather than as a 'hobby'.

To SIR FREDERICK MACMILLAN

MAX GATE, | DORCHESTER. | 25th. September 1920.

Dear Sir Frederick:

I am obliged for the copy of the Golden Treasury Selections, which has reminded me that some time ago I sent you a few corrections to be made whenever you were reprinting the book. These you doubtless sent on to the printer that they may be embodied whenever a new impression comes out.

I suppose the Medici Society may as well have the benefit of them, and accordingly I am enclosing the same list for you to send on to them with the copy they use for printing from—or for you to mark on the copy itself, as may be most advisable.

As I think the list I now send is a more accurate one than the one I first forwarded, I send it in duplicate, that one of the copies may go on to Messrs Clark, in case the first list was not quite so complete as the present. Thus they will easily be able to see if the corrections for many of them have been made.

Yours very truly,
Thomas Hardy.

Text   MS. BL.
Selections: Macmillan (23 Sept 20, Macmillan letterbooks, BL) said he was sending TH a copy of the latest printing of the 1916 *Selected Poems*; see letter of 22 Sept 20.   *to Messrs Clark*: the printers (see letter of 9 Dec 25); Macmillan replied, however (28 Sept 20, Macmillan letterbooks, BL), that one of the copies would be kept until a new printing was called for while the other would go to the Medici Society to enable correction of the Riccardi Press edn.

To ETHEL COWLEY

MAX GATE, | DORCHESTER. | 29 Sept. 1920

Dear Mrs Cowley:
    I hope you will allow me to contribute a little to the cost of reinstating the old Stinsford font? You have shown such commendable zeal in starting it, & taken such trouble, that it will be a great pleasure to me to help in a small way.

Sincerely yours
Th: Hardy.

Text   MS. (with envelope) Canon Cowley.
old Stinsford font: see letter of 15 Aug 20.

To ETHEL COWLEY

Max Gate | Oct 1. 1920

Dear Mrs Cowley:
    It is generous of you to pay for reinstating the old font. But please keep the £2—2—0 for anything in the Church or Churchyard that may want doing. I daresay that to refix the marble font somewhere will be a little expense. But use the subscription as you think best.
    By the way, the marble font has a respectable history. I think it about the date of the Pitt monument, or a little later—perhaps 1730 or so. My impression is that the 2 fonts would rather add to the interest of the church as a record of its history. Mr Cowley would probably be of the same opinion. Sometimes in other old churches one sees the superseded font near the other.

Sincerely yours
Th: Hardy.

Text   MS. Canon Cowley.
old font . . . marble font: see letters of 15 Aug and 29 Sept 20.   *Pitt monument*: the elaborate monument to George Pitt (d. 1734) on the N. wall of Stinsford church.

To SIR FREDERICK MACMILLAN

Oct 6: 1920

My dear Macmillan:
    Here it is signed & returned. Many thanks for your kind attention to it.

Th: H.

Text   MS. BL.
Here it is: Macmillan (5 Oct 20, Macmillan letterbooks, BL) had asked TH to sign a duplicate of the agreement covering Swedish translations of five of his novels; see letters of 27 Apr and 21 May 20.

To SIR FREDERICK MACMILLAN

MAX GATE, | DORCHESTER. | October .9th. 1920.

Dear Sir Frederick:

I have received the enclosed, and cannot remember the length of the term for which the film rights in Far from the Madding Crowd were assigned to the Turner Company. As it seems to have been a failure, and there are other very successful English Companies I believe, I do not quite know whether to wait for an application from one of the latter, or to go on with this Mr Meyrick Milton. Perhaps you have had experience of others since then.

I fancy I have received applications from other companies for this very novel, which I have passed over in the belief that the Turner Company had it.

Yours very truly,
Thomas Hardy.

P.S. Please do not take any notice of this, if it is not worth while. Th. H.

Text MS. (typewritten) BL.
the enclosed: still accompanying TH's letter is an 8 Oct 20 letter to him from Meyrick Milton, a film director, seeking a renewal of the film rights to *Far from the Madding Crowd* previously purchased by him on behalf of the now defunct Turner Film Company.   *a failure*: i.e., the film of *Far from the Madding Crowd* made by the Turner Film Company in 1915 (see V.111); Milton seems to have had no hand in that production.   *P.S. . . . while.*: postscript added in TH's hand.

To SYDNEY COCKERELL

MAX GATE, | DORCHESTER. | Sunday. 17: 10: 1920

Just a line to wish you bon voyage, which is all a stay-at-home can do. However, experience will decide, as the Psalmist says. Let us hear from time to time. Kindest regards from both.

Th: H.

Text MS. (postcard) Taylor.
bon voyage: Cockerell was about to sail to the United States with Alfred Chester Beatty (1875–1968; *D.N.B.*), the American-born mining engineer and art and manuscript collector.
the Psalmist says: it is not clear what (if any) particular passage TH had in mind.

To JOHN MIDDLETON MURRY

Max Gate | Oct. 26: 1920

Dear Mr Middleton Murry:

At last I acknowledge the arrival of "The Oxen" setting, that you so kindly sent. A mysteriously caught cold, which still is hanging on, has thrown my correspondence, such as it is, out of gear (if it ever was in), & there you have a lame sort of explanation. As I have already seen Mr Edward Dent's music I am awaiting the "Lyonnesse" setting, which I know nothing of. Neither do I of "Cinnamon & Angelica", whose acquaintance I shall make with pleasure when it comes.

I hope to be able to find some small poem good enough for the Athenaeum in a month or so. I have sent off only one for a long time anywhere, my chief occupation of late having lain in tearing up ill-written scraps, & listening to my wife's reading of the novels of Jane Austen—all six of them straight through—which I had not read since I was a young man. Please excuse these desultory lines which are made worse by a bad pen.

Always sincerely
Thomas Hardy.

After all I have not thanked you for getting "Lyonnesse" done, which however I do now. Th: H.

Text MS. Berg.
"The Oxen" setting: by Edward Joseph Dent (1876–1957; *D.N.B.*), musicologist and teacher; it was pub. in the *Sackbut*, December 1920. According to Hugh Carey, *Duet for Two Voices* (Cambridge, 1979), 163, Dent refused to pub. it earlier lest it be 'taken up at carol concerts at Christmas in the Albert Hall, with organ accompaniment'.   *"Lyonnesse" setting*: unidentified, but not, apparently, the setting by Charles Speyer (see letter of 24 Apr 20).   *& Angelica"*: Murry inscribed a copy of his verse-play *Cinnamon and Angelica* (London, 1920) to TH in November 1920.   *for the Athenaeum*: see letter of 9 Dec 20.   *sent off only one*: the reference is probably to 'At a House in Hampstead', written in July 1920 for *The John Keats Memorial Volume* (London, 1921); see Purdy, 216–17.   *Austen*: see letter of 5 Aug 20.   *all six*: TH first wrote 'all five'.   *getting "Lyonnesse" done*: see letter of 9 Jan 20.

To ALFRED POPE

MAX GATE, | DORCHESTER. | October 27: 1920

Dear Mr Pope:

I have just heard today of your great loss, & the tidings come so suddenly that I can only offer you my sincerest sympathy in the briefest way as yet. I was not able to get to Wrackleford when I meant to come, as you may know; & have been for the last week or two much out of sorts with a cold; but I was looking forward to your arrival at South Court, when I could call quite easily on you & Mrs Pope. But man proposes! It is a sad satisfaction, however, that my last meeting with her was under such pleasant circumstances, leaving a most attractive memory of her for me to retain. Please convey my sympathy & my wife's to all your family also, & with renewed assurances of how much you have been in my thoughts in your trouble, I am

Very sincerely yours
Thomas Hardy.

Text MS. (with black-bordered envelope) Thomas Hardy Society.
Pope: Alfred Pope, brewer, one of Dorchester's leading citizens; see I.100.   *great loss*: Pope's wife Elizabeth (see IV.286) died 25 Oct 1920, aged 70.   *Wrackleford*: the Popes' house in the country; see V.267.   *South Court*: the Popes' house in Dorchester itself.   *all your family*: the Popes had had 14 children, of whom 10 were still living.

To WALTER DREW

October 30. 1920

Dear Sir:

I am glad to hear that the memorial Tablet is nearly ready. The service I rendered was a very small thing to do for the devoted men whose names appear in the list.

I much value the wish of the Staff & yourself that I should unveil the tablet. But I feel that being already closely associated with it in designing it, & in putting words of my own as the epigraph, it would be better for somebody else to unveil it; also since that for physical reasons, I am never sure of being able to keep an engagement in winter time nowadays. With sincere thanks for the request I am,

Yours very truly
(Signed) T.—H—

Walter Drew Esq. | Post Office | Dorchester

Text MS. (pencil draft) DCM.
Drew: Walter Drew, head district postmaster, Dorchester.   *glad to hear*: from Drew's letter of 29 Oct 20 (DCM).   *memorial Tablet*: TH had composed and designed a memorial to the 11 employees of the Dorchester Post Office who died while serving in the armed forces during the war of 1914–18; the tablet, in marble, can still be seen at the post office, inside the New Street entrance.   *the epigraph*: 'None dubious of the cause, none murmuring', from TH's poem 'Embarcation'.   *unveil it*: the official unveiling, on 16 Nov 1920, was performed by the Surveyor of the Post Office's South-Western Division; FEH was present, but not TH himself.

To FLORENCE HENNIKER

MAX GATE, | DORCHESTER. | All Saints Eve. | Oct 31. 1920

My dear friend:

My thanks for your very nice letter; but before entering into it I write at this particular moment to ask if you are going to the presentation to Mr Gosse on Friday next at 3, at the Steinway Hall? Florence has to be in London the day before, & thinks she can go, as she is not coming home till the evening train of Friday. I cannot go, so she must represent me. As Ld Crewe & Mr Balfour are in it, & the recipient is Gosse, I daresay it will be an interesting ceremony. They say the bust is good, but I have not seen it.

Yes: I have thought of you in your loss of "Milner". I have gone through the same experience in respect of cats. What silly people we are to get so attached to pets whose natural lives, as we well know, must in every reasonable probability finish before our own!

I did not expect much from the electric treatment, but of course if it has made you much better my doubts are answered. I have had a bad cold, but have begun to go out again.

I do hope what you expect of the Council of Justice to be well founded. Here in this stock-breeding county one sees instances continually of what does not exactly amount to legal cruelty, & yet is cruelty.

Fancy your reading that old novel of mine Two on a Tower right through. History does not record whether Swithin married Tabitha or not. Perhaps when Lady C. was dead he grew passionately attached to her again, as people often do. I suppose the bishop did find out the secret. Or perhaps he did not.

We saw the announcement of Mr Shorter's marriage in the Times, & he has written since to us about it. We do not know anything of the lady, except from what he says, that she is young, & in his judgment pretty.

I want you to get this to-morrow morning, & must hastily wind up as the post is just going. I like this mysterious eve of saintly ghosts, & also to-morrow eve, of All Souls—

Ever affectly
Tho H.

This is a mere scrawl. I will write a better letter next time, as I hope. Th: H.

Text MS. DCM.
nice letter: of 24 Oct 20 (DCM).   *into it*: TH wrote 'into into it'.   *presentation to Mr Gosse*: a portrait bust of Edmund Gosse by Sir William Goscombe John, subscribed to by more than 200 of Gosse's friends, was presented to him by Arthur James Balfour (see letter of 7 July 20) on 9 Nov 1920—not on 5 November ('Friday next') as TH seems to have expected. *Steinway Hall*: Balfour was unwell on 9 November and the ceremony was moved to the dining-room of his house in Carlton Gardens.   *Ld Crewe*: Mrs. Henniker's brother, Robert Offley Ashburton Crewe-Milnes, Lord Houghton (see II.3), had been created Marquess of Crewe in 1911.   *"Milner"*: see letter of 28 Feb 20; Mrs. Henniker's letter of 24 October spoke of her grief at her dog's death.   *electric treatment*: it is not clear from Mrs. Henniker's letter what the treatment was for, only that she was '*much* better—having had no pain for some weeks'.   *of Justice*: the Council of Justice to Animals; see IV.143.   *on a Tower*: see letter of 5 Aug 20; TH is responding in this paragraph to Mrs. Henniker's speculations in the 24 October letter.   *Lady C.*: Lady Constantine, a character—like Swithin St. Cleeve, Tabitha Lark, and Bishop Helmsdale—in *Two on a Tower*.   *in the Times*: Clement Shorter's marriage to Annie Doris Banfield, his second wife, was announced in *The Times*, 24 Sept 1920.

To HAROLD CHILD

Max Gate | 11 : 11 : 1920

Dear Mr Child:

I have never heard a sound of this Miss Pond, & it complicates the O'Brien romance considerably. It is, in fact, an eighteenth century novel ready written.

The Armistice supplement makes a very good show. I am afraid I must have been rather obscure, for the writer of the leading article on the subject seems to think I ask, why did the Allies fight? But the meaning is, of course, why did the War originate: why did those who started it, whoever they were, do so.—So far it looks as if they were the Germans, as we have all along supposed.

The Dorchester Dramatic Society is going to perform The Return of the Native next week. The dramatization is entirely the work of our respected Alderman, Mr Tilley—to whom I have given no assistance whatever, beyond letting him have the complete words of the old mumming play from which speeches are quoted in the novel. How it will turn out I haven't an idea. They have got me to promise to go to the dress rehearsal, so I suppose I must. My wife takes a great deal of interest in the performance, & sends you her views—with which, I must own, I am in accord. Perhaps you can make a preliminary paragraph of them. Believe me

Sincerely yours,
Th: Hardy

Text MS. Adams.
O'Brien romance: for TH's long-standing fascination with the marriage of Lady Susan Strangways to the actor and dramatist William O'Brien in 1764 see V.109 and *EL*, 11–12. Miss Pond has not been identified, but she was perhaps alleged to have been O'Brien's mistress. *Armistice supplement*: TH's poem 'And There Was a Great Calm' was first pub. in the Armistice Day Section of *The Times*, 11 Nov 1920; see Purdy, 211. *leading article*: headed 'Armistice Day', *The Times*, 11 Nov 1920. *next week*: specifically, on 18 and 19 November. *Mr Tilley*: see letter of 17 Nov 20. *in the novel*: *The Return of the Native* (Wessex edn.), esp. 157–63. *in accord*: TH's phrasing suggests that FEH's 'views' may in fact have been his own; they no longer accompany this letter but are obviously reflected in the item, 'Return of the Native', *The Times*, 16 Nov 1920, which is largely devoted to the use of the mumming play in the forthcoming production. *preliminary paragraph*: see previous note.

To THE REVD. H. G. B. COWLEY

Max Gate: 11. 11. '20

Dear Mr Cowley:

I have just heard from the Secretary of the Dramatic Society in answer to my application for the 9 seats at a reduced rate. He says the Society agrees to let the Stinsford Choir have them—9 good seats for Friday evening the 19th at 8 (They have been obliged to have this extra performance on Friday on account of the great demand for seats).

If you therefore communicate with him all will be arranged. His address is—H. A. Martin Esq. Sec. Debating Society, Dorchester. I hope they will enjoy the play.

Yours sincerely
T. Hardy.

Text MS. (with envelope) Canon Cowley.
Cowley: the Revd. Henry Guise Beatson Cowley, vicar of Stinsford; see IV.237. *9 seats*: for *The Return of the Native*; see letter of 11 Nov 20 to Child. *Martin*: Henry Charles Austin Martin, a local auctioneer; see IV.57.

To T. H. TILLEY

FROM THO. HARDY, | MAX GATE, | DORCHESTER. |
Wedny morning— [17 November 1920]

Reminder:

To tell Clym & Eustacia to *speak up* very *clearly* when they first exchange words ("Are you a woman?" &c) as it is the key to the whole action—

Text MS. (postcard) DCM. *Date* From postmark.
Tilley: Thomas Henry Tilley, Dorchester alderman, the adaptor and producer of *The Return of the Native*; see IV.115–16 and letter of 6 Oct 24. *Clym*: played by Edgar Wilmot Smerdon, M.D., of High West Street, Dorchester. *Eustacia*: played by Gertrude Bugler; see letter of 2 Dec 24. *very*: added in pencil by TH. *a woman?"*: see *The Return of the Native* (Wessex edn.), 170.

To EZRA POUND

MAX GATE, | DORCHESTER. | 28th. November 1920.

Dear Mr Pound:

Apart from your reason for writing, I am glad to get a letter from such an original thinker on poetry—and *in* poetry, I should add—as yourself: which very few people are nowadays, more's the pity.

As to your question, I have been hunting over some MS. pieces, written and half-written, but have not found anything yet that would exactly suit. I will have a further search.

The difficulty always is that in a periodical, surrounded by practical prose, poems are not screened from the bleak wind of supercilious criticism as they are to some extent when standing all together in a volume. However, as I say, I will try to send something.

I am much obliged for the copy of The Dial, which I have known a little of, and estimate highly.

Sincerely yours,
Thomas Hardy.

Text   MS. (typewritten) Yale.
Pound: Ezra Loomis Pound (1885–1972), American poet and critic.   *reason for writing*:
Pound wrote 13 Nov 20 (DCM), praising TH's verse and prose—especially *The Mayor of Casterbridge* and *A Group of Noble Dames*.   *your question*: Pound sent the November 1920 issue of the *Dial* (New York), of which he was Paris correspondent, and asked TH for a contribution.   *further search*: TH's poem 'The Two Houses' appeared in the *Dial*, August 1921.

To SIR HAMO THORNYCROFT

Max Gate | 28 Nov. 1920

My dear Thornycroft:

I was truly disappointed at being unable to see & hear the presentation to Gosse: & what was equally provoking was that my wife had arranged to attend on the first date that was fixed, & then, when it was altered, she found it too late to change the date of her visit to London, engaged for on the first date. However, from friends that were there we have heard what an interesting occasion it was—as, indeed, it was sure to be. I probably should have gone up with her if the earlier date had been adhered to. Should you be seeing Gosse this might be made clear to him if you don't mind.

The play was an unexpected success (by me, at least). I did not prepare it myself, as you may know, & even tried to dissuade Alderman Tilley (who dramatized the story) from attempting it. The mumming interlude was especially attractive. I wonder if your St. George's play in Cheshire was like ours here (the old Dorset version). The presentation & wording differ in almost every county, though the general groundwork is much the same. Some versions are loaded with all sorts of absurdities, which were shorn off the reading that was used here. No doubt they were "gag" added by the irresponsible performers of past generations.

I am glad Sassoon got back safely: it was rather a risk for him, I think, to go on such an errand. Our kindest regards to you & all your household.

Always sincerely
Thomas Hardy.

Text MS. DCM.
Thornycroft: William Hamo Thornycroft, sculptor; see III.137 and V.217.   *presentation to Gosse*: see letter of 31 Oct 20.   *The play*: *The Return of the Native*.   *mumming interlude*: see letter of 11 Nov 20 to Child.   *in Cheshire*: Thornycroft himself was born in London but his sculptor father, Thomas Thornycroft (*D.N.B.*), came from Cheshire.   *"gag"*: a Victorian term (*O.E.D.* dates it from 1847) for material interpolated by an actor.   *back safely*: from the United States; see letter of 15 Jan 20.   *risk for him*: TH apparently means that Sassoon, known for his opposition to the recent war, might have been received with some hostility.

To AN UNIDENTIFIED CORRESPONDENT

[December 1920]

A friend of mine writes objecting to what he calls my "philosophy" (though I have no philosophy—merely what I have often explained to be only a confused heap of impressions, like those of a bewildered child at a conjuring show.) He says he has never been able to conceive a Cause of Things that could be less in any respect than the thing caused. This apparent impossibility to him, and to so many, has been long ago proved non-existent by philosophers, and is very likely owing to his running his head against a *Single* Cause, and perceiving no possible other. But if he would discern that what we call the First Cause should be called First Causes, his difficulty would be lessened. Assume a thousand unconscious causes—lumped together in poetry as one Cause, or God—and bear in mind that a coloured liquid can be produced by the mixture of colourless ones, a noise by the juxtaposition of silences, etc., etc., and you see that the assumption that intelligent beings arise from the combined action of unintelligent forces is sufficiently probable for imaginative writing, and I have never attempted scientific. It is my misfortune that people *will* treat all my mood-dictated writing as a single scientific theory.

Text Typed transcript (from draft of *Later Years*) DCM.   *Date* From *LY*, 219.
Unidentified: it seems possible that this was not, in fact, a letter addressed to a particular correspondent but a set of self-justifying arguments cast into epistolary form for purposes of publication in *Later Years*.   *has been . . . philosophers, and*: not present in the version pub. in *LY*, 219.

To SIR FREDERICK MACMILLAN

MAX GATE, | DORCHESTER. | Dec 1. 1920

My dear Macmillan:

I suppose Messrs Curtis Brown are reputable agents, (which you would probably know from previous transactions) & assuming this I certainly will take £20 per volume for the Russian translations. I think one of the novels ran as a serial in a Moscow magazine many years ago, but as no exclusive permission to translate was given this would not affect the arrangement I conclude.

I had not noticed till lately that in the Mellstock edition the classification of the volumes is omitted. I suppose there was a bookseller's reason for this, & am personally indifferent about it, but as the classification is referred to in the General Preface there may be a charge of discrepancy from somebody or other. To meet it you may think it worth while to print a synopsis at the end of the last volume, somewhat like that on the dust-cover of the Wessex edition. Or such synopsis might be reserved for the end of any possible future volume, & any grumbler informed that this is the intention.

Sincerely yours
Thomas Hardy.

Text MS. BL.
agents: i.e., literary agents; see letter of 6 Jan 25. Macmillan had reported (30 Nov 20, Macmillan letterbooks, BL) an approach through Curtis Brown for the pub. of Russian translations of TH's books.   *£20 per volume*: as Macmillan had suggested.   *as a serial*: see I.283.   *classification of the volumes*: into 'Novels of Character and Environment', 'Romances and Fantasies', etc., as in the Wessex edn.   *synopsis*: Macmillan replied (3 Dec 20, Macmillan letterbooks, BL) that the omission was unintentional and that the list of vols. did appear on the paper wrappers of the Mellstock edn.

To EZRA POUND

MAX GATE, | DORCHESTER. | Dec 3: 1920

Dear Mr Pound:

Thank you sincerely for these two handsome books, which I have done nothing to deserve. I will not try to express my appreciation of their contents, as I am a very slow reader; & as, moreover, your muse asks for considerable deliberation in estimating her. Believe me

Very truly yours
Thomas Hardy.

Ezra Pound Esq.

Text MS. (with envelope) Yale.
two handsome books: Pound's *Quia Pauper Amavi* (1919) and *Hugh Selwyn Mauberley* (1920), both inscribed to TH.

To WILLIAM ROTHENSTEIN

MAX GATE, | DORCHESTER. | Dec: 4: 1920

Dear Mr Rothenstein:

What an interesting book of portraits this is you send me. My best thanks. I have thought that if you were to collect & publish *all* the portraits you have ever taken—one of each person that is to say—it would be a valuable record, apart from a valuable artistic product.

I fear my books hardly come up to the demands of children! With kind regards

Sincerely yours,
Thomas Hardy.

Text MS. (with envelope) Harvard.
book of portraits: Rothenstein's *Twenty-four Portraits, with Critical Appreciations by Various Hands* (London, 1920); it includes a drawing of TH made in 1916.   *demands of children*: in his letter of 2 Dec 20 (DCM) Rothenstein reported his children as being 'deeply interested' in some stories by TH which he had read to them.

To J. C. SQUIRE

MAX GATE. DORCHESTER. | Dec. 5. 1920

Dear Mr Squire:

I hope some time in the new year to find a poem that may suit The London Mercury—which I am glad to see maintain its high level & interest. My wife is writing about the chance of your coming to Dorchester when convenient. Thanks for your reminder.

Sincerely yours
Thomas Hardy.

Text MS. Texas.
a poem: TH's 'The Woman I Met' appeared in the *London Mercury* (of which Squire was editor), April 1921.

To HOWARD RUFF

Max Gate | Dec. 8. 1920

Dear Sir:

I have to acknowledge the receipt of your letter of the 4th. informing me of the gratifying suggestion of your Committee that I should become an Honorary Vice-President of your now well-known & popular Society.

I am sorry to answer that I have been compelled of late, for reasons I need not trouble you with, to forgo such distinctions; indeed, to withdraw from membership with bodies that I formerly belonged to; so that it will suit me better to remain as before unattached to your Society as to others.

All the same I may be allowed to congratulate its members upon their wise insistence on the word "English" as the name of this country's people, & in not giving way to a few shortsighted clamourers for the vague, unhistoric & pinchbeck title of "British" by which they would fain see it supplanted.

I am, Dear Sir,

Yours very truly

Howard Ruff Esq.

Text MS. (pencil draft) DCM.
Ruff: Howard Ruff (d. 1928), founder and Hon. Secretary of the Royal Society of St. George and editor of its journal, *The English Race*.   *the word "English"*: Ruff's letter (4 Dec 20, DCM) invited TH to become vice-president of 'this English Patriotic Society' and enclosed a copy of *The English Race*; most of this final paragraph of TH's letter was quoted in the magazine's January 1921 issue.

To JOHN MIDDLETON MURRY

MAX GATE, | DORCHESTER. | 9: 12: 1920

Dear Mr Middleton Murry:

Will this do? If the second part shd seem too "pessimistic" (word beloved of the paragraph gents) please leave it out & print the first part only. You will see that the last number of the Athenaeum before the New Year would be the place for the poem—at least so I imagine.

We have read your little "Cinnamon" with much pleasure. (I am writing nearly in the dark.)

Sincerely yours
Th: Hardy.

Text   MS. Berg.
first part only: both parts of TH's poem 'At the Entering of the New Year' appeared in the *Athenaeum*, 31 Dec 1920.   *"Cinnamon"*: see letter of 26 Oct 20.

To CHARLES GIFFORD

MAX GATE, | DORCHESTER. | Dec. 11. 1920

Dear Mr Gifford:

The War Memorial, of which you saw a notice in the papers, was really a mere tablet that I was asked to design & inscribe suitably, & I could not refuse to do it in the circumstances, though I was, naturally, out of practice. The poem "The Oxen", that has taken your fancy, came out in The Times some years ago, during the war.

I was much interested to see that your Naval Recollections were still appearing—at least when I last noticed them. It must have been a pleasure to you to recall them. The difficulty is I think to keep the events in their proper order, & it is tantalizing to find when too late that something which would have given point to a narrative has been accidentally left out. However, perhaps your memoranda were copious.

Your daughter Helen is most energetic. Teaching is a thriving profession nowadays, owing I suppose to the increased anxiety of parents to give their children a good start. How to discriminate between good & commonplace literature is however a secret hard to impart, & hence we see young people wasting their time over second rate productions, & *books about books*, when they should be shown the way to the fountainheads.

The anecdotes of your grandchildren are laughable, & show, as usual, the literalmindedness of children, & their consistency.

We were so grieved to hear of the death of Dr Gifford's daughter Evelyn. When we were at Oxford early this year she went about with us, & seemed so cheerful, & yet she was going to undergo an operation the very next day, which she would not tell us of lest it might be depressing.

My wife sends kind regards. She has just come back from a visit to an old acquaintance of yours, Mrs Arthur Henniker, who used to see a good deal of you & your wife at Southsea, when her husband, Major, (afterwards General) Henniker was living. She liked Mrs Gifford very much.

Always sincerely yours
Thomas Hardy.

Text MS. C. H. Gifford.
War Memorial: at Dorchester post office; see letter of 30 Oct 20.   *some years ago*: on 24 December 1915.   *Naval Recollections*: see letter to Gifford of 12 June 20.   *most energetic*: Gifford's letter of 6 Dec 20 (DCM) reported that Helen Gifford had opened her new school; see letter of 13 July 20.   *your grandchildren*: the children of Gifford's only son, Walter Stanley Gifford; see V.125.   *Evelyn*: see letter of 14 Feb 20. At her death in September 1920 TH wrote the poem 'Evelyn G. of Christminster'; see *LY*, 214.   *at Southsea*: in the early 1890s, when both Mrs. Henniker's husband and Gifford himself were stationed at Portsmouth—the latter as secretary to the Commander-in-Chief of the Royal Navy at Portsmouth; see II.16–17.

To ALFRED NOYES

Max Gate, | Dorchester. | 13th. December 1920.

Dear Mr Noyes:

Somebody has sent me an article from The Morning Post of Dec. 9. entitled "Poetry and Religion" which reports you as saying in a lecture, that mine is "a philosophy which told them (readers) that the Power behind the Universe was an imbecile jester."

As I hold no such "philosophy", and, to the best of my recollection, never could have done so, I should be glad if you would inform me whereabouts I have seriously asserted such to be my opinion.

Yours truly,
Thomas Hardy.

Text MS. (typewritten) Taylor.
Noyes: Alfred Noyes, poet; see III.296 and *LY*, 215–18.   *in a lecture*: according to the *Morning Post* report, Noyes spoke on the future role of literature and poetry at a meeting held to popularize the League of Youth.   *imbecile jester."*: TH has quoted accurately.

To SIR HENRY NEWBOLT

MAX GATE, | DORCHESTER. | Dec. 16: 1920

My dear Newbolt:

I am not going to let you off with a postcard, as you suggest—having thought about you many times lately.

The play would be impracticable anywhere else than here, or among Dorset people, & by the same actors. It has not been printed. They (the Dramatic Society) have done it all themselves, the adapter being Alderman Tilley, one of the company, who has selected scenes here & there, so that the performance can hardly be grasped as a whole by persons not thoroughly acquainted with the book. I had nothing to do with the adaptation beyond giving permission & answering a few questions. Like previous productions of our ambitious society it is entirely a local plant, & would perish if removed.

I, too, thought Rothenstein's book of portraits interesting, & have advised him to continue it till he gets a regular gallery, those that he has chosen being quite arbitrarily selected. I was not aware that you wrote the "appreciation" of my poor self, though I said to my wife "It is the best done of them all, though I am not the one who deserves it."

I suppose the times are past when one could say at the end of a letter anything about wishes for a merry Christmas & a happy new Year, but I do to you & your house as far as permissible.

Always sincerely
Thomas Hardy.

Text MS. Texas.
The play: *The Return of the Native*.   *book of portraits*: see letter of 4 Dec 20.   *the "appreciation"*: the anonymous—and highly eulogistic—account of TH's work on the page facing Rothenstein's drawing of him.

To FORD MADOX FORD

Dec. 19. 1920.

Dear Mr Hueffer:

I am sorry I cannot sign the paper, or say anything about Ireland in the press. If one begins that sort of thing he must be prepared to go on, or to get the worst of it, & at my age I am not able to go on, apart from the fact that I have kept outside politics all my life.

I was faithful to Ireland for 30 years, but my views of late of that unhappy & senseless country have much changed. (I may say this as I have some Irish blood myself.)

Moreover the present Government, though it contains some stupid members, is not inhumane, & I doubt if a new Government would do much better.

Yours sincerely

Text MS. (pencil draft) DCM.
Ford: Ford Madox Ford (formerly Hueffer), novelist and critic; see III.327.   *Mr Hueffer*: although Ford had changed his name in June 1919 he continued to sign himself 'Hueffer' in writing to TH, presumably to make sure that TH knew who he was.   *the paper*: Ford (17 Dec 20, DCM) asked TH to join in signing a letter to the *Manchester Guardian* which would urge the government to seek mediation or arbitration of the Irish situation; the letter did not appear, however, on 29 Dec 1920, the date Ford specified.   *in the press*: Ford also asked TH to speak out independently, 'If you could see your way to write no more than "For God's sake let bloodshed cease!" with your great influence in the nation you would be conferring a boon on civilisation'.   *Irish blood myself*: TH believed a paternal great-great-grandmother to have been Irish; see IV.37.

To ALFRED NOYES

MAX GATE, | DORCHESTER. | December 20th. 1920.

Dear Mr Noyes:

I am much obliged for your reply, which I really ought not to have troubled you to write. I may say for myself that I very seldom do give critics such trouble, usually letting things drift, though there have been many occasions when a writer who has been so much abused for his opinions as I have been would perhaps have done well not to hold his peace.

I do not know that there can be much use in my saying more than I did say. It seems strange that I should have to remind a man of letters of what, I should have supposed, he would have known as well as I—of the very elementary rule of criticism that a writer's opinions should be judged as a whole, and not from picked passages that contradict them as a whole—and this especially when they are scattered over a period of 50 years.

Also that I should have to remind him of the vast difference between the expression of fancy and the expression of belief. My fancy may have often run away with me; but all the same my sober opinion—so far as I have any definite one—of the Cause of Things, has been defined in scores of places, and is that of a great many ordinary thinkers:—that the said Cause is neither moral nor immoral, but *un*moral:—"loveless and hateless" I have called it; "which neither good nor evil knows"—etc, etc—(you will find plenty of these definitions in "The Dynasts" as well as in short poems, and I am surprised that you have not taken them in.) This view is quite in keeping with what you call a Pessimistic philosophy (a mere nickname with no sense in it), which I am quite unable to see as "leading logically to the conclusion that the Power behind the universe is malign."

In my fancies, or poems of the imagination, I have of course called this Power all sorts of names—never supposing they would be taken for more than fancies. I have even in prefaces warned readers to take them only as such—as mere impressions of the moment, exclamations, in fact. But it has always been my misfortune to presuppose a too intelligent reading public, and no doubt people will go on thinking that I really believe the Prime Mover to be a malignant old gentleman, a sort of King of Dahomey,—an idea which, so far from my holding it, is to me irresistibly comic. "What a fool one must have been to write for such a public!" is the inevitable reflection at the end of one's life.

The lines you allude to, "A young man's Epigram", I remember finding in a drawer, and printed them merely as an amusing instance of early cynicism. The words "Time's Laughingstocks" are legitimate imagery all of a piece with such expressions as "Life, Time's fool," and thousands in poetry, and I am amazed that you should see any *belief* in them. The other verses you mention, "New Year's Eve", "His Education", are the same fanciful impressions of the moment. The poem called "He abjures Love", ending with "and then the curtain", is a love poem, and lovers are chartered irresponsibles. A poem often quoted against me and apparently in your mind in the lecture is the one called "Nature's Questioning", containing the words "an Automaton", "Some Vast Imbecility", &c.—as if these definitions were my creed. But they are merely enumerated in the poem as fanciful alternatives to several others, and having nothing to do with my own opinion. As for "The Unborn" to which you also allude, though the form of it is imaginary, the sentiment is one which I should think, especially since the war, is not uncommon or unreasonable.

This week I have had sent me a review which quotes a poem entitled "To my father's violin", containing a Virgilian reminiscence of mine of Acheron and the Shades. The reviewer comments: "Truly this pessimism is insupportable . . . . One marvels that Hardy is not in a madhouse." Such is English criticism; and I repeat, Why did I ever write a line!

However I will go no further. And perhaps if the young ladies to whom you lectured really knew that, so far from being the wicked personage they doubtless think me at present to be, I am a harmless old character much like their own grandfathers, they would consider me far less romantic and attractive.

Yours sincerely,
Thomas Hardy.

Text MS. (typewritten) Taylor. *Date* The version of this letter in *LY*, 216–18, probably taken from a draft, is dated 19 Dec 20.
your reply: of 17 Dec 20 (DCM); it is summarized in *LY*, 216, and given in full in Noyes, *Two Worlds for Memory* (Philadelphia, 1953), 149–50. *than I did say*: in his letter of 13 Dec 20. *"loveless and hateless"*: slightly misquoted from *The Dynasts*, Part Third, After Scene. *"which . . . evil knows"*: slightly misquoted from *The Dynasts*, Part Second, Act VI, Scene 7. *is malign."*: slightly adapted from Noyes's letter. *King of Dahomey*: the kings of Dahomey were specifically associated, in life and at their deaths, with the national 'customs' involving human sacrifice on an extensive scale. *man's Epigram"*: for Noyes the poem 'fairly represented the philosophy' of *Time's Laughingstocks* as a whole. *Time's fool,"*: *1 Henry IV*, V. iv. 81. *"His Education"*: i.e., 'God's Education'. *a review*: not identified. *and the Shades*: the poem refers to the dead as dwelling in the 'Nether Glooms' and 'Mournful Meads'. *ladies . . . you lectured*: see letter of 13 Dec 20.

To THE REVD. HENRY HARDY

MAX GATE, | DORCHESTER. | Dec. 21: 1920

Dear Henry:

My reply to your letter has been delayed by heavy correspondence. Many thanks for your kind congratulations on my good health; but of course my life here is very quiet—much quieter than it used to be in London & elsewhere years ago, which I could not stand nowadays.

I am glad to hear of the well-doing of your son Basil Augustus—(you are right to keep alive your father's name). I knew the former Warden of Keble quite well, but his successor is, I think, a stranger to me. Your visit to Oxford must have been pleasant in the circumstances: we were there last February at the time I received the Hon. degree, & met a good many friends. I hope your boy will not overdo his rowing: I fancy some of the freshmen overexert themselves, & suffer for it afterwards.

I will try to think of something I can send you, but for the moment am at a loss. With the best wishes for Christmas & the new year to you & your household I am

Sincerely yours
Thomas Hardy.

P.S. After a search I have found a book that you may like to have, "Far from the Madding Crowd." It is an old edition, but on that account is sought for by collectors. Th. H.

Text MS. (with envelope bearing name of addressee only) Texas.
Hardy: the Revd. Henry Hardy, rector of Suffield, Suffolk, TH's first cousin once removed; see III.226.   *Basil Augustus*: Basil Augustus Hardy (1901–73), currently a student at Keble College, Oxford; he was later ordained in the Church of England, eventually becoming a canon of Chester Cathedral and headmaster of its Choir School.   *your father's name*: Augustus Hardy; see IV.96.   *former Warden of Keble*: the Revd. Walter Lock; see III.245. He resigned as warden in 1920 upon his election to the Lady Margaret Professorship of Divinity. *his successor*: the Revd. Beresford James Kidd (1864–1948), warden 1920–39.   *a book*: into which this letter, in its envelope, was evidently slipped.   *an old edition*: it was a copy of the 1895 Osgood, McIlvaine edn., with an inscription from TH.

To EDWARD CLODD

MAX GATE, | DORCHESTER. | Dec. 21. 1920 | (Shortest day.)
My dear Clodd:

I must thank your inquisitive friends for being the cause of my getting this letter from you.

No: there is no misprint in the passage you mention.

As to our going to London in the spring, it is a question that has not entered my mind as yet: & we have lately started a telephone, or rather my wife has started one, for I have nothing to do with it (except paying for it) so that she can talk to London people if necessary. This is not quite like seeing their faces, but makes the city seem curiously near us.

Dec. 22.

I had got as far as the above when something happened, & I had to leave off. My letters from the east of England seem to come together: with yours I received one from my cousin Henry H. who is the rector of a parish not far from you. However as I am not likely to persuade you to go to his church I will say no more about him.

Best wishes for Christmas & the New Year.

Yours sincerely
Thomas Hardy.

Text MS. DCM.
passage you mention: Clodd's letter seems not to have survived.   *a telephone*: see letter of 8 Jan 20.   *Henry H.*: see letter of 21 Dec 20 to H. Hardy.   *his church*: an allusion to Clodd's rationalist convictions.

To FLORENCE HENNIKER

MAX GATE, | DORCHESTER. | Dec. 22: 1920
My dear friend:

Fancy my not writing to thank you for that very pretty present, which is on my table at this moment. It shows what ungrateful man is capable of. However I do thank you for it, & think it considerate of you to have chosen it.

I wonder if you are staying in London all this Christmas. I am as stationary as a tree, & don't feel any the worse for it, though whatever moss I may gather is taken away by the tax-collector.

Our Christmas threatens to be quite an old fashioned one. For some reason best known to themselves the Dorchester Mummers & carolsingers are coming here on Christmas night, & we have to entertain them after their performance. I wish you could see the mumming: it is an exact reproduction of the Dorset mumming of 100 years ago, as described in "The Return of the Native". (By the way, the Company is going to London on Jan. 27 next, & will perform the dramatization *including* the mumming before the Dorset Men in L. at the Guildhall School of Music, wherever that may be—so that you *could* see it if you wished.)

It was *very* kind of you to shelter Florence during her late visit. She was so pleased—there is nowhere she likes to go to better than to see you.

Yes: Mr John Drinkwater is good looking: I hope his poetry will turn out to be as good as his looks. I am glad you know Newbolt—I have heard from him this very week. He would be the last to think your manner pushing: I know the much pleasanter word he would use, but I shall not tell you.

F's sister is coming here for Xmas. I think it is more to see the mumming than to see us. The cold has quite gone off here, & this morning was beautiful: we went to Stinsford & put flowers on "our" graves, as we call them. A poem of mine comes out in the Athenaeum on the last day of the year (Friday week). I don't think you will like it.

Ever affectly
Tho. H.

I have omitted to mention best wishes for Xmas—which is why I wrote at this particular time. Th: H.

Text   MS. DCM.
present: unidentified.   *their performance*: see *LY*, 220, and *Friends of a Lifetime* (see letter of 5 Aug 20), 307.   *in L.*: in London.   *her late visit*: at the beginning of December 1920. *Drinkwater*: see letter of 10 Oct 22; Mrs. Henniker said in her letter of 21 Nov 20 (DCM) that she had met him at the presentation to Gosse (see letter of 31 Oct 20).   *Newbolt*: Mrs. Henniker's letter also reported that after attending a lecture by Newbolt she had 'forced' herself upon him 'in a pushing manner'.   *F's sister*: Eva Dugdale; see letter of 6 Jan 20.   *"our" graves*: those of members of the Hardy family, including ELH.   *poem of mine*: see letter of 9 Dec 20.

To EDEN PHILLPOTTS

MAX GATE, | DORCHESTER. | Dec. 22: 1920

Dear Mr Phillpotts:

I was going to tell you last week that we had finished your book, but some trifling thing happened & prevented me. I liked it very much, & was sorry when it came to an end, for I really wanted to know what occurred in the later life of the characters. However perhaps you were right in leaving off where you did, & I am aware that the time-honoured plan of letting the reader know the end of all the personages is quite out of date. There is a point to bear in mind, however, which is that the oldest fashion becomes ultimately the newest; & if I were going to write another novel—which I am not—I should go back to that ancient style, & surprise my readers with a long enumeration of my peoples' fates, as was done in Fielding's time & onward.

Some time ago I was going to mention an idea to you that came into my mind when my wife & I were at Plymouth. I was disappointed to find no case of local MSS. in the Municipal Museum, though Bristol, a much smaller place, has a good show. It struck me that Devon & Cornwall combined ought to be able to get up an interesting group. Perhaps Plymouth is too practical to care for such.

I hope you will have a pleasant Christmas, & with kind regards to Mrs Phillpotts am,

Sincerely yours
Thomas Hardy.

Text   MS. NYU.
Phillpotts: Eden Phillpotts, novelist and playwright; see II.181.   *your book*: Phillpotts's novel *Orphan Dinah* (London, 1920).   *Fielding's*: Henry Fielding (1707–54), the novelist; *D.N.B. at Plymouth*: most recently in 1917; see *LY*, 178.   *to care for such*: in 1923, however, TH presented to the Plymouth Free Public Library the MSS. of three poems with Plymouth settings; these were apparently destroyed by bombing during the Second World War.   *Mrs Phillpotts*: Phillpotts's first wife, Emily (*née* Topham), who died in 1928.

To J. J. FOSTER

MAX GATE, | DORCHESTER. | Dec. 23: 1920

Dear Mr Foster:

I must thank you for this very handsome book, to which my contribution has been so small that I should not have expected you to send me a copy at all, in these times of difficulty for authors.

It is a kind of book to dip into rather than to read through all at once, & I cannot express any real criticism, even if I could make it. Your broom seems to have swept clean so far as it has gone, & as yet I have only missed one name, which you may have purposely passed over. It is that of Pennie the Lulworth dramatist. But, as I say, you possibly weighed him in balances & found him wanting; & would call him a half-worthy only, & ineligible. If not, he & some more that will be sure to occur to you will form quite a respectable rear-guard to some future edition.

I write on the brink of an anniversary, & send you & your house the good wishes of the season; even though anniversaries to people of my age cannot be, in the nature of things, very cheerful occasions.

Sincerely yours
Thomas Hardy.

Text   MS. (with envelope) Eton College.
book, . . . my contribution: see letter of 23 Sept 20.   *Pennie*: John Fitzgerald Pennie, who lived at East Lulworth, Dorset; see I.111 and Millgate, *Thomas Hardy: His Career as a Novelist* (London, 1971), 316 and 409. Foster wrote back, 31 Dec 20 (DCM), to say that he had not known of Pennie.   *found him wanting*: adapted from Dan. 5: 27.

To ALFRED NOYES

MAX GATE, │ DORCHESTER. │ Dec 23. 1920

Many thanks for letter. Yes: the whole scheme is incomprehensible, & there I suppose we must leave it—perhaps for the best. Knowledge might be terrible.

Th: H.

Text MS. (postcard) Taylor.
for letter: of 21 Dec 20 (DCM); see *LY*, 218, and Noyes, *Two Worlds* (see letter of 20 Dec 20), 152–4.

To DOROTHY ALLHUSEN

MAX GATE, │ DORCHESTER. │ New Year's Eve │ 1920.

My dear Dorothy:

Our best wishes for the New Year to you & yours, though the outlook is not very promising as I read it. Many thanks from us both for those you send.

I have known you really a long while—ever since you were quite a child—& I well remember the good times we used to have at Harley Street, & the romping up & down the stairs!

Florence sends her love, & reminds me that I am to tell you Stinsford House (belonging to the Ilchesters) is to be let or sold. It requires a lot of doing up.

Hoping to see you early next year I am,

Your ever affectionate
Th: Hardy.

P.S. I reopen this to tell you what I had nearly forgotten, that there is to be a performance of the "Return of the Native" at the Guildhall School of Music, Victoria Embankment, on Jan 27—under the direction of the Society of Dorset Men in London—(40–43 Fleet St, E.C). It is a curious play, which you may like to see. Th: H.

Text MS. Purdy.
not very promising: TH presumably had chiefly in mind the economic depression, the Irish situation, and signs of political instability in various parts of the world.   *those you send*: in her letter of 29 Dec 20 (DCM).   *Harley Street*: 79 Harley Street, where Mrs. Allhusen lived as a child with her mother Lady Jeune, later Lady St. Helier (see letter of 28 Jan 23), and her step-father; see II.52.   *Stinsford House*: the house, immediately adjacent to Stinsford Church, was not sold but let to another tenant.

To DAISY GIFFORD

MAX GATE, │ DORCHESTER. │ Dec. 31. 1920.

To my cousin Daisy & her mother—
With all good hopes & wishes

from T.H. & F.H.

Text MS. (correspondence card, with envelope) C. H. Gifford.
Gifford: ELH's cousin Margaret (Daisy) Jeune Gifford (1874–1962), elder daughter of Archdeacon E. H. Gifford.   *her mother*: Margaret Gifford; see letter to her of 14 June 20.

1921

To ADA FOSTER ALDEN

Max Gate | Dorchester | January 3, 1921

Dear Mrs. Alden:

(As you will readily believe, I have reached an age at which I am compelled to dictate most of my letters, and therefore make no excuse for the typed form of this.)

Your most natural wish to commemorate by a brief memoir the life and labours of the late H. M. Alden has my great respect. Would that I could join in adding some recollections of his personality to the proposed book. But, alas, I never saw Mr. Alden, and never corresponded with him except on purely business matters.

During this correspondence, though it was of a very intermittent kind, and interrupted by years of silence, it became apparent to me that he was a man of most attractive qualities and considerate nature. This showed especially when our views differed as to the admissibility of particular incidents into novels intended for the magazine of which he was editor for so long. I send you a copy of the only letter from him which I have, as yet, been able to lay hands on, and you will see that it bears entirely on questions of this sort. I dare say mine to him were of the same kind.

If by any chance I should find more—and I fancy I must have more somewhere—and they seem at all interesting, I will send them to you. But they will, of course, bear only on business.

I hope you will be able to get some vivid portraits from people who really knew him. There must be so many still living in America, though perhaps few on this side of the Atlantic.

I send good wishes for the year, if not too late, and am,

Sincerely yours,
Thomas Hardy

P.S. You may of course, use all or any portion of this letter, but I fear there is not much in it. T.H.

Text   Typed transcript (from Mrs. Ada Murray Clarke).
Alden: Ada Foster Alden, *née* Murray (1856–1936), second wife of Henry Mills Alden, editor of *Harper's Magazine*, who had died in 1919 (see I.72); she pub. a vol. of verse in 1910. *proposed book*: Mrs. Alden, writing to TH 6 Dec 20 (DCM), had solicited material for a memorial vol. to her late husband; no such vol. ever appeared, however.   *views differed*: see Alden's letter about *Jude*, 29 Aug 94, in J. Henry Harper, *The House of Harper* (New York, 1912), 530–1.   *the only letter*: dated 23 Apr 94 (information from TH's draft of this present

letter to Mrs. Alden, DCM); it seems subsequently to have been destroyed.   *mine to him*: see
I.72, 180.

To MADELEINE ROLLAND

MAX GATE, | DORCHESTER. | January 8th. 1921.

Dear Miss Rolland:

I was just going to write to you on another matter when your letter came. I will reply to your letter first.

I am glad to hear that a revised translation of "Tess of the d'Urbervilles" is likely to appear, and that you will have an opportunity of printing it in full. If you send me a list of the dialect words I will paraphrase them for you.

So far as I remember there has been no material change in the text since the edition issued by Osgood and Co was published, so that you need not get another.

I do not think "The Mayor of Casterbridge" has been translated. You would probably be able to find out better than I. In any case, you have my permission to do it, if you would like to. I hope you will get something out of it!

I have never seen a translation of "The Woodlanders", "The Return of the Native", or "Under the Greenwood Tree", and you can do as you like about them.

Has "A Pair of Blue Eyes" ever been done into French? It has recently appeared in Spanish, and seems to be a great success. I may say that it is the kind of story that would translate well, and I *think* would attract French readers more than "The Mayor" would.

Perhaps you can find out if it ever has appeared in Paris. If not, and you would like to undertake it, I can send a copy.

I need hardly add that you may translate any of these novels without payment of any fee.

I now come to what I was going to write about. There have been complaints in the press from time to time that my *poems* are practically unknown to French readers, and a plan has occurred to me by which the ice might be broken for them. The plan is that I send you a few of my short poems which I consider of a kind that would be translatable (as you know, some poetry *cannot* be translated), and that you should experiment with them by turning them into French *prose*, arranged in lines, or stanzas, to correspond with the English ones, or as you please; but not rhymed,—in fact, prose (unless you *wish* to rhyme them). Those I should choose would have a sort of narrative or dramatic situation in them which would interest readers apart from their form. You could send one or two to the newspapers, etc, and if the editors would print them you could collect them afterwards into a little volume if you cared to do so.

Well, it is a mere fancy, but I am intending to enclose a few specimens with this letter. Having been published so much more recently than the novels these specimen poems might have some attraction. And I think you might steal a march on the other translators by doing them into terse French prose.

If you would rather not, please don't mind telling me. (No fee would be required by me.)

Forgive my having recourse to the typewriter, which I am compelled to do as I get older.

Ever sincerely yours,
Th: Hardy.

P.S. My wife sends her best wishes, and hopes you will be able to come here this year.

Text   MS. (typewritten) Mme Rolland.
printing it in full: Mlle Rolland's translation of *Tess* was originally pub. in Paris by Hachette in 1901; a new edn. appeared in 1925 (Paris: Editions de la Sirène).   *paraphrase them*: see letter of 14 Mar 21.   *no material change*: TH forgets, or ignores, the restoration of the dance at the hay-trusser's to the Wessex edn. of 1912; see Purdy, 77.   *of Casterbridge"*: see III.95–6, 225–6, for Mlle Rolland's previous experience with this novel; see also letter of 14 Mar 21.   *Woodlanders", . . . Tree"*: none had been translated, although translations of the latter two by Ève Paul-Margueritte did appear in 1923.   *Blue Eyes"*: Ève Paul-Margueritte's translation had appeared in 1913.   *in Spanish*: in 1919; see V.209.   *cared to do so*: it is not clear whether or not Mlle Rolland took up this suggestion, but no such vol. ever appeared. *the other translators*: see letter of 14 Mar 21.   (*No . . . by me.*): added in TH's hand.

To THE REVD. ALBERT COCK

Jan 14. 1921.

[Ansr]

My dear Sir:

I have read with much interest the outline you send of the project which would be carried out in establishing a University for this part of England. That I approve of such a proposal, if practicable, I need not assure you, particularly as you tell me that it would work in harmony with a possible University further West, having it centre at Exeter—an idea which unfortunately is for the present, I believe, in a state of suspension.

That the name of the University should be "Wessex" strikes me as being almost a necessity, no other short & easy name existing, so far as I see, that would denote a sphere of influence roughly conterminous with that of the ancient kingdom of the same title, & covering five or six counties.

That a Chair of English Literature should be founded in my name is a point on which I can express no opinion, but so far as my sanction is needed I cannot of course withhold it, if such a step should be considered advisable at any time in the progress of the University, seeing that it would be truly an honour—though an undeserved one I fear.

In respect of the people of New England, & the appeal for their support that you suggest, there seems to be no reason at all why it should not be made. Closely connected as many of them are by ancestry with this part of old England I think they would be gratified at being considered as sharers in, or at least to have relationship with the scheme, & might give valued support. At all events I hope & trust they will, and will feel even an enthusiasm for it bearing as it does on the intellectual & moral betterment of the counties from which they sprang.

So far as the practical side of the matter is concerned the eminent men who are to address the meeting on Tuesday will be able to form a sounder judgment than I can—who, to be frank, am unable to form any, being now so entirely outside practical life.

From this letter you will be able to inform all whom it may concern that I commend the work, & hope that all good fortune & success may attend it.

Yours very truly
(signed) T.— H—

Professor A. A. Cock. | University of Southampton

Text   MS. (pencil draft) DCM.
Cock: the Revd. Albert A. Cock (1883–1953), Professor of Education and Philosophy, University College, Southampton, 1916–39.   *[Ansr]*: TH's square brackets.   *you send*: with his letter of 12 Jan 21 (DCM).   *establishing a University*: University College, Southampton, was currently a satellite of the University of London.   *it centre*: TH means 'its centre'.   *at Exeter*: the Royal Albert Memorial College at Exeter was in process of being reorganized as the University College of the South West of England; the new memorandum and articles of association were filed in July 1922.   *eminent men*: the principal speakers were Major-General John Edward Bernard Seely (1868–1947; *D.N.B.*), politician and soldier, and Alfred Milner, Viscount Milner (1854–1925; *D.N.B.*), the statesman.   *meeting on Tuesday*: a public meeting held at Winchester, 18 Jan 1921; Cock wrote 19 Jan 21 (DCM) to thank TH for his message of goodwill (i.e., the present letter), read out at the meeting; see *Hampshire Observer*, 22 Jan 1921.

To LUCIEN WOLF

MAX GATE, | DORCHESTER. | Jan 14: 1921

Dear Sir:

My thanks for the copy of "The Jewish Bogey", which I have just read with interest.

Though I know nothing of the question itself I have always been much attracted by the Jewish people, their high literary achievements, & their tragic history.

Yours very truly
Thomas Hardy.

Lucien Wolf Esq.

Text   MS. Central Zionist Archives.
Wolf: Lucien Wolf (1857–1930), journalist and Jewish historian.   *Bogey"*: Wolf's *The Jewish Bogey, and the Forged Protocols of the Learned Elders of Zion* (London, 1920), a reply on behalf of the Jewish Board of Deputies to recent articles in the London *Morning Post*.   *attracted by the Jewish people*: see, e.g., *LY*, 115–16 (a letter written for publication).

To G. LOWES DICKINSON

MAX GATE, | DORCHESTER. | Jan 17: 1921

Dear Mr Lowes Dickinson:

We have lately finished reading your Magic Flute out loud, & though I ought not to have waited till now to acknowledge your kind gift of it I can say how much I was interested in the high flight of your imagination in writing it. The part I liked best was when we forgot the flute & they were all discussing queer things at the Hermitage. (Perhaps I ought not to have confessed this).

It is very good, & Satan a most amusing person whom one would like to have for a week-end.

I could expatiate upon the book ever so much, it being so suggestive, but the hurry-scurry of life's littlenesses compels me to wind up. With warm thanks I am

Always sincerely yours
Thomas Hardy.

Text MS. Celadon August.

Magic Flute: Dickinson's *The Magic Flute: A Fantasia* (London, 1920).   *at the Hermitage*: i.e., 'the hermitage of Jesus', said to be located on the spot where Jesus was tempted by Satan; here, in chap. 3, Satan discusses with representatives of various Christian denominations the implications of a rumoured return of Jesus to earth.

To SIR FREDERICK MACMILLAN

MAX GATE, | DORCHESTER. | 20th. January 1921.

Dear Sir Frederick:

The question to which you allude—which of my novels have been translated into French—was brought to my notice a little time back by the lady who translated *Tess* and *Jude* many years ago—Mlle. Madeleine Rolland, sister of Romain Rolland—an accomplished woman whom you may possibly know, as she is a friend of several of our mutual friends—and Lecturer in English at the Sorbonne. I quote my reply to her:

"I do not think the 'Mayor of Casterbridge' has been translated. You would probably be able to find out better than I. In any case you have my full permission to do it. . . . I have never seen a translation of 'The Woodlanders', 'The Return of the Native', or 'Under the Greenwood Tree', and you can do as you like about them . . . . . Perhaps you can find out if 'A Pair of Blue Eyes' has ever appeared in French . . . You may translate any of these novels."

My reason for writing thus was that, as you know, the matter of translations is a troublesome one: and I know her to be a trusty translator, and in touch with French publishers. Thus, for the present, she has these books in her hands. If the application to you is from some other quarter, I will ask her to let me know whether she means to undertake "The Mayor of Casterbridge" or not (if it has not been done). If not, of course, somebody else might do it.

I enclose a letter I lately received from Messrs Foster, Brown & Co. of Montreal, which I am unable to answer, but you may perhaps be able to reply to.

A lady tells us she cannot get "The Mayor of Casterbridge" or "Wessex Tales" in the "Wessex Edition". I suppose there is nothing in it.

Another item is: Messrs Methuen, to whom it seems I granted permission some years ago to print two or three poems of mine in their anthology, have written for leave to print two more. Remembering your advice I asked them two guineas for one, and, I think, one guinea for the other. They have agreed to pay this, and I have told them to get your consent, which I thought you would be quite willing to give.

Believe me,

Very truly yours,
Thomas Hardy.

Text   MS. (typewritten) BL.
and Jude: although there was talk, in 1897, of Mlle Rolland's translating *Jude the Obscure*, she did not in fact do so; see II.175, 177–8.   *my reply to her*: see letter of 8 Jan 21.   *somebody else might do it*: see letter of 19 Feb 21.   *of Montreal*: Foster Brown Co., Ltd., booksellers, of 472 St. Catherine Street West, Montreal.   *reply to*: see letter of 23 Jan 21.   *nothing in it*: Macmillan replied (21 Jan 21, Macmillan letterbooks, BL) that both vols. were in print and on sale.   *their anthology*: see letter of 6 May 21.   *willing to give*: Macmillan replied (see above) that Methuen claimed to have already arranged with TH for the two additional poems.

To SIR FREDERICK MACMILLAN

MAX GATE, | DORCHESTER. | January 23. 1921.

Dear Sir Frederick:

I am ashamed to say that in empowering Mademoiselle Rolland to translate into French novels of mine that had not yet been translated I had quite forgotten that I had a previous arrangement with you for the same purpose! I will therefore write to her to learn if she will undertake "The Mayor of Casterbridge", and at the same time send her the list you forward as being those not available for her.

In respect of Canadian publication I have looked over my old agreements with and letters from and to the Messrs Harper, and can only find it definitely stated that they have rights in that country in the following books:

Jude the Obscure. (somewhat doubtful, it being in the agreement signed by them, but not in the copy of that signed by me)

The Well Beloved.

Wessex Poems.

Poems of the Past and the Present.

A changed man.

I can find no such stipulation for Tess of the d'Urbervilles. Before Tess, there was no copyright, of course. But I think they used to put in a clause about "Control of the Canadian market" in reference to advance sheets before copyright. That could have meant little, I imagine.

The Foster-Brown Company could be reminded that they can obtain any they want through an English wholesale house, and your own Canadian agency can at any rate let them have all the rest of the books beyond those mentioned above, including the Dynasts and the later volumes of verse. I will leave this to you and not reply to them myself.

If, to make all sure, you would at any time like to read through the bundle of agreements and letters, and see exactly how the case stands, I will send them up with pleasure.

I will investigate the statement of that lady about not being able to get all the Wessex Edition.

Very truly yours,
Thomas Hardy.

Text   MS. (typewritten) BL.
of Casterbridge": see letters of 8 and 20 Jan 21. Macmillan (19 Jan 21, Macmillan letterbooks, BL) reported a request for French translation rights to *The Mayor of Casterbridge*, not on the list of titles available for translation which TH had supplied earlier, and asked for the name of the translator to whom the rights had been assigned.   *Canadian publication*: Macmillan wrote 21 Jan 21 (Macmillan letterbooks, BL) that his firm could not supply Foster Brown of Montreal (see letter of 20 Jan 21) with English edns.—specifically, copies of the Pocket edn.—because Harper & Brothers claimed exclusive rights to the Canadian market.   *leave this to you*: Macmillan (26 Jan 21, Macmillan letterbooks, BL) agreed to write to Foster Brown if TH would return their letter; he added that he was writing to Harper & Brothers to see if they would tolerate the sending of English-printed copies to Canada.   *send them up*: see letter to Macmillan of 19 May 21.   *that lady*: see letter of 20 Jan 21.

To T. H. TILLEY

Max Gate [25 January 1921]

Don't forget to take the Mumming Costumes, swords & staves.

T.H.
(p. FH)

Text   MS. (postcard, entirely in FEH's hand) J. Stevens Cox.   *Date*   From postmark.
to take: to London, for the 27 January performance of *The Return of the Native*.

To DANIEL MACMILLAN

MAX GATE, | DORCHESTER. | 27: 1: 1921

Dear Macmillan:

I send again the Foster Brown Co.'s letter that you may answer it. Do not trouble to return.

If, in corresponding with the Messrs Harper, they claim to have a Canadian right in Tess of the d'Urbervilles (in addition to the books named in my last letter) you can inform them that I say they have not, & should require a copy of my concession of the same if they were to insist. But they probably would be content with my assurance.

Sincerely yours
Th: Hardy.

Text   MS. BL.
Macmillan: Daniel de Mendi Macmillan, publisher; see IV.201.   *Foster Brown Co.'s*: see letters of 20 and 23 Jan 21.   *answer it*: a subsequent Macmillan & Co. letter to Foster Brown (Macmillan letterbooks, BL) indicated that while the firm could not supply British edns. of TH's works through its Toronto office, those same edns. could be ordered from a British wholesaler.
my last letter: that of 23 Jan 21.

To THE REVD. J. B. HARFORD

MAX GATE, | DORCHESTER. | Jan 30: 1921

My dear Sir:

I was glad to learn from the papers that the writing of a Life of Bishop Handley Moule had been entrusted to your hands.

I have no objection whatever to your using in the biography the two old letters of mine of which you send copies. And I have found three of his letters to me, enclosed herewith. Earlier ones are probably lost.

I cannot for the moment recall any incidents of my acquaintance with him & his family that would be likely to interest readers; but if anything suitable comes to mind I will let you know with pleasure.

Believe me, with best wishes for the book,

Yours sincerely
Thomas Hardy.

Revd Canon J. B. Harford.

Text MS. Princeton.
Harford: the Revd. John Battersby Harford (1857–1937), Canon Residentiary of Ripon Cathedral.   *to your hands*: Harford was in fact co-author, with Frederick Charles Macdonald, of *Handley Carr Glyn Moule, Bishop of Durham: A Biography* (London, 1922). *two old letters*: of 11 Feb 80 (see I.70) and 29 June 19 (see V.315), both quoted in the biography, pp. 4, 75–6.   *send copies*: with his letter of 24 Jan 21 (DCM).   *probably lost*: the only letter from Handley Moule to TH now in DCM is dated 21 Nov 13.

To HELEN MACMILLAN

MAX GATE, | DORCHESTER. | Jan 30: 1921

Dear Mrs Macmillan:

Congratulations to you & Mr Macmillan on the event in your son's household. I send this line to you & to them with a sense that I "assisted" at the wedding.

Always yours
Thomas Hardy.

Text Ruth Dudley Edwards, *Harold Macmillan: A Life in Pictures* (London, 1983), 29.
Macmillan: Helen Artie Macmillan, *née* Belles (1856–1937), American-born wife of Maurice Crawford Macmillan, publisher (see III.261).   *the event*: the birth of a son, Maurice, 27 Jan 1921; he died, as Viscount Macmillan, in 1984.   *your son's*: Harold Macmillan (see letter of 16 Feb 21); TH and FEH were present at his marriage to Lady Dorothy Evelyn Cavendish, daughter of ninth Duke of Devonshire, 21 April 1920, and TH signed as one of the witnesses (see *LY*, 211).

To ARTHUR SYMONS

FROM THO. HARDY, | MAX GATE, | DORCHESTER. | 30 Jan. 1921.

Many thanks for good wishes—& criticism of actress in Mr Tilley's play.

Text MS. (postcard) Purdy.
Symons: Arthur William Symons, poet and critic; see II.90.   *of actress*: Symons's letter of 28 Jan 21 (DCM) contains warm praise of Gertrude Bugler's (see letter of 2 Dec 24) playing of Eustacia in the London performance of *The Return of the Native*.

To GEORGE MACMILLAN

MAX GATE, DORCHESTER. | Feb 3. 1921

Dear Mr Macmillan:

As Mr Harry Holmes's "friend away in California" is a very vague personage, not even his name being mentioned, I fear I must decline to sign a book for him. I have, in fact, been obliged to refuse to autograph books for strangers (except in the case of charities), as the books often appear soon after in the lists of second hand dealers, revealing the commercial purpose of the request, which seems one that ought not to be encouraged. So the sponsor of the unknown man had better have his 5/- back. I am sorry you have the trouble of returning it, & am

Always sincerely yours
Thomas Hardy.

Text MS. BL.
Holmes's: Macmillan (2 Feb 21, Macmillan letterbooks, BL) passed on a request from a Mr. Harry Holmes—of whom he knew nothing—for an autographed copy of *The Return of the Native*. An American professor named Harry Nicholls Holmes (1879–1958) pub. two chemistry textbooks with Macmillan's New York house in 1922 and 1925.   *unknown man*: it appears from Macmillan's letter of 4 Feb 21 (Macmillan letterbooks, BL) that the intended recipient was in fact a woman.

To EDMUND GOSSE

MAX GATE, | DORCHESTER. | Feb 5: 1921

My dear Gosse:

The kind thought of presenting me with my portrait, which you are so good as to be interested in, I learnt of some time ago, but quite suddenly, having known nothing of its incubation. And at present I know no more than is implied in the letter you have seen.

If the intention goes on the point is, I suppose, whether M. Blanche's picture is really an honest exhibition of my outside self. And of this I am no judge. Some friends ask if it does not make me too old, or somewhat decayed & senile; some say that it is high art of a very revealing kind, &c., &c. Well, you are the best to give an opinion, & to decide if the painting is worth the trouble of your getting.

You ask as to the portraits of me that exist. Besides Blanche's they are as follows (all of which you may have seen here):

1893. A small oil sketch of head by Strang on a panel: considered good, & interesting as the earliest (except photographs). It is only 10 inches by 8 inches inside the frame.

1895. Half length oil by Miss Winifred Thomson—a delicately painted picture 3 feet by 2¼ feet—as I was then.

1907. Kitcat by Herkomer—2 feet 1 inch by 1 foot 7 inches, inside frame.

Etchings by Strang at different dates.

These are all. So that you see there is nothing of any dignified size in existence, which I imagine to be what you mean.

There is, too Thornycroft's bust, or rather head, on which there is some difference of opinion. He did that of his own accord, & it belongs to him.

If I had anticipated that any friends would have the generous desire to preserve a good likeness of me I would have sat to one of our younger men, such as Glyn Philpot or other modern artist of that sort. But I had no such anticipation, & hence there is nothing available.

Supposing that in the judgment of good critics like yourself Blanche's picture is not strong enough, could he be got to touch it up when he & I are in London? You see how vague I am on possibilities.

I was sorry to be prevented coming to the very interesting function of presenting your bust. But it was owing to the accident of the first date being altered. We fixed a business appointment in London to combine with that occasion, & could not alter it afterwards.

I hope to see you in the spring.

Believe me

Ever your friend
Thomas Hardy.

Text   MS. BL.
with my portrait: the proposal to present TH with the 1906 portrait of himself by Jacques-Émile Blanche (see III.209 and Millgate, 449) seems to have foundered upon TH's and especially FEH's dislike of the image presented; see letter to Gosse of 9 Feb 21. The portrait, purchased directly from the artist by Sir James Barrie, Ernest Debenham (see V.144), Lady Ilchester (see IV.191), and other friends of TH's, was presented to the Tate Gallery later in 1921.   *interested in*: TH is replying to Gosse's letter of 4 Feb 21 (DCM).   *letter you have seen*: Gosse referred to a letter about the portrait written by TH to Ernest Debenham.   *Strang*: William Strang, painter and etcher; see I.284. Portrait now in the National Portrait Gallery.   *Thomson*: Winifred Hope Thomson, artist; see II.79. Portrait (see II.174) now in Dorchester Grammar School.   *Herkomer*: Sir Hubert von Herkomer, painter; see I.255. Portrait now in DCM. *Thornycroft's bust*: see V.82–3; one of the bronze casts is in the National Portrait Gallery, a slightly later marble bust in DCM.   *Philpot*: Glyn Warren Philpot (1884–1937), painter; D.N.B.   *presenting your bust*: see letter of 31 Oct 20.

To GEORGE MACMILLAN

MAX GATE, | DORCHESTER. | 5th. February 1921.

Dear Mr Macmillan:

I have no objection whatever to the map of Wessex being reproduced in Harmsworth's Encyclopaedia.

I wonder which one they mean. That in the "Wessex Edition" is I suppose the best as an advertisement.

Every truly yours,
Th. Hardy.

Text   MS. (typewritten) BL.
no objection: Macmillan wrote 4 Feb 21 (Macmillan letterbooks, BL) to seek TH's approval. *Harmsworth's Encyclopaedia*: if, as appears, the reference is to *Harmsworth's Children's Encyclopedia*, ed. Arthur Mee (10 vols., London, 1922–5), then no Wessex map was in fact included, simply a list of Wessex place-names accompanied by their 'generally accepted identifications'.

To WILLIAM HOWE

MAX GATE, | DORCHESTER. | 6th. February 1921.

Dear Mr Howe:

I have received your letter of the 7th. January.—The question you raise as to the desirability of getting your friend Mr Spicer-Simpson to make a relief-portrait in bronze of myself is one on which, as you will perceive, I am unable to pronounce any opinion, and on which I must defer to your judgment or that of friends in general. But in respect of sitting for such a portrait I am willing to do so, if certain difficulties can be overcome.

One is that I shall not be in London, or at any rate long enough, at any time after Mr Spicer-Simpson's return to England, to give him the necessary sittings there. The other is that if he were to come here, owing to my household arrangements being likely to undergo a change this year, and my space being limited, I could not afford him accommodation in the house, so that he would have to stay at an hotel in Dorchester.

If he should see a way of putting up with these drawbacks there would of course be no difficulty.

Yours very truly,
Th: Hardy.

P.S. It is understood that I should approve of the portrait. T.H.
W. T. H. Howe Esq. 300 Pike Street, Cincinnati.

Text MS. (typewritten, with envelope in FEH's hand) Berg.
Howe: William Thomas Hildrup Howe (1874–1939), publisher and book collector, subsequently president of the American Book Co. of Cincinnati.　　*of the 7th January*: in DCM.　　*Spicer-Simpson*: correctly, Spicer-Simson; see letter to him of 14 June 21.　　*undergo a change*: TH was perhaps anticipating the visit of several weeks paid by Margaret Soundy (FEH's sister; see letter of 2 June 21) and her son Thomas prior to their departure for Canada in May 1921.

To JOHN GALSWORTHY

MAX GATE, | DORCHESTER. | Feb. 7: 1921

My dear Galsworthy:

It was cheering to get good wishes of such far flight from you & Mrs Galsworthy. I can assure you that you also have the same from us. The book, too, came all right, & to judge from its matter so far as I have got in it, deserves my warm thanks, or anybody's, for it becomes more intense at every page. My wife who has read it once, is reading it again.

I almost think you ought to have put a genealogical chart at the beginning, to enable idle ones to grasp the inter-relationships without trouble, since they begin to get complicated. Or perhaps you ought *not* to put a chart, for it would be encouraging the said idle people in their laziness.

How I should like to be in California all of a sudden—say for a week or two—borne thither on the magician's carpet. But to travel all the way there to see & experience its climate & beauties, & through a country where "only the language is different", as somebody says,—no, thank you. My interest in the west coast of the Continent you are on is (beyond its Spanish flavour) largely owing to its looking on the Pacific—that mysterious ocean (to me), which some say the moon came out of: at any rate I like to think it did though I believe geologists & astronomers doubt the possibility of it.

We have had a mild winter here so far (except for an early week or two), & I hope it will end as it is going on. But England & Europe do not look particularly attractive in their political aspects. The extreme party seems to forget that the opposite of error is error still—just as all the revolutionists of history have forgotten it. I suppose such is inevitable: you can't make a pendulum stop in the middle, except after infinite swingings. A friend of mine thinks the great danger is to art & literature, & that a new Dark Age is coming along, in which our books will be pulped to make new paper for football & boxing journals & cinema descriptions.

It will be pleasant to know you have got home when the date arrives, & I hope you will have an easy return. Kindest regards from us both to Mrs Galsworthy & yourself. I hope the change will pick her up entirely.

Always sincerely yours
Thomas Hardy.

Text MS. Univ. of Birmingham.
far flight: Galsworthy had written, 1 Jan 21 (DCM), from Santa Barbara, California.   *Mrs Galsworthy*: Ada Pearson Galsworthy, *née* Cooper (d. 1956), formerly the wife of Galsworthy's first cousin Arthur John Galsworthy.   *The book*: Galsworthy's novel *In Chancery* (London, 1920), one of the Forsyte series.   *as somebody says*: Oscar Wilde; see letter of 15 Jan 20. *The extreme party*: TH seems not to have any specific political group in mind (e.g., the British Labour Party or the Irish nationalists) but to be commenting generally upon the unsettled state of the world in the aftermath of the First World War.   *A friend of mine*: see letter of 5 Apr 21. *pick her up entirely*: Mrs. Galsworthy suffered from rheumatism.

To ETHEL COWLEY

MAX GATE, DORCHESTER. | 9 Feb 1921

Dear Mrs Cowley:

I send herewith the inscription as given in Hutchins, which, as he copied it some 150 years ago, is probably correct, though as even he makes blunders it had better be carefully collated with the old lettering, or what remains of it, on the stone.

As to the font, I find stated in the same volume:

"Here is a neat font of white marble, the gift of the late Mrs Pitt" [probably about 1630–1740].

This is the good lady who did so much mischief in Stinsford, Fordington, Stratton & other churches. I think the Jacob family may have lived in the house now the P.O.—when it was larger.

Always yours sincerely
T. Hardy.

Text MS. Canon Cowley.
the inscription: on one of the monuments in Stinsford church; see John Hutchins, *The History and Antiquities of the County of Dorset* (3rd edn., 4 vols., Westminster, 1861–73), III.566–8.   *the font*: see letters of 15 Aug and 1 Oct 20.   *Mrs Pitt"*: from Hutchins, II.567; for Mrs. Pitt, see letter of 15 Aug 20.   *[probably . . . 1630–1740]*: TH's square

brackets; '1630' is an error for '1730'.   *Jacob family*: the Jacobs, yeomen, lived in Lower Brockhampton at least until 1750, when John Jacob married Rebecca Sparkes (Stinsford registers); see *LY*, 199–200.

To EDMUND GOSSE

MAX GATE, DORCHESTER. | 9: 2: 1921

My dear Gosse:

Since writing to you I have become aware of a strong dislike, among some people who know me well, to M. Blanche's portrait. I do not wish to interfere in anything that may be contemplated, but I think it only right that you should be put in possession of this fact. They are good judges.

Sincerely ever
Th: H.

Text MS. Leeds.
people who know me well: i.e., FEH, who had seen and disliked the portrait in London at the end of January, and Cockerell, to whom she had appealed for advice and support in a letter of 5 Feb 21 (Purdy).   *M. Blanche's portrait*: see letter to Gosse of 5 Feb 21.

To HAROLD MACMILLAN

MAX GATE, DORCHESTER. | 16th, February 1921.

Dear Mr Macmillan:

The post-card you have forwarded set me searching for the packet that was sent by the Mr Barr who wrote, and it was ultimately found amongst a number of such that arrive here. It is now being returned direct to him. I am sorry that these irresponsible people are continually giving you trouble.

Yours sincerely,
Thomas Hardy.

Text MS. (typewritten) BL.
Macmillan: Harold Maurice Macmillan (b. 1894), statesman and publisher, prime minister 1957–63, created Earl of Stockton 1984.   *Mr Barr*: TH's error for 'Burr'; Macmillan (15 Feb 21, Macmillan letterbooks, BL) had forwarded a postcard from a Frederick Burr, of Simla, India, complaining of the non-return of a parcel—presumably containing a book for TH to sign.   *direct to him*: the parcel had originally been sent to TH care of Macmillan & Co.

To SIR FREDERICK MACMILLAN

MAX GATE, | DORCHESTER. | 19th. February 1921.

Dear Sir Frederick:

I have signed the Agreement with the Progress Film Company, and return it herewith. It struck me at first that it might be worth while to insert the following words at page 2, line 17 after "successful film":

"No alteration or adaptation being such as to burlesque or otherwise misrepresent the general character of the novel."

If you think it desirable, in order to run no risk of injuring the sale of the book, will you insert the words at that point? But it may not be necessary.—I assume that I, or yourselves, will receive a duplicate of the agreement signed by the Company.

In respect of the French translation of the story I do not think the one referred to by M. Gallimard can be Mlle Rolland's. But I will ask her, and also let her know that we cannot prevent a rival translation appearing should she determine to go on with hers.—

Yours sincerely,
Thomas Hardy.

P.S. I have inserted 3 words in the agreement that seem necessary. Th. H.

Text MS. (typewritten) BL.
return it herewith: Macmillan (17 Feb 21, Macmillan letterbooks, BL) had sent for TH's signature an agreement with the agents representing the Progress Film Company, covering the film rights to *The Mayor of Casterbridge*; see letter of 22 Mar 21.   *by M. Gallimard*: Macmillan reported that Gaston Gallimard (1881–1975), founder and proprietor of the *Nouvelle revue française*, wished to pub. a translation of *The Mayor of Casterbridge* and obviously could not be prevented from doing so; the translation, by Philippe Neel, appeared in 1922.   *P.S. . . . necessary.*: postscript added in TH's hand.

To VERE H. COLLINS

[Late February 1921]

Dear Mr Collins:

I am honoured by the request from the Oxford University Press to write one of the Prefaces to the series of Shakespeare Plays that is in preparation. I am unfortunately too old for critical writing nowadays—if I ever was capable of it—& am unable to get up the momentum necessary for starting such work. I must therefore decline with regret what would have been an attractive interlude years ago.

It has occurred to me that Mr Birrell might be an excellent hand for one of the Comedies.

With thanks for your letter I am
Very truly yours

Text MS. (pencil draft) DCM.   *Date* Replies to letter of 22 Feb 21.
Collins: Vere Henry Gratz Collins, publisher; see IV.145.   *in preparation*: Collins (22 Feb 21, DCM) had invited TH to write an introduction to a vol. of a new Oxford University Press series tentatively called 'The Poets' Shakespeare'.   *Mr Birrell*: Augustine Birrell, author and statesman; see II.83.   *one of the Comedies*: the series seems not to have materialized, however.

To SIR FREDERICK MACMILLAN

MAX GATE, DORCHESTER. | 1st. March 1921.

Dear Sir Frederick:

I have received the Messrs Bramlins' cheque for £350, for which many thanks. I note that you are paying their commission of £35, and will deduct it, which is all right. It is just as well that you should keep the agreement for reference.

Sincerely yours,
Th: Hardy.

Text   MS. (typewritten) BL.
Messrs Bramlins': the agents for the Progress Film Company; see letter of 19 Feb 21.   *I note*: from Macmillan's letter of 28 Feb 21 (Macmillan letterbooks, BL).   *deduct it*: from TH's royalties account; Bramlins had not taken their 10 per cent commission from the cheque sent TH but asked for a £35 cheque to be paid back to them.

To THE SECRETARY, THE ROYAL LITERARY FUND

MAX GATE, | DORCHESTER. | 3rd. March 1921.

Dear Sir:

I am in receipt of the Report for 1920 of the Royal Literary Fund and am sending herewith a Cheque for £10—10—0 that you may enter my name as a Member of the Corporation.

I note that my name does not appear in the list of contributors for 1920, though I paid £5—5—0 as steward.

I should like to ask whether in the list of "Accumulated Contributions" the sums paid as Stewards' donations in various previous years are included.

Yours very truly,
Thomas Hardy.
per FE.

The Secretary | Royal Literary Fund.

Text   MS. (entirely typewritten except for initials in FEH's hand) Royal Literary Fund.
Secretary: Hugh John Cole Marshall (1873–1947), secretary to the Royal Literary Fund 1919–45; for the Fund itself see Nigel Cross, *The Common Writer* (Cambridge, 1985). *Member of the Corporation*: i.e., life member.   *name does not appear*: Marshall (4 Mar 21, DCM) acknowledged receipt of TH's cheque and apologized for the accidental omission of his name from the previous year's report.   *as steward*: an honorific appointment (associated with the Fund's annual dinner) to which the recipient was expected to respond with a substantial donation.

To MADELEINE ROLLAND

MAX GATE, | DORCHESTER. | 14th. March 1921.

Dear Miss Rolland:

I have explained the words as well as I am able; but, alas, they are old expressions rapidly dying. For instance, nobody in Dorchester would know now the meaning of "glane", though when I was a boy it was known quite well. I am quite beaten over the UR. You must exercise your ingenuity in thinking of a pattern sound. When you come here you shall hear it—unless it is extinct, by no means an impossibility.

I think I should retain "lynchets" untranslated, unless there is a French name for them, which I doubt. They are also called "launches" and "lanches". They are flint slopes in ploughed land, about 2 metres wide, forming terraces, and their origin is unknown. Some people say they were artificially made.

As to a photograph I have no recent one, but I send such as I have.

There was very slight foundation for the story of "Tess"—I once saw a milkmaid something like her—who had a voice also like hers—but her history was quite different—happily! Her father "Sir" John also had a prototype, and some particulars of his history were the same; but not many. A woman was hanged here more than 60 years ago for murdering her husband, but the circumstances were not similar. So I fear you must assume the novel to be but "the figment of a dream".

A translator has lately written from Paris saying he has *finished* translating "The Mayor of Casterbridge" and is about to publish it. As you know I cannot hinder him—the book having been in existence more than ten years—which is the limit of copyright in translations. So that, if I were you, I would not waste time on that novel.

By a curious coincidence I have just had sent me some translations into French prose from my *poems*—not dramatic ones, such as those I sent you, but of the more reflective sort. The translator is a stranger to me. They also have been published more than 10 years.

We both send our kindest regards and hope you keep well.

Always sincerely yours,
Th: Hardy.

P.S. "Tess d'Urberville" is best.

Page—	Line—	Osgood edition.	
17	6	*no clipsing and colling* (clasping and ~~kissing?~~)	putting the arm round the neck
22	20	*larry* (~~lark?~~)	disturbance
22	27	*plim?*	swell, enlarge
22	32	*mampus* (~~heap?~~)	crowd
30	17	*sumple* (supple, soft?)	[Yes]
30	31	*fine figure o' fun* (fine ~~slip of a~~ girl?)	dashing handsome
34	6	Bulbarrow and its *trenches* (Are they Roman earthen-works?)	Yes—ramparts of earth.
44	18	*Austrian* pines	= a large species of pine-tree, imported from Austria
51	last line.	*crumby* girl (~~comely,~~ appétissante?)	[Yes]
136	7 from bottom.	*barton* (farm-yard?)	[Yes]
141	26	*nott* cows (hornless?)	[Yes]

144	9 from bottom. *differing* (I am afraid I made a bad mistake here, translating it: *changeant*, when it must be "which differs from the rest")	different from what his clothes & occupation would have suggested. [It was quite natural that you should have mistaken this, as the ellipsis is too abridged. I was not sure myself at first what it meant!]
159	16	*apple-blooth* (blossom)	[Yes]
163	2 from bottom. "rebellest *rozum*"?	no particular meaning; a sort of onomatopoeia, implying a revolutionary oddity, a non-conforming character.
334	4 from bottom. *glane*?	smile sneeringly
368	8 from bottom. *lynchet* (is it the ground, or the stones?)	a flinty slope in a field, of unknown origin. [I think I should retain the same word]
390	23	*ranter* (I translated—from the dictionary—Méthodiste; but "itinerant preacher" might be more accurate?)	either translation will suit.
431	8	*nammet-time* (collation, goûter?)	Yes. [a light meal in the afternoon, about 4 o'clock].
448	4	*whickered at*?	to whicker is a nearly obsolete dialect work—it means to make a noise like the whinnying of a horse; a soft sarcastic laughter.
14	4, 5, 6 from the bottom. "the characteristic intonation of the dialect being the voicing approximately rendered by the syllable *ur*" I dont know how to explain it to French people??	—I think you could explain it by saying it was something like the UR in "hu*r*ler" or "*ur*gence" "*r*hum", much prolonged & deeper—though this would, after all, be obscure. In English the nearest approach I can think of is "*uhr*" (It is very noticeable in the word "her", which the rustics pronounce "hurrr".)

Text MS. (typewritten, with envelope) Mme Rolland. In the accompanying list Mlle Rolland's questions are typewritten, TH's responses in his own hand; the layout has been standardized.
explained the words: in *Tess of the d'Urbervilles*, of which Mlle Rolland was preparing a revised

translation; see letter of 8 Jan 21.   *woman was hanged here*: Martha Browne, whose public execution in Dorchester TH witnessed at the age of 16; see Millgate, 63.   *figment of a dream*": an apparent allusion to *Hamlet*, II. ii. 258–9 ('the shadow of a dream').   *about to publish it*: see letter of 19 Feb 21.   *translations . . . from my* poems: perhaps those which later appeared as *Poèmes*, trans. J. Fournier-Pargoire (Paris, 1925).   *P.S. . . . best.*: postscript added in TH's hand, apparently in response to a question of Mlle Rolland's as to how the title of *Tess* should be rendered in French.   ~~*kissing?*~~: all cancellations made by TH are so indicated. *[Yes]*: these and all other square brackets are TH's.   crumby: TH's correction of Mlle Rolland's '*crummy*'.   "*rebellest*: inserted by TH.   nammet-time: TH's correction of Mlle Rolland's '*mammet-time*'.   whickered: TH's correction of Mlle Rolland's '*whiskered*'. *dialect work*: TH means 'dialect word'.   "*hurler*": TH first wrote '"coeur"'.   "ur*gence*": TH first wrote '"heure"'.

To EZRA POUND

MAX GATE, | DORCHESTER. | March 18. 1921.

Dear Ezra Pound:

The letter you write from France contains so much that is interesting on literature, critics, etc., that I wish I could reply to it at length. But I am compelled to be brief, and am also compelled to dictate what I do send, as I have just now a weakness of the eyes which I sometimes suffer from, though perhaps not oftener than can be expected for one who has used his so cruelly as I have used mine during a long lifetime.

As to criticising the poems you so kindly sent I am afraid I cannot attempt that without knowing more clearly what you are aiming at. It is to be read only by the select few, I imagine? As I am old-fashioned, and think lucidity a virtue in poetry, as in prose, I am at a disadvantage in criticizing recent poets who apparently aim at obscurity. I do not mean that *you* do, but I gather that at least you do not care whether the many understand you or not.

Thus it is useless for me to say, for instance, as to your "S. Propertius" (on which you make an undeserved deprecatory remark) that all that seems the matter with it in my opinion—barring perhaps a word here and there—is the lack of a few notes for the general reader. I think it really a very fine and striking poem.

By the way, since you call it "confused", don't you think that you give the reader a wrong start at the outset by naming it "Homage to S.P", and not "S.P. soliloquizes", or something of the sort? I may however, have misunderstood the word.

As to the other book "H.S.M.", I don't agree with you at all in thinking it "thin". There is so much packed away in it that it, its racy satire included, can be called very solid indeed by those who really read it. To say that it is not, any more than some other of your poetry, lucid, is as I have stated merely saying that it is not what you don't wish it to be, assuming that I don't misapprehend your aims.

So I refrain from criticising—feeling it best to leave you to the light of your own soul for guidance, and not to be bothered by my "reactions".

As to the poem I hoped to send for The Dial, I have cleared off the others I owed, and will try to have one ready soon. I need hardly say I am much flattered by the request.

I hope you will get home safely and well, and am

Sincerely yours,
Thomas Hardy.

Text MS. (typewritten) Yale.
letter . . . from France: from St. Raphael, undated (DCM); see Patricia Hutchins, 'Ezra Pound and Thomas Hardy', *Southern Review*, January 1968.   *poems you . . . sent*: see letter of 3 Dec 20.   *"S. Propertius"*: Pound's 'Homage to Sextus Propertius', which TH had read in the *Quia Pauper Amavi* vol.   *something of the sort?*: Pound later referred to this suggestion as 'impractical and infinitely valuable'; see *The Letters of Ezra Pound 1907–1941*, ed. D. D. Paige (New York, 1950), 178.   *"H.S.M."*: Pound's *Hugh Selwyn Mauberley*.   *poem . . . for The Dial*: see letter of 28 Nov 20.

To SIDNEY MORGAN

[Ansr]   March 22. 1921.

Will see to the dialect of the titles &c.

The general arrangement seems as good as is compatible with presentation by cinemas—

For guidance I recommend T. H's W. by H. Lea—

Will return scenario in a day or two—

Text MS. (pencil draft) DCM.
Morgan: Sidney Morgan (1873–1946), director of productions, the Progress Film Company; he was director and screenwriter for the film of *The Mayor of Casterbridge* (see letter of 19 Feb 21) which was given its first showing later in 1921.   *[Ansr]*: TH's square brackets.   *the titles*: the film was, of course, silent.   *by H. Lea*: Hermann Lea, *Thomas Hardy's Wessex* (London, 1913); see IV.223. For Lea see letter to him of 3 Oct 24.   *scenario*: Morgan had sent it, requesting TH's help and advice, 19 Mar 21 (DCM); his letter of thanks following its return is dated 2 Apr 21 (DCM).

To GEORGE MACMILLAN

                                      MAX GATE, | DORCHESTER. | 26th. March 1921.
Dear Mr Macmillan:

I am in receipt of your letter about the Copenhagen firm Nyt Nordysk Forlag, who wish to have an option to translate the works of mine they have not yet done, on their guarantee to publish one book a year and to pay for each the sum of £20 on account of a royalty of 7½ per cent on the published price of each copy of their translation. I act on your opinion and accept the offer—it being understood that translating rights only are referred to, and not cinema, dramatic or operatic rights.

(It may be that, as all my books except some of the verse have been published more than ten years, anybody may translate them; so that we cannot guarantee that the option may not be infringed. You will know of this better than I, as will the Danish firm also, and therefore it is not worth mentioning it to them, such an infringement not being likely to happen.)

I have assumed that these translations are to be into the Danish language, and do not interfere in any way with the concession for translating into Swedish, which you may remember we granted to a Stockholm firm some time ago.

Believe me,

Always yours,
Thomas Hardy.

Text MS. (typewritten) BL.
your letter: of 22 Mar 21 (Macmillan letterbooks, BL).   *into the Danish language*: Sir Frederick Macmillan reported 11 Apr 21 (Macmillan letterbooks, BL) that the firm really wanted the German translation rights and was offering £20 on account of a 7½ per cent royalty of any book of TH's they pub. in German; see letter of 13 Apr 21.

To J. H. MORGAN

MAX GATE, | DORCHESTER. | April 5: 1921.

Dear General Morgan:

It is not for want of remembering you that I have not replied to your letter till now, as we often wonder how you are getting on with your Berlin business. Events shift so kaleidoscopically that one can hardly reply on any change before there is another. So that I will leave out conjectures on the politics of Germany & Europe, to which you alluded in your last. I hope you will get done by August or September anyhow, but we must wait & see.

It is, at least, a fine experience for you, & may possibly result in making you a diplomat of the first water. I have said this, forgetting for a moment that diplomacy is, perhaps rightly, regarded as an error by our future masters.

We are in the middle of a coal strike as you will know, which by all accounts promises to ruin the miners no less than the rest of the community. I have no practical knowledge of the dispute whatever; but the real danger in these labour commotions, & in the Labour party's policy generally, lies less in the intention, which may be defensible, but in the method, owing to the ignorance of the majority on what results inevitably follow such & such courses of action, according to the teaching of all history. So that they are like children playing with fire, this illiterate section of the party overpowering by their numbers the thoughtful ones who know how gradually changes should be worked for to avoid a catastrophe to the whole country. A friend of mine, a Professor at Cambridge, in spite of being quite a Radical, says he thinks we are at the beginning of a New Dark Ages centuries long. Absit omen!

I did read that article on Morley in the Lit. Supt but never guessed it was yours. I believe his limited edition is going well.

I envy you your visit to Vienna. I was once on the point of going there when not far off, but something hindered. I like the Viennese love of dancing & music.

My wife is in London, or she would join with me in best wishes for you, & your mission.

Sincerely yours
Thomas Hardy.

Text   MS. Berg.
your letter: of 14 Feb 21 (DCM).   *your Berlin business*: see letter of 28 June 20.   *wait &*
see: Morgan predicted that the disarmament work of the Commission of Control would be
concluded by September 1921 but that Germany would immediately begin to rearm.   *coal*
strike: a national miners' strike began 31 Mar 1921.   *Labour party's policy*: the Labour party
(in opposition) supported the strike.   *Professor at Cambridge*: perhaps John Bagnell Bury;
see IV.155.   *in the Lit. Supt*: an unsigned review, 'The Works of Lord Morley', *Times*
Literary Supplement, 10 Feb 1921, of the 15-vol. *édition de luxe* of Morley which appeared at
intervals throughout 1921.   *not far off*: although TH had travelled in Germany, Switzerland,
and Italy he seems never to have entered Austria.

To C. H. B. QUENNELL

                                                                April 7. 1921.
Dear Sir:

   The commendable interest you take, as is shown by the letter you send me,
in old agricultural implements as valuable relics of the past, I entirely
reciprocate, & were I younger I might assist you in steps towards the
preservation of typical examples. But I am quite unable for one reason &
another to join actively in such a movement. Letters to the papers invariably
bring an overwhelming correspondence, which I cannot cope with at my age.
I trust that you will be able to enlist the sympathies of more active lovers of
such antiquities before it is too late to do anything towards saving them.
   The farm waggon, of which you send a sketch from Country Life, is a
fairly good specimen; but the old ones left hereabout—at any rate till
lately—are more graceful, the curve being very marked, & the floral designs
painted on the front and tail-board very ingenious. This latter feature has
however almost entirely disappeared under a coat of plain paint.

                                                            Yours very truly

C. H. B. Quennell Esq.

Text   MS. (pencil draft) DCM.
Quennell: Charles Henry Bourne Quennell (1872–1935), architect and historian, co-author
(with his wife Marjorie) of *A History of Everyday Things in England*, in Part 3 of which
(London, 1933) this letter of TH's is quoted.   *letter you send me*: of 1 Apr 21 (DCM).
from Country Life: the drawing, reproduced in the work cited above, first appeared in *Country*
Life, 19 Mar 1921, 352.

To SIR FREDERICK MACMILLAN

                                    MAX GATE, | DORCHESTER. | April 13. 1921
Dear Sir Frederick:

   I have signed & am sending back the Agreement with the Nyt Nordisk
Forlag, with a few words added to which they cannot object. I suppose what
they pay for is the authorization, which would have a value even though
others were free to issue translations.
   I have looked up the last returns from the Messrs Harper, & this is a copy
of the list on which they pay royalties:
      Tess

Jude
Woodlanders
Well Beloved
Wessex Poems
Noble Dames
L.L. Ironies
Changed Man

These are all copyright except the Woodlanders. Why they pay on the latter only among the non-copyright books I do not know, unless it is that they took over the earlier ones from Henry Holt when he retired, & consider they owe me nothing on them. But in that case there would be no rights in the Canadian market in respect of them, as I did not guarantee Holt anything.

I may mention that prefaces to all the novels, non-copyright as well as copyright, have been written & published, over there as here, since the International copyright act, & these having copyright in the U.S. though the volume may not would add a value on which something should be paid me, I should think.

In most of my agreements with the Harpers concerning the copyright books in the foregoing list they inserted a clause—"with control of the Canadian market."

If I find anything further that bears on the subject I will let you know.

Yours always sincerely
Thomas Hardy.

I saw that you had been recuperating at Bath, but would not trouble you with a letter of inquiry. I hope the waters & the change set you up right again. Th. H.

Text   MS. BL.
Nyt Nordisk Forlag: see letter of 26 Mar 21; the copy of the agreement accompanying the letter of 22 May 21 (BL) indicates, however, that the rights were subsequently transferred to a German publisher—and the agreement itself cancelled in 1924.   *pay royalties*: Macmillan, returning to the question of Canadian rights (see letters of 23 and 27 Jan 21), reported on 11 Apr 21 (Macmillan letterbooks, BL) that Harper & Brothers claimed all Canadian as well as United States rights on the books by TH that they had pub.; he asked TH to check whether they in fact paid a royalty on all such titles, including those not in copyright in North America.   *the Woodlanders*: which was pub. before the United States passed its copyright act of 1891; see I.222.   *Henry Holt*: TH's first North American publisher; see I.27.   *recuperating at Bath*: from an attack of influenza, as reported in *The Times*, 28 Mar 1921.

To FLORENCE HARDY

[14 April 1921]

My dearest F:

I am glad to hear this morning that you have got through it, so far, & shall hope to see you—or what remains of you—on Friday about 2. I trust the extraction has been for the best, though I don't quite see how the removal of a symptom cures a disease. I hope they did not hurt you much, & am glad Eva was there.

I am writing a line to Mrs Henniker, as I think it very kind of her to put you up. A little parcel has come from Marshal & Snelgroves, & I send on a letter. I posted one from Mrs Vaughan for the 8 o'clock post this morning; I hope you will get this to-night.

If you cannot get back how would it be to go to Enfield for a few days. But you will know best. I have not seen the morning papers yet.

Ever
T.

I am going to the bridge with this to give Wess a run. He has been very good, sleeping on my bed.

I have just seen the papers. It seems that if the strike is not till to-morrow night at 10, you will be able to get home in the morning. T.

Text MS. (pencil, with envelope) Purdy.   *Date* From postmark.
got through it: the extraction of six of her teeth.   *Eva*: FEH's sister, Eva Dugdale; see letter of 6 Jan 20.   *to Mrs Henniker*: see the letter to her of 14 Apr 21.   *Marshal & Snelgroves*: the fashionable London store.   *Mrs Vaughan*: Eleanor Mary Vaughan, of Tarrant Hinton, Dorset.   *cannot get back*: a strike of railwaymen and other transport workers in support of the coalminers' strike (see letter of 5 Apr 21) had been threatened for 15 April, although it was in fact called off.   *Enfield*: where FEH's parents still lived.   *the bridge*: the bridge over the railway on the way into Dorchester; it appears from the 14 April letter to Mrs. Henniker that there was a post-box at the bridge with an earlier collection-time than the one outside Max Gate itself.

To FLORENCE HENNIKER

Max Gate | April 14. '21

My dear friend:

I must write just a line to thank you for so kindly accommodating Florence, & allowing her to make a hospital of your house.

How I wish I could come & see you. When I shall get to London I do not know, what with railway & coal strikes & other things. Those who died before 1914 are out of it, thank Heaven—& "have the least to pay" according to the old epitaph.

I am glad you liked my Keats poem. But almost everything that can be said about him has been said.

F. says that you have a dear & affectionate dog. When are you coming to the Royal H. at Weymouth again. I am sure it picked you up very much last time. I have now to walk a short way with this to catch the early post, & secondarily to give Wessex a run.

Believe me ever

Your Affectte friend
Th: H.

Text MS. DCM.
a hospital: see letter of 14 Apr 21 to FEH.   *the old epitaph*: although TH's source is unknown, the phrase occurs in a 10-line epitaph said in Horatio Edward Norfolk's *Gleanings in Graveyards* (3rd edn., London, 1866) to have been written for a Northamptonshire innkeeper: 'Large is his debt who lingers out the day, / Who goes the soonest has the least to pay'.   *Keats poem*: TH's 'At a House in Hampstead'; see letter of 26 Oct 20.   *affectionate dog*: as a replacement for 'Milner'; see letter of 31 Oct 20.   *last time*: in July 1920; see letter of 7 July 20.

To EDWARD HUDSON

[Mid-April 1921]

Dear Mr Hudson:

I fear that the old type of country waggon, curved & painted on the front & back with conventional flowers, tendrils, &c., has nearly disappeared, if not quite. A person might find a decrepit one by penetrating into the recesses of this county, away from railways. I will try to bear in mind that you want to hear of such a waggon, but as I do not go about so much as I used to do I may not be successful in spotting one. If it should be otherwise I will let you know.

Yours very truly

Text MS. (pencil draft) DCM.   *Date* Replies to letter of 14 Apr 21.
Hudson: Edward Hudson (1854–1936), newspaper proprietor, founder and general editor of *Country Life*.   *nearly disappeared*: Hudson, who had heard from Quennell (see letter of 7 Apr 21), wrote 14 Apr 21 (DCM) to ask where he could obtain for *Country Life* a photograph of such a waggon as TH had described.

To SIR FREDERICK MACMILLAN

MAX GATE, | DORCHESTER. | April 16. 1921.

Dear Sir F. Macmillan:

It would seem reasonable that the Harpers should give you a free hand in Canada with all my books, seeing that they pay no royalty on those that are non-copyright, and that the words "and Canada" in the copyright agreements were not understood by me as meaning that the Harpers only should circulate my books there. Moreover in one case, if not in more, the words "and Canada" were not in the form I signed. But all this happened more than 20 years ago, and I doubt if you will modify their attitude much.

In a letter of theirs of 29 September 1906, in reply to an expostulatory letter of mine, they agreed to pay 10 per cent royalty on the non-copyright books of their complete "Wessex" edition of the novels (your "uniform" edition). But they do not do so. I ought to have complained before, but it is impossible to be always on the alert.

In respect of Messrs Methuen publishing extracts from "The Dynasts" in their School Reader, I cannot find any correspondence about it, but if they say I agreed to it I suppose I must have done so. Perhaps it was through yourselves? Anyhow I rather think such extracts may do more good than harm to the book, so I agree to your suggestion that they be empowered to use them and pay ten guineas for the same.

Yours very sincerely,

Text MS. (typewritten, unsigned) BL.
Harpers . . . Canada: see letter of 13 Apr 21; Macmillan had reported (15 Apr 21, Macmillan letterbooks, BL) that he was taking up the Canadian rights question with Harper & Brothers.   *must have done so*: Macmillan in that same letter said that Methuen claimed to have TH's agreement to their inclusion of several pages from *The Dynasts* in a series of school readers.

To LYTTON STRACHEY

MAX GATE, | DORCHESTER. | April 20: 1921

Dear Mr Strachey:

I have just finished your Life of Queen Victoria, which arrived as a kind gift from you, one that I shall always value. You will by this time be rather tired of comment & criticism, I am sure, so that I will not attempt much of the sort, but just say that I was deeply interested in reading the book, notwithstanding that your subject was a most uninteresting woman, which means that my pleasure must have arisen from your genius in the treatment. Perhaps I ought not to be quite so absolute as to hold that she was uninteresting all through, since during the 20 years of her married life she was certainly more attractive.

I often wished you could have had a more adequate & complicated woman to handle, such as Mary Stuart or Elizabeth. However, Victoria was a good queen, well suited to her time & circumstances, in which perhaps a smarter woman would have been disastrous.

Your remark on her mother's domination is curiously corroborated by what my mother once told me: that on one of her progresses through the west of England when she was a child (which my mother chanced to see) little Victoria stood up in the carriage, the better to acknowledge the homage of the people, whereupon the Duchess promptly pulled her down into her seat by her skirts.

With my thanks for the book believe me

Yours very truly
Thomas Hardy.

Text MS. (with envelope) Texas.
Strachey: Giles Lytton Strachey (1880–1932), scholar and biographer; *D.N.B.* *Life of Queen Victoria*: Strachey's *Queen Victoria* (London, 1921). *her mother's domination*: Strachey makes several observations to this effect in the early part of his book. *my mother chanced to see*): since Jemima Hand (as then she was) came from Melbury Osmond, this must have been the journey from Weymouth to Melbury House which the Princess Victoria made with her mother, the Duchess of Kent, on 29 July 1833.

To ST. JOHN ERVINE

MAX GATE, | DORCHESTER. | 21st. April 1921.

Dear Mr Ervine:

I am much impressed by this intention of the literary group you represent, which you bring to my knowledge quite unexpectedly, and which makes me ask myself why such a kindly recognition should have been supposed to be deserved.

As to the book your friends and you propose to present me with, my feeling is that you are too liberal in thinking of one of so much value as a first edition of a Keats volume, since any book, or no book, would be amply sufficient in my case. But I must leave this entirely to the personal wishes of the begetters of the idea, merely saying that I think I should feel less responsibility in accepting some less rare work. I am at present looking for an old book entitled Winkle's Cathedrals of England, which would please me equally well if you were to light on it, and substitute it for the one you name. But, as I say, the wishes of the promoters are mine.

We shall be happy to welcome the deputation or if more convenient to yourselves to receive the presentation by post.

Sincerely yours,
Thomas Hardy.

Text MS. (typewritten) Texas.
Ervine: St. John Greer Ervine (1883–1971), playwright and author. *group you represent*: Ervine wrote 18 Apr 21 (DCM) to announce that a group of younger writers proposed to honour TH on his next birthday by presenting him with the first edn. of a work by Keats; see letter of 3 June 21. *Cathedrals of England*: *Winkles's Architectural and Picturesque Illustrations of the Cathedral Churches of England and Wales . . . With descriptions by T[homas] M[oult]* (3 vols., London, 1836–42); TH owned a copy at his death.

To SIR ALGERNON METHUEN

MAX GATE, | DORCHESTER. | May 6: 1921

Dear Sir A. Methuen:

It is a charming book: not too big, not too small, & the selections—wise & characteristic—reflect great credit on your discrimination. My thanks for the copy, & for the kind dedication.

Yours very truly
Thomas Hardy.

Text MS. T. Trafton.
Methuen: Sir Algernon Methuen Marshall Methuen, Bt. (1856–1924), publisher; *D.N.B.*
charming book: *An Anthology of Modern Verse*, chosen by A. M. (i.e., Algernon Methuen), introduced by Robert Lynd (London, 1921); it contained seven poems by TH. *kind dedication*: 'To | Thomas Hardy | Greatest | of the Moderns'.

To HAROLD MACMILLAN

May 7. 1921.

Dear Mr Macmillan:

I am much obliged to the Bedford gentleman for pointing out the misprint. I find that it occurs in every edition of "The Dynasts" except the first in three volumes, where it was correct—so that the printers are guilty, & not I; though of course I should have noticed it. For convenience I send the page & line in each case:

1 volume edition.
page 523, bottom line—for despise read despite.

Wessex edition—Verse, Vol. III,
page 254, line 2 from top—ditto . . . ditto.

Mellstock edition. Dynasts Vol III,
page 267, line 2 from top—ditto . . . ditto.
Many thanks for letting me know. I return his letter.

Sincerely yours

Text MS. (pencil draft) DCM.
Bedford gentleman: A. Mitchell Innes, of Bedford, whose letter to the Macmillan firm had been
forwarded by H. Macmillan 6 May 21 (DCM).   *read despite*: the passage, spoken by the
Spirit of the Pities, thus correctly reads, 'So did we evermore sublimely sing;/So would we now,
despite thy forthshadowing!' (*The Dynasts*, Part Third, After Scene.)

To J. C. SQUIRE

MAX GATE, | DORCHESTER. | May 18: 1921

Dear Mr Squire:

I am flattered by this request, but alas, I shall be in London only 2 or 3
days—not being able to stand now what I used to get so much of, & in a way
enjoy—I mean London racket. This really settles the question, but between
ourselves I was never much up to these things, & am now not up to them at
all.

We are going to lodge at Barrie's, who has a marvellous trick of belonging
to the most public & most advertised of professions, & living in the most
public of places, & yet being quite a hermit. I cannot understand how he does
it: it is "wrop in mistery."

Always yours
Thomas Hardy.

P.S. Here is a curious coincidence: last night from 9 to 10 my wife was
reading aloud to me your poem to a bull-dog, & she could hardly keep from
crying: as for me—ahem! Th: H.

Text MS. Colby.
this request: Squire (16 May 21, DCM) asked TH to make the presentation of the Hawthornden
Prize (for the best work of imaginative literature by an English writer under 41) for that year,
although he acknowledged later (21 May 21, DCM) that he had not really expected TH to
agree.   *at Barrie's*: see, however, letter of 22 May 21.   *most public of places*: it is not clear
whether TH means London or, more specifically, Adelphi Terrace (see V.221).   "*wrop in
mistery.*": 'My ma wrapped up my buth in a mistry', from Thackeray, *The Yellowplush Papers*
('Miss Shum's Husband', chap. 1).   *poem to a bull-dog*: Squire's 'To a Bull-dog (W. H. S.,
Capt. [Acting Major] R.F.A.; killed April 12, 1917.)', from *The Lily of Malud and Other Poems*
(London, 1917).

To DOROTHY BOSANQUET

MAX GATE, | DORCHESTER. | May 19: 1921

Dear Mrs Bosanquet:

Your letter is most welcome, as it starts my writing to you, which I had put
off doing for a few days—or rather writing to Mrs Moule—having thought
that she would get so many letters that mine could wait. I hope she is well:
please remember me to her.

I had, of course, known your dear father—off & on—nearly all my life, &
the news of his death was like a bereavement. As you surmise, my thoughts

went straight to the fact that he was the last of "the seven brethren"—as they used humorously to call themselves—*all* of whom I had the felicity to know, (long before you were born!): & I have many recollections of him of a personal kind. This weather brings back to me in particular one—of our hiring a boat at Weymouth, being rowed out into the Bay, diving off, swimming about, & then having great difficulty in getting back into the boat. At another time we agreed to go to Ford Abbey, which we had not seen. Reaching the place we found it was not the show day, & were turning away when the owner rushed out, said it did not matter, showed us all over the building himself, & gave us a sumptuous lunch.

However, all that is past, & I am old likewise, & the shadows are stretching out. I daresay I shall recall other experiences with him from time to time. One other, by the way, is that I happened to be at Fordington Vicarage when the news came of his fellowship.

If you ever condescend to Dorset, please come & see us. Believe me with kind regards

Sincerely yours
Thomas Hardy.

Text MS. Henry Moule.
Bosanquet: Dorothy Mary Cautley Bosanquet, *née* Moule (d. 1962), wife of Vivian Henry Courthope Bosanquet, daughter of TH's old friend Charles Walter Moule (see I.84). *Your letter*: of 16 May 21 (DCM). *Mrs Moule*: Mary Dora Moule, *née* Cautley, Charles Moule's widow. *news of his death*: it occurred on 11 May 1921. *"the seven brethren"*: the sons of the Revd. Henry Moule, vicar of Fordington; see I.70 and Millgate, 65–7. *Ford Abbey*: usually spelled Forde; situated in N.W. Dorset, it is a medieval building with seventeenth-century additions. *his fellowship*: Moule was elected to a fellowship at Corpus Christi College, Cambridge (of which he eventually became president), in 1858. *condescend to Dorset*: Mrs. Bosanquet wrote from Cambridge.

To SIR FREDERICK MACMILLAN

MAX GATE, | DORCHESTER. | 19th. May 1921.

Dear Sir Frederick:

On receipt of your letter I hunted up my agreements with Messrs Harper in respect of two of the novels, and send you a copy of all I can find in them that affects Canada. You will see that in the case of "Tess" nothing was said about Canada, and in the case of "Jude" Canada was not mentioned in the form I signed, but was mentioned in the form signed by them.

I am hoping to be in London for a day or two next week—and if so, I will endeavour to call on Thursday the 26th. about half past two. As, however, it appears that nothing can be done in the above matter, and as I have no particular business to call about, I hope you will let me take my chance of finding you in.

Believe me,

Yours sincerely,
Thomas Hardy.

Text MS. (typewritten) BL.
your letter: of 18 May 21 (Macmillan letterbooks, BL); it sought TH's response to Harper &
Brothers' claim that they had an agreement with TH covering the Canadian market. See letter of
16 Apr 21.   *a copy*: this one-page typed summary still accompanies the letter.   *next week*:
see, however, letter of 22 May 21.

To ST. JOHN ERVINE

MAX GATE, DORCHESTER. | 21st. May 1921.

Dear Mr St. John Ervine:

Anything that you and your comrades propose to do on or about my
birthday that is satisfactory to yourselves will be agreeable to me and Mrs
Hardy. Your calling on June 3rd on your way to Beer is a quite convenient
proposal. I still feel I do not deserve that first edition you mention.

Of the terms of the address I will not say anything now, except that I wish
my writings may bear out on examination the estimate you and your friends
have formed of them!

Yours sincerely,
Thomas Hardy.

Text MS. (typewritten) Texas.
about my birthday: see letter of 21 Apr 21.   *on your way to Beer*: Ervine (19 May 21, DCM)
sent a copy of the 'Address' from the younger writers and suggested that, rather than trouble TH
with a deputation, he could himself present the Keats vol. when on his way to Beer, Devon, in
early June; see, however, letter of 3 June 21.

To SIR FREDERICK MACMILLAN

MAX GATE, | DORCHESTER. | May 22nd. 1921.

Dear Sir Frederick:

I have now gone through the agreements with the Messrs Harper that
relate to the other books, beyond those I mentioned in my last letter. I send a
synopsis of the result in respect of Canada, which you may find it convenient
to have. As you will perceive, the upshot is that, of the copyright books, I can
find no evidence that the Messrs Harper have the Canadian rights in "Tess"
and "Life's Little Ironies", that it is doubtful if they have in "A Group of
Noble Dames", that they might possibly establish a claim in "Jude", and that
with the remaining copyright books they have Canadian rights. In the case of
the non-copyright ones I have no idea how the law stands with regard to
Canada.

Whether it is worth while to go further in the matter considering that only
two or three of the copyright books are claimable you will know better than I.
Perhaps some compromise could be come to.

I said in my last that I hoped to be in London next week, but I find that I
have to put off my visit for a time.

Sincerely yours,
Th: Hardy.

Text   MS. (typewritten) BL.
synopsis: this one-page typed summary still accompanies the letter.   *go further in the matter*:
Macmillan (20 May 21, Macmillan letterbooks, BL) spoke of notifying Harper & Brothers of his
firm's intention to fill all Canadian orders for TH's books.   *put off my visit*: TH and FEH
were to have stayed with Sir James Barrie (see letter of 18 May 21), but the latter's adopted son
Michael Llewelyn Davies was drowned at Oxford on 19 May 1921.

To SIR FREDERICK MACMILLAN

Max Gate, | Dorchester. | 24th. May 1921.

Dear Sir Frederick:
I am in receipt of your letter of yesterday. If you send any of the non-
copyright books to Canada I shall be willing to accept the royalties of 6d. on
the Uniform & Pocket editions, and 9d. on the Wessex edition, in view of
your explanation.
I find by the way that the Messrs Harper pay, or did pay, a royalty on the
United States sale of *one* of the non-copyright novels—"The Woodlanders"
—without however any reference to Canada in the letter of agreement.
Believe me,

Yours sincerely,
Th: Hardy.

Text   MS. (typewritten) BL.
your explanation: Macmillan (23 May 21, Macmillan letterbooks, BL) took the position that
since Harper & Brothers paid no royalty either in Canada or the United States on the books not
in copyright (see letter of 22 May 21), there was no reason why English edns. of them should
not be supplied to Canada—though prices, and therefore royalties, would have to be kept low.

To EMMA DUGDALE

Max Gate | June 2: 1921

Dear Mrs Dugdale:
Many thanks for your letter of good wishes which I much value as coming
from you. I hope you are well, & will be able to get out of doors during these
long days.
I am including Mr Dugdale in this note. Please thank him for his last
letter, which I meant to reply to at the time. So far, all seems to be well with
Margaret.
Connie will know that she also is thanked for her greetings. Tell her I am
so glad the Pageant went off well & that she was presented to the Princess,
whom neither of us has ever met.
Believe me always

Yours affectionately
Thomas Hardy.

P.S. I have a tune in my head which I cannot get rid of—it is called
"Houghton"—by Dr Gauntlett. I wonder if you ever play it. T.H.

Text   MS. (with envelope addressed to 'Mr & Mrs Dugdale') Purdy.
of good wishes: for TH's 81st birthday, 2 June 1921.   *Mr Dugdale*: see letter of 2 July 20.
Margaret: Margaret Soundy, *née* Dugdale, FEH's youngest sister (see V.212); she had recently

gone to join her husband, Reginald Soundy, in Canada.   *Connie*: Constance Dugdale; see letter of 2 June 25.   *the Pageant*: evidently the Pageant of Youth, organized by the Ministering Children's League, held at King's College, London, and opened by the Princess Mary (see letter of 1 Mar 22).   *Dr Gauntlett*: Henry John Gauntlett (1805–76; *D.N.B.*), organist and composer, wrote many hundreds of chants and hymn tunes.

To ST. JOHN ERVINE

MAX GATE, | DORCHESTER. | June 3. 1921

Dear Mr St. John Ervine:

The precious first edition of Keats's "Lamia, Isabella, the Eve of St. Agnes, & other poems" has come, & I hasten to acknowledge its safe arrival.

The larger acknowledgement of the gift itself I feel quite unable to make in any adequate degree, & I should be depressed on account of it if I did not know almost to a certainty that the donors will be quite able to imagine without any telling how I value this original imprint of undying words, & the depth of my thanks.

I would write a longer letter to you & the illustrious group of young signatories to the message but for a weakness of the eyes (temporary I hope) which forbids my using them for more than a few minutes at a time. I should like to write to each one who signs, but I fear I cannot.

Believe me to be

Most sincerely yours & theirs
Thomas Hardy.

Text   MS. Texas.
precious first edition: it is now in DCM; see *LY*, 221–2.   *its safe arrival*: Ervine did not, as he had planned (see letter of 21 May 21), present the book to TH in person but sent it by post; his letter, of 2 June 21, is in DCM.   *signatories to the message*: the address (DCM; quoted in part, *LY*, 222) bore 104 signatures, including those of Robert Graves, James Joyce, Siegfried Sassoon, and Leonard and Virginia Woolf; Ervine signed on his own behalf and for three additional writers currently out of the country. TH did not receive the document itself until September 1921; see letter of 11 Sept 21.

To NEWMAN FLOWER

Max Gate | 6: 6: 1921.

Dear Mr Flower:

Many thanks for kind congratulations.

Proof returned herewith.

T.H.

Text   MS. Texas.
Flower: Newman Flower, publisher, managing director of Cassell & Company; see II.164.
congratulations: in Flower's letter of 3 June 21 (DCM).   *Proof*: of TH's poem 'The Country Wedding' (an expanded version of 'The Fiddler's Story') as pub. in *Cassell's Winter Annual*, 1921–2.

To THEODORE SPICER-SIMSON

Max Gate, | Dorchester. | June 14th. 1921.

Dear Sir:

We much admire the photographs of the medallions you have enclosed.

Almost any time next week would suit me for your coming here to make one of myself, and I suggest Monday next the 20th. I much regret to say that we are in the midst of household changes which prevent our putting you up for the night, but this house is only a short walk out of Dorchester where there is plenty of accommodation (King's Arms, the Antelope, the Junction etc.) and I feel that you will be more comfortable in one of those than here in the circumstances.

Please let me know which day to expect you.

Very truly yours,
Th: Hardy.

Text MS. (typewritten) Princeton.
Spicer-Simson: Theodore Spicer-Simson (1871–1959), American sculptor and portrait medallist. *enclosed*: with his letter of 12 June 21 (DCM).   *one of myself*: the bronze medallion (now in DCM) reached Max Gate in August 1921; FEH wrote to Spicer-Simson 17 Aug 21 (Princeton), expressing her own and TH's thanks and admiration. See letter of mid-April 22.

To W. H. WAGSTAFF

MAX GATE, DORCHESTER. | June 14. 1921.

Dear Sir:

In reply to your notification that I have been elected a Vice-President of the Society I must thank the Members for the distinction conferred. I regret to add that I fear circumstances will prevent my rendering any service to the Society in that honourable position.

Yours very truly,
Thomas Hardy.

Text MS. (typewritten) Royal Society of Literature.
Wagstaff: William Henry Wagstaff, Hon. Secretary to the Royal Society of Literature; his letter dated June 1921 is in DCM.   *the Society*: the Royal Society of Literature, of which TH had long been a fellow.

To SIR HENRY NEWBOLT

Max Gate | 23 June 1921.

My dear Newbolt:

This is a very interesting job of yours that you tell me of; though its scope & necessary research must be rather appalling—at any rate it would be to me with my weak eyes. Of course such extracts from my humble writings as you may want to place in the background of your galaxy are at your service (the fee which my publishers will probably ask me to impose on your publishers being so small as to be negligible.)

I imagine you to be working at the book in the shades of Netherhampton— if you have any shade. We sat out & had tea this afternoon in what we believed to be shade, but the sun stole round & scorched us. By a curious reversal of customary atmospheric conditions this part of England & all down Devon & Cornwall is, according to the papers, drier & hotter than the Midlands & East.

My wife passed through Salisbury a few days ago on her way to Devizes & back—not for pleasure, but to interview a cook & gardener who might possibly suit us. We could hear of neither any nearer. However she found the journey across the Plain in an open car very exhilarating. Walter de la Mare came to see us last week, & we found him delightful. He is just bringing out a novel: I hope it will attract, but somehow I like to think of him best as writing verse.

With kindest regards to you & your house believe me

Always sincerely yours
Thomas Hardy.

Text   MS. Texas.

job . . . tell me of: Newbolt's *An English Anthology of Prose and Poetry, Shewing the Main Stream of English Literature Through Six Centuries, 14th Century–19th Century* (London, 1921); he sent a prospectus with his letter of 20 June 21 (DCM) and asked permission to include several examples of TH's work.   *Netherhampton*: Netherhampton House, Salisbury, Newbolt's home for many years.   *the Plain*: i.e., Salisbury Plain.   *de la Mare*: see letter of 6 July 21; ne had stayed at Max Gate for two days.   *a novel*: de la Mare's *Memoirs of a Midget*; see letter of 9 Aug 21.

To SIR FREDERICK MACMILLAN

MAX GATE, | DORCHESTER. | 29th. June 1921.

Dear Sir Frederick:

I do not feel any particular objection to letting Mrs Head compile the anthology, nor any great wish that she should do so. Perhaps if she is informed of the only way in which it can be done to make her selected passages fairly representative she may not care to undertake it; the way being to choose impartially from the prose and the verse. Possibly she has thought only of the novels; but a one-sided idea would be given of the series of books as a whole if she were to drop all those written during the last 25 years, covering a time as long as that covered by the prose.

However, she may not mean this, but to browse over all, and the case being one that does not compare well with that of Henry James—where all was level prose—I think we ought to know a little more of how the lady would propose to proceed where met by material of great diversity.

In the event of her explanation being satisfactory the 5 per cent you suggest seems quite reasonable.

Sincerely yours,
Thomas Hardy.

P.S. I hope you have not been incommoded by the late heat. If you ever come westward for air, or for any other reason, we shall be delighted to see you. Th. H.

Text MS. (typewritten) BL.
Mrs Head: Ruth Head; see letter of 21 July 21.   *the prose and the verse*: Mrs. Head's anthology (see letter of 21 May 22) contains both prose and verse.   *that of Henry James*: an allusion to Mrs. Head's *Pictures and Other Passages from Henry James* (London, 1916).   *the late heat*: many parts of England had been experiencing unusually high June temperatures of more than 80°F; drought conditions persisted until 25 July.   *P.S. ... see you.*: entire postscript in TH's hand.

To FLORENCE HENNIKER

Max Gate | 2 July 1921

My dear friend:

This continuous fine weather makes me think that you might do well in trying Weymouth again, before the August trippers come. We have been told this week that the Burdon Hotel, which was until lately used for war-purposes, is now restored to its original state, has had the drains overhauled, & is altogether very comfortable, while not so expensive as the Royal—which some people are beginning to complain of in point of charges.

This morning we have had an odd experience. The film-makers are here doing scenes for "The Mayor of C." & they asked us to come & see the process. The result is that I have been talking to The Mayor, Mrs Henchard, Eliz. Jane, & the rest, in the flesh. The company arrived here at 1 o'clock this morning, & leave again to-morrow. It is a strange business to be engaged in.

I believe I never have thanked you for your kind telegram on my birthday. I don't send you messages on yours, which is rather mean of me, but I send them in a lump now. I remember that you are not far from Lady Randolph Churchill, of whose accident we heard at the time, but imagined it to be one she would get over. She has had a lively life altogether, so her shade must not complain.

As you know, we did not go to London after all, & now it does not seem the sort of place to go to in the drought. We have had a few pleasant people calling—poets mostly: I am getting to know quite a lot of the Young Georgians, & have quite a paternal feeling, or grandpaternal, towards them. Siegfried Sassoon has been, Walter de la Mare, John Masefield, & next week Mr & Mrs Galsworthy are going to call on their way to London. We have also seen the Granville Barkers. All this is by reason of the car fashion of travel, which seems to make us almost suburban.

I hope Lady Crewe got over her attack of measles. Our neighbour Mrs Hanbury is ailing, & her father Mr Jeune (Ld St Helier's brother) is ill at her house.

We have no Sunday post now, so I must send this off to night.

Ever yr affectionate
Th: H.

The cinema actors have just called in a body to wish us goodbye. Th: H.

Text MS. DCM.
trying Weymouth again: see letter of 7 July 20.   *Mayor of C."*: see letter of 22 Mar 21.   *her shade*: an allusion to the death, on 29 June 1921, of Lady Randolph Churchill, *née* Jenny Jerome, widow of Lord Randolph Churchill (see II.53), mother of Winston Spencer Churchill

(see V.38); she had lived at 8 Westbourne Street, a short distance from Mrs. Henniker's 2 Hyde Park Square address.   *de la Mare*: see letter of 6 July 21.   *Masefield*: see letter to him of 30 Dec 22.   *Barkers*: see letter of 19 Mar 22.   *Lady Crewe*: Margaret, *née* Primrose, daughter of the fifth Earl of Rosebery, second wife of the first Marquess of Crewe (see letter of 31 Oct 20), Mrs. Henniker's brother.   *attack of measles*: of which TH had learned from Mrs. Henniker's letter of 15 Apr 21 (transcript, DCM).   *Mrs Hanbury*: of Kingston Maurward House, visible from Max Gate; see letter of 6 Jan 20.   *Mr Jeune*: see letter of 14 June 20 to Margaret Gifford.

To NOWELL SMITH

[Early July 1921]

Dear Sir:

My husband has read your letter to the Vicar of Sherborne, of which you have kindly sent a copy, & he echoes your sentiments on the subject. It is the old difficulty—that of preventing the destruction in the interests of utility of bygone architectural remains that are irreplaceable.

Sherborne Abbey suffered much in the 19th century at the hands of restorers, actuated as they were by the best intentions. To see the monuments of bygone inhabitants crowded on the walls of the present Vestry has given pain to many visitors, Mr Hardy included, & the idea of placing them in a better position, or even putting them back into their old places appeals to him.

As far as he can gather, the plan you outline would seem to be an excellent one, & he says he will support you in it as far as his limited power extends. He suggests that you should draw up a statement on the lines of your letter to the Vicar, which he could join you in signing.

Yours very truly

Text MS. (pencil draft) DCM.   *Date* Replies to letter of 4 July 21.
Smith: Nowell Charles Smith (1871–1961), schoolmaster and author, headmaster of Sherborne School 1909–27; he wrote to FEH 4 July 21 (DCM), enclosing a copy of an open letter to the vicar of Sherborne about proposed alterations to the old Lady Chapel of Sherborne Abbey. *Vicar of Sherborne*: the Revd. Stephen Harold Wingfield-Digby, vicar of Sherborne 1916–32. *Sherborne Abbey*: Sherborne Abbey church, described by the Royal Commission on Historical Monuments as 'the most important architectural monument in the county'; its eastern chapels, sold to Sherborne School in the sixteenth century following the dissolution of the abbey, had been reacquired in 1919 and were about to be extensively restored.   *draw up a statement*: although Smith seems not to have adopted this course the restorations were later discussed in a leading article in *The Times* (23 July 1921) and in the correspondence which followed.

To WALTER DE LA MARE

Max Gate | July 6: 1921

Dear Mr de la Mare:

I am uncivil enough to return the paper unsigned, believing such protests useless, &, in any event, my signature no help to them.

I am glad you liked Queen Victoria. Prince Albert was an underrated man I think. I am old enough to remember the jealousies that attended almost any action on his part in this country, till he took refuge in Great Exhibitions, & these being deemed harmless he was let alone.

We are dried up here, & are puzzled to understand how the blackbirds & thrushes live without moisture. I have just corrected the proof of a wretchedly bad poem, that nobody wanted me to write nobody wants to read & nobody will remember who reads it.

This hasty note is in order to catch the morning post.

Always yours
Thomas Hardy.

We shall be glad to see your face again. Th: H.

Text MS. Eton College.
de la Mare: Walter de la Mare, poet and novelist; see V.284.　　*the paper*: de la Mare (5 July 21, DCM) asked TH to join in signing a protest against the Government's Irish policy.　　*Queen Victoria*: i.e., Lytton Strachey's book (see letter of 20 Apr 21), borrowed from TH.　　*in Great Exhibitions*: Prince Albert (1819–61; *D.N.B.*), consort of Queen Victoria, was the instigator of the International Exhibition of 1851 and deeply involved up to the time of his death in the plans for the International Exhibition of 1862—which TH himself visited (see I.1–2).　　*dried up here*: see letter of 29 June 21.　　*bad poem*: presumably 'Barthélémon at Vauxhall', *The Times*, 23 July 1921.

To RUTH HEAD

July 21. 1921

Dear Miss Head:

In reply to your interesting letter of the 20th I can only say, as I am not a good judge of these matters, that your plan for a selection from my writings seems a wise one, & that I have no objection to your making such a selection, if the publishers can arrange.

As there is really no fundamental difference between the prose & the verse I imagine you would propose to mix the extracts of each form, especially as sometimes, I think, I have written on practically the same subject in both forms; & also as some of the verse was written before some of the prose.

When I know what pieces you intend to select I can perhaps draw your attention to any others that have been mentioned by good judges, in case you might like to consider them.

The difficulty of selections, in poetry particularly, is (if you don't mind my saying it) that though what a woman reader likes a man may usually like, what a man likes most is sometimes what a woman does not like at all. And this especially with my writings.

However we shall see; & I am

Yours sincerely

Text MS. (pencil draft) DCM.
Head: Ruth Head, *née* Mayhew (d. 1939); TH had not yet realized that she was the wife of Henry Head the neurologist (see letter of 21 May 22).　　*of the 20th*: in DCM.　　*plan for a selection*: see letter of 29 June 21.

To SIR JAMES BARRIE

[Early August 1921]

Many thanks, &c &c.

My husband says it is impossible for him personally. He has discovered this year that he cannot go visiting any more—a person over 81 must stay at home—But I could &c

Text   MS. (pencil draft) Princeton.   *Date*   See below.
Barrie: Sir James Matthew Barrie, dramatist and novelist; see I.200.   *Many thanks*: TH's draft is written on the back of the envelope of Barrie's letter to FEH of 1 Aug 21 (Princeton; pub. in *Letters of J. M. Barrie*, ed. Viola Meynell [London, 1942], 146) inviting the Hardys to stay for a few days at Stanway, near Cheltenham, which he had rented for a period.

To RUTH HEAD

August 7. 1921

Dear Mrs. Head:

I have been thinking over your letter of July 23, & now find that I was rather rash in saying that I would let you know if your proposed selection should not include pieces or passages favoured by the best critics. For one thing, I don't know who are the best critics, & for another I don't remember what they have liked. So there you are—thrown back on your own judgment.

To be quite candid I prefer this, & indeed wished after writing to you I had not hinted anything about other judgments; I particularly prefer it now that I learn that your husband is giving a kindly eye to your selections. (This is shockingly ungallant, but how can I be otherwise in a business of this peculiar sort!) In extenuation I humbly add that my writings, particularly in verse—& I don't care an atom what prose you select—suffer from the misfortune of being more for men than for women, if I may believe what people say.

But though I prefer to leave your judgment unbiassed by that of professional critics, there can be no harm in my saying that the selection in Macmillan's Golden Treasury series, *so far as it goes*, is satisfactory, bearing in mind its conditions & limitations—that it is primarily a drawing-room table & birthday book—& that therefore the "strongest" (to use the journalists' word), & more controversial poems had to be omitted. Moreover, as it was published before "Moments of Vision" came out it contains no pieces from the latter book (except two or three taken from the manuscript of it) & so omits many, possibly among the best I have written—such as Near Lanivet, To the Moon, The Duel [a man's poem only!] The Photograph [ditto], It never looks like summer, The Figure in the Scene, During Wind & Rain, etc., etc.

As to the editions: I do not think there is much difference in them as to the prose. But perhaps the safest & certainly the handiest for the verse is the green Collected edition in two volumes: 1 Collected Poems, 2. The Dynasts. In the chosen extracts, however, there may be no amendments.

Believe me, with kind regard,

Yours sincerely

Text MS. (pencil draft) DCM.
of July 23: in DCM; she had asked if TH could specify some of the poems especially admired by critics.   *in saying*: in his letter of 21 July 21.   *your husband*: Henry Head; see letter of 21 May 22.   *Golden Treasury series*: i.e., TH's *Selected Poems* of 1916.   *[a man's ... ditto]*: TH's square brackets.   *Collected edition*: of 1919; see Purdy, 287.

To ERNEST RHYS

August 7. 1921.

Dear Mr Rhys:

I am sorry to say in reply to your inquiry on the best short stories in English that I am quite incompetent to give an opinion. Even if I were a good judge, which I am not, I have read so very few works of fiction during the last five & twenty years that I don't know what may have been published.

As to the question, which short story of my own is the best, I am equally in the dark; but if Mr Dent applies to me when the holidays are over for the right to print any one he may select, I will readily consider the matter.

Believe me

Yours truly
T. . . H. . .

Ernest Rhys Esq.

Text MS. (pencil draft) DCM.
Rhys: Ernest Percival Rhys, author and editor; see II.60.   *in English*: Rhys, 15 July 21 (DCM), said that he had been asked to 'consult' TH about a proposed Everyman's Library vol. of the best short stories in English, one of TH's own stories to be included; see letter of 29 Aug 21 to Macmillan.   *Mr Dent*: Joseph Malaby Dent (1849–1926), publisher; *D.N.B.* *holidays are over*: Rhys said that Dent, 'during a sick-man's leisure', was himself selecting the stories for the vol.

To WALTER DE LA MARE

MAX GATE, | DORCHESTER. | Aug. 9. 1921

Dear Mr de la Mare;

I have finished the book you were so kind as to send me. I should say we have finished it, for my wife (owing to the weakness of my eyes) read it aloud to me except a little which I read myself. Many warm thanks for contributing so to our enjoyment.

As you will be already overburdened with criticisms I shall not attempt to add greatly to them, except by saying (if that is criticism) that I have liked the story very much, & that I think some parts—innumerable parts—of the writing to have so subtle a beauty that it may possibly be wasted on the tribe of ordinary novel readers into whose hands it will fall. I don't see how you can help this waste, though you may avoid repeating it by saving up any such future inspirations to beauty for your poetry—to which remark you will mentally reply, I shall do as my inclination leads me.

The latter part of the book is I think what is called the strongest & most dramatic, but the best developed phases to my mind are those which show the gradual misery caused the poor Midget by her finding she is a joke at Mrs

M's. The dinner-party is also excellent. The most real of the characters to me is Fanny. You can touch her with your hand almost.

That walk with you from the station was certainly very pleasant. Since then I have had to undergo the ordeal of opening a huge Bazaar! Keep the Q. Victoria till you have quite finished with it, & believe me,

Ever sincerely yours
Thomas Hardy.

Text MS. Eton College.
the book: de la Mare's novel, *Memoirs of a Midget* (London, 1921).   *Mrs M's*: Mrs. Monnerie, who adopts the midget as a kind of pet or court dwarf.   *Fanny*: Fanny Bowater, the wayward daughter of the midget's landlady.   *a huge Bazaar!*: a fête held in Dorchester Borough Gardens 20 July 1921 to raise funds for the County Hospital; TH made a short speech on the occasion.   *the Q. Victoria*: see letter of 6 July 21.

To JANE PANTON

MAX GATE, | DORCHESTER. | August 26: 1921

Dear Mrs Panton:

I have been truly sorry to see announced in the papers the death of Mr Panton. I had not met him for many years, but I of course remember his genial & kindly nature, & unobtrusive manner. I think he always remained a Dorset man through his long absence from the country.

I much sympathize with you in your loss after so long a companionship, though I know well that letters of condolence are of little use in such circumstances.

Yours sincerely
Thomas Hardy.

Text MS. Purdy.
Panton: Jane Ellen Panton, *née* Frith, author; see I.145.   *in the papers*: specifically, the 26 August issue of the *Dorset County Chronicle*.   *Mr Panton*: James Panton (see I.145) began as a brewer in Dorchester but later moved to Watford; he died in Bournemouth, aged 79. *so long a companionship*: the Pantons had been married for 52 years.

To DOUGLAS FAWCETT

[Ans. to Mr Douglas Fawcett]   Aug. 29. 1921

Dear Sir:

I must write my thanks to you for your book "Divine Imagining" which you have been so kind as to send me, although I have not as yet given it more than a general glance over, for it is a work that I shall obviously not have read thoroughly till acknowledgement would seem unduly delayed.

It has been very courageous of you to cast the philosophy of the Unconscious entirely aside, the more if it should turn out that you have not established your own more pleasing philosophy in its place as firmly as could be wished.

As I gather, you renounce the creeds which deny life-persistence after physical death, as being "fatuously untrue" because they foredoom all great schemes of social betterment to ruin. I do not follow this reasoning, failing first to see any ground for supposing such a consequence, & second, assuming it, failing to see how it would prove the untruth of such creeds. Thus not having grasped any evidence of the persistence of life after bodily cessation, but fancying that there is presumptive evidence to the contrary, I am compelled to regard your picture of the superior sentients of the world-system coalescing into a God as a bright hypothesis merely. But as I said, I am only beginning to get into your book.

It has, I think, been well-received by the press (if that is worth anything!). "The Dynasts", to which you generously allude, had a rougher reception in 1903. As an instance of how times have changed in 18 years I remember that when in that poem I deposed the He of theology, replacing Him by It, as being less childishly anthropomorphic, I was mildly scolded by the critics for such a daring innovation; but nobody, so far as I have seen, has objected to your use of that capital-lettered pronoun.

Believe me,

Yours very truly

T— H—

Text   MS. (pencil draft) DCM.
Fawcett: Edward Douglas Fawcett (1866–1960), author and sportsman.   *[Ans. . . . Fawcett]*: TH's square brackets.   *Divine Imagining"*: Fawcett's *Divine Imagining: An Essay on the First Principles of Philosophy* (London, 1921).   *generously allude*: in his undated letter in DCM.

To SIR FREDERICK MACMILLAN

MAX GATE, | DORCHESTER. | August 29th. 1921.

Dear Sir Frederick:

Mr Dent, who writes from the house of Messrs Dent & Sons, informs me that he is compiling for Everyman's Library a book showing the development of the short story from the Morte d'Arthur to the present date, and asks to be allowed to use two examples of mine—(either "The Son's Veto" or "The Three Strangers," and the sketch called "Tony Kytes".) If you see no objection to his having them can you suggest what fee he should pay, as I don't remember letting a prose story be used before? I suppose it would be a sort of advertisement, but it might perhaps be sufficient to let him have one only.

Believe me,

Yours sincerely,

Th: Hardy.

The respective lengths are, in the Wessex Edition:

    Tony Kytes—10 pages
    Son's Veto—17½ ..
    Three Strangers   26 pages.

Text   MS. (typewritten) BL.
Mr Dent: see letter of 7 Aug 21 to Rhys; Dent's own letter is not in DCM.   *a book*: pub. as *English Short Stories: Selected to Show the Development of the Short Story from the Fifteenth to the Twentieth Century* (London, 1921); it includes TH's 'The Three Strangers'.

To ST. JOHN ERVINE

MAX GATE, | DORCHESTER. | Sept: 11: 1921

Dear Mr Ervine:

The book has arrived safely, & I must again thank you for the trouble you have taken in getting it finished & out of hand. The binding is perfect, & when I look over the names of so many, whom I shall never see, I feel more than I can tell you.

The illuminated pages are beautifully done, the capitals & penmanship generally being worthy of our best craftsmen in the art, which I thought had almost died out under the influence of machine printing.

We were much interested in your sturdy letter to the Times last week, & hope you are well.

Always sincerely yours
Thomas Hardy.

Text MS. Texas.
The book: i.e., the bound vol. containing the 'address' and signatures intended to accompany the copy of Keats's *Lamia* presented to TH by the group of younger writers; see letter of 3 June 21. Ervine's accompanying letter (8 Sept 21, DCM) explained that the vol. had just come from the binder.   *sturdy letter*: Ervine's long letter, featured on the editorial page of *The Times*, 7 Sept 1921, under the heading 'Ulster and Sinn Fein', presented a hostile analysis of the negotiating position currently being taken by the Irish nationalist leader Eamon de Valera.

To SIEGFRIED SASSOON

Max Gate: | 22 Sept. 1921

My dear S.S.

Many thanks for "Jane Shore", which you should not, however, have taken the trouble to get in such a good edition. It inculcates the duty of leading a moral life, I find, poor Jane being used to point the folly of doing otherwise.

We rather miss you now you have gone.

Always yours
Thomas Hardy.

I wonder if I told you that my wife's aunt was a Rowe, of the same family as Nicholas. Th: H.

Text MS. Eton College.
a good edition: Sassoon had in fact sent a first edn. (1714) of Nicholas Rowe's *The Tragedy of Jane Shore*, a play which TH seems to have associated with Lady Susan O'Brien (see letter of 11 Nov 20 to Child).   *my wife's aunt*: Emlin Gifford, *née* Rowe; see letter of 12 June 20 to Gifford.   *Nicholas*: Nicholas Rowe (1674–1718), poet and dramatist; *D.N.B.*

To ROGER INGPEN

MAX GATE, DORCHESTER. | September 24th. 1921.

Dear Sir:

In reply to your question whether I could write a new sonnet on Shelley I am sorry to say that though in years past I might have done it I feel unable now to go back all of a sudden to old feelings on that greatest of our lyrists. But if you would like to use either of the poems about him to which you allude it is at your service—as well as the prose passage in "Jude the Obscure", which I do not for the moment recall.

Perhaps Browning's well-known lines, and those by other poets, might also serve your purpose.

Yours very truly,
Thomas Hardy.

Roger Ingpen, Esq.

Text MS. (typewritten, with envelope in FEH's hand) Adams.
Ingpen: Roger Ingpen (d. 1936, aged 67), author and editor.   *sonnet on Shelley*: Ingpen, writing (22 Sept 21, DCM) as a director of the publishing house of Selwyn and Blount, had sought such a sonnet for inclusion in a centennial edn. of *Epipsychidion*.   *poems . . . you allude*: TH's 'Shelley's Skylark' and 'Rome: At the Pyramid of Cestius', both pub. in *Poems of the Past and the Present*.   *passage in "Jude"*: see *Jude the Obscure* (Wessex edn.), 294, where Sue applies to herself four lines from *Epipsychidion*.   *Browning's well-known lines*: the first stanza of 'Memorabilia' ('Ah, did you once see Shelley plain').

To HAROLD CHILD

MAX GATE, | DORCHESTER. | Oct. 1. 1921

Dear Mr Child:

I will endeavour to bear with equanimity what you are pleased to represent as a terror—I might add, bear it with gratification.

The lines of your former little book, so far as it deals with the poetry, will be quite safe ones to develop in your new criticisms, I am sure. If there should be any question of fact that you wish to put, don't mind doing it, & I will try to answer it, if brief.

"The Two Houses" will, if all's well, be duly reprinted in any future volume of my poems, but not in any English magazine. I am much pleased that you like it.

Thank you for letting me know about the articles. I should have replied sooner, but have been occupied with all sorts of household affairs. My wife sends kind regards & good wishes, as do I.

Sincerely yours
Thomas Hardy.

Text MS. Adams.
as a terror: Child (25 Sept 21, DCM) reported that he was writing a series of eight articles on TH's poetry for the National Home-Reading Union; they appeared in successive monthly issues of the *Home-Reading Magazine*, October 1921–May 1922.   *former little book*: Child's *Thomas Hardy* (London, 1916).   *"The Two Houses"*: see letter of 28 Nov 20 to Pound; the poem was collected in *Late Lyrics and Earlier* (1922).

To HAROLD SPENDER

6 October: 1921

Dear Mr Spender

I have signed the address with great pleasure, understanding that the other signatories (whom you do not mention) are not limited to one political party or denomination.

Yours sincerely
(Signed) Th. Hardy

Text   MS. (pencil draft) DCM.
Spender: E. Harold Spender (1864–1926), author and journalist; he was on the staff of the *Daily News* 1900–14 and had recently pub. a biography of David Lloyd George.   *the address*: an illuminated address to be presented to Frederic Harrison, the positivist (see letter to him of 24 May 22), on his 90th birthday, 18 Oct 1921.   *do not mention*: Spender (5 Oct 21, DCM) had simply said that the list of signatories would be 'limited to one hundred representative national names'.

To JAMES TUOHY

(Private)   MAX GATE, DORCHESTER. | 18 Oct. 1921
Dear Mr Tuohy:

I am sorry not to send a message on Disarmament, in answer to your kind suggestion; but you will perhaps understand that I prefer not to express an opinion on such a practical question in politics.

Yours very truly
T. Hardy.

Text   MS. (correspondence card) DCM, perhaps never despatched (see below).
Tuohy: James M. Tuohy (1859–1923), Irish-born journalist, London correspondent of the New York *World* since 1897. If this card was never actually sent, as its presence among the Max Gate papers suggests, that may have been because of TH's realization that he had in fact taken a position on this issue in a cable printed on the front page of the New York *World*, 29 Dec 1920: 'Yes, I approve of international disarmament on lines indicated by The World' (see also *LY*, 219).

To SIR HENRY NEWBOLT

MAX GATE, | DORCHESTER. | 21 Oct. 1921
My dear Newbolt:

Your welcome letter finds me virtually reading your Anthology—or more accurately in an interval between two dips into it. It has interested me very much (by the way I don't know why I did not write to tell you this sooner: the vice of procrastination was in me I suppose). I have looked upon it as a successful experiment, & I hope other readers do too. For it is an experiment I should say, & to me novel, in this sense, that though there have been many "Gleanings from Best Authors," &c., the extracts have had considerable length, & what is more important, have not followed any particular scheme showing the pedigree of English literature, or its whole onflowing as a stream of tendency (to use Arnold's phrase).

I was much struck with the rapidity with which you got the work done—a big job, certainly for anybody, & to some extent I should think worrying, in having continually to come to a decision between alternatives—which is said to be I believe truly, the most disquieting of experiences.

I confess I have been using the book rather illegitimately—giving myself surprises in uncovering unexpected passages, & being much struck with my own ignorance in never having read them before. I feel much honoured in being in such distinguished company, & though perhaps my own opinion is not of much value (writers being usually influenced by some accidental fact in the history of their productions which has nothing to do with their quality) I do think you exercised a fine judgment in selecting those particular ones of mine. The only fault I have to find with the volume is that there are none of your own pieces in it. Do you think you should have been quite so modest? I can quite understand a natural reluctance in such a matter; but *some* people are not so scrupulous.

We send our kindest regards, & I am always

Yours sincerely
Thomas Hardy.

Text   MS. Texas.
your Anthology: see letter of 23 June 21.   *Arnold's phrase*: 'That stream of tendency by which all things strive to fulfil the law of their being', first used in Matthew Arnold's essay 'St. Paul and Protestantism', *Cornhill Magazine*, October 1869, 435.   *ones of mine*: Newbolt had included 16 of TH's poems and the whole of chap. 4 of *Under the Greenwood Tree*.

To JOHN GALSWORTHY

MAX GATE, | DORCHESTER. | 24 October: 1921

My dear Galsworthy:

I think I like this the best of the Forsyte chronicles, this last one, & I ought to have written sooner to thank you for the gift of it, but I knew you would give me time, & nowadays my promptness, if I ever had it, is a tradition merely.

I don't pretend to estimate the novel with any critical acuteness, but you have made me feel sorry you have finished with the family. This is strange, considering that I do not like any of its members *very much* personally—except perhaps Jon—so that it must be owing to your handling of them that I regret you are going to tell us no more about them. My wife, by the way, has a sympathy for Soames, whom she considers a touching figure. This I do not altogether share.

The story seems to me more of an artistic organism of natural development than almost any of the others, which is one reason why it appeals to me. I may mention being particularly struck with some special scenes—one in the summer-house at p.175: & the death of Jolyon seemed a remarkably good dramatic stroke: the reader vaguely feels something hanging over, yet is not clear as to the moment when the inevitable will happen.

You have large stage schemes on hand in London, I understand, so by this time you may have gone back there. The Masefields called here on their way to you. We have not heard of them since, & as they left here rather late they may not have done the whole journey the same evening. Renewed thanks for

the book, which we have both read, & kindest regards from both of us to Mrs
Galsworthy & yourself.

Always yours
Thomas Hardy.

Text   MS. Univ. of Birmingham.
this last one: Galsworthy's novel *To Let* (London, 1921).   *Jon*: i.e., Jon Forsyte (Jolyon
Forsyte III).   *a sympathy for*: TH first wrote 'a tender regard for'.   *at p.175*: it is a scene
in which Soames sits alone during a thunderstorm and reflects upon his emotional relationships
and upon life in general.   *stage schemes*: an apparent reference to the season of Galsworthy's
plays (*Justice*, *The Pigeon*, *The Silver Box*, *Windows*) presented at the Court Theatre,
February–May 1922.   *Masefields*: John Masefield (see letter to him of 30 Dec 22) and his
wife.   *to you*: i.e., to the Galsworthys' country house at Manaton, Devon.

To SIR FREDERICK MACMILLAN

MAX GATE, | DORCHESTER. | 8th. November 1921.

Dear Sir Frederick Macmillan:

I am writing to ask your opinion on one or two points that have arisen. The
first is that since Moments of Vision was published in 1917 other poems have
accumulated—several being those issued in The Times, Fortnightly, and
other periodicals, American ones included, which readers say they want in
book form like the rest, and the makers of anthologies also ask for (I don't
suppose the latter means much, however). These poems with many others I
have on hand would, I find, fill a volume quite as thick as Moments of Vision;
and though I am by no means anxious to rush into print again—quite the
reverse, indeed—the question arises whether it would not be advisable to
bring them out—say early next year, or whenever you think convenient—and
not leave them to the mercy of curious collectors, and people who print
things privately and then coolly sell them.

What has made me pause is the consideration that the buyers of the
Mellstock edition would, I suppose, want these new poems also, and that
would mean a new volume in the series.

The above is the most important matter. A minor one is that several
readers, "Georgian" poets, &c., say that they would gladly buy the 2 vols.
(Collected Poems and Dynasts) at half-a-crown more for each volume if they
could get them printed on thinner paper so as to be available for travelling,
&c. I am told that the Oxford Book of English Verse doubled its sale directly
it was reduced in bulk by producing it on thin paper, and I have heard of the
same thing happening to other books. This is a question for your handling
entirely. It seems to me that a feasible plan would be to bring out the volume
of new poems, and when the time comes for incorporating them into the
Collected Poems (where there is plenty of room for more at the end) the whole
volume could be issued on thin paper, and the extra poems would give it a
good start.

One thing more is: I have had several Professors of Literature from
American Universities calling here this past summer, and they all agree in
saying that the American people are getting acquainted with my poetry

almost entirely through the aforesaid Collected edition, as circulated there by your American house, except for which they would hardly know anything about the poems. It therefore occurs to me to suggest that when you are writing to New York it might be well to impress them with the advisability of keeping these two green volumes, the Collected Poems and The Dynasts, before the people of the United States, who are a large and serious reading public. One shrewd Professor remarked of his own countrymen that they are like children, and that they read whatever is put before them without much judgment of their own.

    This is enough for one letter, and I am,

Yours sincerely,
Thomas Hardy.

Text   MS. (typewritten) BL.
bring them out: TH's suggestion resulted in the pub. of *Late Lyrics and Earlier* on 23 May 1922. *Mellstock edition*: see letter of 29 Jan 20; Macmillan's reply (14 Nov 21, Macmillan letterbooks, BL) concurred in TH's assumption, but the edn. was never in fact expanded to include *Late Lyrics* or any of TH's subsequent vols.   *issued on thin paper*: Macmillan accepted this suggestion, too, and thin-paper issues of both the one-vol. *Collected Poems* and the one-vol. *The Dynasts* later appeared.   *shrewd Professor*: perhaps Samuel C. Chew, who had recently called at Max Gate; see letter of 17 Sept 22.

To OSCAR BROWNING

[Mid-November 1921]

My dear Sir:
    I am much obliged to you for your kind note & enclosure about Napoleon, whom I have considered only vaguely since I had occasion to look into his history 25 years ago or so, when I touched on it in a book I wrote just after called The Dynasts which may or may not ever have come under your eye. Curiously enough quite lately I discovered on my bookshelves a copy of the first edition of Antommarchi's *Mémoires*, signed by him in faded ink.
    Believe me,

Sincerely yours
T— H—

Text   MS. (pencil draft) DCM.   *Date*   Replies to letter of 15 Nov 21.
Browning: Oscar Browning (1837–1923), educationalist and historian; *D.N.B.*   *enclosure about Napoleon*: evidently Browning's 'Napoleon', *Giggleswick Chronicle*, 23 July 1921—written, according to his letter of 15 Nov 21 (DCM), at the request of the boys of Giggleswick School; in a subsequent letter (24 Nov 21, DCM) he described the 'paper' as expressive of his matured admiration of Napoleon as 'the greatest man who ever lived in the world except, or shall we say after, Julius Caesar and the best man who ever lived after Jesus Christ'.   *under your eye*: Browning's 24 November letter insisted that *The Dynasts* had not given Napoleon his due. Mémoires: TH's copy of *Mémoires du docteur F. Antommarchi, ou les derniers momens [sic] de Napoléon* (Paris, 1825) is in DCM.   *signed by him*: all copies seem to have been so signed, as a guarantee of authenticity.

To SIR GEORGE DOUGLAS

Max Gate | Nov. 20. 1921

My dear Douglas:

You will not suppose that I did not appreciate your kind letter in that I have been so long answering it. But the prize did not come my way, on account of which I was relieved from some embarrassment as to what should be done with it! It is a consummation I need not dread, if for no other reason than that English poetry is always at a discount on the Continent, barring Byron's: & they appreciate him rather as the wicked lord than as the poet.

Yes: I agree: stern sound criticism of all the arts is the great need of the age—under which the writer you celebrate at your dinner would be valued for his real excellencies instead of for some he never had.

I do not think you need be sorry that some of your lands are shorn off. It is the same everywhere: & after all, in the Middle Ages estates were not very big. A neighbour of mine here, who thinks his property small, owns what were three estates down to the eighteenth century.

I think a poem of mine is coming out in the Decr London Mercury, & by an accidental coincidence another in the Fortnightly for the same month. I am afraid they are not much, but I had promised them.

Sincerely yrs
Ths Hardy.

My wife sends kindest remembrances. She was talking to your Cousin Capt. Thwaites only yesterday, & he asked if you were likely to be down this way. T.H.

Text MS. NLS.
Douglas: Sir George Brisbane Douglas, Bt., Scottish landowner and author, one of TH's oldest friends; see I.166.   *kind letter*: of 8 Nov 21 (DCM).   *the prize*: Douglas had prematurely congratulated TH on the award of the 1921 Nobel Prize for Literature; the recipient, announced in Stockholm 10 Nov 1921, was the French writer Anatole France (see III.53–4).   *writer you celebrate*: Douglas spoke of presiding at the annual dinner of the Robert Louis Stevenson Club; for Stevenson, see I.146–7.   *neighbour of mine*: probably Capt. W. F. Martin of Came House, near Dorchester.   *poem of mine*: 'Voices from Things Growing', *London Mercury*, December 1921.   *in the Fortnightly*: 'A December Rain-Scene', *Fortnightly Review*, December 1921.   *Capt. Thwaites*: possibly Capt. Robert Charles George Thwaites of the Royal Army Veterinary Corps, though the indicated relationship to Douglas has not been established.

To JOHN BUCHAN

MAX GATE, | DORCHESTER. | 21st. November 1921.

My dear Mr Buchan:

I must thank you at once for this very kind gift of your valuable book, as I shall not be able to read it through in time to answer early, my plan being, necessarily nowadays, to read only a chapter or two of historical works at one sitting. I have however looked into the volumes far enough to see what an enormous mass of material they contain, which may, I imagine, make of them a quarry for future students of the events of those years—say a hundred years hence.

I wish I had a book to send you in return, but I have brought out nothing of late, though I may next year. I well remember the date in 1917 to which you allude. What a number of events have passed under your eye since the fateful day in 1914: you must be still a walking kinema of them; though putting them down in a book does in a way get rid of them for a time.

Always sincerely yours
Thomas Hardy.

John Buchan Esq. LL.D.

Text   MS. (typewritten) NLS.
Buchan: John Buchan, author, later Lord Tweedsmuir; see V.220.   *valuable book*: Buchan (18 Nov 21, DCM) sent TH the first two vols. of his *A History of the War* (4 vols., London, 1921–2), a revision of *Nelson's History of the Great War* (24 vols., London, 1915–19).   *date in 1917*: Buchan recalled TH's having declined to visit the front line in France in the summer of 1917; see V.220.

To THE SECRETARY OF THE P.E.N. CLUB

Max Gate, | Dorchester. | November 22nd. 1921.

Dear Sir:

I shall have much pleasure in representing England as Honorary Member of the International Writers' Club as your President suggests—that is, if one who can do nothing in connection with the Club can be said to represent it at all. You will I am sure quite understand that I am past activities of such a kind.

Yours very truly,
Thomas Hardy.

The Hon. Secretary, | International Writers' Club.

Text   MS. (typewritten) Texas.
The Secretary: the first secretary of the international writers' association known as the P.E.N. Club (Poets, Playwrights, Editors, Essayists, Novelists) was Marjorie Dawson Scott, later Watts, daughter of the club's founder Catharine Amy Dawson Scott; her undated letter is in DCM.   *representing England*: the newly-founded club had decided to invite distinguished writers from several different countries to become honorary members; see Marjorie Watts, *P.E.N.: The Early Years 1921–1926* (London, 1971), 19.   *your President*: John Galsworthy.

To THE REVD. H. G. B. COWLEY

MAX GATE, | DORCHESTER. | 26: 11: 1921

Dear Mr Cowley:

Herewith I return the copy of the Register. I found it interesting to notice how many families had come & gone in the time it covers. With the growing shifting of populations names will I suppose be more fugitive still as years go on. My best thanks for the loan, & with kind regards I am

Sincerely yours
Tho. Hardy.

Text   MS. (with unstamped envelope) Canon Cowley.
the Register: of Stinsford parish, from which TH had transcribed details of the births,

marriages, and deaths of eighteenth- and early nineteenth-century inhabitants, most of them members or connections of his own family; see *Personal Notebooks* (see letter of 14 June 20 to Edgcumbe), 43–5.

To SIR FREDERICK MACMILLAN

MAX GATE, | DORCHESTER. | 30th. November 1921.

Dear Sir Frederick:

The two volumes of the Spanish translation have arrived, for which I am much obliged. I am sending a photograph for the use of the publishers as requested.

In respect of Messrs Curtis Brown's inquiry concerning a French translation of A Group of Noble Dames which a client of theirs wishes to make, I am unable to discover that I have ever given an authorization to anybody else for such a translation. Therefore if you have no record of having done so the book is free and Curtis Brown can arrange with their client.

I am not sure if the old ten years' law is still in force, under which any person may translate after that lapse of time? If so this may be called the authorized translation, the use of the word being worth, I suppose, a small fee. But no exclusive right can, of course, be conveyed. I should not like the title of the book altered, but only translated, except for good reasons. By giving the stupid title of "Barbara" to the French version of Far from the Madding Crowd it was made unrecognizable.

My thanks for your letter about the new poems. I am going slowly through the MS., but could send it up almost at a day's notice if it would be any convenience to the printers to have it early.

Very sincerely yours,
Thomas Hardy.

Text   MS. (typewritten) BL.
two volumes: i.e., two copies.   *Spanish translation*: of *The Well-Beloved*; it was translated, as *La bien amada*, by F. Climent Terrer (Madrid, 1921).   *as requested*: Macmillan (28 Nov 21, Macmillan letterbooks, BL) explained that the photograph was needed for advertising purposes. *Curtis Brown's*: the literary agency; see letter of 6 Jan 25.   *"Barbara"*: trans. Mathilde Zeys (Paris, 1901).   *new poems*: see letter of 8 Nov 21; Macmillan, in his 14 Nov 21 letter, had offered to have the vol. printed without delay.

To WALTER DE LA MARE

MAX GATE, | DORCHESTER. | Dec. 13: 1921

Dear Mr de la Mare:

I am delighted to get this new book of your poems from you: how thoughtful & kind of you. Delighted for two reasons: one the mean mercenary collector's feeling of having got a valuable thing for nothing: the other, more respectable, that inside the thing is the valuable intangible essence, your verses.

I have not read them all yet: in fact, only just begun dipping into them. One I much like so far is "Who's that?" Of others I cannot make up my mind on preferences till I have read them again.

I must thank you for getting those lines of mine into the Mercury. I should have supposed them too fanciful for a magazine.

We are going on just as usual, & my wife sends kindest regards & good wishes, as do I. Thanks sincerely for your gift. The return of the other books is quite soon enough.

Always yours
Thomas Hardy.

Text MS. (with envelope) Eton College.
your poems: de la Mare's *The Veil, and Other Poems* (London, 1921).   *into the Mercury*: see letter of 20 Nov 21; in his letter of 5 Dec 21 (DCM) de la Mare said that he had told J. C. Squire about 'Voices from Things Growing' after TH had showed it to him in MS.   *the other books*: Strachey's *Queen Victoria* was presumably still among them; see letter of 6 July 21.

To SIR ARTHUR SPURGEON

MAX GATE, | DORCHESTER. | 13th. December 1921.

Dear Sir Arthur Spurgeon:

I have no objection at all to your publishing the letter in the book you are bringing out.

I may mention that as printed in the page you send I think I notice two errors—either in the copy, or the original: viz.,

Line 5 of letter.. for "first volume" read "one-volume"

.. 15 .... for "or" read "for".

Thank you for your good wishes which we reciprocate,

Yours sincerely,
Thomas Hardy.

Text MS. (typewritten) Purdy.
Spurgeon: Arthur Spurgeon (1861–1938), journalist and publisher, general manager of the London publishing house of Cassell 1905–22; he was knighted in 1918.   *letter in the book*: *The Story of the House of Cassell*, pub. anonymously by Cassell in 1922, includes (159) the text of an undated letter from TH to George Manville Fenn (see I.78) which will appear in Vol. VII of the present edn.   *you send*: with his letter of 13 Dec 21 (DCM).   *two errors*: these were corrected in the book as pub.

To MACKENZIE BELL

MAX GATE, DORCHESTER. | December 19. 1921

Dear Mr Mackenzie Bell:

I have received your kind gift of your Selected Poems, with the inscription you have been so good as to write, & shall read them as soon as the pressure of more sordid matters that this season brings has passed over. At present I have only looked at the verses to which you draw my attention, which I like much. Believe me with all thanks,

Sincerely yours
Thomas Hardy.

Text MS. NYU.
Bell: Henry Thomas Mackenzie Bell, poet and critic; see IV.33.   *Selected Poems*: Bell's *Selected Poems* (London, 1921).   *draw my attention*: Bell's letter to TH has not survived,

but a note on the present MS. indicates that he had mentioned the poem entitled 'Trafalgar' (89–92).

To FLORENCE HENNIKER

MAX GATE, | DORCHESTER. | 19 Dec. 1921.

My dear friend.

I have delayed my reply to your kind letter a few days, to bring it into Christmastide, when I know you like to receive missives, even of such a dull character as mine is likely to be I fear. Thank you for your inquiries: we have recovered & are now as well as two aged people can hope to be (F. will thank me for putting it this way!) I fancy from the brightness of your letter that you are already profiting from the country air, even though you must miss the people you are able to see in London. We are in a drizzle here to day, though the weather has on the whole been good.

Bognor I seem to know quite well from friends, though I have never actually set foot in it—which is very stupid, as I have been to Chichester, Worthing, & all about there several times. The young architect who was the original of Stephen Smith in "A Pair of Blue Eyes" (so far as he had any original) used to be enthusiastic on Bognor & to go there with his family. "Blake's cottage" makes Felpham interesting: but which Blake does it mean? Since writing this question I have discovered that it means Blake the poet. Hayley was a poetaster, Blake's friend, & was ridiculed by Byron in "English Bards." I don't know what "steyne" means, unless it is a paved way.

I have read very little on the Irish situation lately: it was so worrying that I had to give it up. "Irish Free State" does, as you say, sound unromantic. The Ireland Free State, or Irish Freeland would perhaps be less so.

Walter de la Mare has sent us his new poems. They are rather too obscure, I think: but many of them have his own peculiar beauty in them when you get to the bottom of their meaning.

We were at our neighbours' the Hanburys at Kingston Maurward yesterday afternoon. Her father, Mr Symons-Jeune, whom you met, is coming to them to stay over Christmas, so we shall see him. A very mild little poem of mine appears in the Dec. Fortnightly, & to save trouble I send a spare proof of it instead of the heavy magazine. I have also another—a longer one—in the Dec. London Mercury. It would, I think, please you more than this trifling one, but I have neither proof nor magazine. The title is "Voices from things growing (in a churchyard)".

Now I come to wishing you a happy Xmas & New Year: as also does F., & many of them.

Yours affectionately
Th: H.

I had nearly forgotten to say that F. had a letter in last Friday's *Times* (Dec 16.) about squirrels—I wonder if you saw it. Th. H.

Text MS. DCM.
kind letter: of 11 Dec 21 (transcript, DCM).   *country air*: Mrs. Henniker wrote from the Manor House, Felpham, Sussex.   *Bognor*: Bognor Regis, the Sussex coastal resort, to which

Felpham is immediately adjacent.   *several times*: especially in the 1860s, when he visited Eliza Bright Nicholls at Findon, N. of Worthing; see Millgate, 84–5, 94, 100.   *young architect*: apparently William Searle Hicks (1849–1902), architect, of Newcastle-upon-Tyne, son of the Revd. James Hicks, vicar of Piddletrenthide, Dorset, and nephew of TH's Dorchester employer John Hicks (see letter of 12 June 20 to J. G. Hicks); see *EL*, 97.   *"Blake's cottage"*: the house (still standing) in which William Blake (1757–1827; *D.N.B.*) lived 1800–3. *Hayley*: William Hayley (1745–1820; *D.N.B.*), poet, about whom Mrs. Henniker had asked in her letter; he lived at Turret House, Felpham, and provided Blake with the cottage.   *in "English Bards."*: see lines 309–18 of Byron's *English Bards and Scotch Reviewers*. *"steyne"*: Mrs. Henniker had asked about 'The Steyne' as a street-name in both Bognor and Brighton; TH's explanation appears to be correct.   *"Irish Free State"*: the Irish Free State, established by the Irish Peace Agreement of 6 Dec 1921, came officially into being 15 Jan 1922; it became Eire, or Ireland, in 1937.   *his new poems*: see letter of 13 Dec 21 to de la Mare. *the Hanburys*: see letter of 6 Jan 20.   *Symons-Jeune*: see letter of 14 June 20 to Margaret Gifford.   *spare proof*: a corrected proof of TH's 'A December Rain-Scene' (see letter of 20 Nov 21) still accompanies this letter.   *about squirrels*: dated from Max Gate 13 Dec 21, it suggested the possibility of exterminating the intruding grey squirrel in order to protect the 'native red squirrel' and the birds whose eggs the grey squirrel ate.

1922

To SIEGFRIED SASSOON

MAX GATE, DORCHESTER. | Jan 9. 1922

My dear ✗ :

Much obliged. Yours is the first news I have that "Haunting Fingers" has appeared: & as I have seen no proof I daresay there are some bad misprints. However I hope you will be able to see it in a collection some time this year, though I have made no arrangements for publication as yet, of a definite kind.

If it has stimulated your Muse to open her mouth the poem will have done some good in the world already.

Ever yours
T.H.

Text   MS. (with envelope) Eton College.
"Haunting Fingers": first printed in the *New Republic* (New York), 21 Dec 1921.   *misprints*: TH made several revisions before including the poem in one of FEH's privately printed pamphlets; see letter of 14 Feb 22 to Cockerell.   *collection . . . this year*: it appeared in *Late Lyrics and Earlier* (see letter of 23 Jan 22).

To SIR FREDERICK MACMILLAN

Max Gate, | Dorchester. | 23rd. January 1922.

Dear Sir Frederick:

At last I am sending the MS of the new poems under a separate cover. I have been hindered by a chill which has kept me in bed for two or three weeks.

I have been wondering if expense could not be saved by making the first printing of the book in the type of the Wessex Edition, with perhaps a smaller margin or what not, so that afterwards it could be embodied in the Wessex series without further printing. There would be only one extra printing—some copies for the Mellstock edition.

Yours very sincerely,
Thomas Hardy.

Text   MS. (typewritten) BL.
new poems: the vol. *Late Lyrics and Earlier*, pub. by Macmillan four months later.   *a chill*: TH, for once, understates the seriousness of his illness; see letter of 14 Feb 22 to Gosse and letter of 1 Mar 22.   *without further printing*: i.e., without any further setting of type; although Macmillan promised to explore this possibility (24 Jan 22, Macmillan letterbooks, BL) it was not in fact adopted. Nor was the title included in the Mellstock edn.

To JOSEPH ANTHONY

Jan 25. 1922

Mr H. hopes he will get it into the April number. It was going into an English magazine, but Century preferred. Perhaps if it did not come out till the May number (supposing that to be pubd just after the middle of April) it wd not much matter, as the book is not likely to be seen much in America by then.

Anyhow he will not now be able to get it into any other magazine, so leaves the matter in yr hands.

Thanks for the novel. If well enough by the spring will be happy to receive a call—it being understood that such wd not be used for press purposes, as he has declined all interviewers for many years—

F.E.H.

Text MS. (pencil draft) DCM.
Anthony: Joseph Anthony, London manager for *Century Magazine*; he wrote 24 Jan 22 (DCM).
April number: TH's poem 'An Ancient to Ancients' in fact appeared in the May 1922 issue of the *Century Magazine* (New York), where it was accompanied by a two-page headpiece by the American artist Rockwell Kent; see V.319.   *the novel*: Anthony's *The Gang* (New York, 1921; London, 1922).   *receive a call*: Anthony spoke in his letter of taking a walking trip through Dorset in March or April.   *F.E.H.*: initials in TH's hand.

To J. C. SQUIRE

MAX GATE, | DORCHESTER. | 27th. January 1922.

Dear Mr Squire:

I am compelled to dictate my reply to your interesting letter, having caught a chill which, though not severe, is tedious, and keeps me in bed a great deal, though I hope only for a few days longer.

I am excluded from your scheme by the accidental position of my publishing arrangements at the present time. All the MSS. of any account that I possess—that is to say the verse accumulations of the past few years since "Moments of Vision" came out—are in the hands of the Messrs Macmillan, who will I suppose print them some time this spring. The upshot of this is that you will have to trust to younger men and leave me out.

I am not capable of criticizing your idea, never having had much enterprize in publishing. The only thing that occurs to me is that you may find it awkward to mix old matter with new. But perhaps you will not do this.

I liked your collection of Women Poets, though was rather disappointed to find you had omitted Charlotte Mew—the greatest poetess I have come across lately, in my judgment, though so meagre in her output.—I am glad you liked my Mercury poem. I should never have ventured to send it but for Walter de la Mare. My wife sends her kind regards,

Yours sincerely,
Thomas Hardy.

Text MS. (typewritten) Taylor.
interesting letter: it appears not to have survived, however, so that the precise details of Squire's scheme cannot be determined.   *print them*: as *Late Lyrics and Earlier*.   *Women Poets*: A

Book of Women's Verse, ed., with a prefatory essay, by Squire (Oxford, 1921).   *Charlotte Mew*: see letter of 3 Jan 24.   *Mercury poem ... de la Mare*: see letter of 13 Dec 21 to de la Mare.

To CLIFFORD BAX

                                                              [Mid-February 1922]
Dear Sir:

I reply for Mr Hardy to your letter to him, as he is only just recovering from a rather tedious illness which still prevents his attending to affairs more than partially.

He thanks you for your sympathy with his writings in verse, which makes him all the more sorry that he can be of no service in the interesting undertaking you propose, having sent off everything old that might have been available, & being unlikely in present circumstances & at his age to produce anything new of a fit kind.

He would be disposed to think (without meaning it as a suggestion) that some one or more of the younger men who are distinguishing themselves as poets would be safer for your purpose.

He quite remembers enjoying the performance of the Arts League of Service, and your little piece.

                                                              Very truly yours,

Text   MS. (pencil draft) DCM.
Bax: Clifford Bax (1886–1962), playwright and author.   *your letter*: of 10 Feb 22 (DCM). *interesting undertaking*: Bax asked TH to contribute to the first issue of a new quarterly magazine; called *The Golden Hind*, the journal appeared in October 1922 but survived for only eight issues.   *Arts League of Service*: its stated goal was 'To Bring the Arts into Everyday Life'.   *your little piece*: Bax's *Square Pegs*—described in his letter to TH as 'a little rhymed duologue'—was part of the programme presented in Dorchester by one of the League's touring theatrical companies on 12 March 1921; TH's appreciative comments on the performance appeared in the *Arts League of Service Annual 1921–1922*, 14.

To SYDNEY COCKERELL

                                                    Max Gate | Feb 14. 1922
My dear Cockerell:

I write to acknowledge your letter to F. as she is down with influenza which prevents her writing, & speaking almost. However the doctor says she is improving, & he hopes to bring her round in a few days.

The ex-service man & his family that we took in have been the cause, the child, who was sent to school, having promptly brought home the complaint.

Fortunately I am better, having gone out yesterday for the first time. So that we are not as yet quite reduced to the latch-key business you tell of.

It is, of course, owing to this that she has not sent the privately printed poems. Meanwhile the proofs have begun to come for the volume: yet I imagine that the "Two Fantasies" will be able to be put about before the volume appears.

This is almost the first letter I have written since my horizontal two or three weeks of late.

Always yours
Thomas Hardy.

We are glad to hear that you & yours have nearly got through the entanglement of this malady. T.H.

Text   MS. NYU; envelope Berg.
the doctor: Benjamin Gowring; see IV.260.   *ex-service man & his family*: the man's wife, *née* Adolphina Busch, was formerly employed by FEH's parents at Enfield and had recently appealed successfully to FEH for jobs for herself and her partly disabled husband; their son was called Oscar.   *latch-key business*: in the absence, and presumed destruction, of Cockerell's letter to FEH, this allusion remains obscure.   *privately printed poems*: the poems 'Haunting Fingers' and 'Voices from Things Growing' were gathered together as 'Two Phantasies' in a pamphlet printed for FEH by the Chiswick Press, February 1922; see Purdy, 213–14.   *"Two Fantasies"*: i.e., 'Two Phantasies'; see above.   *the volume*: Late Lyrics and Earlier.

To EDMUND GOSSE

Max Gate | Feb 14: 1922

My dear Gosse:

Your kind letter finds me just getting out of an illness, this reply being almost the first line I have written for weeks. Lest I should make you think too seriously of it I hasten to add that it has been a milder attack of that same bladder inflamation you will remember my being laid up with for six months when I lived at Upper Tooting, which repeats itself at intervals of some years, as it has done now. But I went out of doors yesterday for the first time since I got up: &, as you see, can now write an ink letter or two.

Meanwhile Florence is down with influenza, but the doctor says she will get round in a few days, though she can hardly speak as yet. However, she is distinctly better I am happy to say.

Yes: I did fear you were overdoing it, & sent that message. It is a good change that you should go to La Mortola. I am too old ever to go. We were as usual often seeing the Hanburys before they left, & also Symons-Jeune: but we have heard nothing of them since.

You have guessed rightly: I have at last collected the stray verses of the last 5 years, (& some more, earlier & overlooked ones, that I found) & it is likely they will come out in a month or two. I don't altogether jump at the chance of appearing on the literary stage again; but I don't know what else to do. By the way, your letter was most apt: I have now been able to put in among the short prefatory words that "some illustrious men of letters" have asked for the poems. How selfish of me to make use of you in this way!

With kindest regards to Mrs Gosse, in which F. joins, I am always

Sincerely yours
Thomas Hardy.

Text   MS. BL.
kind letter: of 13 Feb 22 (DCM).   *at Upper Tooting*: see I.81, *EL*, 187–8, and Millgate, 214–19.   *La Mortola*: the villa and gardens owned by the Hanbury family in Ventimiglia, Italy.   *Hanburys*: see letter of 6 Jan 20.   *Symons-Jeune*: Mrs. Hanbury's father; see letter

of 14 June 20 to Gifford.   *guessed rightly*: Gosse asked if TH was bringing out another vol. of poems.   *short prefatory words*: the phrase within quotation marks occurs in the second paragraph of the 'Apology' prefaced to *Late Lyrics* (London, 1922), vi.

To SYDNEY COCKERELL

<u>Private.</u>   Feb 15: 1922
My dear Cockerell:

In my hurry yesterday I did not send the enclosed as I had meant. I am sending it to ask your opinion whether I shall prefix it to the new volume or not. I don't *wish* to, & should not at all mind destroying it. It came into my mind mostly while lying in bed during the late weeks, & seemed then almost necessary.

Is it uncalled for, or, if not altogether so, is it too cantankerous in respect of reviewers, &c. for a writer whose books are fairly well received nowadays— even quite well received in general. If I cancel it I can easily print the poems without a preface.

If some parts will pass, but not all, I will cut out the undesirable parts. Please mark any paragraphs that might be so deleted, in the latter event.

I ought to have said that why I am bothering you for an opinion in this way is owing to my judgment being thrown out of balance by these household illnesses. If all were well as usual, I could reach a conclusion in a moment on such a trifling matter.

This morning I had quite made up my mind to destroy it, but I have thought since it would be advisable to consult you. The point is that I do not wish to offend staunch readers by making them suppose I think too much about the objectors who turn up from time to time.

F. is not much better, & can still hardly speak. But we are hoping she is improving.

                                                                                  Always yours
                                                                                  T.H.

I have kept no copy of the MS.
P.S. As you are well aware, a writer himself hears less of real opinion about his works, particularly of objections to his views, &c, than an outsider does. Hence my not knowing the actual weight of objections to mine. T.H.
PPS. I thought "Apology" more piquant than "Preface".

Text   MS. (with envelope) Adams.
enclosed . . . meant: draft of the 'Apology' later prefixed to *Late Lyrics*.   *hardly speak*: see letters of 14 Feb 22.

To SYDNEY COCKERELL

                                        MAX GATE, | DORCHESTER. | 18 Feb. 1922
My dear Cockerell;

The Preface has come back safely. Your two verbal suggestions I shall adopt of course. Meanwhile I am abridging the whole somewhat, in spite of your saying you would not omit a word; for I fancy it is a little long &

iterative. To satisfy you that all essentials are still in it I will, if I can, let you see it again before it goes to press—possibly in MS., as I think there will be time.

Many sincere thanks for your taking the trouble to read it, & so carefully. Good nature always gets imposed upon, so I really think I will take advantage of your offer to read the proofs of the poems themselves, since my eyes are not so good as they were, & misprints have a way of stealing past them in a most mysterious manner. Please do not scruple to remark on any other oversights in them that you may encounter, or to suggest any improvement. F. is too unwell still to be asked to read critically, so that nobody sees them but myself.

She is, however, improving rapidly, I am most glad to say, & came downstairs today into a warm room. This is a hurried letter, on account of the awkwardness of our having no Sunday post.

Always yours
Thomas Hardy.

Text MS. (with envelope) Adams.
Preface: see letter of 15 Feb 22.   *two verbal suggestions*: offered by Cockerell in his letter of 17 Feb 22 (DCM); they each affected only two words.

To SYDNEY COCKERELL

Tuesday night [21 February 1922]

My dear Cockerell:

(You are getting a fusillade of letters from this house just now!) Here are two sheets more. You will understand that the proofs I send you are the duplicates of those returned to the printers for a revise, so that any correction you may make will get to me before their revise comes, & I can insert it.

F. is getting better—slowly. I hope your household is all right now.

I sent the MS. Preface to the printers with the slight abridgement I told you of, which is more than made up by a new paragraph I put in. So that I don't think you will lecture me much for spoiling it. You shall see it in proof.

Always
T.H.

Text MS. Adams.   *Date* Supplied on MS. in Cockerell's hand.
from this house: FEH was also in frequent correspondence with Cockerell.   *two sheets more*: i.e., two proof sheets for *Late Lyrics*.

To SIR FREDERICK MACMILLAN

MAX GATE, | DORCHESTER. | February 21st. 1922.

Dear Sir Frederick:

There are many poems in the forthcoming volume that have not been published, and I can forward them to you to send on to the manager of the American magazine who has asked for some or one of them. But as they go to press with their magazines over there so very early will there be time for the editor to get the poems issued before our book comes out?

I do not know why, but I have had several applications for poems from United States periodicals of late, as if they were suddenly waking up after long indifference. I have supplied some—all of which are now out—and therefore have preceded the volume—except one in the Century Magazine— which, I informed them, should be out by the end of March, to ensure anticipating the volume. It may be that the application you have had is from the same quarter. If so, I imagine that the one I lately sent—a longish one—is enough. If not from the Century it will be well to say that we cannot guarantee keeping back the book till they print the poems forwarded, and please stipulate for use in the periodical only.

The printers have just begun to send the proofs of the volume, and as the corrections are but slight I am sending them straight back to them to save trouble, as you suggested last time, and will go on doing so unless you wish otherwise. As I had to modify and enlarge the Preface, I am sending a new MS. of it, before they get to it, so that they may not waste labour in setting up the old one.

I will, then, forward some verses to you immediately, if I hear that it is a new application, which can fulfil conditions as above.

Many thanks for attending to the matter.

Yours sincerely,
Thomas Hardy.

Text MS. (typewritten) BL.
forthcoming volume: *Late Lyrics and Earlier*.   *American magazine*: Macmillan's reply (22 Feb 22, DCM) reported that the inquiry had been made by A. S. Watt, the literary agent (see letter of 6 Sept 24), on behalf of an unnamed American magazine.   *in the Century Magazine*: see letter of 25 Jan 22.   *from the same quarter*: Macmillan (22 Feb 22) assured TH that the inquiry had not originated with the *Century*.

To SIR FREDERICK MACMILLAN

MAX GATE, | DORCHESTER. | February 23. 1922.
Dear Sir Frederick Macmillan:

The 16th. of May as the date of publication is quite satisfactory to me.

I am sending copies of some poems—six in number—available for the American periodical. They are entitled:

Weathers
Summer Schemes
The Garden Seat
I was not he
The Selfsame Song
The Children and Sir Nameless,

and shall be glad for you to complete as you think best the arrangement for the serial publication, if practicable before our date here. If not, perhaps it will be as well to let the matter drop through. And if, supposing terms concluded, we should inadvertently anticipate the magazine, well, I could return the payment or a part of it, as I imagine the chief advantage of letting the poems be published serially over there is the publicity they will obtain, and the attention it will draw to the volume.

Believe me,

Yours sincerely,
Thomas Hardy.

Text   MS. (typewritten) BL.
date of publication: Macmillan (22 Feb 22, DCM) suggested that since a considerable sum of money might be obtained from the American magazine interested in TH's poems (see letter to Macmillan of 21 Feb 22) the pub. date of *Late Lyrics* might be put back a few weeks to 16 May 1922.   *drop through*: it appears that these poems were not in fact printed in the U.S. prior to their inclusion in *Late Lyrics*.

To SYDNEY COCKERELL

28: 2: '22

My dear Cockerell:

Here are two sheets more of what you will soon begin to call those villanous proofs. If busy, don't tire yourself by reading them: I shall understand.

Don't mind scribbling your suggestions on them, if less troublesome than writing on a separate sheet.

I have adopted all your corrections—except one or two, where the readings had already got known as they stand, or where I was not convinced.

I hope you were entertained by your Americans; & enjoyed St John's banquet.

Yours very greatly obliged
Th: H.

P.S. I am not expecting much from these poems, now I read them over. *Writing* verse gives me great pleasure, but not publishing it. I never did care much about publication, as is proved by my keeping some of the verses forty years in MS. Th. H.

Text   MS. (with envelope) Adams.
all your corrections: to the proof sheets returned with Cockerell's letter of 25 Feb 22 (DCM).
your Americans: Cockerell's letter spoke simply of 'My three Americans'—evidently visitors to the Fitzwilliam Museum.   *St John's banquet*: Cockerell said in his letter that he would 'feast' at St. John's College that evening.

To FLORENCE HENNIKER

MAX GATE, | DORCHESTER. | March 1. 1922

My dear friend:

I am writing at (I hope) the end of a series of household calamities, which have thrown my doings out of gear for some weeks past. They began by my having a return of an old complaint—internal inflammation—which, though not violent, has been extremely tedious, & though not absolutely gone as yet, is practically so. Then the whole house had influenza, F.'s being a particularly sharp attack, her voice being very weak & husky still. But, as I say, I believe we are gradually getting normal. I hope you have not suffered from any such visitation.

We had no echoes here of yesterday's wedding—except an invitation to Lady Astor's party, which of course we could not accept. Siegfried Sassoon writes to Florence saying the bridegroom looked worried; but then, bridegrooms always look as if they had got the worst of it, don't you think?

I fancy you knew Lulu Harcourt, did you not? I regretted to hear of his death. He used to come here sometimes, & I was at his wedding. But he never looked strong. Did you see in the papers also the death of Charles Gifford last week?—Emma's first cousin—whom you used to know at Southsea, &, I think, liked. So friends & acquaintances thin out, & we who remain have to "close up".

I have collected most of the poems of mine that have been written since the last volume came out five years ago, & they are to be published anon—about the middle of May, I understand. It is no pleasure to me to appear again in print; but I really did not know what to do with them: a good many having already been printed in magazines, &c., about which people were continually writing to know when they could be got in a volume. In the book there will also be some very old ones, which I had overlooked in making previous collections.

I was sorry to hear that you had lost "Brush"—but that is a frequent unhappy contingency with pets. Our Wessex is as ill-behaved as ever, & acts as if he were quite the master of the house, which indeed he is.

I am directing this to Felpham, where I imagine you still are, though I am not quite sure. Affectionate regards from F. & from me.

Ever yours
Tho. H.

Text MS. DCM.
internal inflammation: see letter of 14 Feb 22 to Gosse.   *yesterday's wedding*: of Princess Mary, only daughter of King George V and Queen Mary, to Lord Henry George Charles Lascelles, later sixth Earl of Harewood.   *Lady Astor's party*: Nancy Witcher Astor, Viscountess Astor, *née* Langhorne (1879–1964), American-born politician and hostess, the first woman to sit in the House of Commons; *D.N.B.* She gave a dinner-party on 28 February followed by a reception 'to meet Mr. Balfour' (i.e., Arthur James Balfour; see letter of 7 July 20). *Harcourt*: Lewis Harcourt, first Viscount Harcourt (1863–1922), politician; *D.N.B.* He died suddenly on 24 Feb 1922.   *come here*: i.e., to the Dorchester area; see *LY*, 25.   *his wedding*: in July 1899; see *Personal Notebooks* (see letter of 14 June 20 to Edgcumbe), 253. *Charles Gifford*: a brief notice of his death appeared in *The Times*, 21 Feb 1922.   *at Southsea*: see II.26.   *"Brush"*: one of Mrs. Henniker's dogs.   *Felpham*: see letter to Mrs. Henniker of 19 Dec 21; Mrs. Henniker replied from there 10 Mar 22 (typed transcript, DCM) but returned to London shortly afterwards.

To SIR FREDERICK MACMILLAN

MAX GATE, | DORCHESTER. | 4th. March 1922.
Dear Sir Frederick:

I am glad to hear that you are negociating for the magazine publication in America of the poems I sent up; and any agreement you may come to with Nash's, or Cassell, for two of them in England, will be satisfactory to me.

I have received a letter from a Monsieur H. Bonnaire, of 20 High Holborn,

Agent-General in Great Britain for the Société des Gens de Lettres, Paris, (of which I am an Honorary Member) asking, at the request of the Society, which of my novels are still available for Cinema purposes, and on what conditions for World-rights.

I don't know if this is worth attending to, and if I should send him a note inquiring what means the Society have for entering into a business of this sort, seeing that they are not a Cinema company, but a body of French authors. Or would a line from yourselves to the same effect be better? If so, and you don't mind the trouble of writing it, I shall be obliged.

Yours sincerely,
Thomas Hardy.

Text   MS. (typewritten) BL.
poems I sent up: see letter of 23 Feb 22; Macmillan (3 Mar 22, Macmillan letterbooks, BL) reported sending off 'copy' of the six poems to the International Magazine Co. of New York. *two . . . in England*: TH's 'Weathers', first pub. in *Good Housekeeping* (London), May 1922, and 'The Children and Sir Nameless', first pub. in *Nash's and Pall Mall Magazine*, May 1922. *Bonnaire*: Henri Bonnaire's letter of 24 Feb 22 is in DCM.   *be better?*: Macmillan suggested (7 Mar 22, DCM) that TH should himself reply along the lines indicated here, and a draft letter to Bonnaire, dated 10 Mar 22, is in DCM.

To SYDNEY COCKERELL
Monday, 6 March 1922

My dear Cockerell:

Yours is a rare eye for misprints & other errors. But I am putting in the note as to the real name of "Bet Greensleeves", not for literary reasons, but because all the other names are real in the verses, except hers.

It was quite as well not to say anything to Squire about the review. If I were to mention it myself it wd be not on my account, but to ask him why a magazine from which we were told to expect new twentieth-century ideas, should have printed an article which might have been written by an old-maiden teacher in a Sunday school in Victorian times—all its objectings being to the comparatively new ideas, & all its approvals being of the old ones.

I am sending 2 more sheets.

Ever sincerely
Th: H.

I had written to him before the Mercury arrived. Th: H.

Text   MS. Adams.
"Bet Greensleeves": in TH's 'Voices from Things Growing in a Churchyard', as pub. in *Late Lyrics*, she is called 'Eve Greensleeves', with a footnote identifying her as Eve Trevillian or Trevelyan; see *Personal Notebooks* (see letter of 14 June 20 to Edgcumbe), 45.   *the other names*: see *The Complete Poetical Works of Thomas Hardy*, II, ed. Samuel Hynes (Oxford, 1984), 514–15.   *the review*: 'The Poetry of Mr. Hardy' by the Irish writer Joseph Maunsell Hone (1882–1959), in the *London Mercury* (of which Squire was the editor), February 1922. *sheets*: of the proofs of *Late Lyrics*.

To SYDNEY COCKERELL

Max Gate. 10: 3: 22

My dear Cockerell:

Received up to p. 160, so here are two more sheets. All your remarks are useful, &, of course, your corrections. Only think: three of them were of errors made by the printer, & were not in the MS., e.g. I wrote "Thence"—they printed "Hence," &c. But on the whole they are fairly correct.

I have altered a word or two in the first verse of "The Chapel Organist", to make it clear that she is indulging in those reflections on the *last* night—immediately before her suicide—not, as it seemed to you, on a later occasion. Of course, it is all inferential, since nobody could *know* the final thoughts of a woman who was dead when they found her: but this is a recognized licence in narrative art, though it should be veiled as much as possible.

I don't mind your telling Squire if you meet him again that I wished he had put me into the hands of an able thinker instead of those of a conventional R.C. But it really does not matter.

As you perceive, the poems are mixed up, light & heavy, indiscriminately. I wonder if I should have classified them a little.

The effigy of Sir Nameless I have dated back a hundred years further, to get rid of the doubt about the ruff. I *fancy* it was worn when real armour had ceased, & dress-armour was in fashion; but I am not sure—though I studied & copied Strutt's plates many years ago when an archt's pupil.

I think the reason why the scenes of many of the poems are churches & ch. yards is that I used to spend much time in such places sketching, with another pupil, & we had many pleasant times at the work. Probably this explains why ch. yards & churches never seem gloomy to me.

I hope that chicken-pox has come to nothing.

Ever yours
Th: H.

Text   MS. Adams.
altered . . . Organist": as pub. in *Late Lyrics* the first line was much revised from the MS. version and ended with the words 'to play never again'.   *conventional R.C.*: i.e., Joseph Hone; see letter of 6 Mar 22.   *doubt about the ruff*: i.e., the question, evidently raised by Cockerell on the proofs, as to when ruffs ceased to be worn; before the vol. appeared TH not only changed 'Two hundred years' to 'Three hundred years' in line 17 of 'The Children and Sir Nameless' but took the additional precaution of changing 'ruff' itself to 'casque' in line 15. *Strutt's plates*: Joseph Strutt (1749–1802), antiquary and artist; *D.N.B.* TH probably refers to Strutt's *A Complete View of the Dress and Habits of the People of England*, first pub. in two vols., 1796–9.   *another pupil*: Henry Bastow, TH's fellow-pupil and close friend at the time of his apprenticeship in the late 1850s to the Dorchester architect John Hicks; see Millgate, 55, 63–5. *that chicken-pox*: presumably among Cockerell's children (his preceding letter to TH has not survived).

To ANDREW BENNETT

15 March: 1922

Dear Sir:

I am in receipt of your letter informing me that the Senatus Academicus of St. Andrews have decided to confer on me the Honorary Degree of Doctor of Laws, & I tender my thanks to the Senate for their feeling, & for holding me worthy of this distinction. But I much regret to say that it is next to impossible for me to travel such as distance as to St Andrews to receive the degree. An illness, from which I am recovering, is expected by my doctor to leave me weak till the summer; & apart from that the fatigue of the journey there & back would I fear, be rather too trying to a person over eighty years of age. Therefore I cannot have the pleasure of receiving the degree in person, & if this should be a Sine qua non—on which point I am uncertain—it would put the honour out of my reach.

I am, Dear Sir

Yours very truly

Andrew Bennet Esq. | The University | St Andrews.

Text   MS. (pencil draft) DCM.
Bennett: Andrew Bennett (d. 1958, aged 86), secretary and registrar of the University of St. Andrews.   *your letter*: of 13 Mar 22 (DCM).   *out of my reach*: the degree was, however, conferred on TH in his absence; see letter to Bennett of 6 May 22.

To W. M. COLLES

MAX GATE, | DORCHESTER. | 18th. March 1922.

Dear Mr Colles:

I am obliged to you for suggesting that you could act for me in treating for the filming of novels. As you suppose, some have been done already. But it is a kind of representation which is quite unliterary, and I am not keen upon it.

I should have been glad to pay any fee you might have charged for letting me know of The Century. The poem is, I believe, to appear in the May number.

Yours truly,
T. Hardy.

Text   MS. (typewritten) Taylor.
suggesting: in his letter of 16 Mar 22 (DCM).   *glad to pay . . . Century*: Colles declined to accept any fee for arranging the *Century* pub. of TH's 'An Ancient to Ancients'; see letter of 25 Jan 22.

To HARLEY GRANVILLE BARKER

Max Gate, | Dorchester. | March 19. 1922.

Dear Granville Barker:

My practical knowledge of the subject of your new book, which I am reading, is of the most elementary kind, so that the humour shown in its pages is at present the greatest attraction to me. I have only had one idea about the theatre, and I wrote a letter to the papers thereon nearly 40 years ago:—that I should like the pit to be level with the stage, and the actors to walk out upon it, so that we could see all round them. But as nobody took any notice of my letter my interest ended.

I daresay you treat of all this when I come to it. Meanwhile thank you very warmly for the book.

I hope you have had a pleasant time in the south, and that we shall hear about it when you come back.

With kindest regards to Helen

Believe me,

> Always sincerely yours,
> Thomas Hardy.

Text   Typed transcript DCM.
Barker: Harley Granville Barker, actor, producer, dramatist, and critic; see V.51.   *new book*: Barker's *The Exemplary Theatre* (London, 1922).   *letter to the papers*: specifically, to the *Weekly Comedy*, where it appeared 30 Nov 1889; see I.213 and Millgate, *Career* (see letter of 23 Dec 20 to Foster), 309.   *Helen*: Barker's second wife, *née* Helen Gates (d. 1950), whom he married in 1918 after his divorce from Lillah McCarthy (see IV.100) and hers from Archer Huntington had been finalized.

To SYDNEY COCKERELL

Max Gate | 22: 3: '22

My dear Cockerell:

I am sending the last ones, as you will be glad to discover. Will you let me know if you wd like to read the Preface, when the proof of it comes?

You will also see that I have thrown in a good many old pieces towards the end: also some quite trivial ones.

I know very little about the younger generation of the Moules; but if one is a musician he is carrying on the talent of his uncle Horace, who was devoted to music.

I think there may be a revival of country dancing. People call these dances folk-dances; but they are not that. They succeeded the folk-dances which I can remember. I have hundreds of country dance figures.

> Always sincerely
> T.H.

Bitter east wind. Three new servants.

Text   MS. Adams.
last ones: i.e., the last proofs of *Late Lyrics*.   *a musician*: evidently Henry Charles Cautley Moule (b. 1893), subsequently a lecturer in music at Cambridge University; he was a son of Charles Walter Moule (see letter of 19 May 21 to Bosanquet).   *uncle Horace*: TH's long-dead friend Horace Moule; see I.2.   *they are not that*: TH's views on the distinction between folk-dances and country-dances were expressed in print in 1927; see Purdy, 323, and Millgate, *Career* (see letter of 23 Dec 20 to Foster), 55–6.   *Three new servants*: a cook, a housemaid, and a between-maid to wait on the cook; in her letter to Cockerell of 2 Apr 22 (Purdy) FEH explained that the cook had made the employment of a between-maid a condition of her own coming.

To CLAUDE HOUGHTON

FROM TH. HARDY, | MAX GATE, | DORCHESTER. | 30: 3: 1922

Dear Sir:

Many thanks for your tragedy "Judas", which I have not read as yet, but mean to do so soon. The subject would seem to be a striking one, if well treated.

Very truly yours
T.H.

Claude Houghton Esq.

Text   MS. (correspondence card, with envelope) Texas.
Houghton: pseudonym of Claude Houghton Oldfield (d. 1961), novelist.   *"Judas"*: Oldfield's play *Judas: A Tragedy in Three Acts* (London, 1922).

To ROBERT BRIDGES

MAX GATE, | DORCHESTER. | April 12. 1922

Dear Mr Bridges:

As a supporter of the S.P.E. I am indeed a backslider; but my energies are so much on the wane that I am no longer, I fear, of much service to anybody or anything. I am sending a small donation, & should like to send an article, though I daresay books have been written of late years that have anticipated what I might think of telling.

I do not know of a single English grammar that answers such obvious questions of the student as, what about the "split infinitive" that third-rate editors make sport of? what about the relative pronoun: should it be in the same case as the antecedent, or only in the same gender & number? &c. (Perhaps modern grammars do, after all, explain these things, but they did not when I was a boy, or a young man even.)

Could the Society be in any way affiliated with the English Association?

I am also an unworthy member of that, but I don't know how it is getting on at present.

Believe me,

Yours sincerely
Thomas Hardy.

Many thanks for the pamphlet. I see things advertised on the back that I know nothing of. T.H.

Text   MS. Lord Bridges.
Bridges: Robert Seymour Bridges, poet, Poet Laureate since 1913; see II.50.   *S.P.E.*: Society for Pure English, which TH had joined shortly after it was founded by Bridges and others in 1913; see IV.305.   *small donation*: of a guinea, for which Bridges thanked TH 13 Apr 22 (DCM).   *an article*: TH never contributed any such article, although Bridges in his 13 April letter suggested he should write on 'the *value of common speech dialectal words* that are in danger of being lost to the language'.   *English Association*: see letter of 18 Sept 22 to Houghton.   *pamphlet*: probably S.P.E. Tract No. VIII, *What Is Pure French?* (Oxford, 1922), written by Bridges and his wife under the pseudonym of 'Matthew Barnes' and pub. 9 Mar 1922.   *on the back*: other S.P.E. publications.

To THEODORE SPICER-SIMSON

[Mid-April 1922]

Dear Mr Spicer Simson:

I am writing for my husband, who writes very few letters now, to say that he is much obliged for the photographs. The one of Meredith is very striking.

No doubt you could make a very successful portrait of Sir James Barrie but unfortunately he has expressed to us that he objects to sit for his portrait. So that it would be advisable for you to get an introduction to him for that purpose through some other of your sitters—such as Mr Galsworthy or Mr Shaw. We do not know what his objection is.

If you visit us again this summer please let us know. Mr Hardy's difficulty in seeing people who come here as it were just to call, is that they print an interview with him. We shall understand therefore that nothing of that sort will appear in the book you mention—but that if it speaks of him at all it will be confined to remarks on his writings.

We hope you are enjoying your renewed visit to London—

Yours &c.
[F.H.]

Text MS. (pencil draft) DCM. *Date* Replies to letter of 15 Apr 22.
photographs: of medallions made by Spicer-Simson. *Meredith*: George Meredith, novelist and poet; see IV.23. *Shaw*: George Bernard Shaw, dramatist; see IV.235. Medallions of Shaw, Meredith, and Galsworthy (but not Barrie) are reproduced in the vol. mentioned below. *visit us again*: Spicer-Simson's letter of 15 Apr 22 (DCM) expressed a hope of renewing acquaintance with TH. *book you mention*: referred to in Spicer-Simson's letter as *Prominent Authors*, eventually pub. as *Men of Letters of the British Isles: Portrait Medallions from the Life by Theodore Spicer-Simson*, with critical essays by Stuart P. Sherman (New York, 1924). The brief essay accompanying the Hardy medallion is evocative of TH's work rather than of his personality. *[F.H.]*: initials and square brackets supplied by TH.

To HAROLD MONRO

MAX GATE, | DORCHESTER. | 2 May. 1922

Dear Mr Monro:

I am letting you know that I have received your poems "Real Property", as I may not read all of them for some time, & will not delay till then my thanks for the gift. So far the one I like best is, I think, "The Silent Pool"; but I may find more that win me.

Always yours truly
Thomas Hardy.

Text MS. (with envelope) David Holmes.
Monro: Harold Edward Monro, poet and editor; see V.332. *"Real Property"*: TH's copy of Monro's *Real Property* (London, 1922), with presentation inscription by Monro, a pencil mark against 'The Silent Pool', and a few other markings, is in the collection of David Holmes.

To ANDREW BENNETT

May 6. 1922

Dear Sir:

The valued Diploma has arrived, & I thank the University Authorities for their considerateness in conferring the degree *in absentia*.

I have hardly gone outside my premises here for the last twelvemonth, &, as I think I mentioned to you, had an illness in the latter part of the winter; or I should have enjoyed a trip to the north to receive the degree in person.

Yours truly

Andrew Bennett Esq. | Secretary to the University of St Andrews

Text   MS. (pencil draft) DCM.
arrived: Bennett's letter of 4 May 22 (DCM) asked TH to acknowledge the arrival of the diploma for TH's honorary LL.D. degree; see letter of 15 Mar 22 and, for the ceremony in St. Andrews, Peter W. Coxon, 'Recollections of Thomas Hardy in St. Andrews', *Thomas Hardy Year Book* 8 (1978), 10–11.

To JOHN BUCHAN

MAX GATE, | DORCHESTER. | May 6: 1922

My dear Mr Buchan:

Thank you very warmly for sending me the third volume of these valuable books. I have not read a line of it yet, but mean to do so, as I did the previous volumes, & continue the absorbing tragedy. I shall look forward to the fourth with interest.

Believe me

Sincerely yours
Thomas Hardy.

Text   MS. NLS.
these valuable books: Buchan (2 May 22, DCM) sent vol. III of *A History of the Great War* (see letter of 21 Nov 21), pub. May 1922.

To MARY DE LAUTOUR

(Copy)   MAX GATE, | DORCHESTER. | May 9. 1922.

Dear Miss de Lautour:

I have had much pleasure in receiving the graceful Greeting from the Bournemouth Poetry Centre, and send my best thanks to the Society for the very charming collection of their verse of which I find myself the possessor.

I am ashamed to say that till now I was not aware, so far as I remember, that there was an altar consecrated to the Muse so near me as at Bournemouth, and it is a delight to find the town to contain so many students of poetry.

I have not yet been able to read carefully all the Poems, so will not attempt to express myself in detail about them; but so far as studied they seem to be alive with feeling and actuality.

With renewed thanks I am

Yours most sincerely,
(Signed) T . . . . H . . . .

To Miss M. T. de Lautour | Hon. Sec. Bournemouth Poetry Centre.

Text MS. (typed draft) DCM.
de Lautour: Mary Thérèse de Lautour (1881–1950), Hon. Secretary of the Bournemouth Poetry Society; a 'Prose-poem' by her appeared in the first no. of the *Wessex Review* (see letter of 20 July 22) and a selection of her writings, *What Is There to Remember: Poems and Impressions* (Bristol, 1951), was pub. posthumously.   *(Copy)*: a pencil addition—perhaps at a later date—in TH's hand.   *collection of their verse*: not, apparently, a pub. vol. but an album put together specifically for presentation to TH; see letter of 20 July 22.   *To Miss . . . Centre.*: added in ink in TH's hand.

To SYDNEY COCKERELL

MAX GATE, | DORCHESTER. | Thursday. [11 May 1922]

Thoughtful of you to send the books. Best thanks. Am pleased to have them. Poems to be published the 23rd.

Th. H.

Text MS. (postcard) Taylor.   *Date* From postmark.
the books: unidentified.

To NEWMAN FLOWER

MAX GATE, | DORCHESTER. | 11th. May 1922.

Dear Mr Newman Flower:

It is a great pleasure to be asked by you to dine and meet the distinguished men you mention, all of whom are friends and acquaintances of mine, as well as yourself. Also to be offered such kind accommodation as you suggest providing. But alas, as you will probably be not unprepared to hear, I cannot be there, for physical reasons. The illness I had in the winter, though I have quite recovered from it, has made it necessary that I should limit my doings very considerably for a time; and although I had intended to be in London this May I have been obliged to postpone the intention indefinitely.

I wonder if we shall see you in Dorset this summer. As you were looking for a house here some months ago I may mention that there is a quiet little retreat at Portesham for sale by Duke and Co, or was a few days ago.

With many regrets, and best thanks believe me

Sincerely yours,
Thomas Hardy.

Text MS. (typewritten) Texas.
distinguished men: Flower (10 May 22, DCM) invited TH to 'a very private little dinner party' at the Savoy Hotel, the others present to include Sir Frederick Treves (see letter of 27 Dec 22), Edmund Gosse, H. G. Wells (see letter of 25 Mar 23), and Leonard Rees.   *kind accommodation*: Flower offered to place a suite of rooms at the Savoy at TH's disposal.

Portesham: a village SW of Dorchester.   *Duke and Co*: Dorchester auctioneers; the property in question was presumably Nethergrove, Portesham, advertised in the *Dorset County Chronicle*, 4 May 1922, as a 'most attractive small freehold residential estate'.

To SIR FREDERICK MACMILLAN

Max Gate, | Dorchester. | 11th. May 1922.

Dear Sir Frederick:

I shall be pleased of course to sign a book for any friend of yours, and will do so if you send it on.

I will think of two or three people whom I should like to have a copy of the Poems, and will let you know.

Sincerely yours,
Th: Hardy.

Text   MS. (typewritten) BL.
friend of yours: Macmillan's letter of 9 May 22 (DCM) identifies the friend only as an American who owned a copy of the first edn. of *Desperate Remedies*.   *of the Poems*: Macmillan reported that *Late Lyrics and Earlier* would appear on 23 May.

To HENRY AND RUTH HEAD

MAX GATE, | DORCHESTER. | 21st. May 1922.

Dear Dr and Mrs Head:

The book of "Pages" has come, and has I think a very nice appearance. Many thanks. As I look over passages I had quite forgotten it is rather appalling to see sentences that were forty years apart in the writing suddenly juxtaposed under the limelight, with all their negligences and ignorances, inconsistencies and misfits.

In your arrangement of the selections you trace association of ideas where it never would have occurred to myself, the instances seeming quite distinct; which does credit to the vividness of your imagination.

It may be useful, in the event of a second impression being wanted, to mark on your copy the few misprints we have noticed and set down in the list enclosed. With kindest regards I am,

Yours sincerely,
Thomas Hardy.

Text   MS. (typewritten) Purdy.
Head: Henry Head (1861–1940; *D.N.B.*), neurologist, with whom TH became friendly in his later years (see *LY*, 264); for Ruth Head see letter of 21 July 21.   *"Pages"*: *Pages from the Works of Thomas Hardy*, arranged by Ruth Head, with an introduction by Henry Head (London, 1922).   *misprints*: these were, in fact, numerous, as Dr. Head acknowledged in his reply of 23 May 22 (DCM), and an errata slip was subsequently inserted in copies of the book offered for sale.

To FREDERIC HARRISON

MAX GATE, | DORCHESTER. | May 24: 1922

My dear Harrison:

My real thanks for your letter. Yes: I shall be 82 next week if I live so long. But I rather shrink from the idea of reaching 90, as you have quite coolly done, because I think, from present experience, that I probably should not by then be in so vigorous a condition as to make it worth while. I am, in fact, surprised that I have lived till now, having been a fragile child who was not thought likely to grow up. I have not been to London for two years, & to stay at friends' houses on visits, as you can, I find rather an effort.

I hope you will get home comfortably, & not the worse from your "circular tour" as I may call it.

Believe me

Always yours
Thomas Hardy.

Text MS. Texas.
Harrison: Frederic Harrison, leading British positivist; see I.134.   *your letter*: of 23 May 22 (DCM), mainly devoted to birthday greetings.   *"circular tour"*: Harrison described himself as in the midst of a round of visits to friends and relations.   *Always yours*: in February 1920, however, Harrison's review of *Moments of Vision* had angered TH to the point of deciding that their friendship was at an end; see Millgate, 529.

To SIR FREDERICK MACMILLAN

MAX GATE, DORCHESTER. | May 24th. 1922.

Dear Sir Frederick:

The copies have arrived, and the contents look quite a good quantity for the money, which is what people think most of I fancy. There are two friends to whom I should like you to send copies direct, as from myself, as you suggest:

Lytton Strachey Esq. 51 Gordon Square. W.C. 1.
John Buchan Esq. LLD. 35 Paternoster Row.

With best thanks I am,

Sincerely yours,
Th: Hardy.

Text MS. (typewritten) BL.
copies: of *Late Lyrics and Earlier*.   *Strachey . . . Buchan*: both of whom had recently presented books to TH; see letter of 20 Apr 21 and letter of 6 May 22 to Buchan.

To W. G. BOWMAN

May 27. 1922

My dear Sir:

This morning I found your letter, which I had accidentally mislaid, or it should have been answered sooner; though I do not know that any remarks of mine can be of much service.

The immediate practical question appears to be concerning the proposed monthly magazine. A Wessex man (Dorset) who is literary manager to a large publishing firm, could, I think, give excellent advice on that point, & estimate the probabilities of its success. He is Mr Newman Flower, of Cassells & Co, & he takes much interest in everything that has to do with Wessex. His private address is Idehurst, Sevenoaks, Kent.

Only one thing occurs to me for the moment as being a matter the magazine could take up with advantage—the preservation of local names— which are so muddled & neglected by the surveyors of the ordnance maps as to be disappearing fast. (To give one instance "Swan-knolls" at Cattistock near here, becomes "Sandhills".) I could give a hundred. Believe me

Yours very truly

Text MS. (pencil draft) DCM.
Bowman: William G. Bowman, journalist, of 97 Cranbury Avenue, Southampton.   *your letter*: of 18 May 22 (DCM); it proposed the establishment of a Royal Wessex Society—to 'attempt a Renascence of the South (Wessex)'—and reported that a monthly magazine devoted to the Wessex Movement would shortly begin publication. See letter of 3 July 22.   *give a hundred*: TH, anticipating a possible reply, noted on a separate sheet of paper (DCM) the omission from recent Ordnance Survey maps of names present in earlier maps and the progressive corruption of other names—so that 'Bardolfston Hill, worn down to Bar'ston, is "Basin Hill"' while 'St Conger's Barrow' had become 'Conquer Barrow'.

To EDMUND GOSSE

Max Gate | 28: 5: 1922

My dear Gosse:

I have read to-day your very kind review of the book, for which you have my sincere thanks.

I got over that illness I had in the winter. (It was that which caused the Preface, which I wrote in bed.)

I hope you & your household are well. We have not seen the Hanburys lately, but I believe they are back. I have not been to London for 2 years! You wd have seen me if otherwise.

Always yours,
Thomas Hardy.

I congratulate Sylvia on her picture-show, which, as I gather from the papers, is a great success, or, what is more, a solid achievement. T. H.

Text MS. Leeds.
very kind review: of *Late Lyrics*, *Sunday Times*, 28 May 1922; see, however, letter of 29 May 22.   *Hanburys*: see letter of 6 Jan 20.   *Sylvia*: Gosse's younger daughter (see II.287), currently exhibiting oil paintings and drawings at the Goupil Galleries.   *from the papers*: e.g., from the notice in *The Times*, 23 May 1922.

To FLORENCE HENNIKER

MAX GATE, | DORCHESTER. | May 29: 1922
My dear friend:

I ought to have sent you a copy of the Poems. But I don't send books to women nowadays—not because I despise the sex, far from it! but because I fear they will not like something or other I have written, & will be in the awkward position of having to pretend they do. I am sure some in the present poems will be against your taste, so you can let fly at me freely & without compunction, which you could not otherwise have done.

Yes, Edmund Gosse was very funny about that young man. But then he always writes wittily. I wish he would give himself more time: he would out-Walpole Walpole if he did.

But I am saying nothing on the most delightful part of your letter (received this morning, I ought to have mentioned)—that you are coming to D. on the 26th. We are both so glad, & will certainly show you the country of The Woodlanders, which is only about 12 miles from here. It is, in fact, just beyond where Gen. Henniker's aunt lived, & Mrs Charmond's house is a sort of composite one. However I can tell you all this when you come.

How strange that you should be so countrified at Highgate. If I were obliged to live close to London I should probably live up that way. [*remainder of page excised*] to the gardener's annoyance. I cannot say when, if ever, she will be tired of keeping [*remainder of page excised*]

I get very odd letters. A lady writes today begging me to write one more novel before I "pass on". T.H.

Text MS. DCM.
Henniker: she died 4 April 1923 (see *LY*, 230) and this is TH's last surviving letter to her.   *sent you a copy*: in her letter of 28 May 22 (typed transcript, DCM) Mrs. Henniker said she had ordered a copy of *Late Lyrics* from a local bookseller.   *that young man*: Gosse's review of *Late Lyrics* (see letter of 28 May 22) had in fact criticized TH's 'Apology' for its sensitivity to the criticisms of 'a Roman Catholic young man' (i.e., Joseph Hone; see letter of 6 Mar 22). 'Let that young man be produced and exhibited in a glass case [Gosse wrote], for he is a rare specimen. What in all the earth does it matter what some young Catholic (or some old Protestant, if it comes to that) has been silly enough to say?'   *Walpole*: i.e., Horace Walpole, fourth Earl of Orford (1717–97), author; *D.N.B.*   *coming to D.*: Mrs. Henniker had taken a room at the King's Arms Hotel, Dorchester, from 26 June to 1 July 1922.   *where Gen. Henniker's aunt lived*: Up-Cerne House, occupied in the 1890s by Lady Kerrison, widow of Sir Edward Clarence Kerrison, 2nd Bt.; Sir Edward's sister Anna was the mother of Mrs. Henniker's husband.   *Mrs Charmond's*: Felice Charmond, a character in *The Woodlanders*; Mrs. Henniker expressed a wish to see 'her' house.   *at Highgate*: Mrs. Henniker was currently living at Fairseat, Highgate Hill, London, N.6.   *I get ... T.H.*: postscript in margin of first page.   *A lady*: unidentified.

To ST. JOHN ERVINE

MAX GATE, | DORCHESTER. | 30: 5: 1922
Dear Mr Ervine:

Many thanks for "The Ship", which I have as yet only looked into, but mean to read, since I shall never see it acted but by a miracle! for I don't go to theatres now, naturally. I hope you get about this fine weather: if you do not you ought to before the rain comes.

Believe me

Sincerely yours
Thomas Hardy.

Text MS. (correspondence card) Texas.
"The Ship": Ervine's *The Ship: A Play in Three Acts* (London, 1922); it was performed in Liverpool in November 1922.

To SIR FREDERICK MACMILLAN

MAX GATE, DORCHESTER. | May 30th. 1922.

Dear Sir Frederick:

I am much obliged for the copy of Mrs Head's book of selections, and quite remember the arrangement of a royalty on the sales. It is interesting to see what strikes readers in one's writings.

I imagine that when the edition of "Late Lyrics" has been exhausted you will not print any more of the edition. If however you should do so (or of course any other edition) I send a correction I ought to have made in the Preface.

Sincerely yours,
Th: Hardy.

Text MS. (typewritten) BL.
book of selections: see letter of 21 May 22.   *royalty on the sales*: Macmillan (26 May 22, DCM) reminded TH that he was entitled to such a royalty.   *any more of the edition*: there were, in fact, three impressions of the first edn. of *Late Lyrics*, the second and third incorporating a number of minor changes in the text of the 'Apology' (here called 'Preface').

To THOMAS J. WISE

MAX GATE, | DORCHESTER. | May 31: 1922

Dear Mr Wise:

I am greatly obliged to you for the Catalogue which, I confess, before I opened it I thought would be uninteresting. But I find it a most readable volume, the reproductions of the old titlepages particularly so.

My wife is, I believe, sending with this a pamphlet she promised you.

Believe me

Sincerely yours
Thomas Hardy.

Text MS. BL.
Wise: Thomas James Wise, bibliographer and forger; see V.192.   *the Catalogue*: vol. I of Wise's *The Ashley Library: A Catalogue of Printed Books, Manuscripts, and Autograph Letters* (London, 1922).   *a pamphlet*: presumably *Two Phantasies*; see letter of 14 Feb 22 to Cockerell.

To CLEMENT SHORTER

Max Gate, | Dorchester | June 2: 1922

Dear Clement Shorter:

It is very good of you to congratulate me on another birthday, & I answer at once, for though I always mean to answer such letters I often break down before I have got far. I quite remember calling on you as Editor—a very important personage in those days to me. With many thanks (& for the little book—)

Sincerely yours
Thomas Hardy

Text   Typed transcript (by J. S. Sample).
as Editor: Shorter's letter of birthday greetings (1 June 22, DCM) recalled TH's first visit to his *Illustrated London News* office 30 years previously.   *little book*: not identified in Shorter's letter.

To LADY HOARE

MAX GATE, | DORCHESTER. | June 3: 1922

My dear Lady Hoare:

My sincere thanks for the translation, & for the pilgrim's bottle, which will be admirably adapted for "the doctor's use" in the mumming play, if the company ever do it again, as he says that his unrivalled medical knowledge has been acquired in the east. Also thanks for birthday wishes.

Mine is not the pen of a ready writer nowadays (mainly because my eyes are so weak), or I would fill several pages. My kindest regards to Sir Henry. Believe me

Always yours
Thomas Hardy.

Text   MS. National Trust (Stourhead).
the translation: Lady Hoare (n.d., DCM) had translated part of an article on TH in a French newspaper and sent it 'with my own poor homage, & love, to Our Greatest Poet, *today*, on his *82nd birthday*—'.   *pilgrim's bottle*: i.e., a costrel, 'a large bottle with an ear or ears by which it could be suspended from the waist' (*O.E.D.*).   *mumming play*: TH's recension of the traditional 'Saint George Play', incorporated by the Hardy Players into their 1920 production of *The Return of the Native*; see V.284–5 and Purdy, 212–13.

To ROBERT BICKERSTAFFE

MAX GATE, | DORCHESTER. | June 5: 1922.

Many thanks for letter & interesting verses.

T.H.

Text   MS. (postcard) David Holmes.
Bickerstaffe: Robert Bickerstaffe, bookkeeper, of 34 Sunbourne Road, Liverpool; his letter of 1 June 22 (DCM) asked TH to accept 'the enclosed verses . . . as a testimony of warm interest in yourself and your Kingdom of Wessex'.

To ETHEL COWLEY

Max Gate | 6: 6: 1922

Dear Mrs Cowley:

I am delighted with your pretty present, which has been set up in a conspicuous place in the window. How very thoughtful of you. Florence has gone to London: she says it is very hot there, & wishes she were home—which she will be to-morrow I hope.

Always sincerely
Th: Hardy.

Text MS. (with envelope) Canon Cowley.
pretty present: see letter of 7 June 22.

To FLORENCE HARDY

Max Gate | Wedny morning [7 June 1922]

My dearest F:

I have had your letter, & can't think what made you unwell, unless it was hurrying. I went to the Hanburys yesterday: it was a tennis-party & was pleasant enough, but I wished you had been there to recognize people for me. Lady Christian was one, & the Hursts. The baby has developed wonderfully: a fat healthy girl. Mrs Cowley has sent me a plant all in bloom as a birthday present. Connie is just going to D. so we think you will get this to-night. I have had a nice letter from Clifford Allbutt.

Lady C. said the Williamses had a lunch party on Monday & were disappointed that we could not be there. However, I will tell you when you come.

We thought that by sending on the R.S.L. ticket you might meet the Barkers, & be asked to come back with them.

Always yours
T.

Text MS. Purdy.   *Date* From internal evidence.
to the Hanburys: i.e., to Kingston Maurward House.   *Lady Christian*: Lady Christian Norah Martin, *née* Dawson-Damer (d. 1959, aged 68), daughter of the fourth Earl of Portarlington; she married Capt. W. F. Martin of Came House, Dorchester, following the death of her first husband, Capt. the Hon. Fergus Bowes-Lyon, in 1915.   *the Hursts*: TH probably means Major John Hirst and his wife Kathleen, who had recently moved to Dorchester from Evershot; Mrs. Hirst later played Iseult in *The Queen of Cornwall* (see letter of 11 Nov 23). *The baby*: the Hanburys' daughter Caroline, for whose christening in September 1921 TH wrote the poem 'To C. F. H.'; see Purdy, 245.   *Connie*: FEH's sister, Constance Dugdale (see letter of 2 June 25), who was staying at Max Gate during FEH's absence.   *Allbutt*: Sir Thomas Clifford Allbutt (see III.267), Regius Professor of Physic at Cambridge; his letter of 5 June 22 (DCM) sent birthday greetings to 'the great prophet of our time'.   *the Williamses*: see letter of 14 Apr 23.   *R.S.L.*: Royal Society of Literature.   *meet the Barkers*: Harley Granville Barker and his wife; Barker delivered a paper on 'Some Tasks for Dramatic Scholarship' at a meeting of the Royal Society of Literature 7 June 1922.

To PRINCESS MARIE LOUISE

Max Gate | June 9: 1922

Dear Madam:

In reply to your kind inquiry I can assure you that I am gratified to learn that some of my poems are deemed desirable for the Library of Little Manuscripts for the Dolls' House that is intended as a gift to the Queen.

Three of my poems that would be suitable are I think, "The Oxen", "When I set out for Lyonnesse", & "In Time of the Breaking of Nations." They are all in the volume of my "Collected Poems" (Macmillan).

I regret to say that a weakness of the eyes prevents my writing them out small & clearly. So that if you can get them copied in any way you wish I will sign them with the greatest pleasure—

I am,

Very faithfully yours

The Princess Marie Louise—

Text MS. (pencil draft) DCM.
Marie Louise: Her Highness Princess Marie Louise (1872–1956; *D.N.B.*); christened Franziska Josepha Louise Augusta Marie Christiana Helena, she was the younger daughter of Queen Victoria's third daughter, Helena Augusta Victoria, and her husband Prince Christian of Schleswig-Holstein.   *kind inquiry*: of 7 June 22 (DCM).   *the Dolls' House*: an elaborate and comprehensively furnished model house prepared under the direction of Edwin Lutyens, the architect, presented to Queen Mary in 1924, subsequently exhibited for charitable purposes, and now at Windsor Castle. The Princess—who is said to have written 2,000 letters in her own hand to those involved in the project—asked TH to name 'the three of your poems which you like best' in order that they might be professionally inscribed in a miniature vol. destined, together with similar vols. containing work by other contemporary writers, for inclusion in the Dolls' House library.

To EDMUND BLUNDEN

MAX GATE, | DORCHESTER. | June 11: 1922

Dear Mr Blunden:

This is a belated line to thank you for "The Shepherd" & its kind inscription. I have read some of it with much pleasure, particularly the name-poem; but I shall not be able to read it all, I fear, till a little later on when I get several pressing things done—if I ever do! You will quite forgive a short note, & believe me

Sincerely yours
Thomas Hardy.

Text MS. (with envelope) Texas.
"The Shepherd": Blunden's *The Shepherd, and Other Poems of Peace and War* (London, 1922).
kind inscription: it was inscribed to both TH and FEH.

To SIEGFRIED SASSOON

Max Gate | 11 June 1922

My dear ⤳

I have been waiting for things to go by, so that I could write an adequate answer to your kind letter on my birthday, & about the poems; but what with weak eyes, & other hindrances, I feel I shall never do it: so I send this line all in a hurry just to let you know that we have been glad to hear from you & to gather that you are well.

When are you coming to see us again? I was ill in the winter but have nearly recovered. My wife sends best regards, & I am

Sincerely yours
Thomas Hardy.

You might, for greater freedom, put up at an inn near here, & come out every day. T.H.

Text MS. Eton College.
kind letter: of 1 June 22 (DCM).   *the poems*: Sassoon said that he was trying to review *Late Lyrics* and finding it difficult to express his admiration 'coherently'; it appears from *Siegfried Sassoon Diaries 1920–1922*, ed. Rupert Hart-Davis (London, 1981), 161, that he abandoned the task that same day.

To J. C. SQUIRE

MAX GATE, DORCHESTER. | June 13th. 1922.

Dear Mr Squire:

I am sending something that may suit your new and interesting scheme of "Reprints". If however it should not be deemed of the class you intend, would you kindly return it. There would, of course, be no charge for the poem.

Many thanks for your article in the Observer. We have been much moved by your "Stockyard".

Yours sincerely,
Thomas Hardy.

Text MS. (typewritten) Taylor.
"Reprints": the title given in Squire's *London Mercury* to a series of reprintings of forgotten poems.   *the poem*: 'Ave Caesar', by Horace Moule (see letter of 22 Mar 22); it appeared, together with TH's brief biographical note, in the *London Mercury*, October 1922 (see Purdy, 321).   *in the Observer*: Squire's review of *Late Lyrics* and Ruth Head's *Pages from the Works of Thomas Hardy*, *Observer*, 28 May 1922.   *"Stockyard"*: Squire's poem 'The Stockyard', *London Mercury*, June 1922.

To HAROLD MONRO

Private.   MAX GATE, | DORCHESTER. | 16th. June 1922.

Dear Mr Monro:

I am much honoured by your questions. But I must ask you to spare me from replying, for even if I could answer them, which is doubtful, I have found that such replies bring down a shower of letters from troublesome strangers, and other inconveniences. I think you will find that all I have to say on those and kindred points is said in the Preface to my volume of Poems just published.

Yours very truly,
Thomas Hardy.

Text MS. (typewritten) King's College, Cambridge.
your questions: Monro (10 June 22, DCM) asked whether TH believed poetry was 'a necessity to modern man', what he saw as poetry's 'particular function in modern life', and what chance he thought there was of poetry's being 'eventually displaced by prose'.

To SIR JAMES BARRIE

MAX GATE, | DORCHESTER. | 17: 6: '22

My dear Barrie:
    I have read the two beautiful sonnets. Nobody can say what the writer might have accomplished had he lived. I hope you are well.

Always
T.H.

Text MS. (correspondence card, with envelope) Colby.
beautiful sonnets: *The Times* of 17 June 1922 reprinted from the *Eton College Chronicle* two sonnets on the Scottish island of Eilean Chona written by the late Michael Llewelyn Davies, Barrie's adopted son; see letter of 22 May 21.

To VERE H. COLLINS
[Copy]

Max Gate | D . . . . | June 22. 1922.

Dear Mr Collins:
    Your letter from Skye to Mr Hardy was unfortunately mislaid till today and he now thanks you for your remarks on Late Lyrics, and for the list of corrections.
    He can express no opinion on your intention to translate Mr Hedgcock's book, which is a dozen years old, and considering that Mr Hardy has now written verse for 27 years, and prose only 25, is naturally out of proportion. Besides, creditable work as it is and carefully written, it is sprinkled with errors of minor detail in the biographical part, of no great importance in a French book, but wh wd stand out prominently in an English one, the besetting fault of the writer being to go to the novels for facts in the author's life—e.g. none of the statements in a Pair of Blue Eyes about Stephen Smith are those of Hardy's life or character beyond that he was an architect: yet Hedgcock takes it for granted that they are. (p. 31) Smith was in fact drawn from an architect's pupil whom Mr Hardy knew, much younger than himself. I might mention a great number of such errors in these identifications.
    It was Mr Hardy's plan always in his fictions to avoid facts of his own life, though not, of course, those he had witnessed in others' lives.
    As to the opinions and criticisms of Mr Hardy's works as art, when the critic does not attempt to get behind them at the writer, Mr Hardy does not

mind them at all, adverse or otherwise, unless wrong as to quotation, &c. When the book came out, a few corrections of these were sent to Mr Hedgcock: probably he has these still.

We shall be at home if you call when at Swanage, if you let us know beforehand. I hope that you had a pleasant holiday in Scotland. I am glad that the rose cuttings struck. The cotoneaster plant I promised looks rather queer, as if it might be going to die, but I hope not.

Yours sincerely,
(signed by F.E.H.)

Text   MS. (carbon typescript) DCM.
[Copy] : word and brackets in TH's hand, as is the address; it appears that the ribbon copy was typed on headed stationery and that this MS. may thus be a carbon of the letter as actually sent. *letter from Skye*: of 14 June 22 (DCM).   *list of corrections*: this still accompanies Collins's letter.   *Mr Hedgcock's book*: *Thomas Hardy, penseur et artiste* by Frank Hedgcock (see letter of 12 July 22), pub. in Paris in 1911 (see IV.37); Collins reported that he had been asked to translate it for Blackwell's, the Oxford publishers.   *wh wd stand out*: TH's revision of the typescript's 'standing out'.   *architect's pupil*: probably William Searle Hicks; see letter of 19 Dec 21 to Mrs. Henniker.   *as to quotation, &c.*: TH's revision of the typescript's 'as to fact'.   *when at Swanage*: Collins did visit Max Gate from Swanage in August 1922; see his *Talks with Thomas Hardy at Max Gate 1920–1922* (London, 1922), 65–85.   *rose cuttings*: taken from Max Gate.   *cotoneaster plant I promised*: during Collins's last visit to Max Gate, 29 Oct 1921, FEH—the ostensible author of this letter—offered to send him a cotoneaster seedling; see *Talks with Thomas Hardy*, 47.   *(signed by F.E.H.)*: added in what appears to be TH's hand.

To VERE H. COLLINS
[Copy]   Max Gate | Dorchester | June 24. 1922.

Dear Mr Collins:

I have received your letter this morning, saying you will not proceed with the book till you hear more. As Mr Hardy told you by telegraph, he disapproves of its publication in England as it stands, and this is the case even if it be brought up to date by adding a chapter. For on examining it further he found that the dissection of his supposed personality in the first chapter or two (he has not examined the book through) and the advancing it as fact, is of a particularly pointed and even prying kind, not at all in good taste when the subject of the assumed dissection, or vivisection, is still alive. And this would be so, even if the analyses were true, and not as in the present case based mainly on incidents in the romances and poems that are pure inventions. Fancy using the absolute fabrications of a novelist (which they were), quoted at pp. 17, 19, 29, 31, 32, 33, 34, 35, etc. and such erroneous inferences as at pp. 4, 17, 26 etc. as facts in the history of the writer!

Therefore Mr Hardy asks me to say that he cannot consider the question of your publishing a translation at all, unless on an undertaking that these pseudo-biographical analyses are omitted, and, speaking generally, most of the personal matter except a few necessary data. To the legitimate literary criticism he has of course no objection.

You must excuse his speaking so plainly. At the time of the book's appearance in French he did not think it worth while to take these things

seriously, as he understood it to be but a thesis in connection with
M. Hedgcock's Paris lectures. He says, in respect of the above passages, that
he would imagine M. Hedgcock himself would dislike at this date to have
personal quizzing of that immature kind revived as his work.

You probably have not as yet noticed these passages, as we feel convinced
you would not wish to do anything that might be unliterary and annoying.

Yours sincerely,

Text   MS. (carbon typescript) DCM.
[Copy]: word and brackets, like the address, in TH's hand; this MS. is apparently a carbon of
the letter as sent, presumably over FEH's signature.   *your letter*: to FEH, of 23 June 22
(DCM).   *the book*: Hedgcock's *Thomas Hardy, penseur et artiste*; see letter of 22 June 22.
by telegraph: at the foot of the 22 June 22 letter TH noted down the text of a telegram sent to
Collins's London address the morning of 23 June, 'On examining Hedgcock's book I disapprove
of publication in English as it stands. Letter follows. Hardy.'   *pp. 17, . . . 35, etc.*: these are
passages which identify TH with such fictional characters as Stephen Smith, Edward
Springrove, and Clym Yeobright.   *4, 17, 26 etc.*: these passages make direct biographical
assertions.   *take these things seriously*: it seems possible that TH did not work his way
through the book until June 1922 and that the extensive markings in the margins of the DCM
copy belong to this date; see IV.165, letter to Collins of 2 July 22, and Simon Gatrell, 'Hardy
and the Critics', *Cahiers Victoriens & Édouardiens*, October 1980, 24–5.

To JOHN LANE
[Copy]   MAX GATE, | DORCHESTER. | 29th. June 1922.
Dear Mr Lane:

We are much obliged for your letter, and have nothing to say for or against
your reissue of Lionel Johnson's book with additions. A literary friend who
has been here says he thinks it a mistake, but that if it must be done the title
should run . . . . . *"by L.J. With an Appendix* (or Supplement) *by"* . . . so
and so.

Mr Hardy says he would have thought the original portrait by Strang
sufficient, but of course wishes to remain passive in the whole matter. Years
ago we should have been most happy to accommodate Mr Hill here in the
house as you suggest, but unfortunately my husband has reached an age
which (especially since his illness in the winter) has compelled us to give up
lodging here even our own friends. However we shall be happy to have Mr
Hill to lunch and tea for the two or three days he is making his drawing, and
this will, I should think, sufficiently enable him to obtain Mr Hardy's
expression. Any time after next week would suit us for his coming in that
way.

The present owner and occupier of Athelhampton Hall is . . . Cochrane
Esq.

Mr Hardy sends many thanks for the book on How to be Happy, which he
will read. I return the letter you enclosed, and am,

Yours sincerely,
F. E. Hardy.

Text   MS. (typed draft) DCM.
[Copy]: word and brackets added by TH in pencil.   *your letter*: to FEH, of 28 June 22
(DCM).   *Johnson's book: The Art of Thomas Hardy*, first pub. 1894 (see II.62).   *with*

additions: i.e., with an additional chapter on TH's poetry by Joseph Edward Barton, headmaster of Bristol Grammar School; the book was reissued thus in 1923.   *literary friend*: Siegfried Sassoon; see *Diaries 1920–1922* (see letter of 11 June 22 to Sassoon), 183–4.   *by Strang*: William Strang, artist (see letter of 5 Feb 21 to Gosse); his portrait-etching of TH was used as the frontispiece to *The Art of Thomas Hardy* in 1894.   *accommodate Mr Hill*: Vernon Hill, illustrator; see IV.328. Lane asked if Hill could be invited to Max Gate for a 3-day weekend and thus 'become more familiar with Mr. Hardy's expression'.   *coming in that way*: Hill's portrait of TH, used as the frontispiece to the 1923 reissue of *The Art of Thomas Hardy*, is dated July 1922.   *Cochrane Esq.*: George Cochrane purchased Athelhampton Hall (near Puddletown, Dorset) from Alfred C. de Lafontaine (see II.305) in 1918.   *How to be Happy*: Arthur Lapthorn Smith, *How to be Useful and Happy from Sixty to Ninety*, just pub. by Lane (London, 1922); it contains no reference to TH and was presumably sent as a joke.   *letter you enclosed*: from J. E. Barton (see above).   *F. E. Hardy.*: originally signed 'Florence Hardy' in FEH's hand; TH has struck through 'Florence' and substituted 'F. E.' The letter as sent (Taylor) is signed 'F. E. Hardy'.

To G. JULIUS CAESAR

[Late June 1922]

Dear Sir:

I regret to say in reply to your letter asking for Mr Hardy's advice on your stories that he is able to give very little, knowing nothing of what publishers require in fiction since he left off writing it between 20 and 30 years ago. Your best plan is to have nothing to do with advertised agencies, & to submit your manuscripts to the editors of respectable magazines, who are always anxious to obtain good work.

Yours truly

Text MS. (pencil draft) DCM.   *Date* Replies to letter of 28 June 22.
Caesar: George Julius Adelmare Caesar (1887–1969), a Weymouth chemist active in local government and education; he wrote 28 June 22 (DCM) to ask where he could obtain constructive criticism of the short stories he was writing but could not get accepted. No published work of his has been traced.

To EDWARD CLODD

MAX GATE, | DORCHESTER. | [Late] June, 1922

My dear Clodd:

I have delayed acknowledging your kind letter on my birthday till I could make my reply fit in with something more adequate than bare thanks—the date of your appearance also in the world, of which I wish you as many returns as you care for. I wonder if you find, as I do, that as your own interest in your birthday decreases the interest of other people in it seems to get stronger.

Your energy seems very remarkable. I had the impulse strong enough to take me to Holland 40 years ago, but do not feel it now. However, you were, I think, always more of a globe-trotter than I, & your journey was probably a survival of that instinct. Yet an old lady—a distant relative of mine, who is, I think, 86,—writes airily from some peak in Switzerland to congratulate me. Believe me, with kind regards from both,

Sincerely yrs
Thomas Hardy.

You infer rightly that I am well, & are very good to be glad thereat. But I had an illness in the winter which kept me in bed three weeks, & indoors two months. T.H.

Text MS. Leeds.   *Date* Inferred from 1 July date of Clodd's birthday.
your journey: Clodd and his wife travelled in Belgium and Holland 21 April–10 May 1922 (Clodd diary, Alan Clodd).   *distant relative*: Margaret Symons Gifford, the widow of ELH's uncle E. Hamilton Gifford.

To VERE H. COLLINS

[Copy]   Max Gate | Dorchester | July 2. 1922.

Dear Mr Collins:

Your letter of the 27th. June makes your intention clearer and less unwelcome, so that though Mr Hardy does not wish for a translation of Dr Hedgcock's book he is willing to remain passive in its production on the understanding that you carry it out as you say—omitting the personal surmises from passages in the books, and confining the biographical passages to the barest of known facts, (which would be, roughly speaking, those that appear in "Who's Who" and other such annuals). A revision of the literary criticism in many places would be desirable, and probably Dr Hedgcock, in his own interest, would recast it in the light of his maturer knowledge, since some of it is amateurish and stale, and must seem so even to himself, a fault that affects him more than it does the subject of his criticism. He would probably state on the titlepage that it was revised.

I have copied on another sheet some notes that Mr Hardy made on the margin of his copy of Dr Hedgcock's volume when looking it through, which you may like to have.

Mr Hardy being quite passive on your publication of the translation, you will not, of course, state anything in the book as to his approving of it, or mention him at all on the question of its being issued.

Yours sincerely,

Text MS. (carbon typescript) DCM.
[Copy]: word and brackets added, like the address, in TH's hand.   *less unwelcome*: Collins's letter (DCM) reported that Hedgcock was already revising the biographical section of his French text and he himself, when translating the book, would ensure 'that nothing will appear of the sort that you take exception to'.   *confining . . . facts*: this formulation is taken over from Collins's letter.   *another sheet*: although no copy of this seems to have been retained TH's comments in the margins of the book itself can be seen in DCM.   *like to have*: a short paragraph—'You will not, of course, state anything in your translation as to Mr Hardy approving of it, or mention him at all on the question of its publication'—has been struck through at this point.

To G. HERBERT THRING

[Ansr]   Max Gate | Dorchester | 2nd. July 1922.

Dear Mr Thring:

I am much obliged to you for letting me know of the publication in Czecho-Slovakia of the translation of a book of mine, which must be "The Romantic Adventures of a Milkmaid"—the heroine's name being Margaret. I do not remember authorizing it, though I am not quite sure whether such a project was ever mentioned to me. In the circumstances, and as the story is a short one, I prefer to do nothing in the matter.

As I am writing it occurs to me to make an inquiry I have often been going to make—are the Society's solicitors Messrs Field and Roscoe accustomed to undertake private practice—such as making wills, etc: Ordinary solicitors usually know nothing of literary questions like the disposal of copyrights, etc. and it struck me that they might be available for such a purpose, if necessary.

Yours sincerely,
(Signed Th H—

Text MS. (carbon typescript) DCM.
[Ansr]: word and brackets added, like the date, in pencil in TH's hand.   *being Margaret*: the Czech title, as retranslated in Thring's letter of 30 June 22 (DCM), was *Margaret's Romantic Adventures (Markétčino romantické dobrodružství)*; the translation, by Zdenek Mach, appeared in Prague in 1921.   *a short one*: first pub. in 1883 (see Purdy, 47–9), it was frequently pirated in the United States before being collected into *A Changed Man* in 1913.   *making wills, etc*: Thring replied (4 July 22, DCM) that Messrs. Field, Roscoe & Co. were expert in literary and copyright matters and would be dependable advisers in the making of a will; on 24 August 1922, however, TH signed a will drawn up by the Dorchester firm of Lock, Reed and Lock. *(Signed Th H*—: all in TH's hand.

To W. G. BOWMAN

[Copy]   July 3. 1922

Dear Sir:

Mr Hardy has been so embarrassed by the pressure of his correspondence that he has been unable to reply to your letter, & now can only do so by deputy. All that has occurred to him about the Prospectus you send of the proposed magazine is that—

1. He would include Somerset, & also Devon, to make it cover all the six counties of the old kingdom (which included a great part of Devon).

2. The word "Royal" seems superfluous in the title, suggesting a holiday char-a-banc. However he has no personal objection to it.

3. He feels strongly that the sub-title should be, "A Magazine devoted to the Wessex Movement" only, omitting his own name, which would certainly prejudice some people against it.

4. He would say "Forward the South-west" instead of "The South"—the latter including Kent, & Sussex.

5. Sir Henry Newbolt & Mr Eden Phillpotts (both Wessex men) might be asked to contribute. But this is only a suggestion.

Unfortunately Mr Hardy's age is too advanced & his energies too limited for him to contribute; but he hopes for the success of the magazine if it really takes shape, although he does not know what its prospects may be.

Yours very truly

F. E. H.

Text   MS. (pencil draft) DCM.
[Copy]: TH's square brackets.   *your letter*: to TH, of 2 June 22 (DCM).   *Prospectus*: in DCM; the declared aim of *Wessex Life: A Popular Magazine Devoted to the Wessex Movement of Thomas Hardy* was 'to bring the Wessex Movement into the Homes of the People . . . to help to make Royal Wessex a strong, independent Province having its own Art, Literature, Songs and Industries'.   *word "Royal"*: not, in fact, in the title of the proposed magazine (see previous note) but certainly in the proposed title of the sponsoring organization; see letter of 27 May 22.   *omitting his own name*: see note on *Prospectus* above.   *instead of "The South"*: the main heading of the prospectus reads 'FORWARD THE SOUTH'.   *what its prospects may be*: it seems never to have appeared; see letter of 20 July 22.

To THE DUCHESS OF HAMILTON

[Ansr]   July 5. 1922

Dear Duchess of Hamilton:

I am unfortunately unable to be present at the meeting, but I can say that slaughterhouse reform has my hearty support. A quick exit, with the minimum of suffering (mental & physical) is a right to which every victim is entitled, & if skilfully ensured may be less painful than the animal's natural death from age or infirmity—which is the only justification for killing such fellow-creatures at all. I fear that what among other things stands in the way in respect of many animals, such as pigs is the belief that they must "die slow" to produce a "well-blooded" carcase—which of course really impoverishes the meat. I should welcome legislation that enforced humane killing.

Believe me

Sincerely yours

(Signed) Thomas Hardy.

Text   MS. (draft) DCM.
Hamilton: Nina Mary Benita Douglas-Hamilton, Duchess of Hamilton and Brandon, *née* Poore (1878–1951), wife of the thirteenth Duke of Hamilton; she was an active campaigner in the causes of antivivisection and slaughter-house reform.   *the meeting*: the Duchess (3 July 22, DCM) sought a message of encouragement for a meeting called to protest against 'the present horrible methods of killing animals for food'.

To VERE H. COLLINS

MAX GATE, | DORCHESTER. | July 9. 1922.

Dear Mr Collins:

In answer to your letter of the 5 July I can only say that Mr Hardy is merely compelled by obvious circumstances to be neutral towards your proposal for translation; and if the corrections and alterations that I have detailed in previous letters were to be made he would not have any objection to the publication of the volume.

He thinks however that it might be advisable to delay publication for a few months, as he is told that Lionel Johnson's book, brought up to date, is to be reissued shortly, and another past book of the kind, also brought up to date, is to appear from another publishing house. Neither publication is desired by Mr Hardy, who is passive in the matter, the decision to enlarge and reprint them having been come to without consulting him (though he has certainly been asked if he wishes for any modifications).

So that to let these pass by might be to the advantage of your book, a point on which you will be the better judge.

Yours truly,
[signed] F. H. . . y

Text MS. (carbon typescript) DCM.
your letter: Collins (5 July 22, DCM) told FEH that, in the face of TH's disapproval, he had withdrawn from his agreement to translate Hedgcock's book; he added that Hedgcock would, in the circumstances, be unlikely to seek an alternative translator.   *Johnson's book*: see letter of 29 June 22.   *another past book*: the reference is perhaps to *Wessex* (1906), with paintings by Walter Tyndale and text by Clive Holland; Holland (see letter to him of 25 Aug 23) wrote to FEH, 10 June 22 (DCM), in an unsuccessful attempt to arrange to talk with TH about a new edn. of the book.   *[signed] F. H. . . y*: all in TH's hand.

To F. W. SLATER

(Copy)July 11. 1922

Dear Mr Slater:
  Will your New York house kindly explain why it is that, though the "Anniversary Edition" of my books in 21 volumes was published by them in June 1921, & received important reviews in the leading American papers about that time or in July, I find no returns for that edition in their account of sales to December 31, 1921, or royalties for the same.

Yours very truly

F. W. Slater Esq. | Messrs Harper Brothers | 45 Albemarle Street | London W.

Text MS. (pencil draft) DCM.
Slater: Frederick William Slater, London representative of Harper & Brothers.   *"Anniversary Edition"*: the trade edn. of the U.S. version of the Wessex edn.; see Purdy, 286.   *important reviews*: e.g., Ernest Brennecke's review in the *New York Times Book Review*, 5 June 1921.   *or royalties*: Slater replied (12 July 22, DCM) that he would write immediately to Harper & Brothers' head office in New York.

To FRANK HEDGCOCK

[Copy]July 12. 1922

Dear Sir:
  I have received your letter of the 9th, & am much obliged for your explanation of the circumstances in which a translation of your book on Mr Hardy has been proposed.

Mr Hardy is quite assured that the erroneous biographical passages were written by you in good faith. But the fact is that much of the personal detail that has appeared about him in the press in past years has been absurdly untrue, being written by irresponsible journalists, and he does not wonder that you were misled by it. As to your remark that they were not contradicted, I may say that attempts at contradiction are hopeless: the untruth is never overtaken by the correction. And Mr Hardy's note that some of the passages in your book, based on these newspaper reports, seemed inquisitive & prying as written of a living author, referred not to you personally, but to the impression such passages produced on a reader's mind, which he supposed that you yourself now in your maturer years would object to as much as he, even supposing they were true.

You probably quite agree with him that the book really requires to be re-written, or at least largely revised, before translation, a study of the poetical works being given at least an equal space with that of the prose, & personal details to be omitted except those authenticated by Mr Hardy in handbooks like "Who's Who." Lionel Johnson's study is an admirable example of how the personal side should be avoided, though his book is only concerned with the earlier half of Mr Hardy's writings.

In respect of the parts of your volume that are distinctly a literary study, some of them, as he has already said, are excellent, & all of them above the average. I have already told Mr Collins that, in the event of a revision of the book on the lines suggested, there would be no objection whatever to its publication in English, though for obvious reasons Mr Hardy must be neutral in the matter.

Believe me,

Yours very truly
[signed] F. E. Hardy

Dr F. A. Hedgcock.

Text   MS. (pencil draft) DCM.
Hedgcock: Frank Arthur Hedgcock, critic and teacher; see IV.109   *[Copy]*: TH's square brackets; his addition of Hedgcock's name at the head of the letter is apparently of later date and has not been reproduced.   *your letter*: in his letter of 9 July 22 (DCM) Hedgcock sought to explain his position but said that he had written to Collins to withdraw his permission for the translation to be made.   *personal detail*: TH first wrote 'personal gossip'.   *told Mr Collins*: see letter of 9 July 22.   *[signed]*: TH's square brackets.

To NICHOLAS MURRAY BUTLER

[Mid-July 1922]

Dear Sir:

In reply to Dr N. M. Butler's invitation to the Conference of Professors of English next year I write for Mr Thomas Hardy to thank Dr Butler for his letter & for the kind offer of accommodation in the University buildings.

Mr Hardy regrets to say, however, that increasing age forbids his crossing the Atlantic, even for such a good purpose. The Conference is, indeed, urgently required; for the English language is in danger of utter ruin, largely as it seems by the multiplication of half-illiterate publications.

I am, Dear Sir,

Yours very truly

for Thomas Hardy

F.E.—Sec

The Secretary, | Conference of British & American Professors | Columbia University. | New York. U S A

Text MS. (pencil draft) DCM. *Date* Replies to letter of 23 June 22 from New York. *Butler*: Nicholas Murray Butler (1862–1947), president of Columbia University 1901–45. *invitation*: Butler (23 June 22, DCM) asked TH to take part in a conference of British and American professors of English to be held at Columbia 13–15 June 1923. *the English language*: Butler said that the conference would consider 'many aspects of that most important subject—the English Language and Literature'. *Conference . . . Columbia . . . New*: TH inserted paragraph signs before each of these words to indicate the intended layout of the address.

To J. C. SQUIRE

[Ansr] M.G.D. | 17 July 1922

Dear Mr Squire:

I feel very strongly the generous considerations that prompt the Architectural Club & yourself to propose to instal me as Honorary President.

Have you really remembered that I have reached an age which quite prevents my doing anything worthy of such a position, or indeed doing anything at all? So, since I should have to be a deadhead, absolutely, would it not be more beneficial to the Club to choose some one who would act, & not a feeble person who could never be in London, eat dinners, make speeches, or write on architectural subjects? The tempting nature of the honour has not been able to hinder me in reminding you of all this.

If, when it has been thought over, the Committee is still of the same mind, I am your man. But please don't have any compunctions about withdrawing the offer, if reconsideration makes you dubious.

Sincerely yours

(Sgd) T— H—

Text MS. (pencil draft) DCM.
[Ansr]: TH's square brackets. *Architectural Club*: correctly, Architecture Club. This newly established society, run from the offices of Squire's *London Mercury*, was open to architects, writers, and others; its declared purpose was 'to enlarge public appreciation of good architecture and the allied arts, and especially of the best work of to-day'. See *London Mercury*, August 1922, and Patrick Howarth, *Squire: 'Most Generous of Men'* (London, 1963), 160–1. *as Honorary President*: Squire (14 July 22, DCM) reported that the first action of the club committee had been to ask TH—'as in a manner the most eminent of architects!'—to become Hon. President.

To DOROTHY ALLHUSEN

MAX GATE, | DORCHESTER. | 19 July 1922

My dear Dorothy:

We are delighted to hear the news about Madeleine & Geoffrey Congreve. From what you say there appears to be every prospect of their venture turning out well. After all, sailors go & come so quickly nowadays that their wives have much less loneliness than in the days of sailing ships when owing to adverse winds & slow voyages they were exiled for an interminable time very often.

We, too, wish Dorchester were nearer Stoke Court. Though a journey here & back in a day is not an impossible feat for a good car.

That illness I had in the winter went off by degrees, & I am now quite well, though my eyes are weak. Many thanks for inquiries. We truly hope you keep active & vigorous as usual & I am still

Yours affectionately
Thomas Hardy.

Text MS. (with envelope) Mrs. Stewart-Mackenzie.
the news: the engagement had just been announced of Mrs. Allhusen's elder daughter Madeleine to Geoffrey Cecil Congreve, R.N., who was created a baronet in 1927; they were married 14 Oct 1922.   *Stoke Court*: Mrs. Allhusen's home at Stoke Poges, Bucks.; see II.222.

To ROGER INGPEN

MAX GATE, | DORCHESTER. | 19 July 1922.

Dear Sir:

I am rather late in thanking you for your kind considerateness in giving me the handsome edition of Epipsychidion that you send, which I shall prize not only for itself, but as coming from a writer so well-known as you.

I remember Browning saying casually to me one afternoon at Mrs Procter's ("Barry Cornwall's" widow) many years ago, that he had been reading Epipsychidion all the morning. I always think the line "Sweet Benediction in the Eternal Curse" the grandest compliment ever paid to womankind.

Yours sincerely
Thomas Hardy.

Roger Ingpen Esq.

Text MS. (with envelope) Adams.
handsome edition: the Selwyn & Blount edn. of Shelley's *Epipsychidion* (London, 1921); TH's copy, with an inscription by Ingpen dated 8 July 1922, was sold after his death.   *Browning*: Robert Browning, poet; see I.176.   *Mrs Procter's*: Anne Procter (see I.114), the widow (when TH knew her) of Bryan Waller Procter, who wrote under the pseudonym of 'Barry Cornwall'.   *"Sweet . . . Curse"*: TH quotes accurately, except that the initial letter of 'eternal' is normally printed in lower-case.

To PRINCESS MARIE LOUISE
July 19. 1922

Dear Madam:

I have felt rather uncertain in carrying out your request to choose nine more poems for the little book which is to help furnish the Queen's Miniature House, though I need hardly say that any of them are at your service.

I think the following extra ones might be suitable—in view of the object of the selection:—

"V. R. 1819–1901." page 77 of "Collected Poems" (1 vol. Macmillan)
"The Temporary the All" ...... 5 ....
"Friends Beyond" ....52 ....
"The Souls of the Slain" .....84 ....
"Song of Hope" .... 120 ....
"The Darkling Thrush" ...... 137 ....
"The Dead Quire" .... 240 ....
"Let me enjoy" .... 222 ....
"A King's Soliloquy" .... 350 ....

Should any of the above be too long, or unsuitable in other ways, some of the following might be substituted:

"Mute Opinion" .... page 115 ....
"The Man he killed" .... 269 ....
"A Church romance" .... 236 ....
"Men who march away" ...... 506 ....
"A call to National Service" .. 514 ....

I am sorry that the state of my eyesight prevents my copying out the poems myself in the small handwriting required.

I am,

Dear Madam,
Yours sincerely

H. H. Princess Marie Louise

Text MS. (pencil draft) DCM.
your request: of 16 July 22 (DCM).   *little book . . . House*: see letter of 9 June 22; a total of nine poems by TH was eventually included.   *small handwriting required*: the poems were, of course, professionally transcribed and in *The Book of the Queen's Dolls' House*, ed. A. C. Benson and Sir Lawrence Weaver (London, 1924), TH is quoted as telling Princess Marie Louise, in a letter of 1 Dec 22, 'I am much pleased with the look of the miniature book, in which I have put my name. It makes one wish to have a whole library of such books!' (146).

To FRANCIS MACNAMARA

[Ansr]   Max Gate. | July 20. 1922

Dear Sir:

In reply to your letter I write for Mr Hardy, whose correspondence is more than he can cope with at his advanced age. He desires me to say that he has no idea what the prospects of the contemplated "Wessex Review" may be. The development of a utilitarian Wessex is entirely beyond the scope of his past conceptions & writings, which have been merely of a dreamland roughly resembling & conterminous with the six counties that now cover the old kingdom. Moreover everything that he has written about Wessex for the last twentyfive to thirty years has been, not in prose fiction, but in verse, as you will see by referring to lists of his works in "Who's Who" & similar publications.

He is very sorry that, apart from these considerations, his time of life does not allow him to take up this new idea. But of course he does not object to having his portrait drawn, if any good can result from it.

He has heard, by the way, of another "Wessex" periodical of the kind which it is proposed to launch shortly from another city of the same region. Whether it would be advisable for the two enterprizes to join their forces he cannot say. In any case he hopes that what is intended, if carried out, may result in complete fulfilment of its projectors' wishes & aims.

> Yours very truly
> for Thomas Hardy
> F.E.H.

F. Macnamara Esq. | Bournemouth.

Text MS. (pencil draft) DCM.
Macnamara: Francis Macnamara, poet and translator; he wrote (15 July 22, DCM) from the 'Office of the Wessex Review', 82 Old Christchurch Road, Bournemouth. *[Ansr]*: TH's square brackets. *"Wessex Review"*: three issues of this magazine appeared, dated Christmas 1922, Lady Day 1923, and Midsummer Day 1923; the first issue included three poems (one of them by Macnamara) headed 'Homage to Hardy. (From an album sent by the Bournemouth Poetry Society)'—presumably the 'collection' referred to in the letter of 9 May 22. *his portrait drawn*: Macnamara asked TH if he would sit to Augustus John (see V.222) for a portrait-drawing; the one used as the frontispiece to *Wessex Review* no. 3, however, is by Henry Lamb (1883–1960; *D.N.B.*). *another "Wessex" periodical*: see letters of 27 May and 3 July 22.

To LEONARD REES

MAX GATE, | DORCHESTER. | 24th. July 1922.
Dear Mr Rees:
I did not realize that the Sunday Times was so old. Unfortunately I collected into my late volume all the poems of any account that I had; and I have reached a stage of life when I cannot write a suitable thing off-hand, or indeed anything. So, though I will try to find a contribution for your centenary number, if I do not send one you will know how it arises, and that it is not intentional.

We read the paper every week, and are much edified. My wife sends kind regards.

> Sincerely yours,
> Thomas Hardy.

Leonard Rees Esq. | Sunday Times.

Text MS. (typewritten) Yale.
so old: Rees (20 July 22, DCM) asked TH for a poem to commemorate the 100th anniversary of the paper's founding, 20 Oct 1822. *a suitable thing*: TH's draft of this letter (DCM) reads, 'a

smart suitable thing'.   *not intentional*: TH did not, in fact, send a contribution; see letter of 15 Oct 22.

To DAISY GIFFORD

MAX GATE, | DORCHESTER. | 26 July: 1922

My dear Margaret:

I am glad to know that you liked the verses on dear Evelyn. I wrote them offhand, when I had heard you had lost her; but I did not think them so good as they ought to have been: so I did not tell anybody.

I hope you & Mrs Gifford are all the better for your sojourn in Switzerland. My wife sends her love, & I am

Ever yours sincerely
Thomas Hardy.

Text MS. Mrs. Sheila Mannion.
glad to know: from Miss Gifford's letter of 22 July 22 (DCM).   *dear Evelyn*: Miss Gifford's younger sister, Evelyn Hamilton Gifford, whose death TH had commemorated in his poem 'Evelyn G. of Christminster'.   *not tell anybody*: the poem was first pub. in *Late Lyrics* and Miss Gifford said that she and her mother had only just seen it.

To LADY GROVE

MAX GATE, | DORCHESTER. | 16 Aug. 1922

My dear Lady Grove:

I am sorry I am unable to be interviewed by the young woman. I have many such applications to obtain personal details, which are quite unnecessary for writing a "thesis", that should be based on published works alone of course. So that I am depriving her of nothing of value in the least.

Please excuse a short note, my eyes being very weak. My wife is writing to you. We have also heard from Dorothy.

Always yours
Thomas Hardy.

Text MS. Purdy.
Grove: Agnes Geraldine Grove, author, wife of Sir Walter John Grove, Bt.; see II.92.   *young woman*: Lady Grove's letter has not survived and the thesis-writer remains unknown.   *from Dorothy*: Dorothy Allhusen; she and Lady Grove were first cousins.

To DOROTHY ALLHUSEN

Dorchester | Tuesday [Late August 1922?]

My dear Dorothy:

I write a quick line to say I have received your letter & enclosures. I will see what can be done, but fear that in this neighbourhood it will not be a great deal.

We hope to see you at some time or other when you are coming this way. Affectionately to all

Yours ever
Th: Hardy.

Text MS. Purdy.

letter & enclosures: apparently the letter of 28 Aug 22 (DCM) with which Mrs. Allhusen, writing as a member of the Ladies Committee of the Southern Irish Loyalists' Relief Association, sent a duplicated appeal for accommodation to be given to Irish loyalist refugees from the newly created Irish Free State.

To JOHN BUCHAN

MAX GATE, DORCHESTER. | 8 Sept: 1922

Dear Mr John Buchan:

I must congratulate you on having tackled your big job at last—&, I need hardly say, thank you for Vol IV. of it. Altogether they make a goodly row & a valuable acquisition, which (beyond dipping into a few tempting pages) I am saving for the winter evenings now fast approaching.

With best wishes for the book & yourself believe me

Sincerely yours,
Thomas Hardy.

Text MS. NLS.

Vol IV. of it: i.e., of Buchan's *A History of the Great War*; see letter of 21 Nov 21 and letter to Buchan of 6 May 22.

To SIR FREDERICK MACMILLAN

Max Gate, | Dorchester. | September 13th. 1922.

Dear Sir Frederick Macmillan:

I have received the enclosed document (in quadruplicate) from the Harpers through Mr Slater, concerning the film rights in Tess of the d'Urbervilles, and though signing them is stated to be only a matter of form I have thought it necessary before doing so to ask you to refer to what you signed when the Metro Corporation bought the rights in 1919, so as to ascertain if these forms sent me are word for word the same as that. I also enclose the explanatory letters that have been sent with the forms.

The only clause that it occurs to me to question is the one conveying the right "to adapt and change the said work and the title thereof"—under which the Corporation would have power to distort or burlesque the novel, to the possible injury of the book here in England as elsewhere; though as a matter of fact I don't imagine they would do any such thing. What do you think? However, if the clause was in the agreement that you kindly executed for me there is, of course, no more to be said, and I will sign the forms.

I don't know why the Harpers should be so keen to learn when I have signed that they wish the information to be cabled. Nor why I should sign before "the American Consul". How am I to get at any such dignitary?

Sincerely yours,
Thomas Hardy.

P.S. If you have to print any more copies of "Late Lyrics" please let me know, and I will correct the few words I mentioned.

Text   MS. (typewritten) BL.
enclosed document: evidently a form of contract for the renewal of the film rights to *Tess*; see V.307–8.   *Metro Corporation*: the film of *Tess of the d'Urbervilles*, with Blanche Sweet as Tess, was produced by Metro-Goldwyn Pictures in 1924.   *in the agreement*: Macmillan (14 Sept 22, Macmillan letterbooks, BL) sent a copy of the original agreement to show that the adaptation clause had indeed been included.   *"the American Consul"*: Macmillan first advised TH to tell Slater that he could only sign the contract before an ordinary commissioner for oaths, but in a second letter of 14 Sept 22 (Macmillan letterbooks, BL) he reported that Slater had undertaken to get the document stamped by the American consul in London. *words I mentioned*: Macmillan, in his first letter of 14 Sept 22, agreed not to reprint *Late Lyrics* without giving TH an opportunity to make corrections.

To MARY WEBB

Sept 15. 1922

Dear Madam:
    I write for Mr Hardy to say that he will be pleased to accept the dedication of your novel.

Very truly yours

. . . .

Text   MS. (pencil draft) DCM.
Webb: Mary Gladys Webb, *née* Meredith (1881–1927), novelist; *D.N.B.*   *your novel*: Mrs. Webb (5 Sept 22, DCM), addressing TH as 'the greatest exponent of the wild human heart since Shakespeare', asked if she might dedicate to him her forthcoming novel, *Seven for a Secret: A Love Story* (London, 1922); the dedication reads, 'To the illustrious name / of / Thomas Hardy, / whose acceptance of this dedication / has made me so happy'. On 29 Nov 22 (DCM) she wrote again to say that she had sent a copy of the book and hoped TH would 'accept it as you would a child's stalkless daisy—valueless, but given with enthusiasm and sincerity'.

To SAMUEL CHEW

17 September 1922

Dear Mr Chew:
    I am enclosing herewith the notes for the new edition of your book as promised. Being but cursory, & not by any means thorough or careful, they are sent on the understanding that they are kept private as to their present shape, & that you do not mention anything about how you came by the details they give, or that you state them on authority: though of course you may embody the whole of them in the corrections of errors of fact in your volume, & they do not presume to attempt any interference with your judgments.
    Mr Hardy has looked them over, & says they are quite correct—indeed, they are based entirely on his own remarks. He also says that you will find the criticisms unceremonious, but that you do not want compliments in such a case.
    We hope you & Mrs Chew will have reached home & settled down comfortably by the time you get this, & that she has quite recovered.

Yours sincerely

Professor S. C. Chew | The College | Bryn Mawr | Pennsylvania | U.S.A.

Notes on Professor Chew's Book.
by F.E.H.

Page 1.   line 1. If exactitude were desired (which it may not be) the
              description would run: a rambling seven-roomed cottage with
              two gardens, horse-paddock, sand and gravel-pits, now filled
              up, and outbuildings now pulled down. The house and
              premises, of a little under two acres, were held on lives
              renewed from time to time, and were built and laid out by
              T.H's great-grandfather.
... ..   line 5. His father was a small master-builder and mason,
              employing about half a dozen workmen—sometimes several
              more. His condition, etc. had no resemblance to Smith's
              father's in "A Pair of Blue Eyes", this being the invention of
              journalists.
... ..   line 16. for "great estate" read "landed estate".
... ..   (bottom) "*mediocre* instruction", etc. Well; it included Latin
              and French, geometry, and algebra.
Page 6.   for "Hardy entered the office" read "became premiumed
              pupil".
... 7   "like Stephen Smith" is superfluous
... 8   "Self-portraiture" . . . . . "yearning for academic distinction",
              etc. It must be said that this is quite inaccurate. There would
              have been no insuperable difficulty in his going to Cambridge,
              and the question was discussed, and particulars obtained from
              one of the colleges. But it was thought unnecessary for an
              architect.
· · · · · · · "The tragedy of Jude Fawley", etc. A suggestion without
              foundation. Jude was a working-man, not at all in Hardy's
              position of a young man with a profession. There is not a word
              of autobiography in "Jude the Obscure".
· · · · · · · "The character of Knight", etc. (further down). Quite
              inaccurate. Knight was an absolute invention. Stephen Smith
              was drawn from an architect's pupil 8 or 9 years younger than
              T.H. "A Pair of Blue Eyes" is only autobiographical in respect
              of some of the external accessories at the beginning, and after
              the first 2 or 3 chapters there is not a word of real experience
              even in the accessories. It is only in the character and
              temperament of the heroine that there is some resemblance to
              a real person.
Page 25.   "The feeble London portions of "A Pair of Blue Eyes" . . . .
              and weakness of the attempts to portray that world in "The
              Hand of Ethelberta", etc. It is amusing to confront this (very
              frequent) assertion of reviewers with the facts. The London
              portions of the former book were all studied on the spot.
              Rotten Row, the Park Drive, etc. being frequented by T.H.

hundreds of times for years during the height of the season; and in respect of "Ethelberta," a well-known society Countess obtained an introduction to the author solely because this novel was the only one she had met with "which showed people exactly as they were". The plot called "impossible" by many, was used 30 years after in a play with great success and no sense of improbability.

..... 17–23   In dwelling on Hardy's view of the world, the grave, etc., it is curious that a certain kinship to Donne is not noted.

Page 26.   for "in May 1869" read "the latter part of 1868".

.... .   for "It is still in existence", read "And the manuscript was ultimately lost."

..... 33.   "Her (George Eliot's) success in delineating the peasantry of Warwickshire suggested to Hardy", etc. to bottom of page. It was Shakespeare's delineation of his Warwickshire clowns (who much resemble the Wessex peasantry) that influenced Hardy most. He found no clowns i.e. farm-labourers or rustics, anywhere in G. Eliot's books, and considered her country characters more like small townspeople than peasantry. And he had never read "Lorna Doone". Nobody "guided him into Wessex". He had always been there.

.... 42   "The courting of Elfride by Stephen . . . indubitably drawn from the writer's own experiences". etc. Not at all—it is invented. Stephen, though furbished up with a few external and travelling details, landscapes, etc., that were like some in the experience of the writer, had an imagined courtship quite fictitious. And Cornwall, familiar to Stephen, had never been visited by T.H. till he paid a professional visit. As to the heroine, there are in her, as above stated, some resemblances in appearance and manner to Miss G., but Elfride's experiences were fabulous, T.H's engagement to Miss G. being of the most uneventful kind, and her whole life likewise.

.... 44   "He moved from Weymouth" etc. should run "He moved from Weymouth to Sturminster-Newton, thence to London, where he lived for several years; later he removed to Wimborne, and finally in 1885 to the outskirts of Dorchester, but taking a house or flat in London for many months each year during about 25 years."

..... 45   "Supposed drowning of Troy", etc. This is inaccurate. He is not really supposed drowned by the chief actors in the story, and such belief is not necessary to the plot. It was introduced to illustrate Troy's character. G. Moore's "Confessions" originated the untruth.

..... 47   The scene in the church-vault, whatever it may resemble, was drawn from one witnessed by T.H. when he was a boy of 15.

.... 52   "Lords and ladies quite wooden". *vide* note to p. 25.

.... 73   "The setting reminds one of the opening of Conrad's", etc. It

should be *vice versâ*, "The Distracted Preacher" having been
written thirty years before the other.

.... 76   "Hardy borrows the theme", etc. If this means that the
incident of not attempting to save a drowning person is
borrowed from "D. Deronda" it is an error: kindred incidents
are common to hundreds of novels.

.... 95   This page appears to mean that all a writer's books bear some
resemblance to each other. Is such a commonplace fact worth
stating?

... 97   "Attacks on marriage" etc. By the characters more frequently
than by the author, it should be added. Hardy had, in fact,
little more than an academic opposition to the institution in
itself, rendered necessary *pro tem.* to carry out the scheme of
the story: though he has always had, of course, objection to
the permanency of distinctly bad and cruel unions.

Page 98.   "We are a little", etc. The remark of a character, not of the
author as the critic implies.

.... 100   Top of page. Amusing exaggeration.

.... 103   "turned to poetry" should be "turned back to poetry".

..... 104   line 5. for 1904 read 1903.

....   The list of volumes would now be lengthened.

.... 106   after "summaries of plots of novels" in M. Hedgcock's book,
should be mentioned a still worse fault, viz, errors of
attribution, in efforts to discern realities under fictional
scenes, and so making biographical facts out of pure
inventions.

.... 107   line 7 for "December 1912" read "November 1912"

..... 139   "Reade and Collins". This as to his dialogues is news to T.H.
And, if anybody, it should be surely Dumas père?

.... 141   "He follows the Brontés" etc. Surely, if anybody, Fielding
(whose scenes and characters are Dorset and Somerset), and
Scott? T.H. has never to this day read one of the Bronté
books except Jane Eyre, he is ashamed to say.

..... 176   "It is the writer who speaks here", etc. The writer certainly
jests there: but has no consciousness of ever holding any such
opinions. This is a typical error of criticism.

.... 191.   The Poems. The criticisms rise to a higher level from this
point, and would bear lengthening.

... 192.   line 3 from bottom. for 1904 read 1903.

... 193   Alter "latest volume."

Pages 226   Hardy unfortunately had not read G. Meredith's
and 232.   "Ode" when he wrote "The Dynasts".

.... 255.   *dele* that the MS. of the first novel is in existence.

Generally—a disproportionate analysis of the novels by comparison with the
poetry, the latter being the work of more years than the former; (novels about

27 years; poetry between 28 and 29). This disposes of the cuckoo-cry that T.H. being new to poetry expresses himself clumsily in verse, his verse good or bad being, as his long practice would suggest, and the best critics acknowledge, more finished than his prose, except where intentionally rough-hewn.

Text MS. (pencil draft) DCM; 'Notes' (typescript) Adams.
Chew: Samuel Claggett Chew, American professor and critic; see V.251. *your book*: Chew had presented TH with a copy of the original edn. of his *Thomas Hardy: Poet and Novelist* (Bryn Mawr, 1921) about a year previously; the revised and expanded edn., incorporating many of the changes here suggested, was pub. in New York in 1928. TH has written in the left-hand margin of this draft, alongside the opening paragraph, 'Professor Chew—"Study" of T.H.' *on his own remarks*: as is made clear by TH's marginal annotations to the first edn. of Chew's book (DCM) and by his extensive holograph additions to the 'Notes' here printed in the form of a postscript. *Notes ... Book*: i.e., the first edn. The top copy of the typescript in the Adams collection accompanies the 17 Sept 22 letter as sent out over FEH's signature; a carbon typescript is in DCM. *the description*: of TH's birthplace. *"landed estate"*: as a description of the social position from which the Hardy family had descended. *premiumed pupil"*: of John Hicks; see letter of 12 June 20 to J. G. Hicks. *"Self-portraiture"*: seen by Chew in the characters of Clym Yeobright, Angel Clare, and Jude Fawley. *Knight"*: in *A Pair of Blue Eyes*, described by Chew as 'the most autobiographical of all the novels'. *architect's pupil*: see letter of 19 Dec 21 to Mrs. Henniker. *society Countess*: Lady Portsmouth; see I.128. *in a play*: Shaw's *You Never Can Tell*. *latter part of 1868"*: date of submission of *The Poor Man and the Lady*. *ultimately lost."*: i.e., the MS. of *The Poor Man*. *"Lorna Doone"*: by R. D. Blackmore; see I.37-8. *Miss G.*: Emma Lavinia Gifford, TH's first wife (ELH). *T.H's engagement ... likewise*: one of the passages added in TH's hand. *the untruth*: an apparent reference to pp. 269–70 of George Moore, *Confessions of a Young Man* (London, 1888); Moore, however, while criticizing the ending of *Far from the Madding Crowd* for not coming 'within the range of literary criticism', says of Troy only that 'he went down to bathe and was carried out by the current'. For Moore see letter of 28 Mar 24. *in the church-vault*: in *A Pair of Blue Eyes* (Wessex edn.), 278–87. *before the other*: i.e., Conrad's and Ford Madox Hueffer's *Romance*. *drowning person*: Chew was commenting on TH's 'A Tragedy of Two Ambitions'. *"D. Deronda"*: George Eliot's novel *Daniel Deronda*, pub. in 1876. *worth stating?*: Chew had asserted that, in *Jude*, 'A certain stiffening of the imagination is apparent in the repetition of situations from the earlier novels'. *Amusing exaggeration*: Chew found in *Jude* a prevailing 'miasma of despair'. *read 1903*: as date of pub. of *The Dynasts*, Part First. *list of volumes*: in the Wessex edn. *"November 1912"*: as ELH's date of death. *as to his dialogues*: Chew attributed to the influence of the novelists Charles Reade (1814–84; *D.N.B.*) and Wilkie Collins (1824–89; *D.N.B.*) what he saw as the excessive use of dialogue in *A Pair of Blue Eyes*. *Dumas père*: see *EL*, 31. *such opinions*: the reference is to a passage from 'A Tragedy of Two Ambitions' in which one of the brothers speaks of the routes to success within the Church of England. *G. Meredith's "Ode"*: George Meredith's 'Odes in Contribution to the Song of French History', said by Chew to have influenced TH's presentation of Napoleon. *except ... rough-hewn.*: added in TH's hand.

To A. V. HOUGHTON

Sept. 18. 1922.

Dear Sir
    Mr Thomas Hardy encloses cheque for £1=5=0 in accordance with your information this morning that the amount is owing, which is much to his surprise & regret, as he can never before have been informed of it; for

whenever a notice for the year's subscription has reached him he has paid. Please send notice every year in future.

Yours truly
for T. Hardy
F.E.

Text   MS. (pencil draft) DCM.
Houghton: Arthur Villiers Houghton, secretary for twenty-six years of the English Association, founded in 1906 'to foster and develop the study of English as an essential element in our national education' (*The Times*, 27 Apr 1906); see Arundell Esdaile, 'A Half-Century of the English Association', *Essays and Studies, 1956*.

To SIR FREDERICK MACMILLAN

MAX GATE, DORCHESTER. | 18 Sept. 1922.

My dear Macmillan:
Many thanks for letting me know how matters stood in respect of the movies, for I was in doubt if the Company had or had not inserted new conditions. I return herewith the form you signed.

Sincerely yours
Thomas Hardy.

Text   MS. BL.
in respect of the movies: see letter of 13 Sept 22.

To LOUIS UNTERMEYER

MAX GATE, DORCHESTER. | 23rd. September 1922.

Dear Mr Untermeyer:
By chance I have taken up your volume of "Modern British Poetry" published two years ago, of which you kindly sent me a copy, and have been looking into it. It reminds me that I probably did not thank you for it at the time, so I do so now; if I did, there is no harm in my doing it again.

Yours very truly,
Thomas Hardy.

Text   MS. (typewritten) Indiana Univ.
Untermeyer: Louis Untermeyer (1885–1977), American author and editor.   *your volume*: Untermeyer's anthology *Modern British Poetry* (New York, 1920); he subsequently sent TH a copy of the enlarged edn. of 1925 (see letter to Untermeyer of 8 July 25).

To STANLEY GALPIN

MAX GATE, | DORCHESTER. | 25th September, 1922.

Dear Mr. Galpin,
I should much like to oblige you by agreeing to your request to express my opinion of Charles Dickens's writings. But apart from the fact that I am a bad estimator of novels, it is almost impossible for me to criticize Dickens without, on the one hand, being considered invidious if I am as frank on his faults as on his genius; and, on the other hand, being considered to express

eulogistic commonplace if I am discriminating, so I will ask you to excuse me from saying anything, and leave it to those of your friends who stand in a more independent position, and are much better able to estimate him, or to yourself.

Yours very truly,
Th. Hardy.

Text *Society of Dorset Men in London: Year-book, 1928*, 9.
Galpin: Stanley Ingram Galpin (see IV.179), a founding member of the Society of Dorset Men in London.   *Charles Dickens's writings*: Galpin (21 Sept 22, DCM) explained that he would shortly be presiding at a dinner of the City of London Pickwick Club and wished to be able to cite TH's opinions, as 'the greatest living novelist', on Dickens and his work.   *discriminating*: the DCM draft of this letter, in FEH's hand and probably taken down from TH's dictation, reads 'indiscriminating', clearly the word intended.

To DOROTHY ALLHUSEN

Max Gate. | 27 Sept. 1922.

My dear Dorothy:
    I am sending you a pretty joyous old tune they used to sing a hundred years ago in this county, set to cheerful words that *might* suit a wedding service. The tune at any rate would suit, though professional musicians would of course smile at the old-fashioned nature of the melody. But that is what you want & expect them to do, I imagine. The words are merely those of Psalm 106, which is now scarcely ever used in churches in its metrical form—nobody knows why. Other words might perhaps be found for the tune, though I don't see that these I send are at all ill-suited to a wedding.
    Anyhow, if what I enclose does not please, throw it aside without compunction.
    I hope everything will go well, & am ever

Yours affectly
Th: Hardy.

Text MS. Mrs. Richard Tyler.
joyous old tune: 'Wilton'; still accompanying this letter are the music—annotated by TH, 'An old fashioned tune, suited to feasts and bridals'—and the words for the first five verses of the Tate and Brady version of Psalm 106.   *wedding service*: Mrs. Allhusen (23 Sept 22, DCM) wrote to seek TH's advice in choosing hymns for her daughter's wedding (see letter to her of 19 July 22); *The Times* report of the service (16 Oct 1922) mentions that the hymn, 'chosen for the occasion by Mr. Thomas Hardy', was sung during the signing of the register.

To JANE POPHAM

6 October 1922

Dear Mrs Popham:
    (I am obliged on account of age to get my letters typewritten whenever I can, which please excuse.)
    I remember your sister Mrs Reeve very well, & how faithful she was to Dorsetshire. My letter to her that you mention may have been concerning either The Trumpet Major, or The Mayor of Casterbridge, both of which were

written shortly before that date; but I have no recollection which. Of the T.M. I remember her telling me that your father when a boy of nine saw the soldiers ride down to the spring at Sutton Poyntz just as I describe in the opening of the story.

The letter from Berlin I return, since you ought to keep it for family reasons. Your sending it singularly coincides with the arrival of one from a friend of ours who is one of the Commission of Control in Berlin in which he speaks of the militarism there now as your father did more than 100 years ago.

Your being so sadly interested in the dead past of your sister, now that such interest can avail nothing, is, of course, the experience of most of us, & the penalty we pay for not dying early. This month I have published in the London Mercury the poem of a long-deceased friend of mine who wrote it exactly 60 years ago, to whom it would have been a keen pleasure to know what he is sublimely ignorant of—that his verses had been preserved to be read to-day.

Many thanks, I am as well as 82 can hope to be. My wife wonders if you ever come to Dorchester, & could call.

Sincerely yours

Text MS. (pencil draft) DCM.   *Date* It appears from a transcript (DCM) that the final version of the letter was not sent until 9 October.
Popham: Jane (Jeanne) Susanna Popham, of Bournemouth; see V.1.   *Mrs Reeve*: Christina Reeve, wife of Henry Reeve, editor of the *Edinburgh Review*; see I.149. In her letter of 4 Oct 22 (DCM) Mrs. Popham referred to the experience of reading through her sister's (actually her half-sister's) papers.   *My letter to her*: evidently that of 28 June 86 (I.148–9), referring to *The Mayor of Casterbridge*; *The Trumpet-Major* was pub. six years previously.   *your father*: George Tilley Gollop of Netherbury, Dorset; see I.189 and V.1.   *letter from Berlin*: written by George Gollop in 1815, partly quoted in TH's letter of 12 Oct 22; it is now in DCM.   *friend of ours*: J. H. Morgan; see letter of 12 Oct 22.   *friend of mine*: Horace Moule; see letter of 22 Mar 22.

To JOHN DRINKWATER

MAX GATE, DORCHESTER. | 10th. October 1922.

Dear Mr John Drinkwater:

I have pleasure in letting you use "An Ancient to Ancients" in the volume of poetry you tell me of. You need not trouble yourself to write to the publishers, as I have an understanding with them on the point. But they advise me to charge a small fee for such permissions, to cover a conceivable loss on the original edition thereby, which I accordingly do—the sum of two guineas.

We have seen "Mary Stuart"—in the picture papers only!

Yours always truly,
T. Hardy.

Text MS. (typewritten) Yale.
Drinkwater: John Drinkwater, poet and playwright; see IV.34.   *volume of poetry*: Drinkwater's *An Anthology of English Verse* (London, 1924); it includes TH's 'An Ancient to Ancients'.   *in the picture papers*: the *Sphere* of 7 Oct 1922 carried three pages of photographs

of the current production of Drinkwater's play *Mary Stuart* at the Everyman Theatre, Hampstead.

To J. H. MORGAN

MAX GATE, | DORCHESTER. | 12 Oct. 1922

Dear General Morgan:

I had already begun a reply to your interesting letter from Berlin, which opened up so many points that had engaged me 20 years ago, but had rather faded in my memory. Now that you are at home I will write it in a more succinct form, for it is not likely that amid the many details you have to attend to after your absence you will want to think much about Napoleonic times.

I cannot for my life recall where I obtained the idea of N's entry into Berlin by the Potsdamer-Strasse, though I don't think I should have written it without authority. However, you have to remember that the events generally in The Dynasts had to be pulled together into dramatic scenes, to show themselves to the mental eye of the reader as a picture viewed from one point; & hence it was sometimes necessary to see round corners, down crooked streets, & to shift buildings nearer each other than in reality (as Turner did in his landscapes); & it may possibly happen that I gave "A Public Place" in Berlin these convenient facilities without much ceremony.

You allude to Leipzig. That battle bothered me much more than Jena or Ulm (to which you also allude)—in fact more than any other battle I had to handle. I defy any human being to synchronize with any certainty its episodes from descriptions by the historians. My time-table was, I believe, as probable a one as can be drawn up at this date. But I will go no further with these stale conjectures, now you are in London.

I have quite recently been reading a yellow old letter written from Berlin in June, 1815 by a Dorset man whose daughter is a friend of ours, & who lately sent it to me. The writer says what is oddly in keeping with your remarks on the arrogance of Prussian officers.—"Buonapare has rendered Germany completely military; at the inns & post-houses a private Gentleman exacts not half the respect exacted by a soldier. This contempt for those who wear no swords displays itself in no very pleasant shape to travellers. About 3 weeks ago I might have died of damp sheets if my German servant had not taken upon him to assure a brute of a Post-master that I was an English General travelling for my health. . . . I have since girded on a sabre, got a military cap, & let my moustache grow: soldiers now present arms as we pass."

It would be strange to find that Napoleon was really the prime cause of German militarism! What a Nemesis for the French nation!

Well, I have gone back to Boney again after all: but no more of him. I hope you find the change to London agreeable, & keep well in your vicissitudes.

Sincerely yours
Thomas Hardy.

Text MS. Berg.
20 years ago: i.e., when he was writing *The Dynasts*.   *by the Potsdamer-Strasse*: in *The*

Dynasts, Part Second, Act I, Scene 6; see also the directions at the beginning of Act I, Scene 5. *Leipzig*: see *The Dynasts*, Part Third, Act III, Scenes 1–5.   *lately sent it to me*: see letter of 6 Oct 22.   *Buonapare*: TH means 'Buonaparte'.   *Thomas Hardy*: at the end of the typed transcript of this letter in DCM TH has written, '[May be included in Materials]'; see *LY*, 228–9.

To LEONARD REES

MAX GATE, DORCHESTER. | 15 Oct. 1922

Dear Mr Rees:

Please let me off. I am so bad at such things, & have been too much in print lately!

We hope you will drop in upon us as you did, in that pleasant way—say next summer.

Yours sincerely
Thomas Hardy.

Text   MS. Yale.
let me off: Rees (13 Oct 22, DCM) had repeated (see letter of 24 July 22) his request for a poem on the occasion of the centenary of the *Sunday Times*.

To LADY GROVE

MAX GATE, | DORCHESTER. | 20 Oct. 1922

My dear Lady Grove:

I am glad to hear that you like the Poems, which after all are a very mixed lot, though the reviewers have been civil enough about them. As to the "Apology", one never can tell beforehand how a writer's meaning may be misapprehended, & I find some people gather from it that I have become strictly orthodox (rather funny, this!) when I thought my meaning to be clear enough that some form of Established ritual & discipline should be maintained in the interests of morality, without entering into the very large question of what that form should be: I should say offhand that it might be some ethical service based on the old liturgy.

Yes: the Romanists had a fine chance, but let it slip: & I fear the English Church may do the same if it doesn't mind. The mediaevalists are the danger: if they succeed in harking back to transubstantiation, plenary inspiration, etc. the Church becomes a sect, & all is undone. I don't know whether you are old enough to have known a friend of mine now long dead—St George Mivart—He was one of the new Catholics; but was extinguished.

Amusing things happen if you write poems: a critic—an old friend of mine by the way, who has grown cantankerous of late—Maurice Hewlett, said that "The Wood Fire" was "revolting": almost at the same time that a quite old fashioned rector near here told me he was interested in it because it was "probably what happened"—seeing nothing shocking in it at all, & thinking it the view of a sturdy Protestant that would tend to counteract any belief in fragments of the "true Cross."

I wonder if you went up to the wedding of Dorothy's daughter: Florence did, but I did not, & she saw all sorts of people there she knew.

Ever affectionately

Thomas Hardy.

Text MS. (with envelope) Purdy.
the Poems: *Late Lyrics and Earlier.*   *a fine chance*: from the reference to Mivart later in the paragraph it appears that TH was assenting to the view that the Roman Catholic Church had begun to move towards a more liberal theology but then reversed itself. TH is reported as making a similar comment in his interview with Frédéric Lefèvre, *Nouvelles Littéraires*, 21 Feb 1925.   *Mivart*: St. George Jackson Mivart (1827–1900), biologist; *D.N.B.*   *extinguished*: Mivart was excommunicated, shortly before his death, for his public repudiation of ecclesiastical authority.   *Hewlett*: Maurice Henry Hewlett, novelist and poet; see II.291. In his review of *Late Lyrics* in *The Times*, 8 June 1922, he spoke of being 'fairly revolted' by some of TH's poems and said that 'The Woodfire' would 'offend many, and gratuitously . . . I think that you shall as well scoff at a man's mother as at his religion'.   *old fashioned rector*: possibly the Revd. George Cecil Niven, rector of St. Peter's, Dorchester; see letter of 5 Oct 24.   *the wedding*: see letter of 27 Sept 22.

To JOHN LANGDON-DAVIES

25 Oct 1922

My dear Sir:
   I have received your letter informing Mr Hardy & myself that Tess of the d'Urbervilles is about to be filmed in England. This, of course, will be a great advantage to the pictures, the former film, being American made, having failed to carry conviction over here.
   Mr Hardy says that he will give any hints he can, but that you will not find much difficulty in locating the scenes, most of them lying within a few miles of this house, so that we could direct you to the points. A guide-book to them will, however, save you time, & the most accurate one is "Thomas Hardy's Wessex" by Mr Hermann Lea (Macmillan).
   He does not quite like the idea of being photographed moving about the garden or house, but he will have no objection to an ordinary fixed photograph.
   The Messrs Macmillan act as Mr Hardy's agents in respect of films, & would give any information of a business nature that may be required, but as to characters, places, &c, it can, as I have said, be had here.

Yours very truly

F. E. Hardy

John L. Davies Esq. | Goldwyn Pictures, Limited.

Text MS. (pencil draft) DCM.
Langdon-Davies: John Langdon-Davies (1897–1971), anthropologist and author, then working in the promotion department of the London office of Goldwyn Pictures.   *your letter*: to FEH, of 23 Oct 22 (DCM).   *the former film*: starring Minnie Madern Fiske; see IV.265. *by Mr Hermann Lea*: pub. 1913; see letter of 22 Mar 21.

To SIR FREDERICK MACMILLAN

MAX GATE, | DORCHESTER. | 28th. October 1922.

Dear Sir Frederick Macmillan:

I am delighted to hear that you are going to print a new edition of the Collected Poems, to include Late Lyrics; and also a thin paper edition. People have told me that they would not mind paying a little more for the latter. (I hope the paper will not be so thin as to make it difficult to turn over the leaves, as with Browning's verse).

There are no new poems to include, as I am obliged to keep the few I have by me for periodicals. But I send by separate post a copy of the Collected Poems as they stand, marked with the corrections that have been made from time to time. Most of these are old ones, and I believe are already embodied in the type; but at any rate if the printers go through the pages before going to press, and make them correspond, there will be no mistake.

For the Late Lyrics now to be added to the volume I enclose the list of changed words I mentioned as having ready, that the printers may mark them on their copy before beginning. But I think I had better read the proofs of this additional part all the same, since in all human probability I shall never do so again.

Yours very truly,
Thomas Hardy.

P.S. Having cut up the only copy of Collected Poems that I had by me I have none for reference. If you can send me one so much the better, but this is not important. T.H.

Text MS. (typewritten) BL.
to hear: from Macmillan's letter of 26 Oct 22 (Macmillan letterbooks, BL).   *include Late Lyrics*: this expanded edn. appeared in 1923.   *thin paper edition*: first pub. 1923. *Browning's verse*: TH apparently has in mind *The Poetical Works of Robert Browning* (8 vols., London, 1906); see IV.4.   *list of changed words*: see postscript to letter of 13 Sept 22. Macmillan acknowledged receipt of this list and of the corrections to *Collected Poems* 30 Oct 22 (DCM).

To SIR FREDERICK MACMILLAN

MAX GATE, DORCHESTER. | 30th. October 1922.

Dear Sir Frederick:

I have just received the cable message I enclose, and imagine that the answer should be that neither Tess of the d'Urbervilles, nor the Mayor of Casterbridge, is available for motion pictures, but that any other novel is available if required (I am not sure what has happened to Far from the Madding Crowd by the way). As you may know something of the company that inquires, which I do not, I have thought it best to send you the telegram to treat as you think advisable. I do not know why they should be so impatient.

A troop of people are down here just now getting up the scenes for the Tess films.

Yours sincerely,
T. Hardy.

Text   MS. (typewritten) BL.
cable message: from the International Story Company of New York; see below.   *of Casterbridge*: Macmillan (1 Nov 22, Macmillan letterbooks, BL) confirmed that the rights to the *Mayor* were already held by the Progress Film Company (London) Ltd.; see letter of 19 Feb 21. *Madding Crowd*: see letter of 9 Oct 20.   *so impatient*: Macmillan offered to write on TH's behalf, but TH himself wrote, 1 Nov 22, suggesting 'The Distracted Preacher' and 'The Romantic Adventures of a Milkmaid' as especially suitable for filming. The letter, addressed simply to 'The Secretary, International Story Company, New York', was returned from the Dead Letter Office and is now in DCM.   *Tess films*: see letter of 25 Oct 22.

To JOHN DRINKWATER

Max Gate: 2: 11: 22

Dear Mr Drinkwater:
     I have received the little book. Many thanks. In spite of your suggestion I shall be sure to read it shortly.

Sincerely yrs
T.H.

Text   MS. (correspondence card) Yale.
little book: presumably Drinkwater's *Preludes 1921–1922* (London, 1922).

To ROBERT BRIDGES

FROM TH. HARDY, | MAX GATE, | DORCHESTER. | 4 Nov. 1922

Have read your article in this month's *Mercury*, & found it *excellent*. I hope it will tend to save our young poets from the woeful fogs of free verse worship.

Always yrs
T.H.

Text   MS. (correspondence card) Lord Bridges.
your article: Bridges' 'Humdrum and Harum-Scarum: A Paper on Free Verse', *London Mercury*, November 1922, seeks to show that free verse involves the renunciation of the 'advantages of the metrical system, the value of which is so great that it is difficult to believe that they can have been duly appreciated by the men who would cast them contemptuously away' (59).

To ROSALINE MASSON

FROM TH. HARDY, | MAX GATE, | DORCHESTER. | 10 Nov. 1922

Many thanks for the copy of the R.L.S. book, which I shall read with interest.

T.H.

Text   MS. (correspondence card) Yale.
Masson: Rosaline Masson (d. 1949), author and historian, daughter of David Masson

(1822–1907; *D.N.B.*), the Scottish biographer and editor.   *R.L.S. book: I Can Remember Robert Louis Stevenson*, ed. R. Masson (Edinburgh, 1922), includes a short contribution by TH; the copy sent by Miss Masson, with an inscription dated 4 Nov 1922, is in DCM.

To LUCY CLIFFORD

11 November. 1922

Dear Mrs Clifford:

Alas, you are asking me to do what is mentally—& almost physically— impossible to a person of 82. It would be, in fact, beyond my powers even if I were familiar with your once much discussed book; but I am ashamed to confess that I have never read it! What you heard must have been the version of the circumstance that Lord Houghton was enthusiastic about the novel, & that I was going to read it immediately. I remember the Jeunes' dinner-party when he was eulogizing it all round. I had never heard of it till then, & my intention was to get it at once. But we know where there is a pavement of good intentions.

It is as much as I can do nowadays to find energy to put out a small poem once in a while, & I have to get the greater part of my correspondence done by another. Thus to read the story critically now for the first time would be beyond me.

So you will see that it is not a question of willingness or otherwise, but of practicability, & not one of the many requests for the same kind of thing that I get have I declined with such regret. Your publisher is probably right in saying that a preface would help a new edition, but I think he is in error in supposing that it being by myself is of any importance, as I have been outside the world of novels for more than 25 years, & know nothing of present movements in it. One of the young advanced novelists would be the man for you.

Thank you much for kind inquiries. We have been fairly well, though with slight colds. The history of the adventures of your first book, & the Browning incident, is most interesting. In my own similar case I lost all my labour & £15 in money!

With our kind love & good wishes.

Yours very sincerely

The book & reviews shall follow in a day or two. My wife is reading the former. T.H.

Text MS. (pencil draft) DCM.
Clifford: Lucy Clifford, novelist, usually known as Mrs. W. K. Clifford; see II.109.   *you are asking me*: in her letter of 8 Nov 22 (DCM) Mrs. Clifford asked TH to write a preface for a proposed reissue of her anonymously pub. first novel, *Mrs. Keith's Crime* (2 vols., London, 1885).   *What you heard*: Mrs. Clifford recalled hearing that both TH and Lord Houghton (see I.118) had praised the novel while dining with Francis and Mary Jeune (later Lord and Lady St. Helier; see letter of 28 Jan 23).   *Your publisher . . . importance*: according to Mrs. Clifford, her prospective publisher, Gerald Duckworth, had said that only TH's name would be 'big enough' to ensure commercial success; another publisher, Eveleigh Nash & Grayson, in fact brought out 'a new and revised edition' of the book, without a preface, in 1925.   *the Browning incident*: Mrs. Clifford recalled Robert Browning's congratulating her, warmly and publicly, on

having written a 'splendid' book that he wished he had written himself.   *my own similar case*: for the fate of TH's first pub. novel, *Desperate Remedies*, see Purdy, 4–5.   *The book &* *reviews*: Mrs. Clifford sent a copy of the Tauchnitz edn. of *Mrs. Keith's Crime* and two early reviews but asked for them to be returned.

To SIR FREDERICK MACMILLAN

MAX GATE, | DORCHESTER. | 12th. November 1922.

Dear Sir Frederick:

I return your correspondent's letter. The word "Patagonians" in Chapter 23 of The Trumpet Major is not a misprint. If he will consult any English Dictionary he will learn the meaning of the word, and by looking into a Biographical Dictionary for "Frederick William the First" he will see the applicability of the epithet to the tall soldier of the story.

I enclose a letter from Messrs Harpers' London manager for you to look over, as I have not the slightest idea about it, which seems a trade matter. I should personally, I think, prefer to have the sheets pulped rather than "remaindered", but I don't know.

Sincerely yours,
Thomas Hardy.

Text MS. (typewritten) BL.
your correspondent's: Macmillan (9 Nov 22, DCM) referred simply to 'our correspondent from Peckham Rye' (in S.E. London).   *"Patagonians"*: in *The Trumpet-Major* (Wessex edn.), 196, Festus Derriman is described as 'a man who would have been a match for one of Frederick William's Patagonians'. The Patagonians were once believed to be the tallest people in the world; hence, 'a giant, a gigantic specimen' (*O.E.D.*).   *"Frederick William the First"*: King of Prussia (1688–1740), whose Potsdam guard was composed of tall men recruited from all over Europe. *trade matter*: Macmillan (14 Nov 22, DCM) returned F. W. Slater's (see letter of 11 July 22) letter and agreed with TH that unsold copies of *A Changed Man* would be better pulped than sold at a very low price for a negligible royalty.

To THE REVD. E. M. WALKER

MAX GATE, | DORCHESTER. | 14 Nov. 1922

My dear Sir:

It is with genuine pleasure that I learn from your letter of the distinction with which Queen's College has determined to mark me; & I need hardly say that, old as I am, I readily accept.

The only sort of hesitation I have had has been on this score of age, which prevents my doing anything whatever in recognition of my election, however much I might be prompted by my feelings to show some small sense of it in the way of visits, or what not, from time to time, with respect not only to its living members but its historic associations. I fear, indeed that I cannot even get to Oxford in this winter weather (though that I may be able to do so next summer is of course a possibility as it is certainly a hope); & I am not sure that attendance is not expected at the formal election; which is what has caused me the hesitation I mention. Of this you will kindly let me know, & if it can be dispensed with or postponed.

Believe me to be

Yours most truly
Thomas Hardy.

Revd E. M. Walker LL.D.

Text MS. Queen's College, Oxford.
Walker: the Revd. Edward Mewburn Walker (1857–1941), classical scholar and chaplain to the King, currently Pro-Provost, later Provost, of Queen's College, Oxford.   *your letter*: of 10 Nov 22 (DCM).   *the distinction*: election to an honorary fellowship.   *next summer*: for an account of TH's first, and only, visit to Queen's College, in June 1923, see *LY*, 231–4.

To ALFRED POPE

MAX GATE, | DORCHESTER. | 19 Nov: 1922
Dear Mr Pope:

I have as yet learnt no particulars of the fire, & possibly it may not affect you much practically since your retirement from the firm, but in any case it must be a worry to you, & I send this line of sympathy from my wife & myself.

Yours sincerely
T. Hardy.

Text MS. (with envelope) Thomas Hardy Society.
the fire: a fire on 18 Nov 1922 resulted (according to the *Dorchester County Chronicle*, 23 Nov 1922) in the virtual destruction of the Dorchester Brewery of Eldridge, Pope, and Co.

To SIR FREDERICK MACMILLAN

Private.

MAX GATE, | DORCHESTER. | 22 Nov: 1922
My dear Macmillan:

Have you, in your large experience of authors, any idea of the general practice of that irritable genus in respect of autographing books for strangers? I am pestered by large parcels of my own volumes from unknown people for this purpose. For instance I have just received a package of half a dozen from Lady Sackville, a total stranger (Christian name Victoria—I fancy I recall a law-suit in connection with her) & she intends to send them *all* by degrees (!), the request being that I write in each "To Lady Sackville—Thomas Hardy", as if she were a dear friend.

In these cases the alternatives are to throw them into a cupboard & take no notice (which brings a pelting of letters of inquiry), to send them back unsigned, or to say that I will sign them (with autograph only; I could not say they are from me, as I did not present them) for a fee of a guinea, or half a guinea, each to be given to our County Hospital here, of which I am a governor, or to some other charity I choose. I have adopted each plan at various times; but as these parcels increase I have to reconsider methods, which is why I write.

There is an amusing side to it all, of course; & don't trouble to answer till you are inclined to.

Sincerely yours
Thomas Hardy.

Text MS. BL.
Sackville: see letter of 25 Nov 22.   *a law-suit*: Lady Sackville was the central figure in two famous cases. The first was in 1910, when one of her brothers failed in an attempt to establish his legitimacy and so claim the title, but TH is presumably remembering the second, in 1913, when she successfully defended her right to receive a considerable fortune together with valuable furniture and pictures under the will of Sir John Murray Scott. See Susan Mary Alsop, *Lady Sackville: A Biography* (London, 1978), 135–8, 155–82.   *the request being*: it was made in Lady Sackville's letter of 18 Nov 22 (DCM).   *till you are inclined to*: Macmillan replied at once (23 Nov 22, DCM), approving the idea of charging a guinea in support of County Hospital funds; see letter of 25 Nov 22.

To GEORGE MACMILLAN

MAX GATE, | DORCHESTER | 24 Nov. 1922

Dear Mr Macmillan:
I have no objection at all to your inserting the circular of Wilfrid Gibson's poems in the Collected volume of mine, & in the one or two others that suggest themselves to your judgment, which is better than mine on the point.
I hope you keep well in this foggy weather, & am

Always yours sincerely
Thomas Hardy.

I send back the copy, as it has corrections marked. T.H.

Text MS. BL.
Gibson's poems: Macmillan (23 Nov 22, DCM) asked permission to insert into copies of TH's *Collected Poems* (see letter of 28 Oct 22) an announcement of *Krindlesyke*, a play in blank verse by Wilfrid Wilson Gibson (1878–1962; *D.N.B.*).

To LADY SACKVILLE

[Copy]   Max Gate | Dorchester | 25th. November 1922.

Dear Madam:
Mr Hardy's correspondence is such a burden to him at his age that I reply for him to your letter requesting him to autograph, as from him to you, the five books you send. These requests from strangers are so numerous that if he signs at all he does not do so without payment of a fee for the benefit of some charity, and he asks you half a guinea for each autograph, the amount to go in this case to the Dorset County Hospital (of which he is one of the Governors, and which is in need).
He is also unfortunately obliged to make it a rule not to inscribe a book as a presentation copy unless he really gives it, so that he will put his name only. Neither can he inscribe the volume of extracts, which is not of his own compiling, some of them being such as he would not have chosen. But on receipt of the amount for the four (£2—2—0) he will send it on to the Hospital, and duly return the books with the signatures.

The story your daughter has written will be very acceptable to him whenever you are pleased to forward it.

Very truly yours,
for Thomas Hardy,

. . . .

[To Lady Sackville]

Text MS. (carbon typescript) DCM.
Sackville: Josephine Victoria Sackville-West, Lady Sackville (1862–1936); the illegitimate daughter of Lionel Sackville Sackville-West, a distinguished diplomat, later second Baron Sackville (*D.N.B.*), she married her cousin Lionel Edward Sackville-West, who succeeded his uncle as third Baron in 1908.   *[Copy]*: word and brackets in TH's hand, as is also the address.   *volume of extracts*: presumably Ruth Head's *Pages from the Works of Thomas Hardy*; see letter of 29 June 21.   *with the signatures*: Lady Sackville replied (3 Dec 22, DCM) that she was only too pleased to send two guineas for TH's charity; on 23 Mar 23 (DCM) she sent another two guineas and four more books for TH to sign.   *story your daughter has written*: *The Heir: A Love Story* (privately printed, 1922) by Lady Sackville's only child Victoria ('Vita') Sackville-West (1892–1962; *D.N.B.*), the writer and gardener.   *[To Lady Sackville]*: words and brackets in TH's hand.

To SIR FREDERICK POLLOCK

[Late November 1922]

Many thanks. It came as a romantic surprise to me (Oxford being the romantic University as Cambridge is the intellectual).

Text MS. (pencil draft) DCM.   *Date* Replies to letter of 24 Nov 22 (DCM).
Pollock: Sir Frederick Pollock, 3rd Bt. (1845–1937; *D.N.B.*), whom TH had known for many years; see, e.g., *LY*, 86, 111, 198. He was the actual recipient of TH's letter of 4 Apr 93, incorrectly identified at II.6 as having been written to his father Sir William Frederick Pollock, 2nd Bt. (see I.126).   *It came*: i.e., his election to an honorary fellowship at Queen's College, Oxford (see letter of 14 Nov 22), on which Pollock had written to congratulate him (24 Nov 22, DCM).

To SIR FREDERICK MACMILLAN

MAX GATE, | DORCHESTER. | 28 Nov: 1922

Dear Sir Frederick:

I think I said that I should like to look through the proofs of the part added to the new edition of "Collected Poems", viz. Late Lyrics—as they appear for the first time in small type, & there may be errata. I am in no hurry, but only remind you.

Many thanks for your hints on autographs which I am acting upon.

Yours sincerely
T.H.

Text MS. (correspondence card) BL.
I think I said: in his letter of 28 Oct 22.   *hints on autographs*: see letter of 22 Nov 22.

To EDWIN STEVENS

                                   28 Nov. 1922

[Ans]

Dear Mr Stevens:

I have looked at Mr Crickmay's sketch for the Gloucester that you have been kind enough to send, & it appears to be quite suitable for the purpose designed.

I have also read the historical notes written by Mr Pouncy, & can suggest nothing further to be said, Mr Pouncy having evidently got up the details thoroughly. The sketch & typoscript are returned herewith.

                                   Very truly yours

                                   T. Hardy.

Text MS. (pencil draft) DCM.
Stevens: Edwin John Stevens, Dorchester civil servant and amateur actor; see IV.190–1. *[Ans]*: TH's square brackets. *Mr Crickmay's*: Harry W. Crickmay, current head of the Weymouth architectural firm for which TH himself had once worked; see *EL*, 83–4. *sketch for the Gloucester*: a design for a commemorative plaque to be placed on or near the Gloucester Hotel, Weymouth, the building at which King George III used to stay when visiting Weymouth during the Napoleonic period (see letter of 8 Jan 20); TH had for some years been advocating that the hotel's historic associations be recorded in this manner (see IV.294–5 and V.183–5, 244–5). *kind enough to send*: Stevens, a director of the Gloucester Hotel company, wrote 25 Nov 22 (DCM). *notes written by Mr Pouncy*: Stevens asked TH to read through, before it was printed, an account of the hotel's history prepared by Harry Pouncy (see letter of 20 Nov 23).

To THE MAYOR OF DORCHESTER

                                   29 November 1922

Sir:

In view of the measures that are being adopted here & elsewhere to provide useful labour for the unemployed I venture to suggest a slight improvement in the approach to Dorchester by the Wareham Road, which would be highly valued by pedestrians in that direction, & would cost comparatively little.

It is to construct a side-walk from the old toll-house at Max Gate to the railway bridge by the steam-plough works, such as exists beside almost, or quite, all the other highways into Dorchester. At present it is dangerous to go to the town on foot after dark & to some extent by day, by reason of the difficulty of keeping out of the way of motor-cars & bicycles—so dangerous as almost to forbid attendance at meetings, etc. in the evening, except by a vehicle.

It happens that on the south side of the highway, between the trees & the wire fence, there is a space wide enough for such a purpose, which only requires a little levelling.

                                   Your obedient servant

To His worship the Mayor of Dorchester.

Text MS. (pencil draft) DCM.
Mayor of Dorchester: Ernest Lorenzo Ling (1853–1949), director of printing firm. *little levelling*: it appears from the Borough Council records that the raised footpath along the south

side of the Wareham Road ('from Max Gate Toll-House to the Southern Railway Bridge, Alington Avenue') was constructed in response to this letter during the summer of 1923. The section of the path immediately opposite Max Gate survived the extensive road works carried out on Alington Avenue in 1985.

To THE REVD. G. B. CRONSHAW

6 December 1922

Dear Mr Cronshaw:

My sincere thanks for the invitation, & for your sending particulars of the Gaudies, which must be quaint enough. I feel proud of the privilege of attending, & should without doubt do so if I were twenty or even ten years younger.

I find that Queen's has owned property at Gussage All Saints in this county, ever since the time of Edward III.

Believe me

Yours most truly

The Bursar | The Queen's College | Oxford

Text   MS. (pencil draft) DCM.
Cronshaw: the Revd. George Bernard Cronshaw (1872–1928), fellow and bursar of Queen's College, Oxford, later principal of St. Edmund Hall.   *invitation*: Cronshaw (1 Dec 22, DCM) invited TH, as an Honorary Fellow, to attend all Gaudies (i.e., college feasts) on Christmas Day and New Year's Day.   *I find*: evidently in his copy (DCM) of Hutchins's *Dorset* (see letter of 9 Feb 21 to Cowley), III.490. Queen's College, founded in 1340–1, was named for Philippa, Edward III's queen-consort.

To SIR FREDERICK MACMILLAN

MAX GATE, | DORCHESTER. | 15th. December 1922.

Dear Sir Frederick:

I enclose a letter from a cinema agent concerning the Return of the Native. I do not know whether he is merely trying to get a job, or whether he is authorized to inquire by some cinema company, which however one would have thought could inquire themselves. I should imagine it would be better to deal directly with a producing company; but I send on the letter in case you have any favourable experience of the agency.

I am not at all anxious to get the Return of the Native filmed, unless a very good offer should come along.

Sincerely yours,
Thomas Hardy.

Text   MS. (typewritten) BL.
cinema agent: still accompanying this MS. is a letter of 5 Dec 22 from Robert Whitehouse (of the Roma June Bureau, Ltd., Leicester Square, London) inviting TH to employ him as an agent in dealing with a producer known to be interested in the film rights to *The Return of the Native*. *experience of the agency*: Macmillan replied (18 Dec 22, DCM) that it was, indeed, better to deal directly with principals in such situations and that Whitehouse was being sent a negative response. Whitehouse wrote again to TH (14 Dec 22, DCM) and TH drafted (15 Dec 22, DCM)

a note—to be sent over FEH's signature—to the effect that his earlier letter had been forwarded to Macmillan.

To NEWMAN FLOWER

23 December 1922

Dear Mr Flower:

I think it a liberal suggestion that you put to me for a Preface to the Nature book, & possibly I might have had the temerity to try my hand on it 20 or 30 years ago. But it is rather beyond my energies nowadays, & anyhow somewhat outside my compass, for I know really nothing about Nature scientifically, & it seems to me that the foreword ought be by a man who is at home in the subject.

So, while thanking you & the firm for writing to me about it I unhappily must decline the attempt. If I may add a word I would say that I think it ought to be done by a younger man—some English Einstein—if you could find one! But perhaps I have misapprehended the drift of the proposed work, the outline of which, however, I have looked over; & return herewith.

Yours very truly
T.H—

Text MS. (pencil draft) DCM.
Preface to the Nature book: Flower (21 Dec 22, DCM) asked TH to write 'a sort of foreword' to a proposed work entitled *Living Nature* which Cassell would pub. in 24 to 48 fortnightly parts; the scheme seems eventually to have been abandoned. *Einstein*: Albert Einstein (1879–1955), physicist; see V.353 and *LY*, 128.

To MADELEINE ROLLAND

MAX GATE, | DORCHESTER. | 27th. December 1922.

Dear Miss Rolland:

It is very kind of you to write such an interesting letter to me and my wife for Christmas and the New Year, and I am glad to find that Switzerland suits you so well. The neighbourhood of Geneva has many pleasant memories for me, but I shall never see it again. The famous English surgeon Sir Frederick Treves (who, if you remember, operated successfully on King Edward) lives there almost all the year, finding that his health is better there than in England.

Your discoveries of the ways of Nature are amusing. But you are not alone in being ignorant of some of them till now. I have often asked Australian visitors if it does not seem strange to see the sun go from right to left instead of, as in the northern hemisphere, from left to right; and they say they have never noticed it!

Last week I received a request from a Parisian dramatist and novelist to let him adapt "Jude the Obscure"—which I think you translated—for the French stage. I have told him I don't object, though I have ceased to take much interest in the theatre, and have no idea how he is going to carry out his idea. He says his reason for wishing to do it is that they have in Paris a splendid actress for the part of "Sue". I don't suppose I shall hear anything more about it, theatrical matters being so uncertain. His name is M. Claude Anet. I wonder if you know anything of him as a writer.

I am obliged to send typewritten letters nowadays, which I hope you will excuse.

If you come to England I hope you will let us know. Best wishes for the New Year to you and your brother from my wife and myself.

Believe me,

Sincerely yours,
Thomas Hardy.

Text   MS. (typewritten, with envelope in hand of FEH) Mme Rolland.
interesting letter: of 23 Dec 22 (DCM).   *pleasant memories*: though TH was in fact ill during his one visit to Geneva, with ELH, in 1897; see *LY*, 70.   *Treves*: whom TH had known since childhood; see III.53.   *ways of Nature*: Mlle Rolland confessed that, now that she was living in the country, she had for the first time realized that the sun got lower in the sky as winter approached and higher again in the spring.   *think you translated*: Mlle Rolland did not in fact translate *Jude*; see letter of 4 July 20.   *Anet*: 'Claude Anet' was the pseudonym used by Jean Schopfer (1868–1931), Swiss-born French novelist, playwright, and historian; TH had already given permission for the adaptation of *Jude the Obscure* but it seems not to have been staged.   *your brother*: Romain Rolland; see letter of 4 July 20.

To JOHN MASEFIELD

FROM TH. HARDY, | MAX GATE, | DORCHESTER. | Dec 30: 1922.

Best New Year's wishes to all. Many thanks for Xmas poem. Nothing new, alas, to send of that sort.

T.H.

Text   MS. (correspondence card) Texas.
Masefield: John Masefield, poet; see IV.189.   *Xmas poem*: unidentified, and perhaps not a pub. item.

To ALFRED POPE

MAX GATE, | DORCHESTER. | 30th. December 1922.

Dear Mr Pope:

Respecting my re-appointment as a Governor of the Grammar School I am in the hands of the Court of Quarter Sessions, if they think my very meagre services will be of any use during the next three years, when I shall be getting still more useless I fear. Also I may be considered to have become too cautious in respect of the rebuilding. Remembering the fate of the County School I have lately held the opinion that transference to the new site should not be largely proceeded with till building conditions have settled down a little more. As you know, materials and construction have already fallen considerably in cost, and will probably go further.

If you consider these views to be no objection, and that a younger man would not be preferable, I shall readily accede to your nomination.

We are sorry to hear of the sprained ancle, of which I learn now for the first time, and send best wishes for the New Year.

Sincerely yours,
Thomas Hardy.

P.S. I am compelled to resort to the typist, having rheumatism in one arm which makes writing irksome. T.H.

Text MS. (typewritten) Thomas Hardy Society.
my re-appointment: Pope (28 Dec 22, DCM) wrote on behalf of the Board of Governors of the Dorchester Grammar School to ask TH to accept reappointment to the Board for a further three-year term.   *Quarter Sessions*: TH was technically a 'Representative Governor', appointed by the Court of Quarter Session—of which he was a member by virtue of his position as a Justice of the Peace; see Edward C. Sampson, 'Thomas Hardy—Justice of the Peace', *Colby Library Quarterly*, December 1977, 269–70.   *the rebuilding*: TH in fact laid the foundation stone of the school's new building in July 1927; see *LY*, 254–6.   *the County School*: a public school established in 1863 for 'the sons of Yeomen, Tradesmen and Professional men'; originally situated in the middle of Dorchester (TH himself lived in the former headmaster's house in Shire-hall Lane 1883–5), it closed in 1895 after moving to new premises outside of the town.

To SIR ROBERT PEARCE EDGCUMBE

MAX GATE, | DORCHESTER. | 31 Dec. '22

Many thanks for paper. Have read it with interest. Happy N.Yr.

T.H.

Text MS. (postcard) Gordon N. Ray.
paper: unidentified.

1923

To J. J. FOSTER

Max Gate | Dorchester | Jan 2. 1923

Many thanks for good wishes, which are reciprocated.

F. & T.H.

Text MS. (postcard) Eton College.
Foster: TH, addressing this card, calls him 'J. A. Foster'.   *F. & T.H.*: all in TH's hand.

To SIR HAMO THORNYCROFT

Max Gate | 8 Jan: 1923

My dear Thornycroft:

I am much interested in the photograph of your model that you have sent—also in the illustrations showing the Memorial at Dunstable. The figure at the top is striking, & forms, of course, the best finish to such designs: but unfortunately few corporations can afford it.

Curiously enough the model of Charing Cross illustrates the part of London with which I was most familiar for between 5 & 6 years when I was a young man. I knew the spot when Hungerford Market was still standing (where Charing Cross Hotel is now,) & used to lunch there. It was quite Dickens's London in those days. I saw the iron bridge built, from the windows of 8 Adelphi Terrace where I was, & saw the first barge load of earth thrown into the water to form the Embankment.

I don't gather whether your plan would sweep away that Terrace, so familiar to me; but some plan or other will, no doubt, before very long. Old Northumberland House went to make room for the Avenue—destroyed unnecessarily, it was said afterwards.

You will probably develope your model still further. If I were you I should put in more detail, so as to make it clearer to the man in the street. However you will know best about that.

My wife has just come home from Surrey, & joins with me in sending best New Years wishes to you & the household. We have not heard from Gosse for ages, but conclude that he is flourishing, as he always is.

Always sincerely yrs
Thomas Hardy.

Text MS. DCM.

photograph . . . sent: Thornycroft's letter of 5 Jan 23 (DCM) enclosed a photograph of a model of a proposed new layout of the entire Charing Cross area of London; the model was later displayed, together with other such models and plans, at an exhibition arranged by the London

Society in March 1923. See Elfrida Manning, *Marble & Bronze: The Art and Life of Hamo Thornycroft* (London, 1982), 184.   *Memorial at Dunstable*: Thornycroft also sent a Bedfordshire newspaper containing photographs of a new war memorial for which he had been largely responsible; it was not, however, at Dunstable but at nearby Luton. See Manning, 206. *between 5 & 6 years*: i.e., 1862–67, when he worked for Arthur Blomfield (see I.3) as an assistant architect.   *8 Adelphi Terrace*: where Blomfield had his office; see I.3–4.   *before very long*: Thornycroft replied, 9 Jan 23 (DCM), that his scheme did not affect Adelphi Terrace—which was, however, pulled down in 1936.   *the Avenue*: i.e., Northumberland Avenue, running from Trafalgar Square to the Embankment.   *from Surrey*: she had been visiting Mrs. Henniker at Epsom.

To SIR FREDERICK MACMILLAN

MAX GATE, | DORCHESTER. | 10th. January 1922 [1923].

Dear Sir Frederick:

A cheap edition of some of the novels for India, on which you write, has I conclude been well considered by yourselves and I agree to the four you mention appearing experimentally, with the introductions as you suggest, at a ten per cent royalty on the published price, which I assume to be as much as you think you can afford to pay.

To the other matter—the extract from Tess of the d'Urbervilles—there can be no objection.

As I am writing I may mention that whenever you bring out the Collected Poems complete, either on thin or thick paper, I think it will not be worth while to send it, or any further volume of my poetry, to the Spectator. They gave me such a mean notice last time that their reviews are not worth a copy.

I am, sincerely yours,
Thomas Hardy.

P.S. I enclose two letters I have just received on the same matter of extracts—which perhaps it would be better for you to answer? I suppose they may be permitted to make the extract, if they are willing to pay a fee? T.H.

Text MS. (typewritten) BL.   *Date* See notes below.
you write: Macmillan (9 Jan 23, Macmillan letterbooks, BL) made a proposal for cheap Indian edns. of some of TH's novels with introductions by John Henry Fowler (d. 1932, aged 72), formerly a master at Clifton College.   *four you mention*: *Far from the Madding Crowd, The Mayor of Casterbridge, The Return of the Native*, and *The Trumpet-Major*.   *no objection*: Macmillan sought TH's agreement to a charge of two guineas being made for inclusion of an 86-line extract from *Tess* in an anthology of nineteenth-century prose.   *last time*: A. Williams-Ellis, reviewing *Late Lyrics and Earlier, Spectator*, 8 July 1922, described its contents as 'almost all more or less the raw materials of poetry; poems might be made of nearly all of them, but they have not been made. . . . [Hardy] can really descend to extraordinary ineptitudes'.   *for you to answer?*: see letter to Macmillan of 13 Jan 23.

To J. C. SQUIRE

FROM TH. HARDY, | MAX GATE, | DORCHESTER. | 11 Jan 1923

Dear Mr Squire:

If your paper is too moral to sympathize with a wicked woman, will you return the enclosed? which I send for the February number.

T.H.

Best wishes for the New Year.

Text MS. (correspondence card) Taylor.
the enclosed?: TH's poem 'On the Portrait of a Woman about to be Hanged', dated 6 Jan 1923, three days before the execution of Mrs. Edith Jessie Thompson for the murder of her husband. TH, like many others, was distressed by Mrs. Thompson's conviction and sentence—she was only 28 and the extent of her participation in the murder remained very much in doubt—and in a letter to Sydney Cockerell (16 Jan 23, Purdy) FEH said that on 9 January he drew her attention to the fact that the hour of the execution had passed.   *February number*: of Squire's *London Mercury*; Squire replied (15 Jan 23, DCM) that he would be glad to pub. the poem. TH later inserted into one of his scrapbooks (DCM) an article from the *Daily Express*, 21 Feb 1923, which accused him of treating Mrs. Thompson as a Clytemnestra figure when she was in fact 'the Tess of our time'.

To EDWARD DUGDALE

MAX GATE, | DORCHESTER. | 13 Jan. 1923

Dear Mr Dugdale:

Many thanks for the paper with the article about Enfield old Palace, which I remember visiting with you. I do not know who the cheery inhabitant may be who professes to be so well acquainted with Florence & myself, or when he called here, but I fear he will not get me to join in a campaign for the preservation of Enfield relics. The Society for the Preservation of Ancient Buildings might show an interest in the matter.

My love to Mrs Dugdale, & best wishes for the year. Florence had a meeting of influential inhabitants here yesterday on the question of slaughterhouses.

Sincerely yours
Thomas Hardy.

P.S. F. says that somebody else is the sender of the paper!—but it does not matter. T.H.

Text MS. (with envelope) Purdy.
Enfield old Palace: an important Tudor building in Enfield, Middlesex (where FEH's family lived); it was pulled down in 1927. The article may have been 'Enfield Palace Sold', *Enfield Gazette and Observer*, 5 Jan 1923.   *cheery inhabitant*: unidentified.   *meeting . . . slaughterhouses*: although the precise occasion has not been identified it was presumably related to the current consideration of Humane Slaughtering by-laws by the General Purposes Committee of the Dorchester Borough Council.

To SIR FREDERICK MACMILLAN

FROM TH. HARDY, | MAX GATE, | DORCHESTER. | 13. I. '23

Letter received. I don't at all wish Mrs Dawson Scott to be given permission—or the other man.

Text MS. (postcard) BL.
Letter received: of 12 Jan 23 (DCM), written in response to TH's letter of 10 Jan 23. *Scott*: Catharine Amy Dawson Scott, founder of P.E.N. (see letter of 22 Nov 21); Macmillan advised against her being given permission to include one of TH's short stories in a proposed anthology for schools, saying that it would gain TH neither reputation nor money. *other man*: referred to by Macmillan as Mr. Glover—and as someone whose request for Hardy extracts should certainly be refused.

To W. M. COLLES

17 January 1923

Dear Mr Colles:

In reply to your inquiry I am sorry to say that all the available pieces were printed in the volume which appeared last summer, & that there are no more written at present which would suit a periodical.

Yours truly
Thomas Hardy

Text MS. (pencil draft) DCM.
your inquiry: of 15 Jan 23 (DCM). *the volume*: Late Lyrics and Earlier.

To HAROLD MONRO

MAX GATE, DORCHESTER. | 17th. January 1923.

Dear Mr Monro:

At last I send up one—a very poor thing—for the March number. Unfortunately I raked together all those I thought the best for the volume published last summer. If you don't like this one please send it back, and I will look for another.

Yours sincerely,
T. Hardy.

Text MS. (typewritten) Colby.
March number: TH's poem 'The Church and the Wedding' appeared in the *Chapbook*, edited by Monro, March 1923.

To AUSTIN HARRISON

MAX GATE, | DORCHESTER. | 21 Jan. 1923

Dear Mr Austin Harrison:

I write a line to add to the numerous letters you must have received, to let you know how much I regretted to hear of your father's death, he having become such a permanent institution, as it were, of these days. I had not heard lately from him, my own powers of correspondence not being what they were. But I had known him for probably a longer period than you may be aware of: from the time when he was living in Westbourne Terrace, & I was a resident in a London suburb, you being then a boy. Your mother I knew also, & remember interesting conversations with her. This must have been more than 40 years ago. I was, of course, quite familiar with the lectures at Newton Hall.

My sympathies are with you & your sister in your loss, & I am

Sincerely yours
Thomas Hardy.

Text MS. Texas.
Harrison: Austin Harrison, editor of the *English Review*; see IV.71.   *your father's death*: Frederic Harrison died 14 Jan 1923.   *not heard lately from him*: they had, however, corresponded the previous year; see letter of 24 May 22 to F. Harrison.   *Westbourne Terrace*: Harrison lived almost continuously at this Paddington address 1870–1902.   *London suburb*: TH apparently means Upper Tooting, where he lived 1878–81.   *Your mother*: Frederic Harrison's wife, and cousin, Ethel Bertha (d. 1916).   *Newton Hall*: the Positivist Society's centre for meetings and lectures; see I.134.   *your sister*: Olive Harrison.

To HAROLD MONRO

MAX GATE, | DORCHESTER. | 24th. January 1923.

Dear Mr Munro:

I am compelled to dictate my reply to your letter as I am in bed with a bad cold. I think that upon the whole the poem is as good as any I shall be able to find and I will insert another verse that occurred to me after I had posted your copy and this will I think, improve it.

Yours sincerely,
Thomas Hardy.
pp. F.E.H.

Text MS. (FEH's initials in her hand, remainder typewritten) Colby.
improve it: TH continued to revise 'The Church and the Wedding' (see letter to Monro of 17 Jan 23) until it was collected in 1925; see letter of 22 Feb 23 and Purdy, 241.

To LADY ST. HELIER

MAX GATE, | DORCHESTER. | Sunday – Jan 28 – 1923

My dear friend:

(I am obliged to write this in pencil, as I am kept in bed by a bad cold which came on a few days ago—but it appears to be going off.) How very good of you to take such trouble to find out all about G. Gifford's position with the County Council, & with such excellent results. It is, of course, most reassuring for him, & I need not say how grateful he will be.

We shall be delighted to see you down here, & you must let us know when the spirit moves you. I think I told you what a good time we had with Dorothy—& how charming Elizabeth was. I had no idea such a delightful girl had grown up all of a sudden.

I hope you are almost out of the hands of the dentist—& will be all the better for what you have been made to undergo. Florence sends her love & I am always

Yours affectionately
Thomas Hardy

I send back Mr Topham Forrest's note. T.H.

Text MS. (pencil) Purdy.
St. Helier: Mary, widow of Lord St. Helier and one of TH's oldest London friends; see I.144. Long famous as a fashionable hostess, she had in more recent years been active in social work and as an alderman of London County Council.   *such excellent results*: Gordon Gifford (see V.27), ELH's nephew, feared he might lose his position as an architect with the London County Council as a result of predicted staff cuts; Lady St. Helier, at TH's request, had obtained from E. Topham Forrest (d. 1945), chief architect to the L.C.C., an assurance that Gifford's job was in no danger.   *Dorothy . . . Elizabeth*: Dorothy Allhusen and her daughter Elizabeth (see letter to her of 7 Jan 24) visited Max Gate in early November 1922; see *LY*, 229.   *Forrest's note*: to Lady St. Helier, forwarded by her when writing to TH 7 Jan 23 (DCM); a copy in FEH's hand is in DCM.

To SIR FREDERICK MACMILLAN

MAX GATE, | DORCHESTER. | February 6. 1923.

Dear Sir Frederick Macmillan:

I have received the letter I enclose with this, the question being rather one for you than for me, that you may decide what answer shall be returned.

As far as the *literary* side of it is concerned, I should not mind their including "A Pair of Blue Eyes" in the series, this being one of the short novels, on the condition that I read the proofs. Or, if poetry will suit them as well as prose, "Wessex Poems" which, including "Poems Past and Present", make one volume in the Wessex Edition. I mention these instances in case you think it worth while, from any practical considerations, such as advertisement, etc, to come to terms with the publishers of the "Everyman" series. But I have no feeling on the point either way, further than that I should, of course, like to do what is best for keeping the books before the public.

Yours sincerely,
Thomas Hardy.

Text MS. (typewritten) BL.
letter I enclose: from Ernest Rhys (4 Feb 23, DCM), proposing the inclusion of one of TH's novels in the 'Everyman' series.   *what answer*: Macmillan (8 Feb 23, Macmillan letterbooks, BL) urged TH to decline the suggestion as not to his financial advantage, and on 9 Feb 23 (draft, DCM) TH wrote to Rhys to that effect.

To HELEN GIFFORD

MAX GATE, | DORCHESTER. | 11th. February 1923.

Dear Miss Gifford:

I don't at all mind your using your French version of the sonnet entitled "Hap" in your school magazine or in an educational competition. It seems to me to keep pretty close to the original, except perhaps in the last line or two;

but my criticism is of course worthless, and none but a French man or woman who is master of English could really criticize it, as French poetry.

I am obliged to dictate my letter as I have been laid up with a chill, and am only just recovering.

Believe me, with best wishes,

Sincerely yours,
Thomas Hardy.

Text   MS. (typewritten) C. H. Gifford.
your French version: Miss Gifford, who had read French at Oxford, sent the text of her translation, entitled 'La Hasard', with her letter of 8 Feb 23 (DCM).   *school magazine*: that of the Marie Souvestre School, Sutton, Surrey, which she had recently founded; see letter of 13 July 20.   *educational competition*: a possibility mentioned by Miss Gifford herself.

To THE REVD. E. J. BODINGTON

[Copy]   MAX GATE, | DORCHESTER. | 12th. February 1923.
Dear Sir:

Somebody, I know not who, has kindly sent me the Jersey Morning News for 6th. Feb., containing a report of a lecture you gave at St. Heliers on my novels and my personal history; and I write a line to thank you for the high appreciation you show of the novels, especially as they were all finished nearly 30 years ago, and have been superseded in the view of critics by the more important half of my work, the verse, published during the last 25 years.

The personal details you give have amused us as being rather imaginative, though since they are what was commonly gossiped when I came to live here after an absence of half a lifetime, (coinciding with the date when you were curate here) it is natural that you believed them. It would have interested your audience if they could have been told that my forebears came from the very isle you were lecturing in. But it would have spoilt your theory of my line of descent, and perhaps it was as well that you did not know it.

Believe me, with renewed thanks,

Yours truly,
Signed T. Hardy

The Ven. E. J. Bodington. M.A.

Text   MS. (typed draft) DCM.
Bodington: the Revd. Eric James Bodington (1862–1929), Archdeacon of Wiltshire, formerly (1886–9) curate of West Fordington, Dorchester.   *[Copy]*: word and brackets in TH's hand.   *report of a lecture*: 'Thomas Hardy, Novelist', Jersey *Morning News*, 6 Feb 1923.   *personal details*: e.g., 'Mr. Hardy came from a line of unmixed peasants. He was a rural peasant with a rural mind.'   *from the very isle*: for TH's insistence on his family's Jersey origins see, e.g., *EL*, 5.   *Signed T. Hardy*: all in TH's hand.

To HARRIET MONROE

FROM TH. HARDY, | MAX GATE, | DORCHESTER. | Feb 13: 1923

Proof returned. As one of the poems would be nonsense, & the other thrown out of rhythm, if printed uncorrected, the corrections must be made, or the poems not printed at all.

T.H.

Text MS. (correspondence card) Univ. of Chicago.
Monroe: Harriet Monroe (1860–1936), American editor, founder (in 1912) and editor of *Poetry: A Magazine of Verse*.   *Proof*: of the two new poems (making six in all) to be included in a new and enlarged edn. of *The New Poetry*, ed. Harriet Monroe and Alice Corbin Henderson (New York, 1923), first pub. 1917. TH had given permission in April 1922 for the addition of 'In Time of "the Breaking of Nations"' and 'The Two Houses'.

To J. C. SQUIRE

MAX GATE, | DORCHESTER. | 13: 2: '23

Many thanks for circular, etc. of the A.C. Will do my best. Am driven to post-carding, which please pardon.

T.H.

Text MS. (postcard) Taylor.
the A.C.: the Architecture Club; see letter of 17 July 22. The 'circular' (DCM) includes the statement of the Club's aims, etc., cited in the notes to that earlier letter.   *do my best*: Squire (12 Feb 23, DCM) asked TH to help publicize the exhibition, 'Twenty Years of British Architecture', which the club would be organizing in London in March.

To SIR FREDERICK MACMILLAN

MAX GATE, | DORCHESTER. | 15 February 1923.

Dear Sir Frederick:
   In respect of the inclusion of "An Ancient to Ancients" by Mr Jonathan Cape in a volume to be called "The Best Poems of 1922", on which you inquire, I find that though I have had no correspondence with him, and know nothing of him, I gave permission to Mr Thomas Moult (who appears to be a responsible man of letters) to include the poem in a book with the above title that he said he had in preparation, on payment of a fee of two guineas, and your having no objection. I now gather that Mr Cape is his publisher.
   I have found that one has to overcome one's first instinct not to allow any of these people to use poems, etc., for if they are refused the reading public invariably conclude that one's work is not good enough to be in such anthologies, and that it is therefore negligible by a purchaser. (I have had experience of this, and other authors tell me the same thing as being theirs). So when the request comes from responsible persons I agree, asking, as you recommended, a fee. The irresponsible ones are mostly thus choked off.

Sincerely yours,
T. Hardy.

Text   MS. (typewritten) BL.
of 1922": *The Best Poems of 1922*, ed. Thomas Moult (London, 1923); it did include TH's 'An Ancient to Ancients'.   *you inquire*: Macmillan (14 Feb 23, Macmillan letterbooks, BL) asked if TH had given Cape permission and suggested that he should, in any case, insist on payment. *Moult*: Thomas Moult (d. 1974), poet, author, and editor, president of the Poetry Society 1952–61.

To JOHN MIDDLETON MURRY

Feb 15. 1923

I have just seen your address in the Lit. Suppt, & am glad to be able to send on a letter I wrote to you in Jan., which was returned through the dead letter office. I hope you are well.

Ever yrs
T.H.

MAX GATE, | DORCHESTER. | 21 Jan. 1923

Dear Mr Middleton Murry:

I am sending this at a venture, not knowing where you are. But I thought I should like to tell you of my deep sympathy, & my wife's, with you in your loss. I have passed through the same experience as that you are now undergoing, & I know how very useless letters are at such times. But we go on writing them just the same.

We were, of course, quite familiar with Mrs Murry's books, which are what the world regrets to have no more of: yet to the inner life such things count for little. Believe me

Always yours
Thomas Hardy.

Text   MS. Berg.
in the Lit. Suppt: Murry's letter requesting copies of his late wife's letters appeared in the *Times Literary Supplement*, 15 Feb 1923.   *your loss*: Murry's New Zealand-born wife Kathleen, *née* Beauchamp, who wrote under the pseudonym of Katherine Mansfield (1888–1923; *D.N.B.*), died of consumption 9 Jan 1923.

To THE REVD. E. J. BODINGTON

[Ansr]   . . . . [Mid-]February 1923

Dear Dr Bodington:

I send a line to assure you that your errors in your lecture as to my personal history were of a very harmless kind. So many imaginary biographies have been given that I have become case-hardened, & do not contradict them.

As for the Hardys, It is noticeable that families with a Norman name are never found in "a line of unmixed peasants" (to quote your words). If such names are found among the peasantry—i.e., farm-labourers, they are borne by families which have been forced by misfortune into that class.

It was remarked during my father's lifetime that he was the only one of the name left who owned landed property in Dorset, though so many Hardys had been proprietors here of estates (not large) after they crossed the Channel from the 16th. century onwards. And he did not own much—a farm, a dozen houses or so, a brickfield, kilns, &c,—all which he preferred to let, having such a liking (to his own inconvenience, being an employer of labour) for the dilapidated old homestead built by his grandfather, which you appear to have seen—though the stabling & other outbuildings have been pulled down since his time. With thanks for your letter I am

Yours truly

The Ven. Archdeacon Bodington: | Calne.

Text MS. (pencil draft) DCM.   *Date* Replies to letter of 13 Feb 23.
[Ansr]: TH's square brackets.   *harmless kind*: Bodington (13 Feb 23, DCM) had replied apologetically to TH's letter of 12 Feb 23 and declared himself to be a great admirer of TH's work.   *Hardys, It*: 'As for the Hardys' was an afterthought.   *quote your words*: see letter of 12 Feb 23.   *homestead*: i.e., the Hardy cottage at Higher Bockhampton.

To HAROLD MONRO

FROM TH. HARDY, | MAX GATE, | DORCHESTER. | 22: 2: 1923

Dear Mr Monro:
   I think that to lengthen it would be inadvisable, so return the proof with a slight correction, or rather improvement, only. My cold is very slowly going off, thanks.

Sincerely yrs
T.H.

Text MS. (correspondence card) Colby.
proof . . . improvement: the proof of 'The Church and the Wedding', showing changes to the second stanza, still accompanies this letter; see letter of 24 Jan 23.

To HARLEY GRANVILLE BARKER

Max Gate, Dorchester. | 5 March 1923.

This may reach you when you get back from Rome. I was interested to know your feeling about the Eternal City. I remember that mine, after being there a few days, was a growing oppressiveness from the grinning decay around—rendered more insistent in that the ruins had lately been stripped of their creepers. Now I believe they have grown again.
   I trust you are both well. Kindest regards to Hn.

Sincerely yours.
Th. H.

Text Typed transcript DCM.
from Rome: where Barker and his wife had spent much of the winter.   *a few days*: in 1887.
stripped of their creepers: see EL, 246–50, esp. 247.   *Hn*: Helen, Barker's second wife; see letter of 19 Mar 22.

To AMY LOWELL

MAX GATE, | DORCHESTER. | 7th. March 1923.

Dear Miss Amy Lowell:

"I do remember my faults this day".—Never have I acknowledged receiving that book of American Poetry at the end of last year with your charming inscription, although I read as much as I could of it when it arrived. This "could" by the way, has a sinister ambiguity that I did not mean; I merely alluded to spare time. I read all *your* pieces anyhow, and much like "The Swans".

Edna Millay seems the most promising of the younger poets, don't you think? As to the free verse which appears so frequently in the volume, I suppose I am too old to do it justice. You manage it best; but do you mind my saying that it too often seems a jumble of notes containing ideas striking, novel, or beautiful, as the case may be, which could be transfused into poetry, but which, as given, are not poetry? I could not undergo an examination on why (to me) they seem not. Perhaps because there is no expectation raised of a response in sound or beat, and the pleasure of its gratification, as in regular poetry; which only ancient poetry, like the English Bible, is able to dispense with because of its other character of antiquity.

As for myself, I am rather perplexed by letters I get on whether readers can have a difficulty in obtaining my books of verse in the United States, particularly "The Dynasts" complete in one volume (green, published by Macmillans). If you or any friend should be in a book store any day, and would not mind asking if they keep that edition, or if it is readily obtainable, I shall be greatly obliged. It is so difficult to get information through the publishers and booksellers themselves. With best wishes for your poetry and yourself,

Believe me,

Your affectionate friend,
Thomas Hardy.

Text MS. (typewritten) Harvard.
Lowell: Amy Lowell, American poet and critic; see V.67.   *faults this day"*: an apparent allusion to the Book of Common Prayer version of Psalm 51: 3, 'For I acknowledge my faults'. *book of American poetry*: *American Poetry 1922: A Miscellany* (New York, 1922) opens with seven poems—including 'The Swans'—by Miss Lowell; the copy she sent TH (Cornell Univ.) contains some notes by TH which he appears to have used when writing this letter (see *Studies in the Novel*, Winter 1972, 628–9).   *Millay*: Edna St. Vincent Millay (1892–1950), American poet; eight of her sonnets are included in *American Poetry 1922*.   *particularly "The Dynasts"*: Miss Lowell replied 8 May 23 (DCM) that the one-vol. *Dynasts* was selling well.

To F. R. YERBURY

March 13. 1923

Dear Sir:

I much appreciate the desire of the Council of the Architectural Association that I should become an Honorary Member of that body. But I have lately found it advisable that at this advanced time of my life I should not form further memberships, even if they are merely nominal; & I therefore must forego the honour, especially as I could be of no service to the Association.

I may mention that the Essay prize of the Institute, to which you allude, was won before I became a member of your society.

Please convey my thanks to the Council for their suggestion. With best wishes for the continued prosperity of your now ancient fraternity, I am

Yours very truly

F. R. Yerbury Esq.

Text MS. (pencil draft) DCM.
Yerbury: Francis Rowland Yerbury (1885–1970), architect; *D.N.B.* He wrote 12 Mar 23 in his capacity as Secretary of the Architectural Association.   *Essay prize*: the essay, 'On the Application of Colored Bricks and Terra Cotta to Modern Architecture', with which TH won the silver medal of the Royal Institute of British Architects in March 1863; see Millgate, 79–80. *member of your society*: it appears, however, that TH was in fact elected to membership of the Architectural Association in November 1862; see Millgate, 75.

To SIR FREDERICK MACMILLAN

MAX GATE, DORCHESTER. | 20th. March 1923.

Dear Sir Frederick:

I am sending on a letter from a troublesome anthologist, that you may answer him, since he will not take No from me. He has threatened in previous letters to print without permission such of my poems as have no copyright, and seems to be somewhat eccentric mentally; so that for your firm to send him a refusal in considerate terms would perhaps be best.

Sincerely yours,
Th: Hardy.

Text MS. (typewritten) BL.
troublesome anthologist: A. Ivor Parry, with whom TH had already had an unsatisfactory correspondence in 1921 (DCM). Writing on 7 Mar 23 (DCM) he asked if TH's failure to reply to his previous letter meant that no copyright was being claimed and that his use of, say, 15 or 20 lines from *The Dynasts* would therefore not constitute a copyright infringement.   *perhaps be best*: Macmillan replied (21 Mar 23, DCM) that he was writing to tell Parry that he could not have any of TH's verse for his anthology.

To ST. JOHN ERVINE

MAX GATE, | DORCHESTER. | 22 March 1923

Dear Mr Irvine:

I thank you for your kind gift of Impressions of my Elders—which makes you seem very juvenile to me. I have read with pleasure a good many pages, but not all as yet. I did not realize that you had travelled (mentally) so far outside things theatrical as this books shows you to have done. Please blame weak eyes for such a short letter.

Sincerely yours
Thomas Hardy.

Text MS. Texas.
of my Elders: Ervine's collection of essays, *Some Impressions of My Elders*, pub. in New York in 1922 and in London in 1923.   *this books*: TH means 'this book'.

To H. G. WELLS

MAX GATE, | DORCHESTER. | 25 March 1923

Dear Mr Wells:

The book has come, & we have promptly read it. I was left here alone last week for two or three days, when I tackled the philosophic parts, which interested me very much, though my wife was more interested in the narrative parts. At the same time I admit that Mr Cecil Burleigh is immensely amusing to those who have ever known him. I am glad you kept him alive, though at one moment I was horrified at the idea that he was to be extinguished.

As I may have said before—at any rate I have thought it—I don't know at all how you can manage to keep so fresh, & at such a high level, so continuously.

Sincerely yours
Thomas Hardy.

Text MS. Univ. of Illinois, Urbana.
Wells: Herbert George Wells, author; see V.280.   *The book*: Wells's novel *Men Like Gods* (London, 1923).   *ever known him*: Burleigh—the Conservative leader in the novel who unexpectedly finds himself in Utopia—was a caricature of A. J. Balfour (see letter of 7 July 20).

To C. F. CROSBIE WOOD

[Late March 1923]

Dear Sir:

I write for Mr Hardy, who is much pressed by correspondence, to say in answer to your letter that he is gratified to hear of your interest in the Mayor of Casterbridge & his friend Mr Farfrae. You may not be aware that you will find some real Dorset Characters, & scenes laid at Weymouth, in his drama called "The Dynasts"—written much later than The Mayor.

He is sorry to say that the beet-sugar Industry is outside his province, but that he wishes it success.

Yours very truly
for Thomas Hardy
F E.

Text MS. (pencil draft) DCM.   *Date* Replies to letter of 21 Mar 23.
Wood: Charles F. Crosbie Wood, of West Parade, Weymouth, wrote 21 Mar 23 (DCM) in his capacity as 'Propagandist and Hon. Organizing Secretary' of the Dorset & South-Western Counties of England Sugar Beet & Beet-Sugar Development Association.   *Mr Farfrae*: Wood drew attention to his letter in that day's *Dorset Daily Press* headed 'The Dorset Exodus—Why?'; it cited Henchard and Farfrae as examples of the kind of 'energy and enterprise' that were needed to activate Dorset's stagnant economy.

To JOHN MASEFIELD

MAX GATE, | DORCHESTER. | 3rd. April 1923.

Dear Mr Masefield:

(I am compelled to my regret to dictate my reply, my eyes being so weak that I have to wear a shade). My experience is that the more editions there are the better: the announcement of any new edition waking up readers to the fact that you are still alive. So that I think your publishers are right, as they consider the commercial side of a book very thoroughly. In my case the separate volumes have been issued by the same publishers as the collected volume, and at only about a shilling cheaper; if in your case the little volumes are by other publishers the collected [*two words torn away*] probably stir them up to push the little ones, which is to your advantage.

The British Public is a greedy creature, always thinking of what *quantity* is to be got for its money. My opinion is that Tennyson should have had a collected volume years before he did, and poor Swinburne suffers to this day from there being no one volume collection of him—suffers I think both in popularity and sale. For though the collected volume is the one they buy at the free libraries, and therefore one copy goes a long way among readers, you should I think remember that it is better to be read, even for nothing, than not to be read at all.

I should perhaps remind you that my own verse is in two volumes. 1. the Short Poems, 2. The Dynasts. But I had hoped at first it would all go into one.

So that as you see I agree with your publishers. I am not sure if I have answered you clearly: anyhow, don't mind asking me anything more of the sort, as I have had 50 years experience, and it is a pity it should all "go down into silence" with me.

Our kindest regards to you and your household.

Always sincerely,
Thomas Hardy.

Text   MS. (typewritten) Texas.
my reply: to Masefield's undated letter (DCM) enquiring as to the likely effect of *The Collected Poems of John Masefield* (London, 1923) upon the sales of the preceding individual vols. of his verse.   *Tennyson . . . volume*: the first one-vol. edn. of Tennyson's works appeared in 1878, when he was sixty-nine.   *two volumes . . . Dynasts*: TH's 'Poetical Works' comprised the *Collected Poems*, first pub. 1919, and the one-vol. edn. of *The Dynasts*, first pub. 1910; see Purdy, 287.   *into silence"*: Psalm 115: 17.

To GEORGE MACMILLAN

MAX GATE, DORCHESTER. | 4th. April 1923

Dear Mr Macmillan:

Certainly give the German essayist free permission to print a translation of "A Tragedy of Two Ambitions" with his article.

I am glad to see you are soon going to bring out the thin paper edition of my verse, which my younger readers have been clamourous for for some time, though it remains to be seen if they will buy it.

Believe me,

Yours very sincerely,
Thomas Hardy.

Text   MS. (typewritten) BL.
with his article: Macmillan (3 Apr 23, Macmillan letterbooks, BL) reported that a German publisher (Der Weisse Ritter Verlag, of Berlin) was bringing out an essay on TH's work and wished to include a translation of 'A Tragedy of Two Ambitions'; the author of the essay was not named.   *thin paper edition*: see letters of 8 Nov 21 and 28 Oct 22.

To JOHN MASEFIELD

MAX GATE, | DORCHESTER. | 5th April, 1923.

Dear Mr Masefield,

Since receiving your letter I have looked at the Returns on Sales in past years (which I hardly ever do look at!), and I find that the separate editions have gone on selling since we published the Collected Edition—particularly the Pocket Edition of each separate volume of Poems.

But then, I do not know how much more, or less, these small ones would have sold, supposing that the Collected Edition had not been brought out. And I do not see how this can be discovered, even by yourself, (assuming that you publish the Collected volume), since if the cheap ones decrease in their sales afterwards they may also have done so, owing to some freak of the public, if you had not published the Collected volume. As I said last time, I think the publishers know best.

Thanks, the eyes are no worse. I am saving them as much as I can, as you see.

Always yours,
Thomas Hardy.

Text   MS. (typewritten) Colby.
your letter: apparently the one to which he had already replied on 3 April.   *as you see*: a reference to this present letter's being typewritten.

To VERE H. COLLINS

[Ansr]

7 April [1923]

Many thanks for drawing our attention to the curious blunder in the Literary Suppt wh. ought to be corrected. So that there can be no objection to your saying you cannot understand what they mean by making that statement about a writer who, as you remark has pubd 3 vols. of new verse within 10 years—one of them only last year, with a combative preface—& who frequently publishes in magazines English & American.

Text   MS. (pencil draft) DCM.   *Date*   Replies to letter of 6 Apr 23.
[Ansr]: TH's square brackets.   *curious blunder*: Collins wrote FEH 6 Apr 23 (DCM) to ask if he should write to the editor of the *Times Literary Supplement* to protest the 'disgracefully ignorant' statement in its front-page article of 5 Apr 1923 that 'Mr. Hardy has long since

withdrawn from the arena'; the unsigned article, 'How It Strikes a Contemporary', was in fact by Virginia Woolf (see letter of 20 May 23), who subsequently collected it in *The Common Reader* (London, 1925).   *your saying*: no letter from Collins appeared, however, either because he did not write one or because the editor did not think the matter significant.

To SYDNEY COCKERELL

                                    MAX GATE, | DORCHESTER. | 14 April: 1923

My dear Cockerell:
    The Country Dances have come, but no bill with them. I hope you have not paid for them, as they must have cost a lot, & I can't let you stand the price, which would be a poor result to you from a casual conversation. So please let me know what has happened.
    I have not examined them much yet. Several of the tunes are those I used to play as a boy from my father's & grandfather's books: & several I have not seen before.
    In the Folk-Song book, the one you have marked, called "The Keys of Canterbury" has much the same words as the dramatic performance for three characters that we used to call "O Jan, O Jan, O Jan", which I told you of, & have somewhere written out,
[Domestic interruption of 2 hours (a caller to lunch)]
so far as I could remember it, & will look for some day. The ending, containing the lover's last proposal, which wins her, is much tamer than ours was. Like so many of these old songs & dialogues it had a rather broad double-entendre in it, quite Shakespearean, at which the men used to laugh, some of the women smirk, others stiffen, & wh. others wd paraphrase for domestic performance. As a child I knew only the paraphrase (much like the version you send), but in after years the original dawned upon me, & I no longer wondered why my father smiled when it happened to be enacted in his presence. However I must stop this: the subject can be revived when we meet.
    F. & I want to go to a meeting this afternoon to hear about ominous cracks in Salisbury Cathedral. Christopher & Mrs Moule called yesterday, with Sir R. Williams & his daughter, with whom they are staying. Many thanks for sending the books. I would finish this page but my eyes are giving out.
                                                Always sincerely
                                                Thomas Hardy.

Text   MS. Adams.
The Country Dances: it appears from Cockerell's letter of 12 Apr 23 (DCM) that he had visited Novello & Co., the London music publishers, and arranged for TH to be sent a selection of the country-dance and folk-song music they had in print; Cecil Sharp's *The Country Dance Book*, pub. in six parts 1909–22, was probably included.   *father's & grandfather's books*: the old music-books (DCM) they used as members of the Stinsford choir; see Millgate, 14–15, and *The Dorchester Hornpipe*, ed. Joan Brocklebank (Dorchester, 1977).   *written out*: TH's copy (DCM) of the typescript of 'O Jan, O Jan, O Jan', as prepared for performance by the Hardy Players later in 1923, carries the description 'Being a Recension of a Wessex Folk-Piece, with additions; By Thomas Hardy. (As played in Dorsetshire houses [the reading 'in his childhood at his father's house' has been struck through]—about 1844 to 1847).'   *[Domestic . . . lunch)]*: TH's square brackets.   *Salisbury Cathedral*: the meeting (reported in the *Dorset County*

Chronicle, 19 Apr 1923) was assured that the danger to the spire from heavy road traffic had been greatly exaggerated.   *& Mrs Moule*: the Revd. Arthur Christopher Moule (1873–1957) and his wife Mabel, *née* Wollaston; Moule, the son of Horace Moule's elder brother George Evans Moule (see I.84), was currently vicar of Trumpington, near Cambridge, and subsequently Professor of Chinese Language and History in the Univ. of Cambridge.   *Sir R. Williams*: Colonel Sir Robert Williams, Bt. (1848–1943), of Bridehead, near Dorchester, Conservative M.P. for West Dorset 1895–1922.   *his daughter*: probably the youngest of his five daughters, Dorothy Rhoda, still unmarried at this date.   *staying*: Moule had been curate, 1911–16, of the parish in which the Williamses lived.

To JOHN GALSWORTHY

MAX GATE, | DORCHESTER. | April 20: 1923

My dear Galsworthy:

I fear I am too old to send any distinct message to the Club. But I should have liked to meet the delegates of various nationalities who may be coming to the dinner. The exchange of international thought is the only possible salvation for the world: & though I was decidedly premature when I wrote at the beginning of the South African War that I hoped to see patriotism not confined to realms, but circling the earth, I still maintain that such sentiments ought to prevail. Whether they will do so before the year 10,000 is, of course what sceptics may doubt. I hope you will have a pleasant time, & am,

yrs always sincerely
Thomas Hardy.

Text   MS. Univ. of Birmingham.
the Club: Galsworthy wrote 17 Apr 23 (DCM), regretting TH's absence from the first international congress of the P.E.N. Club (see letter of 22 Nov 21) but hoping for 'a little message of sympathy' that he, as president, could read out at the dinner on 2 May 1923.   *The exchange . . . world*: Galsworthy subsequently reported (6 May 23, DCM) that these words of TH's were 'received with acclamation' when he read them out at the dinner; they are underlined in the MS., together with all but the first word of the preceding sentence.   *circling the earth*: an allusion to the closing lines of TH's poem 'Departure', written October 1899.

To THE REVD. H. R. L. SHEPPARD

Max Gate, Dorchester. | 23rd April, 1923.

Dear Mr. Sheppard,

It is very strange that I should get a letter from St. Martin's Place, close to the Church, for when I was a young man, in 1862–3, I was two doors from your vicarage, (at No. 8), with the late Sir Arthur Blomfield the church architect, and son of the Bishop, and as familiar with St. Martin's bells as one so near well could be, and with the clock face—or rather the half of it visible from our windows. After some months we removed to Adelphi Terrace.

However, this is not to the point. You have my permission to print in the *Review* any poem of mine already published (Collected Poems: Macmillan). But you probably mean that you want a new poem; and this is rather a more difficult consideration, as I am getting too old to write things off-hand as I used to do. But I will see what I can find.

I wish I had something bearing on St. Martin's in those old times, but I fear I have not.

Believe me,

Yours sincerely,
Thomas Hardy.

Text St. Martin's Review, February 1928.
Sheppard: the Revd. Hugh Richard ('Dick') Sheppard (1880–1937), vicar of St. Martin's-in-the-Fields 1914–27, active in Church reform and, later, in the Peace Pledge Union; *D.N.B. a letter*: of 17 Apr 23 (DCM).   *Blomfield*: see letter of 8 Jan 23.   *the Bishop*: the Revd. Charles James Blomfield (1786–1857), Bishop of London 1828–57; *D.N.B.*   *the* Review: the *St. Martin's Review* which, as Sheppard's letter rightly claimed, attempted to 'have a wider outlook than most Parish Magazines'.   *want a new poem*: this is, indeed, clear from Sheppard's letter; TH seems never to have sent such a poem, although 10 lines from 'And There Was a Great Calm' were reprinted in the *Review*, November 1925, in response to Sheppard's letter of 26 Aug 25 (DCM).

To SIR FREDERICK MACMILLAN

MAX GATE, | DORCHESTER. | May 2. 1923.

Dear Sir Frederick Macmillan:

I have received a letter from Princess Marie Louise, asking for permission to print in "The Book of the Queen's Doll's House Library" twelve short poems of mine that she had previously obtained leave to be copied into the miniature volume for the Doll's House. She says: "The published book will be the property of Her Majesty, who will herself decide upon the charitable distribution of the profits . . . We do not wish to do anything without your sanction and that of your publishers. The edition will be limited to not more than 2000 for Great Britain and the Dominions, and possibly 500 for U.S.A."

I suppose there is nothing to be said except that we assent?

I am,

Yours sincerely,
Thomas Hardy.

*Text MS. (typewritten) BL.
"The Book . . . Library": The Book of the Queen's Dolls' House Library*, ed. E. V. Lucas (London, 1924); TH's poems appear on pp. 146–52. For the Dolls' House see letter of 9 June 22.   *not more than 2000*: it was in fact limited to 1500 copies.   *nothing to be said*: Macmillan replied (3 May 23, Macmillan letterbooks, BL) that he did not see how TH could very well refuse permission, especially since he took it 'for granted' that all the other contributors would acquiesce.

To A. C. BENSON

MAX GATE, | DORCHESTER. | 8 May 1923

My dear Dr Benson:

I am much pleased to see your handwriting again, & to know that your health & energies have got into their normal stride. It is very strange—that overclouding of one's mind at times—when one seems to have nothing physically the matter at all. I used to get such clouds more often than I do now. They must of course be based on something corporeal: what you tell me about the attack of neuritis bears out a suspicion I have had for a long time, that diseases transmute themselves, but don't ever take an absolute departure. I have suggested to doctors to write a book on these transmutations for the use of ordinary people; but they don't seem to warm up to the idea.

It is pleasant to hear that the Bp. of Salisbury is to be admitted to an Hon. Fellowship. I should much like to be present, for I hear delightful things about him, & it seems in every way appropriate when we think of his own personal qualifications, & his brother's too early Severance from the offices at Cambridge that he filled so well. Oddly enough, though I have known the occupants of the See of Sarum ever since I was confirmed by one of them, I don't know the new bishop.

I am, "in a manner of spaiking"—as they say here—quite well: nevertheless I feel an increasing burden in little things which have intrinsically no weight at all, & my eyes are often very weak, which is no wonder. Please don't be tempted to put on too much pace now that you feel you can do it. My wife sends her kindest regards, & I am,

Always yours
Thomas Hardy.

Text MS. (with envelope) NYU.
their normal stride: Benson reported (6 May 23, DCM) that his depression had lifted; see letter to Benson of 8 June 20.   *transmute themselves*: Benson speculated that his last violent attack of neuritis had 'shifted the poisonous elements away from the brain into the much less important leg'.   *Bp. of Salisbury*: the Revd. St. Clair George Alfred Donaldson (1863–1935), Bishop of Salisbury 1921–35.   *Hon. Fellowship*: of Magdalene College, Cambridge, of which Benson was master and TH himself an honorary fellow.   *filled so well*: the Revd. Stuart Alexander Donaldson had been master of Magdalene and vice-chancellor of the university; see IV.260.   *confirmed by one of them*: the Revd. Edward Denison (1801–54), Bishop of Salisbury 1837–54; *D.N.B.*

To G. HERBERT THRING

9 May. 1923

Dear Mr Thring:

I am unable either personally, or by a personal representative, to participate in the proposed Congress, under the auspices of the Authors' League of America, for formulating the artistic principles to be observed in the development of the motion-picture industry—about which I have received particulars from you this morning.

The matter appears to me to be one which mainly concerns those younger members of the Society who are writing novels at the present time, & hence are largely interested in cinema productions.

Yours very truly
Thomas Hardy
per. . . .
Sec

Text MS. (pencil draft) DCM.
proposed Congress: the International Congress on Motion Picture Arts, held in New York 7–8 June 1923.   *particulars from you*: Thring (8 May 23, DCM), acting on a cable received from

the Authors' League of America, asked TH, as president of the Incorporated Society of Authors, if he wished to attend the Congress as one of the two representatives of the Society whose expenses Adolph Zukor, the producer, had offered to pay.

To GEOFFREY BESANT

MAX GATE, | DORCHESTER. | 13 May 1923.

Dear Mr Besant:

I think I remember seeing you as a little boy, though I cannot remember the Authors' dinner. However I knew your father very well.

In respect of the matter on which you write, you may be aware that I take no active part in the management of the Society of Authors, which is left to a Committee; so that I have not heard that an Assistant Secretary is or will soon be required, and if such is the case I should not think it would be a very remunerative post, the funds of the Society being small. But I will send on your application to the Committee, who will hardly need reminding (though I will do so) of your father's services which I am sure will win for you a sympathetic hearing whenever the question comes on.

Many thanks for kind wishes, and believe me

Yours very truly,
T. Hardy.

Text   MS. (typewritten) NYU.
Besant: Geoffrey Barham Besant (1879–1965), author and publisher, son of Sir Walter Besant (see I.63).   *Authors' dinner*: Sir Walter Besant had been the most active and influential of all the early members of the Incorporated Society of Authors; see I.191.   *(though I will do so)*: inserted in TH's hand.   *sympathetic hearing*: Besant was not appointed, however.

To SIR FREDERICK MACMILLAN

MAX GATE, | DORCHESTER. | 17th. May 1923.

Dear Sir Frederick:

Many thanks for the copies of the new editions of the poetry. The thin-paper form is very attractive.

I have received the enclosed inquiry from the Société des Films Albatros, about their producing The Return of the Native. I don't remember that the novel has been used in this way as yet, but I know nothing of the Company. If you should have heard of them, and think them worth answering, would you kindly do so? The only consideration is of course a commercial one (there being nothing literary in films), and any good it may do in making the book known to readers, etc.

As I am writing I will also enclose another letter—one from a Berlin translator. Whether he is a responsible person I cannot say, or whether he expects to be paid for his translations. It would be more satisfactory to hear from the publishers themselves whom he mentions that they really are prepared to carry out the job, as there are so many translators who are seized with the idea of doing some book, but have no means of making it practicable.

Believe me,

Sincerely yours
Thomas Hardy.

Text MS. (typewritten) BL.
thin-paper form: of the 1-vol. *Collected Poems.* *Films Albatros*: a film company established in France by a group of Russian *émigrés* led by Alexandre Kamenka (1888–1969); its productions included many of the best silent films of Jacques Feyder and René Clair. *kindly do so?*: Macmillan replied (23 May 23, DCM) that he knew nothing of the company but would write to say that the rights to *The Return of the Native* were available for purchase; see letters to Macmillan of 11 and 30 June 23. *Berlin translator*: Dr. Kurt Busse, who wrote to TH from Berlin 6 May 23 (DCM). Macmillan reported, however, that the German rights to TH's books had been negotiated through Curtis Brown in 1921 and were satisfactorily in the hands of Dr. Edwin Magnus of Berlin, and TH annotated Busse's letter 'Unanswered'.

To VIRGINIA WOOLF

20 May 1923

Dear Mrs Woolf:

It was a pleasure to me to see the name subscribed to your letter, as being that of the daughter of one who influenced me in many ways when I was a young man.

That the Nation is now to be edited by Mr Woolf raises expectations, & I am sure conducting it will be interesting to him & to you.

As for your kind suggestion that I should contribute something, alas I have fallen into the sere & yellow leaf, & fear I am unable to undertake writing now: indeed I doubt if I can redeem one or two promises rashly made a long time ago. But there are plenty of young pens available, & I shall, just the same, take much interest in the paper.

Yours sincerely

Text MS. (pencil draft) DCM.
Woolf: Adeline Virginia Woolf, novelist and critic; see V.77. *your letter*: of 17 May 23 (DCM). *one who influenced me*: Leslie Stephen; see I.27. *Mr Woolf*: Virginia Woolf's husband Leonard Sidney Woolf (see V.77) was literary editor of the *Nation and Athenaeum* 1923–30. *sere & yellow leaf*: an allusion to Shakespeare, *Macbeth*, V. iii. 23, somewhat ironic in light of the letter of 7 Apr 23.

To ALFRED NOYES

MAX GATE, | DORCHESTER. | 5 June 1923
My dear Mr Noyes:

I feel very undeserving of your moving lines in the Sunday paper, & am still less able to be worthy of them in any answer I can make at this moment by reason of a bad cold, which, as you will know, has a stupefying effect on one. I am, however, getting better. I hope & indeed conclude from your being able to dash off those verses so perfectly, that you are in the full vigour of health & creativeness, & am despite this inadequate reply

Always yrs sincerely

Thomas Hardy.

Text   MS. (with envelope) Univ. of Kentucky.
Sunday paper: the London *Sunday Times*, 3 June 1923; though not specifically titled, the poem appeared together with a prose tribute by Edmund Gosse (see letter of 6 June 23) beneath the heading 'To Thomas Hardy. / On His Eighty-third Birthday.'

To EDMUND GOSSE

Max Gate | 6: 6: 1923

My dear Gosse:

I send a line to supplement Florence's grateful letter to you on your very kind paragraph, which she wrote when my eyes (never of the best now-a-days, naturally) were obscured by rheum. They are now better.

As I may have told you before, I read these things said about me by generous friends as if they were concerning some person whom I but vaguely know, & whom they have mistaken for me. When I saw in the newspapers that you were at the Academy Private View I regretted my feebleness of will in not going. We had told several friends that we hoped to be there; but at the last moment stood shivering on the brink like Dr Watts's timorous mortals, & stayed at home.

We read your articles in the Sunday Times: & cannot think where your energy to write them comes from.

Always yours

Thomas Hardy.

Text   MS. (with envelope) Leeds.
Florence's grateful letter: of 3 June 23 (Leeds).   *kind paragraph*: Gosse in fact contributed four short paragraphs as his *Sunday Times* birthday 'tribute' of 3 June 23 (see letter of 5 June 23), saluting TH as 'the first of living men of letters in the world'.   *Private View*: Gosse and his wife were among those listed in *The Times*, 5 May 1923, as attending the Private View of the Royal Academy the previous day.   *Watts's timorous mortals*: an allusion to the fourth verse of Isaac Watts's hymn 'There is a land of pure delight' ('But timorous mortals start and shrink / To cross this narrow sea, / And linger shivering on the brink, / And fear to launch away.'). See III.144.   *in the Sunday Times*: where he was the principal reviewer; see Ann Thwaite, *Edmund Gosse: A Literary Landscape* (London, 1984), 483–7.

To MACLEOD YEARSLEY

MAX GATE, | DORCHESTER. | 7 June: 1923

Dear Mr Yearsley:

Thank you & Mrs Yearsley very sincerely—though of necessity briefly—for your kind letter of congratulation on my birthday. It would have been pleasant if you could have alighted when you were passing through Dorchester recently. My wife & I had of course no idea that you were so near.

I think she has corresponded with you on the advisability of removing the gland in her neck. I naturally feel anxious about it, & you will forgive my asking in my ignorance of these things if such an operation would be quite within your province, & also if there would be much danger in it, or risk of further complications. To tell the truth I rather wish it could be dispensed with altogether, if you think no further harm would arise beyond the slight disfigurement it causes, which we do not mind; & I am sure you will give a disinterested opinion.

   With kind regards I am

Yours always truly
Th: Hardy.

Text   MS. (with envelope) Eton College.
Yearsley: Percival Macleod Yearsley, surgeon and author; see V.100.   *Mrs Yearsley*: Yearsley's wife Louise, who became a friend of FEH's.   *letter of congratulation*: of 1 June 23 (DCM).   *through Dorchester*: Yearsley said in his letter that he had passed through Dorchester by train on his way home from Jersey in late May.   *disinterested opinion*: Yearsley saw FEH in London on 14 June and wrote TH that same day (DCM) to report that the 'little gland' had not 'altered in size appreciably' and that he had advised FEH against having it operated on for the time being.

To ETHEL COWLEY

MAX GATE, | DORCHESTER. | 11 June 1923

Dear Mrs Cowley:

   How very kind of you to send this nice handkerchief & letter of congratulations. I am unfortunately forced to reply in a few very mean & meagre lines which you will readily understand the reason of, I am sure.

   I hope you are having a pleasant time at Torquay. I think I have got over my cold at last. My wife sends her love, & I am

Always yours sincerely
Thomas Hardy.

Text   MS. (with envelope) Canon Cowley.

To SIR FREDERICK MACMILLAN

MAX GATE, DORCHESTER. | 11 June 1923.

Dear Sir Frederick Macmillan:

   I am much obliged to you for finding out about the "Albatross" Film Society in Paris, and getting a definite offer from them for the film rights in "The Return of the Native". I am quite willing to accept it, being of the same opinion as you in the matter, and therefore ask you to finish the transaction. Please pass on charges to me.

Sincerely yours,
Thomas Hardy.

Text   MS. (typewritten) BL.
of the Native": see letter of 17 May 23 and letter to Macmillan of 30 June 23.

To LUCY CLIFFORD

MAX GATE, | DORCHESTER. | 15: 6: 1923

Dear Mrs Clifford:

Many thanks for good wishes. I wish I could write more, but you will understand why I send such a mean, brief reply, with bad eyesight & old age!

Ever yours
Thomas Hardy.

Text MS. (correspondence card, with envelope) NYU.
good wishes: in her letter of 2 June 23 (DCM).

To THE MAYOR OF DORCHESTER

15 June 1923

Dear Sir:

My sincere thanks to you & the Aldermen & Councillors of Dorchester for your good wishes on my birthday.

Although I enter the Town rather less frequently than I formerly did I take great interest in its gradual development, & in noticing the frequent surprise of London visitors at finding it so busy & thriving a place.

Yours very truly

His Worship the Mayor, | Dorchester.

Text MS. (pencil draft) DCM.
Mayor: E. Lorenzo Ling; see letter of 29 Nov 22.   *good wishes*: in a letter of 13 June 23.

To J. C. SQUIRE

MAX GATE, | DORCHESTER. | 16 June 1923

My dear Mr Squire:

I just acknowledge the receipt of the book of poems you have been so kind as to give & dedicate to me—though I have not really read it carefully yet.

Nevertheless I have read again "The Stockyard"—which has a paralyzing attraction. After that terrible piece I have gone on to the more pleasant things—that do not compel reflections on the awful welter of the world in which we live—to such poems as "A London Sunset", "The Lover" & "The Journey" all of which I like. Also your reflections at the end, called "Descendants". But I shall name them all if I go further.

With sincere thanks I am

Ever yours truly
Thomas Hardy.

I cannot tell how you find time to do so much. T.H.

Text MS. Texas.
dedicate to me: Squire's *American Poems and Others* (London, 1923) is dedicated 'To / Thomas Hardy'.   *"The Stockyard"*: see letter of 13 June 22.   *"The Lover"*: i.e., 'The Lover Comforts Himself'.

To JOHN MASEFIELD

MAX GATE, | DORCHESTER. | 17 June 1923

Dear Mr Masefield:

What with a bad cold, & weak eyes, & a mounting tale of years, I have left "King Cole" & your kind birthday wishes unacknowledged till now.

I like the circus part of the poem very much—I mean the real part—the scene of the people in the rain & mud, for I have loved circuses all my life, & you have brought them back vividly in your pages. Of the shorter pieces "The Rider at the Gate" arrests me most. But I have not read the book yet as carefully as I mean to do, when I shall be able to make up my mind upon "K.C." as a whole.

I don't know whether Oxford will see me after all this summer. Not that I find locomotion difficult, but I feel a growing disinclination to move about. Kindest regards to Mrs Masefield: also from my wife; & believe me

Always yours
Thomas Hardy.

Many thanks for kind invitation. T.H.

Text MS. (with envelope) Columbia Univ.
"King Cole": Masefield's *King Cole, and Other Poems* (London, 1923).   *circus part*: i.e., the description (51–7) of the circus performance in 'King Cole' itself; for TH's love of circuses see Millgate, 62.   *kind invitation*: evidently issued in general rather than specific terms; see letter of 24 June 23.

To JOHN MIDDLETON MURRY

MAX GATE, | DORCHESTER. | 19 June 1923

Dear Mr Middleton Murry:

I am ashamed of myself for not having answered you sooner, & still more ashamed at not sending anything to the new periodical (a copy of which I received: thanks). But I have seemed dried up of late:—"it is almost time!" you will probably remark—& beyond copying out an old production I don't think of printing I have done nothing. Much success to "The Adelphi" (good title *I* think having passed 5 years there—). If anything does occur to me I will send it.

Always sincerely yrs
Thomas Hardy.

Text MS. Berg.
new periodical: the *Adelphi*, edited by Murry; the first issue was dated June 1923.   *old production*: see letter of 2 July 23.   *5 years there*: see letter of 8 Jan 23.   *send it*: TH contributed one poem, 'A Leader of Fashion', to the *Adelphi*, November 1925.

To JOHN MASEFIELD

Max Gate | Sunday. 24. 6. '23

Dear Mr Masefield,

Having just told you there was no chance of our getting to Oxford this year, lo, a friend comes along with his car, & insists upon motoring us there to-morrow for a day or two. I let you know this in case we should be able to call on you for a few minutes as we go by, to or fro, our road being from Wantage to the city of learning, & therefore passing by Boar's Hill a little to the W.

While in Oxford we shall be in the hands of the Provost & Vice-Provost of Queen's, & we also have to call on some relations; & have to be back here by Wednesday evening. So that if we should seem uncivil & not be able to drop in upon you, you & Mrs Masefield will, I am sure, make allowance for our situation.

Always yours
Thomas Hardy.

Text MS. (envelope) Texas.
just told you: see letter of 17 June 23.   *a friend*: William Watkins; see III.129.   *a day or two*: specifically, 25 and 26 June 1923.   *of Queen's*: the Revd. John Richard Magrath (1839–1930), provost of Queen's College since 1878; it was the pro-provost, the Revd. E. M. Walker (see letter of 14 Nov 22) who wrote (18 June 23, DCM) to invite TH and FEH to visit Queen's.   *some relations*: Margaret Gifford and her daughter Daisy.   *drop in upon you*: TH did visit the Masefields at their house just outside Oxford; see *LY*, 233.

To WALTER DE LA MARE

MAX GATE, | DORCHESTER. | 28 June: 1923

My dear Mr de la Mare:

We have just returned from a sojourn in "the home of lost causes"—Oxford, & I find, among other of my negligences, that I have not yet answered your letter of the 14th—in which you very kindly point out to me a channel through which I may possibly extend the circulation of my verses in America. It happened very oddly that just after your letter had arrived a literary gentleman from the U.S. called here, & I enquired of him how my poetry books were getting on over there. He says that within the last twelvemonths their circulation has much improved, & that they are quite accessible everywhere now, though till lately they were not—a statement corroborated by Miss Amy Lowell, to whom I had put the same question a short time back. So that at present I think I may as well leave things alone & see what happens. If I should want another publisher on that side the one you mention would seem to be excellent.

We should immensely like you to be at Weymouth for a few days. A good many trippers are there in August, but after all they are a harmless folk: & we could show you some lodgings in quarters they don't frequent.

As to what friends say about "Seaton's Aunt"—well, I shouldn't listen to them. It is a *splendidly gruesome* story: & I always feel that a man should write what he can write best: if you have a bass voice they must accept bass from you, & not be perpetually wanting you to sing treble. That's my plan, anyhow.

We enjoyed ourselves at Oxford very much—living in College (Queen's) &

we went there & came back entirely by road. My wife sends her love to Mrs de la Mare, & I am always

Sincerely yours
Thomas Hardy.

We called on Masefield at Oxford. He lives on Boar's Hill, a little way out, & has *a haunted house* immediately opposite him! T.H.

Text MS. Eton College.
of lost causes": TH had invoked in *Jude the Obscure* (Wessex edn., 94) this phrase from the Preface to Matthew Arnold's *Essays in Criticism* (1865).   *in America*: de la Mare (14 June 23, DCM) reported that his own publisher, Alfred A. Knopf, would like to pub. a selection of TH's poems in the U.S., especially since he felt they were not being adequately promoted by Macmillan.   *literary gentleman*: unidentified.   *a short time back*: see letter of 7 Mar 23.   gruesome *story*: de la Mare's 'Seaton's Aunt', first pub. in *London Mercury*, April 1922, had recently been collected in *The Riddle and Other Stories* (London, 1923); he complained to TH that reviewers had tended to call his work 'morbid' and that Sydney Cockerell had entreated him to mend his ways.   *entirely by road*: for the Oxford visit see letter of 24 June 23.   *Mrs de la Mare*: Constance Elfrida de la Mare, *née* Ingpen (d. 1943); she was the sister of Roger Ingpen (see letter of 24 Sept 21), who married de la Mare's sister.

To EDWARD CLODD

MAX GATE, | DORCHESTER. | 30 June: 1923

My dear Clodd:
   On my way back from Oxford (where we have been staying for a few days) it came into my head that your birthday drew near; & I send this line to wish you as many happy returns of the same as you care to have—perhaps another score or so?—but that I leave to you.
   Our kindest regards to you & yr house.

Sincly yrs
Thomas Hardy.

Text MS. (correspondence card) Leeds.
another score or so?: Clodd was just 29 days younger than TH himself.

To SIR FREDERICK MACMILLAN

MAX GATE, | DORCHESTER. | 30 June: 1923

My dear Macmillan:
   I don't see that it matters at all about the scenes & characters of The Return of the Native being made French instead of English. I imagine that the life of these films is not a long one, & even if otherwise it only amounts to a sort of translation of the story. So that I have no objection.

Sincerely yours
Thomas Hardy.

Text MS. BL.
instead of English: Macmillan reported (29 June 23, Macmillan letterbooks, BL) that the Société des Films Albatros (see letter of 17 May 23) had agreed to pay £250 for the film rights to *The Return of the Native* but wanted to be sure that TH had no objection to the settings and characters being transferred to France. The film seems not to have been produced, however.

To HARLEY GRANVILLE BARKER

Max Gate. | Dorchester. | 2. July 1923.

My dear Granville Barker,

I am sending with this a little thing I have had lying about for years in outline, and have lately finished to please our Dorchester Amateurs, who want something new. Do you think they could do it—I will not say well, but middling? The only virtue it possesses in a seriously dramatic light is its unity of line and place, which, so far as I am aware, not one of the many renderings of the old story has ever attempted.

Make any remarks about it you please—I should never have ventured to trouble you to read it if my wife had not told me you were interested in hearing I had such a matter in hand.

We spent some days in Oxford last week—going and returning by road, and living in College while there. I hope you are both well, and am

Sincerely yours,
Thomas Hardy.

Text   Typed transcript DCM.
little thing: a copy of *The Queen of Cornwall* (see letter of 30 Aug 23).   *Dorchester Amateurs*: the Hardy Players; see Purdy, 351, 353.   *unity of line*: this is the reading of the transcript, but TH probably wrote 'unity of time'.

To SIR GEORGE DOUGLAS

Max Gate, | Dorchester. | 8 July 1923.

My dear Douglas:

Here's a nice time of day for me to answer your letter of June 1. But you will, I am sure, know how it has happened. Many thanks for your good wishes, which I know are genuine.

I am interested in the fact of your nephew being in the 15th. Hussars, as I think I must already have told you: of my knowing a man of that regiment who fought under Wellington? Thomas Young of Sturminster Newton: you will see all about him in The Dynasts, Part III. Act II. Sc. I.

I agree with you in holding that the best of Keats lies in his poetry: the painful facts of his life rather injure the dreams and fancies raised by his verse. I have to cut short my letter because of 2 Americans who are calling. My wife sends her kindest regards and I am,

Ever sincerely yours,
Thomas Hardy.

Text   Typed transcript DCM.
of June 1: in DCM.   *your nephew*: Capt. George Francis Valentine Scott Douglas (see V.248), son of Douglas's younger brother Francis—whom TH had known in Wimborne in the early 1880s.   *Thomas Young*: Thomas Young (1798–1853), soldier, who appears (as TH says) in *The Dynasts*, Part Third, Act II, Scene 1, and is there identified in a footnote. It seems improbable that TH knew him personally, although he did know his nephew Robert Young ('Rabin Hill', the Dorset dialect poet), who provided information about his uncle in a letter of 2 Nov 96 (DCM).   *facts of his life*: Douglas said that he had been bored by Sidney Colvin's biography of Keats (see V.31) and felt that 'Lives of poets are a mistake'.   *2 Americans*: unidentified.

To HARLEY GRANVILLE BARKER

Max Gate, | Dorchester. | 9 July: 1923.

My dear Granville Barker:

Just a hasty line on the arrival of the play and your kind and valuable notes on the little job of which I had, and have, no very high opinion, but wished to get out of hand after long delays. So I did not hope for such a careful reading, and such wise counsel on the details of staging—a business quite out of my province, as you could see from my blindness to all but the effect of the tragedy as read in a book.

I shall not go carefully through each item you have marked, reviewing it by the light of your comments—which I have only as yet scanned rapidly—doubtless adopting all you recommendations—or as many of them as I have energy left for adopting this hot weather!

We are very sorry to hear of the loss of your and Helen's friend. I have never lost so many in a similar space of time as I have this year. Good wishes to both—F. would include hers but she is out for the afternoon—and believe me

Always sincerely
T. Hardy.

Text   Typed transcript DCM.
valuable notes: Barker's letter of 6 July 23 (DCM), largely devoted to *The Queen of Cornwall*, runs to 10 pages.   *not go ... all you*: evidently transcription errors for 'now go' and 'all your'.   *your and Helen's friend*: James Gray, London solicitor, described in Barker's letter as 'a good and close friend' and as his wife's 'lawyer and counsellor and man of business'.

To KATHARINE HARDY

Wedny 18th [July 1923]

My dear Katharine:

Florence has been to ask the Mayor whether Stinsford Hill is a good place for you, H., &c. to see the Prince pass—& he says that as the cars will turn off sharp into the ewelease (where the Exhibition was) which may possibly be closed to the public, S.H. is not a good place. You will see from the route I enclose that they do not come straight down Stinsford Hill into Dorchester, but go round to Lower Burton, so as to come up Grove Buildings. This is done because places for the school children have been arranged on the green slopes of the North Walk, so that when the Prince's route from Mere was altered to Blandford way instead of Sherborne way, as first intended, the entrance to the town had still to be in the same place.

I think that the bottom of Cuckoo Lane would be a nice quiet place to see H.R.H. pass, or inside the plantation close by—or opposite Higher Kingston— or near Birkin House, where the cross road from Stinsford church comes into the London road; or at the bottom of Yellham Hill—

As we told you, you can of course come here & stay in the bedroom behind the jessamine—you would then see him come, & go: we could probably send you up a snack of something to eat during your hour's wait. If I had known you would have cared to be at the Drill hall I could easily have got you tickets, but now none can be obtained, as they have issued 1000, & the hall will only hold about 500—at least so it is said. The Mayor says it will be as hot as the Black Hole of Calcutta. A police cordon is to be set all round our premises, so that nobody will be able to get over the wall, but the highway will not be stopped. If you do come here get here before 12, as nobody will be allowed to enter our gate after that without a police pass—or one from us.

Our neighbours are very kind in offering to lend us anything. There will be 6 men & 7 women to have a meal in the kitchen & side room—& they will have theirs early (except the Prince's chauffeurs) to have it over before our lunch-time.

Eva left for Lyme Regis this morning, & I rather miss her. She says she is glad to be out of our little entertainment.

Yes: H. can hoist the union-jack if he likes to—they are putting up barriers in Dorchester, I hear.

Ever affectionately

T.

Text   MS. (pencil) Mary Jacobus.
Hardy: Katharine Hardy, TH's surviving sister; see II.124. She wrote 17 July 23 (DCM) to ask where and when she could best see the Prince of Wales when he visited Dorchester.   *the Mayor*: see letter of 29 Nov 22.   *H.*: Henry Hardy, TH's younger brother; see I.31.   *the Prince*: Edward, Prince of Wales (1894–1972), later King Edward VIII; for his visit to Dorchester, 20 July 1923, see *LY*, 234, and Millgate, 548–9.   *(where the Exhibition was)*: the field (on the N. side of the Dorchester–Puddletown road opposite the turning off to Stinsford) where the Bath and West of England Show had been held in the past.   *H.R.H.*: His Royal Highness.   *the Drill hall*: the main ceremonial function of the Prince's visit was the official opening of this building at the headquarters of the local Territorial (i.e., part-time) army units. *Eva*: Eva Dugdale, FEH's sister; see letter of 6 Jan 20.   *hoist the union-jack*: Henry Hardy had asked his sister to ask TH if it would be 'all right' to fly the Union Jack from the flagpole at Talbothays, their house near West Stafford, Dorset.

To HAMLIN GARLAND

FROM TH. HARDY, | MAX GATE, | DORCHESTER. | 8: 8: 1923

Dear Hamlin Garland:

Any afternoon between next Friday & the following Tuesday inclusive I shall be delighted to see you. It will be well to let me know which date you choose, that I may not be out. I am glad to hear that you have had a pleasant time.

Sincerely yrs

T. Hardy.

Text   MS. (correspondence card) Univ. of Southern California.
Garland: Hamlin Garland (1860–1940), American novelist; his visit to Max Gate, on Saturday, 11 August, is recorded in his *Afternoon Neighbors: Further Excerpts from a Literary Log* (New York, 1934), 85–93.

To DOROTHY ALLHUSEN

MAX GATE, | DORCHESTER. | 17 Aug: 1923
My dear Dorothy

I am glad to learn that you are well & have been on a visit. We are not going anywhere this month except to places a few miles round here.

In respect of the appeal for Stoke Poges church, as I cannot propose reconstructions in any church that I have not personally inspected, & even then repairs only—having written frequently against restorations, & being a Member of the Society for the Protection of Ancient Buildings—I think a good plan for you would be to write to the Society (A. R. Powys, Sec. 20 Buckingham St. Adelphi), & ask their support in the matter. They would probably inspect the building, & if the case is one of urgent necessity, would I am sure write to the papers about it. A letter from the Society would carry great weight.

The question of the adjoining land is beyond me, & must be tackled by people who know the spot well, & the probabilities of its ruin by invasion.

We have not heard when, or if, your mother is coming; but she will probably write soon.

Always affectionately
Th: Hardy.

Text MS. C. J. P. Beatty.
to learn: from her letter of 16 Aug 23 (DCM).   *on a visit*: to her mother, Lady St. Helier, at Cold Ash, near Newbury.   *for Stoke Poges church*: Mrs. Allhusen asked TH to write to the *Daily Telegraph* in support of an appeal for the restoration of the spire of Stoke Poges church. *A. R. Powys*: see letter to him of 25 Aug 23.   *the adjoining land*: a report of the appeal in *The Times*, 6 Oct 1923, spoke of preserving 'the rural surroundings and peaceful charm of the "country churchyard," made famous by Thomas Gray, by the purchase of land surrounding it'. The Allhusens' own land extended along one side of the churchyard.   *write soon*: Lady St. Helier wrote 17 Sept 23 (DCM) to say that she would arrive at Max Gate on 4 or 5 October.

To CLIVE HOLLAND

(Not for publication.)   MAX GATE, | DORCHESTER. | 25th. August 1923.
Dear Mr Clive Holland:

I should not think it worth while for you to come here for an article while you have better material at hand in prefaces and notes to volumes I have published. However, I have no objection to your taking a few photographs of this house and garden, if you wish to do so. But I should object to being photographed personally, and to anything like an interview for press purposes. Such interviews have brought so much fabrication and misrepresentation in the past that I have been compelled for years to decline them, having moreover written no novels for nearly 30 years, or anything to pique the curiosity of the man in the street.

If you read the thin paper volume called "Collected Poems"—one of the two containing all my productions of the latter time (the other volume being

"The Dynasts") you will gather more personal particulars than I could give you in an interview, circumstances not being so veiled in the verse as in the novels.

Yours truly,
Thomas Hardy.
T.H.

Text MS. (all except TH's initials typewritten) Adams.
Clive Holland: pseudonym of Charles James Hankinson, novelist and journalist; see II.177.
come here: Holland (20 Aug 23, DCM) asked if he could visit Max Gate to take some photographs for an article on TH, his books, and the region of Wessex.

To A. R. POWYS

MAX GATE, DORCHESTER. | 25th. August 1923.

Dear Mr Powys:

I am informed that Stoke Poges Church is in need of repair, and am requested to support a movement to obtain funds. If the repairs are so urgently needed as is represented I should be quite willing to do this, but I am unable to inspect the building personally to assure myself on the point. If you know anything about the matter, and could give me the benefit of your opinion, I should be obliged.

I enclose herewith a copy of the information that has been received by a friend of mine who lives there, which please let me have back.

Yours truly,
Thomas Hardy.
T.H.

Text MS. (all except TH's initials typewritten) SPAB.
Powys: Albert Reginald Powys (see V.296), architect and secretary of the Society for the Protection of Ancient Buildings.   *support a movement*: see letter of 17 Aug 23.   *friend of mine*: Mrs. Allhusen; she had written again, 22 Aug 23 (DCM), urging TH to be more active in his support.

To ERNEST BRENNECKE

27 August 1923

Dear Mr Brennecke:

I write for Mr Hardy, owing to the pressure of his correspondence, to say that the typoscript essay has arrived. He is unfortunately not able to read it with sufficient care to authorize it in any way, as was, he believes, explained to you on your last visit.

This, perhaps, is no misfortune for the critical book you contemplate. The Art of Thomas Hardy by Lionel Johnson, though now somewhat out of date, was a model of what such a work should be; & he never met or communicated with Mr Hardy till long after his book was issued.

As far as Mr Hardy can gather, you appear not to have stumbled into the pitfall which has been the undoing of some previous critics—that of assuming his inventions to be real personifications & experiences of his own. For instance (as he may have told you) Jude the Obscure, often quoted as autobiographical, contains not a page of his own experiences—as may be readily discovered by looking into Who's Who—& no portrait from the real, except as to some characteristics of the young woman Sue.

Since Mr Hardy cannot discuss any points of the essay with you, or consent to your using the visit for press purposes, you will perhaps feel that there is little use in coming here, though we shall be happy to see you if your call is not to be made use of *practically*.

Text   MS. (pencil draft) DCM.
Brennecke: Ernest Brennecke, Jr. (1896–1969), American critic and university teacher; he first wrote to TH (from New York) 24 May 23 (DCM).   *typoscript essay*: evidently the typescript of all or part of Brennecke's *Thomas Hardy's Universe: A Study of a Poet's Mind*, first pub. 1924.   *somewhat out of date*: see letter of 29 June 22.

To SIR FREDERICK MACMILLAN

MAX GATE, | DORCHESTER. | August 30th. 1923.

Dear Sir Frederick Macmillan:

I am about to startle you by sending up with this, for you to consider, a short MS. of a one-act play—quite a different production from anything I have sent before. The circumstances are these: I have written it, or rather finished it (for it has been more or less in existence for a long time) for our local dramatic society, who are going to act it about the middle of November. I did not at first mean to publish it at all, but as the acting may attract some attention, which it has already done before, although only by amateurs, I have thought whether it would be worth while to print the play as a thin volume, and publish it on the day it is produced here.

It is, in a way, a novelty in one feature, for though for acting, it announces itself as requiring no theatre or scenery, and no modern author, so far as I know, has thrown down the gage to the scene-furniture-maker before. So that, as there are so many collectors about, an edition might go off.

The question would be, what kind of book to make of it? Though so short I think it would be better not to lengthen it by mixing it up with any poems I could collect from magazines, &c. It might be published in stiff paper covers, or do you think a 4/6 cloth volume better? Perhaps the illustrations I have drawn at the beginning would be some help to it.

It would, of course, ultimately go in with any miscellaneous MSS. I may collect, or leave behind me.

Sincerely yours,
Thomas Hardy.

Text   MS. (typewritten) BL.
one-act play: TH's verse-play *The Famous Tragedy of the Queen of Cornwall*, pub. by Macmillan 15 Nov 1923.

To ROGER LOOMIS

MAX GATE, DORCHESTER. | 3rd. September 1923.

Dear Sir:

I must apologize for not having acknowledged the arrival of the book that you were so very kind as to send me, but unfortunately parcels get overlooked sometimes, and possibly it was so in this case.

I shall be here, so far as I know, on the 12th. and 13th. Sept. if you like to call on either afternoon, letting me know which a day or so before, that I may not be out. I will endeavour to have read the book before you come.

Yours very truly,
Thomas Hardy.

Roger S. Loomis Esq. | c.o. American Express Company. | Haymarket.

Text MS. (typewritten) Adams.
Loomis: Roger Sherman Loomis (1887–1966), American medievalist, editor of *Arthurian Literature in the Middle Ages: A Collaborative History* (Oxford, 1959). *the book*: Loomis's trans. of *The Romance of Tristram and Ysolt*, by Thomas 'the Troubadour' (New York, 1923); Loomis had sent it the previous May but wrote again 30 Aug 23 (DCM) to renew his request to visit Max Gate.

To SIR FREDERICK MACMILLAN

MAX GATE, | DORCHESTER. | September 5th. 1923.

Dear Sir Frederick:

The style of production you suggest seems as good as any, and please announce it whenever you choose. As the titlepage is probably the most original feature of the play the more of its wording you make known the better I should imagine.

The small view of the exterior of the Castle is a reduced photograph of the actual drawing I made, which is 14 inches by 11, and of course much clearer: if the illustrator would prefer to have that to work from I can send it, as it rolls up easily.

I have promised our stage-manager here not to anticipate his date, which is about the middle of November. I will find out the exact day and let you know.

Sincerely yours,
Thomas Hardy.

Text MS. (typewritten) BL.
you suggest: in his letter of 4 Sept 23 (Macmillan letterbooks, BL). *the titlepage*: a facsimile of the MS. title-page of *The Queen of Cornwall* was used on the dust-wrapper of the first edn. *exterior of the Castle*: TH's drawing was used as the frontispiece to the first edn. *stage-manager here*: i.e., of the Hardy Players; TH apparently meant T. H. Tilley, the producer. *his date*: i.e., the date of the first performance; see letters of 18 Sept and 27 Oct 23.

To MACMILLAN & CO.

MAX GATE, | DORCHESTER. | 8 Sept. 1923

The Drawing mentioned in letter of the 5th is sent by this post—

T.H.

Text   MS. (postcard with address in FEH's hand) BL.

To SIR FREDERICK MACMILLAN

MAX GATE, | DORCHESTER. | 10 September 1923.

Dear Sir Frederick:

We have been looking with great interest at the specimen page you send, which seems all that can be desired. I suppose the opposite page will bear as heading "The Famous Tragedy of", unless there is any reason for printing the same headline to every page.

The original drawing of the exterior of the Castle I sent on Saturday, since it may be more convenient for reproduction than the little photograph of the same.

The rough sketch of the interior, which was also attached to the MS., was made merely for the use of the scene-painter here, but Mr Granville Barker, who happened to see it, says it is a great help to reading the play; hence I don't know whether it ought not to be included as a second illustration, even though so badly drawn. You can probably get expert opinion on this matter.

The other point you allude to, our agreement forms, is as you imply, and as I have often casually thought, not very intelligible, and I shall be very glad to have the various items codified into one agreement, which please draw up as soon as you choose. I remember that some of the changes, on account of the war, were not very favourable from an author's point of view, so that any improvements you can make in that respect will be welcome.

Believe me,

Yours sincerely,
Thomas Hardy.

P.S. I am reminded to mention, what I have often been going to say, that if ever you want to ask anything suddenly you can call us up by telephone— "Dorchester. 43."

Text   MS. (typewritten) BL.
specimen page: for *The Queen of Cornwall*, sent 6 Sept 23 (Macmillan letterbooks, BL).
same headline: Macmillan had evidently forwarded a right-hand page, headed 'THE QUEEN OF CORNWALL'; the left-hand pages of the first edition are indeed headed 'THE FAMOUS TRAGEDY OF'.   *on Saturday*: see letter of 8 Sept 23.   *Granville Barker*: for his interest in the play see letters of 2 and 9 July 23.   *second illustration*: it faces p. 4 of the first edn.   *agreement forms*: Macmillan pointed out in his letter that since TH's publishing agreements with the house of Macmillan, first entered into in 1902 (see III.11–14, 15–16), had since been expanded and modified 'almost beyond recognition', it might be sensible to draw up a new consolidated agreement.   *by telephone*: this had been installed in late 1919; see letter of 8 Jan 20.

To JOHN HAY BEITH
11 September, 1923

Dear Mr Hay Beith:

I should very much like to dine with the Society again, after so many years of absence from its dinners. And I feel I ought to do so, since it honours me by retaining me as its President still. But the undertaking is impossible for several reasons, the greatest being the physical one, as you will infer.

But while this is unfortunately the case, the Committee & yourself may be sure that I value the kind thought which suggested the request, & that some distinguished persons should be invited to meet me.

I have not been in London for more than two years, & am much in doubt on when I shall see that noisy but in some respects enjoyable city again.

Believe me to be

Yours most sincerely

Ian Hay Beith Esq. C.B.E.

Text MS. (pencil draft) DCM.
Beith: John Hay Beith (1876–1952), author of novels and plays under the pseudonym of 'Ian Hay'; *D.N.B.* He wrote 8 Sept 23 (DCM) in his capacity as chairman of the Committee of Management of the Incorporated Society of Authors to request TH's presence at the Society's annual dinner in London on 23 November.   *invited to meet me*: Beith promised to invite 'a few eminent guests whom I know would appreciate the distinction of being associated with you on this occasion'.

To MACMILLAN & CO.
FROM TH. HARDY, | MAX GATE, | DORCHESTER. | 13th Sept. '23.

Letter & enclosures received. Will read & return Memorandum in a day or two.

Text MS. (postcard, entirely in FEH's hand) BL.
enclosures received: see letter of 18 Sept 23; TH there refers to this present item as '[m]y postcard', despite its being in FEH's hand, and it was certainly sent in his name.

To SIR FREDERICK MACMILLAN
MAX GATE, | DORCHESTER. | 18 September 1923.

Dear Sir Frederick Macmillan:

I find that about November 15th—(8 weeks from this)—will suit our Dramatic Company here for the publication of "The Queen of Cornwall".

The proofs have arrived from the printers, and I am about to read them.

My postcard will have let you know that I duly received the account of sales and the form of Agreement.—I think as you do that the sales are very satisfactory.

Being much interested in the proofs, and occupied with hearing the performers read through their parts, I have only had time as yet to glance at the codified Agreement, but I shall be able to do so in 2 or 3 days. Meanwhile will you let me know if I am right in assuming that my copyright in *all* my books, early-written ones and late, will extend to 50 years after my death? It is very stupid of me not to be quite sure (especially as I am President of the Society of Authors, which is always dealing with the subject!)

Yours sincerely,
Thomas Hardy.

Text MS. (typewritten) BL.
My postcard: of 13 Sept 23.   *very satisfactory*: Macmillan reported (12 Sept 23, Macmillan letterbooks, BL) that TH's royalties for the year ended 30 June 1923 totalled £2,526, approximately £200 more than for the previous year.   *my copyright*: Macmillan (19 Sept 23, Macmillan letterbooks, BL) explained that the current (1911) copyright law granted unrestricted copyright for 25 years after the author's death and that there was a further 25-year period during which anyone could reprint the author's work upon payment of a 10 per cent royalty on the published price.

To SIR FREDERICK MACMILLAN

MAX GATE, | DORCHESTER. | 22 Sept: 1923

My dear Macmillan:

   You & your partners will be quite aware that the suggestions I have made in the detailed letter I am posting with this are (supposing my books to have any sale in the future) in view only of possible contingencies, such as personal changes in your firm, or my affairs being in the hands of executors. Were the same individuals to be directors of Macmillan & Co for 25 or more years ahead, or descendants of theirs, I should take no sort of trouble about words in an Agreement, knowing that things would readily be set right if wrong. My bringing the books to you in 1902 was almost entirely for personal reasons; so may I assume or hope that some or other of the family are likely to remain in the firm, which has now become famous!—at any rate that there is no intention of their becoming dissociated from the direction of it?

Yours most sincerely
Thomas Hardy.

Text MS. (typewritten) BL.
bringing the books to you: it was indeed TH who took the first steps towards an agreement with the house of Macmillan; see III.11–12.   *from the direction of it?*: Macmillan responded (24 Sept 23, Macmillan letterbooks, BL) that there was no prospect of the firm's going out of the family, especially since his brother Maurice's two sons, Daniel (see letter of 27 Jan 21) and Harold (see letter of 16 Feb 21), were 'very clever fellows and keenly interested in their occupation'.

To SIR FREDERICK MACMILLAN

MAX GATE, | DORCHESTER. | September 22nd. 1923.

Dear Sir Frederick Macmillan:

   Many thanks for information upon the term of copyright. I have now read the codified Agreement form you sent, and approve of it except in some minor particulars, viz:—

   Clause 1. Upon the whole I should like the words "are to be written," (though unimportant, considering my age), to be omitted. In respect of poetry, plays, or fiction they are of no moment, as it is in my interest that such work should go with the rest. But if I should ever want to publish, for instance, an essay or preface to another author's works (as I did on Barnes the poet) it might be necessary that it should be in a list with, or attached to, the subject treated of.

Clause 3. "Translation of the works." You will probably agree that the word "translation" should be left out, as it contradicts the sentence which follows it.

Clause 4. I do not see why fractional parts of the published price as in the old Agreement are not retained, as they would in my opinion render this clause fairer to both parties. So I suggest that after the words "the following schedule" there be added: "If any of the published prices should be changed, the royalty to be paid shall be changed to bear the same proportion to the new prices that the royalties scheduled bear to the present prices," (or something to that effect).

I am not sure if we ought not to insert the following provision, considering that the Agreement will be in force for at least 25 or 30 years, and that executors may have to represent us: "In the event of a dispute on any question arising out of this Agreement, the parties agree to abide by the decision of an Arbitrator or Arbitrators mutually approved by the said parties." What do you think?

As to the United States. Do I rightly understand that things over there are as follows: that all the prose is published by Harpers, and all the verse, including The Dynasts, by yourselves, except that in their Wessex edition (which they call "Anniversary" I think) they necessarily include the verse to make it complete?

Believe me,

Yours sincerely,
Thomas Hardy.

P.S. If you approve of my suggestions I will send back the form for you to insert them.

Text   MS. BL.

term of copyright: see letter of 18 Sept 23.   *"are to be written,"*: Macmillan & Co.'s standard printed agreement, which TH had been sent (see letters of 18 and 27 Sept 23), referred to the works 'which have been or are to be written, compiled, or edited by the Author'; in the agreement as signed (BL) this entire passage has been struck through in favour of an inserted reference to TH's works 'at present issued by [the publisher] in various editions'.   *on Barnes the poet*: see letter of 15 Feb 24 to Drinkwater.   *sentence which follows it*: in the standard agreement the requirement that the author should not permit 'any abridgement or translation of the works' without the publisher's consent was immediately followed by the sentence, 'All rights of translation or dramatization shall remain the property of the Author'; in the signed agreement the words 'or translation' were struck through.   *to insert them*: Macmillan replied (24 Sept 23, Macmillan letterbooks, BL) that he gladly agreed to TH's suggested modifications of the codified agreement.

To SIR FREDERICK MACMILLAN

FROM TH. HARDY, | MAX GATE, | DORCHESTER. | 25: 9: 1923

Agreement form returned for corrections according to letters exchanged.

Text MS. (correspondence card) BL.
letters exchanged: i.e., TH's second letter of 22 Sept 23 and Macmillan's reply of 23 Sept 23.

To CLEMENT SHORTER

FROM TH. HARDY, | MAX GATE, | DORCHESTER. | 25: 9: 1923

Many thanks for letter. Am sorry to say that I am quite unable to answer your question on what I meant in the novel.

T.H.

Text MS. (postcard) Berg.
your question: Shorter (23 Sept 23, DCM) had questioned the references in *A Laodicean* (Wessex edn., 27) to painters called 'Sir Geoffrey' and 'Sir Thomas', pointing out that Kneller's first name was Godfrey and that Gainsborough was never knighted; later issues of the Wessex edn. read 'Godfrey' for 'Geoffrey' but retain 'Sir Thomas', probably because TH had Sir Thomas Lawrence in mind.

To SIR FREDERICK MACMILLAN

MAX GATE, | DORCHESTER. | 27 Sept. 1923

Dear Sir Frederick:

I return the Agreement signed, with the first draft, on which a clause was deleted that you overlooked in the fair copy, & which I therefore struck out.

I am very glad to know that the Macmillan Co. have all the verse in the United States. Readers over there tell me that they can now get The Dynasts & the Collected Poems without trouble in the large towns, which shows that your Company have put them about more actively than when complaints were made.

Yours very sincerely
Thomas Hardy

Text MS. BL.
return the Agreement: the Memorandum of Agreement between TH and Macmillan & Co. still accompanies this letter; dated 26 Sept 1923, it covers all the works then in print except for *Under the Greenwood Tree*, of which the copyright was still owned by by Chatto & Windus.   *struck out*: apparently Clause 7, 'The Author agrees to pay all costs of corrections and alterations in proof sheets exceeding 25 per cent. of the cost of the composition of the works.' For TH's earlier objections to such a clause see III.80.   *in the United States*: TH had raised this point in his second letter of 22 Sept 23 and been reassured by Macmillan's reply.

To THE REVD. G. CURRIE MARTIN

28 Sept. 1923

Dear Sir:

I much appreciate the suggestion of the Committee of the London R. L. Stevenson Club that I should become an Honorary Member, even though as a matter of fact I am not what would be called a Stevensonian in the full sense in which that expression could be applied to so many, probably all, of the Club's members.

However, the question of my sufficiency does not really arise. I have now reached a great age, one at which I find it necessary to abstain from further association with Societies, even if only of an Honorary kind, flattering as the connection may be; & therefore I must decline the distinction of being elected one of the London branch of the Club.

Yours truly

. . . .

Prof. G. Currie Martin. M.A. | ["Vailima" | 30 Ambrose Avenue | London. N.W. 11]

Text   MS. (pencil draft) DCM.
Martin: the Revd. George Currie Martin (1865–1937), lecturer and author, chiefly on religious subjects; he wrote 27 Sept 23 (DCM), as secretary of the Robert Louis Stevenson Club of London, asking TH to send his 'benediction' for the club's inaugural meeting on 5 Oct 1923 and offering to elect him as an honorary life member. This reply, though negative, was read out at the meeting and pub. in *The Times*, 9 Oct 23.   *Stevenson*: see letter of 20 Nov 21. *["Vailima" . . . N.W. 11]*: TH's square brackets.

To MACMILLAN & CO.

FROM | TH. HARDY, ESQ., | MAX GATE, | DORCHESTER. | 2 Oct 1923

Proofs of the "Queen of Cornwall" to end, returned herewith for press.

Messrs Macmillan

Text   MS. (printed stationery with 'Memorandum' heading) BL.

To EDWARD CLODD

MAX GATE, | DORCHESTER. | 4 Oct. 1923

My dear Clodd:

Many thanks for sending on Mr Shansfield's letter on Westminster Hospital, & for kind enquiries. Just now I am rather troubled by diarrhoea, which, as you know, is enervating; but I don't think it will last much longer.

I had heard before that the Hospital was in sad need of renovation inside, it having been, I believe, the most backward in equipment in London.

I hope you will be able as usual to face the east wind off the sea when it comes.

Yours sincerely
Th: Hardy.

Text   MS. (with envelope) Leeds.
Shansfield's . . . Hospital: see letter of 4 Oct 23 to Shansfield.   *off the sea*: Clodd, now retired, was living permanently at Aldeburgh, on the Suffolk coast.

To SIR FREDERICK MACMILLAN

MAX GATE, | DORCHESTER. | 4 October 1923.

Dear Sir Frederick:

I like the look of the book immensely, and the reproduction of the drawings. I am sending the whole back, as the specimen may be useful to show what the volume will be like.

There is, I see, room for the titles of the illustrations at the bottom of the list of Characters, which is a suitable place, as you say.

I thought, too, that the outside of the Castle would be the better one for the frontispiece. The other would naturally follow the description of the stage on page IV.

As to the price, 6/- will not, I imagine—seem too much, now that I see how the book will appear. I hope readers will not think I have been rather stingy in the quantity of matter!

Yours sincerely,
Thomas Hardy.

Text MS. (typewritten) BL.
the book: *The Queen of Cornwall*; Macmillan (3 Oct 23, Macmillan letterbooks, BL) sent proofs of the illustrations and a dummy of the vol. as a whole.   *on page IV*: in the vol. as pub. the page facing TH's drawing of the Castle's interior (see letter of 10 Sept 23) has the arabic numeral '4'.   *As to the price*: Macmillan said in his letter that the handsome appearance of the vol. justified an increase in price from five shillings to six shillings.

To W. N. SHANSFIELD

4 October 1923

Dear Mr Shansfield:

I am writing for my husband, who is unwell, though not seriously; yet sufficiently so to experience a great lack of energy. He has received your letter & read it with interest, but unhappily is compelled to say that he cannot undertake to write a preface or foreword to the booklet that is intended to be issued. Apart from the circumstance I mention above he feels himself too old & too far from the scene of operations to write such a thing satisfactorily.

Knowing also so little of the hospital details, & never having been inside it in his life, he thinks it would be unfair to such a noble institution that it should not have a better advocate than himself, when there must be many who could set forth its claims quite adequately.

He is nevertheless honoured by having been asked to help in a cause which he really has at heart. He is also glad that your request has been the means of bringing him a letter from Mr Clodd, from who he had not heard for years.

I am, with many regrets

Yours very truly
F. E. Hardy.

W. N. Shansfield Esq. | South of Ireland Publications | 180 Fleet Street | London | E.C. 4.

Text MS. (pencil draft) DCM.
Shansfield: William Newton Shansfield, journalist, formerly Hon. Secretary of the Whitefriars Club (see *LY*, 89–90). *your letter*: of 2 Oct 23 (DCM), requesting TH to write a brief foreword to a proposed booklet supportive of Westminster Hospital's appeal for public donations. *letter from Mr Clodd*: see letter of 4 Oct 23 to Clodd; Shansfield's letter to Clodd, asking if he thought TH would help, is also in DCM.

To SIR FREDERICK MACMILLAN

MAX GATE, | DORCHESTER. | 9. October 1923.

Dear Sir Frederick:

The Queen of Cornwall.

The opening page giving the list of characters is quite correct.

I had not thought of doing anything with the manuscript of the play. But now that the question has arisen we have decided to keep it for the present in case any museum which cares for such things should want it, as has happened on former occasions. But I will bear in mind Mr Sachs's inquiry, and let him know through you if this idea should be given up and the MS. be available. His letter is returned herewith.

Yours very sincerely,
Thomas Hardy.

Text MS. (typewritten) BL.
quite correct: Macmillan (8 Oct 23, Macmillan letterbooks, BL) sent a revised proof of the page containing the list of characters, to which had now been added the list of illustrations; see letter to Macmillan of 4 Oct 23. *returned herewith*: Macmillan forwarded an inquiry received from Howard J. Sachs (1891–1969), American investment banker and book collector, as to whether TH had considered selling the MS. of *The Queen of Cornwall*; a letter to Sachs from Macmillan & Co., conveying the substance of TH's message, was sent 10 Oct 23 (Macmillan letterbooks, BL).

To FORD MADOX FORD

MAX GATE, | DORCHESTER. | 18th. October 1923.

Dear Mr Madox Ford:

I have received your interesting letter, and quite admire your purposed attempt to start the publication you describe, which, as you imply, seems rather a venturesome step. I have no sort of opinion on how the scheme will work out, but at any rate I hope it will do well.

Don't you think you should invite young men more particularly, and keep out old men like me? However, that is for you to decide. There is really nothing I can find at present which would suit, and unhappily I don't want to appear in print in any new place till next year, as, without having quite anticipated doing it, I am bringing out a short play next month, and people will be pretty sick of my writing (if they are not already), should I inflict more upon them just yet.

But, apart from this, as I said above, I fancy that some vigorous young pens who may be available would perhaps suit you better.

I am obliged on account of increasing age to get most of my letters typewritten nowadays, which please pardon.

Yours sincerely,
Th: Hardy.

Text   MS. (typewritten) Cornell Univ.
Ford: i.e., Hueffer; see letter of 19 Dec 20.   *interesting letter*: it appears not to have survived but must have included a request for a contribution to the first issue of the *Transatlantic Review*; see letter of 30 Oct 23.

To LEONARD REES

20 October 1923
Dear Mr Rees:
   I write for my husband who has been indisposed these last few days, though not seriously, & has got behind with his letters. He says you are welcome to print either of the "War & Patriotism" poems on Sunday November 11. He thinks the one entitled "His Country" (p. 507, Collected Poems) might suit the peaceable views we have, or say we have, nowadays. If not that one "Often when warring" (p. 513) might do, or "According to the Mighty Working" (p. 541). Whichever seems appropriate in your opinion is at your service.

Text   MS. (pencil draft) DCM.
Sunday November 11: Rees (19 Oct 23, DCM) made it clear that he would prefer a special message from TH for the Armistice Day issue of the *Sunday Times* but would be glad, in any case, to reprint one of the 'Poems of War and Patriotism' from *Moments of Vision*; following this letter, however, Rees chose 'According to the Mighty Working', first collected in *Late Lyrics*.

To LONSDALE DEIGHTON

FROM TH. HARDY, | MAX GATE, | DORCHESTER. | 22 October 1923.
No objection to reproduction of contribution to British Legion Autograph Album.

Text   MS. (postcard) Gordon N. Ray.
Deighton: E. Lonsdale Deighton, compiler of *The British Legion Album in Aid of Field-Marshal Haig's Appeal for Ex-Service Men of All Ranks* (London, 1924); he wrote 20 Oct 23 (DCM) to ask if TH would agree to the reproduction in facsimile of the contribution—one and a half lines from 'I Met a Man'—he had already submitted.

To HARLEY GRANVILLE BARKER

Max Gate, | Dorchester. | 23 Oct. 1923.
My dear Granville Barker
   I don't think those letters will matter much, though it is very good of you to feel as you do about them. I have had worse cases—one in which a dear friend who was, as I thought, dying, sent off my epistles to a dealer immediately they came. The whole time of the next generation will be

occupied in reading the old letters of this, if it justifies the present craze for "collecting".

We shall be glad to see you Thursday, though I tremble to think what a trifle you are coming to see—a reed shaken with the wind! I wish I had taken more trouble over it.

Tell Helen that at last I have secured a dream for her—a poor thing, but mine own. However it is waiting her arrival in an envelope just as if it were the most important reality in the world.

Always yours sincerely,
Thomas Hardy.

Text Typed transcript DCM.
those letters: Barker (22 Oct 23, DCM) expressed his distress at discovering that some letters TH had written him about the 1914 production of *The Dynasts* were being offered for public sale; they had been in the hands of A. E. Drinkwater (see V.59), the manager for that production.   *dear friend*: unidentified.   *coming to see*: evidently a rehearsal of the Hardy Players' production of *The Queen of Cornwall*.   *with the wind!*: Matthew 11: 7.   *Helen . . . a dream for her*: for the dream which TH described for Mrs. Barker see Millgate, 551 n. *a poor . . . own*: adapted from *As You Like It*, V. iii. 57–8.

To SIR FREDERICK MACMILLAN

MAX GATE, | DORCHESTER. | 27 October: 1923.

Dear Sir Frederick:

From what you say I see that Thursday, November 15th. would be the better day for the publication of "The Queen of Cornwall." Therefore please fix it so. The performances here do not begin till November 28th. I thought it advisable that the publication should antedate the acting, rather than the other way. In this the Society agrees with me, thinking it will help them if people have become a little familiar with the story, in which opinion they may possibly be right.

Mr Martin is the President for this year, and also the Hon. Secretary. He is getting up the programme, and says he has a blank page to fill up. I told him he might write to you if he wished, and that you would probably be able to help him in that matter.

It has just struck me whether it would be worth while when you announce the book to add the words: "As it will be performed by the Hardy players at Dorchester on the 28th–30th. November".

Believe me,

Sincerely yours,
Thomas Hardy.

Text MS. (typewritten) BL.
better day: it was, in fact, the date TH had first suggested; see letter of 18 Sept 23.   *Mr Martin*: see letter of 11 Nov 20 to Cowley.   *help him in that matter*: a Macmillan & Co. advertisement for *The Queen of Cornwall* and TH's other works occupies the inside back cover of the Hardy Players' programme for *The Queen of Cornwall* as performed together with *O Jan! O Jan! O Jan!* and *The Play of St. George* on 28, 29, and 30 Nov 1923.

To HARLEY GRANVILLE BARKER

Max Gate, | Dorchester. | Monday 29: 10: '23.
My dear H.G.B.

I have to-day received your letters and the proof, but have not been able to go into them yet. I am afraid you have taken a lot of trouble! I have sent on Mr Tilley's to him, and he is no doubt by this time much exalted at thinking his company worthy of such consideration.

The wind you speak off blew our trees into curses not loud but deep. Barrie says he would have the sea sound all through the play and get over the difficulty of Brn. not seeing the bodies by making it dark.

Kind love to Helen, and believe me with many thanks,

Yours ever,
Th. H.

P.S. The book has gone to press, so cannot be altered: but the acting version can.

Text   Typed transcript DCM.
letters and the proof: Barker's letter of 28 Oct 23 (DCM) refers to 'some notes' for T. H. Tilley, the producer of *The Queen of Cornwall*; the 'proof' was evidently of the *Queen* itself.   *speak off*: so the transcript reads.   *curses . . . deep*: *Macbeth*, V. iii. 27.   *Barrie*: who had perhaps attended the same rehearsal.   *Brn. not seeing the bodies*: Barker had mentioned potential production difficulties with the scene (xx of the original edn.) in which Brangwain, entering, sees Tristram's body at once but not the equally visible body of King Mark; he wrote again (30 Oct 23, DCM) to approve Barrie's expedient and this was in fact adopted in the revised edn. of 1924, added stage directions serving to stress the 'gloom' and 'semi-darkness' of what was now scene xxii.

To FORD MADOX FORD

October 30: 1923
Dear Mr Madox Ford:

As Mr Hardy continues rather unwell—which he has been the last fortnight, though not seriously, except on account of his age—I reply to your last letter that you may not be inconvenienced by further delay.

In the circumstances he fears he can do nothing beyond sending the general message that, believing International understandings should become thorough for the good of mankind, he wishes every success to the Transatlantic Review, since it may help such understandings.

The play to which you allude is in the press, & will be out on November 15. It did not occur to him to send it to any periodical.

Yours truly
F. E. Hardy.

Text   MS. (pencil draft) DCM.
your last letter: of 21 Oct 23 (DCM); it was signed 'Ford Madox Ford'. Ford recalled the founding of the *English Review* in 1908 (see III.327, 331) and begged TH to help get the *Transatlantic Review* (see letter of 18 Oct 23) off to a good start by sending 'a small message in a letter'; the present letter, though sent as if from FEH, was printed, except for its third paragraph, in the first issue of the review, January 1924.

To HAROLD CHILD

MAX GATE, | DORCHESTER. | November 11. 1923.

Dear Mr Child:

It is very good of The Times to think of sending such a competent critic as yourself for the performance of my little play on Nov. 28. and I only can hope that you will not be disappointed in it.

The criticism will be a comparatively easy job, as the play is to be published by Messrs Macmillan on the 15th. (three days after you get this), so that you can be familiar with it beforehand. A copy would naturally be sent to the Supplement for review—must have been, in fact, sent by this time—but I should like you to read it for your self, which will take only a quarter of an hour, being but in one act.

The points that will probably strike you are these (if any!)—that the unities are strictly preserved, whatever virtue there may be in that. (I myself am oldfashioned enough to think there *is* a virtue in it, if it can be done without artificiality. The only other case I remember attempting it in was The Return of the Native). The original events could have been enacted in the time taken by the performance, and they continue unbroken throughout. The changes of scene are denoted by the change of persons present on the stage, there being no change of background.

My temerity in pulling together into the space of an hour events that in the traditional story covered a long time will doubtless be punished by the reviewers of the book. But there are so many versions of the famous romance that I felt free to adapt it to my purposes in any way—as, in fact, the Greek dramatists did in their plays—notably Euripides.

Wishing it to be thoroughly English I have dropped the name of Chorus for the conventional onlookers, and called them Chanters, though they play the part of a Greek chorus. I have also made them ghosts (I don't for the moment recall an instance of this in a Greek play), and it will be amusing to see how our local amateurs here will acquit themselves in this very difficult business. Whether the lady ghosts will submit to have their faces whitened I don't know! They have by the way, got a very promising lady, Mrs Hirst, to take the part of the Queen, who though a cultivated woman is strictly a local amateur. They have also a very good Tristram in the person of a local doctor.

I have tried to avoid turning the rude personages of, say, the fifth century, into respectable Victorians, as was done by Tennyson, Swinburne, Arnold, &c. On the other hand it would have been impossible to present them as they really were, with their barbaric manners and surroundings.

It is the first time I have ever written a play for the Dorchester players, but I had promised them one for years, and so made this piece serve the purpose. You will see that I have flown in the face of custom by saying on the title page that no theatre is required! Our players here, however, will have none of that, as they love all the conventions of the stage, and will duly maintain them.

They tell me there is to be a full-dress rehearsal about 8 on the Tuesday evening preceding the first performance on Wednesday night the 28th. You will be welcome at either or both. I don't know which evening you will come, but my wife says I am to tell you that we shall be glad to see you here to tea on either afternoon, or to an early dinner (no dress), or both. We wish we could put you up for the night, but unfortunately our servants are in rebellion, and we are largely dependent on charwomen, added to which I am in a worse state of health than I have been in all the year, though it is nothing serious.

Any particulars that I am ignorant of will be given you privately by the Hon. Secretary Mr H. A. Martin, 4 Alexandra Villas, Dorchester—also programme—I enclose the advertisement in the local paper.

Sincerely yours
Th: Hardy.

P.S. Mr Martin has just called here. He says that there will be also a rehearsal on Monday the 26th. at 7.30. Should you be able to come to that he thinks it would be quieter than on the Tuesday, when they are invaded by photographers etc. I shall be at the Monday one. On that night, by the way, we could accommodate you without inconvenience.

He also says that if you come to a rehearsal only, and not to the first night, he could telegraph the fact that the performance actually took place, &c. T.H.

Text MS. (typewritten) Adams.
Child: after TH's death FEH gave Child the original pencil draft of this letter (now Adams); she also mentioned (20 Aug 29, Adams) that TH's insertion of the carbon of this typewritten version into his 'Memoranda II' notebook (see *Personal Notebooks* [see letter of 14 June 20 to Edgcumbe], 75–6) showed that he 'thought the letter of importance'. The letter is partly reproduced in *LY*, 235–6.   *The Times*: Child's review of the Dorchester production of *The Queen of Cornwall* appeared in *The Times*, 29 Nov 1923.   *for review*: an unsigned review was pub. in the *Times Literary Supplement*, 17 Nov 1923.   *Mrs Hirst*: Kathleen Mary Hirst; see letter of 7 June 22.   *local doctor*: E. W. Smerdon; see letter of 17 Nov 20.   *Tennyson, Swinburne, Arnold, &c.*: TH presumably alludes to Tennyson's *Idylls of the King*, Swinburne's *Tristram of Lyonesse*, and Matthew Arnold's 'Tristram and Iseult'.   *the Monday one*: Child replied (12 Nov 23, DCM) that he proposed to attend this rehearsal.

To EDWARD CLODD

MAX GATE, | DORCHESTER. | 12. Novr 1923

My dear Clodd:

I was much interested in your letter—or rather succinct survey of the present state of religion in this country, indeed, in all countries for that matter. I should have liked to answer it at length. But I am not quite out of the wood of this lingering indisposition (for it does not deserve to be called illness) which has the effect of making me behind hand in correspondence, though I get most of mine typed nowadays—am, in fact, obliged to. So I must content myself with hoping to discuss your views at a future time. To be sure, I have, to a small extent dealt with the same subject in the preface to my last volume of poems.

I quite agree with you in holding that meeting together at least once a week in the cause of some religion or other is indispensable. I trust this east wind does not find you out on that east coast.

Sincerely yrs
Th: Hardy.

Text MS. Leeds.
your letter: of 6 Nov 23 (DCM).   *state of religion*: Clodd commented sceptically and at some
length on current trends in religious thought and argument.   *last volume of poems*: i.e., in the
'Apology' to *Late Lyrics*.   *meeting together*: Clodd expressed a wish to know TH's 'feeling on
the question of some possible reconstruction of the Creeds whereby those who, like myself,
regret the non-assembling of ourselves together, could cease our Exile'.

To THE DUCHESS OF HAMILTON

[Ans.]   [Mid-November 1923]

Shd be delighted, if it does not commit me to absolute anti-vivisection . . . .
May be cases in wh. a very small amount of suffering, such as a human being
wd submit to, may lead to enlightenment on some point of great value in
relieving the future suffering both of men & of the animals themselves. So I
don't know what to say. Pps you cd suggest—Say title, "Animal defence &
Controlled Vivn Soc." or "A. Defence Soc." alone, & I wd join. . . .

Text MS. (pencil draft) DCM.   *Date* Replies to letter of 10 Nov 23.
[Ans.]: TH's square brackets.   *absolute anti-vivisection*: the Duchess of Hamilton (10 Nov
23, DCM) invited TH to become a vice-president of the Animal Defence and Anti-Vivisection
League, of which she was president.

To SIR FREDERICK MACMILLAN

MAX GATE, DORCHESTER. | 15. November 1923.

Dear Sir Frederick:
    Many thanks for the books, which have come today. I don't think I told
you how much I liked the appearance of the volume, which I did not expect
to look so well.
    I hope it will go off all right, and am

Very Sincerely yours,
Thomas Hardy.

The bookings for the play on Nov 28 are proceeding rapidly, many of them
being from London & other distant places. T.H.

Text MS. (typewritten) BL.
the books: i.e., the copies of *The Queen of Cornwall*.   *The bookings . . . T.H.*: postscript added
in TH's hand.

To SIR FREDERICK MACMILLAN

MAX GATE, | DORCHESTER. | November 17th. 1923.

Dear Sir Frederick:
    I enclose a letter from the British Broadcasting Company which I am quite
at a loss to answer. Will you kindly decide the question, and reply for me? I
am really quite indifferent whether the offer is declined or not. The question
is, I suppose, of its influence upon the circulation of the book? Also, do these
broadcasting people pay a fee for permission?
    There are pourparlers for the production of the play at a London theatre

later on, though nothing definite has been said. I imagine that this possibility would not be affected either way by the broadcasting proposal.

Anyhow I shall be glad if you will settle what is the best course and adopt it,

Sincerely yours,
Thomas Hardy.

P.S. The dramatic company, I am sure, would have no objection. T.H.

Text MS. (typewritten) BL.
a letter: it no longer accompanies the present letter.   *reply for me?*: Macmillan (19 Nov 23, Macmillan letterbooks, BL) proposed that if, as appeared, the Bournemouth station of the B.B.C. wished to broadcast the first Dorchester performance of *The Queen of Cornwall*, permission should be given and a fee of £5 charged; the Macmillan letterbooks also show that a letter in these terms was written to Bertram Fryer, B.B.C. Bournemouth, the same day. On the night in question, however, the Bournemouth station linked up with the Manchester station to broadcast a performance of Mendelssohn's *A Midsummer Night's Dream*.   *at a London theatre*: this idea did not materialize, although the Hardy Players gave a single performance in London 21 Feb 1924; see *LY*, 237.

To ALFRED NOYES

MAX GATE, | DORCHESTER. | 17 Nov. 1923

Dear Mr Noyes:

How kind of you to take the trouble to write an article on my little play—53 years in contemplation, 800 lines in result, alas!

Thank you very much. I envy you the dispatch by which you could do it in a few hours.

Believe me

Yours sincerely
Thomas Hardy.

Text MS. Texas.
an article: Noyes (15 Nov 23, DCM) sent a copy of the review of *The Queen of Cornwall*, headed 'Hardy, the Master', pub. in the London *Evening News* that same day; though generally positive the review was somewhat critical of the quality of the verse in the play.

To HARRY POUNCY

FROM TH. HARDY, | MAX GATE, | DORCHESTER. | 20 Novr 1923

Letter received: many thanks. Also lecture enclosed therewith.

T.H.

Text MS. (correspondence card) Gordon N. Ray.
Pouncy: Harry Pouncy, Dorchester journalist and lecturer; see III.247.   *Letter received*: Pouncy wrote 19 Nov 23 (DCM) to report that he had recently lectured on 'Thomas Hardy and His "Wessex": An Evening in Hardyland' to a large and appreciative audience in Liverpool.

To RUTLAND BOUGHTON
                        MAX GATE, | DORCHESTER. | 25 Nov. 1923.

Dear Sir:
   I should be delighted at your making a music-drama of the Queen of
Cornwall, for though, unhappily, I don't know much about music I do know
of your reputation, & that the Queen will be in good hands with you. But
please don't let it take you two or three years, for I may be dead.
   Many thanks for enclosures, which I have read with much interest.
                                            Yours very truly
                                            Thomas Hardy.

Rutland Boughton Esq.

Text MS. BL.
Boughton: Rutland Boughton (1878–1960), composer and founder (in 1914) of the Glastonbury
Festival; *D.N.B.*   *your reputation*: TH probably had chiefly in mind the popularity of
Boughton's music-drama *The Immortal Hour*; see letter of 12 Feb 24.   *enclosures*:
Boughton's letter has not survived and its 'enclosures' remain unidentified.

To ERNEST BRENNECKE
                                [Early] December . . 1923

Dear Mr Brennecke:
   I am glad to hear of your satisfaction with a probable publication of your
essay.
   The point you submit in your letter concerning a breach of the
understanding that nothing roughly pencilled on the MS. for your private
information should be used in the book, except indirectly for correcting
errors, your authority not being mentioned, is one on which I cannot reply
till I know what comment of mine it is that you desire to print. I may remind
you that, apart from the comment itself, if it were quoted as my words it
would be fatal to the sense of detachment that you must convey to the reader
to inspire a belief in your criticisms. I glanced over only a very few pages of
the composition, & do not remember what I said about Schopenhauer, Mrs
Hardy having written most of the remarks I think, or suggested them.
   The utmost it would seem safe for you to do would be to speak indirectly:
e.g. "Mr. H is understood to hold the opinion," &c, &c—Anyhow, before
any remark of mine is alluded to I must know exactly what it is.
                                            Yours very truly

Text MS. (pencil draft) DCM.   *Date* Replies to letter of 3 Dec 23.
your essay: *Thomas Hardy's Universe*; see letter of 27 Aug 23.   *about Schopenhauer*: in his
letter of 3 Dec (DCM), written from Paris, Brennecke referred to TH's pencillings in his MS.
and sought permission to quote one which praised him for 'pointing out that [TH's] ideas
present a definite step in advance of those of Schopenhauer'.

To A. R. POWYS

MAX GATE, | DORCHESTER. | [Early] December 1923.

Dear Mr Powys:

In reply to your enquiry I may say that I know of Winterborne-Thompson Church, though I do not remember seeing it, and that it is a most interesting little building, having apparently been left (unless tampered with recently) just as it was when the parishioners went out of it 50 years ago after the last service.

I recall that Mr Hermann Lea, of Ten Oaks, Linwood, Nr. Ringwood, visited it and was much interested in it, some time ago, and would no doubt give you particulars of it if you were to write to him. He *might* be able to draw up a report on it, being a very intelligent man, though he is not an architect.

As to the question of some one hereabouts who would be a member and local reporter to the Society I can think of nobody for the moment. Some member of the Dorset Antiquarian Field Club might do so, and you might get a name suggested to you by writing to Capt. Acland, M.A., County Museum, Dorchester. Possibly the Hon. Sec. of the Club might undertake it (though I have no authority for saying this.) His name is Vere L. Oliver, F.S.A. of Greenhill House, Weymouth.

Yours very truly,

T.H.

Text MS. (typewritten) SPAB. *Date* Replies to letter of 5 Dec 23.
your enquiry: of 5 Dec 23 (copy SPAB). *Winterborne-Thompson Church*: usually spelled Winterborne-Tomson; a small Norman church NE of Bere Regis, Dorset. A memorial tablet to Powys inside the church records that he is buried in the churchyard, 'as he desired', and that the restoration of the church was made possible by the sale of Hardy MSS. (formerly in the possession of the Society for the Protection of Ancient Buildings; see S.P.A.B. *Annual Report*, June 1928). *Lea*: see letter to him of 3 Oct 24. *Acland*: the curator of the Dorset County Museum; see letter to him of 12 June 20. *Oliver*: Vere Langford Oliver (1861–1942), antiquarian and local politician, Hon. Secretary of the Field Club 1922–9.

To SYDNEY COCKERELL

Max Gate | 9 Dec. 1923

My dear Cockerell:

I return herewith Swinburne's letter, with many thanks. It is amusing to have him writing that he means "to adhere sternly to Fact & Reality" in his version of Tristram, as if the ascertaining of such (supposing there were any at all) could be possible in that romance of irreconcileable discrepancies.

I enclose with that letter one I had from him about "Jude the Obscure" shortly after it was published. As you have the MS. of the novel in the Fitzwilliam it has crossed my mind that you might care to have this letter as a sort of companion-document. If so you are welcome to it. It was written in the early days of my friendship with Swinburne, when the newspapers were howling me down & suggesting that I should have two years' hard for writing the story. He had of course gone through the same experience.

Ever sincerely
Thomas Hardy.

Text   MS. Berg.
Swinburne's letter: Cockerell (6 Dec 23, DCM) sent TH a letter from Swinburne to Edward Burne-Jones which had just been presented to the Fitzwilliam Museum; see *The Swinburne Letters*, ed. Cecil Y. Lang (New Haven, Conn., 1959–62), II.50–2, where it is dated 4 Nov [1869?].   *his version of Tristram*: Swinburne's *Tristram of Lyonesse* (1882).   *one I had from him*: dated 5 Nov 95 (Fitzwilliam Museum); see *The Swinburne Letters*, VI.91, and *LY*, 39–40.

To SIR FREDERICK MACMILLAN

MAX GATE, DORCHESTER. | 9 December 1923.

Dear Sir Frederick Macmillan:

I have signed and return herewith the Memorandum of Agreement with Messrs Haase & Son for translations into Danish-Norwegian. Considering the precarious nature of arrangements in general with translators, this seems promising. Many thanks for seeing to the matter.

Yours very sincerely,
Th: Hardy.

Text   MS. (typewritten) BL.
return herewith: Macmillan (7 Dec 23, Macmillan letterbooks, BL) recommended acceptance of the offer made by Haase & Son, of Copenhagen, for the Scandinavian rights of all TH's books; they would pay £35 for a first printing of 3,000 copies of each book and a further £10 for every additional printing of 1,000 copies.

To SIR FREDERICK MACMILLAN

MAX GATE, | DORCHESTER. | 17th. December 1923.

Dear Sir Frederick:

I have received a complaint from a reader that the Globe Publishing Company—who are, I suppose, a distributing firm—advertise a "complete edition" of my books for so much money, when, in fact, the edition does not include one of my most important works "The Dynasts", or "Late Lyrics", or the volume you have just published. I do not know about this, but perhaps you do. I suppose the company should be warned against announcing their edition as complete, which perhaps you are not aware of.

Yours sincerely,
Thomas Hardy.

Text   MS. (typewritten) BL.
a reader: unidentified; Macmillan (19 Dec 23, Macmillan letterbooks, BL) suspected that it might be someone seeking TH's autograph.   *distributing firm*: the company was, in fact, a Macmillan subsidiary, selling books directly to the public on the instalment plan. Macmillan acknowledged that the Pocket edn. (the one handled by Globe) did not include *The Dynasts* and promised to see that future advertisements were not misleading; two vols. containing *The Dynasts* and *The Queen of Cornwall* were added to the Pocket edn. in 1924.

1924

To CHARLES LACEY

Many thanks for the reprint, & for good wishes.

T.H.

Text MS. (correspondence card, with envelope) J. Stevens Cox.
Lacey: Charles Lacey, proprietor of the *Dorset County Chronicle*; see II.237.   *reprint*:
probably of 'Thomas Hardy. Interesting Lecture by Mr. H. Harding', a report occupying four
columns of the *Dorset County Chronicle* of 27 Dec 1923; for Harding see III.241.

To MADELEINE ROLLAND

Max Gate, Dorchester. [1 January 1924]

With best New Year's wishes from

T. & F. Hardy.

Text MS. (picture postcard of Maiden Castle, with envelope, all in TH's hand) Mme
Rolland.   *Date* From postmark.

To CHARLOTTE MEW

MAX GATE, | DORCHESTER. | 3 Jan. 1924

Dear Miss Mew:

What I did was really infinitesimal: Others did more than I.

You are merely to think the little event happened—a very small one.

Our kindest regards & best wishes for the New Year.

Sincerely yours
Thomas Hardy.

Text MS. Univ. of Kentucky.
Mew: Charlotte Mew, poet; see V.336.   *more than I*: TH was responding to Mew's letter of
thanks (1 Jan 24, DCM) for his part in securing her a Civil List pension of £75 a year. The
application, initiated by Cockerell, had also been supported by John Masefield and Walter de la
Mare; see *Siegfried Sassoon Diaries 1923–1925*, ed. Rupert Hart-Davis (London, 1985), 46.

To SIR GEORGE DOUGLAS

MAX GATE, | DORCHESTER. | 4 Jan. 1924

My dear Douglas:

Many thanks for good wishes which we reciprocate. Also our kind regards
to your sister.

As for "The Queen of Cornwall", it has been obstructing the way for a long time: & I am glad it is finished—though I own I liked doing it, the place & its associations being so familiar.

A shadow has been cast over the opening of the year for me by the funeral of Frederick Treves, who, as you know, was a Dorchester man, he having been also a friend of many years' standing. The rain came down in torrents. He might have lasted another ten years at least if he had taken care of himself.

I am afraid I don't remember Dickens's novels well enough to discuss their various love-interests at this distance of time from reading them. Miss Ternan was, of course, a friend of his. I knew some of *Mrs* Dickens's family, & they always blamed *him* for the separation.

I hope you will keep up your lectures this year, & with renewed wishes for your well-doing I am

Always sincerely
Thomas Hardy.

Text MS. NLS.
your sister: Mary Helena Henrietta Douglas (d. 1932).   *so familiar*: the play's setting is Tintagel, Cornwall, close to St. Juliot, where TH first met Emma Gifford in 1870.   *Treves*: see letter of 7 Jan 24 to Flower.   *Miss Ternan*: Ellen Lawless Ternan, later Robinson (1839–1914), apparently Charles Dickens's mistress during his last years.   Mrs *Dickens's family*: Dickens married Catherine Thomson Hogarth (1815–79) in 1836; they separated in 1858. TH's connection with the Hogarth family has not been traced, although he did once receive a visit at Max Gate from one of the Dickens sons.   *your lectures*: TH apparently refers not to a series of lectures but to Douglas's frequent acceptance of invitations to address Scottish cultural institutions and other local bodies; in June 1925, e.g., he unveiled a tablet in honour of William Julius Mickle (see letter of 25 July 24), the Scottish poet whom TH had read in his youth.

To AMY LOWELL

MAX GATE, | DORCHESTER. | January 4. 1924.

Dear Miss Amy Lowell:

We have received your New Year's cabled message, and that wakes me up to my delinquencies. However we reciprocate your good wishes heartily, and you will remember that our air over here is not so stimulating as yours, which makes us slower in starting things—at least, so I fancy.

I have not gone into the question of free verse lately—to which you allude in your letter of last summer,—and on this side of the Atlantic it seems to have sunk into a calm for a while. I am sure it would make all the difference if I could hear you read it as you do at your lectures.

Those young interviewers who take notes without one's knowledge are a pest: but their conduct is what is called over here "a fat trouble"—and one is apt to have thrown back in one's face—"better a fat trouble than a lean one". Well, I don't know.

I hope the Keats book is finished. Who would have supposed a little more than a hundred years ago that that young man's private life and affairs would become so interesting to the world. Of course if you do come over this year you will call down and see us.

I read the poems when they came: many thanks for them. I think I liked the Rosebud Wall-paper best. But it is impossible to go appreciating verses in a letter, and I won't attempt it.

My wife sends her best love, and I am

Your affectionate friend,
Thomas Hardy.

Text   MS. (typewritten) Harvard.
letter of last summer: TH apparently refers to Miss Lowell's letter of 8 May 23 (DCM), written in response to his own letter of 7 Mar 23.   *young interviewers*: Miss Lowell had complained in her 8 May 23 letter about the 'reprehensible' behaviour of Llewelyn Powys (see IV.266) in this respect; for Powys's attitude to Miss Lowell see his *The Verdict of Bridlegoose* (New York, 1926), 27–8, 30.   *Keats*: corrected from the 'Keat's' of the typescript, although TH uses the latter form in his holograph letter to Miss Lowell of 6 Mar 25. For the book itself, see that same letter.   *Wall-paper best*: Miss Lowell sent with her 8 May 23 letter a copy of her dramatic monologue 'The Rosebud Wall-paper' cut from the *North American Review*, February 1923.

To ELIZABETH ALLHUSEN

MAX GATE, | DORCHESTER. | 7 January 1924

My dear Elizabeth:

I hope you will get well soon, & come to Dorset in the spring, when it is very lovely.

Ever yours affectionately
T. Hardy.

Text   MS. (correspondence card) Purdy.
Allhusen: Dorothea Elizabeth Allhusen, Dorothy Allhusen's younger daughter; see V.241.
get well soon: she died in 1926, however.   *come to Dorset*: as she had done in November 1922; see letter of 28 Jan 23.

To NEWMAN FLOWER

MAX GATE, | DORCHESTER. | 7 Jan: 1924

Dear Mr Newman Flower:

I am so glad you liked my hasty tribute to our friend in Saturday's *Times*. Longer reflection would have made a better thing of it, no doubt, but I had no proof from them—the editor printing it immediately.—I omitted a few thoughts in writing it, not necessary for newspaper publication when all was fresh in the memory; but they will be included whenever I reprint the verses.

I was, & am, none the worse for the rain, the slight rheumatism, which I had before, not being aggravated at all. We hope to see you again soon.

Very sincerely yours
Thomas Hardy

Text   MS. (with envelope) Texas.
tribute to our friend: Flower's letter of 5 Jan 24 (DCM) had expressed his admiration for TH's poem 'In the Evening', written in memory of Sir Frederick Treves (see letter of 27 Dec 22) and pub. in *The Times*, 5 Jan 1924.   *reprint the verses*: a revised and expanded version of the poem appeared in *The Dorset Year-Book* for 1924 and, later, in *Human Shows*.   *the rain*: at

Treves's funeral in Dorchester, 2 Jan 1924; TH chose the hymns at the service and Flower represented Lady Treves. See *LY*, 236–7, and Flower, *Just As It Happened* (London, 1950), 124–6.

To SIR HAMO THORNYCROFT

MAX GATE, | DORCHESTER. | 10 Jan: 1924

My dear Thornycroft:

I am sending a belated answer to your good wishes for the New Year, which we echo to you & yours. Also to thank you for the photograph, in which I recognize the characters in the group. I had no idea that you were so near Oxford: we motored there last summer across the Downs, & enjoyed the visit.

I shall never forget that run down from Hampstead through the rain & wind when your son kindly steered us. What changes we have seen since then!—& though we have certainly not yet gained the peace of God, it is what passeth all understanding.

Whether & when we shall go to Oxford again is doubtful, but I will not forget Coombe if we do.

Good wishes to your household as to yourself.

Always sincerely
Thomas Hardy.

Text MS. DCM.
good wishes: in Thornycroft's letter of 1 Jan 24 (DCM).   *photograph*: of his family and friends in the front garden of The Old Farmhouse, Coombe, Oxfordshire, where he was now living; Thornycroft had said that TH might recognize his wife and son.   *motored there last summer*: see letter of 24 June 23.   *steered us*: i.e., TH and FEH, in May 1915; see V.97.

To SIR HAMO THORNYCROFT

MAX GATE, | DORCHESTER. | 11 Jan. 1924

Letters have crossed. Many thanks. The picture was done not at my request, but is said to be good.

T.H.

Text MS. (postcard) DCM.
The picture: Augustus John's portrait of TH was reproduced in *The Times*, 9 Jan 1924, on the occasion of its presentation to the Fitzwilliam Museum by T. H. Riches.

To GEORGE DEWAR

13 Jan: 1924

Dear Mr Dewar:

At last I am sending the poem I mentioned, for your use in the Nineteenth Century & After, which I hope you will like. Any month you put it into will please me, as I am not printing it anywhere else at present.

As to price, I don't know what to say, so will leave it to you to judge what will be fair.

If you don't like the poem, will you let me have the copy back early?

Yours very truly

Text MS. (pencil draft) DCM.
Dewar: George Albemarle Bertie Dewar (see IV.139), editor of *The Nineteenth-Century and After*; he wrote to TH 2 Jan 24 (DCM).   *the poem*: 'Xenophanes, the Monist of Colophon', pub. in *The Nineteenth-Century and After*, March 1924.

To ROGER LOOMIS

                              MAX GATE, DORCHESTER. [Mid-January 1924]
Dear Mr Loomis:
I am glad to know that you are home and at work upon the Christmas mumming plays.
I have great pleasure in permitting you . . . to reprint the recension of the "Play of St. George" that I managed to concoct from my memories of it as acted in my boyhood.

Sincerely yours,
Th. Hardy.

Text Fragment, Thomas Hardy, *The Play of St. George* (New York, 1928), [5].
Date Loomis's reply to this letter is dated 15 Jan 24 (DCM).
memories . . . boyhood: TH first drew on these in *The Return of the Native* (Wessex edn., 157–9, 162–3) and later developed them into *The Play of 'Saint George'*, which was prepared for the Hardy Players in 1920 and pub. as a privately-printed pamphlet in 1921 (see Purdy, 212–13). Loomis, visiting TH in 1923 (see letter of 3 Sept 23), evidently suggested the pub. of the more widely available edition of 1928, which also included Loomis's own modernized version of the play.

To RUTLAND BOUGHTON

                    MAX GATE, | DORCHESTER. | January 16th. 1924.
Dear Mr Rutland Boughton:
I shall be here all next week, and shall be pleased to see you. I do not know how the trains serve (if you come by train), but if lunching here about one o'clock will be any convenience to you it will be no trouble to us, if you let us know the day.
As to the Queen, it had to be brought out rather in a hurry at the last moment, to be in time for the actors here, and I have always meant to revise it a little, to bring it roughly to the average length of Greek plays. The enlargements are already written, the chief one being at page 46, after "O Knight of little cheer."
I don't know about page 47, the expression there seems full enough. But two verses can certainly be added at page 27, and a verse at page 65.
The press has been very civil to the play—indeed eulogistic. But unfortunately most of the critics have missed its chief aim—compactness and continuity without a moment's break in the action—characteristics that have never been imparted to the story before—old as it is.

Yours sincerely,
Thomas Hardy.

Text MS. (typewritten) BL.
to see you: see letter of 28 Jan 24.   *at page 46*: all page references in this letter are to the first
edn. (1923) of *The Queen of Cornwall*; TH's changes for the second edn. of 1924 included the
insertion of an additional scene at this point.   *page 47*: the second edn. made no change in
this passage.   *two verses . . . page 27*: only one was in fact added to the second edn.   *at
page 65*: this addition was made.

To J. H. MORGAN

MAX GATE, | DORCHESTER. | 16 Jan: 1924

Dear General Morgan:
    We had already written down The Quarterly in our book-list to get your
article, & now it comes by your kind forethought. I have only looked at it as
yet, but shall read it this evening.
    How very true it is that "the truth never overtakes the legend." I hope you
are well, & am

Sincerely yours
T. Hardy.

Text MS. (with envelope) Berg.
your article: 'The Personality of Lord Morley. I', *Quarterly Review*, January 1924.   *your
kind forethought*: Morgan forwarded a copy with his letter of 15 Jan 24 (DCM).   *the
legend."*: on the first page of his article Morgan quoted from a letter of Morley's which insisted
that attempts to correct misstatements about the past were never successful and that ' "History"
always misleads'.

To ST. JOHN ERVINE

MAX GATE, | DORCHESTER. | 27 Jan: 1924

Dear Mr Ervine:
    After inexcusable delay I just write to thank you for "The Lady of
Belmont," which you have been so kind as to send me. When I get through
the thicket of infinitesimal affairs at present round me, I am going to read
the book—I am sure with much pleasure.

Sincerely yours
Thomas Hardy.

Text MS. Texas.
of Belmont,": Ervine's *The Lady of Belmont: A Play in Five Acts* (London, 1923).

To J. H. MORGAN

MAX GATE, | DORCHESTER. | 27 Jan. 1924

Dear General Morgan:
    I have received your book on The Present State of Germany & am going to
begin reading it as soon as possible, since I feel sure that you have really
something to say on the matter, by the light of your long experience over
there. I need hardly say how much I thank you for the gift.

Sincerely yours
Th: Hardy.

234   *27 January* 1924   ætat 83

Text MS. Berg.
of Germany: Morgan's 107-page *The Present State of Germany: A Lecture Delivered in the University of London* (London, 1923).   *experience over there*: see letters of 28 June 20 and 5 Apr 21.

To RUTLAND BOUGHTON

MAX GATE, | DORCHESTER. | 28th. January 1924.
Dear Mr Boughton:
   Your letter from London arrived this morning, and as it has been nearly three days coming I reply at once to a question in your previous one that you may want answered quickly as is practicable, though I have not as yet had time to do more than glance at the form of agreement you send today, which I have no doubt will suit me very well.
   I have no objection at all to your introducing the songs from my poems that you mention, at the places you point out, if any musical improvement can be gained thereby, provided no words that are not mine are introduced. I quite see that the two versions will not clash if the musical version of the words is always accompanied by the music itself, as I understand it will be. But I will reply on this and other business-details when I have read through the form of agreement.
   Whenever you do come here we shall be glad to see you. If you thought of next Monday, and the strike should be still going on, or even if not, would it help you at all to stay here Monday night? We can easily put you up.
   (I am obliged to type-write most of my letters, on account of weak eyes.)
   Believe me,

Sincerely yours,
Thomas Hardy.

Text MS. (typewritten) BL.
form of agreement: see letter of 12 Feb 24.   *songs from my poems*: the many modifications made for *The Famous Tragedy of the Queen of Cornwall . . . Set as a music-drama* (London, 1926) included the replacement of Scene viii of the first edn. by TH's poem 'When I Set Out for Lyonesse' and the introduction into Scene xi of the first four stanzas of 'Beeny Cliff'.   *still going on*: a settlement in the national rail strike was in fact reached 29 Jan 1924.   *stay here Monday night?*: Boughton wrote (30 Jan 24, DCM) to accept this invitation for 4 February, and on 7 Feb 24 (Purdy) FEH told Cockerell that she and TH had been swept off their feet by their visitor, TH claiming to like him better than anyone he had ever met.

To JAMES BONE

. . . . [Early] February 1924
Dear Mr Bone:
   Many thanks for the numbers of Country Life containing your articles on Portland Stone, which I have read with interest.
   I have naturally, as a Dorset man, noticed the indebtedness of London to Portland ever since I first lived in London more than 60 years ago; & in my Presidential Address to the Society of Dorset Men in London, in 1908–9, I made that my topic, entitling it "Dorset in London". I regret that I have not a

copy of the Address, & it has never been reprinted; but you can see it, if you care to, in the Year Book of the Society, by applying to Mr William Watkins, the Secretary, 274 Gresham House, Old Broad Street.

I have heard rumours of the "Best Bed" in Portland—that used by architects hitherto, who *know*—being nearly exhausted by the enormous demands upon it, but I don't answer for the truth of the rumour—if so, the inferior beds will be used as there is an unlimited quantity, which look just the same to the uninitiated (that is to say everybody, architects included, who have not had close experience of the beds). If so Portland Stone will lose its reputation for weathering.

Yours very truly

Text MS. (pencil draft) DCM.   *Date* Replies to letter of 31 Jan 24.
Bone: James Bone (1872–1962), London editor of the *Manchester Guardian* 1912–45; he wrote 31 Jan 24 (DCM).   *on Portland Stone*: Bone's 'Portland Stone in London' and 'The Matrix of London. A Visit to the Portland Quarries', pub. in *Country Life* 29 Dec 1923 and 5 Jan 1924; they were later drawn upon for the second chapter of Bone's *The London Perambulator* (London, 1925).   *the Year Book*: for 1908–9; the address is reprinted in *Thomas Hardy's Personal Writings*, ed. Harold Orel (Lawrence, Kansas, 1966), 218–25.   *Watkins*: see III.129.   *"Best Bed"*: Marcia Bencomb's father in *The Well-Beloved* is founder of 'the Best-Bed Stone Company' (Wessex edn., 23).

To SIR FREDERICK MACMILLAN

MAX GATE, | DORCHESTER. | 5 February 1924.

Dear Sir Frederick:

I have thought for some time that it would not be amiss to include "The Dynasts" in the Pocket Edition.

The two volumes which it will make can hardly be divided anywhere except at the end of Part II—although this will give a greater number of pages to the first volume. But there will in the future be an advantage in having the second volume thinner than the first, since if "The Queen of Cornwall" should later on be included in the Pocket Edition (and I suppose readers will wish it to be) it will go very well in the spare room at the end of the second volume of "The Dynasts"—thus keeping the dramatic writings together.

Yours very sincerely
Thomas Hardy.

Text MS. (typewritten) BL.
in the Pocket Edition: as proposed by Macmillan in his letter of 4 Feb 24 (Macmillan letterbooks, BL).   *dramatic writings together*: Macmillan replied (11 Feb 24, Macmillan letterbooks, BL) that TH's suggestion for the inclusion of *The Queen of Cornwall* would be adopted, even though it would mean delaying pub. 'until, say, next September'.

To SIR FREDERICK MACMILLAN

(Enclosure)   MAX GATE, | DORCHESTER. | 12. February 1924.

Dear Sir Frederick,

I leave to you entirely the date for publishing the pocket edition of The Dynasts with the Queen of Cornwall put in at the end. By September, the time you suggest, I suppose the present edition of The Queen will not be in demand. If you will let me know when they are going to print the latter, I will send up a copy for them to work from, with corrections of the errors and omissions inevitable in a first edition.

If it should turn out that it would be more convenient to divide The Dynasts at another point than at the end of Part II, I don't see at present that it would matter much. But upon the whole that seems the most convenient place.

I have to write about another question in connection with The Queen of Cornwall. Mr Rutland Boughton the composer wants to make an opera—or, as he calls it, a music-drama—of the play; just as he has lately done with Gilbert Murray's Alcestis, and Sharp's Immortal Hour. I have told him there is no objection to his doing so, and he has sent me his form of Agreement with Mr Gilbert Murray, as he supposes a similar one would do for The Queen. I enclose herewith a copy of it with some words changed to suit The Queen of Cornwall. If it appears all right to you will you return it please.

I shall be glad to make over to you any royalty that you may think your firm ought to claim as your proportion for his use of the words in the publication of his opera, if such would be proper in the circumstances. As you will see, he has no right to print the words except as an accompaniment to the music, so that the play as you publish it will not be competed with. And with the music added it will make a very bulky affair (to judge from Murray's Alcestis, which he showed me), and only of use to musicians.

If the music-drama should be such a success as The Immortal Hour has been, which of course we cannot reckon on, it will, I imagine, cause a renewed demand for the play.

Very sincerely yours,
Thomas Hardy.

Text MS. (typewritten) BL.
(Enclosure): added in TH's hand.   *at the end . . . suggest*: see letter of 5 Feb 24.
Murray's Alcestis: Boughton's *Alkestis*, with a text based on Murray's trans. of Euripides's tragedy, was first performed at Glastonbury 26 Aug 1922. For Murray, see IV.144.   *Sharp's Immortal Hour*: Boughton's *The Immortal Hour*, with a text adapted from the writings of 'Fiona Macleod' (William Sharp; see I.277), was first performed at Glastonbury 26 Aug 1914 and in 1922–3 had an enormously successful London revival.   *accompaniment to the music*: see letter of 28 Jan 24.

To RUTLAND BOUGHTON

MAX GATE, | DORCHESTER. | 15 February 1924.

Dear Mr Boughton:

I return herewith the form of Agreement you lent me, and also a draft copy I have had made by my secretary with the names and slight details that have occurred to me changed to suit our arrangement, so that if you find it all right you may be able to get it written out in duplicate for us to sign, as in the other case. The terms, &c, there mentioned, which I have copied into ours, are quite satisfactory to me. If there is any error in the wording as I have put it, please let me know.

I hope you will soon feel inspired to set about your glorification of the play.

Sincerely yours,
Thomas Hardy

P.S. Mrs Hardy hopes you duly received the ticket for the performance on Feb. 21. T.H.

Text MS. (typewritten) BL.
performance on Feb. 21 : the single London performance of the Hardy Players' production of *The Queen of Cornwall*.

To JOHN DRINKWATER

15 February 1924

Dear Mr Drinkwater:

I don't see any reason why you should not include in your series a selection of poems from William Barnes—either those you mention as published in aid of Winterborne Monkton School (which I have never seen or heard of, to my recollection), or any others from the Collected edition of his verses published by Kegan Paul & Co., whether I may have chosen some of the same ones or not. As to those issued in aid of the School, I do not know if they are marked "privately printed",—probably not, but if they should be, the copyright would I suppose still be the property of his representatives. Otherwise it will long ago have expired.

My selections & introductions—one a volume for the Oxford University Press & the other a section in Ward's English Poets—were merely made at the request of the respective editors, & not by any authority of the family.

If you were to inspect a file of "The Dorset County Chronicle" 1850–1870 at the British Museum, you would find in the Poets' Corner many by him that have never been reprinted—some as good as those which have been gleaned from the same pages.

With best wishes for the "Little Classics" I am

Very Sincerely yours

Text MS. (pencil draft) DCM.
your series: Drinkwater (13 Feb 24, DCM) spoke of the possibility of including a Barnes selection in a series (tentatively called 'Little Classics of the Nineteenth Century') which he was editing for Basil Blackwell, the Oxford publisher; the vol., *Twenty Poems in Common English* by William Barnes, with an introduction by Drinkwater, appeared in 1925.   *in aid of . . .*

School: i.e., William Barnes, *A Selection from Unpublished Poems* (Published at the School, Winterborne Monkton, Dorchester, 1870); the little vol. originated with, and was sold by, Barnes's son, the Revd. W. Miles Barnes (see I.155), who, as rector of Winterborne Monkton, was seeking to raise funds for the improvement and enlargement of the village school. See *Dorset County Chronicle*, 22 Sept 1870.   *Oxford University Press*: *Select Poems of William Barnes*, ed. by TH (London, 1908); see III.292–3, etc.   *English Poets*: *The English Poets*, Vol. V, ed. Thomas Humphry Ward (London, 1918), 174–6; see V.181.

To SIR FREDERICK MACMILLAN

MAX GATE, | DORCHESTER. | 20 February 1924.

Dear Sir Frederick:

I am much obliged for your reading through the Agreement about setting The Queen of Cornwall to music. I have inserted the note that the words of the play itself are published by your house.

I am sending herewith the copy of the play for the pocket edition, or any other edition that may be required in the future, containing the few words here and there that I have written in since seeing it acted. I think that perhaps I had better read the proofs through for safety.

Yours very truly,
Thomas Hardy.

P.S. Whenever done with, will you please let me have back the two drawings used in the illustrations, as I have no copy of them. T.H.

Text   MS. (typewritten) BL.
Agreement: see letter of 12 Feb 24.   *by your house*: as Macmillan had stipulated in his letter of 13 Feb 24 (Macmillan letterbooks, BL).   *pocket edition*: see letter of 5 Feb 24.   *the two drawings*: they are now in DCM.

To EDEN PHILLPOTTS

MAX GATE, | DORCHESTER. | 23 Feb: 1924

Dear Mr Phillpotts:

We are reading the Devon story you have been so kind as to send, & so far I rather like your heroine, though perhaps she will turn out to be a bit of a minx later on. One never knows with these women. Many thanks for the book. I hope you are getting through the winter as comfortably as you can expect. With kind regards I am,

Sincerely yours
Thomas Hardy.

Text   MS. NYU.
Devon story: Phillpotts's novel *Cheat-the-boys* (London, 1924).   *bit of a minx*: Gilyan, the heroine, is indeed the 'cheat-the-boys' of the novel's title.

To THOMAS J. WISE

MAX GATE, | DORCHESTER. | 1 March 1924

Dear Mr Wise:

I have received Volume IV., & am greatly obliged for the copy of what will be a valuable record. Also I am glad to find that you are getting on towards the end of your rather heavy job. With kind regards I am

Sincerely yours
Thomas Hardy.

Text   MS. BL.
Volume IV: of Wise's *The Ashley Library* (see letter of 31 May 22), pub. 1923.

To RUTLAND BOUGHTON

MAX GATE, | DORCHESTER. | 6 March 1924

Dear Mr Boughton:

I have received your letter, & have referred to Clause 5 of the form I based on your agreement with Mr. Murray. As for the musical settings of the songs, please omit them from the Clause. And in fact you can also omit the Chanters' parts if you care to, for, alas, I don't suppose I shall ever want them at my time of life. However, perhaps the fairest plan will be to let the Society of Authors settle the form. I am quite indifferent to details, being vastly more interested in your forthcoming "Structure of tones" (as Browning would have called it) than in any practical result.

We have heard nothing of any lady of the name you mention. But I have had a request from a composer for leave to turn another of my writings into a kind of folk-opera. His name is Mr Hubert Bath, of the Carl Rosa Opera Company, & says he has successfully done Buchanan's "Wedding of Shon Maclean." Perhaps when you are writing you can tell me if he has any standing in the musical world, & needs encouragement.

I am,

Yours sincerely
Thomas Hardy.

Text   MS. BL.
with Mr. Murray: see letter of 12 Feb 24.   *"Structure of tones"*: apparently an allusion to the opening line of Robert Browning's 'Abt Vogler', 'Would that the structure brave, the manifold music I build', and perhaps also to line 53, 'Consider it well: each tone of our scale in itself is naught'.   *the name you mention*: in the absence of Boughton's letter the lady remains unidentified.   *Bath*: Hubert Charles Bath (1883–1945), composer and conductor; he wrote 23 Feb 24 (DCM) asking permission to produce a one-act opera based on TH's story 'The Three Strangers' and explaining that he planned to use 'a deal of simulated folk-music'. It appears that Bath did write such a piece but that it was never pub. or performed.   *Shon Maclean.*": Bath's cantata *The Wedding of Shon Maclean: A Scottish Rhapsody* (London, 1909), based on the poem 'The Wedding of Shon Maclean. A Bagpipe Melody' by Robert Williams Buchanan (1841–1901; *D.N.B.*), poet and novelist.

To GEORGE MACMILLAN

MAX GATE, | DORCHESTER. | March 8. 1924.

Dear Mr Macmillan:

I am inclined to let Messrs Falkner & Co print the card for three guineas, as I don't see that any harm can be done by it; so that perhaps you will kindly let them know.

Last week I was asked by a local lecturer, whom I know very well and to whom I gave permission to read some of my poems to his audience, if I would object to his broadcasting some of them with the rest of his lecture. I told him I saw no objection, but that I would ask you what you thought about it. It seems to me that whatever effect broadcasting may have upon novels, it can do no harm to poems: it would in fact advertise them. If you agree I will inform him that he must name the volume he quotes from, but I will not communicate with him till I hear from you.

With kind regards I am,

Very sincerely yours,
Thomas Hardy.

Text MS. (typewritten) BL.
Falkner: perhaps a typing error; see next note.   *print the card*: Macmillan reported (7 Mar 24, Macmillan letterbooks, BL) that C. W. Faulkner & Co., London fine art publishers, wished to pub. TH's poem 'The Oxen' as a Christmas card but declined to pay a fee of more than three guineas.   *let them know*: the Macmillan letterbooks show that Faulkner & Co. were so informed on 10 March.   *local lecturer*: presumably Harry Pouncy.   *hear from you*: Macmillan (10 Mar 24, Macmillan letterbooks, BL) agreed that the poems could be broadcast free of charge.

To FLORYAN SOBIENIOWSKI

. . . . [Mid-]March, 1924

Dear Sir:

I write for Mr Hardy in reply to your letter marked "Urgent" received March 13th, & requesting an answer by the 14th, to inform you that the pressure on his time & energies prevents him investigating your circumstances with the necessary care & promptitude, which would only be practicable for persons acquainted with you—such as the dramatists whom you have translated—who are on the spot in London & not strangers at a distance.

In no case could he advance you £100=0=0 in order that you may take a boarding-house.

It would seem that you are in an exceptionally good position to be English correspondent to Polish newspapers.

The copies of testimonials are returned herewith.

Yours very truly
for Thomas Hardy

. . . .
Sec.

Mr F. Sobieniowski | 41 Guilford Street | London. W. C.

Text MS. (pencil draft) DCM.
Sobieniowski: Floryan Sobieniowski, minor Polish *littérateur* currently living in London; according to Antony Alpers, *The Life of Katherine Mansfield* (New York, 1980), he translated some Shaw and Galsworthy plays into Polish, had 'a love-affair, of sorts' (101) with Katherine Mansfield, blackmailed Middleton Murry into buying back her letters, and died in Warsaw in 1964 at the age of 73.

To SIR FREDERICK MACMILLAN

MAX GATE, | DORCHESTER. | 20th. March 1924.

Dear Sir Frederick:

It does so happen that since you published my last volume of poems some more have accumulated—as was inevitable—and I do not want to bring out another volume till there are enough to make it worth while. So that some of them may very well be printed in periodicals. I have promised two or three to English editors, but none to America (except vaguely to The Century) so far as I remember.

I will therefore send you copies of a few, and I shall feel obliged by your distributing them to the American agent on whatever terms you think best.

By the way I find that by stating clearly that the price is for serial use only—American, English, or both, as the case may be—it saves the trouble of asking afterwards for permission to republish in book form.

The poems shall reach you in a few days.

Believe me,

Sincerely yours,
Thomas Hardy.

Text MS. (typewritten) BL.
printed in periodicals: Macmillan wrote 19 Mar 24 (Macmillan letterbooks, BL) to report an enquiry from a North American source as to the availability of new poems by TH.   *the American agent*: Macmillan was, in fact, corresponding with the London literary agent A. S. Watt (see letter of 6 Sept 24), who seems to have been acting for Ray Long, editor-in-chief of the International Magazine Co. of New York.

To SIR FREDERICK MACMILLAN

MAX GATE, | DORCHESTER. | 23 March 1924.

Dear Sir Frederick:

I am sending herewith 7 poems—of different lengths and styles—which I hope will suit. Use them how and when you think fit.

I am

Sincerely yours,
Thomas Hardy.

Titles. A Night of Questionings.
  The portraits.
  The Carrier.
  The Son's Portrait.
  The Last Leaf.
  Vagrant's Song.
  "Any little old Song."

Text MS. (typewritten) BL.
think fit: 'The Last Leaf' appeared in *Nash's and Pall Mall Magazine*, November 1924, followed by 'The Portraits' (later retitled 'Family Portraits') in the same journal a month later and 'Vagrant's Song' in January 1925; no American periodical publication for any of these poems has been traced, however.

To J. C. SQUIRE

MAX GATE, | DORCHESTER. | 25 March 1924

Dear Mr Squire:

   In reply to your inquiry for another poem I can only say I am honoured by your wish, & will bear it in mind. But I want to hold my tongue for a few months, having been rather too obtrusive lately I fancy, & there are some short pieces of mine floating about America, which I will wait to see disposed of before I venture into the Mercury again. But, as I say, I will get ready a suitable one for your pages.

   When are you going to call upon us again.

Always yours
T. Hardy.

P.S. I hope you got the portrait back. T.H.

Text MS. Texas.
floating about America: see letter of 23 Mar 24.   *the Mercury again*: TH in fact pub. two poems, 'Waiting Both' and 'An East-End Curate', in the *London Mercury*, November 1924. *the portrait*: unidentified.

To JOHN MIDDLETON MURRY

MAX GATE, | DORCHESTER. | 28 March 1924

Dear Mr Middleton Murry:

   I am not sure whether you have started yet, or not, on your circular tour of our little lump of earth; probably not. (I remember that as a child I used to think a journey round the world, which appealed much to my imagination, meant that the traveller went in an exact circle the exact distance of 24,000 miles. What a pity that we lose these ideal views.)

   However, that is not what I am sending you a line upon, which is to say that we have been much interested in your brilliant little article in The Adelphi about Mr George Moore; though it is rather like the amber enclosing the fly, for till lately I had only heard of him & his doings very vaguely, & I have not seen this book of his. Nor have I set eyes on him more than once or twice in my life; but I once answered a letter of his, about, I think, copyright, with great civility, as I supposed. Yet this attack is obviously personal. And I know hardly anything of his writings, for one makes, half unconsciously, a mental list of writers that are negligible, & I included him among them—with great relief, under the growing pressure of books that *must* be read.

   I doubt if he was worth such good powder & shot as you give him!

   I have occasionally wondered why the English press is so afraid of Mr Moore. It speaks of him always with bated breath, when I should have thought him to be the most tempting sport among present day detractors for robust critics. Somebody once called him a putrid literary hermaphrodite, which I thought funny, but it may have been an exaggeration.

The reviewers, so far as I have seen, have timidly waited till you came along to show at any rate that (to change the image) this lion, so great at roaring, is only Snug the Joiner: so perhaps the press will no longer be terrified.

To return to where I began, I hope you will have a good journey, whenever it may come off, & whithersoever it may be. I am,

Always sincerely yours
Thomas Hardy.

Text MS. Berg.
your circular tour: Murry's letter of 5 Apr 24 (DCM) reported the abandonment of his projected round-the-world tour—an idea which seems to have been connected with D. H. Lawrence's departure for North America in early March 1924.   *George Moore . . . book of his*: George Moore, the novelist (see IV.133), whose *Conversations in Ebury Street* (London, 1924) offers a series of hostile comments on TH and his work; Murry had defended TH and attacked Moore in 'Wrap me up in my Aubusson carpet', *New Adelphi*, April 1924. FEH re-emphasized TH's gratitude in a letter to Murry of 30 Mar 24 (Berg) and in a letter of 11 Apr 24 to Cockerell (Purdy), partly reproduced in *Friends of a Lifetime* (see letter of 5 Aug 20), 310–11.   *letter of his*: see IV.133.   *obviously personal*: as was TH's own hostility to Moore; see Millgate, 553, 571.   *lion . . . the Joiner*: *A Midsummer Night's Dream*, V. i.

To GEORGE MACMILLAN

MAX GATE, | DORCHESTER. | 29 March 1924

Dear Mr Macmillan:
I have finished looking over the new printing of the Queen of Cornwall to see that it accords with the old proof, & send up the latter as promised, which I am most happy to do, though it is rather dirty.

I shall be returning the new proofs in a day or two.

Always sincerely yrs
Thomas Hardy.

Text MS. BL.
new printing: i.e., the revised and enlarged second edn.; it was not pub. until September 1924, however.   *as promised*: Macmillan asked (24 Mar 24, DCM) if he might have the proofs of *The Queen of Cornwall* with TH's autograph corrections; on 4 Apr 24 (DCM) he acknowledged the arrival of the proofs and said that they had been put in the hands of a binder. Their present whereabouts are unknown.

To EDWARD FAIRHOLME

5. April 1924

Dear Captain Fairholme
I send back the proof of the "Compassion" Ode corrected by Mr Hardy. As the original copy was written in great haste, & these corrections are very necessary, please let him have a revised proof as soon as you can.

My husband will be pleased for you to send the verses to the Times for publication on the Centenary day, June 16, as it will probably help the cause as greatly as anything. He suggests (though leaving it to you) that you should put "No copyright" under the poem being willing to waive his claim to copyright in order that other newspapers may be able to reprint the Ode in the interest of animals.

Yours

The Secretary | R.S.P.C.A.

Text MS. (pencil draft) DCM.
Fairholme: Edward George Fairholme (d. 1956), chief secretary of the Royal Society for the Prevention of Cruelty to Animals 1905–33.   *in great haste*: Fairholme originally asked FEH (5 Jan 24, DCM) if TH would write a celebratory ode that could be set to music and sung at the international conference to be held to mark the centenary of the R.S.P.C.A. in June 1924; and TH sent off the MS. of 'Compassion' 23 Jan 24 (draft, DCM). On 4 Apr 24 (DCM) Fairholme reported to FEH that no suitable composer had been found but sent a proof of the poem itself as it would appear in *The Times*; see *LY*, 238, and Purdy, 231–2.

To RUTLAND BOUGHTON

MAX GATE, | DORCHESTER. | April 7th. 1924.

Dear Mr Boughton:
    As I have told you in my telegram, I know nothing about anybody, except yourself, setting The Queen of Cornwall to music, and if any composer is doing it, it must be for his or her private pleasure, as it cannot be publicly performed without permission, the play being copyright. Nobody has communicated with me on the matter, and if somebody were to, I should naturally refuse permission in my own interest whilst yours is on the stocks.
    So you need not entertain any wish to change the title of your version. In any case it would be the greatest mistake in the world to do so, the title as it stands being a novel one that attracted attention, as well as the arrangement of the play itself, the two Iseults having never before been brought face to face on the Tintagel stage. And though your music would excite interest with any words, there would, if I may say so, be an added interest by the public knowing that the words were those lately published as The Queen—which was very popular—and it would be a pity to sacrifice the popularity already gained. "The Two Iseults", "Tristram and Iseult" &c., have all been used as titles for the subject in its old form, before my innovation, and people are *so* stupid that they would not realize the difference when they saw it advertised.
    Please let me know particulars, and my publishers will stamp out this intruder. By the way pupils of the Royal Academy of Dramatic Art have performed the play, and somebody or other composed music for the songs. But this was not a public performance—though they might have asked permission as a matter of civility; but I knew nothing about it till afterwards.
    I am delighted to hear you have plunged into the work. Of course you can come here and try over a part at any time. We must try to motor to Glastonbury in August, and hear it. (My eyes are so weak that I am obliged to send a typed letter.)

Yours very sincerely,
Thomas Hardy.

Text MS. (typewritten) BL.
music for the songs: this performance of 1 Apr 1924—briefly reported in the *Daily Telegraph*, 5 Apr 1924—was precisely the source of Boughton's concern; see letter of 8 Apr 24 to Barnes and *Friends of a Lifetime* (see letter of 5 Aug 20), 310.   *Glastonbury in August*: TH and FEH did attend a Glastonbury Festival performance of Boughton's version of *The Queen of Cornwall* on 28 Aug 1924; see *LY*, 239.

To KENNETH BARNES

8 April 1924

Dear Sir:

Mr Hardy has received the programme of his play "The Queen of Cornwall" & the preceding Operetta "O Jan, O Jan", as performed by members of the Academy of Dramatic Art on the 1st of this month, specially set to music. It is sent by a friend who was invited to the performance, & is the first intelligence Mr Hardy has had of any such production. Would you kindly inform me why he was not apprised of it, since having himself made arrangements with another composer for the music, it has placed him in an awkward position. I was in London at the time, & should have wished to see the performance.

Yours very truly
F . . . . H . . . .
(Mrs Thomas Hardy)

Kenneth R. Barnes Esq. M.A. | Royal Academy of Dramatic Art | Soho. London. W.

Text MS. (pencil draft) DCM.
Barnes: Kenneth Ralph Barnes (1878–1957), principal of the Royal Academy of Dramatic Art 1909–55; *D.N.B.*   *specially set to music*: by A. Davies Adams, whose work (along with the direction of Claude Rains) was particularly praised in the *Daily Telegraph* notice (see letter of 7 Apr 24). In a letter to TH of 15 Apr 24 (DCM) Adams said that he had intended to have a private performance of his music and then, if all went well, approach TH for permission to perform it publicly; TH's draft reply of 3 May 24 (DCM) is sympathetic but non-committal. *a friend*: unidentified.   *in London at the time*: it is not clear that this was so, since FEH dated at least one letter—to Kathleen Lion (DCM)—from Max Gate on 1 Apr 24.

To SIR HENRY NEWBOLT

MAX GATE, | DORCHESTER. | 8 April 1924

My dear Newbolt:

I don't at all mind your quoting the whole of each of the four poems you mention, in the book you are preparing—which sounds rather an interesting one by the way—& I don't think the publishers will mind either, as the pieces are among those you included in your previous book. If they say anything I will explain, but I am sure they won't.

/ Personally I prefer the whole of a poem to be quoted. A d—d good natured reviewer who was bent on proving me a pessimist—blessed word—at all costs, cooked up my little love-poem called "I travel as a phantom now" into one of irreligious despair by leaving out the last verse, a bit of ingenuity which did him credit if you leave honesty out of the argument.

Whenever you are motoring in this direction later in the spring you must of course call here. We are still living on in the same dull way, to outsiders, & shall be delighted to see you.

As to my views on things in general, everything is so uncertain in Politics, Literature, Religion, Science, & Art (to use the words they display at the head of Reviews) that I have forsworn opinions, & merely wait to see what happens. It saves a lot of trouble, & is a waiting that cannot, in the circumstances, be so long as to be tedious.

Our kindest remembrances to you both. I am

> Always sincerely yours
> Thomas Hardy.

Text   MS. Texas.
book you are preparing: Newbolt's anthology *The Tide of Time in English Poetry* (London, 1925), in which only two of TH's poems are in fact included; see letter to Newbolt of 28 May 25. *your previous book*: *An English Anthology*; see letters of 23 June and 21 Oct 21.   *good natured reviewer*: the reference is apparently to the unsigned review of *Moments of Vision*, *Spectator*, 16 Mar 1918, 287.   *on things in general*: Newbolt (8 Apr 24, DCM) expressed a strong desire to 'know your feelings about politics—English and European'.

To SIR HENRY NEWBOLT

MAX GATE, | DORCHESTER. | 9: 4: '24
P.S.
In "Men who march away", line 5 of first & last verses:
  for "To hazards whence no tears can win us"
  read "Leaving all that here can win us"
(which is how it appears in later editions.)

> T.H.

Text   MS. Texas.
P.S.: to his letter to Newbolt of 8 Apr 24, but evidently posted separately.   *"Men who march away"*: one of the TH poems Newbolt did include in his new anthology.

To JOHN MIDDLETON MURRY

MAX GATE, | DORCHESTER. | 9: 4: 1924
Dear Mr Middleton Murry:
We are glad to hear that you are not, at present at any rate, going to do such a commonplace thing as travel round the world.

Certainly call upon us in the car when you come this way.

As for that ludicrous blackguard G.M. my concern has been for the unfortunate gentlemen his disciples. What a disgrace for them. They must be a timid lot, not to protest, & remind me of performing dogs in a show, obeying their master with fear & trembling lest they shd get the hot iron behind the scenes.

> Always sincerely
> Thomas Hardy.

Text MS. Berg.
to hear: from Murry's letter of 5 Apr 24 (DCM); see letter of 28 Mar 24.   *G.M.*: George
Moore; see letter of 28 Mar 24.   *his disciples*: TH—who had apparently not yet read
Conversations in Ebury Street—evidently had in mind Edmund Gosse, Walter de la Mare, and
the others whom Moore had identified as conversing with him; see *Friends of a Lifetime* (see
letter of 5 Aug 20), 310–11.

To J. H. MORGAN

MAX GATE, | DORCHESTER. | 21 April: 1924

Dear General Morgan:

I have read the second article, & of course was much interested in it. You
raise up the shade of J.M. as vividly as the Witch of Endor did Saul's.

You will not expect me to agree with all his views & yours. For instance,
there is in my opinion a real hope that the League of Nations may result in
something—for a reason which, apparently (I say it with great deference)
neither Lord M. nor yourself perceived, or at least cared to consider—the
self-interest of mankind. Principalities & powers will discern more & more
clearly that each personality in them stands himself to lose by war,
notwithstanding a promise of gain at first, & this thought will damp prime
movers down to moderation. Neither do I think with Ld M. that the poverty
of Ireland is entirely, or mainly, owing to the English. At bottom it is the
temperament of the people that has caused it, & will, I fear, perpetuate
it—much as I regret my conclusion, for they are a romantic & generous
people.

Many thanks for the Review. I hope you keep well, & am

Sincerely yours
Thomas Hardy.

Text MS. Berg.
second article: Morgan's 'The Personality of Lord Morley. II', *Quarterly Review*, April 1924;
for the first article see letter to Morgan of 16 Jan 24.   *did Saul's*: TH's slip for 'Samuel's'; see
letter of 30 June 20.   *for the Review*: Morgan had promised a copy in his letter of 9 Apr 24
(DCM).

To JAMES ISMAY

MAX GATE, | DORCHESTER. | 22: 4: 1924

Dear Mr Ismay:

I shall have much pleasure in signing the portrait for your villge Club-
house if the members care for me to do it. These village clubs which have
sprung into existence of late years seem thriving very hopefully, & to be
affording a nucleus for local centralization in opposition to the tendency
towards the towns: if so, it is a good thing.

Sincerely yours,
Thomas Hardy.

Text MS. R. Greenland.
Ismay: James Hainsworth Ismay (1867–1930), retired businessman, former High Sheriff of
Dorset.   *signing the portrait*: Ismay (21 Apr 24, DCM) asked if TH would sign a

reproduction of the Augustus John portrait of himself for hanging in the Village Club at Iwerne Minster, Dorset; the reproduction, signed by John as well as by TH, is framed with this letter. *your villge*: TH means 'your village'.

To HARLEY GRANVILLE BARKER

Max Gate, | Dorchester. | 28. 4. 1924.

My dear Mr Granville Barker:

The particulars about Kean have arrived, and I am greatly obliged. They agree with what I have always heard, except as to the play itself (which after all was mere hearsay) and I feel sure they are true. I have now inked in the title-page of the visitors' book for Mr Godwin, and no doubt he will get some shillings by exhibiting the place.

I can hardly imagine a sadder spectacle than poor Kean, weary, with the boy at his back, trudging into the town on that, for him, memorable occasion.

With all good wishes I am

Sincerely yours,
Th. H.

Text Typed transcript DCM.
about Kean: i.e., Edmund Kean (1787–1833; *D.N.B.*), the actor, who was acting in Dorchester in 1813 when seen and hired by Samuel Arnold, the manager of the Drury Lane Theatre; in 1902 TH had entered into correspondence about Kean's connection with Dorchester in the columns of the *Dorset County Chronicle* (see *LY*, 98–9).   *have arrived*: in Barker's letter of 27 Apr 24 (DCM).   *the play itself*: *LY*, 98, identifies the play as *Coriolanus*, but Barker said (correctly) in his letter that Kean had taken the part of Octavian in *The Mountaineers* (by George Colman the younger).   *visitors' book . . . the place*: the visitors' book was to record the names of those who came to inspect the building in High West Street, Dorchester, which was then occupied by Mr. John Thomas Godwin's china-shop but still retained many features of the theatre it had formerly been. TH's pencilled draft (on Barker's letter) of his description of 'The Old Theatre' is closely similar to the wording of his headnote to the visitors' book itself (now DCM).   *the boy at his back*: Kean's son Howard, who died in Dorchester and is buried there; see *LY*, 98.

To NELSON RICHARDSON

Max Gate, Dorchester. [Early May 1924]

Dear Mr. Richardson,

I am sorry to have to say in reply to your kind letter that I do not feel capable of presenting the prize to His Honour J. S. Udal, glad as I should have been to do so in other circumstances, as he is a friend of mine. I have an inflammation of one eye and rheumatism in the neck and head (both probably from the same cause), and am unequal to a function of any sort, as, indeed, I am at most times. I do not doubt that you will find a better man, and am much pleased that Mr. Udal has been successful. Many thanks for kind inquiries.

Very sincerely yours,
Thomas Hardy.

Text   *Proceedings of the Dorset Natural History and Antiquarian Field Club*, 1923–4, lxxiv–v.
Date   From internal evidence.
Richardson: Nelson Moore Richardson (see II.268), then in his twentieth year as president of the Dorset Natural History and Antiquarian Field Club.   *Udal*: John Symonds Udal (see I.136), retired colonial judge; he had been awarded the Club's Mansel-Pleydell Medal for his essay, 'Armorial Bearings in the Old Houses of Dorset'.   *a better man*: Richardson himself made the presentation at the Club's annual meeting on 6 May 1924.

To SIR FREDERICK MACMILLAN

MAX GATE, | DORCHESTER. | May 4 1924.

Dear Sir Frederick:
    There has been no agreement for the publication of a German translation of "The Dynasts", and if Bruckmann the Munich publisher seems to be a responsible man I should not be at all averse to his producing one. The drama was written before the war, as you are aware, and, as I gather from German reviews, &c, has interested German critics, that country showing up rather well in it as our allies of those days. Therefore if you can enter into some arrangement with this publisher so much the better.
    The terms I will leave to you, suggesting that they should be rather easy ones. Ten percent, as you say, as a royalty upon the German published price, seems fair enough.
    Believe me,

Sincerely yours
Thomas Hardy.

Text   MS. (typewritten) BL.
fair enough: Macmillan, who had passed on the enquiry from F. Bruckmann A.-G. in his letter of 30 Apr 24, replied 5 May 24 (both in Macmillan letterbooks, BL) that he would write to Bruckmann in these terms; the translation seems not to have materialized, however.

To RUTLAND BOUGHTON

MAX GATE, | DORCHESTER. | 6 May 1924

Dear Mr Boughton:
    I am glad to hear that you are getting on with The Queen.
1. As to omitting the Prologue and Scene I. from the music. Although I should have supposed such introductory music to be essential, my amateur opinion is really of no account, & I must leave the question to you. As the musical version will never be published without the accompanying score, it will not affect the Tragedy as published to be spoken.
2. The same as to the omission of the words at page 26.
3. The same as to the re-arrangement of the people on the stage & slight abridgements, at pp. 27, 32, 35.
    It will be most interesting to hear it played over when you come, though I am a poor judge.

Yours very truly
Th: Hardy.

Text MS. BL.

leave the question to you: Boughton did begin his music-drama (see letter of 28 Jan 24) at the opening of TH's Scene ii.   *at page 26*: TH had already read the proofs of the second edn. of *The Queen of Cornwall* (see letter of 29 Mar 24) and seems to have used that edn. (in proof or advanced copy) when writing to Boughton 18 June 24; whether he did so on this occasion is rendered unclear by the fact that the pages mentioned are identical in the two edns. Boughton later recalled (*Musical News*, 15 Feb 1928) TH's transferring the added passages into Boughton's copy by hand.

To RUTLAND BOUGHTON

                                        MAX GATE, | DORCHESTER. | 8: 5: 1924
Dear Mr Boughton:

I must have given you a wrong impression, as I quite approve of your doing what is best for the music: so you need have no mercy on the Prologue & Epilogue, as Merlin is outside the story.

As to the Messenger: he is so impersonal that if he is not wanted, slay him: or at any rate, in that particular scene you mention. I don't mind so long as you don't puzzle the audience about what is happening. In haste

                                                Yours sincerely
                                                      T.H.

Text MS. BL.

have no mercy: see letter of 6 May 24.   *outside the story*: Merlin is the speaker of the Prologue and Epilogue of *The Queen of Cornwall* but has no role within the play itself.   *in that particular scene*: i.e., Scene viii, the only one in which the Messenger speaks; Boughton in fact omitted the entire scene.

To ALEC PRIDHAM

                                                      12 May 1924
Dear Sir:

I write for Mr Hardy, who has received your letter, to say that he is sorry to be unable, on account of age, etc. to read from his works, or make a speech, at the intended Garden Party, for the benifit of the Dorset Nursing Association.

As however the Association requires encouragement he is willing to let his writings be used in any way on the occasion, & suggests that any member of the Dorchester Dramatic Society should be invited to read scenes from the books, or 2 or 3 members read a scene in combination.

He also gives permission to the "Hardy Players" (a section of the same Society—Mr Tilley, manager) to act any of the pieces from his novels that they have previously acted, or any short new adaptations by Mr Tilley from the same books, suitable for acting on a lawn without scenery. Mr Tilley has already done some of this sort with great success. His address is

                        T. H. Tilley Esq
                            Gordon
                            Dorchester

As to your programme Mr Hardy doubts if people who come in char-a-bancs will pay 5/- for admission.

Yours truly

. . . .

Sec.

Text   MS. (pencil draft) DCM.
Pridham: John Alexander Pridham (1891–1965), physician, District Medical Officer for the Weymouth area of Dorset.   *your letter*: of 11 May 24 (DCM), asking TH to make a speech or read something from his works at a garden party in aid of the Dorset County Nursing Association to be held at Ilsington House, Puddletown, on 31 July 1924.   *Mr Tilley*: see letter of 17 Nov 20; the Hardy Players, including Gertrude Bugler, in fact performed 'Bathsheba Everdene and Her Lovers', episodes from *Far from the Madding Crowd* adapted not by Tilley but by Harry Pouncy (see letter of 20 Nov 23 and III.279–81).   *5/- for admission*: Pridham, referring to the occasion as 'a big social affair', said that the admission had been set at five shillings in the hope that 'only people of some education will be present'; in the event the admission price was reduced to two shillings and sixpence.

To G. HERBERT THRING

MAX GATE, | DORCHESTER. | 13 May 1924.

Dear Mr Thring:

The Return of the Native. Czech rights.

I am quite willing to accept the terms proposed by the Prague publisher for the Czech translation, and agree to the deduction of 10% for the Society's lawyer, and 5% for collection.

I have not to my knowledge parted with the said rights; though I am not sure if I am in strictness entitled to demand any fee for a book that has been published more than 10 years. Foreign publishers however, prefer to pay something as a sort of authorization.

I should be obliged by your attention to this small matter as you kindly suggest.

Yours truly

Thomas Hardy.

G. Herbert Thring Esq.

Text   MS. (typewritten) BL.
the Czech translation: *Rodákův návrat*, trans. by L. Vymětal, pub. in Prague in two vols., 1924–5.

To E. B. POULTON

MAX GATE, | DORCHESTER. | 20 May 1924

Dear Mr Poulton:

The story you allude to must be "The Superstitious Man's Story" in *Life's Little Ironies*. The incident of the "miller moth" flying out of a man's mouth at the moment of his death—supposed to be his soul—is or was a belief of this county.

The spot whereon the particular instance of it that I had in mind is assumed to have occurred was a place called "Buttock's Spring" in the parish of Melbury Osmund.

How old the superstition may be I do not know. The old lady who told it to me said it happened in her childhood, & that would have been about 1820.

The common white moth is still called a "miller's soul" by the peasantry, for obvious reasons.

Very truly yours,

Th: Hardy.

Text MS. (draft) DCM.
Poulton: Edward Bagnall Poulton (1856–1943), zoologist; *D.N.B.*   *you allude to*: Poulton (18 May 24, DCM) asked whether the 'miller-moth' superstition was common in England and what TH felt about the possibility that the ancient Cretans associated white butterflies with the human soul. On 11 July 24 (DCM) he sent TH a copy of a projected article on the 'soul butterfly'.   *The incident*: it occurs on pp. 218–19 of *Life's Little Ironies* (Wessex edn.).   *assumed*: TH first wrote 'supposed'.   *old lady*: almost certainly TH's mother, Jemima Hardy (see I.163), who was born in 1813 and spent her childhood in Melbury Osmond, in NW Dorset.

To STEPHEN GRAHAM

MAX GATE, | DORCHESTER. | 23 May 1924

My dear Sir:

I have received from Messrs Putnams your Life of Wilfred Ewart, & write to thank you for getting them to send it.

It enables me to know more of a young man whose death I much regretted, but whose diffidence had hindered our getting well acquainted. Your well-written & interesting book is an excellent reminder of him. With renewed thanks I am

Sincerely yours

Thomas Hardy.

Text MS. Purdy.
Graham: Stephen Graham (1884–1975), travel writer and authority on Russia.   *of Wilfred Ewart*: Graham's *Life and Last Words of Wilfred Ewart*, pub. in London and New York by G. P. Putnam's Sons in 1924; during the First World War Graham was, despite his inferior rank, the close friend of Wilfred Herbert Gore Ewart (1892–1922), author of the successful novel *Way of Revelation: A Novel of Five Years* (London, 1921).   *diffidence*: the obituary of Ewart in *The Times*, 5 Jan 1923, refers to his 'apparent stiffness of manner, due to a modesty which was in no way affected by his sudden fame'.   *getting well acquainted*: Ewart visited Max Gate in 1920; see his posthumously pub. *Scots Guard* (London, 1934), 215.

To J. C. SQUIRE

MAX GATE, | DORCHESTER. | 3 June 1924

Dear Mr Squire:

A short time ago I was inveigled into setting up Wireless, & did not know what was going to happen. Last night we heard your lecture—every word, beautifully delivered we thought—& I must thank you for taking the trouble to give it.

I have not forgotten that I mean to send a poem. But I have been so blatant lately that I must keep quiet awhile for decency's sake.

My wife desires me to say that when you are down this way again we could put you up for a night with pleasure.

Sincerely yours
Thomas Hardy.

P.S. Our dog listened attentively.

Text   MS. Texas.
your lecture: Squire broadcast 'An Appreciation of the Life and Work of Thomas Hardy' over the London and Bournemouth stations of the B.B.C., 2 June 1924 (TH's 84th birthday). *send a poem*: see letter of 25 Mar 24.   *Our dog*: Wessex; see letter of 28 Feb 20.

To EDWARD CLODD

Max Gate | 4 June 1924

My dear Clodd:

Many thanks for birthday letter. I also must thank Mr Putnam, whom I met 2 or 3 weeks ago by accident, for giving a good account of my state of health, though I was not aware that he noticed. I have, in fact, nothing to complain of, though I may have already remarked to you, & you no doubt have felt, that birthdays in the eighties are not quite the same as the one at eight: but at any rate a person feels at the greater age that he has less to get through than he had at the lesser.

I cannot remember whether Putnam said he had been to see you, or was going. He told me that he had visited England 60 times, which must be, I should think, a record.

Clement Shorter called me, or, at any rate, this household, on the telephone on Monday, but I fear I did not make him hear any reply from me, though he got a reply of some sort. I am bad at it myself.

I am the first, probably, to wish you (in your own words, I think) as many returns of your coming birthday as you require. I also send kind regards to Mrs Clodd, whom, as well as yourself, I hope did not suffer from the east winds of last spring. My wife would join me in this if she were here, but she is just now in London—partly to see "Saint Joan".

Always yours sincerely
Thomas Hardy.

Text   MS. BL.
birthday letter: of 31 May 24 (DCM).   *Mr Putnam*: Clodd's friend George Haven Putnam (1844–1930), head of the American publishing house of G. P. Putnam's Sons.   *your coming birthday*: on 1 July.   *"Saint Joan"*: Shaw's play, first performed in London 26 Mar 1924, was still playing at the New Theatre; FEH went with Sydney Cockerell.

To EMMA DUGDALE

MAX GATE, | DORCHESTER. | 4 June 1924

My dear Mrs Dugdale:

Many thanks for birthday letter. Florence has answered a good many, but I have kept you for myself. She is in London just for the day, returning this evening, & now it is turning out wet I see.

You will know that we have had a good batch of correspondence this week! Best wishes to you & Mr Dugdale.

Ever affectionately
Thomas Hardy.

(We are expecting Connie).

Text MS. (with envelope) Purdy.
just for the day: see letter of 4 June 24 to Clodd.   *Connie*: Constance Dugdale; see letter of 2 June 25.

To THE REVD. G. CURRIE MARTIN

. . . . [Early] June 1924

Dear Sir:

You are right in supposing that "Under the Greenwood Tree, or the Mellstock Quire" was never rejected by any publisher. Mr Meredith advised Mr Hardy not to publish a first novel that was submitted to him, & consequently it never was published, "Desperate Remedies" being substituted, which was of a less controversial nature, & cleverer as a mere tale.

If you refer to "Who's Who", & to the Prefaces to the "Wessex Edition" (Macmillan) of the several books—particularly to the General Preface, Vol I. of that edition—you will find all necessary information, both on Mr Hardy's verse & prose.

With thanks for good wishes

Yours very truly
for Thomas Hardy

. . . .

Rev. G. Currie Martin, M.A.

Text MS. (pencil draft) DCM.   *Date* Replies to letter of 3 June 24.
right in supposing: Martin (3 June 24, DCM) sought confirmation of his opinion that J. C. Squire was wrong in saying during his broadcast (see letter of 3 June 24 to Squire) that *Under the Greenwood Tree*—rather than TH's unpub. first novel—had been rejected by George Meredith. *first novel*: *The Poor Man and the Lady*.

To J. W. MACKAIL

MAX GATE, | DORCHESTER. | 5 June: 1924

My dear Mackail:

I have read the lecture on Bentley's Milton. I had a decent respect for Bentley for some years, but now I conclude that I don't think much of him. I had no idea that he tampered with Paradise Lost to that extent. It is extraordinary that he should have stood so high as a critic when he had not the primary qualification for good criticism—the will & power to meet a poet half-way in his enterprize. Unless the reader does half the business in any poem, the poor poet—even a Milton—is nowhere. But Bentley was one of those—how well I know them—who stand rigid as a handpost, & say, "Do it all: it is your business, not mine".

I am suddenly appalled at having said this to a professor of criticism! But I
hope you will pass it by lightly, exclaiming "It is only Hardy's fun".

Well, I repent. To leave Bentley groaning in limbo, I wish an eminent
literary judge & writer like you would do an article some day on the influence
of scholarship on creativeness in literature. If Shakespeare had been a scholar
like Milton, could he have been Shakespeare? Well, we don't know—not
even Sidney Lee.

I am greatly obliged for the pamphlet, & for your good wishes, & hope you
will be coming down here again. We send kindest regards to you & your
house.

Yours sincerely
Thomas Hardy.

Text MS. Yale.
Mackail: John William Mackail, critic and civil servant; see V.174.   *the lecture*: Mackail's
Warton Lecture on English Poetry, pub. as *Bentley's Milton* (London, 1924).   *Bentley*:
Richard Bentley (1662–1742; *D.N.B.*), scholar and critic; his edn. of *Paradise Lost* appeared in
1732.   *Lee*: Sidney Lee, Shakespearean scholar (see III.237); his *A Life of William
Shakespeare* was first pub. 1898.   *the pamphlet*: i.e., the lecture.

To VIRGINIA WOOLF

MAX GATE, | DORCHESTER. | 6: 6: 1924

Dear Mrs Woolf:
    In the nebulous disguise of "The Hogarth Press" I recognize the daughter
of my old friend Leslie Stephen, & send this line of thanks to her for his Early
Impressions, which cover a time not so very much earlier than my own. I
shall have great pleasure in reading the book & am

Sincerely yours
Thomas Hardy.

Text MS. (with envelope) Berg.
Early Impressions: Stephen's *Some Early Impressions* (London, 1924), pub. by Leonard and
Virginia Woolf at the Hogarth Press.   *a time . . . my own*: there is, indeed, a brief reference in
the book (150) to the *Cornhill* serialization of *Far from the Madding Crowd*.

To LEWIS HIND

8 June 1924

Dear Mr Lewis Hind:
    I am so sorry to have left your letter over till now, & not to have thanked
you for "The Bermondsey Book", which one would not have guessed from its
title to be of such a high quality. But alas for me, I am now of an age at which
I cannot promise anything to any publication. Nevertheless I sincerely hope
that this particular one will make its way in the literary world.
    It is very good of you to be my reader still, & I am

Most truly yours

Text MS. (pencil draft) DCM.

Hind: Charles Lewis Hind, author and editor (see II.155), wrote 31 May 24 (DCM) on behalf of the proprietors of *The Bermondsey Book* (a new literary quarterly) to suggest that a contribution from TH would be much appreciated. Although this letter was clearly not intended for publication, a brief extract from it appeared in *The Bermondsey Book*, September 1924; TH's poem 'The Weary Walker' appeared there December 1925.

To WALTER OAKESHOTT

17 June 1924

Dear Mr Oakeshott:

I am much interested in your plans for touring this part of the country with the Oresteia of Aeschylus that you kindly let me know of. If the weather should be fine the Amphitheatre here will be an ideal place for the performance (though I don't know how it will be for sound). To be sure, it is not Greek, but it is almost certainly Roman, & the crimes that have been committed within its circle would I think match in horror those of the house of Atreus.

It is very good of you & the company to offer to play the trilogy in this garden, & to tell the truth it is doubtful if (on account of rheumatism, &c) I should be able to go to Maumbury Rings. But then there is the question of giving the players the labour of doing the thing twice over in one day, for which the tea my wife would be glad to invite you to would prove but a poor recompense. So that it seems rather selfish for me to say that I should be delighted to have you do it here. Still, I leave that physical question to yourselves, merely letting you know how pleased we shall be if you can come.

I should add that this lawn is a very sheltered & level one, & of course you can all rest in the house afterwards.

I am compelled to send a machine-written letter, owing to the weakness of my eyes.

Sincerely yours

P.S. By a very odd coincidence your letter came at the same minute almost as the copy of the Times containing some lines of mine in which occurs a rough paraphrase of some words in the Agamemnon.

Text MS. (pencil draft) DCM.

Oakeshott: Walter Fraser Oakeshott (b. 1903), at this date an undergraduate at Balliol College, Oxford, subsequently an authority on medieval art and rector of Lincoln College, Oxford, 1953–72.   *your plans*: i.e., those of the Balliol Players, an undergraduate theatrical group; Oakeshott wrote 15 June 24 (DCM) to invite TH to attend either the group's public performance in Dorchester the evening of 1 July 1924 or a private performance to be presented at Max Gate itself.   *Oresteia*: it was in fact an abridgment of the English version by R. C. Trevelyan. *Amphitheatre here*: i.e., Maumbury Rings, the Roman amphitheatre on the outskirts of Dorchester; see TH's article 'Maumbury Ring', *The Times*, 9 Oct 1908, collected in *Personal Writings* (see letter of early Feb 24), 225–31.   *the crimes*: notably the public burning of Mary Channing early in the eighteenth century; see *Personal Writings*, 228–30.   *if you can come*: the play was performed at Max Gate on 1 July as proposed; see *LY*, 238–9.   *words in the Agamemnon*: a reference to the third stanza of TH's 'Compassion' (see letter of 5 Apr 24), as pub. in *The Times*, 16 June 1924, '"Ailinon," / Outcalls one great of old: "May good have rule!"'.

To RUTLAND BOUGHTON

MAX GATE, | DORCHESTER. | 18 June 1924.

Dear Mr Boughton:

I have been unable to find in the "Collected Poems" any lines exactly suitable for Whitehands to sing to herself while awaiting Tristram on her arrival at the Castle—(to follow her words:

"To one I would not harm the littlest jot"

which I think is the place where you wish to insert the song). The nearest I have come across are these:

"Between us now and here—
    Two thrown together
Who are not wont to wear
    Life's flushest feather—
Who see the scenes slide past,
The daytimes dimming fast,
Let there be truth at last
    Even if despair."

("*Between us now*". "Collected Poems" page 124.)

Tristram would then enter. One objection to these is that, in the lyric, they are supposed to be said by a man. But perhaps that is of no consequence. However you must judge. The second verse of the same lyric might be added if wanted, but the third would not do.

The only other one I found, that might do, is this short extract from "The Minute before Meeting" (Collected Poems, page 219.)

"The grey gaunt days dividing us in twain
Seemed hopeless hills my strength must faint to climb,
But they are gone: and now I would detain
The few clock-beats that part us; rein back Time!"

In the second case, that of some words for the drunken revellers, the only ones I can find are the following from "The Trumpet Major", (also printed in Collected Poems, page 15):

"Rollicum-rorum, tol-lol-lorum,
Rollicum-rorum, tol-lol-lay."

I am sorry to be able to do no better.

I hope you got through your London business, and am

Yours sincerely,
Th: Hardy.

Text MS. (typewritten) BL.

"*To one . . . jot*": these words occur only in the second edn. of *The Queen of Cornwall* (London, 1924), 49.   *But . . . consequence.*: added in TH's hand.   *you must judge*: Boughton did not in fact introduce any additional lines at this point.   *for the drunken revellers*: Boughton did not supply words for the drinking chorus at the point corresponding to p. 59 of TH's second edn.   *from "The Trumpet Major"*: Wessex edn., 35.   *London business*: Boughton had evidently gone on to London following his 11–13 June visit to Max Gate; see *Friends of a Lifetime* (see letter of 5 Aug 20), 313.

To THE REVD. J. H. DICKINSON

MAX GATE, | DORCHESTER. | 19 June: 1924

Dear Mr Dickinson:

I am rather late in thanking you for your kind letter of congratulation on my birthday, & the good wishes of yourself & the parishioners. It is a pleasant surprise that they know anything about me, since it is scarcely likely that many are left who were there when I used to stay at the rectory.

I am glad to hear that the union of St. Juliot with Lesnewth has been a success.

I am reminded that the west gable of the former was damp when I last came, & that you thought of doing something to cure it. I should be pleased to contribute towards payment of the expense, the old part of the church being so interesting.

We often think we should like to pay the place & yourselves a visit again, but I am doubtful when we shall get so far.

With kindest remembrances to Miss Dickinson, in which my wife joins I am

Yours sincerely
Th: Hardy.

Text   MS. Berg.
kind letter: of 4 June 24 (DCM).   *parishioners*: of St. Juliot, Cornwall.   *many are left*: TH first wrote 'any are left'.   *Lesnewth*: the neighbouring parish; see letter of 15 June 20. *last came*: in September 1916; see *LY*, 172–3.

To THE REVD. WILLIAM PERKINS

19 June 1924

Dear Mr Perkins:

I send a word of thanks for your very kind wishes on my birthday.

I quite remember you as being at Dorchester more than 60 years ago, as well as your two brothers, when I was an architect's pupil, & you were an undergraduate of Aberdeen.

You say nothing about yourself, so that I do not know if you have remained in the Baptist ministry for which I think you were intended, like your eldest brother.

I hope you are well, & am

Very truly yours

Text   MS. (pencil draft) DCM.
Perkins: the Revd. William Henry Perkins (1843–1928), Baptist minister, third son of the Revd. Frederick Perkins, Baptist minister in Dorchester 1858–60. See *LY*, 237.   *very kind wishes*: in Perkins's letter of 2 June 24 (DCM).   *your two brothers*: Frederick, eldest of the three brothers, appears to have been a Baptist minister in Stafford in the mid-1860s; the second brother, Alfred More, who died young, is mentioned in Perkins's letter as having been TH's particular friend. See *EL*, 38–40.   *Baptist ministry*: the last of Perkins's several pastorates were in Bournemouth, 1899–1918, and Henley-on-Thames, 1918–22; he wrote to TH from Bournemouth, where he was living in retirement.

To ERNEST BRENNECKE

MAX GATE, │ DORCHESTER. │ 21st. June 1924.

Dear Mr Brennecke:

I am sorry to find that I did not acknowledge to you the receipt of your book, as well as to the publisher. My secretary said she believed I had done so, but her memory must have been at fault.

As for the book itself, I should imagine that it had been fairly well received in this country, and probably will be in America. I saw a criticism which remarked that it was a little too much like a treatise on Schopenhauer with notes on Hardy, and though that was a humorous exaggeration, what the critic meant, I suppose, was that Schopenhauer's was too largely dwelt upon to the exclusion of other philosophies apparent in my writings to represent me truly—that, as my pages show harmony of view with Darwin, Huxley, Spencer, Comte, Hume, Mill, and others (all of whom, as a matter of fact, I used to read more than Sch.) my kinship with them should have been mentioned as well with him. Personally I have nothing to say on this point, though I share their opinion to some extent.

You are quite right in asserting in the footnote at page 71 that I have never been influenced by Bergson. I had written a good deal before Bergson was heard of, and I have never accepted him as a thinker, his views seeming to me to be only a re-hashing of the old creed of Dualism.

By the way, a passage which struck me as odd was on page 70 where you state that I make great men "give utterance to the tendencies of the Will", and quote Pitt's words as an instance. You will be surprised to hear that those words of Pitt were literally those he used!—his last public ones—before Schopenhauer was heard of.

The paragraph on pp. 75, 76, which states that a principle of Schopenhauer was adhered to in my use of small incidents, &c. seems an attempt to trace imitation of him in a purely accidental resemblance (if any). Such details were given because I possessed them, with no thought of any philosophy. This tendency to find influence in chance likenesses occurs frequently elsewhere, as for instance, at page 15. The "Overworld" scenes were a pure invention: I had no knowledge of anything of the sort in Schopenhauer. Also p. 67. "His fondness for endowing inanimate objects", &c. But every poet and every child does it!

You must not, however, suppose that I am telling you all this by way of complaint. By comparison with the extraordinary things that are said about books of mine by others, yours are venial sins. I simply mention them in case you should ever recast your volume.

I enclose a list of a few misprints which caught my eye, as you may like to have them pointed out.

If you come to England again we shall be pleased to receive a call from you, and with thanks for the book I am

Yours very truly,
Thomas Hardy.

Text MS. (typewritten, with envelope in TH's hand) Columbia Univ.
to the publisher: Brennecke wrote from New York (9 June 24, DCM) to express the hope that TH
had received a copy of his *Thomas Hardy's Universe: A Study of a Poet's Mind* from its English
publisher, T. Fisher Unwin; Unwin's covering letter of 21 May 24 and TH's draft reply are both
in DCM.   *My secretary*: May O'Rourke; see letter of 5 Oct 24.   *old creed of Dualism*: as
TH had argued in writing to Caleb Saleeby in 1915; see V.78–9. Brennecke's footnote, however,
is chiefly devoted—like the rest of his book—to stressing the influence of Schopenhauer.
words of Pitt: in *The Dynasts*, Part First, Act V, Scene 5.   *principle of Schopenhauer*: defined
by Brennecke (75) as 'the portrayal of the smallest incident as a true mirror of the government of
the universe'.   *page 15*: which insists that 'the "Overworld" scenes of *The Dynasts* could not
possibly have been composed if Schopenhauer had not previously written *Die Welt als Wille und
Vorstellung*'.   *inanimate objects", &c.*: Brennecke linked with Schopenhauer's 'teleological
view of nature' TH's 'fondness for endowing even inanimate objects with personalities and
making them as essential parts of his stories as the human agents'.   *few misprints*: a typed list
of seven such items still accompanies this letter.

To SIR FREDERICK MACMILLAN

MAX GATE, DORCHESTER. | 21st. June 1924.
Dear Sir Frederick:
    I enclose a letter to which the answer had better perhaps come from you. I
think that I should like the poem asked for to be in the high schools' textbook,
and leave you to suggest the fee if you agree with me,

Yours sincerely,
Th: Hardy

Text MS. (typewritten) BL.
a letter: it no longer accompanies this letter but appears from Macmillan's reply (23 June 24,
Macmillan letterbooks, BL) to have contained a request from Francis C. Walker, a professor at
the Univ. of British Columbia, for the inclusion of TH's 'The Souls of the Slain' in an anthology
intended for use in the high schools of British Columbia.

To J. H. MORGAN

FROM TH. HARDY, | MAX GATE, | DORCHESTER. | 22: 6: 1924
Shall be highly honoured by dedicn. Eyes too weak to write more, as I shd
have wished (can hardly see paper, but getting better).

T.H.

Text MS. (correspondence card) Berg.
dedicn.: the dedication to Morgan's *John, Viscount Morley* (see letter of 1 Dec 24) reads,
'To / Thomas Hardy, / O.M.'

To THE MAYOR OF WEYMOUTH

MAX GATE, | DORCHESTER. | 24th. June 1924.
Dear Sir:
    A delay in my reply to your letter has been caused by my large
correspondence of late. I send my thanks to yourself and the Townspeople of

Weymouth for your good wishes on my birthday and your kind words of appreciation.

Yours very truly,
Thomas Hardy.

To the Mayor of Weymouth.

Text   MS. (typewritten) R. Greenland.
of Weymouth: Frank Walter Henville Peaty (1877–1961), the current mayor of Weymouth.

To G. HERBERT THRING

FROM | TH. HARDY, ESQ., | MAX GATE, | DORCHESTER. | 24 June 1924

"R. of Native". Czech rights agreement.

One copy signed & returned herewith—a couple of words being added to make the meaning clear. Many thanks.

To Sec. Society of Authors

Text   MS. (printed stationery with 'Memorandum' heading) BL.
Czech rights: see letter of 13 May 24. .

To C. E. S. CHAMBERS

27 June 1924

Dear Mr Chambers:

    I am flattered by being asked for something to print in Chambers's Journal on the Jubilee of my first appearance in its pages. I cannot lay my hand at the moment on a little poem that would suit, but I will examine further & let you know if I can find one.

    Your letter on that early contribution in 1865 (which was written to amuse some architect's pupils I was associated with) brings back the occasion to me, & also an advertisement I have lately been told of that the story is on sale by a publishing club the copyright having been purchased by the advertisers or words to that effect. I did not know that I sold the copyright when I accepted payment (£3..15..0 I think) for the contribution, & in ignorance of this sale I should have included it in my miscellaneous works if I had not thought it too trifling. Will you kindly send me a copy of the transfer, if I did sell it, that I may know if these people are right?

    I am sorry to give you this trouble, but you will see why I do so.

    I have not been to the Athenaeum for a long time, or in London, disliking the turmoil of the streets.

Sincerely yours

Text   MS. (pencil draft) DCM.
Chambers: Charles Edward Stuart Chambers, Scottish publisher; see IV.9.   *first appearance*: Chambers (21 June 24, DCM) recalled that TH's first publication, 'How I Built Myself a House', had appeared in *Chambers's Journal*, 18 March 1865, and invited him to send a contribution to mark 'the Diamond Jubilee of your reign as an author'.   *find one*: see letter of 5 July 24.   *architect's pupils*: those of Arthur Blomfield (see I.3), for whom TH worked as an assistant architect 1862–7; see *EL*, 62.   *publishing club*: see letter of 5 July 24.   *the*

transfer: see letter of 5 July 24.   *Athenaeum*: Chambers remarked that he had not seen TH at the Athenaeum Club (of which they were both members) 'for a long time'.

To SIR RENNELL RODD

MAX GATE, | DORCHESTER. | 27 June: 1924
Dear Sir Rennel Rodd:

I am interested in your information & enclosure, & am much obliged to you for sending it. I give my name & support to the proposed letter to The Times with pleasure. Whatever Byron's bad qualities he was a poet, & a hater of cant, & I have often thought some memorial of him should be at Westminster. The defect of the Abbey is, of course, that it is denominational, which a herōon should not be; but that cannot be helped (till an Annexe is built!)

I have nothing to object to in the wording of the draft. I should prefer the Latin form of the inscription to the Italian: & I think the word "Westminster" should be inserted, the public being such an obtuse animal. I have pencilled what I mean on the draft, which is returned herewith.

Would that Shelley & Keats could be comprised in the same memorial! or commemorated separately. But they no doubt must wait.

Sincerely yours
Thomas Hardy.

Text   MS. Keats-Shelley Memorial Association.
Rodd: Sir James Rennell (misspelled by TH) Rodd (1858–1941), diplomat and scholar; *D.N.B. enclosure*: i.e., the draft letter, sent with Rodd's letter of 26 June 24 (DCM).   *proposed letter*: an appeal, signed by TH and 12 others (including H. H. Asquith and Rudyard Kipling), for the dedication of a memorial to Byron in Westminster Abbey in his centenary year (d. 19 April 1824). Pub. in *The Times*, 14 July 1924, it was rejected in a letter from the dean of Westminster, pub. 19 July 1924. See TH's poem 'A Refusal' and Purdy, 243.   *Annexe is built!)*: see IV.22–3.   *returned herewith*: TH's suggestions appear to have been adopted; the appeal as pub. in *The Times* mentions Westminster and invokes both the Italian (*implora pace*) and the Latin (*implorat pacem*) forms of the proposed inscription. The wording eventually used was entirely different.   *Shelley & Keats . . . wait*: Shelley and Keats were in fact commemorated in the Abbey in 1954, Byron not until 1969.

To THE REVD. J. H. DICKINSON

MAX GATE, | DORCHESTER. | 28: 6: 1924
Dear Mr Dickinson:

It is a satisfaction to hear that the damp in the West gable of St. Juliot appears to be cured.

I should like to give something towards the expense of the re-pointing, so I enclose a small contribution. I hope you will have enough visitors this summer to pay the rest!

Believe me with kind regards

Yours sincerely
Th: Hardy.
I am much interested in hearing about Mrs Sandercock & the mittens. T.H.

Text MS. (with envelope) Berg.
the damp: see letter to Dickinson of 19 June 24.   *& the mittens*: Dickinson (24 June 24, DCM) reported that Mr. Sandercock, the current sexton of St. Juliot church, had a wife 20 years older than himself who remembered Emma Gifford (later ELH) and still owned a pair of mittens worked by her.

To C. E. S. CHAMBERS

5 July 1924

Dear Mr Chambers:

I am sending in response to your request for a little poem the only one I can find that seems at all suitable, though it contains no reference to the Journal.

I am much obliged to you for letting me know the form of receipt I signed for that early sketch of mine. It shows the fair dealing of your late father, since if he had said "for the copyright", & it had concerned an important MS. I, as a young man quite ignorant of such matters should no doubt have signed it readily. Being one so insignificant it did not of course really matter what the form was.

I find that the paragraph I spoke of as being in some newspaper was not quite as I put it. It was in the "Literary Letter" of *The Sphere* for June 28, & merely stated that the sketch had been reprinted in a Magazine called *The First Edition & Book Collector*. Also that it was reprinted in *The Review of Reviews* by courtesy of the owners of the copyright.

I hope you will think the contribution apposite that I send for your use in the Journal, but I fear it is not.

Yours sincerely
Signed Th. H . . . .

Text MS. (pencil draft) DCM.
little poem: as TH notes on the MS., this was 'A Bird-Scene at a Rural Dwelling', pub. together with 'How I Built Myself a House' in *Chambers's Journal*, January 1925.   *letting me know*: in his letter of 1 July 24 (DCM).   *form of receipt*: it assigned to W. & R. Chambers the right to pub. 'How I Built Myself a House' in *Chambers's Journal* 'and any other of their works'; the original document remains in the possession of the firm and is reproduced in Millgate, opp. 145. *your late father*: William Chambers (1800–83), proprietor of *Chambers's Journal* in 1865; *D.N.B.*   *"Literary Letter"*: written by Clement Shorter, editor of the *Sphere*, it criticized the recent first issue of the *First Edition and Book Collector* for claiming that its reprint of 'How I Built Myself a House' was the only one since 1865—the *Review of Reviews* having reprinted it 15 May 1922. Chambers mentioned in his letter to TH that his firm had recently given *First Edition* permission to reprint.   *Signed Th. H . . . .*: all in TH's hand.

To GEORGE MACMILLAN

MAX GATE, | DORCHESTER. | 8 July 1924

Dear Mr Macmillan:

I am willingly sending in the accompanying parcel the MS. of "The Queen of Cornwall" which probably, as you say, will be the most appropriate for lending to the Toronto Exhibition. As to its value, I have no idea, or rather I have no idea what collectors would value it at. However in view of the present passion for collecting I agree that it should be insured—for how much you probably would know better than I. Perhaps from £50 to £100? But fix it as you best judge.

Believe me

Yours always sincerely
Thomas Hardy.

Text MS. BL.
as you say: in his letter of 7 July 24 (Macmillan letterbooks, BL).   *Toronto Exhibition*: the MS. was on view at the Canadian National Exhibition, August–September 1924, as part of a display mounted by the Macmillan Co. of Canada.   *to £100?*: the MS. was insured for one hundred pounds.

To SIR FREDERICK MACMILLAN

MAX GATE, | DORCHESTER. | 12 July 1924.

Dear Sir Frederick:

I must write a line to say that I read your history of Net Book Agreement when it was sent, though I don't think I thanked you for it, or told you how unexpectedly interesting I found what at first I thought was going to be a rather formidable array of figures. Certainly I did not guess that the affairs of authors, publishers, and booksellers could have had such dramatic episodes. Perhaps I ought to hope that for their general good their history will be duller henceforth.

I had intended to make several other comments on what interested me when reading it; but you will have had so many that it is not worth while to add to them.

Believe me,

Yours very sincerely,
Thomas Hardy.

Text MS. (typewritten) BL.
history . . . Agreement: Macmillan's privately printed *The Net Book Agreement 1899 and the Book War 1906–1908: Two Chapters in the History of the Book Trade* (Glasgow, 1924); for Macmillan's role in the establishment and defence of the Net Book Agreement (requiring that books be sold at their published price without discounting of any kind) see his own account (above) and Charles Morgan, *The House of Macmillan (1843–1943)* (London, 1943), 177–81, 193–207.

To CHARLES SPEYER

[Ansr copy]   14 July 1924

Dear Sir:

Your enquiry of the 11th is to hand. Mr Hardy finds that the music of Tristram's Song which you sent last month with a letter duly arrived, but amongst the number of other letters & parcels must have been overlooked or forgotten. After some search the manuscript & letter have been found. Mr Hardy is much obliged for the song. As the copy is very beautifully written & you may have no other it shall be returned on request.

As he informed you when you inquired last February, he did not, as you asked, send the words to you when the song was finished, being of opinion that it would not be effective or intelligible except as part of a composition including the whole tragedy, & he suggested you might try instead another of his lyrics, if any. And in fact an opera of the whole, which has been announced for the last two months, is as you may have seen to be produced next month. What the result will be none knows, but Mr Hardy could not consent to your publication of the song with your setting just now, since, for one thing, the two might ruin each other by clashing. Whether he will be able to consent later on it is, of course, impossible to say at present.

Yours truly

. . . .

Sec.

C. A. Speyer Esq.

Text MS. (pencil draft) DCM.
[Ansr copy]: TH's square brackets.   *of the 11th*: in DCM.   *Tristram's Song*: beginning 'Let's meet again to-night, my Fair', in Scene xi of the first edn. of *The Queen of Cornwall* (40–1).   *have been found*: Speyer's letter of 10 June 24 (DCM) is annotated by TH as having been left deliberately unanswered.   *inquired last February*: Speyer's letter of 18 Feb 24 and the draft of TH's reply of 20 Feb 24 are both in DCM; Speyer requested the text of the additional stanza TH was said to have written but TH, concerned to protect Boughton's position, refused to send it.   *an opera*: Boughton's, soon to receive its first performance at the Glastonbury Festival.

To A. H. EVANS

. . . . [Mid-]July 1924

Dear Mr Evans:
Your letter of July 14 has been received by Mr Hardy, who is now compelled reluctantly to do most of his correspondence through a Secretary, owing to weakness of sight, etc.

He is glad to hear that your son Maurice is showing some talent, a possession that is really very rare.

The inquiry he makes, that Mr Hardy will allow the arrangement of "The Woodlanders" made for the Dorchester Players many years ago to be performed in London, is not so simple as it may seem, & he is obliged to his regret to refuse such permission for good reasons, with which, however, it is not necessary to trouble you. Its performance here was agreed to only on the understanding that it should be by the Dorset players only, & should take place nowhere else except before the Dorset Society in London at that date.

The dialect would be a great difficulty except for Wessex players, & a drawback to a London performance, & Mr Hardy thinks your son might exercise his skill on a less local play by some London writer.

Yours very truly

Text MS. (pencil draft) DCM.   *Date* Replies to letter of 14 July 24.
Evans: Alfred Herbert Evans (see IV.22), former Dorchester chemist and dramatizer of TH's novels, currently living in Stamford Hill, London.   *of July 14*: in DCM.   *your son*

Maurice: Maurice Evans (b. 1901), later a well-known actor.   *inquiry he makes*: also of 14 July 24 (DCM); he sought permission for the Hornsey Players (of which he was a member) to produce his father's adaptation of *The Woodlanders*, first performed in Dorchester by the Hardy Players in 1913.

To C. E. S. CHAMBERS

25 July 1924

Dear Mr Chambers:

I find that you asked me how much you ought to pay for printing the little poem in your Journal. Really it does not matter if you pay nothing, but as you will like the matter to stand on a business footing (as Meredith used to say) shall I say five guineas?

However, to mention this is not my immediate object in writing. Do you ever see, on the second hand bookstalls in Edinburgh, the poems of that neglected Scotch poet, W. J. Mickle (1735–1788). If you should, will you ask them to send it on to me. He was not great, but I used to be much interested in him when I was a boy.

Sincerely yours

Text   MS. (pencil draft) DCM.
asked me: in his letter of 11 July 24 (DCM).   *little poem*: see letter of 5 July 24.   *Mickle*: William Julius Mickle, Scottish poet and translator of Camoens; *D.N.B.*

To SERGE YOURIÉVITCH

27 July 1924

Dear Mr Youriévitch:

I have received your letter, but I fear I am not able to buy a portrait-bust of myself at present, though I have no doubt that it would be an excellent one, executed by a sculptor of the school of Rodin (which I am told you are). And I do not like to occupy your time in modelling me without due payment.

I never go to London now on account of the distance.

If you should ever be staying in this neighbourhood, & should have nothing better to do, I would not mind giving a few sittings.

Yours very truly

Mr Serge Youriévitch. | 9 Regent Street | London. S.W

Text   MS. (pencil draft) DCM.
Youriévitch: Serge Youriévitch, sculptor, born in France of Russian parents.   *your letter*: of 21 July 24 (DCM).   *told you are*): Sydney Cockerell told FEH (23 July 24, DCM) that he had visited Youriévitch and found him to be 'a nice man, a pupil of Rodin's and very strongly under his influence'.   *And I do not*: TH has struck through the immediately preceding sentence, 'Moreover I should have no room for it in my small house.'   *a few sittings*: TH did sit for the bust in August 1924 (see *LY*, 239) and FEH told Cockerell (7 Sept 24, Purdy) that she had helped to cast it in the Max Gate stable; that plaster cast is now in DCM and a bronze miniature (6½ inches high) is at the University of Texas but the present whereabouts of other versions of the sculpture are unknown.

To J. H. MORGAN

Private.   MAX GATE, | DORCHESTER. | 28 July 1924

Dear General Morgan:
    I am in receipt of your letter of the 25th.
    I am, alas, completely out of court in respect of the Nobel Prize, for Peace or anything. My advocacy would be a red rag to the Committee, & would endanger your cause, possibly ruin it, as I am excommunicated by the Council—(so I am told, anyhow). The clerical party appears to have great sway among them. My opinion of your book is, of course, quite as high as any of those you enclose, & I inwardly support your claim. But I think that outwardly you should get some quite orthodox people to do it, the point being, as I hope you will see, that you should not run any risk by my backing you.
    Believe me
                                                          Sincerely yours
                                                          Th: Hardy.

Text MS. Berg.
letter of the 25th: in DCM; it asks TH to write in support of Morgan's nomination for the Nobel Peace Prize, citing his recent book *The Present State of Germany* (see letter to Morgan of 27 Jan 24).   *those you enclose*: Morgan sent a testimonial from one of his sponsors 'as indicating the sort of thing that would appear suitable'.   *run any risk*: the Peace Prize for 1924 was not in fact awarded.

To C. E. S. CHAMBERS
                                        MAX GATE, | DORCHESTER. | 1 Aug. '24

Dear Mr Chambers:
    Many thanks. I enclose receipt. Please do not take any trouble to find the Mickle, unless you casually come across it: it was just a fancy of mine to get it from Scotland.
    Those pages from the History of Literature you kindly enclose give a useful & succinct account of him.
    As for reprinting "How I built myself a House" in the Journal with the poem I don't mind at all, if you really think it worth while.
                                                          Very truly yrs
                                                          T. Hardy.

Text MS. W. & R. Chambers.
receipt: for Chambers's cheque, sent with his letter of 30 July 24 (DCM).   *the Mickle*: see letter of 25 July 24.   *account of him*: Chambers had sent the pages relating to Mickle from *Chambers's Cyclopaedia of English Literature*.   *with the poem*: see letter of 5 July 24.

To ODIN GREGORY

[Early August 1924]

Dear Sir:

I write for Mr Hardy, who is much pressed by his correspondence, to say in reply to your inquiry that he has no objection to your dedicating your play of "Cain" to him.

He has read it, but is unable to give to it the time necessary for forming a critical opinion. Many thanks for lending him the typoscript copy, which is herewith returned.

The subject is not, of course, a new one, Byron's tragedy, with which you are doubtless familiar, being the first that occurs to the mind. His (as you may remember) is also in three acts, but in a greater number of scenes than yours, & Byron does not use the shorter lined verses that you introduce occasionally. Again thanking you.

Yours sincerely

. . . .

Sec.

Text　MS. (pencil draft) DCM.　　*Date*　Replies to letter of 15 July 24 from New York. *Gregory*: pseudonym of Joseph G. Robin, formerly a prominent American financier who was once gaoled for infringing the banking laws, currently a would-be playwright; Theodore Dreiser wrote an introduction to Gregory's verse-play *Caius Gracchus: A Tragedy* (New York, 1920) and took him as the subject of ' "Vanity, Vanity", Saith the Preacher' in *Twelve Men* (New York, 1919).　　*your inquiry*: of 15 July 24 (DCM).　　*"Cain"*: it appears never to have been pub.; TH (draft, 27 Mar 23, DCM) had previously responded, over FEH's name, to a request from the Colony Press of New York for his comments on Gregory's *Jesus* (New York, 1923). *Byron*: Byron's *Cain*, first pub. 1821 (separately pub. 1822).

To SIR SIDNEY COLVIN

MAX GATE, | DORCHESTER. | 3 August; 1924

My dear Colvin:

I have just read of your loss; & am *very* sorry indeed.
I have gone through it myself, & know what it is.
Don't answer this of course.

Sincerely yours
Thomas Hardy.

Text　MS. Univ. of Kentucky.
Colvin: Sidney Colvin, art and literary critic; see IV.286.　　*your loss*: Colvin's wife, Frances, *née* Fetherstonhaugh, died 1 Aug 1924; as Frances Sitwell, the wife of the Revd. Albert Sitwell, she had been a close friend of Robert Louis Stevenson.

To SIR HAMO THORNYCROFT

Max Gate | 5: 8: 1924

Dear Thornycroft:

I am glad to hear from you, & wish you could have called. My wife was at the performance, but I was not. The players made it up themselves out of my old novel, to their own satisfaction, at any rate; & I hope to that of the spectators.

I don't think you ever told me before that you were a fisher. Contrasting characters follow that "gentle" sport—another friend of mine devoted to it is a City broker. It is called gentle by the way; but probably the fish does not give it that name.

Kindest regards to both.

Sincerely yrs
Th: Hardy.

Text   MS. (correspondence card) DCM.
the performance: Thornycroft (2 Aug 24, DCM) mentioned that while on a brief fishing trip to Dorset he had seen and much enjoyed the performance of 'Bathsheba Everdene and Her Lovers' at Puddletown (see letter of 12 May 24).   *a fisher*: Thornycroft reported that the Dorset trout had liked his 'gay tiny flies'.   *City broker*: unidentified, but perhaps William Watkins (see letter of early Feb 24 to Bone).

To T. H. TILLEY

(Copy)   24 Aug. 1924

Dear Mr Tilley—

We have thought that in meeting the Company of players on Monday evening it might be advisable for you to let them know the conditions on which Mr Hardy agrees to their performing the Tess play, so that if they demur to them on your reading them over the idea of their doing the play can be abandoned, & he will not send the copy.

1. That performance in Dorchester only, is conceded at present, any question of performance elsewhere being left to be agreed on in the future.

2. Every announcement of the play is to include the statement that it was dramatized from the novel in 1894–5, (without stating by whom.)

3. The cast decided on is to have Mr Hardy's sanction, who is to be entitled to reject any actor that in his opinion is unfitted for the part, though this is not likely.

4. Nothing is to be mentioned publicly or allowed to get into the press of its intended production till discussion of "The Queen of Cornwall" opera has died down—say the end of September.

5. No more dialect or local accent than is written in the play is to be introduced by the performers, each part being spoken exactly as set down.

Of course Mr Hardy does not suppose there will be any objection at all to the above, as it is merely what any author expects, and he is reading through the play to see it is all right for your putting it in hand.

Yours very truly
F. E. Hardy

Text   MS. (pencil draft) DCM.
Company of players: the Hardy Players.   *Mr Hardy agrees*: TH first wrote 'I agree'.   *the Tess play*: TH's dramatization of *Tess of the d'Urbervilles*, first prepared in 1894–5, considered for London performance, but eventually put aside; see Millgate, 363–4, 375–6. For the history of the Hardy Players' production and of TH's feelings for Gertrude Bugler, who played Tess, see Millgate, 555–9.   *F. E. Hardy*: this signature is also in TH's hand.

To ST. JOHN ERVINE

MAX GATE, | DORCHESTER. | 25 Aug: 1924

Dear Mr Ervine:

It is very good of you to tell me all about Donaghadee, & very stange that you happened to be there when I wrote the few lines of verse. The fact is that some stranger sent me a letter therefrom about some book of mine, & knowing nothing of the town I scribbled down an impromptu suggested by the letter received, which my wife I am afraid thought too much of. However, I will look it up & send it to you some time or other: it will probably never be printed—at any rate not for years.

I hope the globe-trotting you have in prospect will work itself out successfully. With thanks for your information I am

Sincerely yours
Thomas Hardy.

You will excuse a hasty note; I have to rush off to Glastonbury. T.H.

Text   MS. (with envelope) Texas.
few lines of verse: Ervine wrote from the village of Donaghadee, near Belfast, 21 Aug 24 (DCM), having heard—through a letter from FEH to his wife—that TH had just written a poem called 'Donaghadee'; he went on to describe the village and the meaning of its name.   *some stranger*: for speculation on this point see J. O. Bailey, *The Poetry of Thomas Hardy: A Handbook and Commentary* (Chapel Hill, N.C., 1970), 551–2.   *not for years*: the poem was in fact pub. in *Human Shows*, December 1925.   *globe-trotting*: Ervine spoke of visiting France and, later, South Africa.   *to Glastonbury*: see letter of 12 Sept 24 to Boughton.

To SIR FREDERICK MACMILLAN

MAX GATE, | DORCHESTER. | September 6th. 1924.

Dear Sir Frederick:

I am much obliged to you for letting me know of the application of the literary agent, even though, as you surmised, I could not have sat down and written off hand to order a poem treating of Christmastide.

But after a search I find I have a fairly good one relating to Christmas which I had quite forgotten, but my wife remembered seeing, though it was only roughly scribbled down in pencil a long time ago, and was abandoned for some reason or other. This I can take up, and could send it to you for the agent in a week or two. It is of good length, about sixty lines, of the narrative ballad-kind, and therefore is suitable for a magazine, though perhaps less so for a volume.

I leave it to your judgment whether you inform the agent of these particulars or merely tell him that I will write the Christmas poem he asks for on the terms mentioned for serial right only and deliver it in a fortnight.

The report of my illness had as its only foundation a slight indisposition which made it advisable for me to stay in bed a day or two. The fact is that two correspondents of London papers live in the town a mile from this house.

Believe me,

Yours very sincerely,
Thomas Hardy.

Text MS. (typewritten) BL.
literary agent: the agent, not named by Macmillan in his letter of 3 Sept 24 (Macmillan letterbooks, BL), was Alexander Strahan Watt (d. 1948), second son of A. P. Watt (see I.113); see letter of 20 Mar 24.   *about sixty lines*: as completed by TH 'The Midnight Revel' (later retitled 'The Paphian Ball') was 70 lines in length.   *suitable for a magazine*: *McCall's Magazine* paid $500 for the poem—as Harold Macmillan reported to TH 11 Sept 24 (Macmillan letterbooks, BL)—and it appeared in the December 1924 issue with a 2-page illustration by N. C. Wyeth.   *report of my illness*: Macmillan said that he had been glad to see 'by the papers' that the report of TH's illness was 'without foundation'.

To RUTLAND BOUGHTON

MAX GATE, | DORCHESTER. | 12th. September 1924.

Dear Mr Boughton:

I have received your letter and the agreement-form which you enclose. I will look over the latter as soon as I have got through a job or two I have in hand, and send it on to Mr Thring, &c, as you suggest. I have no doubt that it is all right.

With regard to your paying me anything in the way of fees, when the accounts for the performances at Glastonbury are made up, I assure you that I could not think of taking any. The labour of getting up the production has been so great to you and your assistants that you must certainly keep whatever profit may result, if any. I always meant that this should be the case. We will start fees when you make a practical start with further performances.

I am so glad to hear that the success of the venture encourages you to get on with the score, &c.

With kind regards,

Yours very sincerely,
Th: Hardy.

Text MS. (typewritten) BL.
Mr Thring: as Secretary of the Incorporated Society of Authors; see letter of 6 Mar 24.   *at Glastonbury*: Boughton's version of *The Queen of Cornwall* had received its first performance at the Glastonbury Festival 21 Aug 1924 and TH had driven there to attend a subsequent performance (see *LY*, 239).

To HAROLD MACMILLAN

MAX GATE, | DORCHESTER. | 12 Sept 1924

Dear Mr Macmillan:

Here is the Christmas poem. There was less to do to it than I thought.

I don't know whether the cabling it over will cause mistakes; but I suppose the editor of the Magazine must risk that, & we must hope for luck. Believe me

Sincerely yours
Thomas Hardy.

Text MS. BL.
Christmas poem: see letter of 6 Sept 24.   *cabling it over*: to *McCall's Magazine* in New York.

To REYMOND ABBOTT

MAX GATE, | DORCHESTER. | Sept 16. [1924]

At home Thursday afternoon—

Text   MS. (postcard, addressed in an unidentified hand) Mrs. Michael MacCarthy.
Abbott: James Reymond de Montmorency Abbott, a friend of TH's for many years (see III.24), currently living at Ventnor in the Isle of Wight; he visited Max Gate 17 Sept 1924 in the company of Desmond MacCarthy's (see III.203) son Michael.

To HENRY HEAD

MAX GATE, | DORCHESTER. | 18 September 1924

Dear Dr Head:

I am deeply obliged for your explanatory & assuring letter, which makes me hope with increased conviction that the operation will not be a dangerous or very doubtful one. Florence's general health seems to me to be good, & that, I assume, is an advantage.

I also owe Mrs Head & yourself many thanks for accommodating her so comfortably. She says she has never had such a pleasant time in London.

Anything you may suggest that I can do to make the time easier for her I will do.

With kind regards believe me

Sincerely yours
Thomas Hardy.

Text   MS. (with envelope) Adams.
the operation: FEH stayed with the Heads in London over the night of 16 Sept 1924; the next day Dr. Head took her to see James Sherren, the surgeon, who recommended an operation to remove a potentially cancerous lump in her neck.

To SIR FREDERICK MACMILLAN

MAX GATE, | DORCHESTER. | 19 Sept. 1924

My dear Macmillan:

I am much obliged for the royalty accounts, which seem to me satisfactory enough. I did not expect the Queen of Cornwall to go off so satisfactorily, considering that it was an old subject unlikely to interest modern readers. If Mr Rutland Boughton carries his opera to London, there may be a revival of interest in The Queen. Believe me

Sincerely yrs
Thomas Hardy.

Text   MS. BL.
royalty accounts: for the year ending 30 June 1924; in his accompanying letter of 18 Sept 24 (Macmillan letterbooks, BL) Macmillan remarked that while *The Queen of Cornwall* had brought in less than £400 the general sales of TH's works had 'very materially increased', resulting in a total payment of £1,200 more than the previous year (see letter of 18 Sept 23).

To HAROLD MACMILLAN

FROM TH. HARDY, | MAX GATE, | DORCHESTER. | 23 Sept 1924

Dear Mr Macmillan:
    "The Queen" has arrived, none the worse for her voyage on The Atlantic.
Many thanks for returning the MS. Believe me

Sincerely yours
T.H.

Text MS. (correspondence card) BL.
her voyage: to Canada and back; see letter of 8 July 24.   *returning the MS.*: Macmillan's
covering letter, dated 22 Sept 24 (Macmillan letterbooks, BL), assured TH that the MS. had
been 'of the very greatest interest to literary people in Canada'.

To JOHN DRINKWATER

MAX GATE, | DORCHESTER. | 24 Sept 1924

Dear Mr Drinkwater:
    Certainly—if you really think me worth the honour of having the
forthcoming poems inscribed to me. I shall of course read them with much
interest, especially as my own production of such commodities is (naturally)
getting limited.
    If you send the invitation you speak of, well & good. But the fact is that
nowadays we are getting too much like those spirits of the vasty deep who
don't come when they're called—much to our loss often. Many thanks for
thinking of it, just the same. With kind regards & best wishes,

Very sincerely yours
Thomas Hardy.

Text MS. Yale.
inscribed to me: Drinkwater (23 Sept 24, DCM) sought permission to dedicate his new book of
poems to TH; his *From an Unknown Isle* (London, 1924) is dedicated 'To / Thomas Hardy'.
invitation: though Drinkwater did not explicitly say so, he had in mind his marriage to Daisy
Kennedy (1893–1981), the Australian-born violinist, following the finalizing of her divorce from
Benno Moiseiwitsch.   *when they are called*: *1 Henry IV*, III. i. 52–4.

To RUTLAND BOUGHTON

MAX GATE, | DORCHESTER. | 25th September 1924

Dear Mr Boughton:
    In accordance with your suggestion I sent up the Agreement form to Mr
Thring that he might see if it was in order. Only one point on which he
recommends a slight modification is of any importance—which is concerning
fees in Clause 4. He says that the one-third royalty should be paid on fees or
profits received by you from *publication* and *broadcasting* of the version with
the music, as well as from *performance*. I don't know what you feel about
this: I am quite in ignorance of whether it is due to me or not. Please let me
know how you regard it.

If you agree with him I will get the form copied in duplicate, with the above embodied. Also one or two verbal changes that he suggests.

He says, by the way, that you should secure the United States copyright. This no doubt you have already thought of.

I hope you are setting about the business of carrying the Opera further than Glastonbury.

Sincerely yours
Th: Hardy.

P.S. I can send you Thring's letter, if you would like to see it.

Text MS. (typewritten) BL.
to Mr Thring: see letter to Boughton of 12 Sept 24.   *further than Glastonbury*: it was performed in Bournemouth (see letter of mid-April 25 to Godfrey) and again at Glastonbury in 1925 and in Liverpool in 1927 but not then revived (apart from broadcasts) until 1963.

To SYDNEY COCKERELL

MAX GATE, | DORCHESTER. | 25 Sept 1924

My dear Cockerell

I am very grateful for your letter. It is of course a very depressing time, & I have all sorts of imaginings. But, as you say, there is every reason to believe that the operation is not a dangerous one. As for the length of time that she may be recovering, I don't want her to hurry away too soon: & possibly you may be able to judge by seeing her towards the end of the period if she is getting fit to come away: she may herself think she ought to leave before it is quite advisable, since there will be nobody down here who will be able to attend to her.

She may have told you that she feels she would rather go up by herself. I would of course go with her; but we have concluded that it is imperative that both of us should not be ill, or even ailing, at the same time, & London overthrows me in a day or two: hence I can be of more service here in an active state than I should be there if incapacitated. Many thanks for making those inquiries of the specialist: they are assuring. Believe me always

Sincerely yours
Th: H.

Text MS. Taylor.
your letter: of 22 Sept 24 (DCM), reporting the reassuring comments of a Cambridge specialist on FEH's impending operation (see letter of 18 Sept 24).   *judge by seeing her*: Cockerell replied (27 Sept 24, DCM) that he would call in to see FEH on Monday, 29 September, the evening before the operation; see letter of 3 Oct 24.

To LADY OTTOLINE MORRELL

MAX GATE, | DORCHESTER. | 25 Sept. 1924

Dear Lady Ottoline Morrell:

We have been interested in the photographs you kindly send, which to my surprise are quite clear, for I thought that their being done in such haste would cause them to be failures. I am particularly obliged for the one of the

Poet Laureate, which is exactly like him. My wife sends her thanks for them.

I am pleased to hear that you were won by the beauties of Dorset & adjoining counties, for as you know I dont limit my scenes to the first mentioned.

I very well know those tombs in Puddletown church that so attracted you. They have been badly used in centuries past, & the alabaster one that you photographed stood originally in the middle of the transept. I should like to put it back there. They were all erected to the members of the Martin family of Athelhampton, a fine old building about a mile from the Church.

I don't remember the song you allude to. Believe me

Yours sincerely
Th: Hardy.

Text MS. (with envelope) Texas.

Morrell: Lady Ottoline Violet Anne Morrell, *née* Cavendish-Bentinck (1873–1938; *D.N.B.*); half-sister of the sixth Duke of Portland, wife of Philip Edward Morrell, she was the central figure of an important intellectual and artistic circle.   *the photographs*: of TH himself, taken during a recent visit to Max Gate; see *Lady Ottoline's Album*, ed. Carolyn G. Heilbrun (New York, 1976), 61.   *exactly like him*: since Lady Ottoline suggested in her accompanying letter (19 Sept 24, DCM) that the photograph of Robert Bridges would 'amuse' TH, it was perhaps the one reproduced on p. 85 of *Lady Ottoline's Album*.   *Puddletown church*: which Lady Ottoline had visited after leaving Max Gate.   *of Athelhampton*: Athelhampton Hall (see II.305) was rebuilt by Sir William Martyn (a Lord Mayor of London) in 1493.   *song you allude to*: Lady Ottoline said she had not been able to find 'the Poem you mentioned about The Old Song'; TH had perhaps referred during her visit to his poem 'Any Little Old Song', first pub. in *Human Shows* in 1925.

To A. C. BENSON

MAX GATE, | DORCHESTER. | 27 Sept. 1924

My dear Benson:

I should have answered your welcome letter earlier in the week if it had not chanced to be a week of anxiety with us. My wife has to undergo a surgical operation in the next few days, which, though we are assured it is not dangerous, is serious. We had been hoping it would not be necessary, till lately the doctors have said that it must be done. They are men of the best repute in London, & it is at any rate well to think that there is no alternative, in their judgment. So we must hope for the best.

Although I know by hearsay the house you are in I have never been inside it. I remember thinking it strange that Henry James, who told me once that he could not live at Bournemouth because of the dull clubless evenings, should have gone to what I suppose from a society man's point of view, was a duller place.

Yes: Gosse is wonderfully young for his age. I hope he is not doing too much journeywork, & indeed I don't see why he should turn himself into such a journalist as he has done: his writing is too good & distinctive to be run through quickly in a newspaper.

I am glad to hear that Magdalene is flourishing: if the war had not come how many times I should have visited it! But that senseless event made all my plans gang agley, & after it was over I felt too old to get about much.

The author of the book on Ld Palmerston whom you mention as a bye-fellow, would perhaps be surprised to know that I once heard P. speak in the H. of Commons: not only so but make an atrocious pun, (to which he was much given in his later years).

The early memories of which you write are certainly not so poignant as the intermediate & nearer ones. I am close to the spots of my childish memories (though far from my middle-age scenes), & I revive them very often by going to "a slope of green access" about a mile from here, finding no pain in so doing.

I trust you will get back to Cambridge with renewed vigour, & am

Most sincerely yours
Thomas Hardy.

Text MS. (with envelope) Texas.   *Date* The envelope is in fact postmarked '26 SEP 24'. *welcome letter*: of 20 Sept 24 (DCM).   *surgical operation*: see letter of 18 Sept 24.   *the house*: Lamb House, Rye, formerly the home of Henry James (see III.90).   *young for his age*: Benson described Gosse as 'very well & juvenile'.   *such a journalist*: see letter of 6 June 23.   *Magdalene*: i.e., Magdalene College, Cambridge, of which Benson was still master. *visited it!*: in his capacity as an honorary fellow of the college.   *gang agley*: an allusion to Burns's 'To a Mouse'.   *a bye-fellow*: Basil Kingsley Martin (1897–1969; *D.N.B.*), editor of the *New Statesman and Nation* 1931–60, was currently a bye-fellow of Magdalene College and author of *The Triumph of Lord Palmerston* (London, 1924).   *heard P. speak*: see *EL*, 67.   *early memories*: Benson spoke of revisiting his old home for the first time in many years, adding, 'One ought not to be afraid of memories. They drop their bitterness as a stream drops its silt!'   *of green access"*: Shelley, *Adonais*, stanza 49, line 7; the reference in the poem is to the Protestant Cemetery in Rome, but TH of course had in mind the Hardy family graves in Stinsford churchyard.

To RUTLAND BOUGHTON

MAX GATE, DORCHESTER. | 29 September 1924

Dear Mr Boughton:

I accept your opinion that you should pay no fee for the use of the words in publication with the music, as I don't think it a point that matters much; and accordingly I send in duplicate a copy of the Agreement you sent on to me, without any alteration except the addition of the few words you yourself wrote in. If you will sign the two and send them back I will do the same, retaining one, and returning the other for you to keep.

I hope you are getting on with the score and am

Sincerely yours,
Thomas Hardy.

Text MS. (typewritten) BL.
the Agreement: see letter to Boughton of 25 Sept 24.

To HENRY HEAD

MAX GATE, | DORCHESTER. | 30 Sept. 1924

Dear Dr Head:

How kind of you to send the telegram. I am much relieved, & thank you & Mrs Head very warmly.

I hope Florence will not try to come home before she is quite fit. I can get on without difficulty, & it is important that she should have supervision as long as necessary.

London is really better than the country when the autumn is wet like this one. With kindest regards

Sincerely yours,
Thomas Hardy.

Text   MS. Univ. of Bristol.
the telegram: reporting that FEH had come through her operation earlier that day. See *Personal Notebooks* (see letter of 14 June 20 to Edgcumbe), 84.

To J. C. SQUIRE

FROM TH. HARDY, | MAX GATE, | DORCHESTER. | 1 Oct. 1924

Dear Mr Squire:

Thanks for your flattering request. Would the enclosed suit?—or one of them, for they have no relation to each other.

I hope your holiday was beneficial.

Sincerely yrs
T.H.

Text   MS. (correspondence card) Taylor.
flattering request: for a contribution to the *London Mercury*, contained in Squire's letter of 25 Sept 24 (DCM).   *the enclosed*: TH sent two poems, 'Waiting Both', and 'An East-End Curate', both pub. in the *London Mercury*, November 1924.   *your holiday*: it apparently included a visit to Max Gate, for Squire wrote, 'I enjoyed my night with you as much as any night of my life'.

To SYDNEY COCKERELL

Max Gate | Dorchester | 3 Oct 1924

My dear Cockerell,

It is most good of you to do all you are doing to relieve my anxiety. I get no *definite* information except through you, and have not heard from F. herself yet. I almost wish I had gone up, but the difficulty was leaving here. Her dog Wess would have broken his heart (literally) if we had both gone away. I think I may run up and back in one day to fetch her when she returns. I doubt if that will be next Friday the 10th as she prophesied. I am so glad that the pains have ceased, but feel very helpless to aid her, being down here.

Always yours
T.H.

Text   Transcript (by Cockerell himself) Purdy.
relieve my anxiety: Cockerell had visited FEH both before and after the operation (see letters of 18 and 30 Sept 24) and reported to TH on 30 Sept, 1 Oct (twice), and 2 Oct (all DCM).   *no definite information*: although James Sherren, the surgeon, wrote 1 Oct 24 (DCM) to report a 'quite satisfactory' operation in which the whole of the tumour had been successfully removed.

To HERMANN LEA

MAX GATE, | DORCHESTER. | 3 October 1924.

Dear Mr Lea:

In respect of the question you raise, I can say that, judging from my own experience, the handier a book is the better it seems to sell, and your volume is rather a heavy one for a tourist to carry about. I should therefore accept the proposal to produce it in the Highways and Byways Series.

A royalty on copies sold is in my opinion a better arrangement than a profit-sharing one. Ten per cent would have been considered low in pre-war times, when publishers used to pay a sixth, that is, about sixteen per cent. But I don't think you can get more nowadays than they offer.

I should, I think, in accepting, ask them whether they propose to bring the book up to date by adding a supplementary chapter, or appendix, of places introduced into the Wessex volumes since your book was published. Such an appendix need have no illustrations (though it would be better with some), merely giving a few words on each place mentioned: I fancy, however, they do not mean to do that till I have done writing; and, after all, it is not of great importance, even though it would enable them to advertise "New & enlarged edition".

I am sorry to say in reply to your kind enquiries that Mrs Hardy is in a London nursing home, recovering from an operation. She is getting on excellently they say, but of course it is an anxious time.

Yours sincerely,
Thomas Hardy.

Publishers' letter returned herewith.

Text MS. (typewritten) DCM.
Lea: Hermann Lea, photographer; see II.232. Many of his photographs of Dorset scenes and people are reproduced in John Fowles and Jo Draper, *Thomas Hardy's England* (London, 1984).   *question you raise*: Lea (1 Oct 24, DCM) sought TH's advice on a proposal by Macmillan to reprint his *Thomas Hardy's Wessex* (see letter of 22 Mar 21) in a smaller format, approximately the same size as the Pocket edn. of TH's works. Lea's letters of 1 and 4 Oct 24 appear in *Thomas Hardy Through the Camera's Eye* (Beaminster, Dorset, 1964).   *enlarged edition"*: no changes were in fact made for the book's reappearance in 1925 as a vol. in Macmillan's 'Highways and Byways' series; the last TH vol. covered thus remained *Time's Laughingstocks* (1909).

To FLORENCE HARDY

Sunday—noon— [5 October 1924]

My dearest F:

I have been out with Wess, who is submitting with a good grace to the force of circumstances. Did I tell you that a telegram came from the W. Dispatch asking you to give my reasons for my keeping back the Tess play for 30 years?—Miss O'R shall answer tomorrow that you are unable to reply as you are away from home. I don't know how you feel as to *when* you can return. If you feel you cannot at the end of this week (& I imagine it will be rather too early) shall I write to the gardener & his wife saying that they are not to come for a few days, but will be paid from date just the same?

K. came in to tea last evening. She thinks the idea a very good one that H. & Voss shd fetch you, & went on home to discuss it with H. There may be a letter from her by this same post telling you further what they think. She says H's car is so well springed that it wd not shake you. If this is carried out the idea of my fetching you by train wd fall through, of course.

Mr Niven called yesty aftn to inquire. I did not see him, but Nelly told him you were getting on well. Mr Tilley called in the evening to discuss Tess play. He doubts if he will not have to put it off till February, on account of possible general election, & difficulties with the parts. Gertrude B. is rather dismayed at the bigness of hers—& says she does not like the Tess of the play so well as the Tess of the book (which is intelligent criticism). Tilley says the physical strain on her will be very great, & we are thinking of the possibility of giving her some rests between.

I hope the envelope I posted yesterday with several letters &c. in it, & mine, did not burst? I ought to have used a stronger one.

I do not know whether H. & Voss cd go up for you & back in one day. T. H. Tilley says they *could* do it, but it wd be a heavy journey. They *might* go up the afternoon before, & stay at the West Central Hotel. But as they cd start from here at daybreak I think they cd do it in the same day. I will finish this later.

4.0 p.m. It has come on to be a very wet afternoon though it was a beautiful morning on Froom Hill. Nobody has called, & W. is on the hearthrug & I by the fire. There is a disabled motor-van by the gate between the cottage & the directing post. Two collided at 10 o'clock last night, but nobody seems to have been injured, though I am not sure—The leaves are beginning to come down rather fast, & Caddy has planted the little macrocarpus in the corner we looked at. I hope you sleep well. I must have an umbrella to post this.

Ever
T.

Text MS. (pencil, with envelope) Purdy.   *Date* From postmark.
Wess: the dog Wessex (see letter of 28 Feb 20); in this letter's final paragraph he is referred to as 'W'. *W. Dispatch*: the *Weekly Dispatch*, a London Sunday newspaper for which FEH occasionally wrote (see Millgate, 545–6). *the Tess play*: see letter of 24 Aug 24; its forthcoming production by the Hardy Players had been recently announced. *Miss O'R*: May O'Rourke, poet, occasional secretary to TH and FEH at Max Gate; see V.271. *the gardener*: Walter William Caddy (named later in this letter). *K. . . . H.*: TH's sister Katharine and brother Henry; see letter of 18 July 23. *Voss*: Harold Lionel Voss, chauffeur; see his *Motoring with Thomas Hardy* (Beaminster, 1963). *H's car*: apparently, at this date, a Sunbeam open tourer. *Mr Niven*: the Revd. George Cecil Niven, rector of St. Peter's, Dorchester, 1919–29; see *LY*, 224. *Nelly*: Ellen Elizabeth Titterington (d. 1977, aged 78), the Max Gate parlourmaid since 1921; see her *The Domestic Life of Thomas Hardy (1921–1928)* (Beaminster, 1963). *general election*: a general election was indeed held on 29 Oct 1924, earlier than Tilley seems to have feared. *Gertrude B.*: Gertrude Bugler; see letter of 2 Dec 24. *West Central Hotel*: a temperance hotel which TH had himself been accustomed to use in the past. *not sure*: the accident was not serious enough to be reported in the *Dorset County Chronicle*. *corner we looked at*: evidently in the paddock, adjoining the original Max Gate property, which FEH purchased from the Duchy of Cornwall in 1923; of two macrocarpus trees there, one had died by 1971 while the other was blown down in a gale the following year, blocking the road for several hours.

To FLORENCE HARDY

Monday 1 o'clock | 6 Oct. 1924

My dearest F.

I have had a note from Katie this morning telling me what she has probably told you also, that Henry is delighted with the idea of fetching you, & suggesting that I should let Tilley know early what we contemplate, lest Voss shd be booked for something else. I accordingly have called at Tilley's this morning to inquire, though I was unable to let him know when. He was very obliging about it, & says that in the circumstances he will put off anything to let Voss go, even at short notice. I was afraid you might be cold in the car, but he says it is a warm one, & that you could have a hot water bottle if necessary. K. asks me to send on some rugs to Talbothays beforehand, which I am going to do.

Tilley says that if they start from here at 8 in the morning they can easily arrive about 12, & come back in the afternoon. Henry however is for starting at a preternaturally early hour; but that will not be necessary. It can be done in one day without sleeping.

Tuesday—12.30—

It is all "fixed up" (American language). H. has been here this morning, & went on to Tilleys, coming back here, & telling me the arrangements. He & Voss are to start from Talbothays about 8, Thursday morning, & they will come Salisbury way, going back New Forest as you suggest. He says the journey up will take not much less than 5 hours, & I have given him a map of London with the route marked on it from Hammersmith (which will be the way he arrives) round by Kensington Palace Gardens, Bayswater Rd, Grand Junction Rd—& Marylebone Rd—to F. Square—But of course Voss will go which way he likes. H. has taken to Talbothays in his car the black fur rug, the brown, the plaid, & 2 cushions—so as to have all ready. He will also take an empty hot water bottle wh. I daresay they wd fill at the Home. He & Voss will get something to eat before they call, which will be probably about 1, if all goes well. You must, of course, have your lunch before you start.

On second thoughts I telegraph that they are coming, that you may know early.

5 p.m.

Wet afternoon again. As H's car is not an absolutely closed one, you will have to keep the wind from the wound. I so hope you won't get cold. If anything else occurs I will write tomorrow, not otherwise.

Mr Tilley called last night with his miniature models for scenery of Tess. He is really a most ingenious man.

Ever yrs
T.

Text MS. (pencil) Purdy.
note from Katie: dated 5 Oct 24 (DCM).   *Henry is delighted*: she added that he kept putting 'the hour of starting earlier & earlier, like father used to do in quite a merciless way. Do you remember?'   *Tilley*: Thomas Henry Tilley, the producer of the Hardy plays (see letter of 17 Nov 20), was a garage proprietor who not only sold and repaired cars but also hired out both vehicles and drivers; Harold Voss was one of his employees.   *Talbothays*: see letter of 1 Sept

20.   *F. Square*: Fitzroy Square, the London nursing-home (established by Sir Frederick Treves) at which FEH was staying.   *H's car*: see letter of 5 Oct 24; Cockerell (6 Oct 24, DCM) was perhaps reflecting FEH's own concerns when he suggested that the journey to Dorchester might best be made by train.

To HERMANN LEA

MAX GATE, DORCHESTER. | 8 October 1924

Dear Mr Lea:

I rather imagined the publishers would not wish to go any further at present. But you can store up the new place-references and photographs, and there may be another volume forthcoming later on, which would suggest more. If you should meet with a copy of The Queen of Cornwall programme, produced by the Dorchester players last autumn, you will find in it a photograph of Tintagel Castle as at present. I should like you to save that in case it should be wanted. It would be the only illustration the play would require. (Or you could yourself photograph the original drawing, which we have here—or the original spot if you were travelling that way.)

Many thanks for inquiries. Mrs Hardy proposes to come home to-morrow by car.

Yours sincerely,
T.H.

Text MS. (typewritten) DCM.
any further at present: see letter to Lea of 3 Oct 24; Lea reported (7 Oct 24, DCM) that Macmillan & Co. showed no interest in expanding the scope of *Thomas Hardy's Wessex*. Lea's letters of 7 and 12 Oct 24 are in *Thomas Hardy Through the Camera's Eye* (see letter to Lea of 3 Oct 24).   *photograph of Tintagel Castle*: it was in fact a photograph of a water-colour of the castle by Emma Gifford (ELH), captioned 'From a Water Colour Drawing in the possession of the Author'.   *by car*: see letter of 6 Oct 24.

To J. B. PRIESTLEY

MAX GATE, | DORCHESTER. | 15 Oct. 1924

Dear Mr Priestley:

I should have acknowledged the receipt of your kind gift a little sooner if it had not happened that I was in bed for a few days with a bad cold. I have now only read one of the essays—that on my friend Mr A. E. Housman, which I think an able estimate of his genius. By a coincidence we came across in the Mercury just before the arrival of the book your paper on J. M. Barrie, which we—my wife & I—both liked.

I am, of course, going to read the others in the volume, & with many thanks believe me

Sincerely yours
Thomas Hardy.

Text MS. Texas.
Priestley: John Boynton Priestley (1894–1984), novelist, dramatist, and critic. He wrote 10 Oct 24 (DCM) to send a copy of his *Figures in Modern Literature* (London, 1924).   *Housman*: see IV.321; the essay oocupies pp. 77–102 of *Figures*.   *paper on J. M. Barrie*: 'Sir James Barrie', *London Mercury*, October 1924.   *others in the volume*: these did not, however, include one on TH himself.

To JACQUES RIVIÈRE

22 October 1924
Dear Sir:

In reply to your inquiry received the 21st. inst. I write for Mr Thomas Hardy to say that he is much obliged for your letter, but that on account of increasing age he is unfortunately unable to send to the Nouvelle Revue Francaise an appreciation of the life & work of the late Joseph Conrad. Mr Hardy regrets to add that though he was an admirer of Mr Conrad he did not know him personally.

Yours truly
M O'R
Secretary.

M. Jacques Rivière | 3 Rue de Grenelle | Paris.

Text MS. (pencil draft) DCM.
Rivière: Jacques Rivière (1886–1925), French critic and novelist, editor of the *Nouvelle Revue Française*. *the 21st. inst.*: Rivière's letter is, however, dated from Paris 3 Oct 24 (DCM). *an appreciation*: for inclusion in the special 'Hommage à Joseph Conrad' issue of the *NRF*, December 1924. *not know him personally*: a 1907 meeting between Conrad and TH is, however, recorded in *LY*, 124.

To THOMAS J. WISE

MAX GATE, | DORCHESTER. | 24 Oct: 1924
Dear Mr Wise:

Many thanks for the fifth volume. It is, I think, the most interesting of the lot, including as it does such two extremes as Shelley & Sheridan. Mary's letter, with its spectral details of her home experiences when Shelley was drowned, is engrossing & moving.

You probably know that Mr Sheridan who lives near here—the direct descendant of R.B.S., has the manuscripts of all his plays.

Very truly yours
Thomas Hardy.

Text MS. (with envelope) BL.
fifth volume: of Wise's *The Ashley Library* (see letter of 31 May 22), pub. 1924. *Mary's letter*: Mary Shelley's letter of 15 Aug 1822 to Maria Gisborne is quoted in full in *The Ashley Library*, V.32–8. *Mr Sheridan*: Algernon Thomas Brinsley Sheridan, of Frampton Court, near Dorchester; see I.184. *R.B.S. . . . his plays*: for the eventual fate of the Sheridan MSS. see *The Dramatic Works of Richard Brinsley Sheridan*, ed. Cecil Price (Oxford, 1973), I.22–4. Wise's letter to TH of 25 Oct 24 (DCM), requesting Mr Sheridan's full name and address, is annotated '[Unansd]' in TH's hand.

To SIR FREDERICK MACMILLAN

MAX GATE, | DORCHESTER. | 29 Oct. 1924

Dear Sir Frederick:

The Dynasts have, or has, come, & we like the appearance of the volumes. I will bear in mind that I can have extra copies if required. With thanks

Believe me

Sincerely yrs
T.H.

Text   MS. BL.

the volumes: Macmillan (27 Oct 24, Macmillan letterbooks, BL) sent two copies—one bound in cloth, the other in leather—of the two-vol. Pocket edn. of *The Dynasts* (with *The Queen of Cornwall*), to be pub. the following day.

To JOHN GALSWORTHY

MAX GATE, | DORCHESTER. | 30 Oct. 1924

My dear Galsworthy:

I have heard of a Green Dragon; (there is one a mile from here)—I have heard of a Red Lion—(one 5 miles off) & of a Black Bear (8 miles away) but I have never before met with a White Monkey. This means that your kind gift has come, & I write to acknowledge it before you go abroad, which I believe you are on the brink of doing.

We hope that Mrs Galsworthy is better, & that all will go well: also that you are not driven "frantical" (as they say here) by the elections.

Ever sincerely
Thomas Hardy.

Text   MS. Univ. of Birmingham.

a mile from here): the nearest Green Dragon public house appears, in fact, to have been in the Piddle Valley, some four miles from Max Gate.   *Red Lion*: at Winfrith, about seven miles away.   *Black Bear*: at Wool, about nine miles away.   *White Monkey*: Galsworthy had sent a copy of his novel *The White Monkey* (London, 1924).   *go abroad*: to Italy and North Africa.   *the elections*: the general election held on 29 Oct 1924 had resulted in a large Conservative majority.

To ERNEST BRENNECKE

[Ansr]   Nov 1 or 2—1924

Dear Mr Brennecke:

As Mr Hardy's correspondence is so heavy he asks you to excuse him for replying to your letter of the 20th by proxy.

In respect of the inquiry you make he regrets to say that he cannot authorize anything of the nature of a biography of himself to be published. He has only a vague recollection of the typoscript pages you speak of wishing to utilize, that were not printed in "Thomas Hardy's Universe", and in which some passages about his life were given, & remarks on them pencilled by Mrs Hardy, so that he does not remember what errors were corrected, & what may have been overlooked, the remarks having been of a cursory kind.

Many thanks for the little edition of Mr Middleton Murry's article. Mr Hardy heard about Mr George Moore's book, but he did not read it, except as to some quotations from it by its reviewers, who all seemed to satirize its extreme foolishness.

Also thanks for the cutting from the newspaper.

Yours very truly

. . . .

Ernest Brennecke, Jr., Esq. | Sunday "World" Office | 63, Park Row, New York. U.S.A.

Text   MS. (pencil draft) DCM.
[Ansr]: TH's square brackets.   *of the 20th*: written from New York.   *biography of himself*: Brennecke reported that his New York publisher (Greenberg) wanted to pub. as a separate vol. 'the short biographical sketch which formed part of the rather huge MS I brought over to you last year'; he added that since TH had gone over the sketch and checked its factual statements perhaps he or FEH could give permission for it appear as 'an authorized biography, at least as far as the main facts are concerned'. TH seems not to have replied to Brennecke's letter of 17 Nov 24 (DCM) announcing that he now planned to make the book 'rather a descriptive critique of your poetical work' and requesting permission to use three or four of the illustrations from *Wessex Poems*, but see letter of 28 Jan 25.   *little edition*: a separate, limited printing by Greenberg of Middleton Murry's *New Adelphi* article, 'Wrap me up in my Aubusson carpet' (see letter of 28 Mar 24).   *Moore's book*: *Conversations in Ebury Street*; see letter of 28 Mar 24 and letter of 9 Apr 24 to Murry.   *the cutting*: it contained a review of the recent film version of *Tess of the d'Urbervilles*.

To SYBIL THORNDIKE

2 November: 1924

Dear Mrs Casson:

(Physical difficulties compel me to send a typewritten letter which please pardon)

Yes: as you have heard, your sister Mrs Ewbank & my wife & I had a pleasant talk about the possibilities of your producing the play of "Tess", an event which would be an interesting thing to me solely from the fact that it is you who would or might like to do it. Apart from that I have no particular wish to get the play acted on the regular stage at all—indeed, I should never have thought of it again since the time when many years ago I was inclined to try it as an experiment.

As you probably are aware, the performance here by the Dorchester amateurs is for our local entertainment only, & has nothing to do with the question whether it is a good play or a bad one. But I shall have pleasure in sending you a copy of it to read when I have got it made & have looked it over. Whether it would be better before sending it to wait till the production here has taken place I don't know: perhaps you will be able to judge.

It would certainly be desirable that Mr Casson, or anybody else you can think of if he should be unable, should see one of these performances, as I daresay that a practised eye could gather from the inexperienced acting an idea whether the adaptation was successful as a turning of the tragedy from narrative to dramatic form. The dates will be Wednesday evening Nov 26, Thursday the 27th, afternoon & evening, & Friday & Saturday evenings 28 & 29.

Please don't mind sending the play back when you have read it, if you are not quite sure you wish to take it up, as you will guess from what I have told you that I am very vague about its practicability. I was not, of course, aware that you had been impressed by the story, or I would have hunted up the play for you to read years ago.

It is disgraceful that I have never seen you in any character! However, to compensate for this shortcoming in me I hasten to add that my wife has been amongst your delighted audiences, & has long recognized your powers.

Sincerely yours—

[Mrs Sybil Thorndike Casson | 6 Carlyle Square | Chelsea | London SW.]

Text MS. (pencil draft) DCM.
Thorndike: Sybil Thorndike (1882–1976), actress.   *Mrs Ewbank*: Eileen Ewbank, *née* Thorndike (1890–1954), actress.   *many years ago*: in 1894–5; see letter of 24 Aug 24. *the Dorchester amateurs*: i.e., the Hardy Players.   *Mr Casson*: Lewis Casson (1875–1969), actor and producer; he married Sybil Thorndike in 1908.   *see one of these performances*: Miss Thorndike replied (5 Nov 24, DCM) that her husband would come to Dorchester on 29 November but wished to read the play first; on 11 Nov 24 (DCM) she acknowledged receipt of a copy of the play.   *[Mrs . . . SW.]*: TH's square brackets.

To VERE H. COLLINS

MAX GATE, DORCHESTER. | 11th. November '24.

Dear Mr Collins:

I am willing to let the Oxford University Press print the poems you mention—"Friends Beyond", "Weathers", and "When I set out for Lyonesse" —in their forthcoming selection for schools on the following terms: two guineas for the first-named, and a guinea each for the other two. My publishers will also be willing I know.

Yours very truly.
Th. Hardy.

Vere Collins. Esq. | Oxford University Press.

Text MS. (typewritten) Texas.
selection for schools: the three poems mentioned are included in *A Book of Modern Verse*, ed. J. C. Smith (Oxford, 1925).

To HAROLD CHILD

MAX GATE, | DORCHESTER. | November 13th. 1924.

Dear Mr Child:

I am glad to hear that you are to come to see the Tess play, as you enter so ably into our local attempts, and also will have mercy on the shortcomings of a job I undertook entirely by request 30 years ago—a job I should not think of doing now, which the company are going to act unaltered.

There will be two dress rehearsals, the first on Monday the 24th at half past 7, and the second on Tuesday at the same time. I dare not go to the second one (to which the management have, I think, invited newspaper critics in general) because of the snapshotters and gossiping paragraphists who are sure to be there, so I am going to the Monday one. I do not know which would suit you best, but no other critic will be present but yourself on Monday if you come to that—in fact, the door will be strictly guarded. The only other person present from outside will be Barrie, who has asked to come then instead of to the public performance, for the same reason as my own. Of course at these rehearsals, as you know, though the players will be in costume, they will not be made up in face and head, and a slightly bald Angel Clare will perhaps damage your estimate of him. However that cannot be helped.

(I am compelled to use the typewriter, on account of weakness of sight.)

Ever sincerely yours,
Th: Hardy.

Of course we shall hope to see you to tea whichever day you come. F.H.

Text   MS. (typewritten, with postcript in FEH's hand) Adams.
see the Tess play: Child wrote 12 Nov 24 (DCM) to say that he had been asked to review the play for *The Times* and would prefer to see the dress rehearsal, as when he had reviewed *The Queen of Cornwall* (see letter of 11 Nov 23).   *bald Angel Clare*: the part was played by Dr. E. W. Smerdon (see letter of 17 Nov 20).

To JOHN DRINKWATER

MAX GATE, │ DORCHESTER. │ 16 November 1924

My dear Mr Drinkwater:

My real thanks for "An Unknown Isle", which I am beginning to read, though as yet I have only gone through two, very sweet ones. Also for the distinction of having it inscribed to me.

As you know, the best wishes for your future accompany this note.

Very sincerely yours
Thomas Hardy.

Text   MS. Yale.
Unknown Isle": see letter of 24 Sept 24.

To A. M. PARRATT

17 November 1924

Dear Sir:

In reply to your letter of 11 Oct. to Mr Thomas Hardy I much regret to state that although a troublesome search has been made, no trace of the letter or photograph of which you speak can be found.

From the tone in which you write you are obviously unaware of what the correspondence of an author can be like. Were Mr Hardy to answer the mass of letters he receives from strangers like yourself he would have no time whatever for any work of his own, or even for taking rest.

Yours truly

M—O'R.

Secretary

Mr A. M. Parratt | Yarram | Victoria.

Text MS. (pencil draft) DCM.
Parratt: Arthur M. Parratt, schoolteacher; he wrote (11 Oct 24, DCM) from the Higher Elementary School, Yarram, Victoria, Australia, to demand the return of the photograph of his 'book' (apparently an autograph album) which he had sent to TH the previous February together with a request for his autograph.   *tone in which you write*: e.g., 'I think as a matter of courtesy from one gentleman to another I was entitled to the return of my photo.'

To JOHN MASEFIELD

MAX GATE, | DORCHESTER. | 18 Nov: 1924

Dear Mr Masefield:
   We have been much interested in your theatre ever since we heard of it—indeed we were wondering about its construction only a day or two ago; & now you add to the interest by writing on the subject. I am honoured by your thinking of The Queen of Cornwall as a piece for it, & of course consent.
   As to my coming, how I should like to; but, alas, I am getting to be a mere vegetable in point of immobility.
   Curiously enough I happen as well as you to be mixed up with stage matters just now. Our local players asked me to let them have something for this year, & to save trouble I hunted up an old play I carpentered out of a novel 30 years ago. Instead of trouble being saved I find myself insensibly drawn into the details of production, which I must say is, for a change, very entertaining. Our best wishes to you both.

Sincerely yours

Thomas Hardy.

Congratulations on your fine novel Sard Harker. T.H.

Text MS. Texas.
your theatre: in the large music room he had built in the garden of his house on Boar's Hill, Oxford.   *writing on the subject*: in an undated letter (DCM) supplied by TH with the date of 17 Nov 24 Masefield asked permission to stage *The Queen of Cornwall* in his theatre; a sketch-plan of its layout was included in Masefield's undated letter of reply (DCM).   *Curiously . . . you both.*: this paragraph is represented as comprising the entire text of the letter in the 'facsimile' pub. in the *Countryman*, July–September 1936, 528.   *Sard Harker*: Masefield's *Sard Harker: A Novel* (London, 1924).

To PHILIP PEARCE

26 November 1924

Dear Sir:
   In reply to your letter I write for Mr Hardy to say that he is much pleased at your request that he should write a funny verse in the Dorset dialect for the

forthcoming Dinner to the members. He regrets to say, however, that it is quite beyond his powers to produce such a verse, but hopes you will be able to find a poet somewhere in the county who can successfully do it for you.

Yours truly

. . . .
Secretary

Philip Pearce Esq. | Albert Street | Blandford.

Text   MS. (pencil draft) DCM.
Pearce: Philip Pearce, of the North Dorset Conservative Association; he wrote from Blandford 25 Nov 24 (DCM) to ask if TH 'would kindly write—gratis—a funny verse in the Dorset dialect bringing in the four conservative M.P.s' names of Dorset'; he explained that the verse would appear on the front of the list of toasts for a 'smoker' at which the four recently elected Members of Parliament would be present and added that an 'early reply' would be much appreciated.

To SIR JOHNSTON FORBES-ROBERTSON

29 November 1924

Dear Sir J. Forbes-Robertson:

I am flattered by the wish of Lady Forbes Robertson. As you may guess I have no great desire at my time of life to see the Tess play acted in London; & in fact it has been lying in a cupboard almost forgotten since ever so long ago, so that she might have had it for the asking any time these last dozen years. It happens, however that now it has come to life it may be out of my power to hand it over to her. The matter stands thus: that if any manager wishes our girl here—Mrs Gertrude Bugler—to do the part in London with a professional company that he would provide, I am morally bound to let her do it, seeing how well she has served us. Should that not come off there is an understanding with Sybil Thorndike (who asked to read the play 2 or 3 weeks ago) that she may have it, though I have not definitely assented: & some managers & critics who have been down here think that the part would not suit her. If she should be also of this opinion, & Mrs Bugler also should not be able to go to London, the play would be free, & I would entertain with great pleasure the question of Lady Forbes Robertson presenting the character, as I am already aware of her great abilities.

Alas: years & years ago, you ought to have been Angel Clare, & she Tess! How well you would have carried the thing off.

Always yours sincerely
[Signed] T— H—

P.S. I am compelled to send a typewritten reply, on account of weak eyesight.

Text   MS. (pencil draft) DCM.
Forbes-Robertson: Johnston Forbes-Robertson, actor and manager; see II.83. He was knighted upon his retirement from the stage in 1913.   *Lady Forbes Robertson*: the American actress Gertrude Elliott (1874–1950) whom Forbes-Robertson married in 1900; as the latter explained in his letter of 27 Nov 24 (DCM), she was eager to play the role of Tess.   *Thorndike*: see letter of 2 Nov 24.   *Angel Clare*: Forbes-Robertson had in fact considered producing *Tess* in 1894 but seems to have found the part of Angel Clare unattractive; see II.82–3 and III.107. *[Signed]*: word and brackets in TH's hand.

To SIR FREDERICK MACMILLAN

MAX GATE, | DORCHESTER. | 29 November 1924

Dear Sir Frederick:

I have thought over the idea that the dramatic version of "Tess" might be published; and certainly, in one aspect of the matter, it would be worth while to do it. But owing to the fact that the play is made up more largely from the novel than in many adaptations for the stage—containing pages of the story almost word for word—I feel its publication might injure the novel, by being read as a short cut to the gist of the tale, saving the trouble of wading through the much longer narration of it. For this and other reasons I should not like to have it printed.

As I am writing I will ask you to oblige me by sending two copies of Tess in the uniform edition.

Sincerely yours,
Thomas Hardy.

Text MS. (typewritten) BL.
might be published: Macmillan (27 Nov 24, Macmillan letterbooks, BL) raised the possibility, suggesting that it would sell well if pub. in a format similar to that used for *The Queen of Cornwall*.

To J. H. MORGAN

MAX GATE, | DORCHESTER. | 1 Dec. 1924

Dear General Morgan;

The Morley book duly arrived, & I have read it through. I would not write till I had done so, &, as you may have guessed from the newspaper reports of the play just produced here, we have been much occupied with rehearsals, &c., for though I did not mean to have anything to do with the staging I was insensibly drawn in. However it was an amusing little experience, & I don't regret it.

I see Morley more clearly in your pages than I could do in his own reminiscences, which seemed to aim at keeping him invisible. There is a good deal more, I find, in this volume than in the Quarterly articles. I don't notice any error to speak of in your report of my words: I believe I said "The Sporting Times" instead of "The Pink 'Un", but that is the merest trifle. I may mention that "Frederic Harrison" is misprinted "Frederick Harrison" on p. 17.

As for Gladstone, who fills large spaces on your paper, you leave the question of his theology as much of a mystery as ever. It is almost impossible to believe a man with his intellectual curiosity & penetration to be blind to the puerilities that stare out from dogma when investigated, & yet by some sort of super-casuistry he upheld them. Even those who do not admire Mr G. can hardly think his eccelesiasticism a mask, to retain the church party politically.

Now that Morley is gone I wish I had visited him oftener. How well I remember his look—quite boyish—when I first met him in his chambers in 1868 or 1869.

With my thanks for the book & the inscription believe me

Sincerely yours

Thomas Hardy.

Text   MS. Berg.

Morley book: Morgan's *John, Viscount Morley: An Appreciation and Some Reminiscences* (London, 1924); see letter of 22 June 24.   *the play*: the Hardy Players' production of *Tess*. *his own reminiscences*: John Morley, Viscount Morley of Blackburn, *Recollections* (2 vols., London, 1917); TH read them in 1918 (see V.248).   *Quarterly articles*: by Morgan; see letter to him of 16 Jan 24 and letter of 21 Apr 24.   *merest trifle*: both were newspapers devoted to sporting (mainly horse-racing) news; on p. 31 of Morgan's book TH is quoted as saying of Morley, 'He seemed to draw an invisible ermine about him as though he were a sporting peer who never read anything but the *Pink 'Un'*.   *Gladstone*: William Ewart Gladstone (1809–98), statesman and author; *D.N.B.*   *1868 or 1869*: in *EL*, 79, their first meeting is assigned to January 1869.

To GERTRUDE BUGLER

MAX GATE, DORCHESTER. | 2 December: 1924

My dear Mrs Bugler:

I forgot to enclose the promised Chant in the book-parcel, & send it on with this, for of course you must have a copy of it. The piano will do to try it on, but you should hear it on an organ; so give my compliments to the organist & ask him to oblige me by playing it over to you: or ask the vicar to get him to do so.

I hope you & the baby got safely home, & that all is well after your exertions to please the public. They are grateful to you, I am sure. Let me know if I can do anything for you.

Sincerely yours

Thomas Hardy.

Text   MS. Mrs. G. Bugler.

Bugler: Gertrude Adelia Bugler, *née* Bugler (b. 1897), Dorset actress; she married her cousin, Ernest Frank Bugler, M.C. (1888–1956), farmer, in 1921. See letter of 17 Nov 20, also her *Personal Recollections of Thomas Hardy* (Dorchester, 1964) and Millgate, 510, 535–6, 555–8. *promised Chant*: on a separate sheet still accompanying this letter TH wrote out a few bars of music headed '*Langdon in F*. (Tess's favourite chant.) from T.H. to G.B.' See *Tess of the d'Urbervilles* (Wessex edn.), 107: 'the old double chant "Langdon"'.   *the book-parcel*: it had contained the copies of the Osgood, McIlvaine edns. of *Tess* and *The Return of the Native* which TH inscribed, respectively, 'To / Gertrude Bugler / the impersonator of "Tess"— / with affectionate regard / from / Thomas Hardy. / Dec. 1924.' and 'To / Gertrude Bugler / the impersonator of "Eustacia". / With affectionate regard / from / Thomas Hardy. / Dec. 1924.'   *organist . . . vicar*: presumably of the parish church of Beaminster, in N. Dorset, where she lived.   *the baby*: Diana (now Diana Toms), born in March 1924.

To HARLEY GRANVILLE BARKER

Max Gate, | Dorchester. | 3 Dec. 1924.

My dear H.G.B.

I am so glad to get a letter from you, as it implies that you are "still running", and I had been anxious lest you should have got laid up. Many thanks for congratulations on the play, though beyond handing the 30-years-old copy of it on to the company I did not do much towards its production. I should like you to see it acted, nevertheless, for there is a proposal afoot to have it done in London by Sybil Thorndike (if our local Tess cannot get any manager to put it on with her in it), and journalists critics are hinting that the play must be altered and re-arranged, my adaptation not being good enough for Miss Thorndike. (I should add that *she* has not said this). Knowing the difficulties of the dramatization I think it may be made worse it tinkered: and at any rate, if it is announced as my doing I shall not let it be re-written. I am not at all anxious to get it performed in London, and don't mind if it is never done there.

Your judgement on its construction and presentation on the boards would be invaluable, and this has occurred to me. Two performances are to take place at Weymouth on Thursday Dec. 11—to-morrow week—afternoon and evening. Would it be possible for you and Helen, before adventuring to Paris and other noxious places, to go to Weymouth for a few days covering the date of the play, and take up your abode facing the sea, so as to pick yourself up if the doctors have pulled you down, which I expect they have. Anyhow we are saving 2 tickets on the chance of your coming.

Best wishes and kind regards from us to both,

Ever sincerely.
Thomas Hardy.

(Letter to Lawrence sent on. T.H.)

Text Typed transcript DCM.
letter from you: of 2 Dec 24 (DCM).   *our local Tess*: Gertrude Bugler.   *journalists*: so the transcript reads.   *it tinkered*: clearly a transcription error for 'if tinkered'.   *Lawrence*: i.e., T. E. Lawrence, 'Lawrence of Arabia' (1888–1935; *D.N.B.*), currently stationed, as 'Private Shaw', at Bovingdon Camp, near Wool, Dorset; for his friendship with TH see Millgate, 549–50, and Ronald D. Knight, *Colonel T. E. Lawrence . . . Visits Mr & Mrs Thomas Hardy* (Weymouth, 1985).

To GERTRUDE BUGLER

MAX GATE, DORCHESTER. | 3 Dec. 1924

I send along these, though you probably have seen most of them.

Ever,
T. H.

Text MS. Mrs. G. Bugler.
these: cuttings of newspaper notices of the *Tess* play, performed in Dorchester 26–29 Nov 1924.

To SIR FREDERICK MACMILLAN

MAX GATE, | DORCHESTER. | 4th. December 1924.

Dear Sir Frederick Macmillan:

I quite approve of your bringing out an illustrated edition of Tess of the d'Urbervilles printed from the Wessex edition, and shall be happy to see you go on with it. It has often been represented to me by editors, &c, that to illustrate the book would be an attractive venture, but it has never been done, except as to frontispiece, etc.

Miss Gribble's woodcuts (which are returned herewith) seem to convey the atmosphere of dairies and farms, and to have a style of their own, akin to, though not imitative of, the modern methods of drawing. I do not know if you thought of using these same ones. Of course a great deal depends upon Miss Gribble being able to convey the personality of Tess, and the real accessories of her situation. The little sketch I have marked with a red cross is very near to her look. But what I think would be a great help to the artist if she goes on with the work would be to see the young woman who has personified Tess in the play, who is the very incarnation of her. A meeting with her privately, which I could arrange, might perhaps suffice, but a better thing would be for her to see her in dairy costume on the stage. There are to be two more performances of the play a week hence—at Weymouth next Thursday the 11th., at 2.45 and 8. Miss Gribble might perhaps get back to London the same evening if she attended the matinee, but she would probably prefer to stay and see it twice. We can send you a ticket for her if she would care to come.

Well, the above is my idea of procedure: but the illustrations might be done without Miss Gribble coming, although perhaps not so realistically: or by a private sitting to her of Tess's impersonator, as above stated.

Yours sincerely,
Thomas Hardy.

Text MS. (typewritten) BL.
illustrated edition: pub. by Macmillan in 1926, with 41 wood engravings by Vivien Gribble; Macmillan made the proposal, which had originated with the artist, in his letter of 3 Dec 24 (Macmillan letterbooks, BL).   *Miss Gribble's*: Vivien Gribble (Mrs. Doyle Jones), wood engraver and book illustrator; she died in 1932.   *on the stage*: see letter to Macmillan of 9 Dec 24.

To HAROLD CHILD

MAX GATE, DORCHESTER. | 9th. December 1924.

Dear Mr Child:

Here are the few particulars as to dates, &c., that you asked me for. I have, of course, left you to criticize the new books named, which I am sure you will do ably. Any other facts you may wish to know I daresay I can send.

Yours sincerely,
T.H.

"T.H. by Harold Child."

ERRATA, & MEMORANDA.

p.81.   bottom line for 1904 read 1903
  ″ 7   line 3. for twenty read thirty.
  ″ 8   "What the day soon to come", &c, revise.
  ″ 10   revise top line.
  ″ 33   2 line from bot. for "not I believe" read "now I believe".
  ″ 41   line 12 for "Beemy" read "Beeny".
  ″ 87   bot. line for "four" read "six".
  ″ 88   line 5 add Moments of Vision, & Late Lyrics & Earlier.
  ″ 107   line 17. for "eternal" read "external".
  ″ 114   line 5. for "Still" read "Shall".

At or near the end insert account of later books, viz: *Moments of Vision* 1917. *Late Lyrics and earlier* 1922. *The Famous Tragedy of the Queen of Cornwall*, "a new version of an old story", 1923. The novel feature in this play has been left curiously unnoticed by critics, who have regarded it as but one more relation of the old romance as told contradictorily by Malory and others down to Tennyson, Wagner, Arnold, and Swinburne. But the artistic justification for this new version is the dramatic concentration into action no more extended in time than the stage action itself, and into one scene within four walls, of a rambling tragedy covering years, and widely dispersed localities, in its presentation by all previous narrators of it in prose, verse and music.

The two following poems, not yet reprinted from periodicals, may be added if necessary: "Compassion: an ode": published by the R.S.P.C.A. (1924) "Xenophanes the Monist of Colophon": published in the Nineteenth Century (1924).

Also may be added, *if worth while*: that the practical drama never seems to have had a great attraction for this author, his only original work for the real stage being the above criticised Queen of Cornwall tragedy.

Besides this tragedy he once prepared (1893) a dramatic version of "The Three Strangers" entitled "The Three Wayfarers," which has been frequently acted but never published. There may also be mentioned an early dramatization (1894–5) of "Tess of the d'Urbervilles," done by request, and also never published, the author unearthing it for performance on the country stage (1924) merely because chance had led him to encounter in the flesh the first woman who bore a real resemblance to the imaginary figure of his heroine, and who was not born when the book was written. There have been some dramatizations of his works by other hands, but not by his own.

He gave to be performed also (in 1920) a recension of an old Wessex version of the mumming play of Saint George, and (1923) of a little operatic piece he had heard in childhood, known locally as "O Jan, O Jan, O Jan". Neither of these has been published.

(Add the above named books to the bibliography.)

Text   MS. (typewritten) Adams.
few particulars: set out on two separate typewritten sheets still accompanying this letter and printed here as a postscript to it.   *p. 81*: the page references are to the first edn. of Child's *Thomas Hardy*, pub. in London by Nisbet in 1916; see V.143. The ten items in the errata list have been struck through in pencil, presumably by Child; all of them were incorporated, together with most of TH's other suggestions, in the new edn. ('Revised, as to periods of time and works') of 1925, although no attempt was made to expand the critical commentary of the 1916 edn.   *story", 1923*: '1923' originally followed *'Cornwall'* earlier in this same sentence; the lines indicating this transposition and those underlining titles are in ink and perhaps TH's.   *Malory*: there are extensive markings to the Tristram and Iseult portions of TH's copy (Purdy) of Sir Thomas Malory's *Morte d'Arthur* (2 vols., London, n.d.).   *Tennyson, . . . Swinburne*: for the three authors see letter of 11 Nov 23; for TH's response to the music of Richard Wagner (1813–83), whose *Tristan und Isolde* was first produced in 1865, see *LY,* 117, 118.   *from periodicals*: Child, thanking TH for his help (10 Dec 24, DCM), pointed out that there were other poems still uncollected.   *never published*: although six copies of the play had in fact been printed for copyright purposes in New York in 1893; see Purdy, 78–9.   *the first woman*: Gertrude Bugler.   *mumming play*: see letters of 3 June 22 and mid-Jan 24. *O Jan"*: see letter of 14 Apr 23.

To SIR FREDERICK MACMILLAN

MAX GATE, | DORCHESTER. | 9th. December 1924.
Dear Sir Frederick:

The tickets for the two Weymouth performances of the play on Thursday have been posted to Mrs Doyle Jones at the address you gave, and I will aim to see her at the theatre, and perhaps I may be able to help her by a few suggestions. If she comes to Kingston Russell in the Spring she will not be far from the real Tess, who would doubtless be pleased to pose for her in milking attire, &c.

As to the publication: I am quite ignorant of the expense and trouble of getting up an illustrated book of this sort, and acquiesce in your representations that although the price of the book will be higher than in the ordinary Wessex edition the royalty will remain the same.

Yours very sincerely,
Thomas Hardy.

Text   MS. (typewritten) BL.
on Thursday: TH himself attended both performances of *Tess* in Weymouth on 11 Dec 1924. *Mrs Doyle Jones*: see letter of 4 Dec 24.   *address you gave*: Mrs. Doyle Jones's home address (near Colchester), supplied in Macmillan's letter of 8 Dec 24 (Macmillan letterbooks, BL). *Kingston Russell*: Mrs. Doyle Jones was the daughter of George James Gribble, of Kingston Russell House, W. of Dorchester.   *pose for her*: Mrs. Bugler recalled (letter, 11 Mar 1985) that she did visit Kingston Russell to sit (or rather stand) to Mrs. Doyle Jones, although neither the artist's medium (the woodcut) nor—as she acknowledged to Mrs. Bugler—her talents were particularly adapted to portraiture; see letter of 16 Dec 24 to Mrs. Bugler.   *your representations*: Macmillan proposed in his letter that his firm should print at least 3,000 copies of the illustrated edn. and pay TH the standard royalty of one shilling and sixpence a vol.

To THE MAYOR OF BOURNEMOUTH
—[Mid-]December 1924

Dear Sir:

Since the performance of "Tess of the d'Urbervilles" by the Dorchester "Hardy Players" I have received letters from Bournemouth residents asking my permission for the production of the play in Bournemouth by the same players. This I would readily grant, & though I take no active part in the production the company of players would no doubt give such performance in your town in aid of any charity, if asked by the Corporation to do so. The Mayor of Weymouth has made such a request, & they are performing there this week, the profits to go a fund for the unemployed. As most of the Seats are already booked the play having excited great interest, this will probably result in a substantial sum, just as the performances did in Dorchester, the players making no charge for their performance, & only requiring their out-of-pocket expenses to be paid.

The shortest course seemed to me to be to write to you, in case the Bournemouth Council should be inclined to oblige the inhabitants. Any such request should be addressed to the manager & producer of the play:

T. H. Tilley Esq. J.P.
Gordon
Dorchester.

I am, Dear Sir

Yours faithfully

To his Worship the Mayor | Bournemouth

Text MS. (pencil draft) DCM.   *Date* From internal evidence.
Mayor: Frederick Skinner Mate.   *Mayor of Weymouth*: see letter of 24 June 24.   *go a fund*: TH's slip for 'go to a fund'.   *Any such request*: TH received a positive reply to this letter on 15 Dec 24 (see letter of 16 Dec 24 to Mrs. Bugler), but in the event Bournemouth preferred to stage *The Queen of Cornwall* (see letter of mid-Apr 25 to Godfrey).

To FREDERICK HARRISON

13th. December 1924.

Dear Mr Harrison:

(I am compelled to typewrite letters of any length on account of eye-weakness; which I hope you will pardon.)

I have waited to see Mrs Bugler before replying to your note, which I did at the Weymouth performance of the play. She says she will hold herself in readiness for any matinées you may be able to arrange at some time early in the spring. She thinks that perhaps her sister, who plays the child Liza-Lu (a few lines only) might come with her for company, as she does not know London very well. But this is only a suggestion.

I have as yet made no definite agreement for any other production of the play, though I have been asked in two or three quarters. As I think I informed you, I told Miss Sybil Thorndike in answer to her strong wish for the part, that though I did not particularly want the play produced in London at all at my time of life, I should like her to do it. But she has not closed with me, and I gather that her hands are very full at present, so that she may be a long time in taking it up. Moreover her husband Mr Casson came to Dorchester to see a performance after you had been here, and I told him that we owe Mrs Bugler so much that she must have the first chance of London, if she could be offered it and avail herself of it. He thought that her appearance in a series of matinées would not much affect Mrs Casson's production—the audience for matinées being somewhat different from those for evenings.

So the matter stands. I ought in justice to Mrs Bugler to tell you that the Weymouth audiences, though more sophisticated than the Dorchester ones, were much moved by her performance, although it is so artless, or perhaps because of it. In case you should wish to communicate directly with her I may say that her address is,

Riverside Cottage
Beaminster,
Dorset.

In respect of my writing the two little extra scenes to connect the others, I see no difficulty in doing so.

Yours very truly,

P.S. It has struck me that if you should have any difficulty in getting a good Sir John (Tess's father) when making up a company, the one we had here—Mr T. Pouncy—can hardly be bettered. His address is,

Cornhill, Dorchester.

Joan, Tess's mother, was also very good (Mrs Major, Cornhill, Dorchester.) She has had some practice on the stage, as has also Mr Pouncy. But I have not mentioned this to either of them, and of course they might not be able to come.

I suppose that the play would have a better chance if produced before the present interest in it has subsided.

Text   Carbon copy (typewritten) Mrs. G. Bugler.
Harrison: Frederick Harrison (1854–1926), theatrical manager; see II.114.   *matinées*: Harrison proposed to present matinée performances of *Tess*, with Mrs. Bugler in the title-role, at the Haymarket Theatre, London.   *her sister*: Augusta Noreen Bugler (b. 1906), now Mrs. Woodhall.   *Mr Casson*: see letter of 2 Nov 24.   *communicate directly with her*: it was this passage which gave TH the occasion to send Mrs. Bugler the copy of this letter; see letter of 16 Dec 24 to Mrs. Bugler.   *T. Pouncy*: Thomas Pouncy (d. 1936, aged 75), Dorchester saddler and amateur actor.   *Mrs Major*: Ethel Homer Major, *née* Jameson (d. 1951, aged 72), Dorchester confectioner and amateur actress.   *I suppose . . . subsided.*: sentence added in TH's hand.

To G. HERBERT THRING

MAX GATE, DORCHESTER. | 15th. December 1924.

Dear Mr Thring:

The Mayor of Casterbridge.
Czech Rights.

I am quite willing that permission should be given for a Czech translation of this novel.

The terms you suggest—£15 for an edition of 3000 copies—will quite satisfy me, and I shall be pleased if you will inform the Prague lawyer to arrange accordingly.

Yours very truly,
Th: Hardy.

Text MS. (typewritten) BL.
Czech translation: it seems not to have materialized, however.

To GERTRUDE BUGLER

MAX GATE, | DORCHESTER. | 16 Dec. 1924

My dear Mrs Bugler:

I think I ought to send you a copy of the letter I have written to Mr Harrison of the Haymarket Theatre in reply to his, which I read to you when you were here. This will let you know exactly how matters stand, in case he should write to you.

But forgive my saying that I don't quite like the idea of your going to London (if this comes to anything, which it may not). We are so proud of you down here that we wish to keep you for ourselves, so that you may be known as the Wessex actress who does not care to go away, & who makes Londoners come to her. I fancy Capt. Bugler will agree with me in this. However, you must have your own way I suppose.

Mrs Doyle Jones called next morning after Weymouth. She is coming to Kingston Russell at Easter, & will communicate with you about sitting to her. As she has a car there will be no trouble in her getting across to you. She said that why we could not find her after the performance, to introduce her to you, was that her face was so bleared with crying that she was ashamed to let us see her, & ran off to the hotel. That was your doing, young lady! There were a good many other wet handkerchiefs besides hers.

Yesterday I received a letter from the Mayor of Bournemouth informing me that he was going to lay before the General Purposes Committee the question of your giving a performance of Tess in Bournemouth. On this he says he is going to write again.

We hope to see you later on.

Your affectionate friend
Thomas Hardy.

The enclosed scrap from The Times may amuse you. Don't trouble to return either the letter or scrap. T.H.

Text   MS. (with envelope) Mrs. G. Bugler.
to Mr Harrison: see letter of 13 Dec 24.   *Capt. Bugler*: Mrs. Bugler's husband; see letter of
2 Dec 24.   *after Weymouth*: i.e., after the Weymouth performances of *Tess*.   *sitting to
her*: see letter of 9 Dec 24.   *of Bournemouth*: see letter of mid-Dec 24.   *scrap from The
Times*: a photograph, cut from *The Times* of 13 Dec 1924, showing Mrs. Bugler seated next to
TH at a dinner given between the two performances of *Tess* at Weymouth on 11 December.

To THE REVD. H. G. B. COWLEY

MAX GATE, | DORCHESTER. | 16 Dec. 1924
Dear Mr Cowley:
    Yes: regard me as a Parishioner certainly. I hope to be still more one when
I am in a supine position some day. Will the enclosed be any good? it is not
much I am ashamed to say.
    I was so sorry I could not come to see Mrs Cowley the other evening.

Sincerely yours
Thomas Hardy.

Text   MS. (with envelope) Canon Cowley.
a Parishioner: i.e., of Stinsford, although Max Gate is in the parish of Fordington St. George.
the enclosed: presumably a sum of money sent in response to an appeal for church funds.

To SIR JAMES BARRIE

MAX GATE, | DORCHESTER. | 18 Dec. 1924
My dear Barrie:
    Mr Serge Youriévitz, the Russian sculptor, has lately been down here to
make a bust of me, & critics who have seen it pronounce it very good. He has
suggested that I should give him an introduction to you for the same purpose,
& I am very glad to do this. Whether you decide to have it done or whether
you don't, you will find Mr Youriévitz a most interesting artist.
    Believe me

Yours sincerely
Thomas Hardy.

Text   MS. Yale.
Youriévitz: or Youriévitch; see letter of 27 July 24.   *the same purpose*: Barrie seems not to
have acted upon this suggestion, although he told TH (2 Jan 25, DCM) that from a photograph
of the bust he judged it to be 'the best thing of you that has been done'.

To SIR JAMES BARRIE

MAX GATE, | DORCHESTER. | 19 Dec: 1924
My dear Barrie:
    Mr Frederick Harrison seems inclined to try Mrs Gertrude Bugler in *Tess*
at some matinées—(Granville Barker, by the way, says he should put the
play in the evening bill straight off, people being so interested in it on account
of the press notices that it would be a safe venture: however, that is a point
for Mr Harrison's judgment). He, F.H., asks me to refer him to my agent for

terms. Now I am a child in all this, but, as you are an ancient, can you tell me of any agent? Or, if I were not ashamed to trouble you, I should say, will you pronounce *ex cathedra* whatever arrangement would be fair in the circumstances, & so make an end of it.

I don't care much what I get (if anything), so long as she gets whatever can be expected for a novice beyond the chance of a performance in London.

As I may have told you, I have known her from girlhood, & though I don't want to begin playwriting at my time of life, & have no ambition whatever to produce a play, I feel bound to do as much for her as I can. I have told her that I don't like the idea of her trying the professional stage at all, but with little effect; & it is only natural I suppose that she should not want to hide her undoubted personal attractions under a bushel. At the same time she says that she wants to leave everything to my judgment. So there it is, & I feel frightfully responsible.

Don't answer these ruminations if they worry you, but I thought I would communicate first with you before applying to anybody else. Excuse a scrawl owing to weak eyesight.

Always sincerely
Thomas Hardy.

We were much interested in the doings at "Bonnie Dundee."

Text MS. Colby.
matinées: see letter of 13 Dec 24.   *of any agent?*: Barrie (20 Dec 24, DCM) suggested Reginald Golding Bright, with whom TH had already dealt in the past; see letter of 23 Jan 25. *from girlhood*: Gertrude Bugler's first 'Hardy play' was in 1913, when at the age of 16 she played Marty South in *The Woodlanders*, but TH would have seen her when attending rehearsals of earlier productions in premises owned by her father, a Dorchester confectioner; for TH's memories of Gertrude Bugler's mother, Augusta Way, see Millgate, 293–4.   *she should not*: TH first wrote, 'she does not'.   *frightfully responsible*: Barrie in his reply suggested that Mrs. Bugler should be given her chance to show what she could do on the London stage.   *"Bonnie Dundee."*: it was, however, the freedom not of Dundee but of Dumfries (where he lived 1873–8) which Barrie received on 11 Dec 1924; the occasion was reported in *The Times*, 12 Dec 1924.

To J. W. MACKAIL

MAX GATE, | DORCHESTER. | Christmas Eve: 1924

My dear Mackail:

It is so kind of you to send the little Bunyan book. I wish I had something new for you, but I have published nothing lately except in papers. What memories the Pilgrim's Progress wakes in me: the first time of reading it as a boy of 10 walking across a field in the dusk, in an old edition with hideous illustrations that had just been lent me by two old ladies. The picture of Apollyon fighting Christian made me so uncomfortable in that lonely spot that I was compelled to shut the book & not open it again till I reached human society & candlelight (there were candles on earth in those days.)

During the last 2 months I have been drawn into theatrical matters quite unexpectedly, &, indeed, reluctantly, owing to the interest shown in the Tess play, which I dug out of a drawer where it had lain for 30 years, merely to please the players here. Mrs Bugler, to whom you allude, took everybody by surprise, myself not least, as I had no suspicion she could tackle tragedy in the way she did. I am afraid the attention she has drawn upon herself has given her an itch for the regular theatre, & I am old fashioned enough to feel uneasy about it, being to some extent the cause.

Our warmest wishes for Christmas & the New Year. Pardon blotted writing through weak eyesight.

Always sincerely
Thomas Hardy.

Text MS. Yale.

little Bunyan book: Mackail's *The Pilgrim's Progress: A Lecture Delivered at the Royal Institution of Great Britain March 14, 1924* (London, 1924); his covering letter is dated 23 Dec 24 (DCM).   *two old ladies*: possibly Rebecca and Amelia Sparks; see Millgate, 49.   *(there were . . . days.)*: a humorous allusion to Genesis 6: 4.   *to whom you allude*: Mackail had not seen Mrs. Bugler as Tess but remembered her being 'very striking & distinguished' as Eustacia Vye.

To A. C. BENSON

MAX GATE, | DORCHESTER. | 26 December 1924

Dear Dr Benson:

It was not my intention to receive your book of Selected Poems in such silence as this, but I have been carried along by a stream of incidents till the date of its arrival is a long way behind—the incidents in question being some dramatic performances that have been going on here during the last month, which, though I was really outside them, drew me into attendance at rehearsals & a wish to help all I could.

I began reading the poems directly they arrived, & finished them last night. I somehow wish you had reprinted more from Le Cahier Jaune: indeed I almost wish you had reprinted the whole of those you have published from time to time, & have left readers to do the selecting. Perhaps you will some day, for it is more satisfactory: I should then have found one I used to like, "What made you turn your face to me?" in the volume.

We were considering favourites last night among those you have included here. These are some:—Regret: On the Western Cliffs: New Year's Day: A Trio: The Shepherd: Evensong: A Song of Sweet Things. By mentioning these I don't mean to be sure they are better than their neighbours: only that they struck me at the moment.

Cambridge is no doubt as squally as Dorset. We have been as cheerful as may be this Christmas, & I hope you have also. But I long ago entered the region in a lifetime in which anniversaries are the saddest days of the year.

I said "Cambridge" above, but you are almost certainly not there, but at the delightful seaside house of which I have a picture on my mantelpiece.

Many thanks for the book. I am always trying to show young people that they would save time by taking their allowances of literature in poetical form rather than in prose, but they seem not to heed.

My wife sends her kindest regards & I am,

Yours ever
Thomas Hardy.

Text   MS. (with envelope) Texas.
Selected Poems: Benson's *Selected Poems* (London, 1924).   *Le Cahier Jaune*: Benson's
privately printed first vol. of verse, pub. 1892; see I.280.   *face to me?"*: the poem is entitled
'A Midsummer Night's Dream'.   *Sweet Things*: full title, 'A Song of Sweet Things That
Have an End'.   *seaside house*: Lamb House, Rye; see letter of 27 Sept 24.

1925

To CURTIS BROWN, LTD.

MAX GATE, | DORCHESTER. | January 6th. 1925.

Dear Sirs:

I am much obliged by your letter concerning the possible production of Tess of the d'Urbervilles as a play in London and elsewhere.

It happens, however, that nothing has been settled in the matter of such a production, so that I can give no information about it. Possibly your correspondent has been supposing from misleading paragraphs in the newspapers that definite arrangements have been entered into here instead of mere pourparlers on the subject. The right to act a dramatization of the novel, or to submit a copy of the play with a view to such acting, still remains in my hands, no contract with anybody having been made.

I may add that I am not anxious to see it on the professional stage, and the idea of putting it on in America before it has been done in England does not attract me at present.

Yours very truly,
T. Hardy.

Messrs Curtis Brown. Ltd.

Text MS. (typewritten) Adams.
Brown, Ltd.: the well-known firm of literary agents; for earlier references to Curtis Brown himself see III.101 and V.106.   *your letter*: it appears not to have survived, but see letter of 16 Sept 25.   *your correspondent*: Winthrop Ames (1870–1937), American theatrical producer, mentioned by Granville Barker (13 Feb 25, DCM) as being interested in the play; see letter of 16 Sept 25.

To CLEMENT SHORTER

MAX GATE, | DORCHESTER. | 8 Jan: 1925.

Dear Clement Shorter:

Many thanks for New Year's wishes, which I reciprocate. I will bear in mind the kind of poem you want, & will try to let you have it soon. I think the price you offer very fair.

I am obliged to be very short, as my eyes are so weak. The fault of the 'phone was at this end.

Always sincerely,
Thomas Hardy.

Text MS. BL.
poem you want: TH's 'No Bell-Ringing' appeared in the Special Christmas Number of the *Sphere* 23 Nov 1925.   *fault of the 'phone*: for an earlier occasion when TH and Shorter had difficulty in communicating by telephone see letter of 4 June 24 to Clodd.

To JOHN MASEFIELD

Max Gate: 9: 1: '25

Dear Mr Masefield:

It is a very generous thought of yours to send this; but I won't take it, if you don't mind. When you are making a fortune out of a play of mine I will come with a stern demand for a share of profits.

What a strange coincidence of tragedies—out of doors & in. I am glad the play went off well.

Sincerely yours
T. Hardy.

Text MS. (correspondence card, with envelope) Colby.
to send this: evidently a performance fee in respect of Masefield's production of *The Queen of Cornwall* in his private theatre; see letter of 18 Nov 24.   *coincidence of tragedies*: presumably a response to a remark in Masefield's letter, which seems not to have survived; it may be relevant, however, that the performances of the play on 1, 2, and 3 Jan 1925 coincided with a period of gales, heavy rainfall, and extensive flooding.

To R. GOLDING BRIGHT

MAX GATE, | DORCHESTER. | 23 January 1925

Dear Sir:

"The Queen of Cornwall", about which you inquire, is available both for stage performance and for film production. But I am not anxious to have it presented in either form, and would go to no trouble or expense on the chance of getting it so done. However, I am quite willing to put it in your hands for either purpose, both for England and America, if you think anything will result from taking up the matter.

In such an event there would be one or two (literary) conditions that you would have to insist on. 1. That the full title, "The Famous Tragedy of the Queen of Cornwall", be given in all announcements. 2. That the correct version as in the last edition (of which I would send you a copy) be used.

In respect of the "Tess" play at the Haymarket, I will let you know if anything definite arises.

Yours very truly
Thomas Hardy.

R. Golding Bright Esq. | 20 Green Street, | Leicester Square. | London W.C. 2.

Text MS. (typewritten) W. M. King.
Bright: Reginald Golding Bright, theatrical agent; see III.272 and letter of 19 Dec 24.   *at the Haymarket*: see letter of 13 Dec 24.

To G. HERBERT THRING

MAX GATE, | DORCHESTER. | 26th. January 1925.
Dear Mr Thring:

The Mayor of Casterbridge—Czech Rights.

Replying to your letter of the 24th. I can say that I am really more indifferent to the price to be paid for the above than to the interests of literature, if any, in respect of such a translation. So please let the publisher have it for whatever he can afford to pay.

With many thanks I am,

Yours very truly,
T. Hardy.

G. Herbert Thring. Esq. | Incorp: Society of Authors.

Text MS. (typewritten) BL.
such a translation: see letter of 15 Dec 24.

To SIR FREDERICK MACMILLAN

MAX GATE, | DORCHESTER. | 28th. January 1925.
Dear Sir Frederick:

I am writing to ask if you will kindly get the printers to send me a few copies in sheets of The Queen of Cornwall, in the small-type edition in which it is put at the end of the second volume of The Dynasts—beginning at p. 527, and ending at p. 569. It appears that they want to put the play on the stage in America, and I should like them to have a copy with the final corrections, which were not all made in the larger edition.

Also: I enclose a letter from India, which you will know how to deal with better than I. It may possibly contain a little information of a useful kind.

Thanks for your opinions about the biographer.

Yours very sincerely,
T.H.

Text MS. (typewritten) BL.
small-type edition: i.e., the Pocket edn.   *letter from India*: see letter to Macmillan of 3 Feb 25.   *the biographer*: when Ernest Brennecke cabled 25 Jan 25 to repeat his request for the use of illustrations from *Wessex Poems* (see letter of 1/2 Nov 24), TH cabled back, 'Cannot permit reproduction of illustrations or anything copyright. Disapprove of biography altogether. Hardy' (pencil draft, DCM). Macmillan wrote FEH 26 Jan 25 (Macmillan letterbooks, BL) to approve this action, but added that little could be done until the book had actually appeared and they could see 'what the thing looks like'.

To YVONNE SALMON

1 February 1925
Dear Madam:

I have to say in answer to your letter of the 29th January that the 10.30 train from Paddington, arriving at Dorchester at 1.40, which you suggest, would suit Mr Hardy very well for seeing M. Lefèvre & yourself, since it would enable you to get to this house about 2.0 by taxicab, Max Gate being a mile from the station. You could catch the 3.4 train for getting back to London if you keep the cab waiting; but you could hardly do it in time if you walk back from here to Dorchester.

It is to be distinctly understood that no personal details observed at the interview are to be published by M. Lefèvre.

As Mr Hardy has nothing special to communicate on the subject of the Alliance Française, but only to express his wish for its success in general terms, it may be that Mr Lefèvre, on second thoughts, may not think anything will be gained by taking a troublesome journey to see Mr Hardy, & may decide to give it up. However, Mr Hardy will be happy to see him on the above conditions.

Yours truly
F. E. Hardy.

Mlle Yvonne Salmon.

Text   MS. (pencil draft) DCM.
Salmon: Yvonne M. Salmon, lecturer in French at University College, Reading, and author of *Le Général de Gaulle*, pub. by Univ. of London Press in 1943; she wrote 15 and 29 Jan 25 (DCM) in her capacity as secretary of the Fédération britannique des comités de l'alliance française.   *of the 29th January*: it was addressed to FEH.   *M. Lefèvre*: Frédéric Lefèvre (1889–1949), French journalist, editor-in-chief of *Nouvelles Littéraires* (Paris).   *& yourself*: Mlle Salmon acted as interpreter.   *back to London*: Mlle Salmon had explained that she and M. Lefèvre had a dinner to attend in London that same evening.   *no personal details*: Lefèvre's interview with TH appeared in *Nouvelles Littéraires*, 21 Feb 1925, and subsequently in his *Une heure avec* . . ., 3rd series (Paris, 1925), 85–93. Though entirely positive in tone it is not wholly free of the 'details' TH here seeks to proscribe.

To R. GOLDING BRIGHT

MAX GATE, | DORCHESTER. | 3 February 1925

Dear Sir:

I am enclosing herewith the copy of The Queen of Cornwall that I promised to send, for your use in arranging for its production on the stage should that be practicable. You can have another copy or two if necessary. Whether it is worth your while to take it up you will decide for yourself, but you can hardly get much profit out of it at the ten per cent on author's receipts that I am willing to pay on Sir James Barrie's suggestion.

Believe me,

Yours very truly,
T. Hardy.

R. Golding Bright Esq.

Text   MS. (typewritten) W. M. King.
promised to send: see letter of 23 Jan 25.   *Barrie's suggestion*: see letter of 19 Dec 24.

To ST. JOHN ERVINE

MAX GATE, | DORCHESTER. | 3 February 1925.

Dear Mr Ervine:

I welcome a letter from you.

Mr Lewis Casson has written on this same subject of dramatizing Tess, and I can tell you briefly what I had replied to him before your letter came:

That I am too old to do anything more with the play, such as to collaborate in preparing a new version. But that I should be happy to have you do it entirely, in a way different from mine, on condition that it should be announced as your dramatization alone, without mentioning my old one.

But if you would like to make use of mine (supposing it to be of any use) I should be quite willing for you to do so, there being added to the announcement of your version the words "based on Mr Hardy's adaptation of 1894–5."

Since "the Hardy players" (as they call themselves) acted it here, I have written into the play some dialogue from the beginning of the novel as a sort of introductory first act, in case it should be performed again, it having been suggested as desirable, though I did not feel it to be necessary. However, you could have a copy of this short first act if you use my play as a basis as above mentioned.

Thank you, yes, we are both well, and hope that you and Mrs Ervine are. We shall be glad to see you before you go off to South Africa. It is very good of you to like doing the play.

Always sincerely,
Thomas Hardy.

P.S. My wife suggests to me to tell you that Barrie (who came down to the performance) wrote to Mrs G. B. Shaw that the play as acted here "*got home*, again and again in queer, inexplicable ways." (whatever that meant). T.H.

Text MS. (typewritten) Texas.
Casson: see letter of 2 Nov 24.   *dramatizing Tess*: neither Casson's letter nor Ervine's appears to have survived, but for Ervine's account of his involvement in a projected rewriting of the *Tess* play—as urged by Casson and by Sybil Thorndike in her letter of 11 Feb 25 (DCM)—see '*Tess' in the Theatre*, ed. Marguerite Roberts (Toronto, 1950), lxxxiv–lxxxv. *Mrs Ervine*: Leonora Mary Ervine, *née* Davis (d. 1965), whom Ervine married in 1911. *South Africa*: see letter to Ervine of 25 Aug 24.   *Mrs G. B. Shaw*: Charlotte Frances Shaw, *née* Payne-Townshend (1857–1943).

To SIR FREDERICK MACMILLAN

MAX GATE, | DORCHESTER. | 3 February 1925

Dear Sir Frederick:

My best thanks for the pages in small type of The Queen of Cornwall. They make such a nice little book that it might be bound and sold; and, if the play should ever be acted in England, as the book of the words. Also thanks for the Indian editions of the novels. I have told the enthusiastic young Indian schoolmaster that a publication of the short stories by him cannot be permitted, as you are issuing a cheap edition of them, but that he may write what theses he likes about my poetry.

Yours sincerely,
Thomas Hardy.

Text　MS. (typewritten) BL.
nice little book: the sheets (see letter of 28 Jan 25) had been bound in grey paper wrappers; see Purdy, 231.　　*Indian editions*: Macmillan (30 Jan 25, Macmillan letterbooks, BL) sent the 4 vols. already pub., all with introductions by J. H. Fowler (see letter of 10 Jan 23), and said that a fifth vol. was in preparation. Fowler had already sent copies of his introductions to TH, whose draft reply of 19 Jan 25 (with list of suggested corrections) is in DCM.　　*Indian schoolmaster*: N. R. Harihara Iyer, headmaster of a school in southern India, had written to TH on a number of occasions to request permission to pub. a selection of his short stories for the use of Indian university students; in his letter of 8 Jan 25 (DCM) he spoke of writing a doctoral thesis, 'The Poetry of Hardy', for Madras Univ., and in April 1929 he pub. an article on TH's poetry in the *Educational Review* (Madras).

To J. C. SQUIRE

MAX GATE, | DORCHESTER. | February 4th. 1925.

Dear Mr Squire:

　A few years ago I should have welcomed the opportunity of becoming acquainted with the newest things in poetry, which I suppose would happen if I could be one of the judges in the competition you speak of. But the question is settled for me by the fact that I am physically unable to undertake it—my eyes being so weak that I am compelled to limit my reading seriously, and the usual resource of being read to, which I adopt to some extent in the case of simple prose, a growing hardness of hearing prevents with poetry. I am very sorry, but you see how it arises that I must decline.

Sincerely yours,
Thomas Hardy.

Text　MS. (typewritten) Taylor.
competition you speak of: Squire (4 Feb 25, DCM) asked TH to be one of the judges for a £100 annual prize, newly founded by Lady Dorothy Wellesley, for 'a book of poems by a man under 45 or so'. Virginia Woolf noted on 21 Dec 1924 that Lady Dorothy wanted to establish a second Hawthornden Prize for poets only; see *The Diary of Virginia Woolf. Vol. 2, 1920–1924*, ed. Anne Olivier Bell (London, 1978), 326.　　*being read to*: by FEH.

To SYDNEY COCKERELL

MAX GATE, | DORCHESTER. | 6 Feb. 1925

My dear Cockerell:

　I will mark the error in the spelling of "Hoghton" for correction in any new edition of The Dynasts.

　Thanks for saying you will read proofs of any coming volume of poems. As I have nearly given up writing verses, except very brief trifles occasionally, there is no reason why I should not bring out those on hand (some of them years old) except that when editors ask me for a poem I can hunt up one, which I could not do if it had been already published in a volume. "The Absolute Explains" was one I found in that way.

I hope Middleton Murry's lectures are liked. I was rather surprised that not more notice was taken of McTaggart's death.

Always sincerely
Thomas Hardy.

Text MS. Adams.
spelling of "Hoghton": Cockerell sent with his letter of 5 Feb 25 (DCM) a partial transcription of a letter he had received from a member of the family of Major General David Hoghton (d. 1811 at the battle of Albuera; *D.N.B.*) complaining that in *The Dynasts*, Part Second, Act VI, Scene 5, the name was spelled 'Houghton'; TH made the correction in the large-paper edn. of *The Dynasts* pub. in 1927.   *"The Absolute Explains"*: pub. in the current (February 1925) issue of the *Nineteenth Century and After*.   *Murry's lectures*: the Clark Lectures at Cambridge, subsequently pub. as *Keats and Shakespeare* (Oxford, 1925).   *McTaggart's death*: J. McT. E. McTaggart, the philosopher; see III.208. He died 18 Jan 1925 and an obituary appeared in *The Times* the following day.

To GERTRUDE BUGLER

MAX GATE, | DORCHESTER. | 7 Feb: 1925

Dear Mrs Bugler:

I had just heard from Mr Harrison of your decision not to go to London to play Tess at the Haymarket Theatre, when your letter arrived. He is now sending back the script of the play which he had borrowed for arranging the scenery & choosing the others in the cast.

No doubt you have come to a wise conclusion, though I think he is a little disappointed. Although you fancy otherwise, I do not believe that any London actress will represent Tess so nearly as I imagined her as you did.

I have not up to now entered into any definite agreement with Miss Sybil Thorndike, but since you have declined the part I can do so, though I do not think her production of the play is coming on till next autumn or winter. With best wishes

Believe me,

Yours Sincerely
Thomas Hardy.

Text MS. (with envelope) Mrs. G. Bugler.
your letter: of 4 Feb 25 (DCM), citing her young daughter and her husband as the reasons for her decision to decline Harrison's offer (see letter of 13 Dec 24); she had in fact been more strongly influenced by a private and intensely personal appeal made to her by FEH (see Millgate, 557–8).   *I can do so*: see, however, letters of 10 and 19 Feb 25.

To ANNIE LANE

MAX GATE, | DORCHESTER. | 7 Feb. 1925

Dear Mrs Lane:

In common with innumerable friends, no doubt, who must sympathize with you, I send a line to express my deep regret at your loss.

Though I never had a business connection with Mr Lane as a publisher, his being a native of a part of the West of England that was of much interest to me, brought us to a knowledge of each other many years ago, as you must know. I always enjoyed his geniality when we happened to meet. I am sorry to say that I did not hear of his illness till I saw the announcement of his death. I trust that you are not too heavily tried in the present sad circumstances.

Sincerely yours
Thomas Hardy.

Text MS. Allen Lane Foundation.
Lane: Annie Eichberg Lane (see II.198), widow of John Lane, the publisher (see I.239), who died of pneumonia 2 Feb 1925. *West of England*: Lane was born in the N. Devon village of West Putford. *many years ago*: they met at least as early as 1891.

To ST. JOHN ERVINE

MAX GATE, | DORCHESTER. | 9th. February 1925.

Dear Mr Ervine:

I have received your letter of the 6th., and have thought that instead of sending the short First Act of Tess by itself I would send the whole play as it now stands. It therefore accompanies this letter. You will see that all I have done is to put in a little prefatory matter from the novel, and at the end of Act V restore the situation as written in the novel. The play was thus in the original draft, but I cut out the pages to shorten it.

I shall be pleased for you to do as you choose—either make a play of your own, or keep to my scheme. My only fear is that if you adopt the former plan and make drastic alterations the critics will out of sheer cussedness exclaim against your changes, however vast the improvement—an astonishingly large number of them, from London, Manchester and Glasgow, having witnessed one or other of the eight performances here and at Weymouth. However, you are the best judge.

I know how pretty a battle of flowers can be. I hope you are getting good weather.

Believe me,

Sincerely yours,
Thomas Hardy.

P.S. When you have quite done with the previous copy of the play would you kindly let me have it back? T.H.

Text MS. (typewritten) Texas.
by itself: as TH had proposed in his letter to Ervine of 3 Feb 25. *keep to my scheme*: Ervine replied (12 Feb 25, DCM) that he was 'very anxious' to keep to TH's scheme 'as far as possible' and proposed only 'to use what technical knowledge I have to correct any little clumsinesses in stage construction due to your lack of acquaintance with plays'. *battle of flowers*: Ervine and his wife were staying at Cannes.

To HARLEY GRANVILLE BARKER

Max Gate, | Dorchester. | 10 Feb. 1925.
My dear H.G.B.

I was beginning to think that I should like to get a letter from you. As to the *Tess* play. Curtis Brown has also written to me on sending it to America, and I will consider the matter. I am asking Sybil Thorndike if she minds their doing it over there before she does it here—supposing she does it at all. She appears to be postponing it indefinitely.

She and her husband propose either a re-dramatization from the novel, or a modification of my version—in either case by Mr St. John Ervine. I told her I did not much care what was done with it, but one or two considerations have arisen since. First, her original request was to produce *my play*, and to this I gave a favourable answer; nothing being said about a new rendering from the novel. Second, Mr. Frederick Harrison (who was going to put on Mrs. Bugler in the part till she was compelled to abandon it for domestic reasons) wrote to me that the public would be far more interested in my own dramatization than in any other: thus there seems to be a commercial reason for sticking to mine. The minor point that the public would assume my dramatization to be unactable I should not much mind, though the critics who saw it here agreed that the story was well adapted.

It will be pleasant to see you both again. I don't know that I care *much* for Paris in the winter, though at this time you have the advantage of hearing French spoken there, which you hardly would get in the streets and hotels in summer time.

With sincere regard believe me

Yours always.
Th: Hardy.

Text   Typed transcript DCM.
postponing it indefinitely: she wrote again 11 Feb 25 (DCM) to say that she understood TH to have agreed to the necessity of certain changes.   *Paris in the winter*: Barker and his wife had been there since the middle of December.

To SAMUEL KARRAKIS

[Ansr]   . . . .[Mid-]February: 1925
Dear Sir:

Mr Hardy acknowledges the receipt of the play you have constructed on his novel The Hand of Ethelberta.

He has not had sufficient time at his disposal to criticize it closely, but, so far as he has looked into it, it seems to contain much irrelevant matter that is not in the novel, & trifling episodes which however amusing in themselves, hinder the progress of the action. Yet almost every speech in a well-constructed play tends to help on the issue.

Ethelberta herself seems to be seldom on the stage, Act I is rambling the arrival of the guests in Act II seems confusing & long-winded, & the lengthy conversation between Ethelberta & Neigh could not possibly be held while guests are arriving.

These, however, are only casual remarks.

Mr Hardy could not entertain the question of authorizing & protecting this adaptation (or a re-written one in which the play is pulled more closely together) by sending the necessary letter to the Registrar of Copyrights, until he receives an offer from the manager of a New York Theatre of good standing to put the play on the stage within a reasonable time.

He can in no event consent to the publication of the play, or to any motion pictures being made from it, as they would have to be drawn from the novel itself, as in other of his stories, & the right to such obtained from him.

The copy of the play is retained till you request its return, enclosing the necessary postage. With thanks for sending it, I am,

Yours very truly

. . . .

Secretary.

To | Karrakis (Paul Kay) | 1632 East 21 Street | Brooklyn, New York.

Text MS. (pencil draft) DCM. *Date* Replies to letter of 28 Jan 25 from New York. *Karrakis*: Samuel Karrakis, calling himself simply Karrakis, also known as Paul Kay, a young American with aspirations as an actor, producer, and playwright; in his letter of 28 Jan 25 (DCM) he gave his date of birth as 1894 and claimed to have 'had the honor to be associated in London with my own production of your Mr. John Drinkwater's fine play, ABRAHAM LINCOLN'. A vol. entitled *Symphonic Prose, Series No. 1*, by Samuel Karrakis, was pub. in Los Angeles by 'P. Kay' in 1951. *[Ansr]*: TH's square brackets. *letter to . . . Copyrights*: as Karrakis had requested.

To SIEGFRIED SASSOON

MAX GATE, | DORCHESTER. | 18 Feb: 1925

My dear ♔ :

I am glad you like the verses; though perhaps the evergreenness you allude to is not quite so vivid as you fancy, for they were written in 1922. My wife has spotted you in the London Mercury, though I did not: yet I had read the sonnet, & thought it a good one.

Always yrs

ℋ

Text MS. (correspondence card, with envelope) Eton College. *the verses*: presumably 'The Absolute Explains'; see letter of 6 Feb 25. *spotted you*: Sassoon's sonnet, 'At the Grave of Henry Vaughan', appeared in the *London Mercury*, February 1925, over the initials 'Z.A.'; for TH's interest in Vaughan see V.194.

To ST. JOHN ERVINE

MAX GATE, | DORCHESTER. | 19 Feb: 1925

Dear Mr Ervine:

I have just written to Miss Sybil Thorndike to tell her that so many difficulties have cropped up against having the play re-cast, or revised, or announced as any but my own adaptation, that I have decided to withdraw it if she wants it altered at all except to the extent of the minor changes I had decided on. I hasten to add that you must not suppose I think my version better than one you could make, far from it!—but the present one has got known (there were eight performances) & the audience at Weymouth were largely London people, & the critics here well-known London critics; & there would be a feeling against its abandonment. Moreover a complication lies in the circumstance that in America they want to do my version verbatim, & the Berlin performance (if ever carried out) is to be from a German translation of the play as it stands. I don't, however, jump at these developments, being too old.

Thus you see how the matter stands. My consolation in giving up your assistance is that, according to my experience of the theatre, provided a play has a good story at the back of it, the details of construction are not important. And there remains the fact that I do not much care to have the play produced at all. The dramatization of a novel is really only a piece of ingenious carpentry.

I let you know this as early as I can, that you may not begin work on the play. Let me have my copy back at your convenience, & I have asked Miss Thorndike to return hers when she gets it from you, in the event of her throwing up the production—which I shall be very sorry for, as I hear on all sides what a charming woman she is.

I wonder when you start for the Cape, & how you are getting on with your book. We wish you were at Beer still.

Sincerely yours
Thomas Hardy.

Text   MS. Texas.
critics here: i.e., the critics who attended the Dorset performances of *Tess*.   *my version verbatim*: Granville Barker, 13 Feb 25 (DCM), said that Winthrop Ames (see letter of 6 Jan 25) wanted TH's own dramatization of *Tess*, and rightly so.   *Berlin performance*: no such performance has been traced, nor any German translation of the play version of *Tess*.   *gets it from you*: Ervine himself returned both copies 22 Feb 25 (DCM).   *the Cape*: of Good Hope; see letter of 25 Aug 24.   *your book*: Ervine's *Parnell*; see letter to Ervine of 8 July 25.   *at Beer*: Ervine often stayed at Seaton, near Beer, on the south Devon coast.

To SIR FREDERICK MACMILLAN

MAX GATE, | DORCHESTER. | 28 February 1925.

Dear Sir Frederick:
I am sending back Mr Watts's book signed, in a separate parcel. As I am writing I am reminded to ask if you will be so kind as to let me have half a dozen more copies of the small-type "Queen of Cornwall" stitched up in paper, as last time?
Believe me,

Sincerely yours,
Th: Hardy.

Text MS. (typewritten) BL.
Mr Watts's book: Macmillan (27 Feb 25, Macmillan letterbooks, BL) asked if TH would sign
A. S. Watt's copy of the first edn. of *The Dynasts*, Part First; he added that Watt (see letter of 6
Sept 24) had been helpful in getting good prices for TH's poems from American magazines.
stitched up in paper: see letter to Macmillan of 3 Feb 25.

To AMY LOWELL

MAX GATE, | DORCHESTER. | 6 March 1925

My dear Cousin Amy:

It has been a great pleasure to me to receive this valuable book, your life of
John Keats, & I don't know how to thank you enough for it. I have not been
reading it straight on—I should say we, for my wife has read it aloud on
account of the weakness of my eyes. I am quite amazed at the skill & industry
you have shown, & to me at any rate, every page is interesting.

Not Shakespeare himself, I should think, has been so meticulously (is that
the right use of the word? I never know) examined as it has fallen at last to
poor neglected Keats's lot to be. If he could only have known! How you have
sifted out the legends for & against him. It was in one respect fortunate for
him that his brother went to America, as it has rendered accessible to you
many papers, &c., that would otherwise have been buried here in England or
lost.

By the way, did it never occur to you that the words "pure serene" in the
Chapman's Homer sonnet may have been an unconscious memory of the line
in Gray's Elegy ending, "purest ray serene"? This seems to me more probable
that Paget Toynbee's suggestion of it having come from Cary's Dante.

My wife's mother, who grew up at Enfield, Middlesex, knew the Clarke
schoolbuilding of which you give an illustration. Her maiden name was
Taylor, & there is every reason to believe that she & the publisher Taylor
were of the same family.

Another thing: I may be wrong, but for many years I have fancied that the
Grecian Urn which inspired the poem is actually one in the British Museum:
at any rate I remember standing before one & concluding that it must have
been the same Keat's looked at. But you have probably thought all that out.

I am sorry to say I cannot write all I would write about the book. You must
not take any notice of what our funny men of the newspaper press say about
the size of it, &c. That's how they are; & it never makes any difference.

My wife sends her love, & believe me

Affectionàtely yours
Thomas Hardy.

Text MS. (with envelope) Harvard.
Cousin Amy: TH was remembering (if not very appropriately) Tennyson's 'Locksley Hall'; see
V.293.   *of John Keats*: Lowell's *John Keats* (London, 1924).   *Toynbee's suggestion*: Paget
Jackson Toynbee (1855–1932; *D.N.B.*), Dante scholar; his letter to the *Times Literary
Supplement*, 16 June 1921, is quoted in *John Keats*, 180–1.   *wife's mother*: Emma
Dugdale.   *Clarke schoolbuilding*: the Enfield school conducted by John Clarke and attended
by Keats as a boy; a sketch of the building is in *John Keats*, opp. 20.   *publisher Taylor*: John
Taylor (1781–1864; *D.N.B.*), proprietor of the *London Magazine*, Keats's first publisher.   *in
the British Museum*: for possible 'originals' of Keats's urn see Ian Jack, *Keats and the Mirror of*

Art (Oxford, 1967), 214–24.   *our funny men*: TH probably has in mind Leonard Woolf's
hostile review in the *Nation and Athenaeum*, 18 Feb 1925.

To ARTHUR McDOWALL

MAX GATE, | DORCHESTER. | 7 March 1925
Dear Mr McDowall:

Your kind note has travelled on to me & I just send a line to say I am much
pleased that a critic I think so highly of as yourself should have been attracted
by that poem in the Nineteenth Century. Alas, it was written between two &
three years ago, although I seem to have done it quite lately. But

"The more we live, more brief appear
Our life's succeeding stages."

I have, I am glad to say, got over that cold, though this wind does not favour
getting out of doors. I hear you are going to set up your tabernacle at or near
Avebury—or *a* tabernacle in addition to your town one. It is a romantic spot,
& the air is decidedly bracing. I think I have written about the Marlborough
Downs somewhere: you will not be far from that famous haunted house
Littlecote. With best wishes to Mrs McDowall I am

Sincerely yours
Thomas Hardy.

Text MS. (with envelope) T. R. M. Creighton.
McDowall: Arthur Sydney McDowall, critic and author; see V.248.   *travelled on to me*:
McDowall's letter of 26 Feb 25 (DCM) is addressed to FEH.   *that poem*: 'The Absolute
Explains'.   *succeeding stages."*: from the first stanza of Thomas Campbell's 'A Thought
Suggested by the New Year'.   *Downs somewhere*: in the story 'What the Shepherd Saw', first
pub. 1881.   *Littlecote*: a house in Wiltshire with a reputation for being comprehensively
haunted; it is the subject of a long note to Canto V of Scott's *Rokeby* (1813).

To G. HERBERT THRING

MAX GATE, | DORCHESTER. | 16th. March 1925.
Dear Mr Thring:

The Return of the Native.

Please let the lawyers do whatever they can in respect of the rendering of
the above in Czecho-slovakian, at a 10 per cent fee. I have not parted with
any rights over there, though strictly, I believe translators may appropriate
freely any book that has been out more than ten years. But publishers like to
have a sort of authorization.

Yours very truly,
T. Hardy.

Text MS. (typewritten) BL.
in Czecho-slovakian: presumably the same translation referred to in the letter of 13 May 24.

To SIR GEORGE FORREST

MAX GATE, | DORCHESTER. | 21st. March 1925.

My dear Forrest:

The only thing I can lay my hand on at the moment that might at all suit your purpose is the description I gave of Anne in the "Trumpet Major," which Mrs Procter herself said was a portrait of her when she was young, at a little after the date of the story. As she often signed notes to me afterwards "Anne Loveday" (the name of the heroine) it is evident that the portrait had struck her as being very much like herself in those early days. She believed I had taken it from her, and I certainly had her in mind. To save you trouble I quote the passage:

"Anne was fair, very fair, in a poetic sense; but in complexion she was of that particular tint between blonde and brunette which is inconveniently left without a name. Her eyes were honest and inquiring, her mouth cleanly cut and yet not classical, the middle point of her upper lip scarcely descending so far as it should have done by rights, so that at the merest pleasant thought, not to mention a smile, portions of two or three white teeth were uncovered whether she would or not. Some people said that this was very attractive. She was graceful and slender, and, though little above five feet in height, could draw herself up to look tall. In her manner, in her comings and goings, in her "I'll do this," or "I'll do that," she combined dignity with sweetness as no other girl could do; and any impressionable stranger-youths who passed by were led to yearn for a windfall of speech from her, and to see at the same time that they would not get it. In short, beneath all that was charming and simple in this young woman there lurked a real firmness, unperceived at first, as the speck of colour lurks unperceived in the heart of the palest parsley flower."

I fear this is not of much value, but I send it for what it is worth. The "real firmness" combined with charm alluded to in the above passage, was exactly like her.

I am sorry to hear that you have been ill. I also have been laid up this winter with influenza, though only for a short time. I have long been compelled to dictate letters through "the detestable machine" you speak of, my reason being mainly weakness of sight.

Believe me,

Sincerely yours,
Thomas Hardy.

Text MS. (typewritten, with envelope in hand of FEH) Purdy.
Forrest: George W. D. S. Forrest, historian of India; see III.268. He was knighted in 1913.
suit your purpose: in his letter of 17 Mar 25 (DCM) Forrest said that he was contemplating a selected edn. of the letters of Mrs. Anne Procter (see letter of 19 July 22 to Ingpen), whom TH had known in the 1870s and 1880s.   *the passage*: TH quotes the entire second paragraph of *The Trumpet-Major* (Wessex edn., 1–2).   *machine" you speak of*: Forrest apologized for having been forced by illness to use a typewriter in writing to TH.

To SIR FREDERICK MACMILLAN

MAX GATE, | DORCHESTER. | March 24th. 1925.

Dear Sir Frederick:

I have heard of The Nonesuch Press, though I don't know anything about it. I am disposed to let them, or it, have the poems at the price you suggest of two guineas each—(the four "She to him" sonnets to be reckoned as one poem which they are—) because I find some people are induced to buy an author by reading snatches of him by chance.

What they call the "last Chorus" from The Dynasts means, I think, what the reviewers call by that name, viz., the last 26 lines of the book, beginning "Last as first the question rings". So that the Nonesuch Press can be asked the same price of two guineas for that one also.

Therefore please answer them to this effect, and request them for the sake of correctness to print from the small two-volume edition of the Collected Poems and The Dynasts.

Sincerely yours,
Thomas Hardy.

Text MS. (typewritten) BL.
Nonesuch Press: founded in 1923 by Francis Meynell, in partnership with Vera Mendel and David Garnett.   *price you suggest*: in his letter of 23 Mar 25 (Macmillan letterbooks, BL). *snatches of him*: the anthology in question, *Great Names*, edited by Walter James Turner (see letter of 15 Jan 20), was in fact pub. in New York in 1926 by the Dial Press under an arrangement with the Nonesuch Press; the Hardy section consisted of a brief introduction by Siegfried Sassoon, the closing 26 lines of *The Dynasts*, 'The Impercipient', and 'She, to Him. I'.

To THOMAS LOVEDAY

25th March, 1925.

Dear Mr. Loveday:

I feel it to be a high distinction that the Senate and Council of the University should be willing to confer on me the Honorary Degree of Doctor of Letters, and I should be gratified to accept this kind offer on June 10th but for a physical difficulty. Unfortunately I shall by that time have reached my 85th birthday, and I could not without some discomfort be at Bristol to attend the ceremony, as I go hardly anywhere nowadays. So that I fear I must forgo the honour. With many thanks, nevertheless, for the possibility held out.

I am

Sincerely yours
Thomas Hardy

Text *Hardyana*, ed. J. Stevens Cox (St. Peter Port, Guernsey, 1967), 7.
Loveday: Thomas Loveday (1875–1966), Vice-Chancellor of the Univ. of Bristol 1922–44; he wrote 23 Mar 25 (DCM) to notify TH that the university wished to confer upon him an Honorary D.Litt. degree.

To SIR FREDERICK MACMILLAN

MAX GATE, | DORCHESTER. | 27th. March 1925.

Dear Sir Frederick:

I have received the enclosed letter within the last few days, and have posted a line to the writer merely to say that it has been sent on to you. In some ways his proposal seems attractive, in others not. Perhaps you will reply to him at your convenience, or send me suggestions for a reply,

Sincerely yours,

T.H.

Text MS. (typewritten) BL.
enclosed letter: still accompanying this letter is a detailed proposal from the Revd. E. J. Thompson for a series of sixpenny booklets of verse by contemporary poets (i.e., the 'Augustan Books of Modern Poetry') which he was to edit for the publishing firm of Ernest Benn. *suggestions for a reply*: Macmillan (30 Mar 25, Macmillan letterbooks, BL) reported that Macmillan authors were being advised to refuse permission, and a letter of refusal was subsequently sent to Thompson on TH's behalf.

To C. BORLASE CHILDS

1 April. 1925

Dear Mr Childs:

I have received your letter, & will propose you whenever you may decide that it will be desirable.

The history of the prominent people in the Childs pedigree, that your uncle has in mind, would be amusing. Christopher the landowner in Charles the First's time would have to figure in it I suppose.

As I am writing I may mention that the American author, whose book entitled "T.H.'s Universe" you issued in England some time ago, has now brought out a large biography of me, as if it were an authorized Life. I would caution you in respect of it in case he should ask you to take it up for England, as it is a mass of unwarranted assumptions & errors that are at times ludicrous, & has been published in New York in the face of my protests against such an impertinence.

Sincerely yours

Text MS. (pencil draft) DCM.
Childs: Christopher Borlase Macrae Childs, publisher, a remote cousin of TH's, one of whose great-grandmothers on his mother's side was born Maria Childs. *your letter*: of 31 Mar 25 (DCM). *propose you*: for election to the Athenaeum Club, as had been requested by Childs's father, Christopher Childs (1846–1928), formerly a physician in Weymouth (see V.216) but currently living in retirement in Cornwall; Childs was not elected, however. *your uncle*: John Frederick Childs, of Looe, Cornwall. *Christopher the landowner*: TH was perhaps confusing his great-grandmother's family (see letter of 14 June 20 to Edgcumbe) with his great-grandfather's family, the Swetmans, who also lived in Melbury Osmond; a Christopher Swetman is recorded as owning land in Melbury in 1635. *you issued in England*: Childs's firm, T. Fisher Unwin, had pub. the English edn. of Ernest Brennecke's *Thomas Hardy's Universe*. *authorized Life*: see letter of 4 Apr 25. *take it up for England*: Childs replied (3 Apr 25, DCM) that T. Fisher Unwin had in fact just received Brennecke's book, together

with his compilation of TH's non-fiction prose (see letter of 4 Apr 25); in view of TH's comments, however, they would proceed no further with the biography but return it immediately.

To A. C. BENSON

MAX GATE, | DORCHESTER. | 2 April 1925

My dear Benson:

I must at least send a brief line to thank you for your new book, which we are going to read as soon as one in hand is finished.

I am glad to hear your news, & that the stay at Lamb House is so beneficial.

Always yours
Th: Hardy.

Text   MS. (with envelope) Colby.
new book: Benson's novel *The House of Menerdue* (London, 1925).   *Lamb House*: see letter of 27 Sept 24.   *so beneficial*: Benson died, however, in June 1925.

To SIEGFRIED SASSOON

MAX GATE, | DORCHESTER. | 2 April 1925

Safely received. Much thanks—Shall read with interest.

Text   MS. (postcard) Eton College.
Safely received: see letter to Sassoon of 15 Apr 25.

To SIR FREDERICK MACMILLAN

MAX GATE, | DORCHESTER. | 4th. April 1925.

Dear Sir Frederick:

A copy of "The Life of Thomas Hardy" by Ernest Brennecke, which my wife mentioned to you, has arrived from its New York publisher Greenberg, although I cabled to the author my disapproval of its publication. It is a large volume, announcing itself on the cover as: "The first biography of England's novelist-poet; a work which will probably always stand as the most authoritative and comprehensive book on the subject. Mr Brennecke records every known fact of Hardy's life . . . . This biography is the result of ten years of research and personal contact."

The first five chapters are the biographical part (the remainder being mostly criticism of my writings, and although often erroneous, it is unobjectionable so far as I have noticed). The biographical chapters are made up of: (1) what can be learned from books of reference & newspapers; (2) extensive assumptions that narrations in the novels and poems are truth, though given as fiction; (3) notes taken when the writer got into this house under the pretence of being a student of German philosophy, and not an interviewer; (4) what he picked up in the neighbourhood from photographers, tradespeople, servants, etc.

The biographical part is thus mainly guesswork, and, though quite eulogistic, ridiculously incorrect; but as long as the book remains in America it does not much matter I suppose. But I have heard from Fisher Unwin & Co, who published the writer's "T.H.'s Universe", that it has just been offered to them for issuing in England, and on my informing them of its misstatements and that it is unauthorized, and contains copyright matter, they have refused it. But it will probably be offered to other firms who may not know it is so highly conjectural and without authority in its biography; so I thought I would tell you of its advent, in case anything ought to be done to caution them. The quizzing impertinence of its remarks on one's appearance, clothing, household details, &c. would warn some firms, but perhaps not all, that the apparent authorization might be untrue and would be contradicted. I should add that the book is a fairly able one from a literary point of view, & I should not have the slightest objection to the publication of the critical part without the personal details. In that case, however, the type would be so cut about that it would have to be re-set in England. T.H.

I can let you see the book whenever you may wish to, to judge upon the copyright matter (mostly poems)—in case the author should get it published here.

He has lately brought out a book through the same American publishers, entitled "Life and Art: By T.H."—as if it were a new volume by me. But it is made up of miscellaneous writings of mine before the international copyright act of 1891, with letters to newspapers at different times, &c. This he has also tried on Fisher Unwin; but here in England it is all copyright, of course.

Yours very sincerely,
Thomas Hardy.

Text   MS. (typewritten) David Holmes.
cabled to the author: see letter of 28 Jan 25.   *England's novelist-poet*: the front of the dust-wrapper of Brennecke's *The Life of Thomas Hardy* (New York, 1925) in fact reads 'England's foremost novelist-poet'; the passages TH selects for quotation are otherwise accurate.   *of German philosophy*: especially of Schopenhauer; see letter of 21 June 24 to Brennecke. *refused it*: see letter of 1 Apr 25.   *in its biography*: added in TH's hand.   *to caution them*: Macmillan (6 Apr 25, Macmillan letterbooks, BL) suggested that a letter be sent to *The Times*, and on 9 Apr 25 (also BL) he reported that he and Sydney Cockerell had concocted such a letter—which was pub. in *The Times* 11 Apr 1925.   *& I should . . . details.*: added in TH's hand.   *In that . . . T.H.*: added in TH's hand at end of letter but marked by an asterisk for insertion at this point.   *new volume by me*: it was pub. as Thomas Hardy, *Life and Art: Essays Notes and Letters Collected for the First Time*, with an introduction by Ernest Brennecke, Jr. (New York, 1925).   *tried on Fisher Unwin*: see letter of 1 Apr 25 and letter of 18 Apr 25 to Childs.

To GERALD MAXWELL

9 April 1925

Dear Mr Maxwell:

I well knew your mother "Miss Braddon" (as she always was to us), & have a faint recollection of my meeting you at Mrs Henniker's.

I am sorry to say that for very good reasons I have been compelled during many years past to decline interviews for the press. In the present case, however, that point is immaterial, for I know nothing whatever of the English theatre of to-day, & could have told you nothing, not having been inside one for many years except our small local buildings. Believe me

Yours very truly

Text   MS. (pencil draft) DCM.
Maxwell: Gerald Maxwell, journalist; see III.133.   *"Miss Braddon"*: Mary Elizabeth Braddon, novelist; see I.51. She married John Maxwell, a publisher, in 1874.   *at Mrs Henniker's*: Maxwell recalled such an occasion in his letter of 7 Apr 25 (DCM).   *theatre of to-day*: Maxwell asked if TH could spare a few minutes for an interview designed to discover his views 'on the outlook of the British theatre today'. Maxwell's novel *The Star Makers* (London, 1925) has a theatrical background.

To HAVELOCK ELLIS

MAX GATE, | DORCHESTER. | 15 April 1925

Dear Mr Havelock Ellis:
   I have been so hindered in my affairs by a chill caught in the latter part of the winter, & by other causes, that I have only just now cut the pages of the Sonnets & Folk Songs you were so kind as to send me, & have not thanked you for the gift. However I do so at last, & shall enjoy reading it.

Sincerely yours
Thomas Hardy.

Text   MS. Yale.
Ellis: Henry Havelock Ellis, psychologist; see I.118.   *the gift*: Ellis's *Sonnets, with Folk Songs from the Spanish*, pub. by the Golden Cockerell Press of Waltham St. Lawrence, 1925.

To SIEGFRIED SASSOON

MAX GATE, | DORCHESTER. | 15 April 1925

Dear S

We have been reading "Lingual Exercises", & I think them an advance on your previous poems. I like particularly "To an old Lady, Dead" which I am inclined to think the best—

Ever yrs

Text   MS. (correspondence card, with envelope) Eton College.
"Lingual Exercises": Sassoon's privately printed *Lingual Exercises for Advanced Vocabularians* (Cambridge, 1925).

To SIR DAN GODFREY

.... [Mid-]April. 1925

Dear Sir Dan Godfrey:

Many thanks for your letter about "The Queen of Cornwall" opera. I hope to be present with Mrs Hardy at a performance—the Saturday afternoon one, as I cannot very well be out at night.

We should prefer to come quite privately, like any other people in the audience, particularly as the musical work is Mr Rutland Boughton's & not mine.

For the above reasons I am quite willing to write for tickets & pay for them, unless the management prefers to send them.

Sincerely yours

Sir Dan Godfrey. R.A.M.

Text MS. (pencil draft) DCM.   *Date* Replies to letter of 14 Apr 25.
Godfrey: Sir Dan Godfrey (1868–1939), orchestral conductor, director of music to the Corporation of Bournemouth 1893–1934.   *your letter*: of 14 Apr 25 (DCM), inviting TH and FEH to attend in the Winter Garden Theatre, Bournemouth, one of the first performances with full orchestra of Rutland Boughton's version of *The Queen of Cornwall.*   *Saturday afternoon*: i.e., Saturday, 25 Apr 1925.   *quite privately*: according to the London *Sunday Times*, 26 Apr 1925, the Hardys were 'received' by the Mayor and Mayoress (see letter of mid-Dec 24) before the performance and 'entertained' by Godfrey afterwards. See also Boughton, 'A Musical Association with Thomas Hardy', *Musical News*, 15 Feb 1928, 34.

To THE REVD. ALBERT COCK

.... [Mid-]April 1925

Dear Professor Cock;

I am delighted to learn from you that the tide has turned in favour of a University for Wessex, which must be owing to the exertions of others than myself, who am nearly *hors de combat* by this time in such matters, as you may imagine.

Certainly use in the proposed Wessex Supplement the message I sent the other day, if it will serve any purpose.

As to your idea of founding a Chair of English Literature associated with my name, my impression is that it would be more effective if the name were attached to the foundation after my death. I personally should of course have no objection to the honour, but you have to consider people's prejudices, & many dislike commemorating a person whilst he is alive. I fancy I do myself!

So far as I know I shall be here the first week in May—indeed I hardly ever go away except for a few hours, so please fix date & time most convenient to yourself.

I will bear in mind the public meeting at Winchester on May 22, though I shall not be able to attend it—being obliged to forgo such functions however tempting, on account of increasing age.

Sincerely yours

P.S. Many thanks for the newspaper.

Text MS. (pencil draft) DCM. *Date* Replies to letter of 15 Apr 25; MS. has '18th' added in ink in another hand.
University for Wessex: i.e., the establishment of University College, Southampton, currently a part of the Univ. of London, as an independent university; see letter to Cock of 14 Jan 21. Cock wrote 15 Apr 25 (DCM) to announce that Austen Chamberlain (1863–1937; *D.N.B.*), the Foreign Secretary, would speak in support of this cause at a public meeting in Winchester on 22 May 1925.   *Wessex Supplement*: apparently a publicity sheet for insertion in copies of local newspapers; Cock said that it would be circulated throughout the S. of England.   *the message*: presumably the one-paragraph statement by TH which was read out at the Winchester meeting and reported in *The Times*, 23 May 1925.   *convenient to yourself*: Cock asked if he could call on TH to discuss the idea of a Thomas Hardy chair; see letter of 18 May 25.

To C. BORLASE CHILDS

18 April 1925

Dear Mr Childs:

I am so sorry to have forgotten your inquiry about "Life & Art: By Thomas Hardy", issued in America by the authority of Mr Ernest Brennecke.

I have had no hand in compiling any such book, & know nothing about it, or its title, though the announcement reads as if it were a new book by me published under my own direction.

The list of contents you kindly sent shows me that the volume is ingeniously made up of articles, &c., all copyright in England, but having been mostly printed before 1891, not copyright in America, together with letters to the papers, & other raked up scraps.

I shall never publish such an olla podrida in England as it stands, but for a long time I have discussed with the Macmillans when my miscellanies (which would include the major part of the said "Life & Art") shall be published in the uniform series of my works, for the sake of completeness. But we have postponed doing it as yet, though it must ultimately be done. This therefore disposes of the question you put to me.

Kind regards to yourself & Mr Unwin.

Sincerely yours

Text MS. (pencil draft) DCM.
your inquiry: see letter of 1 Apr 25; Childs wrote again 17 Apr 25 (DCM) to say that while his firm had sent back Brennecke's *Life* they were still awaiting TH's comments on *Life and Art*. *my own direction*: see letter of 4 Apr 25.   *olla podrida*: unsavoury hotchpotch; literally, 'rotten pot' (Spanish).   *my miscellanies*: i.e., those works of non-fiction prose which TH wished to collect and preserve; a proposal for such a vol., complete with a list of contents and typescripts, proofs, or tearsheets of the principal items, was later prepared by TH and submitted to Macmillan but never pub.   *disposes of the question*: Childs replied (20 Apr 25, DCM) that in view of TH's letter *Life and Art* would of course be returned to its American publisher.   *Unwin*: Thomas Fisher Unwin, publisher; see II.144.

To CHARLES MORGAN

MAX GATE, | DORCHESTER. | 18 April 1925

Dear Mr Morgan:

The book has come, & we shall both read it—I won't say *when*, but as soon as two or three other books have been got out of the way. I am afraid you have wasted the copy upon me, for I am quite ignorant of the Neo-Georgian(?) principles of novel-writing.

I well remember your coming down here for the play. With many thanks,

Sincerely yours

Thomas Hardy.

Text MS. (correspondence card) Roger Morgan.
The book: Morgan's novel *My Name Is Legion* (London, 1925).   *for the play*: the reference is presumably to the O.U.D.S. production of *The Dynasts* (see letter of 25 Jan 20), although it is not clear that Morgan visited Max Gate beforehand.

To THE DUCHESS OF HAMILTON

26 April 1925

Dear Duchess of Hamilton.

In reply to your letter I can say that I have made & am making as many efforts as I can to urge the humane methods of slaughtering upon butchers. Of course no movement to that end will be absolutely successful till we get public slaughter-houses, & I think all animal protection societies should make that their object above all others.

Incidentally I may mention a practice that was customary among butchers when I was a boy, & may be customary still—that of setting their young apprentices to learn the art of killing—or sticking as they called it—by beginning upon sheep—considerable cruelty naturally resulting from the boys' inexperience. I suppose inexperience must begin somewhere before it can grow to experience; but it would be well to ascertain if this is still the case.

Text MS. (pencil draft) DCM.
your letter: of 10 Apr 25 (DCM), asking TH to write to the *Daily Mail* in support of legislation to make the use of mechanical humane killers compulsory in all slaughterhouses.

To G.HERBERT THRING

. . . . [Late] April: 1925

Dear Mr Thring:

I imagine the copies of one of my books imported from the United States, that were offered for sale by Ortega, to be those of some pirated novel, & think therefore that the best plan will be to destroy them.

If however the book should be called "Life & Art", & consists of miscellaneous papers by me collected without my authorization, please send me a copy, & destroy the rest—

Sincerely yours

Text MS. (pencil draft) DCM.   *Date* Replies to letter of 25 Apr 25.
by Ortega: Thring (25 Apr 25, DCM) reported that the Society of Authors had recently been successful in taking proceedings against 'a man called Ortega' who was offering for sale cheap American edns. of works (including one by TH) in copyright in the United Kingdom; he also asked how TH wished the copies of his own book to be disposed of.

To DOROTHY ALLHUSEN

MAX GATE, | DORCHESTER. | 5th May '25.

My dearest Dorothy:

Words are not needed, I know, to express our very deepest sympathy with you in your sad loss. We feel so much for you & your family. We had no idea that Mr Allhusen had been ill.

With my love always,

Yours affectionately,
Florence Hardy.

My dearest Dorothy:

I sincerely join in the above, & have been thinking of you as the little girl you were when I first knew you. I still have your portrait at that age.

I am losing nearly all my friends.

Ever yours
Thomas Hardy.

Text MS. (first portion in FEH's hand, second in TH's) Purdy.
Mr Allhusen: Henry Allhusen (see II.249), Dorothy Allhusen's husband, died 2 May 1925.

To G. HERBERT THRING

MAX GATE, | DORCHESTER. | 12th. May 1925.

Dear Mr Thring:

I am not quite sure how the question of translation into Czecho-Slovak stands in respect of the novel "Far from the Madding Crowd", upon which I have received the enclosed inquiry; and the best thing for me to do seems to be to send it on to you, to treat as you may think best.

Yours sincerely,
T. Hardy.

P.S. I have done nothing in Cz. S. translations except through the society. T.H.

Text MS. (typewritten) BL.
enclosed inquiry: of 9 May 25 (Society of Authors archive, BL) from Dr. Otakar Vočadlo, who identified himself as a lecturer in Czechoslovak at King's College, London; *Far from the Madding Crowd* had already been translated into Czech, however, under the title *Betsabé Everdenova* (Prague, 1910).

To SIR FREDERICK MACMILLAN
MAX GATE, | DORCHESTER. | 16th. May 1925.

Dear Sir Frederick:

I have read Miss Röhm's letter, and do not see any reason for not letting her print her translation of Life's Little Ironies for £2 in the magazine she speaks of, and later on arranging with her in bringing it out in volume form. So that I should like you to settle this with her on those lines, as you suggest.

I return Miss Röhm's letter herewith,

Believe me,

Yours sincerely,
Th: Hardy.

P.S. Will you kindly return Mr Brennecke's so-called biography when you have done with it. T.H.

Text MS. (typewritten) BL.
Miss Röhm's letter: C. E. Röhm, of Cape Town, had written to Macmillan & Co. for permission to pub. her Afrikaans translation of *Life's Little Ironies* in *Die Huisgenoot* magazine. *settle this with her*: Macmillan & Co. wrote (18 May 25, Macmillan letterbooks, BL) to grant permission, but the translation seems not to have appeared.

To WILLIAM WEBER
MAX GATE, | DORCHESTER. | 16th. May 1925.

Dear Colonel Weber:

I do not at all mind signing the books, if you think it desirable, but I should tell you from previous experience that autographed copies are almost sure to be stolen, owing to the high price they will fetch at sales, so that dealers are on the watch for them, my own fetching about £5—5—0 a volume I believe. So that if you want them read and returned, you will be rather endangering the scheme of the Library. However as I say I will do as you please.

Perhaps I might sign one for you to keep and the inscription in the others be printed.

Yours truly,
T. Hardy.

P.S. I shall be at home Monday the 25th. after 3.30 and pleased to see you as you suggest.

Text MS. (typewritten) R. Greenland.
Weber: Colonel William Hermann Frank Weber (1875–1936), retired army officer, of Birkin House, in the parish of Stinsford; see III.37. *the books*: copies of TH's own works. *the Library*: presumably to be located in, or operated through, the Bockhampton Reading-Room and Club; see *LY*, 198.

To THE REVD. ALBERT COCK

18 May 1925

Dear Professor Cock:

I have been laid up with a chill for a few days or I would have answered sooner.

After your explanation I have no opposition whatever to offer to the idea of a Thomas Hardy Chair, merely hoping that in any steps which may be taken to promote it I may be understood to be quite passive.

Very sincerely yours—

Professor A. A. Cock. B.A.

Text   MS. (pencil draft) DCM.
your explanation: Cock (15 May 25, DCM) insisted that those supporting the proposal for a Thomas Hardy Chair of English Literature (see letter to Cock of mid-Apr 25) wanted 'a living memorial of a living man'; see letter of 28 May 25 to Newbolt. The scheme, however, did not materialize (see *LY*, 242).

To THOMAS LOVEDAY

[27 May 1925]

Dear Mr. Loveday,

I am obliged to you for your letter. Certainly if the Senate and Council feel it to be worth while to honour me a little later in the summer by conferring the Degree by deputation I shall have pleasure in receiving it. I hardly ever go anywhere, and if you let me know when I may expect them I shall be sure to be at home.

Believe me,

Sincerely yours,
Thomas Hardy

Text   *Hardyana*, ed. J. Stevens Cox (St. Peter Port, Guernsey, 1967), 8.   *Date*   From a draft of this letter in DCM.
your letter: of 23 May 25 (DCM).   *the Degree*: see letter of 25 Mar 25.

To SIR HENRY NEWBOLT

MAX GATE, | DORCHESTER. | 28 May 1925

My dear Newbolt:

I was quite startled when I saw in The Times the letter you & some more had signed about the Wessex University. I had heard that there ought to be such a thing, but I did not know that I was to appear personally in it, except perhaps as a friendly ghost after my decease, for I am past active service, alas. It is good of you & others to think of me.

However, we shall see what happens. Meanwhile I have been reading your little book called The Tide of Time, which has interested me much. I think you might enlarge it with advantage some day, as I don't remember anything of the sort before—I mean on the same plan.

We send kind regards to you both, & hope you are well.

Sincerely yours
Thomas Hardy.

Text   MS. Texas.
about the Wessex University: the letter, signed by Newbolt and six others, appeared in *The Times* of 26 May 1925; while supporting the long-term aim of an independent university of Wessex (see letter of mid-Apr 25 to Cock) it argued that the Thomas Hardy Chair should be created without delay.   *of Time*: Newbolt's anthology *The Tide of Time in English Poetry*; see letter to Newbolt of 8 Apr 24.   *on the same plan*: the vol., pub. in Nelson's 'Teaching of English' series, sought to illuminate 'the resemblances and inheritances among the poets we read' (17).

To SIR ARTHUR QUILLER-COUCH

MAX GATE, | DORCHESTER. | 28 May 1925

My dear Q:

I am much impressed & moved by this idea of yours & others of associating my name with the proposed Wessex University, which of course I hope may take shape & mature in some way at some time. I did not know that I was to be mentioned at all in it—at any rate yet. I have never wished to be a millionaire till now, so as to set it going.

You must go up & down to Cornwall rather often, but you have never hitherto called round this way. We hear of you occasionally from Sydney Cockerell, & of your great success with the young barbarians at Cambridge, as M. Arnold called them.

Believe me

Sincerely yours
Thomas Hardy.

Text   MS. Miss F. F. Quiller-Couch.
Quiller-Couch: Sir Arthur Thomas Quiller-Couch, King Edward VII Professor of English Literature at Cambridge, 1912–44; see II.277.   *Wessex University*: Quiller-Couch had also signed the letter to *The Times*; see letter of 28 May 25 to Newbolt.   *to Cornwall*: his home was at Fowey, Cornwall.   *as M. Arnold called them*: though 'barbarians' was certainly an Arnoldian term for members of the upper class it seems to have been TH himself who applied it specifically to undergraduates (see letter of 28 June 20).

To PAUL LEMPERLY

MAX GATE, | DORCHESTER. | 30 May: 1925

Dear Mr Lemperly:

My sincere thanks to you for remembering that my birthday is at hand, and sending good wishes. I express the same for yours when it comes along, and that you may have good health to enjoy it.

Believe me

Yours very truly
Thomas Hardy.

Text   *The Letters of Thomas Hardy*, ed. Carl J. Weber (Waterville, Maine, 1954), 113.
Lemperly: Paul Lemperly, American book collector; see IV.70. He maintained for many years a
correspondence with FEH, whose letters to him are in the Colby College Library.

To JOHN DRINKWATER

Dear Mr Drinkwater: MAX GATE, | DORCHESTER. | 1 June 1925

I am much moved by the poem, & should like to write at length about it,
but alas, cannot. Best thanks.

Sincerely yours
T.H.

Text   MS. (correspondence card) Yale.
the poem: TH had evidently seen Drinkwater's 'To Thomas Hardy. June 2nd, 1925: his Eighty-
fifth Birthday', pub. in the *Sunday Times*, 31 May 1925; it was first collected in *Summer
Harvest* (London, 1933).

To CONSTANCE DUGDALE

MAX GATE, | DORCHESTER. [2 June 1925]

Memento of Malmaison & good wishes just received. Best thanks. We are
quite well. Hope you will have a good holiday. With love from both.

T.H.

Text   MS. (postcard) Purdy.   *Date*   From postmark.
Dugdale: Constance ('Connie') Dugdale, the third of the five Dugdale sisters; see IV.103.
Malmaison: a château near Paris, the residence of the Empress Josephine and, as such, the
setting for *The Dynasts*, Part Third, Act IV, Scene 7.

To SIR EDMUND GOSSE

My dear Gosse: MAX GATE, | DORCHESTER | 3 June 1925

Your good wishes are always welcome, you may be sure. It is true, indeed,
that I don't often meet you now, & many other friends, but the inevitable
results of growing age must be submitted to. I have not been in London for at
least 5 years, & sometimes suppose I shall never go again. I have an
advantage over you in this respect, that I am able to read you every
week—which I do—while you may search in vain on Sundays for any
brilliant article from me.

I have just seen the French translation of some of my verses that you speak
of. I thought they were done with unusual fidelity of statement: I suppose
one cannot expect more. I have been told recently that the translator is an
invalid—a cripple I believe, & that she has worked very hard at them. I hope
she will get something out of them to repay her for her trouble. She is quite a
stranger to me.

We were glad to hear of your so-called honour some months ago; but I thought the honour the other way, & knew you would know I thought so: & did not worry you with a letter.

Kind regards to the household from us both.

Always sincerely yours
Thomas Hardy.

Text   MS. Adams; envelope BL.

good wishes: in Gosse's letter of 1 June 25 (DCM).   *at least 5 years*: TH first wrote 'at least 4 years'.   *never go again*: he never did.   *every week*: as a regular reviewer for the *Sunday Times*; see letter of 6 June 23.   *French translation*: Thomas Hardy, *Poèmes*, trans. by Jeanne Fournier-Pargoire (Paris, 1925); the vol.—a copy of which TH inscribed to FEH in May 1925 (Purdy)—contains prose translations of 61 poems.   *so-called honour*: Gosse received a knighthood in the January 1925 New Year's Honours list.

To T. H. TILLEY

MAX GATE, | DORCHESTER. | June 3rd. 1925.

Most cordial thanks to the Hardy Players for their birthday greetings, which I greatly value.

Thomas Hardy.

Text   MS. (typewritten) DCM.

To A. G. GARDINER

Max Gate | Dorchester. | 5 June. 1925.

Dear Mr Gardiner,

I must thank you for this kind letter—from one whom I have of course known as a name (or mere initials) of distinction for a long train of years, but whom I believe (though I may be wrong) I have never seen in the flesh.

The rebuke you allude to I don't remember to associate with that name, fortunately for my own peace of mind perhaps—particularly now that I hear that you too claim for your own birth the modest date of June 2, as it always seems to me, I suppose because not many people have apparently cared to come into the world on that day, at least not many that I have ever met with.

My reply will not be in time for good wishes this year to you thereon, but it contains them, & they are warranted to keep till next year. Believe me,

Sincerely yours
Thomas Hardy.

Text   Transcript (by Gardiner himself) British Library of Political and Economic Science.

Gardiner: Alfred George Gardiner, editor of the *Daily News* 1902–19; see III.307.   *rebuke you allude to*: Gardiner had evidently recalled TH's writing to him in 1908 to protest against being described as a pessimist; see III.306–7, 308.   *ever met with*: TH perhaps did not know that he was born 100 years, to the day, after the birth of the Marquis de Sade.

To THE SECRETARY, THE ROYAL LITERARY FUND

MAX GATE, | DORCHESTER. | June 10th. 1925.

Dear Sir:

I enclose a letter from the widow of the late David Christie Murray the novelist, asking for assistance. Mrs Murray is unknown to me, as was her husband, and I cannot corroborate her statements, but I send you her application for the Council's investigation.

Yours truly,

Th: Hardy.

The Secretary, | Royal Literary Fund:

Text   MS. (typewritten) Royal Literary Fund.
Secretary: H. J. C. Marshall; see letter of 3 Mar 21.   *Literary Fund*: of which TH was elected a vice-president in 1922.   *widow . . . Murray*: David Christie Murray (1847–1907; *D.N.B.*), novelist and journalist, was twice married, but not to the woman calling herself Marion Christie Murray, mother of four of his children, who wrote to TH 6 June 25 (DCM). Marshall reported (12 June 25, DCM) that her case would not be considered by the Fund, two previous applications having already been rejected because of her inability to produce a marriage certificate.

To R. GOLDING BRIGHT

12 June. 1925

Dear Mr Bright:

I have decided to withdraw the play of Tess of the d'Urbervilles from offer to managers if not for good, at any rate for the present—I therefore will ask you to return the script to me. I hope making inquiries about it gave you no trouble.

Believe me

Yours very truly

R. Golding Bright Esq. | 20 Green Street | Leicester Square

Text   MS. (pencil draft) DCM.
return the script: Bright sent the MS. 15 June 25 (DCM).

To SIR HENRY NEWBOLT

MAX GATE, | DORCHESTER. | 12 June 1925

My dear Newbolt:

Many thanks for your letter. I hasten to say that you must have misunderstood mine, or I must have written obscurely. I highly value the honour of the proposed "T.H. Chair": & only hope that the idea of the Wessex University will mature rapidly. I never wished to be a millionaire till read of the scheme in the Times.

I don't know whether you feel the heat in London as we do here on the south coast: but it prevents my doing anything. Kindest regards.

Always yours
Thomas Hardy.

Congratulations on the Cambridge Litt D. I thought you had it already. T.H.

Text MS. Texas.
your letter: of 11 June 25 (Texas); Newbolt regretted that TH had been 'startled' by the letter in *The Times* and feared that its signatories had been misled into making 'an improper use' of TH's name.   *misunderstood mine*: i.e., his letter to Newbolt of 28 May 25.   *till read*: TH's slip for 'till I read'.   *Cambridge Litt D.*: Newbolt received this honorary degree at a convocation on 9 June 1925.

To ARTHUR KENNEDY

MAX GATE, | DORCHESTER. | 21 June 1925

Dear Mr Kennedy:
Sincere thanks for "Winter Nights", which I am beginning to read with pleasure. Also thanks for birthday congratulations. As to your kind suggestion of a visit from me, I fear I shall never get so far north again.
Being an old Magdalene man you will have regretted the recent death of Arthur Benson—a good friend of mine & of so many.

Yours very truly
Thomas Hardy.

Text MS. (with envelope) UCLA.
Kennedy: Arthur John Clark Kennedy (1857–1926), poet and translator; he wrote to TH (2 June 25, DCM) from Chillingham Castle, Northumberland.   *"Winter Nights"*: Kennedy's verse translation (London, 1923) of Henry Murger's *Les Nuits d'hiver*.   *an old Magdalene man*: as Kennedy had mentioned in his letter.   *Arthur Benson*: he was still master of Magdalene College, Cambridge, at his death on 17 June 1925.

To THOMAS LOVEDAY

24 June 1925

Dear Mr Loveday:
July 15 would suit me quite well to receive the deputation the University has so kindly arranged to meet my difficulty of attending at the proper place. About three o'clock would be convenient. We will have ready an early tea for the deputation.
The journey by road, if you come that way, is a very pleasant one this time of the year. I used to bicycle over it in years gone by.

Yours sincerely

The Vice-Chancellor | The University | Bristol

Text MS. (pencil draft) DCM.
the deputation: see *LY*, 242.   *bicycle over it*: TH's cousin Nathaniel Sparks (see III.38) had lived in Bristol and in the collection of Mrs. Celia Barclay is a scenic route which TH once wrote out for the guidance of Sparks's sons, James and Nathaniel (see II.188), when cycling from Bristol to Dorchester.

To CALEB SALEEBY

MAX GATE, | DORCHESTER. | 5 July 1925

Many thanks for drawing attention to your article in Spectator which I am glad to read. Kind regards

T.H.

Text MS. (postcard) Adams.
Saleeby: Caleb Williams Saleeby, doctor and reformer; see V.70.   *in Spectator*: Saleeby's 'Mother and Baby Week', *Spectator*, 4 July 1925; Saleeby (2 July 25, DCM) asked TH to respond to a reference to *The Dynasts* included in his final paragraph.

To ST. JOHN ERVINE

MAX GATE, | DORCHESTER. | 8 July 1925

Dear Mr St John Ervine:

I am reading the Parnell book with great interest, though I have not yet read it through (my eyes being weak) & I must thank you for so thoughtfully presenting me with a copy.

In avoiding a political tone & style for a human & dramatic representation you have I think adopted quite the right method in respect of a man who is already putting on something of a mythical shape to the new generation. By me, of course, his time & circumstances are remembered in their crude reality.

I hope you are well, & am sending this through the publishers, as I don't know where you are just now. Believe me,

Sincerely yrs
Thomas Hardy.

Text MS. Texas.
Parnell book: Ervine's *Parnell* (London, 1925).

To THOMAS LOVEDAY

8th July, 1925.

Dear Mr. Loveday,

We shall be pleased to receive the very interesting deputation you mention at 3 on the 15th as stated, and hope you will get here comfortably. If it would save you trouble to dispense with robes altogether I shall not mind. But that matter I leave entirely to you.

Sincerely yours,
Th. Hardy.

Text *Hardyana*, ed. J. Stevens Cox (St. Peter Port, Guernsey, 1967), 9.
you mention: in his letter of 6 July 25 (DCM).   *on the 15th*: i.e., 15 July; see *LY*, 242.

To LOUIS UNTERMEYER

MAX GATE, | DORCHESTER. | 8 July 1925

Dear Mr Untermeyer:

I have the pleasure of acknowledging the receipt of your kind gift of "Modern British Poetry," which I have already looked into, renewing acquaintance with forgotten pieces, as well as lighting on some new to me.

I hope the time & thought you have given to making the selection is duly appreciated in America.

Yours very truly
Thomas Hardy.

Text   MS. Indiana Univ.
British Poetry": see letter of 23 Sept 22.

To THE REVD. SYDNEY SMITH

[Mid-July 1925]

Dear Sir:

In reply to your inquiry I am sorry to say that I can find no letter from the late Dr Donald Macleod concerning the story The Trumpet Major which appeared in the pages of Good Words at the time he was editing the Magazine. If I remember my arrangements with him were carried on through Mr Isbister the publisher, though I met Dr Macleod whenever he came to London & discussed small literary points with him, all of which I have forgotten except two: that he asked me to make a lover's meeting, which I had fixed for a Sunday afternoon, take place on a Saturday, & that swearwords should be avoided—in both which requests I readily acquiesced, as I restored my own readings when the novel came out as a book.

You can easily ascertain if other changes were made by comparing the magazine version with the volume version afterwards published, since the latter stands as originally written. Knowing that this would be the case it is quite possible I told him he might modify any magazine passage if he wished to do so. My impression is, however, that, if so, on second thoughts he gave up the idea, or reduced it to infinitesimal proportions.

Should I meet with any letter from him I will send it on to you.

Yours very truly

Revd Sydney Smith | Edinburgh.

Text   MS. (pencil draft) DCM.   *Date*   Replies to letter of 14 July 25.
Smith: the Revd. Sydney Smith, Scottish minister and biographer.   *your inquiry*: Smith wrote from Edinburgh 14 July 25 (DCM) to ask TH for letters or memories of Dr. Donald Macleod, former editor of *Good Words* (see I.66), whose biography he was writing. *Mr Isbister*: William Isbister, proprietor of *Good Words* at the date (July–December 1880) of the serialization of *The Trumpet-Major*.   *on a Saturday*: the day was in fact changed to a Monday, as Smith correctly records when mentioning this episode in his *Donald Macleod of Glasgow: A Memoir and a Study* (London, 1926), 113.   *wished to do so*: Smith quoted (113) a sentence to this effect from what was apparently a letter from TH to Macleod, 'Should you on looking over the MS. as we go on discover any passages out of keeping with the general tone of the magazine, be kind enough to tell me frankly and I will do anything to get it right.'

To PHILIP RIDGEWAY

MAX GATE, | DORCHESTER. | 16th. July 1925.

My dear Sir:

I am sorry to have delayed my reply to your inquiries, and still more that I cannot give you a definite answer on whether the play of "Tess of the d'Urbervilles" is, or will be, available for the stage. It is at present in the hands of a literary friend of mine, and I myself have some literary work on hand which prevents my attending to the play.

As you may possibly guess from it not having been produced in London yet, I have some reluctance in taking active steps towards doing so, partly owing to its being a "star" play, and a satisfactory heroine being almost impossible to find.

I do not therefore see that it could be done so early as September in the circumstances, even if we were to come to terms, so I will ask you to drop the question for the time, and let me inquire of you later on how you stand, which I may be quite glad to do.

Yours very truly,
T. Hardy.

Philip Ridgeway. Esq. | Barnes Theatre.

Text MS. (typewritten) Adams.
Ridgeway: Philip Ridgeway (1891–1954), theatrical producer.   *your inquiries*: on 14 July 25 TH had responded to a telegram from Ridgeway by sending a telegram of his own, 'Will entertain arrangements state further by letter Hardy' (Adams).   *literary friend*: this seems to have been a cautionary or temporizing invention on TH's part.   *so early as September*: Ridgeway's production did open on 7 September, however.

To GEORGE MACMILLAN

MAX GATE, | DORCHESTER. | July 17th. 1925.

Dear Mr Macmillan:

I find that my correspondence with Mr Hubert Foss has been as follows:—

He first wrote and asked permission to perform a musical setting of "The Sergeant's Song", which I granted, and that he might publish his setting on payment of a fee of two guineas.

He later wrote: "I have now completed a cycle of seven songs to poems of yours" (naming those you have named) "which I want to have performed at a Concert. . . . . I should be very grateful if you would grant me permission to have these performed on the same conditions as before. I shall offer these songs for publication by the Oxford University Press". My reply was that I was "willing for you to perform and publish the song-cycle you mention on the same terms as those stated for The Sergeant's Song"—my view being that the songs would be sung as a "cycle", and published in the ordinary way in separate sheets, if at all—which I doubted, as so many of these requests fall through: otherwise I should have consulted you on the matter. I did not know that Mr Foss was Musical Editor to the University Press.

If therefore you think he, or his publishers, likely to be amenable, please ask them for a small royalty; though it is not worth while to contest the matter, as it is a nice point whether my inadvertent words could be held to cover publication in book form. Many thanks for drawing my attention to the matter.

Very sincerely yours,
Thomas Hardy.

Mr Foss's letter returned herewith.

Text MS. (typewritten) BL.
Foss: Hubert James Foss (1899–1953), musician, writer, and publisher; *D.N.B.*   *poems of yours*": Foss's *Seven Poems by Thomas Hardy . . . For baritone, male-voice chorus and piano*, pub. by Oxford University Press, 1925.   *Musical Editor*: Foss had recently been appointed music editor for the Oxford University Press and head of its music department.   *it is not . . . matter, as*: added, like the postscript, in TH's hand.

To R. GOLDING BRIGHT

MAX GATE, | DORCHESTER. | 19th. July 1925.

Dear Mr Golding Bright:
    Having concluded that I would put the "Tess" play aside for a time, and lent it to a friend to do what he liked with it, I get a request for it from Mr Philip Ridgeway of the Barnes Theatre, who seems to be a responsible manager, though I do not know him. Would this request be worth considering, or is the theatre too suburban?
    As you know I am not anxious to stage the play, unless a good place offers.

Very truly yours,
T. Hardy.

Text MS. (typewritten) Adams.
aside for a time: see letter to Bright of 12 June 25.   *a friend*: see letter of 16 July 25.   *worth considering*: TH had already sent Ridgeway a telegram, 18 July 25 (Adams), 'Consider the play available Hardy.'   *too suburban?*: the theatre was in the SW13 postal district, on the S. side of the Thames between Mortlake and Putney.   *unless . . . offers.*: added in TH's hand.

To R. GOLDING BRIGHT

MAX GATE, | DORCHESTER. | July 21st. 1925.

Dear Mr Golding Bright:
    Many thanks for your reply. As I have nothing to lose by the "Tess" play in the event of a failure, and as Mr Philip Ridgeway the manager of the Barnes Theatre seems young and energetic, I was inclined to let him have a chance; but this was of course subject to nothing being discovered of any serious sort against a production at Barnes beyond the objection of its remoteness.
    Should I persist in my idea you probably would not care to see to it for me? But if you would like to, and there is probably not much money in the proposal, I would guarantee that your fee should not be less than twenty-five guineas, if it were performed successfully or otherwise.
    He promises to produce it very attractively. I am going to think it over for a

day or two. Meanwhile you can let me know if you could attend to it, in case it comes to anything and an agent should be necessary.

Yours very truly,
Th: Hardy.

Text MS. Adams.
have a chance: see letter of 19 July 25.

To PHILIP RIDGEWAY

MAX GATE, | DORCHESTER. | 21st. July 1925.

Dear Mr Ridgeway:

(I find it is a day and a half's post between here and Margate.)

I have not yet heard what my friend has done about the play, nor have I decided whether to produce it; so that you will understand that I write provisionally, though for only a few days longer, I trust, while thinking it over.

All would depend upon the two chief characters—Tess and (in a less degree) Angel Clare. I don't know about Hermione Baddeley for the former, never having seen her in tragedy. I enclose an opinion on her sister Angela, who might do. Miss Fay Compton is not too old, but she has, I fear, too many engagements.

In the event of well-known actresses failing, I should like to look about in the provinces for some unknown young woman—there must be several—who combines in her person the following particulars:—

— A fair amount of experience on the stage.
— A bright intelligence.
— Good looks.
— A pathetic voice.

Believe me,

Very truly yours,
Th: Hardy.

Text MS. (typewritten) Adams.
Margate: on the Kent coast; see letter of 23 July 25 to Bright.   *my friend*: see letter of 16 July 25.   *Baddeley*: Hermione Baddeley [Clinton-Baddeley] (1906–86), actress; TH had sent her a note (28 Dec 24, pencil draft, DCM) in response to her telegram of Christmas greetings.   *sister Angela*: Angela Baddeley [Clinton-Baddeley] (1904–76), actress. *Compton*: Fay Compton (1894–1978), actress.   *unknown young woman*: TH presumably had Gertrude Bugler still in mind; see letter of 3 Aug 25.   *on the stage*: added in TH's hand.

To J. C. SQUIRE

MAX GATE, | DORCHESTER. | July 21st. 1925.

Dear Mr Squire:

It has been upon my conscience that I gave short measure last time, so I send a short epitaph I have discovered, if you care to print it in the Mercury any time before November or so, when I hope to include it in a volume. This is, of course, sent gratis.

Ever sincerely,
T.H.

Text MS. (typewritten) Taylor.
last time: see letter of 1 Oct 24.   *short epitaph*: either 'Cynic's Epitaph' or 'Epitaph on a Pessimist', both pub. in *London Mercury*, September 1925; see letter to Squire of 26 July 25.

To R. GOLDING BRIGHT

MAX GATE, | DORCHESTER. | 23rd. July 1925.

Dear Mr Golding Bright:

I am delighted to think you take a sufficient interest in Tess to go on with the business, even if it should not be one to make a fortune with, and I agree of course to ten per cent commission on the author's royalties. I have decided to let Mr Ridgeway have a try.

He has gone down to Granville Court Hotel, Cliftonville, Margate, to get a little air, but he says he is returning in a few days, when his address will be Barnes Theatre. He wants to open with the play in September. I sent him a copy of it to save time.

I will tell you briefly my idea of terms.

I used to hear that 5 per cent on the gross receipts up to £800 and 7½ or 10 over £800 was fair. But as this theatre is a small one, would that be too high? I particularly want to give the manager every chance, with only a secondary regard to my own profit.

Should his licence to perform be for the run of the play at Barnes simply? or, in the event of success, should he have the privilege of putting it on at a first class London Theatre if he can get one?—and of doing it with a touring company? I leave you to settle these points, but I suppose it would be only fair that he should.

I reserve America, as I have half promised a friend over there.

He suggests various damsels for Tess, upon whom the whole thing hangs. I have told him I don't care how obscure a country actress the girl is, if she has—(1) a bright intelligence, (2) good looks, (3) fair experience—(4) a pathetic voice. He suggests Fay Compton, Hermione Baddeley, or Angela Baddeley, &c., but I don't think he will get either of them. Norman McKinnel (if he has a sense of humour) might do for Tess's father, and Marie Tempest for her mother. He says he has been approached by both of these latter.

I suppose you would also like a copy of the play?

It is very kind of you to suggest running down here. It is easy to do it in a day, and I will bear the possibility in mind.

Sincerely yours,
Th: Hardy.

Text MS. (typewritten) Adams.
but I suppose ... should.: added in TH's hand.   *friend over there*: TH perhaps had Winthrop

Ames in mind; see letter of 6 Jan 25.   *Fay . . . Baddeley, &c.*: see letter of 21 July 25 to
Ridgeway.   *McKinnel*: Norman McKinnel (1870–1932), actor.   *Tempest*: Marie Tempest
[Mary Susan Etherington] (1864–1942), actress; *D.N.B.*

To HAROLD CHILD

MAX GATE, | DORCHESTER. | 23 July 1925

Dear Mr Child:

I am much pleased that Marty South's words have been found appropriate
to music. The girl who acted the character here & produced such an
impression (although it was only an adaptation by the players themselves) is
the same one you saw as Tess last winter when you came down.

You may be angry with me for recklessness when I tell you that I have
flown in the face of good advice & consented to let the manager of the Barnes
Theatre—Mr Philip Ridgeway, whom I know nothing about—have the Tess
play for production this autumn. After all, he cannot hurt the book, whatever
happens. Friends say: "You should have it produced in the best manner", &c.
&c. But nothing comes of what they say, & this Mr Ridgeway seems an
energetic young man deserving a chance.

I wonder if you will get back from your delightful excursion north in time
to see it—if it comes off.

Always sincerely
Thomas Hardy.

The Times might have had the kindness to send you south instead of north!
T.H.

Text   MS. Adams.
appropriate to music: Child (21 July 25, DCM) mentioned a performance of Patrick Hadley's
*Scene from Thomas Hardy's 'The Woodlanders'. Set for soprano voice, flute, violin, viola and
pianoforte* (pub. 1926).   *The girl*: Gertrude Bugler; she played Marty South in the
Dorchester production of *The Woodlanders* in November 1913.   *excursion north*: Child said
he would spend the next two months reporting for *The Times* in Scotland and northern England.

To GEORGE MACMILLAN

MAX GATE, | DORCHESTER. | July 23rd. 1925.

Dear Mr Macmillan:

I am much obliged to you for improving the conditions on which Mr Foss
can publish his "Song-Cycle," which is a new thing to me.

As I am writing I may mention that the poems which I have published of
late years in periodicals have, as you may guess, accumulated to such an
extent that, with others still in MS. they would make up a volume of about
the content of "Late Lyrics," etc. In America they are getting copied into
anthologies although we have not printed them as yet in book form. So that it
may be as well to bring them out—say at the end of the year, not to forestall
two or three still awaiting magazine publication, which I should wish to
include.

Should this meet your views I can let you have the MS. at almost any time, if it would be more convenient to get it printed at leisure during the autumn instead of immediately before issuing the volume.

Believe me,

Very sincerely yours,
Thomas Hardy.

Text MS. (typewritten) BL.
improving the conditions: Macmillan reported (22 July 25, Macmillan letterbooks, BL) that Oxford Univ. Press had agreed to pay a royalty of twopence on every copy of Foss's work in which the texts of the seven poems were included; see letter of 17 July 25. *bring them out*: see letter to Macmillan of 29 July 25.

To PHILIP RIDGEWAY

MAX GATE, | DORCHESTER. | 23rd. July 1925.

Dear Mr Ridgeway:

To save time I posted to you this morning a copy of the play.

The one I send is its latest revised form. The sliding flats *could* be left out, and the play begin at Act 2; but Sir James Barrie, who saw it done by our amateur company here, thinks the introductory scenes help the understanding of the plot. You will perceive that the scenery is of the simplest kind, and will not put you to much expense.

I enclose the newspaper opinion on Angela Baddeley's acting. My friend Granville Barker says he likes her better than Hermione. But I leave you to judge.

As I am down in this remote spot I cannot personally go into details about an agreement with you. But Mr Golding Bright (20 Green Street, Leicester Square) who has acted for me occasionally, will see to terms &c. for me. He is a most just-minded man, and you will be quite safe in dealing with him. I have told him I wish to be strictly fair, as I want to give you every chance.

I may add that I think the play will, at the worst, pay its way, for even with the amateur acting we had here it held people to an extraordinary degree. It has, as you know, never been produced in England by a professional company.

I don't *particularly* want Fay Compton unless she really wants to do it. N. McKinnel might do for Tess's father if he has a sense of humour. Mrs Hardy thinks Marie Tempest would do excellently for Tess's mother. Angel Clare is, of course, an austere kind of lover—something as Forbes-Robertson was in his younger days. However, it is of no use for me to make suggestions—times have so changed since I was a theatre-goer.

Yours very truly,
Th: Hardy.

Text MS. (typewritten) Adams.
better than Hermione: see letter to Ridgeway of 21 July 25 and letter of 26 July 25 to Child. *Compton*: see letter to Ridgeway of 21 July 25. *McKinnel . . . Tempest*: see letter of 23 July 25 to Bright. *as Forbes-Robertson was*: see letter of 29 Nov 24 to Forbes-Robertson.

To HAROLD CHILD

MAX GATE, | DORCHESTER. | 26 July 1925

Dear Mr Child:

My thanks for your reassuring note. But I don't expect much from *Tess*: it is not as if it were a new play & I were a young man. Granville Barker was here yesterday, & spoke warmly of you, & amusingly of my prospects as a playwright commencing business at 85. However I hope you will see the production: I shall not—trust me!

Mrs Bugler's husband won't let her go on the regular stage. I cannot *think* of any other Tess. What poor Mr Ridgeway will do to find one I cannot tell; he has suggested Hermione Baddeley. Barker laughs at this, & says the man must be mad. Who shall decide when doctors disagree.

Ever yrs
T.H.

Text   MS. (correspondence card) Adams.
reassuring note: Child's postcard of 24 July 25 (DCM), in which he took a more optimistic view of the forthcoming production of *Tess* than he had done in his letter written earlier that same day (DCM).   *on the regular stage*: see letter of 7 Feb 25 to G. Bugler; in his first communication of 24 July Child confessed to having a prejudice against any actress other than Mrs. Bugler who might attempt to play Tess.   *Who . . . disagree*: the opening line of Pope's *Epistle to Lord Bathurst*.

To J. C. SQUIRE

MAX GATE, | DORCHESTER. | 26: 7: 1925

Dear Mr Squire

I have found another Epitaph (enclosed). If the one I sent last week has gone to press for the August number please return this one: if not, put this with the other (assuming you care to print either) to make up a decent contribution.

In haste
T.H.

Text   MS. (correspondence card) Taylor.
another Epitaph: see letter to Squire of 21 July 25.

To R. GOLDING BRIGHT

MAX GATE, | DORCHESTER. | 27th. July 1925.

Dear Mr Golding Bright:

My thanks for your note this morning. Mr Granville-Barker was here Saturday, and I mentioned the play to him. He suggested first that, as I never had dealt with Mr Ridgeway before, I should let him have it for the run at the Barnes Theatre only; but when I said I might give him a further chance he agreed that there might be an understanding that if the run were a success and he could put the play on elsewhere he should have the option of doing so, on condition that I should be satisfied with the theatre, the cast, and the general circumstances; but that as we are so much in the dark I should not transfer to him absolutely at the present time the command of the play for England till I knew further what was going to happen.

I have thought it as well to let you know this opinion of his.

Very truly yours,
Th. Hardy.

P.S. I am sending a copy of the play, which perhaps you will let me have back again when this business is over. T.H.

Text   MS. (typewritten) Adams.

To R. GOLDING BRIGHT

MAX GATE, | DORCHESTER. | 29th. July 1925.

Dear Mr Golding Bright:

I approve the Agreement, and return it signed, as I suppose Mr Ridgeway wants to get on. Will you please have it stamped. In haste,

Yours truly,
T.H.

Text   MS. (typewritten) Adams.
the Agreement: for Ridgeway's production of the *Tess* play, dated 29 July 1925 (Adams).

To GEORGE MACMILLAN

MAX GATE, | DORCHESTER. | 29th. July 1925.

Dear Mr Macmillan:

Acting on your suggestion I am about to send off the MS., which I have called for want of a better title, "Poems Imaginative & Incidental: with Songs and Trifles." I hope you think it will do.

Meanwhile it so happens that the play of "Tess of the d'Urbervilles" which our amateurs produced down here last December, is to be put on the stage at (of all places) the Barnes Theatre, in September or October, and possibly in a leading London Theatre later on, if it succeeds. Do you think this may injure the poems? I do not expect much from the play, but of course one never knows. Anyhow I have thought I would put you in possession of the verses, to print them just when you choose, and we can consider the question of their date of publication later on, when more is known about the play.

Believe me,

Very sincerely yours,
Thomas Hardy.

Text   MS. (typewritten) BL.
your suggestion: Macmillan (24 July 25, Macmillan letterbooks, BL) welcomed the prospect of a new vol. from TH (see letter to Macmillan of 23 July 25) but remarked on the need for early action if publication before Christmas was to be achieved.   *think it will do*: the title was subsequently changed, however; see letter of 25 Aug 25.   *injure the poems?*: Sir Frederick Macmillan, replying in his cousin George's absence (30 July 25, Macmillan letterbooks, BL), dismissed this possibility.

To PHILIP RIDGEWAY

MAX GATE, | DORCHESTER. | August 3rd. 1925.

Dear Mr Ridgeway:

On second thoughts I send a postscript to my last letter, to say that if you have any great difficulty in finding a good Tess you might write a line to

Mrs Gertrude Bugler,
Riverside Cottage,
Beaminster. Dorset.

telling her that as matter of courtesy, since she was so successful with the character down here, you just put the question to her whether she will take it. You have seen what the Times, etc, said about her, and she is not altogether an amateur—only she wants a little drilling. The real trouble about it was her domestic arrangements till lately, as she had a young baby. But now there is no difficulty it seems.

You may however by this time have settled it. Anyhow in case of a hitch there will be Mrs Bugler to fall back upon.

[*remainder excised*]

Text   MS. (typewritten) Boston Public Library.
my last letter: presumably, though not necessarily, that of 23 July 25.   *the Times*: Harold Child's review of the *Tess* play in *The Times*, 27 Nov 1924, had described Mrs. Bugler's performance as 'full of the right sort of simplicity and breadth, and of a most moving sincerity and beauty—more beauty, one imagines, than could have been achieved by one or two of the many eminent professional actresses who have longed to play this character'.   *fall back upon*: in a letter to Cockerell of 8 Aug 25 (Purdy) FEH reported that Ridgeway, '*thank Heaven*', had not taken up TH's suggestion; she added that TH had not for a long time been as happy about anything as he was about the play.

To PHILIP RIDGEWAY

MAX GATE, | DORCHESTER. | 4th. August 1925.

Dear Mr Ridgeway:

Please keep the press notices till you have quite done with them.

I think I should like to leave the whole production in your hands, if you don't mind, it being five years since I was in London. I have the less reluctance to do so now I find that you are setting about it so diligently, and I don't really know much about these things. You have a big job in finding a Tess! Whoever takes her part might be able to run down here for a few hours, when I can read it over to her. I will pay her expenses down and she can easily get back the same evening.

I will ask the Society of Authors if the new short act at the beginning should be submitted to the Censor, but I should hardly think it necessary to submit the play again.

I am sending up the only other copy of the play.

I need hardly say that in mentioning Mrs Bugler's name I did not wish to influence you at all unless you were in great difficulties.

Yours very truly,
T. Hardy.

Text MS. (typewritten) Boston Public Library.
new short act: see letter of 18 Aug 25 to Golding Bright.

To HAROLD MACMILLAN

MAX GATE, | DORCHESTER. | August 5th. 1925.

Dear Mr Macmillan:

In respect of your inquiry this morning on copyrighting the poems in the United States I think it best to do so, as your New York firm suggest. I understand that all my verse is increasing in circulation in America, which makes the point rather more important than it was.

Yours very sincerely,
Thomas Hardy.

Text MS. (typewritten) BL.
in the United States: Macmillan (4 Aug 25, Macmillan letterbooks, BL) asked if TH would agree to the proposal of Macmillan New York that they copyright TH's new vol. of poems instead of simply buying copies of the English edn.

To GWEN FFRANGÇON-DAVIES

[13 August 1925]

Dear Miss Ffrangcon Davies

I quite approve of your adding the few words from the novel in Act III—& therefore send back your draft of it for your use.

As for the Stonehenge scene I am more in doubt, but have embodied the words from the novel, & as there are other trifling changes I send my arrangement instead of returning yours. You will find they differ very little. I thought at first that by making the pair enter in this way after the curtain has risen, the repose of the scene is lost that you have if they are discovered there as in the script. But really it is not important—Please consult Mr Filmer on this.

Yours sincerely

Text MS. (pencil draft) DCM. *Date* See letter of 13 Aug 25 to Ridgeway and note below.
Ffrangçon-Davies: Gwen Ffrangçon-Davies (b. 1896), actress and singer; she had been cast as Tess in Ridgeway's production. *send my arrangement*: see letter of 18 Aug 25 to Bright; Miss Ffrangçon-Davies (14 Aug 25, DCM) thanked TH for his note and said that the new material was being copied for the other members of the cast. *Mr Filmer*: A. E. Filmer, stage-director and producer; he is listed as 'producer' in the programme of the Barnes Theatre production of *Tess*.

To PHILIP RIDGEWAY

Max Gate, | Dorchester. | 13th. August 1925.

Dear Mr Ridgeway:

Miss Ffrangçon-Davies wished one or two of the Tess speeches and entries shifted, and as there was not the slightest objection to this being done I have had a copy of the play modified accordingly. I send it on for her, and also that you may mark the changes in your copy, which I think will do away with two flats, and save Mr Filmer some trouble.

Your note has just come, and I will answer on the points in a few days. We were glad to find you got back comfortably.

Yours sincerely,
Th: Hardy.

Text MS. (typewritten) Boston Public Library.
got back comfortably: Ridgeway and Gwen Ffrangçon-Davies had visited Max Gate on Sunday, 9 August, in order to discuss the play with TH.

To HARLEY GRANVILLE BARKER

Max Gate, | Dorchester. | 14: 8: 1925.

Dear H.G.B.

You will have seen from the papers the footlightery into which I have unfortunately stumbled. But I must see the courageous little company through the business somehow, and only hope they won't suffer.

One thing I should like to know is, and probably you can tell me in a moment: is it *customary* to enter into an agreement, or anything else, for production abroad before the result of the production in England is known? My inclination is *not* to do so, but if it is usual and expected of play-wrights, well and good.

Don't write more than a line or two in reply as your hands must be pretty full. We send love to Helen.

Always yours
Th. H.

Of course we see you have all sorts coming on. Th. H.
H. Granville-Barker, Esq. | Netherton Hall, | Devon.

Text Typed transcript DCM.
line or two in reply: see letter of 22 Aug 25.   *Helen*: Barker's second wife; see letter of 19 Mar 22.   *all sorts coming on*: see letter of 12 Nov 25.   *H. Granville-Barker . . . Devon.*: added in FEH's hand; it was apparently she who typed this and other transcripts of TH's letters to Barker, subsequently deciding to record the forms of address used on such envelopes as had survived. Though part of the transcript, therefore, these words probably did not appear on the letter as sent.

To R. GOLDING BRIGHT

MAX GATE, | DORCHESTER. | August 15th. 1925.

Dear Mr Golding Bright:

Mr Ridgeway has written to say that he wants to make "some arrangements ahead which I think I shall be able to do to advantage now . . . regarding my doing the play in the Colonies & Foreign Countries and in New York in a big way".

But is it not unusual to be rushed thus? My own idea was to see what happens in England before doing anything at all further.

Yours very truly,

T.H.

Text   MS. (typewritten) Adams.

To SIR FREDERICK MACMILLAN

MAX GATE, | DORCHESTER. | 15 August 1925.

Dear Sir Frederick Macmillan:

I am not sure I quite understand your proposal of the 14th., but I believe I am right in looking at it thus: that it refers only to the leather-bound copies of the thin-paper pocket-edition sold by canvass by the Globe Publishing Co., and not through the booksellers; that the extra royalty on these of one-third per copy (i.e. 3d., the retail price being 1s. 6d. above the cloth) is to be taken away.

You will admit that a reduction of 18,000 threepences—£225 a year (taking last year's figures) is rather a big jump. If it had been half-way—from 1/- to 10½d instead of to 9d—I would have agreed off-hand. Is it possible that instead of the Globe sale last year being 17,092 leather, and 1792 cloth, as you state, the amounts were the other way? I am led to ask this by noticing that in the regular sales by booksellers the cloth copies always largely preponderate.

Believe me,

Yours sincerely,

Thomas Hardy.

Text   MS. (typewritten) BL.
your proposal of the 14th.: it was Harold Macmillan who wrote the letter of 14 Aug 25 (Macmillan letterbooks, BL) which asked TH to accept a royalty of ninepence rather than one shilling upon leatherbound copies of his books sold directly to the public through the Globe Publishing Co., a Macmillan subsidiary; see letter of 17 Dec 23.   *agreed off-hand*: see letter of 21 Aug 25. *other way?*: the figures were correct; see letter of 21 Aug 25.

To R. GOLDING BRIGHT

MAX GATE, | DORCHESTER. | 18th. August 1925.

Dear Mr Golding Bright:

Thanks for your views on foreign rights in the play, which coincide with what I remember from years past.

Mr Ridgeway and two or three of the cast are coming down here next Sunday to go through some of the scenes, and if he alludes to the subject I shall have a clearer notion of how to regard it, without being unfair to him. If I don't like the reception of the play here I shall refuse to have it done in America at all. As you know, I have been reluctant to let it be produced anywhere, having written it so many years ago.

In respect of the alterations to which you allude, they were suggested by Miss Davies, as making her part easier, and are very slight and unobjectionable, being re-arrangements only, the substance of the play being untouched.

They are as follows:—

Act First is turned into a Prologue, and instead of being in two parts is run into one by not letting Tess enter, which she does not, in fact, in the novel. Act Second is thus Act First, Third is Second, Fourth is Third, and Fifth is Fourth, the sliding-flat at the latter part of the Fifth being left out, and the conversation thrown into the After Scene.

The result upon the stage-setting is that the two short scenes are got rid of which I had not in the original manuscript. If you like to send me your copy I will get the changes marked on it, and return it to you next day.

Believe me,

Yours very truly,
Th. Hardy.

Text   MS. (typewritten) Adams.
suggested by Miss Davies: see letter of 13 Aug 25.

To PHILIP RIDGEWAY

MAX GATE, | DORCHESTER. | 18th. August 1925.

Dear Mr Ridgeway:

I am glad to learn that the rehearsals are progressing well. Next Sunday 23rd. August, will be quite convenient to us for you and Mr Filmer to come, bringing the three chief characters. (It is understood that no reporters or photographers will be present, and nothing about myself or Mrs Hardy in the papers.)

In respect of your inquiry on the production of the play abroad, I cannot do anything towards it as yet, as I find it would be a leap in the dark before knowing what results from its production in England, and would not, in fact, be customary in such a case. As for America, I am not anxious to produce it there at all. I hope and imagine however, that if you manage to put it on at a West End Theatre I shall be able to give you an option respecting the Colony you asked for, viz., South Africa; and possibly Australia.

But, as I said, I cannot agree to anything now further than our contract extends which includes provincial production in England Scotland and Ireland—an option I wished you to have in consideration of your enterprize in taking up the play.

I am,

Yours sincerely,
Th: Hardy.

Text   MS. (typewritten) Boston Public Library.
Mr Filmer: see letter of 13 Aug 25 to Ffrangçon-Davies.   *three chief characters*: i.e., Gwen Ffrangçon-Davies (Tess), Ion Swinley (Angel), and Austin Trevor (Alec).   *in the papers*: there were references to the visit in the press, however, notably Gwen Ffrangçon-Davies's 'The Task of Playing "Tess"', *John o' London's Weekly*, 5 Sept 1925.   *the play abroad*: Ridgeway's letter appears not to have survived, but see letter of 16 Sept 25.

To SIR FREDERICK MACMILLAN

MAX GATE, | DORCHESTER. | August 21st. 1925.

Dear Sir Frederick:

I just write to confirm the agreement that the royalty on the leather-bound pocket edition sold by the Globe Publishing Company and not through the regular booksellers shall be 10½d. instead of 1s., the royalty on all cloth copies remaining as before.

A curious question raised by these sales through the Globe Company is what sort of people they are who buy leather copies so largely in preference to cloth, the purchasers through book-sellers being so much of a different mind.

Yours very sincerely,

Th: Hardy.

Text MS. (typewritten) BL.
the agreement: Macmillan (19 Aug 25, Macmillan letterbooks, BL) accepted the suggestion made by TH in his letter of 15 Aug 25.

To HARLEY GRANVILLE BARKER

Max Gate, | Dorchester. | 22 August 1925.

My dear H.G.B.

What you say makes the whole position plain as the sun at noon, and I am infinitely obliged to you, though I did not mean you to take the trouble to set it out so fully. It quite agrees with my uninformed reasoning. I shall now get along I hope with this sudden and unexpected business, which plays ducks and drakes with my natural doings, but brings some curious and amusing experiences for us here. This afternoon some of the company are coming, with manager, producer, &c., to rehearse over scenes. We shall be able to tell you both about it when we meet.

Always yours

Th. H.

Text Typed transcript DCM.
What you say: Barker's letter of 16 Aug 25 (DCM) warned TH against parting with the overseas and especially the American rights to the *Tess* play; see letter of 14 Aug 25.

To SIR FREDERICK MACMILLAN

MAX GATE, | DORCHESTER. | 25th. August 1925.

Dear Sir Frederick:

I should like your opinion on the substitution of the enclosed title for the Poems instead of that I sent up, "Poems Imaginative & Incidental". I have no preference myself; but it may be that this one is not quite so commonplace— moreover, easier for readers and booksellers to remember, as in the shops the book will be called merely "Human Shows". If you think the new one better practically, will you please send it on to the printers, and ask them to let me have back the MS. of the old one: if otherwise, return the one I enclose.

Perhaps you or some of your firm will be able to remember if "Human Shows" has been used before. If so, of course I will abandon it.

Yours very sincerely,
T.H.

Text MS. (typewritten) BL.
enclosed title: i.e., *Human Shows, Far Phantasies, Songs, and Trifles.*   *better practically*: Macmillan replied (26 Aug 25, Macmillan letterbooks, BL) that he did think *Human Shows* an improved title.

To PHILIP RIDGEWAY

MAX GATE, | DORCHESTER. | August 27th. 1925.

Dear Mr Ridgeway:

I don't know that there would be anything special for you to say on my account on the first night. If it should be a genuine call after a successful result you might tell them that my not being present was not owing to any want of interest on my part, but that it was not considered advisable for me to come so far, and be out at a night performance.

I enclose a tracing of the milking-pail drawing that Mr Filmer expressed a wish to have.

Yours sincerely,
Th: Hardy.

Text MS. (typewritten) Adams.
Mr Filmer: see letter of 13 Aug 25 to Ffrangçon-Davies.

To SIR FREDERICK MACMILLAN

MAX GATE, | DORCHESTER. | 2nd. September 1925.

Dear Sir Frederick:

I quite agree that the first and second lines of the title should be of one length. I send back the proof. Thanks for returning the other title.

I am rather behindhand in reading the proofs the printers are sending, owing to correspondence, &c., about the Tess play they are going to produce at Barnes—with what success Heaven only knows; (though I am told that the Duke and Duchess of York have signified their intention of being present). But when that is under way I shall be able to get on with the proofs, which require very little correcting.

Yours sincerely,
Thomas Hardy.

Text MS. (typewritten) BL.
of one length: on the title-page as pub. the first line, 'HUMAN SHOWS', and the second 'FAR PHANTASIES', are of exactly the same length; Macmillan advocated this layout in his letter of 1 Sept 25 (Macmillan letterbooks, BL).   *the other title*: i.e., the MS. of the abandoned title-page; see letter of 25 Aug 25.   *proofs . . . sending*: of *Human Shows*.   *of York*: later King George VI and Queen Elizabeth; they were apparently not present at the first night, however.

To R. GOLDING BRIGHT

MAX GATE, | DORCHESTER. | 10 September 1925

Dear Mr Golding Bright:

I am much obliged to you for your information on the production of the play at Barnes. I gathered from the visit of some of the company to me here that Mr Ridgeway was sparing no pains to present the tragedy worthily.

He has mentioned over the telephone the question of American rights, but, as you will see, there would be no use in my transferring them to him that he might sell them to an American manager. However, I will write to you as soon as I know definitely what it is he wants. It can hardly be that he thinks of taking his English company over there.

I am glad to hear that the play may be removed to a West End theatre: indeed there are reasons which would make this transfer so desirable that I would promote it even at a little sacrifice commercially.

Sincerely yours,
Th: Hardy.

R. Golding Bright, Esq. | 20 Green Street, | Leicester Square, | London. W.C. 2

Text MS. (typewritten) Adams.
the play at Barnes: the first performance, 7 Sept 1925, had received generally favourable reviews. *visit . . . here*: see letter of 18 Aug 25 to Ridgeway. *West End theatre*: it was transferred to the Garrick Theatre, Charing Cross Road, 2 Nov 1925.

To SYDNEY COCKERELL

MAX GATE, | DORCHESTER. | 12 Sept: 1925

My dear Cockerell:

I have received the proofs you sent back, & am forwarding the remainder—but don't stress yourself to read them if you are busy. As before I am correcting the oversights you point out, & adopting some suggestions: others not. There are astonishingly few misprints this time.

I hope you enjoyed your trips with Christopher—& that he did: of the latter there is not much doubt.

All the people who have seen the play testify to one experience: how much they were moved by it. The critics in the papers seem to have been like little children—expecting the whole novel: though the tone of the supercilious ones seems to be mainly exasperation that an intruder should splash in among the regular dramatists, in whose interest some of them appear to write. However they need not be alarmed at a production which is the result of the merest accident, & which I do not dream of following up. My wife saw it on Thursday, & says the audience was in tears: so the remark of the critic who says "everybody went to be moved, but nobody was"—is rather brazen. Florence went with the Heads, staying with them that night.

W. C. Whetham & daughter called this afternoon—& Sir A. Fripp is coming to-morrow. I wonder if you know him. Kindest regards to the household.

Always yours
Th: H.

Text   MS. Taylor.

proofs: of *Human Shows*, returned with Cockerell's letter of 11 Sept 25 (DCM); he sent back an earlier batch of proofs 25 Aug 25 (DCM).   *Christopher*: Cockerell's son, subsequently Sir Christopher Cockerell, inventor of the hovercraft (see V.218); father and son had been visiting Oxford and the surrounding countryside together.   *but nobody was"*: evidently a reference to the *Daily Chronicle* review, 8 Sept 1925; headed 'Strangest First Night. Expectant Audience That Was Never Really Moved', it contrasted a 'curious expectancy in the atmosphere' before the curtain rose with the play's having 'apparently moved no one to tears'. FEH, interviewed in the *Daily News* 11 Sept 1925, also referred to the critic who said that no one in the audience cried. *the Heads*: Henry and Ruth Head lived at 52 Montagu Square, W. 1.   *Whetham & daughter*: William Cecil Dampier Whetham, Cambridge scientist and Dorset agriculturalist (see V.324); he had five daughters.   *Fripp*: Sir Alfred Downing Fripp (1865–1930), Surgeon-in-Ordinary to the King; he was born in Dorset and had a house at West Lulworth, Dorset.

To BARON D'ERLANGER

MAX GATE, | DORCHESTER. | 13 Sept 1925

Dear Baron Frederic d'Erlanger:

So far from having forgotten you I can say that we were talking of you & your beautiful opera within the last few days, & wondering whether it would ever be revived, accidental circumstances having cut short its career at its first appearance in London. The music was very haunting & I for one should like to hear it again.

Many thanks for your congratulations on the present production of "Tess"—though as you probably may know, the play is one I wrote a long time back.

Yours very sincerely
Thomas Hardy.

Text   MS. DCM.

d'Erlanger: Baron Frédéric d'Erlanger, composer; see III.204.   *forgotten you*: as d'Erlanger had suggested in his letter of 9 Sept 25 (DCM).   *beautiful opera*: d'Erlanger's *Tess*, performed at Covent Garden in 1909 and 1910; see IV.30–6.   *accidental circumstances*: the death of King Edward VII, 6 May 1910, disrupted the London 'season' during the second, and final, year of the opera's Covent Garden production; see IV.230.   *hear it again*: the opera has not been revived on the stage since 1911, although an English translation under the supervision of the composer was broadcast by the B.B.C. in 1929; see Desmond Hawkins, *The Tess Opera* (The Thomas Hardy Society, 1984), 19–20.

To ST. JOHN ERVINE

MAX GATE, | DORCHESTER. | 13 Sept. 1925

Dear Mr Ervine:

I must write & thank you sincerely for the indulgent criticism of the Tess play which I have read to-day in The Observer:—moreover for its literary quality—a feature sadly to seek in most dramatic criticisms.

I have not seen the play myself, & possibly never shall, though it seems to be getting along very well. It belongs to a far past time in my life, & no doubt if I had to dramatize the novel now I should do it differently—a perception which made me feel when we corresponded about it that it was best to let it stand as it was, with all its imperfections.

Your article reminded me of another thing—that some time ago you gave me lights on the pronunciation of "Donaghadee", & that I promised to send you the little song I had written about the place, which had inspired my question. Here it is, if you will accept it—though it is only a thin jingle, which may go very well with a lot of other poems that I am bringing out in a volume in a month or two, but will hardly bear your scrutiny on a sheet by itself. However I am glad I have not forgotten to let you have it—such as it is.

Our kindest regards to both. We hope you will get a house at Beer some day, & start again as country folks.

Always yours
Thomas Hardy.

Text MS. (with envelope) Texas.
in The Observer: Ervine's review, 'At the Play. "Tess of the d'Urbervilles"', *Observer*, 13 Sept 1925.   *"Donaghadee"*: see letter of 25 Aug 24.   *sheet by itself*: TH had written out the poem in his own hand; Ervine (15 Sept 25, DCM) sent his thanks for the 'precious gift'. *at Beer*: see letter of 19 Feb 25.

To HENRY ARTHUR JONES

MAX GATE, | DORCHESTER. | 13 Sept. 1925

Dear H. Arthur Jones:

It was with much pleasure that I received your letter telling me of your visit to the Barnes theatre for the performance of the Tess play. An experienced judgment like your own has a settling effect upon the chaos of opinions I have read in the newspapers as to the general aspect of the production, though of course I make allowance for your indulgence towards the manifold defects in the construction of the play. As you probably know, it was written thirty years ago, when both you & I were younger, & our views of the theatre—at any rate mine—were not quite the same as they are now. If I had adapted the novel in these days I daresay I should have done the job differently; but when, quite by accident, & at the request of the amateur players here, I looked it up, I found I could not get back to the subject closely enough to handle it anew. However, all independent observers agree with you in saying that it did not fail to move the emotions, which is quite as much as one could expect, though one critic, by the way, said that the audience "all went to be moved, but none were moved", a puzzling statement I pass over in the face of the other testimony. I am quite of your opinion in respect of Miss Ffrangcon Davies. She has been down here, & we liked her very much: her great intelligence, too, was striking, while she was free from the vanities one too often finds among stage people.

It is a long time since we met. I well remember your "Case of Rebellious Susan", &, of course, several of your other plays. I sometimes wonder that new plays from your hand do not appear oftener now that the terrible

Victorian restrictions are removed, & events can be allowed to develope on the stage as they would in real life.

I go to London very seldom, finding that, though I am quite well while here, the least thing upsets me when I am away—which is, I suppose, not unnatural at my age.

I gather from your presence at Barnes that you keep fairly well. My wife can remember meeting you, & sends her kind regards. She went up to the Thursday matinée, but was not at the first night.

How many have disappeared for another stage since we first sat in a theatre!

Yours sincerely
Thomas Hardy.

Text MS. Taylor.
Jones: Henry Arthur Jones, dramatist; see II.31.   *your letter*: of 8 Sept 25 (DCM), pub. in Doris Arthur Jones, *The Life and Letters of Henry Arthur Jones* (London, 1930), 356–8. *none were moved"*: see letter of 12 Sept 25.   *Davies*: Jones spoke of her as 'so unforced, so sincere and restrained. There was not one wrong note in her performance.'   *down here*: see letter of 18 Aug 25 to Ridgeway.   *Rebellious Susan"*: first performed in 1894; see IV.98.

To THE NEWINGTON STEAM TRAWLING CO.

[Ans]

14 Sept. 1925

Dear Sirs:

That the vessel may prosper in all her goings out & comings in is the wish of

Yours faithfully
T— H—

The Newington Steam Trawling Co.

Text MS. (pencil draft) DCM.
Trawling Co.: of St. Andrew's Dock, Hull; the secretary and manager, J. W. Kirby, wrote 12 Sept 25 (DCM) to ask TH for an autographed letter (to be framed and hung in the boardroom) wishing success to the firm's new deep-sea trawler, the *Thomas Hardy*.   *[Ans]*: TH's square brackets.   *the vessel*: built by Cochrane and Sons of Selby, Yorks., she displaced 336 tons and had a 96 h.p. engine; she was wrecked on the Norwegian coast in November 1936 but without loss of life.

To R. GOLDING BRIGHT

MAX GATE, | DORCHESTER. | 15th. September 1925.

Dear Mr Golding Bright:

I am willing that you should deal on my behalf with the inquiry you have had from Hungary about the Tess play, and that you should send the copy you have to the persons asking to see it, telling them to return it if they don't think of taking it up.

There has been a small change made at the end of the Fourth Act—the curtain coming down when Tess goes out silently after the murder, the entry of the landlady being omitted, on the assumption that the audience are sufficiently aware of what has happened, without the landlady's discovery. It may be that such a slight change need not be mentioned now, but if you think otherwise please mark it on the copy.

The first week's returns seem very satisfactory.

Yours very truly,
Th: Hardy.

Text MS. (typewritten) Adams.
from Hungary: the results, if any, of this enquiry are not known.   *returns*: from the Barnes Theatre box-office.

To R. GOLDING BRIGHT

MAX GATE, | DORCHESTER. | 16th. September 1925.

Dear Mr Golding Bright:

I am writing again, having received further inquiries about the American rights in the play: and I think therefore that I can do no better than put you in possession of all the particulars I have received on the point, that you may consider what is best to be done.

The first communication on the American question was from Messrs Curtis Brown on the 3rd. January last, just after the Dorchester performance. They wrote for Mr Winthrop Ames, the New York manager, who had informed them that he was much interested in producing the play, and wished to read it with a view to such production. Mr Granville Barker, who is a friend of Mr Ames, also wrote to the same effect, saying that Ames is a good man to deal with. My reply was that I wished to do nothing before the play had been produced on the professional stage in England.

The next was your informing me in February that you had had an inquiry.

The next was a request from Mr Ridgeway on 12th. August (of which I informed you) that I would arrange with him regarding his doing the play in the Colonies and Foreign Countries—"doing it in New York in a big way" he added. My reply was that I could not do anything on the production of the play abroad as yet, as it would be a leap in the dark before its production in England.

The next was a letter from Curtis Brown on 18 August repeating the request that Mr Winthrop Ames might see the play; to which the reply was the same as before.

The next was another letter from Mr Ridgeway, stating that it was customary for Foreign and Colonial rights to be included in the contract and that he had never made one with such rights omitted. He adds "All I ask is, as far as America is concerned, that if it should be done at all there, I may do it. As far as all the Colonies are concerned I should like to make arrangements as early as possible." To this nothing more definite was replied than before—and only by word of mouth when the company came down here.

The next came yesterday. Messrs Curtis Brown write: "The New York Theatre Guild are very interested in the American rights of Tess, and have asked if it would be possible for them to have a manuscript of the play to consider. As you possibly know, the Theatre Guild is now one of the most important managements in New York", etc. To which I have just replied that as soon as I am in a position to come to a conclusion on the matter I will let them know, which I hope will be in a few days.

So much for how it stands. You will perceive that in addition to the latter request, that of Mr Winthrop Ames has also to be considered, and that neither makes any definite offer—only expressing a wish to read the play. Whether Mr Ridgeway's would be definite I don't know.

The subject is rather worrying, and it has occurred to me to ask you to take it in hand and see what can best be done. As you will gather, I am quite uncommitted. I suppose Curtis Brown is acting both for the Theatre Guild and Mr Ames, and either by seeing or communicating with Curtis Brown you will be able to come to some conclusion as between them, and also as to the third party—Mr Ridgeway—who is on a similar track about the play. If you feel I am putting an undue weight on your agency by these matters will you kindly let me know?

Of course if the play collapses in England all these questions will resolve themselves.

Believe me,

Yours very truly,
Th: Hardy.

P.S. As I have said, I wish to be fair all round, even at my own expense. T.H.

Text   MS. (typewritten) Adams.
3rd. January last: this letter has apparently not survived, but for TH's reply and identification of Ames see letter of 6 Jan 25.   *12th. August*: for TH's response see letter of 18 Aug 25 to Ridgeway.   *came down here*: on 23 Aug 1925; see letter of 18 Aug 25 to Ridgeway.   *New York Theatre Guild*: dedicated to the production of important and especially non-commercial plays; it opened its own theatre in April 1925.

To R. GOLDING BRIGHT

MAX GATE, | DORCHESTER. | 19th. September 1925.
Dear Mr Golding Bright:

Since my last letter to you I have received one from Mr Curtis Brown (who has just returned from America) in which he says that Mr Winthrop Ames "expresses his continued interest in the possibility of his producing *Tess* in America"; moreover has just cabled to him, Mr Brown, "to hurry on the script". I have replied that you are already instructed to act for me in the matter; but to save time, I have posted the play to him direct, for Mr Ames's consideration, though without prejudice to any arrangement I may meanwhile make for America, should a manager offer to contract for the play offhand, on the strength of its success in England, or for any other reason.

I learn from Mr Granville Barker, who knows Ames very well, that he is an excellent man to deal with, and would be sure to put the play on properly. So I wish to give him every consideration.

I have thought it well to put you in possession of these additional facts.

Cheque for fees has arrived: many thanks. I do not send a formal receipt, as I see there is one on the back of the cheque.

Yours very truly,
Th: Hardy.

P.S. Mrs Hardy has this moment received a letter from Mr Ridgeway. It is rather incoherent; he says, "I want to get the contract in existence now, as I wish to communicate with her—[Qy.—Miss Gwen Davies's?] American friends, and also with their [?] foreign and Colonial people with a view to doing it myself in conjunction with the controllers of the theatres of course.... As I have put all my life and soul into this play I want to show it to the world...... I know you will treat me fairly." &c.

I don't know if this means he wants to combine with such a manager as Winthrop Ames, for instance. T.H.

Text MS. (typewritten) Adams.
Mrs Hardy . . . Ridgeway: TH seems not to have communicated directly with Ridgeway after the letter of 27 Aug 25 but to have conducted the subsequent correspondence through FEH; more than 30 letters from FEH to Ridgeway are in the Adams collection.   *[Qy. . . . Davies's?]*: TH's square brackets.   *their [?]*: TH's question-mark and square brackets.

To LADY HOARE

[21 September 1925]

The Cerne Giant's figure was never all over white, like King George's near Weymouth, but only the trenches forming his outline. These are fairly deep, & all that can be done to make his shape clear is to keep the trenches cleaned out & spread white chalk over the bottom of them. This will remain white many years if raked over & weeded now & then. The interior of the Giant's figure was always green.

T.H.

Text MS. Wiltshire Record Office.   *Date* Supplied on MS. by Lady Hoare.
Cerne Giant's: a large turf-cut phallic figure, somewhat resembling Roman representations of Hercules and probably dating from the 2nd century A.D.; it is cut into a hill-side to the NE of the Dorset village of Cerne Abbas. In a covering letter ('Monday', DCM) FEH refers to Lady Hoare's having solicited these comments ('With great pleasure TH has written the few lines you requested. His memory is wonderful, & you may depend upon the accuracy of his statement.'), but the purpose of her request is not clear. A brief note, 'The Giant of Cerne Abbas', *Country Life*, 18 Oct 1924, cites TH as the source of similar suggestions for keeping the Giant's outline sharply visible; although unsigned it was evidently written by the editor, Graham Anderson, who visited Max Gate after inspecting the Giant in August 1924 (see *Siegfried Sassoon Diaries 1923–1925* [see letter of 3 Jan 24], 182–3). L. V. Grinsell (*Somerset & Dorset Notes & Queries*, March 1980) points out that Lady Hoare's husband had endowed the maintenance of the Giant through the National Trust in 1924.   *King George's*: the figure of King George III on horseback, cut into a hillside near the S. Dorset village of Osmington in 1815.

To MAURICE MACMILLAN

MAX GATE, | DORCHESTER. | 21st. September 1925.

Dear Mr Macmillan:

I am willing to let John o' London's Weekly run Tess of the d'Urbervilles once as a serial for £1000 (one thousand pounds) if you think the Proprietors the right sort of people. Also that, as you propose, two-thirds of this amount be paid to me, and one third to yourselves.

It is understood, of course, that the story shall appear just as in the volume, and not with any alterations.

I am much obliged for the copy you send of the paper, which seems of a very good class.

Sincerely yours,
Thomas Hardy.

Maurice Macmillan. Esq. M.A.

Text   MS. (typewritten) BL.
once as a serial: this second serialization of *Tess*, with a new introductory note by TH, appeared in *John o' London's Weekly*, 25 Oct 1925 to 10 July 1926.   *as you propose*: in his letter of 19 Sept 25 (Macmillan letterbooks, BL).   *not with any alterations*: all of TH's conditions were incorporated into the memorandum of agreement, dated 5 Oct 1925 (BL), between Macmillan & Co. and George Newnes, the publishers of *John o' London's*.   *very good class*: the original *John o' London's Weekly*, a literary magazine aimed at a general audience, ran from 1919 to 1954.

To G. M. HARPER

MAX GATE, | DORCHESTER. | 25 Sept. 1925

Dear Sir:

Many thanks for the copy of Scribner's, wherein I have read your article with great pleasure.

I remember you very well as an author, the Life of Wordsworth, published by you some years ago, having as I thought presented him in a more human aspect than any previous life of him had done. Believe me, with renewed thanks

Sincerely yours
Thomas Hardy.

Mr G. McLean Harper:

Text   MS. (with envelope) Princeton.
Harper: George McLean Harper (1863–1947), American scholar and university teacher. *your article*: Harper's 'Hardy, Hudson, Housman', *Scribner's Magazine*, August 1925; Harper sent it, from Princeton, 11 Sept 25 (DCM).   *Life of Wordsworth*: Harper's *William Wordsworth: His Life, Works and Influence* (New York, 1916).

To JAMES SMELLIE

MAX GATE, | DORCHESTER, | DORSET. | 25th. September 1925.

Dear Sir:
    In reply to your letter I send the following lines, which perhaps may suit the Memorial you propose:

> If you think, have a kindly thought,
> If you speak, speak generously
> Of those who as heroes fought
> And died, to keep you free.

Yours very truly,
Thomas Hardy.

Mr Alderman James Smellie. J.P. | Mayor's Parlour | Dudley.

Text MS. (typewritten) West Midlands Library, Dudley.
Smellie: James Smellie, Mayor of Dudley, Worcestershire; he wrote 23 Sept 25 (DCM) asking if TH could improve upon the 4-line inscription he had himself composed for the town's war memorial. For Smellie's letter and an account of the entire episode see William W. Morgan, 'Verses Fitted for a Monument: Hardy's Contribution to the Dudley War Memorial', *Thomas Hardy Journal*, January 1985.   *keep you free*: as Morgan points out, the comma was omitted from the last line of the quatrain as inscribed on the War Memorial Clock Tower itself—and as pub. in *The Times* report (17 Oct 1928) of the formal dedication performed by the Prime Minister, Stanley Baldwin, the previous day.   *Mr Alderman . . . Dudley.*: added in TH's hand.

To R. GOLDING BRIGHT

MAX GATE, | DORCHESTER. | 26th. September 1925.

Dear Mr Golding Bright:
    I sent on a spare copy of the Tess play, that you might do the best you can with it for production in Italy. The Italian translation of the novel has a large circulation in that country.
    I find that Curtis Brown sent the copy I meant for Winthrop Ames to the Theatre Guild of New York (which had also asked for it). This he had no business to do, but I have written to tell Ames that the play was meant for him; so I suppose matters will right themselves over there.
    I have told Ridgeway, who writes nearly every day, that I will do the best I can for him about South Africa and Australia after he has brought the play to the West End, which of course does not commit me to anything definite. But if you find that he really has facilities for those two colonies I should not mind obliging him in some way with regard to them, seeing that he was the first to venture on the play in England. I may mention that an Australian firm—J. C. Williamson, Ltd. has asked me indirectly for it, and that the Manager of the Theatre du Marais, Brussels, (who has produced some of Sir James Barrie's plays) wants to translate it. I have sent the latter a copy.
    Ridgeway is like a child in his wants. He asks for "foreign rights for translation" whatever that means—a matter with which he has nothing whatever to do, and this morning that I will let him "fix up the colonies

forthwith", as he is feeling very disappointed. You may be able to learn his meaning as to the Colonies, and his capabilities in respect of them.

I have thought it best to post you up in these details though perhaps none of them may mean much.

Yours very truly
Th. Hardy.

Text MS. (typewritten) Adams.
Italian translation: *Una donna pura* (*Tess dei D'Urberville*) (Milan, 1904).   *Ames* . . .
Theatre Guild: see letter of 16 Sept 25.   *J. C. Williamson, Ltd.*: the theatrical management company founded by the American-born Australian impresario James Cassius Williamson (1845–1913).   *the Manager*: Jules Delacre (1883–1954), Belgian poet and theatrical producer, founder of Le Théâtre du Marais, Brussels, 1922–6.   *(who . . . Barrie's plays)*: added in TH's hand.   *You may . . . of them.*: added in TH's hand.

To SIR FREDERICK MACMILLAN

MAX GATE, DORCHESTER. | 26th. September 1925.
Dear Sir Frederick:

I am much obliged for the accounts to June 30, and quite understand your explanation of the mistake in those of 1923–24; and that the new rate of royalty on the leather volumes sold by the Globe Company began last July.

I am sending back the proofs of the Poems straight to the Printers, as there is very little correction, and I thought it would save trouble.

I have been thinking that some day you will be able to include in the Wessex Edition a volume containing what has been published since the last volume of that edition, for though I do not imagine there will be much demand for such a volume at first, the edition is a favourite one with literary people, so that it will be worth while to complete it ultimately as the library edition of my writings; for I don't suppose you will ever decide to start another.

Sincerely yours,
Thomas Hardy.

Text MS. (typewritten) BL.
accounts to June 30: FEH reported to Cockerell, 26 Sept 25 (Purdy), that these amounted to £4,404 15s. 5d. for the year.   *mistake . . . 1923–24*: it was Harold Macmillan who wrote 25 Sept 25 (Macmillan letterbook, Birchgrove archive) to explain that in 1923–4 TH had received the standard royalty on pocket edn. sheets sold to the Globe Publishing Co. (see letter to Macmillan of 15 Aug 25) for binding in cloth; since, however, these sheets had in fact been bound and sold in leather a higher royalty was now being retroactively paid.   *new rate*: see letter of 21 Aug 25.   *the Poems*: *Human Shows*.   *since the last volume*: see letter of 8 Oct 25.

To SYDNEY COCKERELL

MAX GATE, | DORCHESTER. | 28 Sept. 1925
My dear Cockerell:

I have sent off the final proofs at last, & must thank you for your list of suggestions as to words here & there. I adopted some—about half I should say—& considered the others carefully. However, you will see when the book comes out. I don't expect much from it: indeed I am weary of my own writing, & imagine other people are too by this time.

I have not seen the play, & don't suppose I shall. It is very odd that I should have drifted into a job which I quite disbelieve in,—a dramatized novel—& did not at all foresee when I gave way to the request of the local players that I would let them have something.

Sincerely yours
T.H.

Text MS. (with envelope) Taylor.
when the book comes out: see letter of 20 Oct 25 to Macmillan.

To H. KETTERINGHAM

29 September 1925

Dear Sir:

Mr Hardy returns the pamphlets on spelling reform as requested. He thinks the rules for simplification too drastic, & as tending to destroy the history of the language. Also that there is greater need for a reform of pronunciation than of spelling. The gradual disappearance of the letter R from London speech—so that boa and boar, daw and door, etc. are sounded alike—is very serious. In the West of England this attrition has not taken place, & these words are as distinct in pronunciation as in spelling.

Yours truly
for Thomas Hardy
. . . .

H. Ketteringham Esq.

Text MS. (pencil draft) DCM.
Ketteringham: H. Ketteringham wrote from Birmingham, 26 Sept 25 (DCM), describing himself as a former schoolteacher and superintendent of registration for the Birmingham Education Committee. *the pamphlets*: unidentified, but Ketteringham in his letter advocated a gradual reform of English spelling, first by omitting letters that were effectively silent and then by making substitutions for letters that were 'wrong'.

To J. C. SQUIRE

MAX GATE, | DORCHESTER. | 29 Sept. 1925

Dear Mr Squire:

It was kind of you to go to the play, which has got upon the stage in such an unexpected manner, & almost against my wish, for I no longer believe in dramatizing novels, & have no dramatic ambitions. Its appearance is entirely owing to the fact that our leading lady down here coaxed me to let her do Tess.

The critics, as you say, were silly. They always put technique first & emotional power last, instead of the reverse. But only one of them, so far as I saw, told a deliberate lie, in saying, "We all went to the play to be moved, but nobody was moved." What his motive was I don't know.

The epigram which, as I stated in the Mercury, I imitated from "the

French" is such an obvious reflection that probably it could be found in every language under the sun. I return your correspondent's letter.

> Sincerely yours
> Th: H.

Text MS. Colby.
leading lady down here: Gertrude Bugler.   *nobody was moved."*: see letter of 12 Sept 25.
The epigram: see letter of 2 Oct 25.

To RUTLAND BOUGHTON

MAX GATE, | DORCHESTER. | 1 October 1925

Dear Mr Rutland Boughton:

My thanks for returns from performances of the Queen. Herewith a formal receipt. I regretted that I was unable to get to Glastonbury this year. However we saw a very good account of the music in the papers. I wish the Glastonbury Corporation (if there is one) would build you a better hall.

Also thanks for congratulations on the play, which has come to light in such an unexpected manner after thirty years.

> Yours very truly
> T. Hardy.

Text MS. BL.
to Glastonbury: Boughton's version of *The Queen of Cornwall* had again been performed at the 1925 Glastonbury Festival.   *a better hall*: the town's Assembly Rooms were used for the Festival's musical performances.

To HENRY BROADBENT

MAX GATE, | DORCHESTER. | 2 Oct: 1925

Dear Sir:

I have no doubt that the epigram you refer to occurs in almost every language upon earth; it having been an obvious reflection for any gloomy person from Cain onwards—though I believe he was not a bachelor. I do not remember what French author I got it from: &, though most things in literature come from the Greek, it is just possible that he was not a plagiarist, the impulse to such an exclamation being so natural to a man in a state of despondency—even if only from a slight headache.

Believe me

> Yours very truly
> Thomas Hardy.

Henry Broadbent Esq. M.A.

Text MS. (with envelope) Univ. of Kentucky.
Broadbent: Henry Broadbent (1852–1935), librarian of Eton College.   *the epigram*: TH's 'Epitaph on a Pessimist (From the French)', *London Mercury*, September 1925; Broadbent pointed out (1 Oct 25, DCM) that the same thought occurred in a well-known epigram in the Greek Anthology and TH subsequently changed 'From the French' to read 'From the French and Greek' (see Purdy, 244).

To SIR FREDERICK MACMILLAN

MAX GATE, | DORCHESTER. | 8 October 1925.

Dear Sir Frederick:

I am glad to hear that you are going to bring out the new Wessex volume without delay, and I send a list of the few corrections. The page-references are to the Pocket Edition, as being the last revised one, which will therefore be the best for the printers to use as copy.

Believe me,

Yours very sincerely,
Th: Hardy.

Text MS. (typewritten) BL.
to hear: from Macmillan's letter of 5 Oct 25 (Macmillan letterbooks, BL), responding to TH's of 26 Sept 25.   *new Wessex volume*: a vol. containing *Late Lyrics and Earlier* and *The Queen of Cornwall* was added to the Wessex edn. in 1926.

To GWEN FFRANGÇON-DAVIES

17 October 1925

Dear Miss Ffrangcon-Davies.

My best thanks for the photograph, which has come safely. You look more thoughtful & pretty in it than in any other that I remember to have seen.

I note what you say as to the suddenness of the transition to the lodging-house after Angel has left Tess, & the desirability of showing more clearly the stress to which she was put before she went back to Alec, & I have been searching for an old draft of the play in which this was shown by a scene or two combining the swede-hacking with the bailiff coming for her mother's furniture. But this was omitted as making the play too long, & the effect was endeavoured to be obtained by substituting Alec's call on Tess on the evening of her marriage, & the discussion of her poverty by her mother & Angel, which I thought made her situation sufficiently clear.

If however, you do not think the substitution emphatic enough the arrangement you send in outline fulfils the same object, & nothing better can be done than that you should adopt it, in consultation with Mr Filmer. The words pencilled you can use or not as you choose—The removal of the play to the West End might be a good occasion for inserting the scene, if Mr Ridgeway approves, as he no doubt would. Unfortunately I cannot find my old draft though I could reconstruct it I think. But yours has the same effect, & does not require more scenery, as my arrangement would have done.

I think you are right in wishing to retain the diamond scene—if Alec's call is omitted.

I return your draft, in case you may not have kept a copy. I hope you do not feel the daily strain to be excessive.

Yours most sincerely
T— H—

P.S. We have heard from Mr & Mrs Granville Barker how much they were moved by your presentation of Tess. Also from other experts in drama. T.H.

Text   MS. (pencil draft) DCM.
the photograph: of Miss Ffrangçon-Davies in her costume for *Tess*, sent with her letter of 14 Oct
25 (DCM).   *Mr Filmer*: see letter to Ffrangçon-Davies of 13 Aug 25.   *reconstruct it*: TH
does appear to have supplied the text for the additional scene between Tess and Alec which was
approved by the Lord Chamberlain's office 18 Nov 1925 (BL).   *retain the diamond scene . . .*
omitted: the play currently had Alec d'Urberville intruding upon the beginning of Tess's and
Angel's honeymoon at Wellbridge Manor; the incident of Tess's putting on the diamonds,
omitted from the Dorchester production, was restored when the new scene (see previous note)
was introduced.

To HARLEY GRANVILLE BARKER

Max Gate, | Dorchester. | 20 October 1925.

My dear H.G.B.

I am much interested to learn that you and Helen have taken the trouble to
go to the play, and seen what I shall never see—Miss Gwen F.D. in the part
of Tess. It is so strange that this resurrection of the character should have
come about, when a year ago I did not dream of such a thing; and it is a pity
that, owing to my not foreseeing it, I had no time to revise the technicalities
of the adaptation, which no doubt I should have done if I had known that my
casual handing over of the old copy to the players here would have extended
so far afield.

She is a charming young woman, we think, and I have had a letter from her
today to say that she will drop down upon us next Sunday and talk over what
has happened. She seems to live in the piece, and I hope will not wear herself
out with it, for it must be a heavy strain, and she is not robust.

The real fact is, as I may have said before, to attempt to put a novel on the
stage is hopeless, and altogether a mistake in art. I should never have thought
of trying my hand on it nowadays; but having been tempted by many
"leading ladies" of the nineties I could not resist. But the courage of managers
did not equal that of the would-be Tesses, and they put the extinguisher on
my effort, in the interest of propriety.

Yes: you are right in thinking the christening scene and the baby-nursing
scene vital parts of the story. Not only could they not be got into the stage-
action for technical reasons, but for moral reasons they were not allowed to be
in the novel when it ran as a serial in 1891. Whether the gentler and more
clinging quality given to the character by Miss F.D. (which I am told is most
moving) than was given her in the book, is consistent with the smouldering
ancestral fire in Tess's nature that broke out in the murder, I of course cannot
judge: Florence says it does not strike a spectator as being out of keeping.

It must be amusing to you to see what they are all doing in London—
histrionically I mean (if I may use such a dignified word in connection with
stage popularities at the present day).

Later.

I have received the lecture: it is kind of you to send it. We are going to read it
to-night after dinner. I am not capable of doing much just now—being only

just recovering from an attack of lumbago. I was boasting a few months ago of never having anything of the sort! Best love to H., and believe me

ever yours.
Thomas Hardy.

Harley Granville-Barker, Esq. | 26 Hill Street, | Mayfair.

Text Typed transcript DCM.
what I shall never see: but see letter of 15 Dec 25.   *as a serial in 1891*: both scenes occur in chap. 14, which was omitted from the *Graphic* serialization; see Purdy, 69.   *the lecture*: Barker's British Academy Annual Shakespeare Lecture for 1925, *From 'Henry V' to 'Hamlet'* (London, 1925).   *Harley . . . Mayfair.*: added in FEH's hand; see letter of 14 Aug 25.

To MAURICE MACMILLAN

MAX GATE, | DORCHESTER. | 20th. October 1925.

Dear Mr Macmillan:
    Many thanks for the Cheque to hand. I should not suppose that the serial publication would at any rate do any harm to the book. The only other case I remember of publishing a story in a weekly magazine so long after its original appearance is that of Scott's Kenilworth.
    This curious coincidence in the production of play, serial, and the forthcoming volume of poems, is of course accidental. Whether it may be bad for the last named I don't know. I have not asked your brother what his opinion is; but if you and your partners have any doubt I should not mind the poems being kept back till the beginning of next year.
    I am just getting over an attack of lumbago: otherwise am well, as I hope you are.

Sincerely yours,
Thomas Hardy.

Text MS. (typewritten) BL.
the Cheque: for two-thirds of the amount received for the *John o' London's* serialization of *Tess*; see letter to Macmillan of 21 Sept 25.   *harm to the book*: Macmillan (19 Oct 25, Macmillan letterbooks, BL) took the view that *Tess*'s readership would be widened as a result of its appearance in 'this rather popular paper'.   *Scott's Kenilworth*: this serialization has not been traced.   *your brother*: Sir Frederick Macmillan.   *kept back*: Macmillan replied (21 Oct 25, Macmillan letterbooks, BL) that the current publicity would, if anything, enhance the sales of *Human Shows*—which was pub. on 20 Nov 1925.

To WALTER LOCK

MAX GATE, | DORCHESTER. | 28 Oct. 1925

Dear Dr Lock:
    The dramatized version of the Three Strangers, which Mr Owen inquires about, has never been published, & I have thought that the shortest way to his getting a copy is to lend him mine. I have pleasure in giving his young men permission to act it, if they care to, & if they will kindly undertake to return my copy when they have had one made for their use.
    To go to quite another subject: I fear I may not have written to tell you how deeply I was interested in your booklet on what came to your mind in the

nursing home, & that I found it food for thought for a long while. Well, better late than never, & I do so now.

Also: your letter has happened to come while I have before me the proofs of some poems that are to appear next month, one of which is a memory of your brother Fossett. I send the page containing it, thinking you may like to read it before the book is out.

Our best wishes to Mrs Lock & yourself.

Sincerely yours
Thomas Hardy.

Text   MS. Mrs. Mildred Wheatcroft.
Lock: Walter Lock (1846–1933), Warden of Keble College Oxford, 1897–1920; *D.N.B.* He was born in Dorchester, younger brother of Arthur Henry Lock, solicitor (see I.73).   *Mr Owen inquires about*: Arthur Synge Owen, a tutor at Keble College; his letter to Lock of 27 Oct 25 (DCM) was forwarded to TH by Lock the same day (DCM).   *lend him mine*: Owen acknowledged its receipt 30 Oct 25 (DCM) and TH's play was performed, together with two by other authors, in Keble College 21 and 22 June 1925.   *your booklet*: Lock's *Personal Religion* (London, 1924); TH's copy, inscribed by Lock, was sold after his death.   *your brother Fossett*: TH's '"Nothing Matters Much"', pub. in *Human Shows*; it refers to Judge Benjamin Fossett Lock (see V.165), who died in August 1922.   *Mrs Lock*: *née* Jane Cecil Campion.

To R. GOLDING BRIGHT

MAX GATE, | DORCHESTER. | 29 Oct. 1925
Dear Mr Golding Bright:
   Many thanks for telegram. We shall watch developments with interest.
Sincerely yours
Th: Hardy.

Text   MS. (correspondence card) Adams.
telegram: contents unknown, but see letter of 3 Nov 25.

To HERBERT GRIMSDITCH

30 October 1925
Dear Mr Grimsditch:
   I have to thank you for the copy of your book of studies on my novels. I have only as yet glanced into it, but mean to read it through—I am sure with interest, to judge from some thoughtful works I have seen—in spite of it being difficult, of course, for one who has been occupied during the last thirty years in the production of more mature works, good or bad, than the novels, to enter into questions concerning his now nearly forgotten art in fiction, the writing of which came to an end last century, in the reign of Queen Victoria.

   As you tell me you are a young man you will not mind my suggesting that if you ever want to read anything more of mine, (which you may not), you might do well to take up my later & more deliberate books. But I thank you nevertheless for thinking it worth while to write about any of them.

Yours very truly

Text MS. (pencil draft) DCM.
Grimsditch: Herbert Borthwick Grimsditch (1878–1971), author, executive editor *The Book of Knowledge* 1951–63; he wrote 27 Oct 25 (DCM).   *your book*: Grimsditch's *Character and Environment in the Novels of Thomas Hardy* (London, 1925).

To DOUGLAS MACMILLAN

1 November 1925

Dear Mr Douglas Macmillan:

In reply to your letter I am sorry to tell you that, although my writings are said to have a good deal of folk-lore scattered about them, whatever there may be of it is merely such as I have met with by accident, the systematic study of folk-lore as a science having been quite outside my pursuits. Hence I cannot make any suggestions upon it that will be of service. At first it occurred to me, seeing that the words "folk-lore" are a modern term which has been appropriated by another periodical that is I believe in existence still (though I am not sure), to ask whether some equally good title for your proposed publication could not be found, such as "OLDTIME LORE: A Dialect, Folk-customs, & past-day Dance & Song Recorder" (the word British seems unnecessary). But this may not express so precisely as "folk-lore" what your paper is going to concern itself with, & I therefore don't recommend it.

I repeat my regret that on the above account, & by reason of increasing age, which prevents my taking up any new subject, I cannot be of service, & am

Yours very truly

Text MS. (pencil draft) DCM.
Macmillan: Douglas Macmillan, poet and writer on Somerset history and folklore, sometimes under the pseudonym of 'D. M. Cary'. He wrote 29 Oct 25 (DCM) to seek suggestions for the title of a proposed new periodical devoted to dialect and folklore.   *another periodical*: *Folklore*, first pub. in 1890.

To R. GOLDING BRIGHT

MAX GATE, | DORCHESTER. | 3rd. November 1925.

Dear Mr Golding-Bright:

I am quite willing that you should send a copy of the play to M. Pitoeff. Unfortunately I have not one by me, but only a very rough draft. I will set about making it clear enough to be typewritten, and send the script to you as soon as I can get it done.

I wonder what M. Delacre of Brussels is doing with his copy. He has never even acknowledged the receipt of it. I think it might be as well to ask him if he means to get on and produce it, and if not to be good enough to return the copy.

Sincerely yours,
Th: Hardy.

Text MS. (typewritten) Adams.
M. Pitoeff: Georges Pitoëff (1887–1939), actor and theatrical producer; born in Russia, he settled in Paris after World War I.   *M. Delacre*: see letter to Bright of 26 Sept 25. *Th: Hardy*: immediately preceding this signature the initials 'R.G' have been written in FEH's hand and then struck through.

To SIR FREDERICK MACMILLAN

MAX GATE, | DORCHESTER. | 5 November 1925.

Dear Sir Frederick:

I enclose herewith an application from the Editor of "Standard Stories", a magazine I know nothing of, and therefore ask you to be kind enough to answer his letter as you judge best, which I have told him you will doubtless do.

I am personally indifferent on the matter, and shall not at all mind if you consider it inadvisable to let him print one of my short tales, as requested. But if you see no objection to such publication I will select one. My only feeling is that I don't want to get over-advertised just now.

Believe me,

Yours very sincerely,
Th: Hardy.

Text MS. (typewritten) BL.
"Standard Stories": a short-lived periodical pub. by Hutchinson and edited by Geoffrey Besant (see letter of 13 May 23).   *his letter*: of 3 Nov 25 (DCM), offering £25 for permission to reprint any one of TH's short stories.   *consider it inadvisable*: Macmillan (6 Nov 25, Macmillan letterbooks, BL) strongly urged that the offer be refused, and permission was in fact denied in Macmillan & Co.'s letter to Besant of 16 Nov 25 (Macmillan letterbooks, BL).

To R. GOLDING BRIGHT

MAX GATE, | DORCHESTER. | 11th. November 1925.

Dear Mr Golding Bright:

I am sending herewith a copy of the play that I have had made, that you may send it to the Paris manager with what remarks you think expedient.

It stands exactly as they have been playing it in London hitherto, but in a few days they think of inserting a short new scene of a few minutes between Acts III and IV, where the transition is said to be rather abrupt. If the Paris request comes to anything I can let them have the scene if desired, though perhaps a French-manager would not think it necessary, as I hardly do.

Yours very truly,
Th: Hardy

Text MS. (typewritten) Adams.
Paris manager: see letter of 3 Nov 25.   *short new scene*: see letter of 17 Oct 25.

To HARLEY GRANVILLE BARKER

Max Gate, | Dorchester. | 12 Nov. 1925.

My Dear H.G.B.

It was very kind of you and Helen to invite F., and she is much disappointed at having been unable to go. But the state of her throat and chest—which are no better to-day—made the journey impossible: moreover the symptoms of influenza that accompany the others might have brought it into your house. She had been diligently studying "The Wild Duck" to be able to follow your lecture: and now has missed it. I trust it was appreciated nevertheless.

The hints are very useful that you send about the Spanish gentleman, who has written twice to me, as you will see from the letters I enclose, and though I have not replied, I might have done so later on, owing to what he says about "Saint Joan". I wonder if it is true, and whether G.B.S. should be warned?

We are full of good hopes for the Madras House, but as it has already proved itself a fine play you need have no misgivings. Best wishes to both;

Sincerely yours
T.H.

(Thank H. for her translation.)
H. Granville-Barker, Esq. | 26 Hill Street, | Mayfair.

Text   Typed transcript DCM.
invite F.: FEH had evidently been asked to stay with the Barkers in London.   *your lecture*: Barker spoke on 'The Technique of Ibsen's *Wild Duck'* to the Royal Society of Literature, 11 Nov 1925.   *Spanish gentleman*: Barker wrote 11 Nov 25 (DCM) to forward some discouraging information about two young Spanish brothers, one of whom, Clemente Fernández Burgas, had written to TH 12 Aug and 10 Sept 25 (both DCM) for permission to translate *Tess* for performance in Spain.   *"Saint Joan"*: see letter of 4 June 24 to Clodd; in his letter of 12 Aug 25 Burgas said he was currently translating the play for production in Spain 'during the next season'.   *the Madras House*: a revised version of Barker's play (first performed 1910) was produced at the Ambassadors Theatre on 30 November; see letter of 19 Dec 25.   *her translation*: it was Helen Granville Barker who translated and wrote out the information about Burgas, received from a Spanish friend, which still accompanies her husband's letter. *H. Granville-Barker . . . Mayfair.*: added in FEH's hand; see letter of 14 Aug 25.

To R. GOLDING BRIGHT

MAX GATE, DORCHESTER. | 18th. November 1925.

Dear Mr Golding Bright:

I will inquire of my publishers if there is any practical reason against a kinema production of The Romantic Adventures of a Milkmaid. I am not aware of one of any other kind. If they don't suggest any objection I will communicate further.

Yours very truly,
Th: Hardy.

Text   MS. (typewritten) Colby.
of a Milkmaid: see letter of 18 Nov 25 to Macmillan.

To SIR FREDERICK MACMILLAN

MAX GATE, | DORCHESTER. | 18th. November 1925.

Dear Sir Frederick:

The theatrical agent who arranged the Tess play—Mr Golding Bright—writes to tell me that he has had an inquiry whether the film rights in "The Romantic Adventures of a Milkmaid" are available. This, as you will recall, is one of the tales in the volume "A Changed Man" and it has never been used for kinema production so far as I know. I see no reason why it should not be so used, as it is a story of rather light nature which I do not much value, and as I suppose this treatment of it would do the published form of it no harm; though I should hesitate if it were a more serious story. You have had a larger experience of the various film-companies than I have had, and you may be able to tell me if there are any to be avoided, or any special stipulations to make. Or, if you would prefer, I could put Mr Bright into communication with you for the purpose.

Very sincerely yours,
Thomas Hardy.

Text MS. (typewritten) BL.
into communication with you: see letters of 20 Nov 25.

To R. GOLDING BRIGHT

MAX GATE, DORCHESTER. | 20th. November 1925

Dear Mr Golding Bright:

I have received a reply from my publishers on the matter of a film-production of "The Romantic Adventures of a Milkmaid." Sir Frederick Macmillan says that if you will communicate with him he will discuss with you any arrangements to that end. As he has had much to do with making similar arrangements and is on the spot I think it better for him to take it in hand than myself.

Yours very truly,
Th: Hardy.

P.S. The story occurs in the volume entitled "A Changed Man" and is about half the length of an ordinary novel. T.H.

Text MS. (typewritten) Colby.
arrangements to that end: no such film has been traced earlier than an Italian production of 1940.

To SIR FREDERICK MACMILLAN

MAX GATE, | DORCHESTER. | 20th. November 1925.

Dear Sir Frederick Macmillan:

I have received the volumes of poems, for which many thanks. I will, if I can get it done before post-time, enclose a list of half a dozen trifling errors to correct, in case a second edition should be wanted.

I have told Mr Golding Bright, (20 Green Street, Leicester Square) to communicate with you about filming the story, "The Romantic Adventures of a Milkmaid". He has acted for me in staging "Tess" (having been recommended by Sir J. Barrie, whose play-business he attends to); so that he will carry out any instructions as to terms that you may give him.

In respect of this same kinema business, I have also had the enclosed letter from the Society of Authors about "The Mayor of Casterbridge". I do not know how the matter stands with the company which bought the film-rights in that novel some years ago. If the company still retains its rights there is of course no more to be said.

Very sincerely yours,
Thomas Hardy.

Text MS. (typewritten) BL.
volumes of poems: copies of *Human Shows*, pub. that day. *second edition*: Macmillan (19 Nov 25, Macmillan letterbooks, BL) reported that almost the entire first printing of 5,000 copies had already been sold; in his letter of 25 Nov 25 (also BL) he promised that the corrections would be made in the second printing, already in hand. *by Sir J. Barrie*: see letter of 19 Dec 24. *enclosed letter*: from G. H. Thring, 19 Nov 25 (DCM). *no more to be said*: Macmillan (25 Nov 25, Macmillan letterbooks, BL) reminded TH that film rights to the *Mayor* remained with the Progress Film Company (see letter of 19 Feb 21) and TH wrote Thring to this effect 27 Nov 25 (draft, DCM).

To SIR JAMES BARRIE

MAX GATE, | DORCHESTER. | 26 Nov. 1925

My dear Barrie:
Sincere thanks for your interest in the play. I am much surprised at what is really the result of the merest accident—a request from our leading young woman here & the rest of the Dorchester company that I would let them try the piece, which I had nearly forgotten.

I hope you don't feel this cold weather in your lofty nest.

Always yours
Thomas Hardy.

Text MS. (with envelope) Colby.
interest in the play: Barrie wrote 24 Nov 25 (DCM) to congratulate TH on the 100th performance of Ridgeway's production of *Tess*. *lofty nest*: in Adelphi Terrace; see letter of 18 May 21.

To R. GOLDING BRIGHT

MAX GATE, DORCHESTER. | 1 December 1925.

Dear Mr Golding Bright:
I am quite willing that Mr Ridgeway should pay only £25 in each case as advance payments for royalties in Australia and South Africa, which I think he should regard as very considerate in the circumstances. In respect of the sliding scale you mention, I must leave that to your judgment of what is reasonable.

I forget if I told you that Sir F. Macmillan will have pleasure in consulting with you about The Adventures of a Milkmaid.

Yours very truly,
Th: Hardy.

Text MS. (typewritten) Colby.
if I told you: TH had done so in his letter to Bright of 20 Nov 25.

To C. J. LONGMAN

3 December 1925

Dear Mr Longman:

I do not remember the incident to which you draw my attention, but I think it very probable that it happened, as I knew Haggard very well. I therefore have no objection whatever to your printing it, if you care to.

I believe we did sit next to each other at that lunch. In those days I used to be in London a good deal, & to go about everywhere, which I am very far from doing now!

Believe me

Yours very truly

C. J. Longman Esq.

Text MS. (pencil draft) DCM.
Longman: Charles James Longman (1852–1934), editor and publisher.   *the incident*: Longman (2 Dec 25, DCM) wrote that he was editing the autobiography of the late Sir Rider Haggard (see I.235) and would like permission to include an anecdote about TH reading a review of one of his novels in the Savile Club and declaring, '"There's a nice thing to say about a man"' and '"Well, I'll never write another novel"'. See Haggard, *The Days of My Life*, ed. C. J. Longman (2 vols., London, 1926), I.272–3.   *that lunch*: Longman recalled sitting next to TH at a lunch given by Andrew Lang (see I.146) at the Oxford and Cambridge Club and thought that Walter Pollock (see I.121) and Rudyard Kipling (see III.90) had also been present.

To SIR FREDERICK MACMILLAN

MAX GATE, | DORCHESTER. | 3rd. December 1925.

Dear Sir Frederick:

I have received the enclosed script of an intended publication, which, though called "a study", is as you will see simply an abridgement of the novel "Tess of the d'Urbervilles". The publishers, or editor, seem to think they are rather exceeding their rights, and so submit it for approval. I do not myself know what the effect of such an abridgement would be upon the original work, but you probably do know, and I have no wish at all to oblige the firm if this concoction of theirs would injure the circulation of the unabridged story. Perhaps you will reply, or suggest an answer.

Mr Golding Bright writes to say that he will call on you about the Adventures of a Milkmaid as soon as he can get particulars of the film-company's proposal.

Would you be so kind as to let me have another copy of "Human Shows?"

Yours sincerely,

Thomas Hardy.

Text   MS. (typewritten) BL.

submit it for approval: John Alexander Hammerton (1871–1949), author and editor, had sent TH a typescript of 'Thomas Hardy, *Tess of the d'Urbervilles*: A Study', by Coulson Kernahan (see V.219), which subsequently appeared in Hammerton, ed., *The World's Great Books in Outline* (2 vols., London, 1926), II.801–8.   *suggest an answer*: Macmillan (4 Dec 25, Macmillan letterbooks, BL) thought pub. of the 'very light' summary of the book could do no harm, and Hammerton wrote TH 7 Dec 25 (DCM) to thank him for granting permission.

To R. & R. CLARK

FROM | TH. HARDY, ESQ., | MAX GATE, | DORCHESTER. | 9 Dec. 1925

"Human Shows."

(If not too late for 2nd impression.)

    page 167, line 3 from bot. *after* Never mind, omit quote. marks

    page 168, top line. omit quot. marks *before* What's the world . . .

To: Messrs Clark

Text   MS. (printed stationery with 'Memorandum' heading) Purdy.

Clark: R. & R. Clark, Limited, Edinburgh printers; they had printed almost all of TH's work since Macmillan became his publishers in 1902.   *for 2nd impression.)*: both corrections—to 'At a Pause in a Country Dance'—were incorporated into the second printing of *Human Shows*.

To MAUD LUCAS

MAX GATE, | DORCHESTER. | 10 Dec. 1925

Dear Mrs Lucas:

    I must thank you very sincerely for this gift of one of your etchings which, though our house is small, must be found room for somewhere. You should not have taken the trouble to frame it.

    I do not remember ever to have met you, though you say you have been my neighbour for half a lifetime. Nevertheless I am

Yours very truly

Thomas Hardy.

Text   MS. Mrs. Norton Downs.

Lucas: Mrs. L. Maud Lucas wrote from 23 Dean Park Road, Bournemouth, 10 Dec 25 (DCM), to present TH with her recent etching of the old Manor House at Wool, the 'scene' of Tess's and Angel's honeymoon.   *my neighbour*: Mrs. Lucas replied (11 Dec 25, DCM) that when she spoke of being TH's 'neighbour' she meant that she lived in the next county to Dorset and knew 'Wessex' intimately.

To SIR FREDERICK MACMILLAN

MAX GATE, DORCHESTER. | 10th. December 1925.

Dear Sir Frederick:

    The story you mention, "Squire Petrick's Lady" was, I believe, one which, like some of the others in "A Group of Noble Dames", (though not all of them) appeared before the copyright with America in 1891, so was pirated over there; and hence no permission was asked for reprinting it in that country.

Though its republication could be forbidden here I agree that the simplest thing to do would be to let the English publisher include it in his Anthology on the payment of a small fee.

Very sincerely yours,
T.H.

Text   MS. (typewritten) BL.
story you mention: Macmillan (9 Dec 25, Macmillan letterbooks, BL) asked if TH had given permission for 'Squire Petrick's Lady' to be included in an American anthology, *Great Short Stories of the World*, of which an English edn. was now being planned.   *English publisher*: the vol., ed. by Barrett H. Clark and Maxim Lieber, was pub. in London by William Heinemann in 1926.

To R. GOLDING BRIGHT

FROM TH. HARDY, | MAX GATE, | DORCHESTER. | 15: 12: '25

Dear Mr Golding Bright:

Mr Ridgeway asks me to agree to half-fees for last week, as the expenses of bringing his company down here were so heavy. I did not wish him to come, but since he did come I don't mind letting him off half.

Truly yrs
T.H.

Text   MS. (correspondence card) Adams.
company down here: see *LY*, 243–4, for an account of the private performance of the *Tess* play given at Max Gate on 6 Dec 1925.

To LADY MILLICENT HAWES

Max Gate, Dorchester, | 16 Dec. 1925.

Dear Duchess of Sutherland,

(As you still are to me.) At last you have written straight, as you might have done long ago if you had chosen. And I was at the point of writing to you about your remarkable novel, which impressed me much. But I did not quite like to invade your privacy after so long.

Do you remember that when I used to come, as a comparatively young man, to your parties at Stafford House, you would tell me that you did not care for the whirl of the life you were in? I would think, "That's what she *says*," and I forgot the matter till I found that you had practically abandoned it, when I thought: "Then, what she said was true," and up you went in my opinion twice as high as before, though you never were low.

But I won't say anything more about this, except that I should like to see you once again, if you ever come this way.

Affectionately yours,
Thomas Hardy.

Text   Colby Library Quarterly, 1952, 93–4.
Hawes: Lady Millicent Hawes (1867–1955), daughter of the fourth Earl of Rosslyn; in 1884 she married the Marquess of Stafford, who became the fourth Duke of Sutherland in 1892 and died in 1913; in 1914 she married Brig.-Gen. Percy Desmond Fitzgerald, and after that marriage was dissolved in 1919 she married Lieut.-Col. Ernest Hawes and lived in Paris. See Denis Stuart, *Dear Duchess: Millicent Duchess of Sutherland 1867–1955* (London, 1982).   *written straight*: it appears from her letter of 15 Dec 25 (DCM) that TH may have sent her an inscribed copy of *Human Shows*.   *remarkable novel*: her *That Fool of a Woman, and Four Other Sombre Tales* (London, 1925).   *come this way*: she wrote again, 23 Dec 25 (DCM), promising to visit TH but adding that she did not know when she would be coming to England.

To SIR FREDERICK MACMILLAN

MAX GATE, | DORCHESTER. | 16th. December 1925.

Dear Sir Frederick:

I find on referring to the matter you mention that I understood the request for the three extracts to come from Mr Walter de la Mare who is editing the Anthology, and as he is a friend of mine I felt I could not very well refuse his wish or ask him a fee, though I rather wondered why he did not write himself. I now gather that I was really dealing with Mr Blackwell.

They are only short prose passages, it is true, which might almost have been quoted without asking; but I think I should have demanded a small fee, or sent him on to you, if I had realized, nevertheless.

Yours very sincerely,
Thomas Hardy.

Text   MS. (typewritten) BL.
matter you mention: Macmillan (14 Dec 25, Macmillan letterbooks, BL) asked if TH had, as the publisher alleged, given permission for the use without fee of extracts from *The Trumpet-Major*, *Tess*, and *The Dynasts* in a series of school readers.   *editing the Anthology*: it was, in fact, a six-book set entitled *Readings*, ed. by de la Mare and Thomas Quayle (Oxford, 1925–6); the extract from *The Trumpet-Major* appeared in Book V, the two others in Book VI. *Mr Blackwell*: Basil Blackwell (1889–1984), publisher; he was knighted in 1956.

To HARLEY GRANVILLE BARKER

Max Gate, | Dorchester. | 19. Dec. 1925.

Dear H.G.B.

I have finished The Madras House which you were so kind as to send me, and though you have probably formed your own opinion about it by this time I should like to tell you how it strikes a contemporary—if I can be considered a contemporary!

I shall horrify you by saying that I am almost sorry you did not write it as a novel. I have read it as one, anyhow. Its subtleties are to my mind largely wasted on the stage which, think what you will, addresses itself to people who are not very perceptive except the few who don't count among the mass. (Thats' why I always feel Shakespeare is largely wasted in acting.) I think it possible that you may ultimately drift into novel writing: I don't see how otherwise you can express all the complications that you discern in life. However, I don't give advice; but bear that thought in mind.

I will only add (what is really a part of the same thing) that your acute judgements of Victorian, and other, architecture makes me hazard that guess that you would have thrived as an architect, or architectural critic.

I hope you have got to Paris without adventure either with snowstorms or anything else. We have none here. You are going on south I hear. Best wishes from us to both of you for the Christmas—not that I believe one atom in Bethlehem of Judea, though I agree with the late Dr. Cheyne in holding that much may be said for Bethlehem in Galilee. (This is a digression.)

Always yours.
Thomas Hardy.

Text   Typed transcript (DCM).
Madras House: Barker had evidently sent TH a copy of the new edn. of the published text of the play (London, 1925); for the new production see letter of 12 Nov 25.   *architectural critic*: although buildings have important representative functions in *The Madras House* TH apparently has in mind Barker's detailed specification of the stage-settings.   *Paris*: Barker replied from there, 23 Dec 25 (DCM).   *Dr. Cheyne*: the Revd. Thomas Kelly Cheyne, biblical scholar; see IV.48.   *Bethlehem in Galilee*: Cheyne frequently challenged—e.g., in the entry on Nazareth he contributed to the *Encyclopaedia Biblica* (1902)—the tradition that Jesus was born in Bethlehem of Judea, arguing instead for Bethlehem in Galilee or, later on, for still other possibilities.

To R. GOLDING BRIGHT

MAX GATE, DORCHESTER. | 22nd. December 1925.

Dear Mr Golding Bright:

I have decided to accept half royalties for the last week at the Garrick Theatre, as I think it will give Mr Ridgeway more spirit for his country tour if he feels we have not been hard upon him in London. So will you please return to him whatever may be required to set the matter straight.

Yours very truly,
Th: Hardy.

Text   MS. (typewritten) Adams.
country tour: Christine Silver took the part of Tess in the production of the play that went on tour early in 1926, following the end of the London run at the Garrick on 12 Dec 1925.

To THE SECRETARY, THE ROYAL LITERARY FUND

MAX GATE, | DORCHESTER. | 23rd. December 1925.

Dear Sir:

I have received the enclosed application from Miss Rosetta G. Spearing, who says she is a distressed writer, but of whom I know nothing whatever. I shall be obliged if you will read it, that your committee may consider if it is a deserving case.

Yours truly,
Ths Hardy.

Secy Literary Fund.

Text MS. (typewritten) Royal Literary Fund.
Secretary: see letter of 3 Mar 21.   *enclosed application*: the letter Rosetta Grace Spearing wrote TH from Weymouth 22 Dec 25 is in her Royal Literary Fund file; it tells a pathetic tale of ill fortune and begs TH's assistance in obtaining financial aid.   *deserving case*: in a letter to Marshall of 28 Dec 25 (Royal Literary Fund) Spearing attempted to explain why she could not supply copies of her work, none of which had been pub. in vol. form; the matter appears to have been closed with Marshall's insistence, 29 Dec 25 (copy, Royal Literary Fund), that submission of such copies was indispensable to any consideration of her case.   *Secy Literary Fund.*: added in TH's hand.

To JOHN PINNEY

MAX GATE, | DORCHESTER. [Christmas 1925?]

DEAR JOHN,
    THANK YOU FOR YOUR CHRISTMAS GIFT. I HAVE LIGHTED THE CANDLES WITH GREAT JOY, AND WISH YOU A HAPPY NEW YEAR,

YOURS AFFECTIONATELY
T. HARDY.

Text MS. Univ. of Bristol.   *Date* See note below.
Pinney: John Pinney (1920–86), youngest son of Maj.-Gen. Sir Reginald John Pinney (1863–1943) and Lady Hester Pinney (d. 1958); he served with H. M. Overseas Service 1941–64 and was awarded the M.B.E. in 1955. Racedown, the Pinney's house in NW Dorset, was visited by TH in August 1925 for its association with William and Dorothy Wordsworth; see *Siegfried Sassoon Diaries 1923–1925* (see letter of 3 Jan 24), 278.   *DEAR JOHN*: TH's use of capitals throughout this letter suggests a date earlier than his April 1926 letter to John Pinney, which is written in a large rounded script.   *CHRISTMAS GIFT*: apparently a miniature Christmas tree.

To J. C. SWINBURNE-HANHAM

[Copy]   31 Dec. 1925

Dear Mr Swinburne-Hanham:
    The term of office for which I was appointed a representative Governor of the Dorchester Grammar School expires at the coming Epiphany Sessions, & I feel I shd like to let you know, in case the question of my re-appointment shd arise (though of course it may not) that I have no wish for such re-appointment, & should, indeed, prefer to retire, my opinion being that a more active Governor than age will, alas, permit me to be, shd take the place I have had the honour of filling for so long as a representative of the magistracy.
    Believe me

Yours sincerely
T— H—

J. C. Swinburne-Hanham Esq. J.P.

Text MS. (pencil draft) DCM.
Swinburne-Hanham: John Castleman Swinburne-Hanham (1860–1935), J.P., chairman of Dorset Quarter Sessions 1923–33.   *[Copy]*: TH's square brackets.   *prefer to retire*: TH was not reappointed; see *LY*, 246.

INDEX OF RECIPIENTS

A General Index will be included in the last volume of the edition.